Ronald Segal

THE BLACK DIASPORA

Five Centuries of the Black Experience outside Africa

The Black Diaspora tells the enthralling story of Africa-descended people outside of Africa. Focusing on a span of more than five centuries, religion and politics, language and literature, music and art, author Ronald Segal yokes together the histories of seemingly disparate societies to show that diaspora culture has an organic and coherent identity.

Beginning with African civilization before slavery, Segal guides us from the horrors of the slave trade to the slave experience, revolt, and eventual emancipation, which removed the fetters of ownership and left those of racism. From Britain and the United States, to the islands of the Caribbean, Guyana and Brazil, Segal's rich comparative method reveals how different responses to abolition continue to exert a profound influence on black lives today.

A groundbreaking work of history and cross-cultural analysis, *The Black Diaspora* is a major contribution toward understanding the politics, the poetry, and the peopling of the Western world.

South African-born RONALD SEGAL left the country with African National Congress leader Oliver Tambo in 1960 for political exile in England. In early 1994, he returned for three months, at the special invitation of the ANC, to take part in South Africa's first democratic election. Founding editor of the Penguin African Library, he is the author of twelve books, including *The Crisis of India*, *The Race War*, and *The Americans*.

Praise for The Race War:

*Brilliantly sustained analysis,
scrupulously documented . . .
encyclopedic knowledge, rare
intelligence and a controlled
urgency before which the most
closed minds surely cannot help
but unclench.*
—NADINE GORDIMER
The Nation

HISTORY
INDEX
6^1/$_8$ × 9^1/$_4$ / 416 pages
0-374-11396-3 / $25.00

THE BLACK DIASPORA

THE BLACK DIASPORA

by Ronald Segal

FARRAR, STRAUS AND GIROUX

NEW YORK

LIBRARY OF CONGRESS CATALOGING-IN-PUBLICATION DATA
Segal, Ronald.
The black diaspora / by Ronald Segal.
p.   cm.
1. Blacks—America—History.   2. African diaspora—History.
I. Title.
E29.N3S44   1995   970.004'96—dc20   94-48707 CIP

Grateful acknowledgment is made to the following for permission to reprint previously published
material: Excerpts from *The Music of Black Americans: A History, Second Edition* by Eileen
Southern, with permission of W. W. Norton & Company, Inc. Copyright © 1983, 1971 by
W. W. Norton & Company, Inc. Excerpts from *Their Eyes Were Watching God* by Zora Neale
Hurston. Copyright © 1937 by Harper & Row, Publishers, Inc. Renewed 1965 by John C.
Hurston and Joel Hurston. Reprinted by permission of HarperCollins Publishers, Inc.
Excerpts from *Brown Girl, Brownstone* by Paule Marshall.
Copyright © 1959 by Paule Marshall. Renewed 1981 by the Feminist Press.
Excerpts from *The Arrivants* by Edward Kamau Brathwaite.
Copyright © 1973 by Edward Kamau Brathwaite. Reprinted by
permission of the Oxford University Press.

IN MEMORY OF

OLIVER REGINALD TAMBO

1917–1993

A great leader in the cause of freedom and a beloved friend

ACKNOWLEDGMENTS

This book would have been impossible to write without the advice, information, and insights provided by many of the people I met on the way. All gave me of their time. Some gave me unexpected and much appreciated hospitality that I hope to have the opportunity one day to return. The purpose of such acknowledgments is to express my gratitude, and I do so in the consciousness that not all recipients may approve of the product with which I am associating them. I trust that these will be soothed by my assurance that they are not to be held responsible for the use that I have made of their help.

I wish to thank, in alphabetical order: David Abdullah; Margaret Walker Alexander; Peter Altman; Andaiye; Walter Annumunthodo; Anthony Appiah; Professor Azevedo; Edwige Balutansky; Ana Mae Barbosa; Clovis Beauregard; Max Beauvoir; Valerie Belgrave; Joby Bernabé; Henri Bernard; Lloyd Best; Pat Bishop; Harcourt Blackett; Jennifer and Salamon Blajberg; Grace and Jimmy Boggs; Julio Braga; Dionne Brand; Ianna Brown; C. C. Bryant; Clementine Burfield; Ezekiel Campbell; Horace Campbell; David de Caries; Martin Carter; Marcus Joaquim Maciel de Carvalho; Yeda Pessoa de Castro; Sharon Chacko; Carole Charles; John Henry Clarke; Oliver Clarke; Max Cointre; Johnetta Cole; Raphael Constant; Robin Coxson; Louis Crusol; Maceo Daley; Roger Desire; Howard Dodson; Jean Dominique; Jocelyn Dow; Bobby Duval; Michael Dyson; James Ferguson; Stanley Fischer; Miles Fitzpatrick; Tony Fraser; Peter Fryer; Paula Giddings; Eddie Gilbert; Michael Gilkes; Professor Glaberman; Marius Gottin; Stanley and Alison Greaves; Freddie Grimm; Beverly Guy-Sheftall; Wilson Harris; Richard Hart; Carlos Hasenbalg; Linda Healy; Michelle Heisler; Errol Henderson; Fred Hermantin; Ronald Heus; Robert Hill; Marc Hofnagel; Bell Hooks; Antonio Ibanez; Max Ifill; Selma James; Carlos Jara; Errol Jones; Klaas de Jonge; João Jorge; Joseline Juca; Eusi Kwayane; George Lamming; Albert Levy; Olive Lewin; Maureen Warner Lewis; Neville Linton; Chokwe Lumumba; Johnny Macalla; Cathy Magones; Haki Mahdubuti; Lucille Mair; Marcel Manville; Daniel Maximin; Ian McDonald; Mike McCormack; Leslie Miles; Peter

Minshall; Rooplal Monar; Antonio Moraes; Mervyn Morris; Andrew Morrison; Petrona Morrison; Richard Morse; Luiz Mott; Trevor Munroe; Ann Musgrave; Abdias do Nascimento; Richard Newman; Rex Nettleford; David Nichols; Renato Orgiz; Hugh O'Shaughnessy; Hans Panofski; Cathy Peters; Gerard Pierre-Charles; Schofield Pilgrim; Veerle Poupeye-Rammelaere; Ken Ramchand; João and Emilia Reis; Alfie Roberts; Gordon Rohlehr; Rupert Roopnaraine; Adalgisia Rosario; Sandi Ross; Selwyn Ryan; Ivaniev dos Santos; Joel Rufino dos Santos; Juanita Elbein dos Santos; Theresa dos Santos; Lloyd Secawar; Nicholas Simonette; Ricky Singh; Richard Small; Munis Sondré; Jeffrey Stanford; Brent Staples; Carl Stone; Yannick Tarrieu; Clive Thomas; Lourdes Teodoro; Patrick de la Tour; Michel-Rolph Trouillot; Frantz Voltaire; Clotel Walcott; Anne Walmsley; Raymond Watts; Claudette Werleigh; John Wickham; Amy Wilentz; Denis Williams; Joan Williams; and Bridget Wooding.

   If I have misspelled any of these names or inadvertently omitted others which should have been included, I apologize. There are also those I must mention as due my special thanks. Shula Marks, the distinguished historian, guided my steps in exploring the African past. Peggy Miller of Farrar, Straus and Giroux has been helpful at all times and become a valued friend. John Glusman, my editor, has been unstinting, in his criticism as well as his encouragement, and I owe much to him for both. I must express my gratitude as well to Robert Hemenway, whose corrections, queries, comments and suggestions have much improved the text. Susan, my wife, has put up with my abandoning her for months at a time while I went on my travels, and with my fluctuating moods at home as I raced or staggered through this book. The best of it is as much hers as it is mine.

CONTENTS

PREFACE

This is a book whose beginning reaches back into my childhood. I was born into a Diaspora myself, the Jewish Diaspora, in a country, South Africa, where Jews occupied both a privileged and a perilous position. Acceptably white, we had title to the top floor in the racial structure. As Jews, we were consigned to the balcony and constantly at risk of being pushed over the railings.

I was born the year before Hitler came to power in Germany, and I was growing up while the "Purified" Nationalist Party of a resurgent Afrikanerdom proclaimed an affinity with much in Nazism, especially its anti-Semitic frenzy. Shortly after the fall of Paris in the Second World War, I was sitting in the public gallery at the House of Assembly when the Nationalist spokesman on foreign affairs, a Goebbels-like figure, rose to gloat at the plight of French Jews and the prospect that Jews in South Africa might come to suffer the same fate.

Our peril was all the more apparent to me because my parents, for all the material success which had disposed other Jews of their class to other preoccupations, were ardent in asserting their Jewish identity and commitment. A succession of like-minded Jewish visitors from abroad to our home kept us informed of the horror that threatened and soon overwhelmed so many millions of European Jews. My two elder brothers were in the armed forces. My sister, ten years older than I, was put on a ship for studies in the United States, so that, if South Africa should succumb, one member of the immediate family might survive.

I acquired from all this a loathing of racism which led me at the University of Cape Town into the student politics of opposition to racial discrimination in all its forms. The Nationalist Party, far from chastened by the defeat of Nazi Germany, though no longer publicly claiming an affinity with much in Nazism, had been elected to power in 1948 and had begun, in what it called apartheid, the ruthless elaboration of established white supremacy.

After the interruption of a few years in studies abroad, I returned home to publish *Africa South*, an international quarterly devoted to confronting racism everywhere, but centrally in South Africa. I had no doubt then, as I have none now, that I owed much of my outlook to the Jewish upbringing I had had. I took from this a sense of identity that was not religious or national, but historical and moral. It brought me to challenge the outlook of the South African Jewish community.

Jewish alarm at the rise of its old enemy to power had been allayed by reassurances that reflected the government disposition to close the white ranks. Jews were individually—and, indeed, disproportionately among whites — opposing apartheid. Yet, as one infamous law followed another, some of them with a more than passing resemblance to the race laws of Nazi Germany, I argued that Jews should be expressing collective outrage. I learned to realize the obvious. Jews come in all kinds. And so do blacks.

I continued to believe then, however, as I believe now, that a people with a past infused by oppression and suffering is charged with a special responsibility, to remember and remind: to redeem that past with a creative meaning; to recognize and insist that we must treat one another as equally human, beyond differences of race or nationality, religion or culture, if we are not to become mere beasts that talk.

Africa South and other activities of mine led the South African government to pay me the compliment of its displeasure. I was banned from all gatherings, stripped of my passport, and subjected to death threats that began as rather alarming and then became simply infuriating. In the immediate aftermath of the 1960 Sharpeville massacre, I drove the African National Congress leader, Oliver Tambo, across the border and took the quarterly into exile. Publication continued until late in 1961, when the resources with which I had been subsidizing it were blocked in South Africa. Penguin Books invited me to start and edit a Penguin African Library. Among the books I decided at the outset to commission was one on the African Diaspora. In the event, the Library would publish more than forty books during its quarter-century of existence. *The African Diaspora* was not to be among them.

My first choice of an author for it turned me down with the comment, "Such a book needs a hundred scholars working for twenty years." I replied that they would end up with a directory, doubtless with its own value, but cautious with consensus, when what I wanted was the adventure of a single mind. I could not persuade him, nor could I persuade any of the potential authors I subsequently approached, as the idea of the book time and again chose to nag me into a new burst of activity on its behalf. At last, in 1987, I began to consider writing the book myself.

The relevant literature at which I looked only confirmed me in my belief that the book I had in mind needed to be written. There was so much material, but scattered, as though the various parts of the body did not belong to one another. Those books that had been written on the Diaspora, when not collections of academic essays, seemed primarily concerned with tracing African tracks. That was part of the subject, but it was not the subject itself, as this took an increasingly distinct form for me. The book should be a study of the Diaspora, from its genesis to its impact, as the story of a people with an identity, vitality, and creativity all its own.

The Diaspora whose development I had determined to describe originated in the Atlantic slave trade which preyed overwhelmingly on black Africa— roughly, that bulk of the continent that lies south of the Sahara. This was one reason for changing the title of the book to *The Black Diaspora*. There was another. The racism which sought to sustain slavery and subsequent forms of subjugation or discrimination based itself increasingly on the black- ness of the Diaspora rather than on its geographical genesis. This blackness came to include lighter complexions and any other features, such as lips, nose, and hair, which revealed traces of a black ancestry. It was crucially, as geography was not, inescapable.

Increasingly, too, though not until well into this century, "black" came to be adopted within the Diaspora itself as a term of dignity and defiance, in revulsion from the use of the word "Negro," with all the abusive and contemptuous associations that this had acquired. "Black is Beautiful" be- came a slogan, and it was in the cause of Black Power that militancy raised a clenched fist. Today some blacks in the United States prefer the term "African-American." Other terms used elsewhere in the Diaspora include "Afro-Caribbean" and "Afro-Brazilian."

People have a right to call themselves whatever they please. For a book on the Black Diaspora, however, to use these different terms would mean cluttering the argument and confusing the issue, without even escaping the risk of causing offense. Is a Barbadian living in the United States an Afro- Caribbean or an African-American? Does one become the other by being granted corresponding citizenship? If the black community in Britain is mainly Afro-Caribbean in origin, what of the many blacks there who had been born in Africa, or whose parents had been? If these are to be termed "Afro-British," the term "Afro-Caribbean" becomes invidious, which is why "Afro-Caribbean" is a description more often used by bureaucrats than by blacks in Britain.

I have used the term "black" throughout this book except where the immediate context requires the use of another. For instance, official statistics in Britain may apply specifically to blacks of Afro-Caribbean origin. Peculiar social divisions and stresses require me to use as well, in dealing with certain parts of the Diaspora, the terms "colored" and "mulatto," since those of mixed black-and-white ancestry were often treated differently from blacks and in their turn often regarded blacks as inferior. The history of Haiti in particular can only be explained largely in terms of this division. Some "colored" people still today prefer to think of themselves as almost white. It is sad that they should do so, without recognizing how much more they are losing than gaining in the process. They are here, nonetheless, regarded as belonging to the Black Diaspora.

The subject of the book excludes the substantial trade in slaves for the Islamic world. The story of what happened to those blacks, I decided early on, would have to be told in another book. The subject I had marked off for myself was enough. This confidence proved to be presumptuous. There was more than enough, I found, than I could manage. Glimpses were given to me not only in the writings of others but in personal encounters. Waiting at the airport in Port-au-Prince for a flight to the north of Haiti, I met an Ethiopian who had been working for the World Health Organization on a project in Colombia. As we exchanged information about each other, he told me of a black community there which I should visit for my book. I never made it to Colombia. I never made it to some other places I should have visited. There were times when I thought that one more wave of information would sweep the book irretrievably out to sea.

This book does not pretend to be comprehensive. Nor does it pretend to be a work of scholarship. It is mainly a work of synthesis that has drawn on the scholarship of others, with observations, a compass, and an argument of my own. It is in no way definitive, except as a match may be definitive in starting a fire. This is, above all, what I looked for from such a book, more than thirty years ago: that it would ignite an interest which others might bring to a blaze of new insights.

When I had written a synopsis for *The Black Diaspora*, I took it to New York. One of the publishers I visited there told me that he was captivated by the project, but then added regretfully, "There is only one problem. You are white." That had not been, I tartly told him, an insuperable obstacle for blacks such as George Jackson, who had, in one of his letters published as *Soledad Brother*, referred to the value of my exercise in rewriting history, *The Race War*. But this was no more than repartee. It was already clear that this publisher and I would not be working together. Happily, I found one who cared nothing about my color and everything about my enthusiasm for the book. I am deeply indebted to Roger Straus for the faith he invested in me. I am as concerned for him as for myself that this investment should not prove to have been misplaced.

I have learned much in the process of writing this book. I did not come unprepared for an encounter with human cruelty and with the indifference to it among those not directly affected. For a Jew in particular, the Holocaust has extended the limits of the horror that can be comprehended. I had read books on slavery. Yet all that was in the past. Nothing prepared me for the desolation of Detroit now or the murder now of black children as a form of street-cleaning in Rio de Janeiro. Nor had I recognized before, as I now came to do, in close-up, the ultimate injustice, that the victims are so often also victimizers of one another and themselves.

And yet, along with all this, I found, in both the past and the present of the Diaspora, so much courage and generosity and grace, so much that has been creative and that has celebrated life, that I came to wonder less at the depths which humanity has plumbed than at the heights its spirit can scale. My late mother used to say that she was in love with the Jewish people. In writing this book, I fell in love with the Black Diaspora. She would not, in her demanding devotion, have appreciated the object of mine, but she would have understood the ways and the reasons by which I reached it.

Ronald Segal

ONE

From Africa
to Slavery

1 | PEOPLE

~~~~~~

There were no slaves in the caves. It took civilization to create the concept of people as property. The supreme paradox of human progress is that it has brought, along with much light, a deepening of the dark.

The civilization of classical Greece, to which modern Western civilization owes so much for the high value it claims to place on individual liberty and speculative thought, was one whose most illustrious philosophers rationalized the exploitation of slaves.

After the fall of the Roman Empire in the west, feudal Europe exploited serfs rather than slaves, but the economic revival that came with the Middle Ages was accompanied by a revival in slavery as well. The very word "slave" came not from *servus*—the Latin word for slave, which developed into "serf"—but from "Slav." For it was from among the pagan Slavs that Western Europeans, reluctant to enslave fellow Christians, turned for slaves, at the great slave markets of Caffa in the Crimea and Tana at the mouth of the Don.[1] Such slaves were sought in particular for the cultivation of sugar, a new economic enterprise that would come to reach across the Atlantic.

In the parts of Palestine and Syria that they had conquered, the Crusaders took over the sugarcane fields from the Muslims. As the Crusaders were driven from their conquests, sugar cultivation was taken westward by Venetian and Genoese investors and colonists—to Cyprus, in particular, which became the main market for slaves in the Mediterranean area.

Still further to the west, on the Iberian peninsula, the Christian kingdoms were conquering territory held by Islam. In the process, they captured black slaves whom their Muslim masters had imported. Although still relatively few in number, "black" slaves, as distinct from "white" ones, began to appear in European records. A will, for instance, dated December 21, 1300, and made by a Genoese colonist in Cyprus, bequeathed a house to a slave identified as "a Negress."[2]

The advance of Islam in the east, by the Ottoman Turks, led in 1453 to the fall of Constantinople and the end of Christianity's Byzantine Empire. Western European rulers, bankers, traders, explorers, and adventurers looked elsewhere, beyond the reach of Islamic power. The search for a sea route to the Indies went southward and found along the way islands in the Atlantic off the African coast. Madeira and later São Tomé became important sugar producers, with the labor of black slaves. Columbus sailed westward and found his Indies in America.

To this New World came Western European conquerors and colonists, along with increasing numbers of black slaves, many of them brought to provide the labor for the cultivation of sugar. The pioneering statistical study of the Atlantic slave trade by Philip Curtin published in 1969 estimated the total of black slaves landed alive in America, by the Atlantic trade up to 1870, at roughly 9,391,000.[3] Subsequent research has raised the total. It is now estimated that 11,863,000 slaves were shipped across the Atlantic, that the overall death rate during the Crossing or what came to be called the Middle Passage was in the range of 10–20 percent, and that the total for those landed alive must accordingly lie somewhere between 9,600,000 and 10,800,000.[4] An intermediate figure of 10,200,000 would seem, for now, to be a reasonable estimate. It is widely conceded that further revisions are more likely to be upward than downward.

While the gender ratio varied from time to time and place to place, overall some 64 percent of the slaves were male and 36 percent were female.[5] Increasingly, the trade was one in children. Before the nineteenth century, children (those under fifteen years of age) constituted on average a little less than 20 percent of all cargoes. In the nineteenth century, this proportion rose sharply, to an average of a little over 41 percent between 1811 and 1870. In the region immediately north of the Zaire (Congo) River, the proportion reached almost 53 percent, and in Angola 59 percent.[6]

Nor was this by any means the limit to the horror. The scholar Joseph Miller has estimated that in western-central Africa, deaths among slaves on the way to the coast may have equaled the number of those who survived to board the ships.[7] Miller calls this a "worst-case assumption," but he evidently excludes those deaths that occurred in the course of raiding and capture. It is, therefore, likely that at least as many people died in Africa itself as a direct result of the Atlantic trade as were carried away from Africa.

Meanwhile, certain Western European states would grow rich and powerful, in important part from the profits of the trade and the colonial production which it made possible. They would make varyingly vast advances in science, technology, and social organization. Britain would take the lead in what came to be called the Industrial Revolution. Influenced by the successful revolt of some British colonies in North America, France would have its own revolution for the Rights of Man.

Slavery would survive, in Brazil and Cuba, until little more than one hundred years ago. It would survive still longer in Africa itself, in a form closer to that developed by the West than any developed in traditional African societies. "The production of slaves for the Americas also produced slaves for Africa. It is difficult to prove that the Atlantic slave trade *caused* the transformation of slavery in Africa, but it is likely."[8] In the region of the French Western Sudan, for instance, as late as the period 1905–13, there were 1,192,000 slaves in a population of 5,134,000.[9]

During all that time, white societies that prided themselves on their moral as well as their material progress excused their exploitation of blacks, first by maintaining that blacks were naturally inferior to whites and then, as this doctrine became increasingly unsustainable, by asserting the cultural backwardness of Africa.

It is by no means self-evident that the culturally advanced are accordingly entitled to subjugate or oppress, let alone enslave, the culturally backward. Moreover, the concept of cultural advance, as of cultural backwardness, begs more questions than it presumes to answer. It is at least arguable that cultural advance involves a moral measure, and that societies which plundered others for their people were, by that measure, correspondingly backward. Yet, even short of such a radical revision, there is evidence that before the beginnings of the Atlantic slave trade, Western Europe was not notably more advanced than parts of black Africa, and that the trade itself created the very conditions on which the Western European view of African cultural backwardness came largely to be based. In fact, since even the more conventional criteria of cultural advance encompass standards of personal security and civil justice as well as material wealth and the extent of territory under centralized administration, the difference may well have been in favor of black Africa.

In the thirteenth century, the Mali kingdom of the Mandingo people began expanding its power through the western savannah until, early in the fourteenth century, it reached from Senegal to the upper Niger. In 1324, Mansa (Emperor) Kankan Musa left his capital on a pilgrimage to Mecca. Along the way, he "spread upon Cairo the flood of his generosity: there was no person, officer of the court or holder of any office of the sultanate who did not receive a sum in gold from him. The people of Cairo earned incalculable sums from him, whether by buying and selling or by gifts. So much gold was current in Cairo that it ruined the value of money."[10]

In 1352, the most widely traveled of the Muslim writers in the Middle Ages, Muhammad Abu Abdullah ibn Battuta, born of a Berber family in Tangier, set out to visit Mali and returned some eighteen months later. He noted "the complete and general safety one enjoys throughout the land. The traveller has no more reason than the man who stays at home to fear brigands, thieves or ravishers." He was patently impressed by "the small number of acts of injustice that one finds there; for the Negroes are of all peoples those who most abhor injustice. The sultan pardons no one who is guilty of it."[11] As the historian Thomas Hodgkin has commented, "Such a judgement could hardly have been passed on contemporary France or England."[12]

Ibn Battuta recorded the wearing of masks by musicians and dancers who performed at the court. Neither in his own writings, however, nor in those of later travelers to black Africa for centuries, was serious attention paid to black African works of art in stone and clay, bone and ivory, wood and metal, examples of which would eventually come to be recognized as among the greatest achievements of the creative spirit. In 1940, decades after such recognition by Picasso and other artists had begun to influence the development of modern art, the first of many terracotta sculptures was found near the town of Djenné along the Niger. Controlled excavations of a mound there during the seventies, with radiocarbon testing of the finds, revealed that the site had been continuously occupied for more than one thousand years before its abandonment in about A.D. 1500. Numerous terracotta figures, of kneeling or standing humans and of various animals, were dated to A.D. 1000–1300.

Advanced in technique and of high artistic quality, the sculptures have a remarkable fluidity of shape. Some of the human subjects are portrayed with an intensity of emotional expression rare in the art of Western Europe at that time. In certain figures, the style of a particular artistic school and even of an individual artist may be identified. One terracotta couple forms a triangle, with knees touching and faces cheek to cheek, in an eloquent rendering of mutual love and need. It might serve as a symbol of the innumerable interdependencies which the slave trade severed.

Mali itself declined in power from the beginning of the fifteenth century, as its main vassals, the kings of the Songhai along the middle Niger, broke from their allegiance and proceeded to make vassals of others. The resulting empire, which took its name from its capital, Gao, on the Niger bend, was even more extensive than that of Mali. It reached further north to include the important salt mines at the southern frontier of what is now Algeria and eastward to Kano in what is now Nigeria, though it never reached as far to the west.

The Gao Empire was at its height in the sixteenth century. Muslim religious leaders and merchants were brought into an administration of provincial governors and also central ministries for such departments as Finance, Justice, Home Affairs, Agriculture, Forests, and even "White People"—the Moors and Tuareg who lived in the Saharan outskirts. Timbuktu was the intellectual center, and the famous university there taught theology, law, rhetoric, grammar, and literature. Its faculty included lecturers from Cairo and Fez along with local scholars. In 1590 the empire was invaded from the north by Moroccan forces armed with cannons and muskets. As an historian in Timbuktu who lived through the ensuing turmoil would record: "From that moment everything changed. Danger took the place of security; poverty, of wealth. Peace gave way to distress, disasters and violence."[13]

Empires on the scale of Mali and Gao were more easily created in the region of the savannah, where armies could use horses or camels for mobility, as could merchants for transport and trade. To the south stretched the vast region of tropical Africa, rich in forest. Here, where travel and trade were generally on foot or by canoe, little foreign influence infiltrated to affect that black African accommodation with the environment informing the animist view of a spiritualized Nature. This was a region of simple village life, of market towns and of city states, with varied artistic traditions that reached far back into the past.

Accidental finds leading to excavations in the valley above the confluence of the Niger and Benue Rivers provided evidence of a notable culture, named the Nok after the village site of the first few finds in 1928. The pottery consists mainly of sculptured human heads and figures. The heads have eyes often triangular in shape, with pupils usually pierced and with stylized eyebrows. The thick-lipped mouths are sometimes open, and the broad noses have pierced wide nostrils. There are various elaborate hairstyles, some of which may still be seen in use by people of the region today. Figures are modeled with decorative dress, hats or caps, and much jewelry. The faces range widely in expression, from the composed and contemplative to the inquiring and awed.

The figures vary greatly in height, and the firing of the larger ones, done without the use of kilns, attests to considerable skill. Those which have survived complete have a head-to-body ratio of 1:3 or 1:4, when the natural ratio is 1:7. "These are the so-called 'African proportions,' still used by many tribes and nations; proving that, amazingly, African aesthetic traditions extend over 2,500 years."[14] The dating of Nok sculpture reaches from 500 B.C. to A.D. 200. Moreover, since the art is highly developed, the likelihood is that it derived from local skills that developed much earlier. Nor was pottery the only medium. Objects made of wrought iron, together with quantities of iron slag from smelting furnaces, have been found and dated back to the fifth century B.C.

How and why the Nok culture came to an end remains a mystery. The Ife culture of the Yoruba people in the region also produced almost life-size pottery figures, and their sculptures have such Nok characteristics as triangular eye shapes and elaborate hairstyles. No evidence of any other kinship between the two cultures has been found, but a common ancestry is possible and seems likely.

The Yoruba number upwards of twelve million today, most of whom live in the southwest of what is now Nigeria, and linguistic evidence points to Yoruba settlement of that area for several thousand years. Their legends credit the town of Ile-Ife with having been founded by the ancestral Odudua, sent by Olorun, God of the Sky, to create the world. Certainly, Ile-Ife became, roughly a thousand years ago, an important city state that was the home of the Oni, or the religious head of the Yoruba. It became, too, an artistic center whose terracotta and copper-alloy sculptured works are among the greatest to have emerged from any culture.

These objects have been dated to a period from the twelfth to the sixteenth century, but radiocarbon testing in the area suggests that the site was occupied some six centuries earlier, and the sculptures are generally so accomplished that a long preparatory phase is probable. The metal figures are naturalistic, though virtually all of them have the head-to-body ratios of the African aesthetic tradition. The faces have such a composed beauty that Leo Frobenius, the German ethnographer, who acquired some Ife works in 1910, could not bring himself to accept that these were black African in origin and postulated that they had been produced by Greeks from the legendary lost city of Atlantis. Frobenius himself found evidence of a substantial glass industry in the area, and excavations have found beads with datings that range from the ninth to the twelfth century.

The wealth of Ile-Ife came in part from the tribute paid to its religious supremacy and in part from its position across the major trade route northward from the forests. In the sixteenth or seventeenth century, it lost its economic importance, while retaining its religious primacy. Power shifted to the city state of Benin among the Edo people and to the Yoruba city state of Owo, situated between Benin and Ife. Both Benin and Owo produced their own great works of art, influenced by the creative style of Ife.

Such states were political and economic centers within a complex of trade routes that connected towns and villages throughout the greater part of West Africa between the Sahara and the sea. Regular markets afforded the exchange of foodstuffs for local manufactures, while the long-distance trade was dominated by Mande and Hausa merchants in the savannah and by Yoruba ones in the forest region. Since most communities grew or manufactured enough for basic needs, and transport in the forest region was difficult and costly, the commodities of the long-distance trade were generally those that had a high value in relation to their bulk. Except for salt, they were luxuries for use by kings and nobles, administrators and the higher military, court artists, and merchants trading either as royal agents or on their own behalf. The states sustaining this class of elevated consumption acquired much of their substance, along with their expansionist dynamic, from the tribute paid by subjects and dependencies.

The West African Sudan or savannah region sent southward salt from the north, horses prized more for the status they conveyed than for any real military use they could have in the forest region, copper and its alloys, cutlasses, cloth from North Africa and the savannah, and cowrie shells imported through Egypt from the edges of the Indian Ocean. In return, the forest region sent northward gold dust, mainly from workings in the interior of what came to be called the Gold Coast; kola nuts, which were the more valuable for being one of the very few stimulants allowed by Islam; ivory, stone, or glass beads; and slaves.

West African societies had slaves: as royal retainers, often in metalworking and other honored occupations, as agricultural labor, and as porters for the trading caravans. References to the export of black slaves to North Africa only begin appearing in the twelfth century, however, and it was only with the mounting European demand from the sixteenth century onward that the large-scale trade in slaves from the forest region developed. This trade would become the dominant factor in politics across much of black Africa. It would set armies marching and have an impact hundreds of miles inland from the coast. Some states would expand, others shrink or vanish, in the engagement to supply the trade. ·

Benin was one city state which initially profited. We have a description of its capital from a Dutchman in 1602 that is especially interesting because it concerns not only the "King's Court," with its "gates upon gates," but a city and suburbs which attest to a large prosperous class.

"The town seemeth to be very great; when you enter into it, you go into a great broad street, not paved, which seems to be seven or eight times broader than the Warmoes street in Amsterdam; which goeth right out and never crooks . . . ; it is thought that that street is a mile long [a Dutch mile, roughly equal to four English ones] besides the suburbs . . . When you are in the great street aforesaid, you see many great streets on the sides thereof, which also go right forth . . . The houses in this town stand in good order, one close and even with the other, as the houses in Holland stand . . . Their rooms within are four-square, over them having a roof that is not closed in the middle, at which place the rain, wind and light come in, and therein they lie and eat their meat; but they have other places besides, as kitchens and other rooms."[15]

Benin was, however, unable to cope with the costs of the disruption and warfare that the slave trade generated. Some of its dependencies, such as Lagos on the coast, successfully rebelled. By the middle of the eighteenth century, it was in marked decline. The Yoruba state of Oyo, with its capital at Katunga near the middle Niger, was now advancing its own imperial ambitions.

Having expanded northward, Oyo power moved south to absorb Lagos and Badagri, both of them important ports of embarkation for the slave trade. Immediately to the west were a number of small states, inhabited by the Fon, Adja, and kindred peoples. Two of these states, Ardra and Whydah (Ouidah), had begun engaging in the slave trade during the seventeenth century, and the quantity of slaves that they supplied was so immense that the area came to be called the Slave Coast. Some seventy miles north was the related state of Dahomey. Its rulers reacted to the success of Oyo by imitating it. By early in the eighteenth century, it had swallowed both Ardra and Whydah.

Further west, a number of small states around Kumasi, in reaction to the threat from neighbors, united at the end of the seventeenth century in the so-called Ashanti Confederacy. By Ashanti tradition, it was Osei Tutu, king of Kumasi, and his chief priest, Okomfo Anokye, who reinforced the alliance with a culminating act of imaginative statecraft. They introduced the Golden Stool of Ashanti, a wooden stool adorned with gold, as the embodiment of a national spirit transcending local affiliations.[16] The new nation became an expansionist one, moving northward to command increasing supplies of slaves for the Atlantic trade and then south toward the ports of embarkation. By early in the nineteenth century, it was disquieting the British, whose interventions would.at last lead in 1874 to Britain's establishment of formal rule over the whole area as the Colony of the Gold Coast.

Recent scholarship has concentrated on the history of western-central Africa, a vast region encompassing Cameroon in the north and Angola in the south and extending to the great lakes in the east. It is a region from which 40 percent or more of all slaves seized by the Atlantic trade are now calculated to have come.

Using mainly the tool of linguistics to identify and date the movement of peoples and developments in culture, one scholar, Jan Vansina, has explored the history of Equatorial West Africa in his *Paths in the Rainforest*.[17] Though "rainforest" is, indeed, generally applied to this vast expanse, it contains, as Vansina stresses, some of the most complex ecosystems anywhere in the world, from permanently inundated forest and mighty rivers to coastal mangroves and dry-soil savannahs sometimes hundreds of miles in extent.

From the Benue Valley in Nigeria, Bantu-speaking farmers and trappers, with a knowledge of pottery, began migrating there in roughly 3000 B.C. The indigenous hunter-gatherers were no match for them and may well have been drastically reduced in numbers by the new diseases which migrated with the newcomers, who also arrived with a ceramic technology that afforded cooked food and accordingly better nutrition. From the fourth century B.C., iron smelting spread through the area, which came to be fully settled certainly by A.D. 1000 and perhaps five centuries earlier. To their new home, the Bantu speakers brought such basic features of their culture as their three interlocking social groups—the House, the village, and the district.

The House, traditionally the unit of food production with from ten to forty members—though old established Houses could encompass hundreds—had at its center the "big man," a term linguistically related to others, such as "fame," "honor," and "to become rich." Essentially involved in the very concept of wealth was the ability to attract followers by way of gifts, in a competitive environment where free men might join one or other House by choice. Different words for "dependent" and "friend" were evidence that the development of a House extended beyond relationships by marriage, though marriage was the key to increasing the number of resident women and attracting young men.

Freedom of choice extended beyond the House. "Each House freely chose which village its members wanted to belong to, and each village freely chose other villages as allies to make up a district."[18] The village was an aggregate of Houses, led by the "big man" who had founded it but assisted by the "big men" of associated Houses in the village council. "Village communities were thought of as a single family whose father was the village headman, and the big men of each House were his brothers."[19]

The district came into being with the association of various villages for common defense, trade, and intermarriage. Essentially, it was an alliance of Houses, which developed into a "clan" or "tribe" with the reinforcement of a common identity through some particular taboo and a tradition of descent from a single ancestor.

The dynamic of alliances for defense presupposed the possibility of attack, and competitiveness did lead to war. This took two distinct forms, each with its own name. The first, "restricted war," had its own set of rules, protective of life and property. The form that was more frequent between one village and another, it was usually stopped by the elders of the belligerent groups after one or two serious casualties. "Destructive war," a term related to the word "to burn," was more frequent between one district and another. It was from such war that "captives" were likely to be taken and become slaves, regarded as dependents without any claims to gifts as a source of allegiance.

Trade developed in such basic commodities as farm produce, metals and metal objects, salt, fish, raffia cloth, pottery, canoes, and redwood powder for skin care, as well as in such luxuries as special shells and furs which enhanced the prestige and authority of their owners. "As to an early slave trade, there is clear linguistic evidence only for pawning in early times, but not for a trade in people as commodities."[20]

The Bantu-speakers believed in a "real" world beyond the apparent one. In this "real" world were the powerful spirits of departed heroes, nature spirits linked to a village domain or a district, and even a "supreme" spirit, sometimes conceived as that of a first ancestor, sometimes as a first Creator. Associated with all this was a belief in charms, as instruments for the exercise of power, and in witchcraft, as an instrument of evil, itself conceived to be always and only the work of humans.

Since witchcraft was generally held to be the product of envy, there was a corresponding recognition of the need to avoid this by sharing rather than accumulating goods. Such sharing harmonized with the practice of attracting and securing the allegiance of followers through gifts and supported an ideology of cooperation despite the social inequalities of "big men" and dependents. Indeed, even those slaves who, in the course of time, became accepted as members of the community, could come to be the recipients of gifts.

Almost everywhere in the region by A.D. 1000, societies were in general no larger than the district composed of four or five villages. Already, however, this equilibrium was coming under pressure, as one or another society grew more powerful than its neighbors by attracting or generating more people to mobilize. In certain instances, this led to a considerable extension in the scale of political entities. In the most notable example, the Kongo to the southwest moved from being societies of 500 members each in A.D. 500 to one of 500,000 by roughly 1400.

Yet this drive to centralization in the cause of security was undertaken at the cost of local autonomy, and an autonomy still so prized that control by the state over the villages remained restricted to a few activities, even sometimes only to the payment of tribute. More significant were the numerous societies which resisted this trend and whose local leaders conceded cooperation only to such specific engagements as trade or occasional military assistance. "That is the distinctive contribution and the special lesson to be learned from equatorial Africa in the world's panoply of political institutions. The inexorable march forward from local community to chiefdom, to principality, to kingdom or state, proposed by unilineal social evolutionists was not the only possible option."[21]

Nor were these by any means static societies. They learned more about their habitats than they needed in order to survive merely as they were. They discovered or encountered and adopted new technologies. They tested new plants and experimented with new medicines. In short, they practiced science, in a productive relationship with their environment.

The Atlantic trade battened on the societies, large and small, of western-central Africa by distorting a crucial element of their functioning. In the competition of "big men" for prestige and authority, the decisive factor was the number of people they controlled, both as the measure of wealth and as the means of producing it, through procreation and labor. People, not goods, were the prize, and the goods acquired through production or trade were invested in acquiring the allegiance or dependence of more people. In kingdoms such as that of the Kongo, powerful provincial lords required correspondingly large gifts to secure their allegiance, though they might then mitigate their obligations by dispatching tribute in return. At the other extreme, those arriving as captives or as refugees from drought and famine required no further gifts for their subordination, since they were already being given their lives.

The Atlantic trade inserted into this system goods not indigenously produced and correspondingly more potent in the competition for prestige and authority by acquiring followers and dependents. Moreover, such goods came not only in considerable quantities but on easy credit terms, so that men previously marginal to the established patterns of trade could leapfrog their way to wealth and power. The catch was that the suppliers of these goods increasingly required in return not other material goods, but people. As Joseph Miller, the historian of the Angolan slave trade, has commented: "The irony, and the tragedy, was that many of these new men found it possible in the long run to maintain access to the goods that gave the power they had won only by sacrificing the very dependents they had set out to keep."[22]

In 1483, the Portuguese arrived from the sea and encountered the kingdom of the Kongo, which extended southward from the Zaire river estuary. They established peaceful relations and supplied, along with missionaries, skilled artisans and even several white women to instruct their Kongo counterparts in Portuguese domestic economy. They also sent their traders, who increasingly took to exchanging their much desired goods for local dependents. Since the provision of these soon proved inadequate to the appetite for slaves, the Portuguese financed *pombeiros* or peddlers who traveled for the purchase of dependents at the major markets on the shores of Malebo Pool, at the terminus of a trade route up the middle Zaire River. Evidence that a trade in slaves had not previously existed there was that commercial slaves subsequently came to be called "persons of *nzimbu*" or "persons acquired with Kongo shell money."[23]

By the late 1560s, the volume of the trade in slaves topped 7,000 a year and was having widespread repercussions. In 1568, the Jaga invaded Kongo and almost conquered the kingdom, in the first attempt by an inland people of the region to exclude intermediaries from the trade route to the coast. They were finally defeated in 1576 only because a Portuguese army intervened to help the Kongo king, but the price was high. The Portuguese carved out of Kongo territory a colony of their own called Angola, with a harbor at Luanda which would soon become the hub of the slave trade.

Regular trading caravans now comprised parties of *pombeiros*, some of them supplied by the Dutch, who initially sought ivory and redwood but were then drawn into the slave trade, and who concentrated their activities at Loango, the coastal city of the Loango kingdom north of the Zaire River. The resource area for the Atlantic trade expanded in direct relation to the demand for slaves, with a front of social turbulence at its edge but with turbulence, too, behind. As more of the trade came to be dominated from Luanda, the financial power of the Kongo kings declined, with their once widely accepted national shell currency subject to severe inflationary pressures. In 1636, the coastal prince of Soyo seceded from the state, which collapsed altogether in 1665, when the Kongo king was killed at the battle of Ambwila against a Portuguese army.

The Atlantic slave trade would continue for more than two hundred years.

It involved in its course the Portuguese, Dutch, British, French, Brazilians, and Spanish Cubans. If the estimate of 40 percent is accepted as the baseline for the proportion of the total trade for which the region accounted, some 4,745,000 slaves were taken on ships from western-central Africa, and at least as many people died as a direct result of the trade before the slaves were brought aboard.

2 | PIECES OF PEOPLE

~~~~~~

The New World encountered by Columbus was duly claimed for Christianity and Spain. Conquest and plunder followed fast. Empire was not designed to be merely patches on a map. Nor was acquiring a host of heathen souls for salvation much more than a pretext, except for those who were professionally engaged in piety. The preoccupation was personal and national enrichment.

The island of Hispaniola, which Spain seized at the start, was slow to provide this. Ornaments worn by the indigenous inhabitants suggested that there were deposits of precious metals to be mined, and the lush vegetation excited interest in the profitable possibilities of agriculture, especially for producing sugar. Yet all this required an investment of labor that the Spanish themselves were more disposed to command than undertake.

The indigenous inhabitants, called Indians under the delusion that Columbus had reached the East Indies from behind, proved to be increasingly unhelpful. They died in multitudes from the diseases, mainly smallpox and measles, which the Spanish brought with them, or from a distress at being subjugated which the promise of having their souls saved by conversion to Christianity did little to relieve.

In 1511, the Crown licensed the dispatch of fifty black slaves to the island for work in the mines. Larger consignments followed, for sugar production on Hispaniola and for gold mining on the island of Puerto Rico, where there were enough slaves by 1527 to mount a formidable revolt. This strain of rebelliousness was regrettable but could be contained by appropriate measures. What mattered was that the blacks were more successful than the Indians at surviving and made, besides, more productive workers while they lived. In fact, they shared with Europeans an acquired resistance to certain diseases, including measles and smallpox, so that if they died from these, they did so in reassuringly smaller numbers than did the Indians, while with their background in intensive African agriculture, they took more easily than did the Indians to the demands of cultivating commercial crops. From the 1520s onward, sugar was produced on Hispaniola as an export commodity, with from eighty to one hundred slaves employed at each *ingenio* or mill.

Indians, nonetheless, possessed one distinct advantage. They did not need to be bought, but were there for the taking. As Spain's American empire expanded from a few islands to more and more of the mainland, so did the fatal consequences for the indigenous peoples within its compass. Crown and Church grew increasingly disquieted. Neither this world nor the next was likely to judge kindly a New Spain whose evident effect on its subjects and converts was to make them extinct. Successive regulations sought to restrict the abuse of Indians.

There stretched an ocean of difference between the commands that issued from Spain and the practices pursued in America. The laws of 1542 which effectively withdrew property rights in enslaved Indians did, however, have an impact, in accelerating the recourse to the use of black slave labor. That black Christians should be viewed as mere property did pose a moral problem. It was avoided rather than solved by a policy of malign neglect. The Crown had early required that in its American domains black slaves should be embraced by Christianity, if only to protect Indian converts from corruption by heathens. This requirement came increasingly to be ignored. The Church, preoccupied with the plight of its Indian converts, left the black slaves to set about their salvation on their own.

In 1500, Portuguese ships reached Brazil, and the Portuguese Crown claimed a territory whose enormous extent it could scarcely suspect. With no evidence yet of precious metal deposits, settlement concentrated on ranching and the growing of grain in the south or on the spread of sugar plantations in the northeast regions of Pernambuco and Bahia.

Initially the Portuguese sought to acquire indigenous Indian labor by a mixture of force and payment in trade goods. But force was cheaper than any form of payment, and trade goods, losing the appeal of novelty, ceased to be an inducement. By the 1540s, the alternative of simple enslavement had been widely adopted. Here, too, both the Crown and the Church soon became concerned about the very survival of their charges. The first Captain-General arrived in 1549 to represent the King and convey his orders that the enslavement of Indians should end. Such intervention was to prove ineffectual. Not until 1758 was the chattel slavery of Indians finally abolished. Meanwhile, Jesuits in the territory took to protective measures of their own. They enclosed within their mission communities as many Indians as accorded with a piety not altogether indifferent to economics. The settlers moved further afield to find Indians for enslavement.

For all the expanse of Brazil and the persistence of the settlers, the demand for labor far outstripped the availability of Indians to supply it. There were too few of them—perhaps less than a million in all—and many of these died from immigrant diseases, ill-treatment, and despair. Even the protection afforded by the Jesuits often proved fatal, since it was accompanied by the insistence that the Indians abandon their habits of nakedness and regular washing for the clothes and accumulating filth of civilized modesty. That they survived at all was mainly due to the reaches of rain forest in which some of them were concealed.

The solution to the labor problem in Brazil was inevitably found in the resort to black slaves, the first of whom were imported in the 1530s, and whose numbers would rapidly increase with the expansion of the sugar industry in the 1570s. For the Portuguese were peculiarly well placed to provide their new colony with black slaves. They were established on islands in the Atlantic, particularly São Tomé, from which they traded for slaves on the Guinea bulge of the mainland, while far to the south they were established on the mainland itself, for a trade spreading through the region of western-central Africa.

Spain, so preoccupied by the expansion of its American empire that it had neglected a trade now dominated by the Portuguese, Dutch, French, and English, turned for slaves to a system of *asientos* or licenses. These were granted to foreign shippers who contracted to supply slaves within a stipulated period. Most of these contracts specified not the number of slaves to be delivered but the quantity of what were termed *piexas de India*, or "pieces of India," which represented units of potential labor in the "Indies" of America. Each piece corresponded to an adult male in prime physical condition. A female, child, adolescent, or adult male beyond his prime was variously valued as a part of the standard piece.

The truth was that considerations of humanity would have made the business of slavery economically unsustainable. Slaves needed to be regarded not as people at all but as pieces of machinery in a productive process, with their value based on the money to be made out of them, minus the capital expended on their purchase and the share of revenue devoted to their operational costs.

The correspondence of status and color facilitated dehumanization. The naturally black came to be identified with the naturally inferior, fit for a form of bondage fundamentally different from that of the indentured whites on whom English colonial settlement in America first relied for its labor force. These whites were individually bound for a stipulated period to their masters, and indentures could be sold by one master to another without the consent of the laborers concerned. The ownership of the service was not, however, the ownership of the servant. The person was not property. This was implicit both in the term of the indenture and in the nature of most indentures as voluntary contracts. In fact, as reports circulated at home about conditions in the colonies, recruitment required the concession of ever shorter terms and became increasingly difficult all the same.

Black slaves had no choice. They were not only property themselves but could procreate it. The child of a female slave became at its birth the property of her owner. There were, to be sure, legal ways for slaves to escape their status. Since owners had property rights to their slaves, they were, outside the obstacles to this that later came to be enacted in the South of the United States, entitled to free them. Moreover, there were provisions, varying in scope and application, for slaves to buy their own freedom. Accordingly, while virtually all slaves were black or, in the course of miscegenation, at least partly so, there were blacks and mulattoes who were free within the slave-owning system. These remained, however, exceptions whose very freedom was circumscribed in practice by the rule that identified race with slavery.

White traders, planters, overseers, and agents were so close to the system that they ceased to see its brutalities for what they were. Yet the paradox was that familiarity bred passion and affection as well as contempt. For slaves were not only property but persons. The measure to which they were viewed as both was often connected to their function. Domestic slaves were generally treated better than were field laborers. There was symbolism as well as convenience and display in the different way servants and laborers were clothed. Women slaves could become the confidants of their mistresses, the concubines of their masters, the mothers of their masters' children. Cast in the role of nannies, they might survive to serve the masters who had clung to them in childhood. Yet, aside from the relatively few so favored as to be given their freedom, they remained property, and passion or affection did not preclude contempt. Most slaves were treated very badly, and even those who were treated well were still victims of their chattel status.

Elsewhere, among the beneficiaries of slavery, it was distance rather than closeness that helped to make the brutalities acceptable. The owners of German factories that sold trade goods to slavers knew little and cared less about the way in which the slaves were captured, taken to the coast, and transported across the Atlantic. British and French investors in slave-trading companies did not consider themselves responsible, if they considered the matter at all, for the treatment meted out to the slaves by their masters in America.

The Spanish definition of slaves as "pieces" was more than a technical term for calculating potential labor. It reflected a view of black people that was the first principle and ultimate abomination of the Atlantic trade in slavery.

3 | MERCHANTS AND MARKETS

~~~~~~

The French empire in the Caribbean began with the activities of French adventurers who established themselves, often as pirates, on tiny islands. With the increasing interest and involvement of the French government, the seizure and settlement of Guadeloupe followed in 1626; of Martinique, in 1635; and, thirty years later, of Saint Domingue, the western third of the island which had once been called Hispaniola and was then renamed Santo Domingo.

French chartered monopoly companies were soon engaged in the supply of slaves not only to the colonies of France but also to those of other Western European states. Spain in 1701 gave France an asiento to deliver some 4,000 "pieces" a year for a fifteen-year period. The existing companies proved incapable of meeting the requirements. The very size of the contract, the mounting demand of the French colonies for slaves, and the outbreak of war in Europe led to such shortfalls in delivery that Spain canceled the asiento and gave one to Britain instead.

The arrival of peace in 1713 was followed by an economic boom, and the French plantation colonies needed so much labor that the French Crown ended the system of chartered monopoly companies in the slave trade. Merchants residing in particular privileged ports were encouraged to enter the trade. Inducements included exemption from export duties on all French manufactured goods that were used in acquiring slaves, and a 50 percent cut in French import duties on sugar and other merchandise from the islands acquired by the sale of slaves there.

By 1741, virtually all French ports had been granted rights to take part in the colonial trade. By then, however, two of them had opened an immense lead: Bordeaux, in general commerce; and Nantes, with the rewards of specialization, in the supply of slaves. From 1700 to 1793, a total of 3,321 French ships collected slaves in Africa and landed just over one million of them in America. Of these ships, 1,143 or over a third came from Nantes alone.[1]

Situated on the River Loire and near the Atlantic, Nantes became, thanks to the slave trade, a town of renowned riches amidst the poverty of the Breton countryside. And here, as in other French ports, the trade was dominated by local merchants whose use of that sophisticated instrument, the company with limited liability, attracted finance from investors and speculators far afield. The largest of such companies in Nantes was that of the partners Riedy and Thurninger, one of whom was a Protestant immigrant from Switzerland and the other a Protestant from Alsace.

Like the Jews, the Protestants, a religious minority subject to intermittent persecution in France, tended to form financial alliances with their coreligionists abroad. Doctrinal differences with Catholic Christianity did not extend to the morality of making money out of slaves. Protestant companies had particularly strong connections with Protestant merchants and bankers in Switzerland, where an ardent desire had been ignited to participate in the profits of the growing trade. Only in La Rochelle, however, among the important French ports engaged in the trade, were most of the major traders Protestant. Despite the primacy of Riedy and Thurninger, the trade in Nantes was dominated by Catholic-owned companies.

The usual practice was to raise separate finance for each slaving expedition, which itself became a company of limited liability. A merchant or more often a merchant company would take responsibility as *armateur* or outfitter and sell shares in the expedition to various investors, who might well be other merchants acting as outfitters for like ventures. Roughly a fifth of all investments made in the Nantes-based slave trade in the period 1783–92 came from the purchase, by local outfitters, of shares in one another's expeditions. Only one tenth came from investors who were not local residents. The large majority of the hundred or so local outfitters retained between 30 and 50 percent of the shares in the expeditions they mounted.

In more than half the recorded expeditions, the captain of the ship acquired a stake, usually 10 percent, and the ship's other officers could also subscribe for shares, though few had the means to buy much of a holding. Many outfitters would press such investments, since this was not only a convenient way of raising money but provided captain and officers with a corresponding inducement to promote the success of the expedition. Local suppliers, too, might be persuaded to accept shares in part or full payment for such provisions as rope or such services as carpentry.

Shares in slaving expeditions were as marketable as were shares in other commercial enterprises. There were blue-chip shares in ships fitted out by leading merchant companies of reassuring repute and resources. There was even provision for preferred shares which commanded a premium of 25 to 30 percent payable as soon as the ship returned home. There developed a thriving business in insurance, with rates that could fall below 5 percent of an expedition's net worth in untroubled times or rise in times of war to as much as 50 percent. In a port as important as Nantes, insurance was available locally, from merchants who combined to form temporary companies for the purpose. There were merchant companies, however, that chose to make their insurance arrangements abroad. Some even insured their ships on the British market while France and Britain were at war. Patriotism was seldom permitted to interfere with the protection of capital.[2]

The slave trade was the basis of an economic activity much greater than itself. The value of sugar and coffee entering French ports, for instance, alone far exceeded the market cost of the slaves provided to produce it. In Nantes, *indiennage*, or the manufacture of printed cloth, was the principal industry. Such cloth was a staple of exchange for slaves in Africa. Nantes was the prime port for shipbuilding. The slave trade was the prime market for ships. A local hardware industry came into being because the outfitting of slave ships required it. The refining of sugar was an obvious industrial development from the vast imports of sugar which, along with other colonial products, the merchants of Nantes took in partial payment for the slaves they sold or which they bought as cargo for the voyage home. Successful local merchants in the slave trade invested in these industries, just as successful local industrialists invested in the slave-trading merchant companies.

The French slave trade was immensely profitable in itself. At its height, some 30,000,000 livres—or around £1,200,000 in sterling equivalent—were annually being committed to it. There were, to be sure, risks involved. Merchants and investors might suffer losses and even ruin through imprudence or misfortune. Yet the rewards were often spectacular enough to excite much speculative investment. It was here that the risks were increased by the system of phased payments for slaves which developed to deal with the chronic indebtedness of many colonial planters, inefficient in their operations or extravagant in their lifestyle. Those who, without capital of their own, borrowed from the banks to invest in a slaving venture might find themselves in trouble merely from the delay in the realization of profits.

Most of the leading slave traders in Nantes came from already established commercial families. Some came from higher up the social scale. Three generations of the aristocratic Espivent family had substantial investments in the trade. Moreover, riches had a levitating quality. Even in the supposedly rigid class structure of France before the Revolution, there were major slave traders who either bought their way into the nobility or—in what was often only another way of putting this—had such status bestowed on them for services to the state. There were also those who rose from the lower reaches of society to riches through the trade. Some began as clerks to outfitters and worked their way into partnership. It helped, however, to have a little capital with which to begin the climb. Louis Drouin in Nantes was given such a beginning with an inheritance from his ship-captain father and made, mainly through slave trading, a fortune estimated at 5,000,000 livres in 1789.

Slave traders were, in fact, among the richest merchants in eighteenth-century France. The worth of the slave trading community in Nantes alone was some 50,000,000 livres or the equivalent of £2,000,000. What such a sum meant in the eighteenth century may be inferred from William Pitt's statement in 1798 that Britain's annual income from its West Indian colonies was £4,000,000 compared to £1,000,000 from the rest of the world.[3] Of the 146 slave traders in Nantes, there were eight each of whom was worth around 2,000,000 livres, and five each of whom was worth at least 4,000,000.[4]

These traders were preoccupied with making their money work for them and were not above haggling over a single sou. A certain Guillet de la Brosse, hardly among the indigent, protested against a tax demand for four livres and 17 sous on one of his holdings. He insisted that one livre would be appropriate and eventually agreed to pay three. Nor were they famous for their charity. On founding a new company with a capital of 150,000 livres, Riedy and Thurninger, who were worth millions, distinguished themselves by donating 100 livres a year to the local poor. It is not surprising that such merchants regarded the slaves in whom they dealt as mere ledger entries.

Large as was the French trade in slaves, the British one was much larger. In the period 1701–1810, British ships transported an estimated 2,467,000 slaves from Africa, while French ships transported 969,000.[5] The early trade was conducted by the Royal African Company, invested with a monopoly in 1672. The Duke of York was Governor of the company and remained so after becoming, as James II, King in 1685. Among the many shareholders was John Locke, the most influential philosopher of the age, not least for his arguments in favor of liberty.

The Glorious Revolution of 1688, which put an end to the reign of James II, put an end as well to the company's monopoly. It became the right of every freeborn citizen to trade in slaves. This was not a right which capital and enterprise were disposed to ignore as the demand for slaves in the sugar colonies soared. In the years 1680–86, the Royal African Company had transported an annual average of 5,000 slaves. In the first nine years after the company's monopoly ended, the port city of Bristol alone accounted for the shipment of some 161,000 slaves, an average annual rate of almost 18,000. In 1771, no fewer than 190 ships, with total accommodation for 47,000 slaves, left British ports.[6] By then, the merchants of Liverpool, through reducing costs and undercutting rivals, dominated the trade. By 1795, ships from the port were accounting for five-eighths of the British slave trade and three-sevenths of the total European one.

The rewards could be enormous. The slaver *Ann*, for instance, left Liverpool in 1751 with an outfit and cargo costing £1,604 and returned to record an extraordinary net profit of £3,287, but profits of around 100 percent were not rare. By the 1780s, the slave trade was estimated to be bringing Liverpool alone a clear annual profit of £300,000. There were risks involved, and difficult times. Between 1773 and 1788, mainly due to the outbreak and impact of the American Revolution, twelve of the leading houses in the trade went bankrupt, and others sustained substantial losses. Yet the proceeds from the easy times more than made up for such reverses, not least for the overall economy. The importance of the slave trade to Britain could scarcely be exaggerated. Malachi Postlethwayt, an eighteenth-century writer on economic matters, described it as "the first principle and foundation of all the rest, the mainspring of the machine which sets every wheel in motion."[7]

The trade contributed mightily to making Britain the leading naval as well as commercial power in the world. There was then much less difference than there would come to be between the merchant vessel and the warship; the one could be speedily adapted to meet the needs of the other. The shipbuilding industry itself correspondingly expanded, as did the ancillary trades. To supply its ships, Liverpool alone had fifteen manufacturers of rope in 1774.

The provision of goods to exchange for slaves promoted the rapid growth of the related industries, notably the manufacture of cotton cloth, which was concentrated at Manchester. By the late eighteenth century, that city was exporting goods to Africa worth some £200,000 a year and employing in their manufacture some 180,000 men, women, and children. Cotton, indeed, provided a classic example of the cumulative profits to be made out of what came to be called the triangular trade. Cotton goods were profitably exchanged for slaves in Africa; the slaves were sold profitably in America, partly in profitable exchange for cotton; and in Britain the cotton was profitably manufactured into cloth.[8]

Trinkets such as brightly colored beads, often made of glass, whether as a commodity in themselves or strung into necklaces and bracelets, were part of any consignment for the African market, just as bottles were a part of any consignment for the colonial one. Bristol, the leading British port for the slave trade until Liverpool rose to dominance, came to be preeminent in the manufacture of glass. The metal industry, too, thrived on the trade. Some products—fetters, chains, padlocks, branding irons—were implements of slavery. Others—copper wire, iron bars, brass pans and kettles, guns— were trade goods for procuring slaves. The gunsmiths of Birmingham accounted the African market their principal customer, though the West Indian colonies, with their own need of guns, were prized customers as well.

The main product of slavery was sugar, and Britain secured for itself the profits from the refining process by the simple expedient of prohibiting the colonies which produced the crude sugar from establishing refineries. Rum, imported from the colonies or produced in Britain, was served not only in moderate quantities to sailors but in immoderate ones to lubricate bargains with African slave traders. One such trader, invited by the captain of a slave ship to dinner and provided with enough rum to induce unconsciousness, awoke to find himself stripped of his clothes and gold, branded and enslaved.[9]

It was the growing challenge to British colonial sugar from cheaper supplies elsewhere in America that first reinforced the moral arguments against slavery with the material ones for free trade. Why, asked the ironmasters of Birmingham and the cotton manufacturers of Manchester, sustain a slave trade that effectively favored the colonial production of commercial rivals and the whole system of closed colonial markets? While Britain wasted money on buying costly sugar from its colonies of declining productivity, other countries bought competitively, from their colonies or from the open market, sugar provided by the labor of slaves that British traders supplied. Yet the very same countries restricted or closed their domestic or colonial markets to British manufactures. A fast industrializing Britain had everything to gain from promoting an end to the slave trade and in due course to slavery itself, for the spread of a free trading system based on waged free labor.

Confirming the argument for free trade at least, British imports from the United States, mainly of slave-produced cotton, rose in value from $9 million in 1792 to $31 million in 1801. In 1785, the exports of British cotton manufactures topped £1 million in value for the first time. In 1830, such exports were worth some £31 million. Britain abandoned the slave trade in 1807, abolished slavery throughout the empire in 1833, and in 1846 ended the preferential treatment it had for so long afforded its colonial sugar.[10]

Having withdrawn from the slave trade, Britain deplored the continuing participation in it by other countries and employed various pressures on them to outlaw it. A British naval patrol, instituted in 1807 to prevent trading in slaves between British possessions, had the effect of driving the trade into the South Atlantic where, in deference to the profitable alliance with Portuguese interests, Britain recognized the trade in slaves between Portuguese possessions.[11] In 1820, Spain at last formally outlawed the trade, and Portugal followed in 1836. The trade would continue in little-diminished volume until 1850, and survive thereafter, though in sharp decline, until 1870.[12] In the period 1811–70, some 606,000 slaves were imported into Spain's American colonies, essentially Cuba, and some 1,145,000 into Brazil.[13]

Portugal was engaged in the slave trade longer than any other European state and for much of the time had the twofold advantage of colonial control over Angola, a major source of slaves, and colonial control over Brazil, the largest market for slaves. Yet, paradoxically, it was not metropolitan commerce that mainly benefited.

In the sixteenth century, while the leading Lisbon merchants were preoccupied with trading for gold in Africa and spices in Asia, the less glamorous business of buying, transporting, and selling slaves was left to others, among them Portuguese "New Christians"—Jews who had been forcibly converted in 1497. Many of them continued to practice Judaism in secret, but were still subject to periodic persecution in Portugal, and came in increasing numbers to seek a more tolerant home in parts of the Portuguese empire or in Protestant Northern Europe. As with the persecuted Protestants in France, their own experience as victims failed to deter some of them from profitable engagement in the slave trade. Even the development of slave-based sugar production in Brazil was financed not by Portuguese capital but by the Dutch, partly through the commercial enterprise of New Christian families with members in both the Netherlands and Brazil.

By 1640, when a weak Portuguese monarchy was restored after a period of Spanish control, Portugal was at the edge of the rapidly developing Atlantic trade system. The extent of its economic and political vulnerability was such that in 1702 it conceded its entire woolen market to England in return for England's preferential treatment of Portuguese wines.

Lisbon trading houses increasingly became agents of British suppliers to the Brazilian market. Those merchants without British connections and corresponding access to the textiles and other goods in high demand in Brazil turned instead to the Angolan trade in slaves, only to find the way largely blocked there. In the second half of the seventeenth century, a succession of Brazilians appointed to govern Angola, several of whom were linked to planter families in Brazil, had employed their powers to increase the supply and control the export of slaves. In this, they had allied themselves with settlers, many of whom were of mixed Portuguese-African descent and had relatives among African traders.

Lisbon, concerned to develop a colonial commerce less dependent on Britain, prohibited governors of Angola from trading in slaves and employed other pressures, such as export duty requirements, to regain control of the slave trade centered at Luanda. By the 1740s it had succeeded, but its success did not last for long. There was ultimately no competing with the mainly British merchandise, augmented by Brazilian sugarcane brandies, brought by the Brazilian slavers who came increasingly to dominate the Angolan trade.

After Napoleon's invasion of Portugal, British ships transported to Rio de Janeiro in 1808 the Lisbon court and the merchants allied with British commercial interests. In return, by a treaty of commerce and alliance in 1810, Britain was granted the right of unrestricted access for its goods to the Brazilian market and, through Brazil, to Angola. For all its official withdrawal from direct participation in the slave trade, it would continue to participate indirectly, by providing the goods and even finance to supply Brazil with slaves.[14]

What took place in Cuba demonstrated the extent to which governments, merchants, and adventurers could mock, by connivance and collaboration, proclaimed morality and law. Between 1820, when Spain formally abandoned the slave trade, and 1865, some 500,000 slaves were imported into the Spanish colony of Cuba. The returns available on slaving overwhelmed other considerations. In 1835, for instance, the cost of a slave in Africa was equivalent to £4, while the price then prevailing in Havana was at least £84, so that a single successful voyage could produce a profit of £20,000 or $100,000.[15] In Havana, there were twenty-two merchants openly engaged in the trade. Most of them had high connections in Spain, and some would retire there with great riches and no evident injury to their social standing.

Pedro Forcade, among them, had access to British capital and even British partners in his slaving ventures. Ships were built in Liverpool to the order of Havana merchants, despite the likelihood that they were to be used for slave trading. Some were fitted out in Cadiz and returned there after the completion of their voyages. Brazilian traders, for the most part engaged in supplying the Brazilian market for slaves, also served the Cuban one.

Most ships in the Cuban slave trade, however, were built in the United States, in New York or Baltimore, often with the involvement of local capital, and New York provided the main insurance market for slave-trading ventures. At no time were the United States laws against the trade used to mount a prosecution; indeed, the trade continued, more or less surreptitiously, to supply the South as well. The ships built in the United States were an important factor in the failure of much British naval policing. They were designed for speed, and the British patrol vessels, loaded with food and armaments, found it difficult to catch them.

Ships engaged in the trade resorted to carrying flags and papers from more than one country, so that they often evaded pursuit or search by changing from one to another form of identity. Deception was still easier once the ships reached Cuban waters. Until 1835, when the British navy was permitted to check the equipment of suspected slaving vessels on the high seas, arriving ships simply landed their cargo elsewhere on the island and then sailed empty to Havana, where the official inspection found no proof of any engagement in the slave trade. Subsequently, other subterfuges, sustained by the complicity of the local United States consul, sufficed. Since trading in slaves within the Western Hemisphere remained legal, suitable United States shipping papers could transform the illegal trade into the legal one. The evidence of successful contravention was overwhelming. David Turnbull, the British consul in Havana, wrote of the years 1838–39:

> As if to throw ridicule on the grave denials of all knowledge of the slave trade which are forced from successive captains-general by the unwearied denunciations of the British authorities, two extensive depots for the reception and sale of newly imported Africans have lately been erected at the further end of the Paseo, just under the windows of his Excellency's residence, the one capable of containing 1,000 and the other 1,500 slaves; and I may add,

that these were constantly full during the greater part of the time that I remained in Havana. As the barracoon or depot serves the purpose of a market place as well as a prison these two have, doubtless for the sake of readier access and to save the expense of advertising in the journals, been placed at the point of greatest attraction, where the Paseo ends, where the grounds of the Captain-General begin, and where the new railroad passes into the interior, from the carriages of which the passengers are horrified at the unearthly shouts of the thoughtless inmates.[16]

In Africa itself, the illegal trade found appropriate instruments. There, from the 1820s to the late 1840s, the dominant trader was a Portuguese mulatto reportedly born in Cuba, Francisco Felix Da Souza, who acquired a monopoly over slave exports from the region ruled by King Ghezo of Dahomey. Theirs was a partnership in greed and brutality which yielded enormous dividends. With Da Souza's help, Ghezo acquired military control over the whole Slave Coast and in a single year received from the export tax on slaves an income equivalent to £300,000.

The passage from Africa to America became more costly of black lives and more terrible in its torments than it had been since the early days. The illegal trade paid no regard to such regulations as had come to govern the legal one. Slaves were crammed into the available space; and to achieve greater speed, especially when pursued, the ships often moved with closed hatches. Diet and medical treatment were minimal. With profits so high, there was no interest in thrifty management of the cargo, let alone compassion. The slave trade had always been a market for turning misery into money. Its late years, like its early ones, were distinguished principally by their more egregious horror.

4 | TO THE BURNING IRON

~~~~~~

The first business of one of our Factors when he comes to Fida [Ouidah or Whydah, on the Dahomey coast], is to satisfie the Customs of the King and the great Men, which amount to about 100 Pounds in Guinea value, as the Goods must yield there. After which we have free Licence to Trade, which is published throughout the whole land by the Cryer . . . For you ought to be informed that Markets of Men are here kept in the same manner as those of Beasts with us.

Not a few in our Country fondly imagine that Parents here sell their Children, Men their Wives, and one Brother the other: But those who think so deceive themselves; for this never happens on any other account but that of Necessity, or some great Crime: But most of the slaves that are offered to us are Prisoners of War, which are sold by the Victors as their Booty.

When these Slaves come to Fida, they are put in Prison altogether, and when we treat concerning buying them, they are all brought out together in a large Plain; where, by our Chirurgeons, whose Province it is, they are thoroughly examined, even to the smallest Member, and that naked too both Men and Women, without the least Distinction or Modesty. Those which are approved as good are set on one side; and the lame or faulty are set by as Invalides . . .

The Invalides and the Maimed being thrown out, as I have told you, the remainder are numbred, and it is entred who delivered them. In the mean while a burning Iron, with the Arms or Name of the Companies, lyes in the Fire; with which ours are marked on the Breast . . .

I doubt not but this Trade seems very barbarous to you, but since it is followed by meer necessity it must go on; but we yet take all possible care that they are not burned too hard, especially the Women, who are more tender than the Men . . .

When we have agreed with the Owners of the Slaves, they are returned to their Prison; where from that time forwards they are kept at our charge, cost us two pence a day a Slave; which serves to subsist them, like our Criminals, on Bread and Water: So that to save Charges we send them on Board our Ships with the very first Opportunity; before which their Masters strip them of all they have on their Backs; so that they come Aboard stark-naked as well Women as Men: In which condition they are obliged to continue, if the Master of the Ship is not so Charitable (which he commonly is) as to bestow something on them to cover their Nakedness.[1]

This account was written by William Bosman, chief factor or agent of the Dutch West India Company at its main trading station of Elmina Castle, in one of twenty letters to a friend in Holland during the first few years of the eighteenth century. It vividly reveals much about the nature of the slave trade at the source of supply.

The Europeans were essentially shippers and retailers, purchasing their stocks from a variety of African wholesalers—kings, chiefs, and merchants. These wholesalers had a manifest motive to pursue and promote whatever activity procured supplies for a market apparently insatiable. Increasingly, therefore, slaves became both the product and the cause of warfare. Moreover, among the very goods for which they were traded, there were those— guns and gunpowder, swords and cutlasses—which assured success in battle for the capture of yet more slaves.

This did not mean that all slaves were prisoners of war. Slave-raiding bands would kidnap the weak or unwary from peaceful villages. One personal account from a victim of such marauding has come down to us. An eleven-year-old boy, son of an Ibo tribal elder, was kidnapped along with his sister in 1756. After a long and painful journey, the boy was sold to an African goldsmith, who treated him kindly before selling him to European traders. Olaudah Equiano or, as he came to be called, Gustavus Vassa, would strike back tellingly at the trade when his autobiography was published almost forty years later.[2]

The journey to the coast was frequently not only painful but fatal. African slaving routes reached hundreds of miles inland. Roped together, slaves were made to march long distances, in the course of which they suffered much from hunger, thirst, and exhaustion. Some might be sold along the way a number of times before they got within sight of the sea. One West African recalled in 1831 that he had been "sold six times over, sometimes for money, sometimes for a gun, sometimes for cloth . . . It was about half a year from the time I was taken before I saw white people."[3]

The market itself was influenced by the preferences of the ultimate consumers, the colonial purchasers, who entertained the prejudices of their proclaimed personal experience or of conventional hearsay. Such prejudices affected not only prices but the choice of catchment areas.

Mandingos, or the Malinke, from Senegambia were considered intelligent and clean in their habits, "genteel and courteous . . . but lewd and lazy to excess." This apparently made them poor field laborers but suitable for crafts and domestic service. The Ibos, a generic term for the Ibibio and Efik as well the Ibo slaves shipped from the Bight of Benin, were held to be tractable but also unhealthy and with a disquieting tendency to commit suicide in captivity. Angolans were believed to be even more unhealthy and inclined to commit suicide, while being without skills and incapable of learning any, so that they could usefully be put only to the most humdrum of physical tasks. The French and Spanish planters considered the Yoruba, shipped from the Bight of Benin, the best slaves of all, while the British attached this distinction to people from the Gold Coast, especially those shipped from Coromantine, who commanded the highest prices.[4]

Such stereotypes now seem absurd. They also became increasingly irrelevant, as soaring demand overwhelmed consumer discriminations. In Jamaica, for instance, from 1702 to 1725, some 22,300 slaves, or almost 35 percent of the total imported there, came from the Gold Coast, and only some 4,800, or 7.5 percent, from Central Africa. From 1792 to 1807, some 13,900, or little more than 8 percent of the total imported there, came from the Gold Coast, and 59,500, or almost 35 percent, from Central Africa.[5]

African rulers, officials, and merchants involved in the trade were not slow to recognize and exploit the competition for supplies. Those who controlled access to the suppliers, whether or not they were also suppliers themselves, exacted "customs duties." Thomas Phillips, of the *Hannibal* from London, reported indignantly in 1694 of having had to pay six slaves' worth of cowries to the King of Whydah and two slaves' worth to each of his officials "for leave to trade, protection and justice," as well as a total of five and one-half slaves' worth to various local officials supervising or assisting the trade. In 1700, James Barbot, of the *Don Carlos* from London, found himself having to pay, in customs duties, 47 pieces of assorted goods to the King of Cabinda and a total of 82½ pieces more to various officials.[6]

The African supplier soon learned the relative values attached by the European traders to the goods they offered and how to press for the best available bargain. When he suspected a more than usual eagerness to acquire adult males, he might charge accordingly for them; or, if he had too many women and children on his hands, agree to sell adult males only as part of a parcel which included more women and children than the trader would otherwise have taken. Not least, he was well aware that European traders, however seemingly heedless of delay, yearned to conclude their business and be gone, so that the more protracted the process of bargaining, the more likely it was that they would yield from sheer impatience. Here, though, the trader had a weapon of his own. He could always set sail for another site of supply. In fact, it was far from uncommon for a trader to visit several sites in the course of an expedition.

Records reveal that trading experience varied widely. On average, a French

ship spent five months in Africa. The captain of the *Duchesse d'Orléans* from
Le Havre, however, took only thirty-two days to acquire a complement of
338 slaves, while the captain of the *Belle Nantaise* from Nantes took twenty-
nine months before leaving at last with a cargo of only forty-five.[7] If some
such extremes were due to variations in the supply of slaves, others might
well have resulted from difficulties in reaching agreement with suppliers.
Paradoxically, the very same European traders who behaved as though blacks
were fit only to be commodities did business with blacks who were plainly
no less fit than they themselves to be commodity dealers.

The conditions in which slaves were often kept at the ports, until sale and
embarkation, were appalling. At Angola and Benguela on the Angolan coast,
they were generally consigned on their arrival to slave pens known as *quintais*,
a word pertinently also applied to farmyards for keeping animals. At Benguela,
these pens were some seventeen meters square and sometimes contained 150
or even 200 slaves, as well as pigs and goats, within high walls. The stench
from such enclosures was such that visitors to the ports who kept their distance
still found it overwhelming. The slaves who died in these conditions were
buried at Luanda in shallow graves for the hyenas to dig up at night. At
Benguela, they were simply dumped, along with sewage, on the beach, until
at the very end of the eighteenth century, the Luanda option of shallow
graves was adopted instead.[8]

Those who lived long enough to be sold were duly branded with the mark
of ownership. Usually in Africa, this was done once. Those passing through
Luanda were more unfortunate. The Afro-Portuguese who were the suppliers
impressed their personal brands on the arms of the slaves before consigning
them to agents or shippers. Early in the eighteenth century, a further brand
was added as evidence that the export duty had been paid. From at least the
late seventeenth century, an official slave brander burned the royal arms
onto the right breast of slaves as a sign of their vassalage to the Crown.
Overlaying this was added a cross brand, as proof of compliance with the
requirement that black slaves be baptized before embarkation.

Reform regulations in 1813 substituted for branding a metal bracelet or
collar that bore the marks instead. This seems, however, only to have made
it simpler for captains to exchange those slaves of their own who died during
the Crossing for healthy slaves owned by others. In 1818, body branding
was restored, though with a refinement probably more evident to the branders
than to the branded. The irons were required to be made of silver.

For the branded, the pain went deeper than that produced by the burning
iron. By widespread tradition in black Africa, the status of people was expressed by the tattooing of designs on their skin. Branding was a corresponding
indignity and humiliation. The deepest injury, however, came from what
the brand was designed to convey: The slave was a commodity, and not a
person.

5 | THE CROSSING

The first object which saluted my eyes when I arrived on the coast was the sea, and a slave ship which was then riding at anchor and waiting for its cargo. These filled me with astonishment, which was soon converted into terror when I was carried on board. I was immediately handled and tossed up to see if I were sound by some of the crew, and I was now persuaded that I had gotten into a world of bad spirits and that they were going to kill me. Their complexions too differing so much from ours, their long hair and the language they spoke (which was very different from any I had ever heard) united to confirm me in this belief . . . When I looked round the ship too and saw a large furnace or copper boiling and a multitude of black people of every description chained together, every one of their countenances expressing dejection and sorrow, I no longer doubted of my fate; and quite overpowered with horror and anguish, I fell motionless on the deck and fainted.[1]

Such was the account of Olaudah Equiano, recalling his impressions as a boy sold to a European slaver in West Africa. Far to the south, in western-central Africa, were many, among them elders honored for their wisdom, who associated the white men at the coast with the followers of Mwene Puto, the Lord of the Dead. That these white men were cannibals, the great copper kettles to be seen on their ships attested. The bodies of the blacks they took were pressed in those regions of the dead across the water by Mwene Puto, for the cooking oil that his followers brought back to Africa for use in their settlements. The blood of the blacks was returned as the deep red wine which the whites sold. The cheeses of the whites were made from the brains of blacks. The very bones of blacks came back to Africa in the form of that ashlike grey powder that emerged in killing fire from the iron tubes.[2] All this was, to be sure, technically untrue. Yet cannibalism of a kind was an apt metaphor for the experience of slavery.

It is no wonder that rebellions and suicides were frequent enough among the newly embarked to require special precautions. Adult male slaves in particular were kept shackled in pairs by the wrist and leg, sometimes with a chain around the neck as well, while sailors with loaded guns stood on constant guard. Such measures were not, however, proof against the desperate who leapt in their shackled pairs from the side of the ship or turned on their guards for what was usually another form of suicide.

When the slaves were packed below, and the ship set sail, vigilance might be a little relaxed. Conditions in the slave quarters were hideous. The height of the hold could be less than four feet in smaller ships and was seldom above five and one-half feet in larger ones. On many ships, most of this space was divided horizontally by shelves, which meant that few slaves could even sit upright, while the packing of slaves was commonly so close as to allow no room for any to lie stretched out on their backs. Special "wind sails" might coax some movement of air through the gratings, but this could have helped little against the prevailing heat. When the ship stood breezeless for days on end, this heat must have become increasingly distressing. No less so would have been the consequences of a strong wind and a heavy swell for the slaves crowded in the hold.

Extremes of weather could be fatal to many or all on board. Ships were occasionally becalmed for weeks and even months; others, swallowed up in sudden equatorial storms. Experience advised which times of the year to avoid, but the weather could veer from its pattern, while delays at the coast in acquiring an adequate cargo might lead to a gamble with the risks of a late start.

Overcrowding was the product of an untamed as well as untrained profit motive. In 1788, British ships were forbidden to carry more than five slaves for every three registered tons up to a total 207 tons, and from that point on at a rate of only one slave per ton. Eleven years later, the restrictions were tightened further, to one slave per ton regardless of the registered tonnage. Such reforms pointed backward to when it was common for a ship with a displacement of 100 tons to carry 200 slaves, and one of 50 tons more than 100. A certain John Knox testified in the late eighteenth century that he had once carried 450 slaves on his ship of 108 tons and that only eighteen lives had been lost on the voyage.[3] If this was true, then the weather, the speed of the crossing, the health and resilience of the slaves, as well as the skill and care of the captain, must all have been exceptional.

British requirements were not necessarily followed by slavers of other nations. "On the Spanish ship *La Panchiata*, active during the late 1820s, the men on the slave deck sat upright in rows in a space so low that none could stand, legs spread and knees raised so that each occupied the space between the limbs of the man behind. A long chain ran through rings on their arms and was attached firmly to fastenings to the side of the vessel. The chain could presumably be pulled through the rings to release a gang of men for feeding or exercise on deck, but at all other times it bound them together in their sufferings."[4]

It was not only the threat or enactment of tighter regulations that produced better conditions on British slavers. Many captains, after the early stages of the trade, came from sheer intelligent self-interest to take measures for reducing the casualties of the crossing. Their payment was partly related to the number of slaves landed alive and salable in the West Indies. Slaves might be consigned to the open deck during daylight while their quarters were scrubbed, disinfected with vinegar and lime juice, and dried by the burning of tar, tobacco, or brimstone. Children and the more trusted of the adults might even be left under guard to stay on deck during the night.

Exercise came to be recognized as essential to the health of the slave, and this took the form of what was called dancing. Dancing, however, had little to do with it. This was no more than a jumping up and down, as free as the confinement of shackles allowed, with a cat-o'-nine-tails or other instrument to encourage participation. Two meals a day became the norm and consisted of yams or rice, beans, barley, corn or biscuit, with a little meat on rare occasions. Pepper, palm oil, or stockfish might be given as a garnish. A mouthwash of lime juice or vinegar was often added at the morning meal to ward off scurvy. One detailed account of the food provided on a voyage in 1789 gave a daily diet of yam (three pounds and ten ounces), biscuit (ten ounces), beans (three and a half ounces), flour (two ounces), a larger than usual amount of salt beef, and a plantain or ear of corn on three out of every five days.

Yet this was likely to have been slaving at its best, and the bad could be very bad indeed. Brazilian slavers lacked the cash to buy American produce. The provisions stocked for months at the African ports were often vermin-infested and putrid. Captains often devoted space meant for food storage to accommodating slaves instead. Most crucial to slave survival was a sufficient supply of clean water, but here, too, storage space was sacrificed to accommodation for slaves, and the water available at Luanda or Benguela was often poor in all but bacteria. Nor was the Brazilian trade by any means the only one that was deficient in providing enough water. By the 1840s, British expert opinion held that a full gallon or a little over four and a half liters of water should be provided per slave per day. In the eighteenth century, Liverpool slavers customarily carried enough for a provision of something over two liters. French slavers were prescribed three liters but might actually have distributed merely three-quarters of a liter. A Portuguese regulation of 1684 set a ration of 1.375 liters. Survivors frequently recollected thirst as the greatest hardship of the crossing.[5]

Even the best treatment, at least by the standards of the time, availed little against the spread of disease. Overcrowding, poor diet and hygiene simply sped its spread and augmented certain diseases with others. From the Eu-

ropean crew came varieties of the common cold virus which could produce
fatal complications when affecting Africans with low resistance. Even diseases
indigenous to Africa could rage in the close packing of slaves from different
areas with correspondingly different degrees of acquired immunity. Most
costly in lives were the various types of dysentery. Both the "bloody flux"
and the "white flux" were rapid in their ravages and insusceptible of treatment.

In any event, medical treatment was no more effective than medical
ignorance, the inferior skills of "surgeons" ready to accept employment on
a slaving expedition, and the outlay of traders who often combined thrift
with fatalism, allowed. The medicines provided even in the later stages of
the trade were mainly sago, cornflower, spices, and wine. The only benefit
that the ill sometimes enjoyed was their removal to better accommodation,
either on deck at the bows, where they might get the best of the breeze, or
in a compartment set aside as a hospital. Less solicitous treatment extended
from leaving the ill where they were or, in seemingly hopeless cases, antic-
ipating the event. In 1781, the captain of the *Zong*, confronted by an epidemic and knowing that his cargo was covered by insurance, dispatched 132
live slaves into the ocean.

It would have been remarkable if, given the nature of the trade, callousness,
cruelty, and sadism had not been demonstrated by some of the captains.
The records reveal numerous instances, and there must have been many
more that went unrecorded. In 1764, for instance, a certain Captain Marshall
flogged a nine-month-old child because it would not eat; treated its swollen
feet by putting them in water so hot that the skin and nails came off; and,
when it died, battered its mother until she threw the body overboard herself.
A certain Captain Williams delighted in flogging slaves who would not eat,
beat slave women who would not sleep with him, withheld food from sick
sailors, and almost killed the cabin boy, who was his son. That his conduct
became public at all was due to his having knocked unconscious the surgeon,
who subsequently brought suit against him in the courts.

Whatever the conditions and the character of the captain on a particular
ship, slaves did not desist from attempting or committing suicide. They
jumped overboard, cut their throats, or hanged themselves if they could find
the means to do so, refused to eat and frantically resisted forced feeding.
They fell into a "fixed melancholy" which might in some cases have been
the result of nutritional deficiencies but in others seems to have been a dying
by effort of will. The very sight of their destination apparently produced a
rise in suicides. As circumstances allowed, they also rose in revolt.

"By a Vessel lately arrived here from the West-Indies," it was reported in
Boston, "we have Advice, that a ship belonging to Liverpool coming from
the Coast of Africa, with about 350 slaves on board, and when in Sight of
the Island Guadeloupe, the Slaves, as 'tis supposed, being admitted to come

upon Deck to air themselves, took an Opportunity . . . and kill'd the Master and Mate of the Ship, and threw fifteen of the Men overboard, after which they sent the Boat with two white Lads and three or four others to discover what Land it was, meanwhile the Ship drove to the Leeward, which gave the Lads an opportunity to discover the Affair to the Commandant of that Quarter of the Island, who immediately raised about 100 Men, and put them on board a Sloop, who went in Pursuit of the Ship, and in a few Hours took her and carried her into Port Louis."[6]

Various scholars of the Atlantic slave trade have provided their estimates for the mortality rates on the ships of particular nations in particular periods. The overall mortality rate for the Crossing throughout the trade remains so uncertain that current scholarship seems confident only in proposing the wide range of from 10 to 20 percent. Even at the lower end of the range, this would represent more than a million lives lost on the slave ships. At the higher end, it would represent more than 2,200,000.[7]

History itself has a hold crammed with horrors. There is something indecent about conducting a contest in holocausts. It is enough to assert that, by any standards, the Crossing must be accounted among them. Nor does the tally of the dead, whatever it may be, exhaust the extent of the suffering involved. Between five and ten times the number who died survived to be sold. The experience of those who did entered the collective consciousness of the Black Diaspora, as memory, myth, metaphor: often submerged, but never lost.

6 | THE WEALTH OF THE INDIES

~~~~~~

In 1493, Pope Alexander VI drew a vertical line on the map. To the west of this, he recognized Spanish rights over territories in the New World; to the east, Portuguese. The two imperial parties then agreed on their own to adjust the line in a way that enabled Portugal subsequently to claim the expanse of Brazil. None of this geometry impressed other European states.

Francis I, himself a Roman Catholic, but also King of France, dismissed the authority of the Pope in sustaining Spanish claims to America. "I should very much like to see," he commented, "the clause in Adam's will that excludes me from a share in the world." Still less were these claims acceptable to the Dutch, in the process of wresting their Protestant independence from Spain, or to an English Crown in command of its own Church.

As Spanish acquisitiveness advanced through America, to take Mexico in 1519 and Peru in 1526, it seized treasure in such heaps as to seem, especially in the view of those who were denied access to it, virtually limitless. Even after the brazen embezzlement which was a feature of Spain's colonial government, the galleons of Spain brought home dazzling riches. From a trickle worth 8,000 ducats in 1503, the cargoes in the record year of 1587 were worth some 6,500,000.[1]

Plundering the Spanish treasure in America by land and by sea became a form of private enterprise backed by the state and often financed by international venture capital. At the Isthmus of Panama, Drake captured three mule trains of treasure from Peru in an exploit that yielded forty-seven times the cost of the expedition's original investment. Organized smuggling breached Spain's trade monopoly with help from the indolence or corruption of Spanish officials. Above all, Spain's European rivals snatched pieces of the New World for themselves, especially in the Caribbean, where Spanish naval power was stretched too thin for more than occasional assertions of sovereignty.

It was the English who were most seriously engaged in colonizing the Caribbean, and at least 30,000 of them are estimated to have settled on various islands there during the reigns of James I and Charles I in the first half of the seventeenth century.[2] A number of ventures succumbed: some to Spanish or indigenous Carib assault; some to fever; some to the perversity of climate or terrain for settlers intent on re-creating the English countryside. The first English settlement to succeed was on St. Christopher, where English and French joined forces in 1624 to massacre the island's Caribs, beat back Spanish attacks, and share the possession uneasily between them for eighty years. Most successful was the settlement in 1627 of Barbados, where climate and terrain favored agriculture, hostile Caribs were absent, and neither Spanish nor French chose to invade.

The French were soon otherwise occupied in settling Guadeloupe and Martinique, islands with large and undocile Carib populations which it would take the colonists many hard years to subdue and eventually extinguish. Meanwhile, the Dutch, whose large navy and small population made trade more attractive than settlement, seized a few tiny islands, notably Curaçao in 1634, to batten on the nearby colonial trading communities of rivals.

On Barbados, the English settlers used indentured servants to support an agricultural economy of tobacco and a little cotton. When one planter had sent his first shipment to England in 1637, he was informed: "Your tobacco of Barbados of all the tobacco that cometh to England is accompted the worst." A few years later, in 1646, another planter was able to report: "There is a greate change on this island of late, from the worse to the better, praised be God."[3] It was the Dutch, however, rather than God, to whom the praise was due. They had taught the settlers on the island how to make marketable sugar.

With less than 100,000 acres of arable land in all on the small island, individual holdings had yet to be large enough for the capital cost of investment in a sugar mill. In a short period of rapid change, some 200 major sugar producers, with some 200 acres as the average holding, emerged from a series of land purchases, while many hundreds of minor proprietors raised sugar or other crops on remaining, often economically marginal, plots. Trees were so heedlessly felled for sugar land that by the 1650s there was a timber shortage. There was so little arable land left for food production that the island became vitally reliant on supplies from England or the English colonies of North America.

The supply of indentured servants from England was soon inadequate to meet the labor needs of the sugar industry. In Bristol, where many officers of the law were variously associated with sugar interests, a scandalous enthusiasm developed for convicting alleged offenders and sentencing them to service on the plantations in Barbados. Since even this did not suffice, English and Irish youths were simply kidnapped for shipment to the island, in a practice so notorious that the word "barbadosed" entered the language of the seventeenth century as a generic term for the victims of kidnapping.

There were still too few available whites; and among these, too many found their working conditions unacceptable and responded by rebelling or absconding. One favored local punishment was to suspend offenders by their hands and burn matches between their fingers. This did not solve the labor problem either. It was the Dutch again who came to the rescue. They not only informed the planters of how well black slave labor would serve the purpose but proceeded to provide the necessary slaves at a competitive price.

By 1645, George Downing, a visitor to Barbados, was reporting that the islanders "have bought this year no lesse than a thousand Negroes; and the more they buie, the better able they are to buye. For in a yeare and a halfe they will earne (with gods blessing) as much as they cost."[4] In the period 1698–1707, some 36,400 slaves would be landed, or an average of 3,640 a year; and overall, from 1640 to 1807, some 387,000 would be imported, or an annual average of 2,300.[5]

The ratio of black to white steeply increased. In 1655, there were some 20,000 slaves to some 23,000 whites. By 1712, the respective figures were 41,970 and 12,528.[6] Scarcely less remarkable was the growth in the concentration of ownership in both land and slaves. Some forty years from the start of the sugar industry, not quite 7 percent of proprietors owned over 53 percent of all land and over 54 percent of all slaves on the island. Planters predominated in the Council, the Assembly, the courts, and the command of the militia.[7] The slave-owning interest could hardly have been in more effective control, and the slave hardly worse situated for some form of protection.

Indeed, as one slave trader reported in 1693, Barbados became to the black "a more dreadful apprehension . . . than we can have of hell."[8] The estimate of a net natural decrease in the slave population of 6.7 percent a year in the period 1645–72 and of 5 percent a year in the period 1684–1756 speaks forcefully enough of the conditions under which labor was exacted from the slaves.[9] It was, the planters calculated, cheaper to lose slaves from overwork, poor diet, or other ill-treatment and replace them from new imports than to keep more of them alive by more humane methods.

The calculation was sustained by the extent of wealth that brutality generated. In 1661, Charles II created thirteen baronets on this tiny island in a single day. Not one of these had an income of less than £1,000 a year, and some of them had incomes of at least £10,000, an enormous sum that very few in the England of that time could match. There was, however, a cost beyond the unregarded one in slave lives. Intensive cultivation without thought of nourishment impoverished the soil. In 1736, it took two slaves to produce one hogshead of sugar; in 1748, three slaves; and in 1783, six. By 1769, the situation was already considered to be so serious that a ship was engaged to import rich soil from Surinam. But the cargo contained an uncommissioned complement of wood ants which did so much damage to the ship that the engagement was not repeated.

By 1750, the four tiny Leeward Islands of Antigua, Montserrat, Nevis, and St. Christopher were together exporting three times as much sugar as Barbados. The delay in the development of their sugar industry was due only in part to the more difficult terrain. The islands were prizes in an Anglo-French rivalry that erupted in three wars. St. Christopher itself changed hands seven times. Yet these were merely interruptions in a process whose profits had proved so great as to command imitation.

From the 1670s, when Leeward Islanders with the necessary cash or credit took to serious sugar production, development followed the pattern set in Barbados some three decades before. White servants and small-scale farmers departed, while black slaves arrived in increasing numbers. The successful sugar producers augmented their landholdings along with their control of government. In 1672, there were some 4,200 slaves on the Islands. In 1774, there were 81,300. That number emerged from slave imports at an annual average of almost 2,500, or a total of some 339,000 in little over a century. As with Barbados, the slave population of the Leeward Islands suffered a net natural decrease year after year, for a labor deficiency which only the diligence of the slave traders could repair.[10]

In 1655, Jamaica, soon to be the prize among England's Caribbean possessions, was seized from Spanish colonists whose economic activity there had been largely listless. Nine years later, systematic English settlement began. Some of the new colonists were drawn from among the poor whites of Barbados. Others were rich ones in search of fresh soil for sugar. Indeed, sugar was virtually from the outset envisioned as the principal crop, and land grants were correspondingly generous. An ordinary white settler with a wife was given ninety acres; a capitalist with one hundred slaves, three thousand acres. The results were predictable. A sugar industry based on slave labor and dominated by a few plantation magnates was soon flourishing. By 1703, Jamaica had 45,000 slaves. By 1778, it had 205,300. Yet, between 1703 and 1775, the island had imported 469,893 slaves, or well over two slaves for each one added to the population. The development of Jamaica into Britain's prime sugar producer made a few people hugely rich, but at the price of killing a multitude more.

During the eighteenth century, Britain added considerably to its West Indian possessions. The Seven Years' War of 1756–63 with France brought it Dominica, Grenada, St. Lucia, St. Vincent, and Tobago. Of these, only Grenada had already become a sugar island, with a substantial French settlement and many slaves. Now all were soon producing sugar with the labor from sizable slave populations. A late prize was that of Trinidad, seized from the enfeebled hold of Spain in 1797, when the island had roughly 10,000 slaves. Within five years, that number had virtually doubled.[11]

In 1776, Adam Smith wrote: "The profits of a sugar plantation in any of our West Indian colonies are generally much greater than those of any other cultivation that is known either in Europe or America."[12] During the first half of the seventeenth century, West Indian sugar plantations provided an annual return overall of roughly 20 percent on capital invested, though this rate then dropped to below 12 percent in 1775, below 8 percent in 1790, and below 6 percent in 1810. Throughout the period of slave labor, the West Indian planters are estimated to have made an aggregate profit of over £150,000,000, at an average annual rate of £1,000,000 during the eighteenth century.[13]

These were prodigious figures for an era when the purchasing power of the pound was so very much higher than it is today and the usual return on good English farming land was around 3.5 percent. Jane Austen, whose appreciation of contemporary financial values was an important element in her novels, allowed Mr. Darcy, the impressively rich hero of *Pride and Prejudice*, an annual income of £10,000. The actual West Indian fortune of William Beckford, in the eighteenth century, dwarfed such fictional riches. He inherited one million pounds, which, even at the low rate of return on English farming land, would have represented an annual income of £35,000. *The West Indian*, a popular play presented in 1771, regaled London audiences with the dazzling wealth of the sugar planter. "He's very rich," one of the characters reported, "and that's sufficient. They say he has rum and sugar enough belonging to him, to make all the water in the Thames into punch."[14]

Jamaica's trade alone was worth more in 1773 than the trade of all Britain's plantation colonies on the North American mainland. Yet the greater production of wealth in the sugar colonies promoted no disposition to invest there in diversified economic activities and no general attachment among the beneficiaries to the islands that were the source of these benefits. The sugar planters treated the colonies much as they treated their slaves, with an interest only in extracting as much from them as possible. Already in 1689, the Agent for Barbados in England had written:

> By a kind of magnetic force, England draws to it all that is good in the plantations. It is the centre to which all things tend. Nothing but England can we relish or fancy: our hearts are here, where ever our bodies be. If we get a little money, we remit it to England. When we are a little easy, we desire to live and spend what we have in England. And all that we can reap and rend is brought to England.[15]

No such centers of education as came to grace the North American colonies were established in the Caribbean ones until much later. The rich of the islands sent their young to Britain for schooling or simply departed with their families to live in Britain themselves, leaving white attorneys, overseers, and bookkeepers to manage the estates and dispatch the revenues. Between 1747 and 1793, the number of British West Indian absentee owners trebled. By the middle of the eighteenth century, absentee ownership had become the rule rather than the exception.

Such absenteeism often proved costly. Jane Austen's *Mansfield Park* has among its main characters the members of the Bertram family, whose fortune is founded on West Indian interests. In an essential part of the novel's dramatic development, the head of the family, Sir Thomas Bertram, is required by the poor returns from his Antigua estate to pay a protracted visit there. Yet the costs of absenteeism did little to arrest the migration of the rich West Indian planters to Britain. Paradoxically, the view of Britain as home was one which would come generations later to inform the minds of many among the descendants of the slaves.

Paradoxically too, the engenderment of so much wealth was based on a grossly inefficient use of labor. A modern exercise in measuring the productivity of the slave-worked sugar plantation in the 1790s found that this might have been as little as one-fifth that of cane cutting by wage labor employing similar implements on a piecework system. [16]

The profitability of sugar production relied on the threat or application of punishment to extract the maximum amount of labor. The organization of laborers in gangs was designed to ensure that the supposedly lazier or stubborn kept up with the productive pace of the more industrious or compliant. But labor under the lash was reluctant labor, and the more that the lash was applied to counter resistance, the more that reluctance found ways of making its protest. The gang system itself could operate in reverse, if the selected leaders chose to set a slower pace.

If slave labor, however resistant, was still overworked, it was also underemployed. Sugar production was seasonal, so that there were times of the year when slaves might profitably have been put to other productive purposes. There was, however, no serious undertaking on any of the islands to develop a market in slaves for hire. Nor was there that diverse economic activity which provided slaves with so many other occupations in the cities of Brazil or even the plantation belt of North America. In 1775, for instance, some 95 percent of the British West Indian slave population lived outside the towns; some 75 percent of them on sugar estates. The legacy of the concentration on sugar was not only dependence on a single market but a black population possessed of few skills beyond the requirements of plantation labor.

Slaves were too cheap, and profits were correspondingly high enough already. For much of the eighteenth century, new slaves were available at between £38 and £45 each. Those with special skills, such as distillers and masons, were scarce and proportionately expensive. One of these might cost £200. But far from promoting further mechanization, the high cost of skills discouraged planters from any development which looked likely to make them more dependent on skilled labor.

With new supplies of unskilled slaves so easy and cheap to obtain, there was no incentive even to nourish a natural increase in the slave population. The island planters bought substantially larger numbers of male than of female slaves. They gave scant attention to the welfare of childbearing slave women unless it was their own children who were involved and even this was not always a guarantee of their solicitude. They regarded slave children in general as less of an investment than an economic drain. Only as the movement against the slave trade gathered strength would the price of replacement slaves rise to a level at which greed created an interest in providing care.

In preserving the system, its prime beneficiaries recognized that the racial factor was of crucial importance. The presumptions of innate white superiority promoted a solidarity in domination which submerged any differences on other issues between leading planters and other whites. The colonial legislatures, though subject to the imperial government, were left largely free to make laws for which there were no counterparts in Britain and which were designed specifically to deal with the status and management of slaves.

The colonial codes were based on the contention that blacks were not British citizens entitled to the rights guaranteed by British law, but constituted property purchased from among prisoners-of-war and other prisoners in Africa. Legislators employed the very value of liberty, so often invoked to confront the power of the Crown at home, in a form of reverse moral leverage, so that it applied only to the rights of proprietorship and excluded even such rights for the slave as Roman law had allowed in conceding that slaves were people as well as property.

Yet slaves were property with a difference. Unlike real estate or furniture, they were capable of expressing discontent with their owners or their treatment. It was fear of just such expression that promoted successive punitive laws, immediately excited or made more severe by instances of slave restiveness or revolt. In 1730, following a slave revolt, the authorities in Bermuda, where the white population was double that of the black, reduced to a mere fine the punishment for the murder of a slave by a white. The harshest laws were passed in colonies where blacks outnumbered whites many times over. There, the punishments exacted for revolt came to be as cruel as fear and revenge could conceive. Of those punished for complicity in the rebellion of 1736 in Antigua, "six were gibbeted, five broken on the wheel, and seventy-seven burned alive."[17]

The codes came to contain so many offenses which slaves could commit that the law seemed bent on exhausting every possibility of intimidating or punishing disobedience, in the cause of saving the proprietor from his own property. There were provisions to punish with varying severity any infringe-

ment of restrictions on the assembly, movement, diversions, and even dress
of slaves, as well as assault, theft, and other conventional crimes whose
victims were whites. Criminal charges against slaves were tried before special
courts, whose judgments might be given by a single justice or by a jury
composed of three white men. Often, however, charge was pronounced,
verdict decided, and punishment applied by the slave owner or some surrogate, without the participation or even knowledge of the courts.

Denied such concessions or opportunities to buy their freedom as existed
in the laws and customs of Portuguese Brazil or the Spanish colonies, slaves
in the British West Indies had little hope of legal escape from their condition.
By the late eighteenth century, free blacks numbered fewer than 15,000 in
all, representing less than 6 percent of the population in Jamaica, 3 percent
of that in Antigua, and less than 3 percent of that in Barbados.[18] Nor was
there as much meaning to their freedom as whites expected from their own.

The Jamaican Maroons,[19] fugitive slaves and their descendants, had succeeded in resisting subjugation to the point where they had been conceded
certain privileges, but only for as long as they kept to their fastnesses in the
interior. Other free blacks on the island—such as those lucky enough to be
liberated for their loyalty by their owners, or those whom their owners had
fathered and chosen to acknowledge suitably—were nonetheless subject to
legal discrimination of various kinds. They were denied the right to trial by
jury and could not serve in the militia. By a law of 1717, they were required
to wear a blue cross on their clothing, supposedly to distinguish them, in
moving about the island, from fugitive slaves. By a law of 1761, they were
prohibited from inheriting property of a value above £2,000: since wealth
beyond that figure might destroy the distinction that it was considered im-
perative to maintain between whites and blacks or their offspring.

On other British islands as well, free blacks were subject to more or less
severe discrimination. In Bermuda, the Extirpation Act of 1730 even provided
for the expulsion of all free blacks within six months of being freed, and
only the recognition that the law was likely to be more trouble than it was
worth led to its being scrapped. In Barbados, the law paid little attention to
free blacks, but only because it came effectively to preclude the freeing of
blacks altogether. Almost everywhere, measures were taken to inhibit the
participation of free blacks in trade.

White racism, confronted by the consequences of a miscegenation it had
never cared to prevent, distinguished four degrees of color for blacks: negro
(wholly); mulatto (half); quadroon (quarter); and mustee (eighth). But pragmatism, that supposedly peculiar British virtue too often perversely absent
in matters of race, could on occasions intervene. In Jamaica, the huge
·numerical superiority of blacks and the high incidence of miscegenation left
the whites feeling dangerously exposed. A law of 1781 classified all blacks
"three degrees removed from the Negro ancestor exclusive" as whites and
accordingly free.

Living conditions for the vast majority of slaves were much as was to be expected from a system whose only concern for its human machinery was to keep its running costs to a minimum. On the estates, slaves were required to construct their own shelter, which was usually close to the stench of the sugar factory. Made of wattle and daub with thatching, the small huts had no windows. They admitted any cold and damp without providing relief from the prevailing heat. A Jamaican law of 1744 laid down that groups of huts in the vicinity of towns should be encircled by a seven-foot fence with a single gate. This security arrangement might well have been the origin of the "house-crammed 'yard' in modern West Indian towns."[20] Given the risks of fire, cooking was generally done in a lean-to, itself close to the crude privy. The resultant hazard to health was increased if, as was often the case, the water for cooking and washing came from a nearby pond rather than a river.

Slave owners were scarcely more generous with the provision of clothing, except for those domestics required to wear livery or other suitable dress for attending to the needs of the white family. Field and factory slaves often worked only in a breechcloth, though some might possess a little relative finery made by themselves for Sunday and holiday wear. Laws were eventually passed for the issue of clothing to slaves, but even then many owners merely provided some coarse cloth and blanketing.

The standard slave diet might have been designed to invite disease. Protein was provided in the form of pickled herring or salt cod, imported in bulk to the islands once or twice a year, so that the fish was often rotting when it came to be eaten. Some slaves were given an opportunity to raise poultry, while many used such time and mobility as they were allowed to trap wild birds, reptiles, and rats. Where they were conceded plots to raise their own crops, they grew such starch-rich foods as yams, cassava, and plantain. Otherwise, they mainly subsisted on rations of imported Indian corn. Issues of sugar, cane juice, and molasses were also supplied, along with rum when the weather turned cold or when excessive demands on labor recommended such liberality.

Deficient in protein and vitamins, it was a diet too often lacking in adequate bulk as well. Yet on this, slaves were required to rise well before dawn and to labor until well after nightfall, either in the close heat and stench of the sugar factories or in the fields, under the tropical sun and rain, with their only protection a hat of felt or straw. Apart, therefore, from diseases of deficient diet such as rickets and scurvy, they fell easy victim to various fevers, spread by the mosquitoes that bred so abundantly on the pools of stagnant water, and to a host of other diseases from the common cold to measles, smallpox, and yaws, which their low resistance frequently made fatal.

The mortality rate was significantly higher among slaves who had insufficient seasoning to the local climate of disease. Contemporary estimates suggest that one in three died within three years of their arrival. Indeed, it was widely accepted at the time that the death rate among newly imported slaves could be reduced by keeping them in quarantine for these years. This would, however, have involved a corresponding sacrifice of their labor, and there were very few planters who did not prefer to risk the loss of life from integrating them with the labor force at once. It was accounted less costly to provide "hot houses" or hospitals on the plantations where the sick might be treated for as long as the prognosis was promising. When it was not, as was believed the be the case for those suffering from yaws, the sick were removed to isolated neglect.

Yet the high mortality rate of slaves on the British West Indian islands was by no means wholly responsible for the startlingly high natural decreases in the slave population that necessitated the continual landing of so many new slaves. There was a substantial gender imbalance until some years after the abolition of the slave trade. In Jamaica at the start of the eighteenth century, for instance, there were three male slaves for every two female, a ratio roughly the same as that on the British slave ships for much of the trade period. This was one factor in accounting for a live-birth rate on the island below 15 per 1,000 of the slave population. There were others. The inadequate diet, overwork, and prevalence of disease undoubtedly reduced the rate of conception and increased that of stillbirths. But there is also evidence of widespread resort to methods of contraception, induced abortion, and even infanticide. Women who endured the horror of slavery themselves were not correspondingly willing to see their children endure it as well.

This was far from being the only form of protest and resistance by slaves. Apart from planned or actual revolts, there was the most common form of rejection, running away. Many slaves merely escaped to the towns, where their very enjoyment of freedom was bound to make their recapture certain. In these cases, owners or their agents, rather than lose working capital by exacting excessive retribution, usually punished offenders with the lash or a period of labor in the harshly supervised "vagabond gangs." Other runaways, who took to the mountains or the forests, presented a more serious threat to the survival of the system. They were hunted down with guns and dogs, and subjected to punishments of exemplary harshness if they were recaptured.

The most common form of protest and resistance, however, was the simple refusal of slaves to provide the amount of labor demanded of them. It was not only poor diet, exhaustion, and disease that accounted for their low productivity. What planters perpetually declared to be the racially inherent laziness of blacks was often the slave's allowance of only as much effort as was needed to evade punishment. Perceptive observers noted that slaves who were permitted their own private plots gave these a measure of application missing from the work for their masters.

Moreover, what so many planters saw as evidence of stupidity or male-volence was essentially the attachment of slaves to the cultural values and expressions of their origins. It is ironic that traditional African beliefs, which mirror modern ecological regard for a coherent Nature, should have been considered less rational than the reckless plunder of the environment in which the planter culture was engaged. Similarly, traditional African therapy, involving an extensive knowledge of herbal remedies and recognizing well in advance of Western medicine the psychosomatic source of much physical illness, was dismissed as ignorance and superstition.

If whites, in the very possession of so much power, so feared for their own survival that they sought to eliminate any slave activity that seemed menacing because it was mysterious, blacks in their very powerlessness clung to such beliefs and practices as offered them some possibility of affecting the course of their lives. Persistent use of the law against obeah—traditional African beliefs and rites which concentrated on medicine and magic—signally failed.

More successful, if not quite with the desired consequences, was the shift in settler attitudes toward the Christianization of slaves. In the early years, both planters and the clergy of the Anglican Church, some of whom were themselves owners of plantations, opposed conversion as likely to foster un-settling convictions through acquaintance with the messages of the Gospel. But then, partly to confront the subversive influence of obeah and partly to preempt the missionary undertakings of such zealous sects as the Methodists and Baptists, planter Anglicanism became more inclined to encourage con-version, at least to a Christianity which would teach the virtues of submission. Many converted slaves, however, drew their own, very different conclusions from the Scriptures.

Slaves preserved their culture, too, in folklore, artifacts, and most creatively in music, where they were quick to use local materials in making suitable instruments. Various types of stringed *banjil*, the prototype of the banjo, were constructed from small gourds or hollowed-out timber covered with skin and with attached necks given strings made of horsehair or the peeled stalks from climbing plants. There were the *goombay* drums that had goatskin membranes and serrated edges which might be scraped with a stick. The trumpet tree provided hollow branches for the flute. Singing was permitted as an accompaniment to labor and as a pleasure during the rare holiday breaks. Drumming, however, was feared to be a means of subversive com-munication, and ordinances were accordingly enacted to restrict or even prohibit it. Traditional African musical expression in song and dance was less susceptible to restraint from edicts and did respond to new influences, from Christian hymns to such European dances as the quadrille.

A less creative influence came from the discriminations that developed within the slave force itself. The planters soon found that, provided with accompanying privileges, slaves made the most effective supervisors of slave labor. Such slave drivers were allowed to carry whips as implements of encouragement and symbols of authority. They received special allowances of food and clothing, along with better housing. Granted larger plots on which to raise their own provisions, they often commandeered for labor in their own behalf the rest time of other slaves. They were joined in the ranks of relative privilege by the few slaves whose traditional skills or particular aptitudes won them the work and status of craftsmen, in the absence of anywhere near enough competent whites to satisfy the demand. Last came the domestics, whose very proximity to their masters secured them better treatment than that meted out to the field or factory slaves, and who accordingly assumed a superiority to the mass of the slave force.

All such divisions were, however, much less significant than the division between white and black. The depth and elaborations of racism went far enough in the British West Indies. They went further still in the French possessions.

In March 1685, the government of France had promulgated the *Code Noir* or Black Code which formulated, more systematically than any other imperial power in America had done, a legal basis for the nature and operations of slavery in the colonies. Influenced by the status and treatment of slaves in Roman law, by the doctrines of Roman Catholicism, and by the interests involved in promoting and securing the regime of sugar production, this was a notable attempt to bring the practices of slavery within the rule of law and establish the rights of the slave as well as the rights of ownership.

Slaves were to be baptized and subject to control only by Roman Catholics. They were to be liberated from labor on Sundays and holy days. They should be encouraged to marry, with the consent of their owners substituted for parental consent; and in any seizure of slaves for the debt of their owners, a husband, wife, and children were not to be sold into separation. White sexual aggression against slaves was made an offense. A master who engaged in sexual relations with one of his slaves was to be penalized by the confiscation of the slave and of any issue, while another free person who did so was liable to a fine. Minimum weekly food and annual clothing rations were prescribed, and slaves not fed or clothed as required had the right of complaint to the King's Agent. Owners were to care for their old and ailing slaves. The torture or mutilation of slaves was forbidden, and owners who engaged in either were to be punished by the confiscation of the slaves involved. Those who killed a slave under their protection or in their charge would be prosecuted under the criminal law. Owners were entitled to free slaves who met certain conditions, such as over twenty years of servitude, and all freed slaves were invested with the same rights and immunities as those possessed by persons born free.

Such provisions were markedly humane for the time. Yet they were accompanied by others that determined the status of slaves as chattels and invested their owners with extensive rights over them. Slaves were forbidden to own property, and whatever they might earn or be given was to be accounted the property of their owners. They could not be parties or witnesses in civil or criminal cases. Much of the Code was devoted to repressive or punitive measures, and the penalties prescribed were often ferocious. Slaves were forbidden to carry arms or even large sticks. Nor might they meet at night with the slaves of other owners. Punishment here ranged from flogging and branding for a first offense to death for repeated transgression. The theft of anything, including even the sugarcane in the midst of which most slaves spent so much of their lives, was punishable by flogging and branding. The penalty for running away might be the cutting off of both ears and the branding of one shoulder; for a second time, by the cutting off of the buttocks and branding of the other shoulder; for a third time, by death. Owners were entitled to flog and to chain their slaves, provided only that they deemed such punishment to be deserved.

Had all the provisions of the Code been scrupulously observed, it would have been bad enough. But in the eighteenth century, a very rage of racism swept the French West Indies. It was fed by three factors: the prodigious riches flowing from slave-based sugar production, most of it in the colony of Saint Domingue; the developing character of the white colonial community; and the obsessively elaborate social distinctions of metropolitan France.

The massive increase in the slave populations of the main French West Indian colonies revealed the nature of the imperial undertaking. In 1664, Martinique had 2,700 slaves; in 1790, it had 84,000. In 1671, Guadeloupe had 4,300 slaves; in 1788, it had 85,500. In Saint Domingue, a slave population of some 2,000 in 1681 had by 1791 become one of 480,000,[21] with a white population of only some 39,000.[22] But then, Saint Domingue was a colonial phenomenon.

Of all sugar production in the Caribbean traded by the French and British, that recorded for Saint Domingue accounted, in the year before the French Revolution, for some 42 percent. And the actual proportion was certainly larger than the recorded one, since quantities of cheaper sugar from Saint Domingue were smuggled into Britain's West Indian islands for subsequent sale in the protected British market. Moreover, some 60 percent of the world's traded coffee came from the colony, and exports of indigo from there exceeded those from all the British possessions in tropical America.[23] In all, Saint Domingue on its own accounted for no less than 40 percent by value of France's total foreign trade, and some five million of the twenty-seven million people in France were directly dependent on trade with the colony.

The vices of an absolute monarchy and its voracious officials in France were magnified in the colonies, where real power resided not in local Councils and Assemblies, as in the British West Indies, but in the representatives of the Crown. The arrogance of these agents was matched only by their dedication to making as much money in as little time and with as little effort as possible, before returning home. Bribery and corruption alone lubricated an otherwise idle administration into movement.

The leading planters or *grands blancs* (big whites) were described by Montesquieu, the French philosopher and essayist, as "ferocious, proud, quarrelsome, voluptuous, and cruel."[24] Between their sense of powerlessness toward an absolute government and their sense of absolute power over their slaves, they devoted themselves to parading their importance in extravagant display. Their principal allies were the local bankers, merchants, and lawyers to whom personally or as agents of French interests they often owed money.

Joining the *grands blancs* in social elevation were younger sons of the French nobility, drawn to the colonies and in particular Saint Domingue by the hope of making or marrying a fortune. Those who failed to become successful planters found employment in commanding the militia or in pursuing such cultural interests as the refinements of etiquette. All but a few soon sank into the prevailing lassitude of the planter class, interrupted only by their pursuit of concubines.

The white wives of this ascendancy were in general no better than their circumstances encouraged them to be. Supplied with a retinue of slaves whose essential function it was to spare them any exertion but that of gossip, they had abundant leisure to brood over the insult to them of husbands who preferred the attractions of black and mulatto women. This did not prevent them from consoling themselves with affairs of their own. A certain Miss Hassall, on a long visit to the colony, wrote to her friend Aaron Burr, former Vice President of the United States: "The Creole lady divides her time between the bath, the table, the toilette, and the lover."[25] Further diversion was available in exercising the prerogatives of race. It was widely reported by contemporary observers that the white women of the colony were even crueler to their slaves than were the white men.[26]

Lower down the social scale came the larger class of *petits blancs* (small whites): shopkeepers, farmers, overseers, artisans, barbers, clerks, along with various adventurers of no fixed occupation, drawn from other countries as well as from France to the supposedly easy enrichment in the colonies and, above all, in Saint Domingue. Despised by the whites above them, they took their revenge by humiliating those whose color set them below.

The relatively liberal provisions of the *Code Noir* came to be swept away by enactments to discourage the freeing of slaves and degrade the free who had any component of color. Unprecedented elaborations were developed to classify the particular racial mix among the 128 parts into which the blood was divided. The *sacatra* had only from 8 to 23 parts of white; the *griffe*, from 24 to 39; the *marabou*, from 40 to 48; the *mulâtre*, from 49 to 70; the *quarteron*, from 71 to 100; the *métis*, from 101 to 112; the *mameluc*, from

113 to 120; the *octoron*, from 121 to 124; and the *sang-mêlé*, from 125 to 127. It hardly mattered, except to those for whom such fine distinctions affected social conduct.

"The taint in the blood was incurable, and spread to the latest posterity."[27] Free persons of color,* whatever the racial mix, were forbidden to hold any public office or practice any profession for which some sort of liberal education was considered necessary. They could not be priests or lawyers or physicians or apothecaries or schoolteachers. A free man of color who struck a white was liable to the punishment of losing his right arm. Yet free persons of color did retain the right to own property. Many of them infuriatingly proceeded with marked success to concentrate on making themselves rich. In 1755, accordingly, the administrators of Saint Domingue sent to the Minister of Marine a request for action to deal with this problem:

> Their economical way of living enables them to lay aside each year a good part of their earnings and thus accumulate considerable capital. When a property is auctioned, they bid it up, until the price has reached astronomical figures. The whites, not possessing as much money as they, cannot buy it, or if they do, find themselves ruined. In many districts the finest estates have fallen into their hands. They are arrogant because they are rich and in proportion to their riches. Unless appropriate measures are taken, the time is not far distant when they will succeed in forming alliances with the most distinguished families in the kingdom, so that a mulatto might actually become a member of the family in which his mother had been a slave.[28]

The French government responded by sanctioning new measures that amounted to systematic persecution. Free persons of color in the colonies were banned from living in France, where they were likely to be treated as equals and might consequently return home with ideas above their station. They were forbidden to assemble on the pretext of weddings, feasts, or dances. They were forbidden to wear swords or even European dress. In churches, theaters, and public conveyances, they were required to occupy special seats. Those who rode on horseback were required to dismount before they entered a town. It was forbidden to address any of them as Monsieur or Madame.

The town council of Port-au-Prince in Saint Domingue was still not satisfied. It proposed banishing all persons of color, up to the degree of *quarteron*, to the mountains and forcing them, along with those who had married them, to sell all their slaves within a year, while the sale of all property on the plains would be forbidden to persons of color, whatever the degree. "For these," the council argued, "are dangerous people, more friendly to the slaves, to whom they are still attached, than to us who oppress

---

* These were overwhelmingly mulattoes, but not exclusively so. It was not illegal to free blacks. "Free persons of color" was the term which included both.

them by the subordination which we demand and the scorn with which we treat them." These proposals, however, threatened to provoke the very rebellion of which the whites were becoming increasingly afraid. They were abandoned.

At Le Cap in the north of the colony, white women successfully agitated for a decree that all women of color should be required to cover their hair with knotted handkerchiefs and be forbidden to wear silk clothing in public. Guards stationed in the streets and outside of churches took to tearing the forbidden finery from offenders. In a momentous instance of resort to the consumer boycott as a political weapon, the colored women of the town stayed at home. The impact on local trade was soon such that the white merchants secured the repeal of the decree. By the late 1780s, relations between the colony's whites and its 27,500 free colored[29] could scarcely have been worse, short of open warfare.

Below all classes of the free population, and despised even by many who were themselves despised for their color, were the slaves, who were treated with increasing harshness as their increasing disaffection was suspected. Something of their condition may be inferred from the fact that it had taken the arrival of 850,000 to produce the 480,000 still alive in Saint Domingue.

"The difficulty was that though one could trap them like animals, transport them in pens, work them alongside an ass or a horse and beat both with the same stick, stable them and starve them, they remained, despite their black skins and curly hair, quite invincibly human beings; with the intelligence and resentments of human beings. To cow them into the necessary docility and acceptance necessitated a regime of calculated brutality and terrorism, and it is this that explains the unusual spectacle of property owners apparently careless of preserving their property; they had first to ensure their own safety."[30]

It was precisely their own safety that the slave owners subverted in the very fervor of their undertaking to ensure it.

7 | ALIENABLE RIGHTS

~~~~~~

The British North American colonies that would rebel to become the United States initially relied on indentured white labor, and more than half of all the early immigrants arrived to serve in this condition. The first blacks were brought by a Dutch warship to Virginia in 1619, but there were only twenty of these, and they were followed by little more than a trickle during the rest of the century, since labor needs could be otherwise met.

Black and white in their shared, if different, bondage worked together, spent together whatever leisure they were allowed, and slept together in or out of wedlock. But already in 1669, Carolina's Lords Proprietors decreed that every freeman should have "absolute power and authority over his negro slaves"; and by the time that more blacks began to arrive, in the eighteenth century, the legal basis of chattel slavery was securely in place. Slaves were to be slaves for life, regardless of their conversion to Christianity, and the issue of slave women were to be slaves themselves. Their status as property and the related rights of their owners were clearly defined. Their very movements were closely circumscribed. Their marriage to whites was prohibited.

As Britain came to be massively involved in the slave trade, increasing numbers of slaves arrived to swell the black population, especially in the South, where a plantation culture prospered on their labor. Their mounting numbers gave commensurate cause for concern. Established planters, eager to restrict competition from new producers, argued for restricting or ending the slave trade. A British government more influenced by the interests of the traders paid no heed.

With the Revolution, the states were free to act; and, beginning with Delaware in 1776, six of them banned the importation of Africans. Then, in 1808, the federal government banned new imports from the trade, while leaving the institution of slavery itself to survive in such states as maintained it and to spread as it might only south of the Ohio River. However hallowed the Declaration of Independence on which the United States had been founded, there were manifestly exceptions to its primary principle that all men were created equal and endowed by their Creator with "certain un- alienable Rights."

By 1860, the slave states together with the District of Columbia had a total population of 12,302,000, of whom 8,098,000 were whites, 3,954,000 were slaves, and 250,000 were "free colored." There were considerable dif- ferences in the proportion of slaves from state to state. Slaves made up 57 percent of the population in South Carolina, for instance, and 55 percent in Mississippi, but only 1.5 percent in Delaware. And only 385,000, or just over a quarter, of the 1,516,000 "free families" in the South owned any slaves at all. Moreover, within this minority, the extent of ownership varied greatly. Well over half of all slaves belonged to those who owned more than twenty each, and a quarter belonged to those who owned more than fifty. Almost half the slave owners possessed fewer than five slaves each and almost three-quarters, fewer than ten. If membership of the planter class required owning a minimum of twenty slaves, only 12 percent of slave owners qual- ified. The planter aristocracy, which stamped its image on the romantic racism of the South, was much smaller still. Defined as composed of those who possessed upwards of fifty slaves each, it encompassed a mere 10,000 families. Fewer than 3,000, or less than 0.2 percent of all free families, were considered very rich, as owners of one hundred slaves or more.[1] Among these, at the summit of ownership, were planters such as William B. Goulden, with one thousand slaves.

The large majority of Southern whites owned no slaves themselves. They were independent farmers, overseers, artisans, unskilled workers in agricul- ture, or those engaged in some form of urban employment. A merely sta- tistical logic might suggest that this Southern white majority would resent the concentration of so much wealth and power in the grasp of so few and seek to challenge the survival of slavery itself. Instead, it was from among those who owned no slaves themselves that the institution of slavery found a mass of impassioned defenders. In some cases, the reasons were obvious. Overseers were inevitable supporters of a system that provided them not only with gainful employment but with the pleasing exercise of power over others, and many in business and the professions saw their own prosperity as insep- arable from that of the planters.

Most Southern whites, however, had no such prosperity to protect. Yet they were encouraged to believe that whatever their particular circumstances, they were the beneficiaries and guardians of a singular civilization, one of stability and harmony and graciousness, whose very existence depended upon the system of slavery. A favorable comparison with the slave-owning culture of ancient Greece affected especially those few who were relatively well educated. On small farms and in workshops, more influential was the favorable contrast between Southern society and the predatory capitalism of the industrial North. More influential still was the connection between slavery and color, which gave to the meanest white, without hope of a single slave to call his own, a sense of superiority to the multitude of blacks.

The Northerner Frederick Law Olmsted, whose accounts of his travels in the South brought him some success before his greater renown as a landscape architect, wrote of seeing a small white girl stop a slave in the road and successfully order him to return at once to his plantation.[2] Only someone from beyond the South would have found the incident worthy of remark. The slave was expected to treat any white with respect and avoid the slightest suggestion of impudence. Moreover, what was expected of slaves came to be expected of all those who were black. "In a well regulated community," wrote one Texan, "a negro takes off his hat in addressing a white man. Where this is not enforced, we may always look for impudent and rebellious negroes."[3]

It was, however, fear as well as the compensations of supposed racial superiority that ensured the support of relatively deprived whites for the institution of slavery. Indeed, the more degraded the whites were in their material circumstances, their lack of adequate education and of marketable skills, the more fearful they were likely to be of any competition from blacks on equal terms. Not least, in a racism that came to be so sexually charged, white men had a particular fear of competition from black men for white women. And beyond all this, for the mass of whites, was the fear bred by the very repressiveness employed to secure slavery. The more that the blacks were made to cringe, the more appalling appeared the retribution that they might exact if they were ever to secure their freedom.

Where much wealth and some education provided self-assurance, whites were less driven by fear and were more inclined to argue, even believe, that the paternalism of Southern slavery was accepted by the slaves themselves as being in their own best interests. For paternalism of any sort, there was little enough evidence in the fields of the large plantations, where overseers were generally responsible for the management of labor. Apologists pointed rather to the close personal relations developed between slave and owner in the town house, on the small plantation whose owner was his own overseer, and in the home of the planter aristocrat where courtesy was enthroned.

This was not altogether a figment of propaganda. Fugitives from slavery in the freedom of the North testified from time to time to the kindness and affection shown by some Southern owners to their slaves. Yet such owners could themselves be sharply selective. James H. Hammond, a South Carolina planter, confided to his diary in 1844 his sadness at the loss of his gardener and plantation "patriarch," described further as his "faithful friend" and "one of the best of men." Of two other slaves who died in the same year, he commented: "Neither a serious loss. One valuable mule has also died."[4]

In fact, favorite slaves might safely reproach their masters or mistresses in terms that would have been regarded as intolerable from servants in the North or in Britain. Even a public display of familiarity was not objectionable. Frederick Law Olmsted wrote of witnessing on a train in Virginia a white woman and a black woman talking and laughing together while their daughters shared a bag of candy, all this with an ease that would have surprised and offended most Northerners.[5]

Such liberties were, of course, allowed only within the limits of an accepted black subservience. There was a strain of contempt in the way even avowed paternalists spoke of their adult slaves as boys and girls, until these were translated at last by long service into uncles and aunties. It is likely that favorite slaves who sometimes scolded their masters or mistresses would have done so only after carefully exploring the extent of the liberties allowed them.

In any event, the selectively benevolent nature of Southern paternalism was an irrelevance to most slaves. The extent of planter dependence on overseers was such that their number in 1860 was virtually the same as was the number of plantations with a force of at least thirty slaves. Few such overseers were disposed to behave as surrogate fathers in any fashion. Since the slaves that they commanded were not their own property to preserve, and since they were themselves commonly judged by the extent of the profits they produced, they tended to whip rather than woo their charges into effort. Court records are replete with cases of overseers who sued their employers after being dismissed for cruelty or of employers who sued overseers for the damage done to slave property. Such cases are unlikely to have reflected the full extent of overseer cruelty or damage to slaves.

The rule of slavery was forced labor, and the South provided no exception. But the degree to which such labor was exacted depended in part upon the kind of production to which it was applied. In 1850, the Superintendent of the Census estimated that of the 2,500,000 slaves employed in agriculture, 60,000 were engaged in hemp, 125,000 in rice, 150,000 in sugar, 350,000 in tobacco, and 1,815,000 in cotton production.[6] The primacy of cotton was such, indeed, that it came to account for almost 60 percent of all exports from the United States and was earning some $190 million a year in the markets of Europe. As elsewhere, sugar production was especially exacting, and slaves in Louisiana were accordingly made to labor up to eighteen hours a day at grinding time. But cotton production was little less exacting. Most slaves engaged in this were roused to be ready for starting work before dawn and, with breaks for meals and rest, were kept to it for fifteen or sixteen hours in the season of cultivation. When cotton was picked, ginned, and packed, slaves labored even longer, often until well into the night.

The mass of Southern slaves were undoubtedly overworked. But this did not mean that their plight was much the same as that of most slaves elsewhere in the hemisphere. Slaves in the South were not in general driven so hard, and their diet was not as poor. Greater care was taken to ensure that they remained fit for work. One reason for this was the mounting pressure from abolitionists in the North. A more crucial one, however, was the rising market price of slaves themselves, with the increasing impact of the ban on such imports from Africa. As one planter commented in 1849: "Negroes are too high in proportion to the price of cotton, and it behooves those who own them to make them last as long as possible."[7] It was economics, probably more than compassion, that led owners to sack overzealous overseers.

Clearly less concerned with preserving the capital value of slaves were those who hired rather than bought them. Among these were farmers without the necessary capital or credit; town families who wanted the use of domestic servants without the obligations of owning them; and industrial enterprises, from cotton factories and sawmills to iron foundries and mines and railroad construction. Such employers, especially the mining companies and the railroad contractors, often exploited their hired slave labor ruthlessly and were charged at a related rate. Those who supplied the slaves—and there were those whose only business this was—had to weigh the risk of damage to their property against the return they were able to command. Commonly, the annual rate ranged between 10 and 20 percent of the slave's market value, with the hirer required to meet all maintenance costs. But those who hired slaves to work as deckhands on the steamers traveling between Galveston and Houston in 1858, for instance, paid as much as $480 a year, somewhere between one-third and one-half the slave's market value.

In other slave systems of the hemisphere, such as those of Brazil and Cuba, slaves were conceded the right to hire themselves out in return for paying their owners a stipulated share of what they earned. It was by such means that many saved enough to buy their freedom. This practice came to be outlawed almost everywhere in the South. There were nonetheless former slaves who had succeeded in buying their freedom when they could still earn money or who had been freed in the wills of generous, grateful, or conscience-stricken owners. And the South increasingly saw the very presence of a freed slave as subversive of the social order. Statutes in various states sought to deal with the danger.

In Tennessee, from 1832, slaves might be freed by their owners only if the freed slave left the state immediately, and from 1855, only if the freed slave was sent to the west coast of Africa. In the Deep South, one state after the other simply outlawed altogether the private freeing of slaves within its borders. For a while, resolute owners found a way around this ban by directing in their wills that the slaves they intended to free should be taken to a free state and freed there. In 1841, South Carolina proceeded to outlaw all deeds and wills directed at freeing slaves before or after departure from the state, and its example was soon followed by Mississippi, Georgia, Arkansas, and Alabama.

Even so, owners across the South could still circumvent the laws by taking or sending their slaves to the North and having them freed there. Very few chose to do so. In none of the slave states did the total number of slaves freed in any one year ever represent more than a small proportion of even the natural increase in the local slave population. In Virginia, for instance, where the testamentary freeing of slaves remained legal and where owners were reputed to be relatively liberal, only 227 slaves out of the half million in the state were given their freedom in 1859.

James Hammond, the South Carolina planter, wondered whether any people in history had voluntarily surrendered two billion dollars' worth of property.[8] If this was a sound estimate of the value attributable to slave property in the South, the measure of wealth involved was enormous. It exceeded the value of all factories in the North, estimated at roughly $1.9 billion in 1860.[9] Mere figures, however, cannot convey the peculiar value attached to slaves in the South.

Elsewhere slaves might be central to the production and display of wealth. In the South, they were this and more: the main substance of wealth, security for credit, and source of status. It was the slave, not the land, that constituted the bulk of capital. If land was secondary, this was because it was both abundant and immobile. With the provision of enough slaves, a viable plantation could be established wherever suitable new lands were being cleared. Slaves were also more reliable collateral for loans, since their price was more likely to rise and was, besides, more easily and quickly realized.

Abolitionists and economists argued that investment in slavery was less secure, less productive, and less profitable than investment in commerce and industry with free labor. They were right, though an investment in slaves was generally profitable enough. The maintenance costs of a single slave remained virtually constant at $35 a year, and such costs, along with the initial capital invested, were substantially more than met by the value earned during an average working life of production. But any such argument was not so much right or wrong as beside the point. As long as the ownership of slaves gave a reasonable enough rate of return on the capital employed, it was to be preferred. Thomas Jefferson himself, the most renowned states- man and philosopher to have emerged from the South, had taught that the agrarian life was more virtuous and honorable than the commercial or in- dustrial one. It was small wonder, then, that successful Southern industrialists and merchants, lawyers and doctors and clergymen, should have invested their savings in the purchase of plantations and slaves, regardless of whether there were more profitable forms of investment available. In the culture of the South, it was the ownership of slaves, and not that of mines or factories or shops, that made the gentleman.

Scarcely less singular, at least for its time, was the attitude of the Southern states to color. Certainly, color prejudice was not limited to the South, but nowhere else in the hemisphere was marriage between whites and persons of color, slave or free, outlawed. This did not mean that miscegenation was rare. On the contrary, the emphasis placed on keeping the races sexually separate seems to have been more an inducement than an inhibition to sexual crossing of the color line. In the Southern census of 1860, over half a million people, equivalent to one in eight of the total slave population, were classed as mulattoes.

There were instances recorded, and inevitably more that went unrecorded, of sexual relations between white women and black men. But this was a practice beyond mere condemnation. It revealed the possibility of a sexually driven white womanhood in the starkest of contrasts to the delicate, decorous vision that floated at the summit of Southern manners. It confronted a patriarchal culture which regarded the act of sex as the use of the female by the male. It roused that sexual jealousy and fear which racism, in its very emphasis on the animal prowess of the black male, promoted. Where such an ultimate breach of the Southern code did occur, beyond the possibility of pressures to end it and pretend it had never taken place, the white woman's innocence was assumed, and the black man was charged with rape.

Altogether differently regarded was the much more common sexual act between white men and black women, a practice essentially acceptable as an assertion of male dominance and white racial prerogatives. It involved white men from every class and calling, though owners and overseers were peculiarly well placed to take sexual advantage of black women.

Young whites often used women slaves for sexual exploration; older ones often sought in women slaves a sexually more satisfying relationship than that provided by their wives. For some, the object was the gratification of the moment. Others formed a more lasting liaison. There were even liaisons that became effectively lifelong marriages, though the implications of these made it necessary to keep them secret, or at least secret enough to be the subject of pleasurable scandal rather than social outrage.

Overwhelmingly, however, sexual relations with slaves were simply rape, and rape without risk, since the law recognized no such crime against a slave. The effect on the black psyche of this can scarcely be exaggerated. Affected were not only the innumerable black women who were immediate victims, but also all the others who lived their lives in fear that they might become such. Moreover, white sexual choice took no account of any existing relationship between a female slave and a male one. Humiliated by their very helplessness, black men had simply to endure the rape of women with whom they had established unions of love and respect.

Why should a society scarcely distinguishable from other slave-owning ones of the hemisphere in the high incidence of miscegenation have gone to such extremes in extending racism beyond the requirements, even the interests, of maintaining slavery? The only historical parallel was with the

French West Indian colonies decades before, when the chief of them, Saint Domingue, was lost in revolution. Certainly, it was not in the South, as it had been in Saint Domingue, a kind of pride. The pride of Southern paternalism was directed quite differently—to the presumption of a benevolent guardianship. Indeed, it may have been guilt, at the practice of a system so at odds with its moral pretensions and, in particular, for the Anglo-Saxon Protestant psyche, at a licentiousness sinful in itself.

Whatever the reason, a veritable rage came to be directed against those few free blacks who personified not only the rupture of the connection between slavery and race but the humanity which slavery so abused. Unsatisfied by successive enactments to outlaw the freeing of slaves, state after state moved to make life as difficult as possible for the already free and even force their return to slavery. Most Southern states, during the last decade before the Civil War, passed laws for the "voluntary enslavement" of free blacks, which conceded them no more than the right to choose their owners. Virginia enacted the sale into "absolute slavery" of any free black convicted of an offense punishable by imprisonment, and Florida applied this to any free black who was "dissolute" or "idle." In 1859, Arkansas offered its free blacks a choice: to leave the state or be hired out as slaves for a year and then be sold into slavery.

Here, then, was the most consistent system of racial enslavement in the hemisphere. And yet here as well was the system least costly of human life. In all, some 400,000 African slaves were landed in North America. In 1860, the slave population of the United States was some 4,000,000.[10] The demographic contrast with other slave-owning societies in the hemisphere could scarcely be starker, and the explanation mainly lies in the Southern view of the slave as not only the dominant form of capital but a procreative one as well. It was this which affected the gender selection of slaves imported for sale and the treatment of slaves themselves. The ratio was roughly 95 female slaves to every 100 males in 1820 and topped 99 to 100 in 1860. In fact, by 1860, the gender ratio across the South was far closer to equality among slaves than among whites, where there were 106 males to every 100 females.[11]

The accusation by opponents that Southern slave owners were widely engaged in the commercial breeding of slaves was indignantly denied by the slave owners and their defenders. It may even have been true that few slave owners were primarily engaged in raising slaves for the market. But it is certain that any natural increase in the number of slaves represented a corresponding increase in capital or, if the slaves were sold, in income. One Virginia planter rejoiced that every infant was worth $200 at prevailing prices and that his slave women were "uncommonly good breeders."[12]

Planters would instruct their overseers to ensure the welfare of expectant or nursing mothers and small children. Planter manuals were packed with advice on the need and value of providing slave women with the right conditions for breeding and rearing. There were doubtless slave women who resisted inducements and were ready to risk being sold as sterile into harsher conditions rather than produce children for slavery. The record suggests, however, that most bore children willingly, some of them influenced by the favor with which fecundity was rewarded. An entry in the journal of Frances Kemble noted the "meritorious air" with which the slave women on her husband's Georgia plantation hastened to inform her of how many children they had produced.[13]

To be sure, there were paternalist planters who never marketed the progeny of people they regarded as their own. Most owners, however, disposed of slaves—whether acquired by purchase or by birth—as need or convenience prompted. Some of these disposals were arranged locally, through private transactions between neighbors, and the slaves involved were not removed from all connection with their families. Far more were arranged through brokers or traders, and the slaves involved might be sold to distant destinations.

The Atlantic and Border states became large exporters of slaves to other parts of the South, in an internal trade much larger than the earlier trade in the importing of slaves from Africa had been. During the period from 1830 to 1860, some 750,000 slaves were dispatched to Alabama, Arkansas, Louisiana, Mississippi, Texas, and states with minor appetites. Virginia alone supplied almost 300,000, virtually the equivalent of the natural increase in its slave population during those years.

Some exports were not the result of sales, but the dispatch of slaves by their owners to new subsidiary plantations in other states or the movement of slaves along with their owners from the developed to the developing South. Most were the material of the interstate slave trade, conducted both by disreputable operators and by such respected firms as Franklin and Armfield, of Alexandria, Virginia, whose partners retired with fortunes of over $500,000 each.

Opponents of slavery made much of a trade which so often involved the disruption of families. This weighed little with the slave states. Only Delaware among them recognized that the trade was "contrary to the principles of humanity and justice"[14] and prohibited the export of any slave, even by the owner, without a permit. Louisiana at least prohibited the sale or importing of slave children under the age of ten who had been separated from their mothers. None of the other importing states enacted even this compromise with compassion. The principal exporting states placed no restrictions whatsoever on separating members of the same family from one another.

If life for the Southern slave was peculiarly long by comparison with the lives of slaves elsewhere in the hemisphere, it was peculiarly distressing as well. Beyond the disruption of families, a regime of repressiveness continually explored new ways of expression. It established the offense of insolence, which might extend from raising a hand against a white to "a look," as one North Carolina judge expounded it: "the pointing of a finger, a refusal or neglect to step out of the way when a white person is seen to approach."[15]

Slaves might not preach, except to other slaves of the same owner and then only in the presence of whites on the whites' own premises. No one, even their owners, might teach them to read or write, give them reading material of any sort, or employ them in setting type for printing. In many places, they were forbidden to beat drums or blow horns, practice medicine, gamble, possess liquor, trade without a permit, or raise cotton, pigs, horses, mules, or cattle. In many towns, slaves were subject to curfews and other restrictions. In Charleston, for instance, they might not swear, smoke, use a cane in walking, or—as though they had much occasion to do so—"make joyful demonstrations."[16]

Their owners were entitled to inflict upon them any violence except malicious maiming or deliberate death. And these two limitations meant little enough in practice. Blacks, slave or free, were not allowed to testify against whites, and whites were generally unwilling to break racial ranks by testifying against one of their number. Furthermore, white juries were generally unwilling to convict whites for crimes against blacks, especially slaves. In addition, there was a host of harsh provisions for punishment in state and local criminal codes. Floggings of up to one hundred strokes at a time on the bare back of a slave were common for such offenses as forging passes, engaging in routs or unlawful assemblies, trespass, or seditious talk. Capital felonies included robbery, arson, or assault of a stipulated seriousness. In Louisiana, for instance, an assault which drew blood from the master, a member of his family, or an overseer commanded the death penalty.

In a system of such rigorous containment and ferocious punishment, revolt was a response which only a fury of defiance might excite. That so many planned revolts should have been recorded was evidence of that irrepressible black spirit which the Southern system recognized in its elaborate endeavors to break it. Individual acts of violence against owners, overseers, and other whites were more numerous. Arson was, after theft, the most common crime of which slaves were accused. Slaves also mutilated themselves as a way of punishing their owners. And there were always those whom despair or revenge drove to suicide. One Texan planter bewailed his misfortune in having lost a slave woman who, after two failures at flight, had hanged herself: "I had been offered $900 for her not two months ago, but damn her . . . I would not have had it happened for twice her value. *The fates pursue me.*"[17]

Thousands of slaves each year tried to find freedom in flight. Most of them were young and male, but female and older fugitives were far from rare. Sometimes they fled from punishment, before or after; sometimes, in protest at being driven too hard; sometimes, to reach members of their family from whom they had been separated. They sometimes fled from owners who prided themselves on treating their slaves with particular consideration. The sheer puzzlement evident in advertisements for the recapture of such runaways suggests with what difficulty white Southerners could allow themselves to realize that a slave might escape simply to be free.

Flight was certainly not a decision to be taken lightly. The more who fled together, the more formidable were the problems in evading patrols and finding food and shelter along the way. Family and friends, therefore, had to be forsaken, for the solitary attempt that added a sense of guilt to one of loss, and both to fear. The use of dogs to track fugitives was no figment of abolitionist propaganda but court-sanctioned practice in the South, and summary punishment was frequently inflicted by letting the dogs savage the found fugitive, if rarely to the point of seriously reducing the value of such property. More delayed retribution included floggings, confinement in chains, or sale to the harsher conditions in the more remote and more secure regions of the Deep South.

Nor was success in reaching any of the free states an assurance of freedom. The Fugitive Slave Act, passed as part of the so-called Compromise of 1850 to save the Union, strengthened the power of slave owners to have their runaways pursued in the North and the repossession of their property enforced by the courts there. Yet slaves persisted in attempts to escape from slavery; and if many failed, enough succeeded to stir others with their example. A Southern judge estimated in 1855 that more than 60,000 had so far been finally lost through escape to the North.

The vast majority of slaves stayed, however, and came to terms with their condition in various ways. Some gave only as much of their labor as they found no possibility of denying. Field slaves on the cotton plantations would put stones in their baskets of pickings so as to produce the required weight. Malingering exploited the reluctance of the owner or overseer to risk the health and related value of the slave. Women slaves in general found it easier than men to provide acceptable reasons for reducing or evading the exactions imposed upon them.

Theft was so common as to be attributed by whites to a racial characteristic. Yet blacks no less than whites disapproved of theft, as they themselves defined it. They simply excluded from the definition the taking of anything that belonged to the owner, since this did no more than transfer one property to the possession of another. Slaves, indeed, developed a morality of their own. It was this which often operated to protect or encourage the defiant. Slaves who themselves never strayed would still recognize a solidarity that kept them silent in their knowledge of some planned escape. The stubborn, whom no amount of whipping seemed able to subdue, enjoyed an admiration from other slaves that the toady, creeping into the trust of the owner, could not command.

Nor were all those who might be taken for toadies really such. Slaves became adept at saying what whites wanted to hear and behaving as whites expected them to behave, in a mocking self-mockery. It was the very exaggeration of the caricature that should often have given the game away, except that it was directed at those who, in their own assumptions, had already made caricatures of themselves.

Nonetheless, it would be merely another of the romantic fictions about the South to portray the slave as invariably a figure, however devious, of defiance. It is a singularly unsuccessful system of subjugation that does not find collaborators from among the subjugated, and the Southern system was in this sense not singular. There were slaves selected to be slave drivers who were notoriously brutal. There were domestic slaves whose essential adherence was to the family of their owner and who were the very creatures of paternalism. There were the informers, from misplaced loyalty or for reward. More slave plots were discovered through their betrayal by slaves than emerged in revolt, and more revolts were cut short by betrayal than developed into serious challenges.

Between revolt and collaboration was another country, and it was here that most slaves probably spent their lives. They did so to endure with some dignity in a system directed at depriving them of any. It was for this rather than out of any allegiance to the interests of their owners or fear of the lash that some of them may have taken such pride in working well, in being stronger or quicker than anyone else in the fields. Yet so many of them who set themselves to endure succeeded only at immense cost.

If rage and humiliation had to be suppressed, this involved an accumulation of pressure that might be intermittently released in violence against those who were closest and most vulnerable. Within the slave quarters, the beating of women by men and of children by fathers almost certainly owed more to this displaced expression of fury and shame than it did to the common incidence of physical violence in a slave labor system. Still more damaging, perhaps, could be a slave's own belief in white supremacy. Frederick Douglass, one of the greatest figures to emerge from slavery in the South, wrote that most slaves were awed by white men and invested their masters with "a sort of sacredness."[18] Daunting as is the authority of Douglass, there is evidence to suggest that such awe may not have been as widespread as he maintained.

The whole anguish of slavery would have been intolerable without some means to make sense and solace out of it, and among these means was the slave tale. There were tellers of such tales who gave their own twist to the text of Genesis. Charles Gentry, a slave who took to preaching, taught that all the first humans were black: "Cain he kill his brudder Abel wid a great big club . . . and God he cum to Cain, and say, 'Cain! whar is dy brudder Abel?' Cain he pout de lip, and say, 'I don't know; what ye axin' me fur? I ain't my brudder Abel's keeper.' De Lord he gits in airnest, and stomps on de ground, and say, 'Cain! you Cain! whar is dy brudder Abel? I say, Cain! whar is dy brudder?' Cain he turn white as bleech cambric in de face, and de whole race ob Cain dey bin white ebber since."[19] Gentry was only retelling in his own way a tale which went back at least as early as the beginning of the nineteenth century. Here was one means by which the presumption of white supremacy was confronted, neatly reversing the repeated white claim of a scripturally sanctioned curse on the black race.

Richest in variety and vividness were the slave tales in which animals were characters. Some of these clearly communicated a strategy of reticence for the slave to follow. In one such favorite, a slave meets an animal that speaks to him and he hurries away to tell his master about it. The master warns him that he will be punished if he is found to have been lying and sets off to hear the animal for himself. But the animal says not a word to the master, and the slave gets to be whipped. When the slave then returns to remonstrate with the animal, it replies, "Ah tol' you de othah day, niggah, yuh talk too much." It was a lesson repeated in such maxims as "De fox wants to know how de rabbit's gittin on" and "Long talk catch run'way nigguh."[20]

Most popular and complex were the slave tales about animals that dealt with the use of some trick to escape from a predicament. These tales derived directly from African folklore, in which certain animals were associated with trickery. In many slave societies of the hemisphere, the animal was Anansi, the spider that figures in the folklore of the Akan-speaking and other peoples in West Africa. In the South of the United States, it was especially Brer Rabbit, related to the hare or rabbit trickster in the folklore of East Africa, Angola, and parts of Nigeria, which came to be used, though Rooster and Pig were among other animals who served this purpose.

In one of these tales, Brer Rabbit gets himself out of trouble by getting somebody else into it.

> Once he fell down a deep well an' did he holler and cry? No siree. He set up a mighty mighty whistling and a singin', an' when de wolf passes by he heard him an' he stuck his head over an' de rabbit say, "Git 'long 'way f'om here. Dere ain't room fur two. Hit's mighty hot up dere and nice an' cool down here. Don' you get in dat bucket an' come down here." Dat made de wolf all de mo' onrestless and he jumped into the bucket an' as he went down de rabbit come up, an' as dey passed de rabbit he laughed an' he say, "Dis am life; some go up and some go down."[21]

The choice of victim here is not accidental. The wolf often appears in slave tales as representative of the strong and predatory. Sometimes it is the strong and predatory who begin the tale by threatening the weak and wily. Nor are the strong and predatory without some wiliness themselves. In the celebrated tar-baby tale, Wolf exploits the curiosity and conceit of Rabbit by making a tar baby and leaving it at the side of the road. Passing by later, Rabbit sees it and greets it and, furious at its refusal to respond, punches and kicks it till he gets stuck all over with tar. Then, having become aware of his predicament, he cries out that he fears most of all being thrown into the briar patch. This is precisely what Wolf proceeds to do, and Brer Rabbit escapes, jubilantly calling back to Wolf, "Dis de place me mammy fotch me up."

A glint of the connection between such tales and the experiences of slavery may be caught in an autobiographical account from Frederick Douglass: "Colonel Lloyd kept a large and finely cultivated garden . . . Scarcely a day passed, during the summer, but that some slave had to take the lash for stealing fruit. The colonel had to resort to all kinds of stratagems to keep his slaves out of the garden. The last and most successful one was that of tarring his fence all around; after which, if a slave was caught with any tar upon his person, it was deemed sufficient proof that he had either been into the garden, or had tried to get in. In either case, he was severely whipped by the chief gardener. This plan worked well; the slaves became as fearful of tar as of the lash."[22]

Indeed, the predatory animal is in some slave tales successful. Fox persuades Jaybird to enter his mouth and remove a bone from his teeth, only to eat him. Buzzard persuades animals to ride on his back and then eats them after dropping them to their deaths. In other tales, it is the predator who comes to an ugly end. In one such, Fox wheedles his way into Pig's house and seeks to cook Pig in the pot of peas on the stove. Instead, Pig tricks him into hiding in a meal barrel and then pours the peas over him, scalding him to death.

If this suggests a certain ambiguity in the slave tales, it came out of the slave experience. Colonel Lloyd was not the only slave owner successful in his stratagems. Brer Rabbit can be both the crafty slave, who survives by his wits, and the crafty slave owner, who uses his wits to keep the slave in subjection. One slave tale, for instance, concerns a trick played on Partridge, certainly no strong predator, by Rabbit, and ends with the lesson: "You nebber kin trus Buh Rabbit. Eh all fuh ehself; an ef you listne ter him tale, eh gwine cheat you ebry time, and tell de bigges lie dout wink eh yeye."[23] One modern scholar, Lawrence Levine, sees in many tales a parody of the whites, with their little work and extensive leisure, their intricate etiquette, their "lofty platitudes" and profession of noble ideals, alongside their dispensing of rewards "not to the most deserving, but to the most crafty and least scrupulous."[24]

More important still to the endurance of the slaves was music, and especially song. Slaves sang at work in the fields and in the factories and on the riverboats, in the houses of the whites and in their own quarters. They sang while picking cotton and hewing wood, while rocking babies and cooking meals. They had songs for every occasion and songs for every mood. They sang to lighten their labor, but also in pain at the plight of their lives, as they rowed on the river:

> Going away to Georgia, ho, heave, O!
> Massa sell poor negro, ho, heave, O!
> Leave poor wife and children, ho, heave, O! . . .[25]

They sang in pleasure at the prospect of night, when the labor would end:

> Nigger mighty happy when he layin' by the corn,
> Nigger mighty happy when he hear dat dinner horn;
> But he more happy when de night come on,
> Dat sun's a slantin', as sho's you born!
> Dat old cow's a shakin' dat great big bell,
> And de frogs tunin' up, 'cause de dew's done fell.[26]

They sang to mock the deceitful promises of the whites and their own gullibility in believing them:

> My old missus promise me
>   Shoo a la a day,
> When she die she set me free,
>   Shoo a la a day.
> She live so long her head git bald,
>   Shoo a la a day.
> She give up de idea of dyin' a-tall,
>   Shoo a la a day.[27]

Many secular songs were composed in the course of the dance, at celebrations which the slaves were conceded by their masters or snatched for themselves from their free time. Some dances were parodies of those that the slaves saw the white folk do, as the cakewalk parodied the parade in the grand march. Most were survivals or adaptations of the dances brought from Africa. Virtually all, in contrast to the relative rigidities of expression among the more elevated classes in Europe and their American imitators, were informed by the improvisation of complex and powerful rhythms. In addition to the stringed and percussive instruments of their own rich musical tradition, blacks adopted from their masters further ones, among them the violin, the guitar, and the clarinet. Sometimes they were given these, so as to be equipped for providing entertainment at white gatherings. Often they made the instruments, or adaptations of them, themselves. And necessarily or not, they could do without instruments altogether, by what was called juba: the clapping of hands together and against knee or shoulder, in an intricacy of rhythms.

The resilience of the slaves was greatly strengthened, too, by the religion which they took from the whites and made their own. The Episcopal Church most closely associated with the dominant planters had little influence on the slaves. Its Southern clergy were rather too reticent in their view of how the glory of God should be celebrated and a good deal too concerned with celebrating the glory of the slave system instead. Evangelical sects had far more appeal, with their emphasis on personal salvation and enthusiasm of worship.

Consigned even by such sects to a dependent role and prevented by the Southern slave laws against assembly from establishing independent churches, slaves contrived to engage in religious celebrations of their own. At these they were able to express themselves more freely, not least in concentrating on those scriptural passages that they found so relevant to their experience. Moses and the exodus from bondage in Egypt, the long journey to the Promised Land, the triumph of David against Goliath, the deliverance of Daniel from the fire in the Old Testament were as vital in their symbolism as the suffering of Jesus and the promise of redemption in the New. From the association of all this with the outpouring of song came the spiritual, perhaps the supreme creative achievement of the slave in the South.

Frederick Douglass confronted the popular white claim that the song of the slave was a sign of contentment: "Slaves sing most when they are most unhappy. The songs of the slave represent the sorrows of his heart; and he is relieved by them, only as an aching heart is relieved by its tears . . . The singing of a man cast away upon a desolate island might be as appropriately considered as evidence of contentment and happiness, as the singing of a slave; the songs of the one and of the other are prompted by the same emotion."[28]

Certainly, sorrow and yearning flowed into the spiritual, but so did joy and hope. Even the darkest of spirituals could suddenly light up, as in "Sometimes I Feel Like a Motherless Child," with the lines:

Sometimes I feel like
A eagle in de air . . .
Spread my wings an'
Fly, fly, fly.

The vividly visualized details of the agony on the cross and the retributions of Judgment Day have the dramatic power of such medieval poems as *Stabat Mater* and *Dies Irae*. "Dey pierced Him in the side . . . Dey nail Him to de cross . . . Dey rivet his feet . . . Dey hanged Him high . . . Dey stretch Him wide." Judgment Day is here also a Day of Wrath. "You'll see de world on fire . . . see de element a meltin' . . . see the stars a fallin' . . . see the moon a bleedin' . . . see the forked lightning." But the Day of Wrath is also a Day of Jubilation. "Hear the rumblin' thunder . . . see the righteous marching . . . see my Jesus coming . . ."

For the spiritual is also clear about what is to be escaped:

No more rain fall for wet you, Hallelujah,
No more sun shine for burn you,
Dere's no hard trials
Dere's no whips a crackin'
No evil-doers in de kingdom.
All is gladness in de kingdom.[29]

Nor was the spiritual concerned only with the release that the next world would provide. The possibility of freedom in this one was also present, in lines such as:

O my Lord delivered Daniel
O why not deliver me too?

Indeed, Frederick Douglass wrote that some slaves had a planned escape to freedom in their minds when they sang:

O Canaan, sweet Canaan,
I am bound for the land of Canaan.

If slaves came to sing of some imminent promise, the implications were not lost on whites. At the time of the slave revolt led by Nat Turner in 1831, there were slaves forbidden to sing

A few more beatings of the wind and rain,
Ere the winter will be over—
Glory, Hallelujah!
Some friends has gone before me—
I must try to go and meet them—
Glory, Hallelujah!
A few more risings and settings of the sun,
Ere the winter will be over—
Glory, Hallelujah!
There's a better day a coming—
There's a better day a coming—
O, Glory, Hallelujah![30]

In 1500, by one of those accidents from which much of history has been made, a Portuguese ship was blown off its course and carried to the east coast of South America. There, on landing, the Portuguese planted their flag, proclaimed the entitlement of their king to this new land, and undertook a tentative exploration. In the jungle they found trees with a wood as red as that which had been imported from the East and become known as *brasil*. The territory acquired a name.

At first the Portuguese Crown took little interest in its new possession. The profits from the trade with India declined, however, as the supply of spices glutted the market, and the expanding textile industry in Europe invested Brazilian dyewood with more importance. Besides, no possession is so dear as one that is coveted by others. Both France and Spain began demonstrating a marked lack of respect for Portugal's claim to sovereignty over Brazil. In 1521, the Portuguese established a garrison at Pernambuco on the eastern bulge of Brazil and in 1530 dispatched five ships to explore the 3,000-mile coast. Two years later, the commander of the expedition initiated the first permanent settlement at São Vicente, near what is now Santos.

In an attempt to extend some control over the vast territory, the king imposed on it a system that had been successfully employed on the islands of Madeira and the Azores. In 1533 he appointed twelve captains, each of whom was granted the equivalent of a private province, with the charge of defending it, attracting settlers for agriculture and trade, and seeing to the spiritual welfare of its inhabitants. The experiment was largely a failure.

The captains were neither equipped nor disposed to do much about spiritual welfare. They were without the resources to secure their respective domains or to promote such economic activity as they could control for their own profit, along with the profit of the Crown. The submissive settlers they wanted were not at all the sort that they got. Those sent to them from the prisons of Portugal were often rebels against Church or State and disinclined to pursue any purpose but their own. Scarcely more tractable were those of means, who had not come halfway across the world to build empires for someone else.

Settlers like these ventured into the interior with the intention of acquiring vast estates and, once having seized them, set about enslaving as many of the "Indians" as they could capture. The indigenous population was not large. This was a land of hunters and gatherers rather than of developed agricultural communities. Imported diseases along with the toll of forced labor drastically reduced the indigenous population within the colonial compass. Crown and Church were uncomfortable with the thought that their spiritual mission, so much proclaimed in support of Portuguese sovereignty over Brazil, was associated with practices likely to end in the extinction of those to whom the mission was directed. The resort to importing slaves from Africa, where the Portuguese were profitably established in the trade, was all too predictable.

In 1549 the king appointed a captain-general to represent the Crown and govern in its name, decreed that Bahia (the present-day São Salvador) should be the capital of a unified Brazil, and sent six ships with a complement of a thousand men, six of them Jesuits. These last soon proved to be troublesome in their preoccupation with the rights of the Indians. By 1580, Brazil was prospering from the export of dyewood, cotton, and especially sugar. It had sixty sugar mills and a "population of between 17,000 and 25,000 Portuguese, 18,000 'civilized' or subjugated Indians and 14,000 Negro slaves."[1]

In that year, the King of Spain seized the vacant Portuguese throne, leaving the Brazilian settlers largely to rule themselves for fifty years. Such vulnerable independence at last became too inviting. In 1630, the Dutch seized Pernambuco and rapidly extended their control northward to near the mouth of the Amazon. Technologically the most advanced people of the time, they introduced new ways of growing and processing sugar, diversified agricultural production, and imported substantial numbers of slaves to provide the labor.

In 1640, when a Portuguese king was once more on his throne, he recognized the Dutch claim to part of Brazil in return for Dutch help against Spain. Brazilian settlers responded by rising in rebellion and succeeded in driving the Dutch from most of the territory they held. By 1654, when the Dutch finally withdrew altogether, the settlers had made it clear that the Portuguese connection could continue only on their own terms.

They defied Church as well as Crown when it pursued policies that they considered objectionable. Prominent among these was the Jesuit practice of protecting Indians by establishing them on mission land, where thousands took to producing sugar that competed with the output of the plantations. When, in 1640, a Papal Bull against any traffic in Indian slaves was issued, riots broke out in Rio de Janeiro, São Paulo, and Santos. The Jesuits were expelled from São Paulo and not permitted to return for fifteen years.

Yet, however the settlers might riot and ignore Papal Bulls, there were never enough Indians to enslave for the plantations and mines. In the sixteenth century, only 50,000 African slaves had been imported. In the centuries that followed, Brazil would import almost 3,600,000 more. Overall, roughly 38 percent of the slaves transported to the hemisphere were landed in Brazil.[2]

In the region from which the Dutch had been driven, the settlers reasserted themselves in their own way. Such was the neglect of crops other than sugar and tobacco that by the eighteenth century Bahia would frequently suffer a shortage of flour. The planters saw no need to preserve the fertility of the soil, as Dutch husbandry had done, by putting back into it the sugar waste. They ignored the lessons such husbandry had taught of the benefits in raising crops and stock together. They took from the land what it could give and then moved on, to devour more.

The bounty of Brazil seemed boundless. Throughout the colonial period, sugar remained the main export commodity, as new forests were burned to provide unexhausted land for production. Gold was discovered in 1693 and diamonds in 1728. Portuguese and other European immigrants were drawn by the prospect of riches, while London secured large returns on the capital investment it provided. One historian has estimated the yield of gold in Brazil during the eighteenth century at well over thirty million ounces and the yield of diamonds at some three million carats.[3] A rising demand for cotton found planters to profit from it, and for most of the eighteenth century, Brazil was the world's leading exporter, until it was overtaken by cheaper production from the United States. A regional expanse congenial to the cultivation of coffee gave Brazil a new export dominance in the nineteenth century.

It was the slaves who overwhelmingly supplied the requisite labor. They planted and cut the sugarcane, ground and boiled the material in the mills. They mined the gold and diamonds, from earth and river. They raised and picked the cotton. They planted and tended the coffee bushes, harvested and transported the beans. They brought with them their skill at cattle raising, to diversify the development of the interior, as well as their skill at metalworking, to establish the first iron forges in Minas Gerais. To the big houses on the plantations and to the towns, they brought a new cuisine, their old crafts, and the rich tradition of their music.

This did not affect the wastefulness with which they were used, almost as though they were part of the limitless land. One nineteenth-century account of land clearance for cotton and rice production in Maranhão gives a vivid view of the human as well as the ecological cost:

At six o'clock in the morning the overseer forces the poor slave, still exhausted from the evening's labors, to rise from his rude bed and proceed to his work. The first assignment of the season is the chopping down of the forests for the next year's planting, using a scythe to hack down the smaller trees. This work normally goes on for two months, depending upon the type of jungle being cut and the stamina of the slaves.

The next step is the destruction of the large trees, and this, like the previous work, continues for twelve hours each day. At night the slaves return home, where evening work of two or more hours awaits them, depending upon the character of the master. They set fire to the devastated jungle, and then they cut and stack the branches and smaller tree trunks which have escaped the fire and which, occupying the surface of the earth, could hinder development of the crop.

These mounds of branches are again burned, and the result is a sad and devastating scene! Centuries-old tree trunks which two months before had produced a cool, crisp atmosphere over a broad stretch of land, lie on the surface of a field ravaged by fire and covered with ashes, where the slaves are compelled to spend twelve hours under the hot sun of the equator, without a single tree to give them shelter.

This destruction of the forests has exhausted the soil, which in many places now produces nothing but grasses suitable for grazing cattle. The temperature has intensified, and the seasons have become irregular. The rains at times damage the crops, and at other times there is no rain at all. The streams and certain shallow rivers, such as the Itapucuru, have dried up or have become almost unnavigable, and lumber for building has become very rare, or is only found at a great distance from the settlements.[4]

Labor was not the only use to which slaves were put. They were sexually used on such a scale that Brazilians would come purposefully to proclaim miscegenation as having been a major factor in the making of their national identity. Gilberto Freyre, the influential Brazilian writer, attributed the phenomenon to various causes: the peculiar Portuguese ethnic and cultural mix of Iberian and North African, which supported a less cramped attitude to color; Portuguese "lubricity" or lust, which the tropical climate of Brazil reinforced; and the shortage of Portuguese women.

There can be no doubting the importance of this last cause. A population in Portugal of no more than a million could scarcely sustain the loss of sufficient families to undertake any serious attempt at colonizing Brazil, even were conditions there conducive to attracting them. Portuguese emigration to the territory during the sixteenth and seventeenth centuries consisted almost entirely of men. These took first Indian and then increasingly African slave women as concubines and wives, with the blessing of authority. By the time that Portuguese women began to arrive in significant numbers, miscegenation was so widespread and so reputable that many of Brazil's most powerful families counted its progeny among their accepted members.

Marriage to Portuguese women was no impediment to miscegenation. Portuguese men were given to regarding their wives as virtual vassals, and the feudal character of the Brazilian plantocracy reinforced such attitudes. In the great houses of the estates, wives did not presume to interfere with the conduct of their men. Their husbands, in patriarchal inviolability, were often proud to acknowledge as proofs of their own virility and power the children of their union with slave women.

That such unions could and often did lead to the bestowal of freedom on children and their mothers made no difference to the exercise of various cruelties, including sexual ones, by masters on their slaves. As Gilberto Freyre chose to describe it, the "furious passions of the Portuguese must have been vented upon victims who did not always share his sexual tastes." A sadism of the conqueror might surface in the sexual use that the son of the great house made of the black boy given to him as his playmate. It was a sadism, in Freyre's view, that was translated with adulthood into a taste for administering thrashings and a penchant "for giving violent or perverse commands," evident even in the university-educated administrative official. It is to this sadism that Freyre attributed the "refinements" with which "the passion for command has always found victims upon whom to vent itself."[5]

One consequence of this imperious sexual appetite was what Freyre called the "syphilization" of Brazil. This was, to be sure, a plague that marked the slave system virtually everywhere in the hemisphere, but nowhere else did it do so to such an extent. By the beginning of the eighteenth century, foreign writers were distinguishing Brazil as the country where the disease was most common. There was evidently little abatement. In 1872, one in six of those serving in the army was found to be infected. The Baron of Lavradio estimated that no less than half the children he had encountered during his service at the Hospital da Misericórdia in Rio de Janeiro had been syphilitic. Here at least was one scourge of the slave system which was visited on slave and master alike, if also on those who were neither.

Slavery was most brutal in phases of expanding production, when the promptings of paternalism were overtaken by predatory greed. The ruin of the sugar industry in Saint Domingue and the disruption to Caribbean trade during the Napoleonic Wars led to a boom in Brazilian sugar production during the early nineteenth century, with a tenfold increase in related exports. This was succeeded by a soaring world demand for Brazilian coffee. The result was that at the very time when various countries were abandoning the slave trade, and some, such as Britain, were ending the practice of slavery in their colonies, slaves were being brought to Brazil in larger numbers than ever and for the harshest exactions of their labor. The average annual number of slave arrivals there during the eighteenth century—the peak one for the world trade—had been 18,910. In the period from 1811 to 1850, when Brazil bowed to pressure from Britain and formally withdrew from the trade, the annual average was 28,550.[6]

In 1828, Robert Walsh, a British clergyman, visited the huge Rio de Janeiro market for slaves along a winding street called the Valongo. In the book he subsequently wrote about his travels in Brazil, he described the scene, which had produced in him a feeling of "morbid curiosity":

Almost every house in this place is a large ware-room, where the slaves are deposited, and customers go to purchase. These ware-rooms stand at each side of the street, and the poor creatures are exposed for sale like any other commodity. When a customer comes in, they are turned up before him; such as he wishes are handled by the purchaser in different parts, exactly as I have seen butchers feeling a calf; and the whole examination is the mere animal capability, without the remotest inquiry as to the moral quality, which a man no more thinks of, than if he was buying a dog or a mule. I have frequently seen Brazilian ladies at these sales. They go dressed, sit down, handle and examine their purchases, and bring them away with the most perfect indifference. I sometimes saw groups of well-dressed females here, shopping for slaves, exactly as I have seen English ladies amusing themselves at our bazaars . . .[7]

Conditions in the countryside, which absorbed some 70 percent of the slaves, varied according to the character of the work. In the backland regions of Pernambuco, for instance, treatment was generally better on the cattle ranches and cotton estates than on the sugar plantations. A great deal, of course, depended on the attitude and conduct of the individual owner.

The British consul in Recife, H. Augustus Cowper, reported in a series of dispatches to the Earl of Aberdeen in the 1840s on his investigations of the slave system. He singled out for praise one owner, Colonel Gaspar de Menezes Vasconcellos Drummond, whose sugar plantations, worked by 400 slaves "and perhaps 50 freemen," were the best governed in the province. The colonel had drawn up a code for his slaves on the principles of martial law; and ensured that only by this code could a slave be tried and, if found guilty, punished for any offense. His slaves were provided with weekly rations, in quantity equivalent to those received by soldiers, and were required to work 18 hours a day during crop time and "14 hours during the season of comparative rest."

If the best seems very far from good, it clearly became almost admirable by contrast with the conduct of which some proprietors were capable. One such, Colonel Antônio Francisco de Rego Barros of the Genipapo sugar estate, worked his slaves, men and women alike, 20 hours a day. He was "in the constant habit of maiming them" and was said to have killed "upwards of 20 in his fury." His favored punishment for female slaves who had offended him was the injection of pepper vinegar into the vagina; and for male slaves, emasculation.

In his dispatch of August 1843, Cowper summed up his impression of the slave owners: "I fear that if there are not many proprietors to be found so brutal as Antônio Francisco de Rego Barros . . . there are still less to be met with so humane as Colonel Drummond." Of the slaves themselves, he reported:

> Their daughters are always debauched when quite children; and their wives (if they are allowed them) only protected by the loss of beauty, brought on by the thousand ills they suffer. They are over-worked. Who can deny it?
> They are ill-fed: even those few who have sufficient in quantity, would die, they could not live long upon the unwholesome and continual salt beef or fish, which is their unchangeable diet, were it not that they rob the precious limited hours allowed them for sleep, to catch rats or crabs for food, or, perhaps worse, become in secret dirt eaters, and die the most horrible of deaths. They are ill-clothed; let us take the most favourable part of my report, Colonel Drummond's property, where they have two suits a year: for the men, a shirt and a pair of trousers; for the women, a shift and a frock. Can persons, constantly hard at work, keep themselves clean with such a wardrobe, and in such a climate? . . . They are denied many of the privileges of beasts, who are at least allowed to tend their young; these men are not. The birds pair at will; these are prohibited, excepting at the will of a capricious master . . . In a word, my Lord, all the worst features of slavery exist in this province; the endeavour of the master is to suppress alike the intellect, the passions, and the senses of these poor creatures, and the laws aid them in transforming the African man into the American beast.[8]

In 1847 Dr. David Gomes Jardim presented a thesis on "Plantation Diseases and Their Causes" to the Medical Faculty in Rio de Janeiro. In it he declared that a third of the slaves in Brazil were dying as a result of the excessive labor demands to which they were subjected:

> We have constantly observed that work is assigned without concern for the strength of the individuals; that the weak and the strong share the work alike. From this lack of consideration can come only one result, that which daily occurs: the weakest are the first to die, and when they do they are completely emaciated. When I asked a planter why the death rate among his slaves was so exaggerated, and pointed out that this obviously did him great harm, he quickly replied that, on the contrary, it brought him no injury at all, since when he purchased a slave it was with the purpose of using him for only a single year, after which very few could survive; but that nevertheless he made them work in such a way that he not only recovered the capital employed in the purchase, but also made a considerable profit![9]

Predictably, the children born in such conditions had little chance of surviving. Pregnant women or nursing mothers among the slaves were not excused from hoeing, since there was no sufficient benefit to be derived in sacrificing their labor so that their children might, after many years, be added to the work force. In 1871, Senator Cristiano Benedito Ottoni of Minas Gerais, in addressing an assembly of Brazilian planters, pointed to the scarcity of adolescent slaves as proof of a high child mortality rate. Even with the improved treatment of slaves accompanying the rise in their price since Brazil had withdrawn from the trade, no more than 25 to 30 percent of the children born into slavery survived to the age of eight. There were no statistics available for the child mortality rate when the price of slaves had been low, but he was certain that at most only 5 percent of slave children had then survived. [10]

Conditions in the mines were rarely much better than those that prevailed on the plantations. Slaves panning for gold were required to stand up to their waists in very cold water while the rest of their bodies were exposed to the tropical sun. They suffered frequently from vomiting and fever chills, dysentery and kidney diseases, while pleurisy, pneumonia, and malaria were also common. Mutilation or death from earth collapses was an obvious danger in underground mining, as was pulmonary disease from working long hours in poorly ventilated tunnels. Safety regulations were inadequate and in any case largely or altogether ignored. Persistent overwork in itself was a major cause of early death or permanent debility. Journeying through Minas Gerais in 1800, Dr. José Vieira Couto noted that a miner expected half of his slave force to die after ten years and the survivors to be no longer capable of heavy labor. [11] Diamond mining involved similar risks and results. Diet was as bad, punishment as harsh, and overwork as general.

In the towns and cities, conditions varied more widely, according to the multiplicity of occupations in which slaves were engaged and which made visitors, even from the South of the United States, marvel. Slaves were used as draught animals, dragging ill-made carts with huge loads through the narrow streets or carrying bags of coffee weighing 160 pounds on bent head and shoulders. Barefoot slaves bore the sedan chairs or hammocks in which the rich reclined, while others, more ornately dressed and wearing shoes, accompanied their owners to carry umbrellas or parcels. Any suggestion of involvement in menial labor was considered so demeaning to the free that even those of modest means needed to be seen with a distinguishing slave or two. The rich had large retinues of slaves, as much for display as for use, with porters, cooks, laundresses, seamstresses, waitresses, and wet nurses, along with children to do odd jobs.

A multitude of slaves, both men and women, peddled a variety of goods through the streets: vegetables, flowers, fruit, chickens, eggs; cakes, pies, and sweets; cutlery, glassware, china, silver; dresses, shawls, bonnets, shoes, handkerchiefs, pins; devotional literature and novels. Their owners usually accompanied those selling the more valuable wares, such as silver and silks, but also bread, which slaves were not permitted to touch. Some male slaves were engaged in skilled occupations as masons, shoemakers, barbers, carpenters. Numerous female slaves were engaged in prostitution, often for the benefit of their owners. Cities and towns generally contained fewer male than female slaves, since men were in demand for plantation labor, while women were preferred for domestic service and certain industrial employment. In 1872, most of the more than fifty thousand slaves in the textile and clothing industries, for instance, were women.

Many suffered harshly. Slaves of both sexes and various occupations might commonly be seen in chains or with iron rings around their necks or even with iron masks on their faces, in punishment for some offense or as an impediment to their getting drunk. Newspapers carried notices that revealed the kind of treatment that provoked some to run away:

> From Dona Constança Umbelina fled a slave named Anna, of the Benguela nation, who is between 18 and 20 years of age, of ordinary height, a thin face, rather pale in color, big lips, and the upper one very elevated, with some sign of a long gash made by an iron instrument on her face under her right eye. She has elevated breasts, legs that are good-looking but a little bowed. She walks fast and is a little snooty (as we say). She is a market woman, and it is supposed that she is going about on certain city streets such as Saco do Alferes, Praia Dom Manoel, etc. . . . Whoever does me the favor of capturing her will be well paid.[12]

Yet the Brazilian slave system had its other side. By the start of the nineteenth century, the free black and mulatto population was already considerable and continued to increase as the century advanced. This was no longer mainly due to the disposition among white owners to free their slave concubines or the children of such relationships. The law allowed slaves to buy their freedom upon payment of a fair price, and owners who were found to be unreasonable in the price they demanded were frequently overruled when slaves exercised their right of appeal to the authorities. Urbanization and economic growth provided slaves with mounting opportunities to buy their way out of slavery.

In the various gold rushes, owners who could not afford the capital to develop a mine might continue in their occupations and send their slaves to work as *fasqueiros* or itinerant prospectors, on condition that these regularly returned to hand over their takings. Some slaves, inevitably, held back part of the gold. In diamond mining, the theft and concealment of stones posed little difficulty, despite the vigilance of overseers and periodic body searches. In gold and diamond areas alike, there were generally whites or free mulattoes and blacks willing to handle stolen property and hold the savings of slaves, in due course to act as intermediaries or financial sponsors for the purchasing of freedom.

In the towns and cities, there were many more opportunities for slaves to buy their freedom. Owners of skilled slaves, whose market price was correspondingly high, could get back the cost and then make a profit by hiring them out, for an agreed division of earnings. Even without the exercise of some ingenuity to shorten the period, such slaves would not take long to save enough for the price of their freedom. Slaves employed in shops and taverns might risk small dealings on their own behalf for the same purpose.

Domestic female slaves might be told by their owners to take trays of cooked meats and other foodstuffs or drinks into the streets for sale, with the slaves allowed a percentage of the proceeds. Inflation then, as now, was a Brazilian disease that could afflict the most highly placed in society. At the end of the eighteenth century, the regius professor of Greek in Salvador remarked on the frequency with which groups of eight or ten women slaves might be seen emerging from the homes of noble families to peddle various wares.[13] Slave women who took to prostitution, at the orders and for the benefit of their owners, could easily enough hold back part of their earnings.

There were also special brotherhoods for those of African descent which supplied slave applicants with loans to buy their freedom. In Rio de Janeiro, for instance, the Brotherhood of Our Lady of the Rosary and Ransom was established precisely for this purpose. Less charitable were owners who freed those of their slaves so old or ill as to be incapable of enough labor and who preferred this way of dealing with them to providing for their upkeep or medical treatment. Finally, there were those slaves who acquired their freedom by taking to their heels and evading recapture.

Formal freedom did not, however, put an end to the plight of many blacks and mulattoes. For despite such tributes as Gilberto Freyre and other Brazilian writers have paid to the laxity of Portuguese racial attitudes, color remained a formidable force of discrimination. The very word "negro" bore the stigma of slavery, as a royal declaration of 1755 demonstrated:

> Among the many regrettable practices and pernicious abuses, which have resulted in the disparagement of the Indians, one prime abuse is the unjustifiable and scandalous practice of calling them *negros*. Perhaps by doing so the intent was no other than to induce in them the belief that by their origins they had been destined to be the slaves of whites, as is generally conceded to be the case of blacks from the Coast of Africa. This abominable abuse, in addition to being offensive to the gentility of the aforesaid Indians, also violates the royal laws prohibiting designation as *negros* of those very persons whom the king wishes to ennoble by declaring them clean of any charge of infamy and thus making them eligible for honorific positions.[14]

It was the whites who made the rules, and the rules, written or not, reflected a presumption of black inferiority. Phrases in common usage revealed the contemptuous equation. A "person of infected blood" (*pessoa de sangue infecta*) or someone possessing a "defect of blood" (*defeito de sangue*) was accordingly a "person of the lowest social standing" (pessoa de ínfima condição). This attitude informed the treatment of free black and free mulatto alike, on a sliding scale of color. Fiscal measures were more rigorously enforced against darker-skinned shopkeepers, and police searches were often directed at property owned by the darker-skinned. There were even municipal laws that specified "freed slaves," a class likely in practice to be identified by their dark skins, for enforcement measures against "undesirables" such as itinerant peddlers. A light-skinned mulatto who had been born a slave and recently been freed was more acceptable than a black whose parents had both been born to freed slaves.

Some of those who were unacceptable for their complexions and had no such exceptional abilities or material means as might make them acceptable all the same, gravitated to certain occupations conceded to be suitably theirs, such as, for women, that of midwife, and for men, that of barber, who not only shaved and cut hair but also pulled teeth and applied leeches. They opened provision stores which operated also as taverns. They engaged in the illicit market which flourished on the frequent scarcity of foodstuffs.

Agriculture provided further opportunities. The growing of tobacco on smallholdings required relatively little financial outlay, and all the necessary labor could be done by members of the family. A rather more precarious independence might be pursued by fishing or by raising pigs and chickens. Those willing to work for others might find jobs as overseers or drovers on cattle ranches; and as artisans, supervisors in the technical processes of sugar production, or overseers of slave labor, on the great estates.

Many former slaves, however, merely drifted from casual labor into begging, prostitution, and petty crime. The long connection between menial labor and slavery promoted among the freed a determination to avoid the one as associating them with the other.

There were also those who acquired wealth or position, to find that such success had a wonderful effect on the way they were seen. Henry Koster, a British visitor who lived in Pernambuco from 1809 to 1820, observed closely the social peculiarities there.

"The degraded state of the people of color in the British colonies is most lamentable," he wrote. "In Brazil, even the trifling regulations which exist against them remain unattended to. A mulatto enters into holy orders or is appointed a magistrate, his papers stating him to be a white man, but his appearance plainly denoting the contrary. In conversing on one occasion with a man of color who was in my service, I asked him if a certain Capitam-mor (Captain major) was not a mulatto man; he answered, 'he was, but is not now.' I begged him to explain, when he added, 'Can a Capitam-mor be a mulatto man?' "[15]

At such elevations, Brazil was kinder or blinder to color than prevailing practice allowed in the North of the United States after the Civil War. André

Rebouças, a mulatto, became in Brazil a successful economist and engineer, highly regarded in particular for his work in the construction of Rio de Janeiro's new docks. In 1873, he visited New York City. He was refused a room at one hotel and only with help from the son of the Brazilian consul was he given a room at another, of the third class, on condition that he never dined in the restaurant. Then, on wishing to attend a performance at the Grand Opera House, he found that "color prejudice" prevented him from doing so. This was not how he was treated at home.[16]

There were others before him who had emerged to renown and respect in Brazil. In the cultural florescence of the eighteenth century, a number of blacks and mulattoes had done so, as composers of baroque music, as architects, sculptors, and painters. Some of these had been free; some had acquired their freedom in recognition of their gifts. Their very success had effectively bleached them, as it would bleach others, during the next two centuries, in the arts and sciences, the professions and politics, the production and accumulation of wealth. Like isolated lights, they interrupted but did not change the dark to which many millions of others were contemptuously consigned.

9 | THE LAST FRONTIER

~~~~~~

When Columbus encountered the island of Cuba in 1492, he described it as "the most beautiful land that human eyes have ever seen." It was not for beauty, however, that Spain valued its new possessions, and it was the island of Hispaniola that held Spanish interest, until the failure to find enough treasure there and the rapid depletion of its indigenous people shifted interest to Cuba. In 1511, an expedition of some one hundred men landed on the island and made short work of the little resistance that was offered.

A few Spaniards, using subjugated indigenous labor, extracted what gold there was along the rivers, and in 1523 credit was provided for settlers to establish a sugar mill. Yet Spain was already becoming preoccupied elsewhere. In 1519, Hernán Cortes had set out from Cuba with his band of adventurers to fall upon and conquer the Aztec empire on the Central American mainland. Here at last was more gold than their experience of the New World had so far led the Spaniards to expect, and settlers in Cuba abandoned their holdings to join in the rush for riches. Cuba became little more than a service station for passing ships, which loaded the salted meat from the cattle raised on the savannahs. By 1544, the island had a population of fewer than 7,000, composed of some 5,000 surviving indigenous Indians, some 660 Spaniards and some 800 black slaves.[1]

Though slaves continued to be imported, the economic activity of the island did not require enormous numbers. Cattle ranching remained the most profitable pursuit for the white settlers throughout the seventeenth century and during most of the eighteenth, as a rising demand for leather in Europe augmented the traditional market in the provisioning of ships. Tobacco, grown on relatively small holdings, was also finding a market abroad. But the sugar industry, that great devourer of labor, was still of small importance. In 1774, there were just short of 39,000 slaves, representing roughly 23 percent of the population.[2] Most of these worked in the countryside; the rest worked as artisans, in construction, at the ports, or in domestic service.

The slave insurrection and ensuing warfare that struck the French colony of Saint Domingue during the last decade of the eighteenth century devastated the predominant sugar industry in the Caribbean, to transform the economy of Cuba. Many French refugees from Saint Domingue arrived on the island and were material there in a rapid development of sugar production. By 1800, Cuba was producing more than 28,000 tons; by 1820, more than 43,000; and by 1830, more than 70,000.

Such large and rapid increases in sugar output involved a corresponding increase in the requisite labor force. In 1791, Spain lifted restrictions on the slave trade to Cuba and reduced the duties payable on such imports. Traders, whatever their nationality, who were engaged in supplying slaves to Cuba were allowed to export from there, free of any duty, rum and other commodities. Between 1790 and 1820, over 225,000 slaves were landed at Havana.[3]

A further, lasting impact on Cuba came from the series of wars, following the French Revolution, which cut off Spain from its colonies and led to increasing trade between Cuba and the United States. Spain itself promoted this by opening the island to the import of United States foodstuffs for slaves. In due course, the United States would become the single largest market for Cuban sugar, and Cuba would become an economic dependency of the United States.

Within Cuba, meanwhile, land reform brought new proprietors into the production of coffee and tobacco as well as sugar. Spain looked to an economic diversification that would loosen the dependence on slave labor. Economic factors disposed otherwise. Coffee farming proved less profitable than sugar, with mounting competition from Brazilian coffee supplies. Tobacco encountered protective tariffs in the United States. Sugar spread over ever more land. The laying of a railroad meant that cane could now be moved more rapidly and less wastefully from remote areas to the mills, and sugar could be moved similarly from the mills to the ports. Mill owners bought up idle land and smallholdings, for a sugar industry of increasing capitalist concentration, based on vast estates with commensurate forces of slave labor.

By 1855, sugar and sugar products were accounting for almost 84 percent of Cuba's exports, in what had become virtually a one-crop economy. From little over 70,000 tons in 1830, Cuban sugar production had increased more than tenfold, by 1870, to 726,000 tons. Within the sixty years from 1811 to 1870, some 550,000 slaves were brought to the island, or a number almost equivalent to the 578,600 brought to the whole of Spanish America in the preceding 110 years.[4]

In some respects, the slave system in Cuba was relatively benevolent. The institution of *coartación*, by which slaves were entitled to buy their freedom at a price agreed upon with their owners, along with the freedom often bestowed on the progeny of miscegenation produced a higher ratio of free black and mulatto to slave than in most slave-owning societies in the hemisphere. By 1872, there were some 107,000 free blacks and mulattoes on the island, alongside 287,000 slaves and 306,000 whites.[5] Spanish law also recognized the legal personalities of slaves in a way which provided far more protection of their rights than that afforded by the slave codes of the Southern United States. Its punitive provisions were less harsh and sweeping; it allowed slaves recourse to the courts for redress against undue abuse; it protected slave marriages.

While very far from disregarding distinctions of color, Cuba was also racially more relaxed than were other parts of the hemisphere during their periods of slavery. Free Cubans of color with appropriate aptitudes made their way into official posts, the university, and the professions, without consequently coming to be considered whites. A number of blacks and mulattoes achieved success as writers. This did not mean that whites took lightly their social domination or the means by which it was sustained. Gathering fears of black rebelliousness in the nineteenth century led to reductions in the number of free blacks permitted to serve in the army.

Yet there was a more gruesome Cuba, to be glimpsed in the demographic record. After slave imports that totaled 770,000, there were in 1870 no more than 394,000 blacks, slave or free.[6] Contributing to this was the limit placed on the natural increase of the slave population by the gender imbalance, as planters concentrated on purchasing males from whom more labor might be exacted. The excess of males over females in the slave force rose from 10,000 in 1792 to the enormous figure of 126,000 in 1841, before falling to just short of 67,000 in 1861.[7] Even where children were born to slaves, the mortality rate was high. On the sugar plantations, this was generally estimated at some 200 per 1,000.

Though the law was elaborate with protective provisions, it did not deal with overwork. In the sugar industry, the conventional wisdom was that a slave needed only four hours of sleep a night. Indeed, one sugar mill which allowed six hours enjoyed the reputation of being peculiarly philanthropic. Visitors to Cuban sugar plantations in the nineteenth century were virtually unanimous in commenting on the incessant labor required to supply the mills at harvest time. The steam engines that had replaced animal or water power to drive the crushing machinery were unremitting in their demands, and slaves worked round the clock at cutting and clearing the cane, feeding the crushers, fueling and filling the boilers. Moreover, the staggering of crops meant that this season often stretched from February to May. From July to October, there was the work of hoeing, weeding, and manuring to be done in the fields. In between, there was the preparing of still more ground for cultivation.

The cumulative effects of overwork and undernourishment were responsible for crippling or fatal accidents at the mills, low resistance to tropical diseases, and the collapse of bodies no longer able to sustain the exactions imposed upon them. One prominent British abolitionist, R. R. Madden, concluded from his personal observation that nowhere else in the hemisphere were slave conditions "so desperately wretched" as those to be seen on the plantations of inland Cuba.[8]

The natural decrease in the slave population that required a continual landing of replacements has been estimated at 4 percent or more a year during the nineteenth century, until the trade, already long illegal, finally ended. Since this overall estimate included losses among urban slaves, who were in general much better treated, and those among other slaves in less demanding sectors of agricultural production, the annual cost in lives among the almost 70,000 on the sugar plantations must have been appreciably higher.

Where brutality is acceptable in the predominant sector of the economy, it is likely to affect attitudes and conduct well beyond the exactions of labor. In fact, for all the protective provisions of the law, slaves were sometimes killed with impunity by their owners in response to trivial offenses. One mill owner killed a slave waitress merely because he had not been served quickly enough. Even a prominent Havana lawyer had a slave flogged to death for suspected theft. Havana itself boasted a special building, outside the old gates of the city, where local slaves were whipped to encourage an obedient disposition.

Brutality, calculated or casual, along with the related disregard of inconvenient laws, would have an influence on Cuban social and political development long after the abolition of slavery in 1886, nearly a quarter of a century after slavery came to an end in the United States.

TWO

The Insurgent
Spirit

~~~~~~

The first revolt of slaves in Spain's New World came hard upon their arrival on the island of Hispaniola. On December 27, 1522, twenty slaves on the estate of Don Diego, son of Christopher Columbus, joined with a similar number of slaves on a nearby estate to attack and kill a few Spaniards. Then they set off to reach the mountain retreat from which Enrique, the leader of indigenous Indian resistance, was conducting guerrilla warfare. Stopping along the way at the estate of Michael de Castro, they killed a Spaniard there, induced one black and eleven Indians owned by de Castro to join them, and camped for the night near a sugar mill which they intended to attack at dawn. Informed by de Castro of their position, Don Diego dispatched a force to deal with them. The one black and eleven Indians belonging to de Castro fled back to him. The rebels dispersed, to be hunted down and hanged.

In 1546, slaves revolted again, to loot the sugar mill of Cepicepi, despite the protection provided by a tower and two crossbowmen. An official report of 1548 stated that the revolt had been crushed "as never before in the history of the island," with "the escaped slaves . . . so dispersed that no memory of them remained." Revolt, or at least the fear of it, apparently persisted, however. In 1552, it was decreed that all sugar mills should henceforth be built of masonry and in the form of forts.

Elsewhere in Spain's spreading American empire slaves were proving troublesome, too. In 1537, the authorities discovered and dealt with a black slave conspiracy in Mexico to kill all the whites. Actual slave revolts broke out there in both 1546 and 1570. In 1548, a formidable slave insurrection struck the San Pedro mining district of Honduras. Puerto Rico in 1527, Panama in 1531, and Venezuela in 1532 experienced slave revolts.[1] In Colombia, rebelling slaves destroyed the town of Santa Marta in 1530, and after it had been rebuilt, seriously damaged it in 1550. In 1548, slaves in the mining district of the Colombian interior killed twenty whites and took 250 Indians along as hostages, while retreating to establish a community of their own beyond the emplacements of Spanish rule.

In Peru, there were two revolts notable for involving the alliance of black slaves and Indians. Near Cuzco in the highland province of Vilcabamba, more than two thousand blacks and a still larger number of Indians had been put to the mining of gold deposits. By 1602, a band of runaways both black and Indian from this labor force was, under the leadership of an Indian named Francisco Chichima, becoming so disruptive in its raids that the governor of the region called on the help of Indian allies. Before such assistance arrived, organized rebellion broke out. Signaling the start, some twenty black slaves on a local plantation burned the buildings there; within a few hours, virtually all the black slaves in the surrounding valley were in revolt, and more than one hundred Spaniards were besieged on one of the estates. Two days later, a large force of Spaniards and loyal Indians rescued the besieged. The rebellion collapsed, and Chichima's band, hunted down in the hills, soon surrendered. When the governor visited the area, the blacks presented him with Chichima's head as a peace offering. The peace was short-lived. Only two years afterward, blacks and Indians together rebelled, but with no more success.

Clearly, Spanish rule would have been far more imperiled if the combination of black and Indian resistance had been more frequent and widespread. This combination was, however, even rarer elsewhere in Spain's mainland American empire than it was in Peru. Justifiably or not, blacks saw in the submission of the indigenous Indians to their conquerors a lack of spirit. Of their own defiance, they left authority in little doubt. In 1615, the overseer of the royal shipyard at the Peruvian port of Callao complained of a slave population in Lima, the capital, "so insolent and daring that one can truthfully say that they are the masters and the masters their servants." If the Indians saw in such insolence and daring a disposition to overthrow white rule only to replace it with a black one, the blacks were partly to blame. Too many of them found relief from the humiliation of their slavery by seeking to humiliate Indians in turn.

They also released the pressure of their rage at the violence against them in violence against one another. A certain Juan Ramos de Guana in Lima protested to the Crown in 1584 that the law officers were not doing their duty and cited the brawls and killings among blacks who, denied access to more usual weapons, would use kitchen knives "to stab one another for the slightest provocation at their dances and drinking parties." Blacks also reacted in other ways to their ill-treatment. The Peruvian chronicler Felipe Guamán Poma de Ayala held the slaveholders responsible for the misconduct of their slaves: "They punish them cruelly, they give them no food, they demand much money from them . . . These are the reasons why they run away and steal."[2]

Running away was, indeed, the most common form of resistance to slavery and the most common of black crimes in Spanish America. Of 502 recorded cases of black crime in Peru in the period 1560–1650, for instance, over half, or 270, were for running away, while theft accounted for 81, assault for 72, and murder for 36.[3] Nor was running away for many the end of resistance. Those who freed themselves often did so in groups or joined others to defend their freedom from fortified retreats. From these, they often went on the offensive to raid white settlements for supplies, kill whites, or stir insurgency among the remaining slaves.

As early as 1544 in Peru, such so-called *cimarrones* or maroons were reported to be attacking people and robbing farms on the outskirts of Lima and Trujillo. In 1545, a force of 120 men was dispatched to deal with a community of some two hundred maroons who had acquired quantities of Spanish arms, held a fortified position in marshland a few miles north of Lima along the coast, and were suspected of having allies among the slaves in the capital. The community was annihilated, but at the cost of eleven Spaniards killed and many others wounded.

The spread and tightening of colonial control in Peru reduced the incidence of maroon activity. Then, in the 1630s, as the local slave population reached a record level, such activities revived. In 1631, a large group of galley slaves escaped from Callao, to be joined in the hills above Lima by other fugitive slaves. The community that they established evaded or successfully resisted all efforts by the authorities to suppress it, until a free mulatto soldier located its hideout and led a detachment of troops there.

Perhaps most remarkable was a group of only thirty maroons who operated nine leagues—roughly twenty-seven miles—from Lima. In November 1633, they ambushed a mule train and captured thirty-six loaded mules. An armed force sent in December to deal with them returned unsuccessful, only to be collectively imprisoned when it became known that the maroons had traded a sizable share of the loot for their freedom. A second expedition, dispatched in early April 1634, returned with nothing; a third, later in the same month, returned with a single captive. A force of Indians finally succeeded in May and sent back to Lima twelve live maroon women and the heads of six maroon men. This spelled the end of only one group, however, and maroon activity continued despite increased police patrols of the capital's outskirts. In 1640, a very large force was dispatched to deal with "the troops of black runaways . . . going about the roads and farms of the countryside," and order of a sort was restored.[4]

The very act of running away involved a defiance that reached beyond any fear of the ferocious penalties attached. As early as 1535, the authorities in Lima had decreed that runaways absent for up to six days were liable to be castrated, while those absent for longer were liable to be executed. Slaves who hid or otherwise aided runaways were subject to one hundred lashes for a first offense, castration for a second, and death for a third. Clearly, the threat of such punishments did not deter some slaves from running away or others from helping them.

What took place in Peru was no less common elsewhere in Spanish America. Among the earliest of maroon communities was one established in 1549 by runaway slave pearl divers from the island of Margarita, off the Venezuelan coast, where the regime was especially harsh. Another substantial community was established in Venezuela during the 1550s, when a Creole slave from Puerto Rico led a revolt of slaves laboring in the gold mines. As King Miguel, he governed eight hundred maroons, whose activities closed the mines until a Spanish military force arrived to extinguish the community. In the 1550s as well, a large community of maroons, led by an African slave who came to be known as King Bayano, flourished on the Isthmus of Panama. In 1572, Francis Drake, reaching Panama at the head of an English raiding expedition, encountered a number of maroon communities with an estimated aggregate population of three thousand, some of whom joined him to plunder the rich town of Nombre de Dios.[5] Drake would invite the help of maroons again in 1586, when they joined him in overrunning Santo Domingo, the capital of Hispaniola.

It was not until early in the seventeenth century that Spain's colonial authorities decided to deal with the more formidable of the maroon communities by coming to an accommodation with them. In 1609, they signed a treaty with a maroon leader called Yanga in the Vera Cruz region of Mexico, by which some one hundred maroons composing a troublesome community were given their freedom and the right to local autonomy in return for a pledge to end all raiding and hand over any future runaways. Such treaties were, however, rare departures from the reliance on force. In the 1690s, for instance, the authorities responded to mounting maroon activities along the northern coast of Colombia with a major military campaign, which eliminated a dozen communities, four of them composed of more than two hundred maroons each, engaged in farming by family units along African lines and governed by kings and religious leaders.

Large slave revolts required corresponding concentrations of slaves and accordingly occurred at the silver mines of northern Mexico and the copper mines of Peru in the seventeenth century, as on the gold fields in the Chocó region of Colombia in the eighteenth. Yet formidable revolts could break out unexpectedly elsewhere. One led by Andresote in the Yuracay Valley of Venezuela in the early 1730s annihilated a force of three hundred Spanish troops before succumbing to a force of some fifteen hundred. At the Venezuelan port of Coro in the late eighteenth century, slaves fired by reports of revolutionary developments in France and by hopes of receiving French aid mounted a rebellion suppressed only by a massive investment of Spanish military force with Indian auxiliaries. In the ensuing repression, there were 171 executions.[6]

The nineteenth-century wars of independence from Spain enhanced the opportunities for slaves to abscond in conditions of disorder. They also involved slaves in the conflict, as the contending forces sought to make use of them, either by recruiting them with the promise of freedom or by inciting them to rebel behind enemy lines. The slaves were not, however, to be easily misled. In Venezuela, for instance, their increasing doubts about the real intentions of the independence movement promoted a shift among them to the royalist side, for help in the crushing of the short-lived first republic.

The lesson was not lost on Simón Bolívar, who engaged the aid of Haiti for another republican attempt in Venezuela by promising that success would be followed by the freeing of the slaves there. While he kept his word by a corresponding proclamation, this met insurmountable resistance from those who were not disposed to be dispossessed of their property. The pressure for abolition continued to increase, however, and there was no extensive slave-based plantation investment on the mainland capable of containing it for long. One after another, the new independent states of Spanish-speaking America would repudiate slavery.

Cuba was a different matter. It was so rich that Spain would cling to it until almost the end of the century; and the plantation interest was so predominant that the colony would keep slavery until 1886. There, too, throughout the centuries, slaves expressed their resistance in revolt.

They did so, indeed, virtually from their arrival. In 1538, they joined forces with the French to sack Havana. In 1731, slaves on the copper mines of Santiago rebelled. Defiance could be solitary. In 1736, for instance, a slave was condemned to death for burning cane fields, though then pardoned, reportedly in response to a sign of intercession from Our Lady of Rosario. Sometimes it was particular conditions that produced an uprising. One large slave revolt in the early nineteenth century on a plantation near Cienfuegos seems to have been at least partly due to the total absence of women among the seven hundred slaves.

By the 1840s, after the freeing of slaves in the British West Indies, the resistance to slavery in Cuba increased sharply. In 1841, slaves building a palace in Havana for a prominent planter rebelled and engaged in battle with Spanish troops. In 1843, a whole series of revolts on various plantations left several sugar mills badly damaged, while slaves on the Cárdenas railroad revolted independently. A large number of slaves were killed, while others fled into the interior. In early 1844, a considerable conspiracy which involved free blacks and mulattoes as well as slaves was discovered and became the occasion for an onslaught from the authorities directed as much at intimidation as at punishment. Some four thousand were arrested, roughly half of whom were free blacks; one hundred or so were whipped to death, and seventy-eight, including the mulatto poet Plácido and the free black musician Roman, were shot.[7]

Throughout the era of Cuban slavery, running away was the most common form of resistance, and the island's professional slave-catchers, or *rancha-dores*, with their specially trained dogs, were renowned across the Caribbean for their ferocious efficiency. They were paid for killing runaways as well as for bringing them back alive, since the loss of property in a dead slave was considered less serious than the danger of marauding maroons.

Esteban Montejo, who had been a runaway in Cuba from 1868 to 1878, survived into the 1960s, to describe the impulse and experience of such defiance in Spanish America:

I have never forgotten the first time I tried to escape. That time I failed, and I stayed a slave for several years longer from fear of having the shackles put on me again. But I had the spirit of a runaway watching over me, which never left me. And I kept my plans to myself so that no one could give me away. I thought of nothing else; the idea went round and round my head and would not leave me in peace; nothing could get rid of it, at times it almost tormented me . . .

One day I began to keep my eye on the overseer. I had already been sizing him up for some time. That son-of-a-bitch obsessed me, and nothing could make me forget him. I think he was Spanish. I remember that he was tall and never took his hat off. All the blacks respected him because he would take the skin off your back with a single stroke of his whip. The fact is I was hot-headed that day. I don't know what came over me, but I was filled with a rage which burned me up just to look at the man.

I whistled at him from a distance, and he looked round and then turned his back; that was when I picked up a stone and threw it at his head. I know it must have hit him because he shouted to the others to seize me. But that was the last he saw of me, because I took to the forest there and then . . .

I didn't want to be taken into slavery again. It was repugnant to me, it was shameful. I have always felt like that about slavery. It was like a plague—it still seems like that today.[8]

11 | GUERRILLA WARFARE IN GUIANA

~~~~~~

As the richer indigenous civilizations of Central and South America were conquered and plundered by Spain, greed came to be directed at the possibility of some still to be discovered empire, full of treasure, in the unmapped interior. The legend of a ruler called by the Spanish *El Dorado*, "the Gilded One," who once a year was covered in gold dust before he plunged into a lake, invested the greed with romance. Sir Walter Raleigh arrived at the belief that the site was somewhere in the mysterious territory east of Venezuela and north of Brazil.

His book *The Discoverie of Guiana*, which followed his voyage there in 1595, excited wide European interest. The Dutch, less inclined to romantic visions, were stirred by the prospect of finding a new trade source of tobacco, since their rebellion against Spanish rule had deprived them of their customary supplies. As early as 1597, a small Dutch party was already trading in the area. Soon afterward, successive groups of English adventurers and settlers arrived, to grow tobacco and cotton as well as search for indications of gold.

The first major colonial undertaking there was an English one in the middle of the seventeenth century, when planters engaged mainly in sugar production were supplied with the necessary black slaves, since the indigenous people resisted demands for their labor by simply retreating beyond reach. One colony led to others, and a few slaves to a vast quantity. Subsequent shifts in sovereignty, as European conflicts affected colonial control in Guiana, complicate the record of slave imports throughout the era of slavery. Together, Dutch and British Guiana may eventually have taken roughly 500,000 slaves according to one authority, Philip Curtin,[1] or roughly 850,000 according to another, Noel Deerr,[2] while French Guiana, the economic laggard, took roughly 50,000.

By 1665, the three rival European nations had settlements in Guiana; and while all three laid claim to the entire territory between the Orinoco and the Amazon, their settlements occupied relatively little space, and were generally confined to the coast or along various rivers. The English colony, situated mainly along the Suriname River, was the largest and encompassed some five hundred plantations. The Dutch settlements were widely scattered, reaching beyond Cayenne in the east and well into what would become British Guiana to the west. The French were clustered at Cayenne and along the Sinnamary River.

In the Second Anglo-Dutch War of 1665–67, the American colonies of the belligerents were both sites and spoils of engagement. By the terms of the treaty which sealed the Peace of Breda in 1667, England acquired from the Dutch a North American colony called New Netherland which came to be renamed New York, while the Dutch acquired the thriving English colony of Surinam in Guiana. By a subsequent agreement in 1674 that brought the Third Anglo-Dutch War to an end, the English colonists in Surinam were given the opportunity to depart with all their transportable assets. Some of the slaves were accordingly transported by their masters, mainly to Jamaica. Others, left behind, seized the opportunity to run away. They comprised the earliest substantial group of so-called Bush Negroes, who sought to assert and secure their freedom in the interior.

The Dutch now devoted much of their attention in Guiana to Surinam and were successful in attracting French Protestants and Jews to assist in the development of the predominantly sugar economy. Inevitably this involved large new imports of slaves. In 1712, during the War of the Spanish Succession (1701–13), a French force of some three thousand men pillaged the colony. The planters fled with their families and slaves into the interior. When the payment of a massive ransom secured the departure of the French force, many of the slaves disappeared into the forests rather than return with their masters. These and the earlier runaways soon came to constitute a considerable disruptive force. They raided outlying plantations, killed settlers, set fire to homes and sugar mills. They took away with them not only whatever weapons they could find but also slaves to augment their numbers. The expeditions of soldiers and settlers sent against them were seldom successful in combating the guerrilla resistance they met in the forests. The Dutch dealt cruelly with any prisoners they took: burning them over slow fires, breaking them on the wheel, or hanging them from hooks driven through their ribs. But if the purpose was to discourage more slaves from running away to join the rebels, it signally failed. Slaves continued to abandon the plantations for the forests, while those who remained often provided intelligence for rebel raids.

In 1730, a slave revolt spread rapidly from one plantation to another, and it took the authorities three years to crush it altogether. Even then, intermittent warfare continued between the settlers and the rebels in the forests, till at last, in 1749, the Dutch effectively sued for peace. In return for promising to restore all future runaways to their plantations, the rebels were offered formal recognition of their freedom. Terms were concluded first with one important rebel leader, Captain Adoe, and then with another, Captain Samsam or Zam Zam. This failed to bring peace, for suspicions persisted on both sides. There were other rebel leaders more difficult to conciliate, and raids on plantations continued for years.

At last, in 1762, the conclusion of a general treaty was celebrated with the parade in state of the rebel representatives through the capital and their entertainment at the Governor's own table. The Dutch acknowledged the freedom of two large black communities, the Seramica and the Ouca. Numbering some three thousand in all, these were also promised a specified annual quantity of arms and ammunition in return for their own promise to be faithful allies of the colony, to deliver up future runaways for due reward, and to keep their own settlements at a proper distance from the capital and the plantations.

This was followed only one year later by the largest slave revolt so far, which came close to ending the life of the colony. Even its eventual failure did not prompt much settler rejoicing, since it led many slaves to flee from the plantations and join the now free blacks in the forests. Attempts by local detachments to recapture them proved so futile that the States-General found it necessary to raise and dispatch a formidable force of soldiers from Holland. Among these was, as a captain of the Scots Brigade in mercenary recruitment, a certain John Stedman, whose subsequent account of a sustained black resistance movement is one of the most vivid and detailed to have come from the era of slavery.[3]

No mere narrator of events, Stedman examined the context: the "trade and intrinsic value of this blood-spilling colony," with its hundreds of plantations producing sugar, coffee, cacao, cotton, indigo, and timber, and the extravagant style in which the white community lived.[4] While citing certain instances of owners who were kind to their slaves, he made it clear that these were overwhelmed by the prevailing ill-treatment, amounting often to cruelty, of which he provided examples in horrified detail.

"By such inhuman usage," he continued, "this unhappy race of men are driven to such a height of desperation, that to finish their days, and be relieved from worse than Egyptian bondage, some have even leaped into the caldrons of boiling sugar, thus at once depriving the tyrant of his crop and of his servant.

"From these sketches can it be a matter of surprize, that armies of rebels are assembled in the forest, and at every opportunity thirsting for revenge?"[5]

By the time of Stedman's arrival, the number of the once rebellious and now recognized free blacks, in formal alliance with the colony, totaled "no less than fifteen or twenty thousand"; and he concluded that, "should the

peace be ever broken, these new allies will become the most dreadful foes
that ever the colony of Surinam can have to contend with." In fact, the
terms of the alliance were only in part being observed by the free black
communities. These had bound themselves to keep the peace, and "the
negroes themselves are uncommonly tenacious of these solemn engagements,
as I never heard of an instance, during all the time I resided in the colony,
of one of them violating his oath."[6] Yet their agreement to deliver up future
runaways in return for arms and reward did not require them to seek out
and capture such runaways. They remained, therefore, effectively neutral,
and this made all the more remarkable the achievement of the new black
rebels in sustaining on their own their commitment to freedom for so many
years.

In their forest retreats, they established agricultural settlements from which
they would emerge to raid individual plantations. Short of weapons, they
would intermingle with the armed among them some who bore only crooked
sticks in the shape of muskets. This appearance of overall strength "more
than once had the effect of preventing a proper defense by the plantation
slaves, when the rebels came to ransack the estates . . ." Against the well-
armed military forces, they employed their developing skills as guerrilla
fighters. They would shoot from behind trees and use spies to track the troops
until these were so weakened by disease or vulnerably positioned as to invite
attack. On one occasion, for instance, "they laid themselves in ambush,
near the borders of a deep marsh, through which the soldiers were to pass
to the rebel settlement. No sooner had the unfortunate men got into the
swamp and up to their arm-pits, than their black enemies rushed out from
under cover, and shot them dead at their leisure in the water."

They were adept, too, at dealing with defeat. When one of their settlements
was about to be taken, they set it on fire. "This bold and masterly manoeuvre
not only prevented that carnage to which the common soldiers in the heat
of victory are but too prone, but also afforded the enemy an opportunity of
retreating with their wives and children, and carrying off their most useful
effects; whilst our pursuit, and seizing the spoil, were at once frustrated both
by the ascending flames, and the unfathomable marsh, which we soon
discovered on all sides to surround us."[7]

The rebels were organized into a dozen communities, each of these under
local leadership, in a strategy that provided against a single mass assault by
government forces, while promoting mobility in both attack and defense.
One rebel leader, Chief Baron, acquired a reputation for clemency, since
he sent back to the capital a number of captured soldiers. In contrast, Chief
Bonny, "a relentless Mulatto, who was born in the forest—his mother had
escaped into the forest from the cruel treatment of her owner, by whom she
was then pregnant—had ordered seven captured soldiers to be stripped naked
and flogged to death."[8]

He apparently exercised a more than local dominance, since other leaders, including Baron, sometimes served, with their forces, under his command. A slave woman captured by the rebels and later recaptured by government troops told the authorities that he demanded the strictest discipline from all he led. Only those who had for some years given him "unquestionable proofs of fidelity and resolution" were entrusted with arms. Yet, she reported, "he *still* was more beloved than he was feared, on account of his inflexible justice and manly courage."[9]

The commander-in-chief of the opposing forces, Colonel Fourgeoud, was certainly more feared than loved. Indeed, his ill-usage of his officers, Stedman amongst them, was such as to provoke from one of the free blacks serving under him the comment: "If in this manner these Europeans treat one another, is it to be wondered at that they should take a pleasure in torturing us poor Africans?" He seems to have been, for all that, courageous, determined, and intelligent in developing a suitable strategy, which prefigured modern counterinsurgency methods of search-and-destroy. Accordingly, "while he killed his troops by scores, without making captures on the enemy, he nevertheless did the colony considerable service, by disturbing, hunting and harassing the rebels, and destroying their fields and provisions."[10]

Such a strategy would, however, almost certainly have failed without the collaboration of the so-called Black Rangers, a recently formed body of slaves who had received their freedom in return for a commitment to fight as soldiers in defense of the colony. These now proved indispensable as trackers and were, besides, the most indefatigable of fighters. The authorities sharpened the commitment by rewarding the Ranger with twenty-five florins for every rebel he killed, fifty for every rebel he captured alive, and one thousand for every rebel settlement he discovered. Yet reward was not all. The conflict bred its own ferocities. The Rangers were regarded as traitors by the rebels and were correspondingly treated if they were captured. The clemency that a rebel leader such as Baron might show to white enemy soldiers was never extended to black ones.

One encounter between colonial and rebel forces made a particular impression on Stedman. On August 20, 1775, a detachment of white soldiers and Black Rangers, some three hundred men in all, was encamped under Colonel Fourgeoud's command close to a rebel settlement. In the middle of the night, the camp was aroused by rebel fire, shouts, and song, followed by an exchange of taunts between rebels and Rangers in the dark. Fourgeoud, using an interpreter, interrupted the exchange to promise the rebels life and liberty if they surrendered.

"They replied, with a loud laugh, that they wanted nothing from him . . . They told us, that we were to be pitied more than they; that we were *white slaves*, hired to be shot at and starved for four-pence a day; that they scorned to expend much more of their powder upon such scarecrows; but should the planters or overseers dare to enter the woods, not a soul of them should ever return, any more than the perfidious rangers, some of whom might depend upon being massacred that day, or the next; and by declaring that *Bonny* should soon be the governor of the colony."

On the morning of August 22, a group of soldiers with Stedman at the head reached the rebel settlement, only to find the thirty homes there deserted and the neighboring fields stripped. "[We] discovered that the reason of the rebels shouting, singing, and firing, on the night of the 20th, was not only to cover the retreat of their friends . . . but by their unremitting noise to prevent us from discovering that they were employed, men, women, and children, in preparing warimboes or hampers filled with the finest rice, yams, and cassava, for subsistence during their escape, of which they had only left the chaff and refuse for our contemplation.

"This was certainly such a masterly trait of generalship in a savage people, whom we affected to despise, as would have done honor to any European commander, and has perhaps been seldom equalled by more civilized nations."[11]

With the readiness of its command to accept a ratio of twenty dead among its own forces to every rebel killed, the military campaign at last succeeded in driving the rebel slaves across the Marawina River into the French-controlled territory around Cayenne. Stedman himself left a supposedly pacified Surinam in March 1777. The rebels then returned, however, reportedly with fresh arms and ammunition supplied by the French, who had their own quarrel with the Dutch. In fact, it would take twenty years from the outbreak of conflict for the rebels in Surinam to be pacified, and then only with the agreement of the colonial authorities to recognize them as free.

Nor was slave rebellion against the Dutch limited to Surinam. To the west was the small colony of Berbice, whose population contained, apart from an unrecorded number of indigenous survivors, 346 whites and 3,833 black slaves. In July 1762, three dozen slaves set fire to their owner's house and escaped into the forest. Most were recaptured and punished. This was only a beginning.

In February of the following year, slaves on two plantations revolted, killing two whites before fleeing up the Corentyne River. From this retreat, they emerged to plunder plantations, kill whites, and gather other slaves to their cause, until they numbered some nine hundred. Panic seized the colony. Many whites fled from their estates, leaving their slaves behind to join the rebels. When news reached Fort Nassau on March 6 that the rebels had overrun the settlement at Peereboom and killed most of its whites, a clamor arose to abandon the colony altogether, with immediate departure on the two slave ships then at anchor in the river.

The colonists were persuaded to stay on the Governor's reassurance that he had already sent an urgent appeal to Surinam for help and on the agreement of the captains to keep their ships at anchor. News of further slave revolts in the near reaches of the Canje River then reignited panic. The secretary to the Council took himself off to the safety of a slave ship. As he would subsequently explain his conduct, he was not obliged to stay and be shot at for twenty guilders a month.

On March 8, a woman arrived at Fort Nassau to report that she had been taken prisoner by the rebels and released to convey a letter from them. In this, they listed their grievances and offered to call off their impending attack if the Governor left for Holland immediately. There ensued a general demand that the fort should be abandoned, and the Governor eventually accepted a proposal that the entire community proceed down the river to the Dageraad (Daybreak) plantation. The guns were spiked. The fort was set on fire. The community, having taken to the various craft at its disposal, in effect left the colony, aside from a few outposts, to the rebels.

Along the way, the retreating settlers saw their estates being plundered and burned by their former slaves. Arriving at Dageraad, they found no reason for hope there either. The captain of one slave ship insisted on being paid at once so that he might set sail for Holland. The secretary to the Council, ignoring all protests from the Governor, declared that neither Governor nor Council was functioning any longer in the colony and left for Holland as well.

The stay at Dageraad was brief. The threat of an imminent rebel attack so terrified the settlers that they insisted on retreating further, to the military post at St. Andries, where they arrived on March 16. There they found only a battery of two rotten cannons and no ammunition for their own few muskets, while the rebels were now reported to number three thousand, with hundreds of muskets, much ammunition, cutlasses, and other weapons. Most of the settlers decided to retreat yet again. On March 27, the Governor let them take the remaining boats, while he stayed with a few stalwarts to await the help he had summoned.

This came on the very next day, in a ship carrying one hundred soldiers from Surinam. The Governor sent some of these to prevent the rebels from crossing the Corentyne River and joining up with the free blacks in the Surinam forests. With most of the rest, he returned to Dageraad, where the force was joined by several hundred blacks who had rejected the rule of the rebel chief Coffy. A message from Chief Coffy now arrived for the Governor. It proposed dividing the colony of Berbice, with the Dutch left undisturbed in one part, while the rebels retreated upriver to live as free people. The Governor rejected the proposal and awaited further reinforcements.

On May 3, two ships brought much needed supplies and 154 soldiers from the Dutch island of Saint Eustatius. Ten days later, rebels attacked Dageraad in force and withdrew after much loss of life. Having waited too long, they now gave up too early. Disease was already spreading so fast through the soldiers at Dageraad that when, on July 7, another ship arrived from Saint Eustatius with four hundred men and supplies, there were not enough left standing to mount an adequate guard.

Developments now increasingly favored the colonial cause. Further west, in the Dutch colony of Demerara, the Governor mobilized a force to prevent any rebels from Berbice crossing the river to spread the revolt or seek refuge and an opportunity to recover. Two ships from Holland were bound for Berbice with 260 soldiers on board. Meanwhile, internal disputes were weakening the rebel forces, dangerously more centralized in Berbice than were their counterparts in Surinam. Chief Coffy was worsted in a quarrel with another leader, Chief Atta, and shot himself. Yet another, Chief Akkara, was stripped of his authority. A set of four new leaders took command, only to increase the conflict.

When a substantial force of government troops advanced upriver on December 9, the rebels were so disorganized as to offer little resistance. Many surrendered, were captured, or were killed. The rest retreated into the forests and, too late, took to guerrilla warfare. By the end of March 1763, less than nine months from the start of the rebellion, some 2,600 rebels were reported to have surrendered or been captured. A number were killed, some by being burned over a slow fire, before a general amnesty was proclaimed at the end of the year.

If the colony was now safe from its slaves, much of it was in ruin. Many of the plantations had been destroyed. One in three of the white population had been killed or had fled abroad. Those who had stayed and survived lacked the resources to restore the colony. The number of black slaves had been halved.[12] The work of repair began, but was soon to be directed by others.

From 1780 onward, British, French, and Dutch disputed possession of the Guiana colonies. In 1795, Britain, already in control of Surinam and Berbice, took control of Demerara and Essequebo as well, shortly before free blacks in the forests there allied themselves with slaves to mount an unsuccessful rebellion. Much capital investment and the arrival of many more slaves promoted thriving exports of sugar, rum, coffee, and cotton. The market for colonial commodities boomed during the Napoleonic Wars, when the value of shipments from the three river colonies in the west amounted to some £2,000,000 a year, with a similar value for shipments from Surinam.

In 1814, Britain was formally ceded the previous Dutch colonies of Berbice, Demerara, and Essequebo, while the Dutch regained possession of Surinam. Britain's withdrawal from the slave trade in 1807 meant that the stock of slaves in its Guiana colonies could not be replenished by new imports, and slave owners there might accordingly have been expected to treat their slave labor force with particular care. Sugar production, however, to which the colonies were increasingly devoted, made its own demands in the pursuit of profit.

Under mounting pressure from the abolitionist movement, and in part to ward off still more radical proposals, the British Parliament in 1823 passed a law to improve the condition of slaves and provide them with certain civil rights. When this was communicated to the colonies in Guiana, the Council of Demerara duly implemented reforms, in particular an end to the flogging of slave women and to the use of the whip in the fields. Meanwhile, however, reports were spreading among slaves in the colony that Britain had decided to give them their freedom but that their owners were withholding it. The center of rebellious sentiment seems to have been on a plantation near to where the Reverend John Smith, a minister of the London Missionary Society and a prominent abolitionist, had his chapel.

A widespread uprising was planned for August 18, and early that morning a mulatto house servant disclosed this to his master. Immediately informed, the Governor called out the local militia and went himself at the head of a party to investigate a reported fire. On the way, he was met by a group of armed blacks. He asked them what they wanted, and they replied, "Our rights." He then ordered them to disperse, but they refused and advised him to withdraw for his own safety. Taking their advice, he then declared martial law, summoned all white adult males to sign on for service, and dispatched detachments to secure the plantations. Though some thirteen thousand slaves were evidently involved in the uprising, it was crushed within a week.

The slaves had seized guns on a number of plantations, but they had made no plans to use them and subsequently demonstrated no disposition to do so, while the whites were soon engaged in repressive violence. The official figure of fifty-eight slaves killed by the army and the militia in restoring order is likely to have been short of the real one. The total of those afterwards sentenced to death or severe flogging reached into the hundreds. The nature and extent of the retribution would excite implicit criticism even from James Rodway, writing early in the twentieth century, whose sympathy with the official line on the rebellion was otherwise undisguised.

"A severe lesson was perhaps wanted," he wrote, "but everyone must regret the necessity for so many executions, the hanging in chains and the heads stuck on poles at the fort and along the public road."[13]

The bullet-ridden body of Quamina, one of the slave leaders, was put on public display. Telemachus, another leader, was executed. But Jack Gladstone, reputed to have been the principal organizer of the uprising, escaped hanging in return for giving evidence, almost certainly perjured, against the Reverend John Smith.[14]

It was generally assumed among the colony's whites that Smith had, at the very least, known of the conspiracy and done nothing to alert the authorities. He was tried by court-martial, convicted, and sentenced to be hanged. Shrinking from the possible repercussions in Britain of carrying out the sentence on their own responsibility, the colonial authorities applied to London for confirmation. The reply was that Smith should be pardoned on condition that he left Guiana and moved to none of the West Indian islands. It came too late. Smith had already died in detention. The news of this did more to promote antislavery sentiment in Britain than all the slave executions.

One early result was a more decisive British government commitment to alleviate the lot of the slave. A special "protector of slaves" was appointed with the charge of ensuring that slaves enjoyed all the rights of free persons except for bondage to a particular master. They were to work no more than nine hours a day and be provided by their masters with food, clothing, housing, and medical attention. In 1831, Berbice, Demerara, and Essequebo were united into the single colony of British Guiana. In 1834, slavery was abolished there, as it was throughout the empire.

~~~~~~

The treatment of slaves in France's prize colony of Saint Domingue was among the most murderous in the Americas. So high was the rate of mortality there that in merely ten years, from 1779 to 1788, some 317,000 slaves, roughly equivalent to two-thirds of the total in the colony, were landed mainly to replace the numbers that had died. On particular plantations, the mortality rate was still higher. At Sucrerie Cottineau, for instance, virtually the entire slave labor force was replaced, three-quarters by new imports from Africa, between 1766 and 1775. It was this that "limited the creolization of the slave population, keeping alive African traditions and an active resistance to *enslavement*, and not simply to *slavery*."[1]

Central to such traditions were religious beliefs and rites whose celebration early engaged the suspicion and alarm of the authorities. The Ordinance of 1704, which prohibited slaves from "gathering at night under the pretext of holding collective dances," was clearly directed against such celebration. It was also clearly ineffective. In 1765, the First Legion of Saint Domingue was formed with the specific function of "breaking up Negro gatherings and *calendas* or night dances." What was coming to be called Voodoo, or Vaudou, a form of traditional African religion that developed features of its own in the new environment, was an ineradicable force of slave life.

Neither the certainty of punishment if they were discovered nor the demands involved in meeting for worship after the exactions of a long day's labor deterred the celebrants. A Swiss visitor to the colony recorded that the slaves started work before dawn: "At eight o'clock they get their dinner; they go back to work till midday. At two o'clock they start again and carry on till nightfall; sometimes right up to ten or eleven p.m."[2] Moreover, as he noted, the two hours allowed for rest and the rare holidays were necessarily devoted by the slaves to cultivating such tiny plots of land as they were conceded, to augment their meager rations of food. Yet whatever the measure of their physical exhaustion, they met at night, often at secret places some distance away, to engage in their ceremonies. Manifestly, they found in these both a brief respite from the anguish of their condition and an assertion of resistance to it.[3]

Such ceremonies were by no means the only expressions of resistance. From the early days of the colony, there were slaves who escaped to the mountains and established themselves in freedom there. Expeditions to capture or kill them were so far from being generally successful that by 1751 there were at least three thousand maroons. From time to time, bands of them would emerge to raid plantations and return to their fortified fastnesses. Nor were they alone in disturbing the composure of the colony.

Slaves poisoned their masters, the families of their masters, the animals of their masters, and even other slaves as a way of punishing their masters. As early as 1726, an official memorandum to the French Minister of Marine declared: "It would be impossible to believe to what extent the Negroes make use of poison if there were not a thousand examples on every hand. There are few colonists who have not suffered loss, and many have been ruined."[4] In 1737, on the Larnage plantation, 100 of the 150 slaves there died of poisoning. The poison itself was easy enough to obtain. Planters held large quantities of arsenic to combat the sugar ant. The household slaves of doctors and apothecaries had access to dangerous drugs. Many slaves were acquainted with the poisonous properties of plants that grew in Saint Domingue as well as in Africa.

The terror excited by actual or suspected poisonings—for poison came to be presumed as the cause of any death not otherwise explained—promoted an increasing cruelty directed at terrorizing the slaves and reassuring the masters of their ultimate power over them. Whipping was stayed midway to inflict more pain by applying salt, pepper, aloes, or hot ash to the open wounds. Mutilation by cutting off limbs, ears, genitals, was common practice. Slaves had burning wax poured over their arms and shoulders or boiling cane sugar poured over their heads, were roasted over slow fires or filled with gunpowder and blown apart, were buried up to the neck with their heads covered in sugar for insects to devour.[5] It was a cruelty that often only promoted a hatred more powerful than terror.

One slave, known as Macandal,[6] worked in the sugar mill of the Lenormand plantation near the northern city of Le Cap and one day lost an arm which was crushed in the machinery. Set to guarding cattle, he escaped, in 1751 or thereabouts, and found his way to a community of maroons in the mountains. His rise to leadership was rapid, and he was soon organizing raids on plantations. His claims to be immortal and to foresee the future, along with his reputation for fearlessness, attracted followers from a wide area, many of whom would walk long distances to attend the meetings he called at night in the forests.

By 1757, he judged the time right for rebellion. He organized the distribution of poison among his followers in the city and on the plantations. On a certain day, the poison was to be appropriately employed, and he would descend with his fighters from the mountains to kill any white survivors. The plan was betrayed, and countermeasures were taken. Shortly afterward, his increasing recklessness led to his capture, and in March 1758 he was burned at the stake. As the flames rose around him, he was seen to wrench himself free of his chains. It was a final act of defiance that helped to engender the myth that he had turned himself into a mosquito and flown away, but would return one day in human form.

The mulattoes, who composed the vast majority of the 27,500 free persons of color in the colony, had reasons enough to resent the treatment meted out to them by the whites. Yet no alliance had developed between them and the slaves. Many of them, indeed, had slaves of their own, on their estates or in their homes, and were not known for treating these with peculiar consideration. Events, however, were to produce a temporary convergence, and mulatto revolt would contribute to slave revolution.

When the States-General of France was summoned to meet in May 1789, for what was to prove the prelude to the French Revolution, the leading white planters in Saint Domingue dispatched representatives to press for the establishment of a Colonial Assembly and an end to the despotic and monopolist control exercised over their institutions and trade. Their eighteen deputies, all of noble lineage, secured from the new French National Assembly a decree which not only established the Colonial Assembly but was so ambiguously worded that the whites of Saint Domingue confidently proceeded to exclude mulattoes from any part in the ensuing election.

Vincent Ogé, a young mulatto whose widowed mother owned a slave-worked plantation near Dondon in the north of Saint Domingue, was living in Paris. He now resolved to return home and raise a rebellion among the mulattoes to secure their civil rights. After visiting London and the United States to seek support, he made his way to Saint Domingue, where he evaded the vigilance of the authorities at Le Cap, who had been alerted to his intentions by their agents in Paris, and reached his mother's plantation. There he was joined by his principal lieutenant, Jean Baptiste Chavanne.

Chavanne argued that the mulattoes were bound to fail if they did not draw the blacks into the rebellion, but was overruled. The rebels recruited some three hundred mulattoes, armed them with muskets brought by a United States ship, and advanced to within a short distance from Le Cap. There they succumbed to a force of fifteen hundred men with artillery. Many of the rebels were captured, and those few, including the leaders, who escaped to the neighboring Spanish colony were arrested on their arrival and delivered to the Saint Domingue authorities. After a trial lasting two months, thirteen rebels were sentenced to serve in the galleys and twenty-one to be hanged.

For Ogé and Chavanne a special punishment was chosen. They were to be broken on the wheel.

The impact made in Paris by the news that such sentences had been executed was enormous. An aroused National Assembly passed the decree of May 15, 1791, which made unequivocal the right of the free mulattoes to vote and stand for membership in the Saint Domingue Assembly. Further, it provided for the dispatch of three commissioners to ensure that the decree was obeyed. When news of this reached the colony, whites reacted with rage. As some took to assaulting, mutilating, and lynching mulattoes, the Governor deemed it necessary to suspend the decree.

Meanwhile, signs of unrest among the slaves were being reported from an increasing number of estates. While planters discussed with their families, their friends, and their guests their own liberation from the shackles of an absolute monarchy, their attendant slaves listened and drew their own conclusions. "Even at table," wrote Baron de Wimpffen in 1790, "surrounded by mulattoes and negroes, they indulge themselves in the most imprudent discussions on liberty, etc. To discuss the 'Rights of Man' before such people—what is it but to teach them that power dwells with strength, and strength with numbers?"[7]

In early 1791, French soldiers arriving at Port-au-Prince embraced blacks with the message that the National Assembly had declared all men free and equal. Soon blacks were arming themselves and rebelling in the neighboring districts. In one of these, it needed the combined efforts of the militia and mobilized local landowners to deal with a force of slaves who surrendered only after all their leaders had fallen. A dozen slaves were hanged.[8]

In the north, between the mountains and the sea, lay the fertile plain that contributed so much to the colony's celebrated riches. There, plans for a mass insurrection of slaves were being communicated and discussed at secret meetings. On the night of Sunday, August 14, 1791, some two hundred blacks met in a glade on the same Lenormand estate where Macandal had once been a slave. The slave forces of more than a hundred plantations were represented by delegates whose leader, a slave who had been brought to the colony from Jamaica, was a gang foreman and Voodoo priest known as Boukman. As a tropical storm raged, the delegates bound themselves together with a blood pact, and Boukman pronounced in Creole a soon legendary summons:

> The god who created the sun which gives us light, who rouses the waves and rules the storm, though hidden in the clouds, he watches us. He sees all that the white man does. The god of the white man inspires him with crime, but our god calls upon us to do good works. Our god who is good to us orders us to avenge our wrongs. He will direct our arms and aid us. Throw away the symbol of the god of the whites who has so often caused us to weep, and listen to the voice of liberty, which speaks in the hearts of us all.[9]

On August 22, starting around ten o'clock in the evening at the plantation where Boukman himself was a slave, the insurrection spread, soon filling the sky with flames. In the next two months, with some 100,000 slaves in rebellion, 220 sugar plantations, 600 coffee plantations, and 200 cotton and indigo ones were destroyed.

There is a graphic account by Bryan Edwards of the scene that greeted him five weeks from the start of the insurrection:

> We arrived in the harbour of Cape François (Le Cap) in the evening of the 26th September, and the first object which arrested our attention as we approached was a dreadful scene of devastation by fire. The noble plain adjoining the Cape was covered with ashes, and the surrounding hills, as far as the eye could reach, every where presented to us ruins still smoking, and houses and plantations at that moment in flames. It was a sight more terrible than the mind of any man, unaccustomed to such a scene, can easily conceive.[10]

Some two thousand whites and ten thousand blacks are estimated to have died in the course of the insurrection. In their hatred and fury, blacks not only killed plantation owners and managers but also committed atrocities against their wives and daughters. The retribution that the whites proceeded to exact as soon as they were able was more deliberate in its cruelty. Many among the hundreds of blacks sentenced to death were broken on the wheel: "a system of revenge and retaliation," Bryan Edwards remarked, "which no enormities of savage life could justify or excuse."

From the window of his lodgings, on September 28, Edwards watched two blacks being killed below him in this way. The first had each of his legs and arms broken in two places before he was dispatched with blows to his stomach. The second, "with his broken limbs doubled up," was then, at the insistence of the attendant mob, bound on a cart wheel to endure his agony without any further blows to shorten it. "French spectators (many of them persons of fashion, who beheld the scene from the windows of their upper apartments), it grieves me to say . . . looked on with the most perfect composure" for forty minutes, until at last a party of British sailors intervened and "strangled him in mercy."[11]

Boukman himself was taken while leading an attack on Le Cap and died at the stake. His head was set on a pike which was placed outside a gate of the city. When the militia were confident enough to patrol the plain, they sought to restore order by shooting all the blacks they encountered and considered not worth the trouble of sending to Le Cap for torture. Many blacks who had so far not joined the rebellion now did so in order to save their lives.

Initially responsible for uniting the rebel bands still scouring the province were Jean-François, a Creole black runaway who had joined a community of maroons, and Biassou, who had been a slave belonging to the Fathers of Charity in Le Cap. The new soldiers would scarcely have made an intimidating show. Some of them wore looted finery or underwear. No more than one in three had a firearm of any sort, while the rest carried machetes or makeshift metal weapons. Their resolve to defend their freedom, however, made them a potentially formidable force, and a rebel now arrived who proved crucial to the transforming of the conflict.

François Dominique Toussaint was born on All Saints' Day in 1744, on the huge Bréda plantation overlooking Le Cap, to a black slave mother and a free black father who was a devout Catholic, literate in French and skilled in traditional medicine. The boy was put to herding cattle by the plantation manager, but his way with horses came to be noted, and at the age of eighteen he was promoted to work in the stables. In 1777, the management of Bréda passed to Bayon de Libertas, a man of liberal disposition, who made Toussaint his coachman and gave him a plot of land for sharecropping. At the age of forty, Toussaint married a relative of his father, who brought with her a young son, Placide, and later gave him two sons of his own, Isaac and Saint-Jean.

How far Toussaint was involved in the planning of the insurrection is uncertain. Evidence had been adduced that the Governor of the colony and his supporters encouraged a controlled slave revolt, to concentrate the minds of those whites who talked of declaring independence from France, and that Toussaint was charged with organizing it.[12] Whatever the case, Toussaint certainly seems to have kept himself in the shadows and the Bréda plantation out of the insurrection until a month after the start. Then, having sent Madame de Libertas to join her husband in Le Cap, he took his own wife and children across the border to the safety of the Spanish colony and proceeded to Grande-Rivière, where the rebel leaders were encamped.

He was appointed to supervise the sanitary services, but rose quickly to command part of the army. He is known, this early in his military career, to have ordered the execution of two subordinates for having committed atrocities against whites. (There is no record of a white in similar authority reacting in such a way to the commission of atrocities against blacks.) Offers from the rebel leadership to discuss terms of a settlement with the white colonists were summarily rejected; the colonists waited for hunger to make the rebels submit. The rebels then went on the attack. In the east they burst through the cordon maintained by government forces and burned the plantations in their path, before turning to capture the Môle peninsula. With each success, more slaves joined the rebellion.

Toussaint increasingly concentrated his efforts on training and equipping the few hundred men under his command for guerrilla warfare. When the two rebel leaders Jean-François and Biassou, apparently unable to resolve their differences, decided to separate, he went with Biassou to establish headquarters at the town of Tannerie, which he fortified on lines of his own devising. For almost a year, there was stalemate in the north of the colony. The rebels were in control of the countryside, while the colonists held Le Cap and the principal fortified towns.

To the west, a different conflict had developed. Reacting to the acts of violence against them from whites infuriated by the decree of May 15, 1791, mulattoes had decided to organize and arm themselves for self-defense. White royalists, in conflict with the white democrats who dominated the garrison of Port-au-Prince, had readily provided officers for what became a mulatto army of four thousand men. Mulatto slave owners had even armed their own slaves and recruited others from among the slaves of white planters, to form a special regiment that came to be called the Swiss.

When at last the two armies fought, the democrats were put to flight. All at once their leaders recognized some merit in the mulatto case. They offered a pact. They would honor the controversial decree and declare that Ogé and other mulatto martyrs had been "the unfortunate victims of passion and prejudice," if the mulattoes agreed to disarm the slaves in their army and send these back to the plantations. The mulattoes agreed.

Some two hundred of the recruited slaves, however, had by now acquired such a rebellious temper that they could not safely be sent back to the plantations. They were consigned in chains to a ship for delivery to the Mexican coast. The ship got as far as Jamaica, where it was turned away, and sailed back to Saint Domingue. There, one night, the slaves were killed and their bodies thrown overboard. The mulattoes were evidently not involved in this massacre, but their initial responsibility became a component in a smoldering black resentment. Nor did the affair secure the new alliance. In one of its many twists, the National Assembly in Paris, concerned at the colonial turbulence, canceled the May decree. The whites repudiated their pact with the mulattoes. In the upheaval that followed, much of Port-au-Prince went up in flames.

In September 1792, three new commissioners, given dictatorial powers and an army of six thousand men, arrived from France. They announced that they had no intention of abolishing slavery and were determined to crush the rebellion, but that they were charged to secure the civil rights of all free mulattoes, in accordance with yet another decree passed by the National Assembly. The army they had brought with them was under capable command, and the rebels were forced to retreat. On the issue of civil rights for free mulattoes, however, the colonists were obdurate. The commissioners dissolved the Colonial Assembly and ordered the arming of the mulattoes.

Then, on January 21, 1793, Louis XVI was beheaded, and the army in Saint Domingue split into republicans and royalists. Some royalist officers deserted to the neighboring Spanish colony, since Spain and Britain were now at war with republican France; others offered their services to black rebel leaders, once more on the attack. Soon troops controlled by the commissioners were at war with troops controlled by the Governor. In Le Cap, where the Governor's troops were victorious, mulattoes were massacred. The commissioners, having withdrawn to the Bréda plantation above the city, sent for the two commanders of a black rebel force encamped a short distance away. They offered these and their followers "all the rights and privileges enjoyed by French citizens," in return for their agreeing to enlist in the service of the republic. The commanders agreed.

On June 21, 1793, according to the contemporary account by Bryan Edwards, "about noon . . . a negro chief called *Macaya*, with upwards of three thousand of the revolted slaves, entered the town, and began an universal and indiscriminate slaughter of men, women, and children. The white inhabitants fled from all quarters to the seaside, in hopes of finding shelter with the governor on board the ships in the harbour; but a body of the mulattos cut off their retreat, and a horrid butchery ensued, a description of which every heart susceptible of humanity must be unable to bear. Suffice it to say, that the slaughter continued with unremitting fury from the 21st, to the evening of the 23rd; when the savages, having murdered all the white inhabitants that fell in their way, set fire to the buildings; and more than half the city was consumed by the flames."[13]

During the night of June 24, some ten thousand white refugees left Le Cap on more than one hundred ships for the United States, most of them never to return.

Of the army that they had brought with them, the commissioners had little left to command. Moreover, since their grant of freedom to the nearby rebel force, they could not rely on help from the free mulattoes, most of whom were hostile to sharing their civil rights with rebellious black slaves. The virtually isolated commissioners extended their previous offer of citizenship to all rebel forces. Jean-François, Biassou, and Toussaint, the three chief rebel commanders, were unimpressed. They were as aware of how vulnerable the commissioners were as were the commissioners themselves. The French National Assembly was far away and fickle. Besides, royalist officers in service with the rebels were confident that the republican government in France would not last much longer against the combined power of the Allies. Spain seemed a better bet.

The neighboring Spanish colony was as poor as Saint Domingue had recently been rich. The inhabitants were mainly cattle breeders, few of whom enjoyed the luxury of bread. Their Governor, on instructions from the Spanish colonial minister, was offering the black rebels of Saint Domingue, in return for an alliance with Spain, not only money and supplies, but their freedom, the rights of Spanish citizenship, and land.

On August 29, 1793, Sonthonax, the dominant French commissioner, resorted to the last measure left to him and formally freed the slaves. On the same day, Toussaint issued his own appeal. "Brothers and Friends: I am Toussaint L'Ouverture. My name is perhaps known to you. I have undertaken to avenge you. I want liberty and equality to reign throughout St. Domingo. I am working towards that end. Come and join me, brothers, and fight by our side for the same cause." And he signed himself "Toussaint L'Ouverture, General of the Armies of the King for the Public Good."[14]

His adoption of this last name, "L'Ouverture" or "The Opening," by which he was apparently well enough known already, has various explanations, but the most obvious seems to be that he saw himself as the one who would open the lives of slaves to freedom.[15] Beginning his independent campaign with only six hundred men, he soon had five thousand under his command, as a series of military successes spread his renown. He was fearless in combat. He lived among his followers, ate the same food, and often undertook the same duties. When he captured a town, he allowed no looting and treated all prisoners, whatever their color, humanely. In consequence, his enemies came to accept defeat the sooner rather than continue fighting from the fear of what might follow their surrender.

It was not long before he broke with both Spain and his fellow rebel commanders. The Spanish authorities, it emerged, had included only the armed rebels in their offer of freedom, citizenship, and land. Biassou and Jean-François were satisfied with this, but Toussaint was committed to ending slavery altogether in Saint Domingue. Furthermore, a new and menacing factor had entered the conflict. Encouraged by a league of planters ready to transfer their allegiance in return for armed intervention to secure slavery, Britain, an ally of Spain's, had decided to take possession of the colony. In September 1793, a British army landed at Jérémie in the south and rapidly advanced to seize Port-au-Prince. Along the way, it restored or reinforced adherence to slavery.

General Laveaux, the commander-in-chief of the French army in Saint Domingue and the Provisional Governor, had little of substance to sustain such titles. His ragged and unreliable force in the north was surrounded by enemies. Toussaint could scarcely have chosen a less promising military ally or a less propitious time to change sides. He did so nonetheless. Defeating a Spanish force on the way, he struck at the camp of Biassou and put Biassou himself to flight. Then, turning to attack the Spanish force at Gonaïves, he took the town together with its large store of supplies.

Having so conspicuously proved his value, he proceeded to place himself under Laveaux's orders. Duly appointed to his own command, he succeeded, within a few months from April 1794, in wresting control over much of the west and north. He moved with astonishing speed, often arriving with his forces at the very place where he was least expected. His own record for a march across mountainous terrain was sixty-four kilometers in a single day, compared to Napoleon's of fifty-two. He had an intelligence network that kept him informed of conditions and developments in the enemy camp. Few of his soldiers were adequately clothed, and all of them from time to time went hungry, but they were hardened, disciplined, and ardently loyal. In a surprise attack, he dealt with Jean-François as he had dealt with Biassou. He was now without rival as leader of the colony's blacks.

Only one indigenous leader stood formidably in his way. André Rigaud, born to a French nobleman and a black mother, commanded the most efficient force of mulattoes in the south, where he had resisted British control and established his own mulatto regime. This he intended to extend throughout the colony, but he needed first to remove the obstacle presented by Laveaux, with his firm support for Toussaint. His one promising ally in the north was the mulatto general Villate, whom Laveaux himself had appointed to command the largely black forces at Le Cap, but whom he was now confronting with charges of corruption.

Incited by an emissary from Rigaud, Villate sent a detachment of mulatto troops on March 10, 1796, to arrest and imprison Laveaux. The mulatto-controlled municipal council immediately declared Laveaux stripped of office and Villate his successor as Provisional Governor. Encamped at Haut-du-Cap within sight of the city was Pierre Michel, the black colonel of the four thousand black troops there, nominally under Villate's ultimate command. He immediately sent a report to Toussaint, who ordered six thousand of his soldiers to join Pierre Michel's, while his representatives roused thousands of armed cultivators on the northern plain to make their way into Le Cap.

Threatened both by the augmented military force above the city and by the augmented black populace within, the municipal council went in a body to release Laveaux from prison and express loyalty to him. On March 28, Laveaux and Toussaint, at the head of ten thousand troops, rode through Le Cap to the cheers of whites as well as blacks. At the beginning of April, Laveaux announced that he was appointing Toussaint, whom he called the black Spartacus, to the post of Lieutenant Governor.

The revolutionary executive or Directory that now governed France decided that Toussaint was growing too powerful. It dispatched three new commissioners, effectively led by the former commissioner Sonthonax, along with a supply of twenty thousand muskets, to curb Toussaint's power and assert their own authority. Meanwhile, Toussaint himself was increasingly persuaded that only independence from France would guarantee the end of slavery. Yet here he recognized that he needed to proceed cautiously.

It was not only Sonthonax who stood in the way. Laveaux himself was ultimately bound to France. Toussaint set out to remove both men as smoothly as possible. Elections to the new French Chamber of Deputies and Senate were due, and the colony had been given the right to elect representatives of its own. With a little help from a detachment of his troops in the vicinity, Toussaint persuaded the Electoral Assembly of Saint Domingue to select Laveaux and Sonthonax. In a letter to Laveaux, he explained that he wished to spare him "that great unpleasantness" which he foresaw as in store for "this unhappy land."[16] Loyal to Toussaint and exhausted by the exactions of his service in the colony, Laveaux accepted the chance of rejoining his family in France. Sonthonax stayed.

While appointing Toussaint commander-in-chief of the army and offering him an alliance, Sonthonax set about undermining him. He arranged to have the twenty thousand muskets distributed among the black cultivators in his own name, won over the garrison at Le Cap by increasing its pay, and promoted disaffection elsewhere in the army by withholding supplies. Toussaint, however, had noted each development and taken appropriate precautions. He had seen to it that the twenty thousand muskets were collected even as they were being distributed. He had measures ready to deal with disorder and, when mutiny surfaced in the army, suppressed it with ease.

On August 16, 1797, he arrived with a large force of soldiers at Petite-Anse, close to Le Cap, and from there ordered Sonthonax to leave the colony for his elected duties in France. Sonthonax demanded an interview and was granted one. It served only to enrage Toussaint, who shouted at one point, "Whenever some scoundrel, be he white, mulatto or black, has some dirty work he wants done, he incites the Negroes to do it for him!"[17] On August 27, Sonthonax and his family, after a ceremonial farewell, left on a frigate for France.

Toussaint now turned his attention to the British, who occupied a long strip of land, secured by a line of forts, along the western seaboard from Jérémie in the south to Môle St. Nicholas in the north, as well as the peacetime colonial capital of Port-au-Prince. They had already lost some forty thousand men, mainly to yellow fever, but had repeatedly received reinforcements and still had an army of twenty thousand, well-trained and well-equipped. Against them, Toussaint had sixteen thousand soldiers, inadequately fed and equipped but battle-hardened, and his own strategic flair.

Early in February 1798, he began his assault, striking with all his forces at one point of the fortified line after another. Within a month he had taken most of the line and looked likely to take what remained virtually at his pleasure. Brigadier General Maitland, who commanded the British forces, offered to withdraw from all but the two ports of Jérémie and Môle St. Nicholas, if Toussaint would guarantee an amnesty for Britain's local allies and allow the British to remove their artillery. Toussaint rejected the second condition, and Maitland complied. Britain had spent five years of effort, the lives of forty thousand men, and £20 million for very little.

On April 14, Toussaint entered Port-au-Prince to the jubilation of the massed inhabitants, especially the blacks, who owed him their freedom, but also from whites reassured by the way he had treated others of their kind along the route of his victories. Most whites would soon forget any gratitude they might have felt, but a few, including the rich merchant and planter who was mayor of Port-au-Prince, would stay faithful to the last.

Toussaint was determined to secure a British withdrawal from the two ports that they still held. He warned them that he would attack if they insisted on keeping their prizes. At the end of August 1798, Maitland met him to communicate a set of proposals from the British government. Britain would surrender the two ports, recognize Toussaint as king of an independent state, and protect that state against France if he would sign a commercial treaty with Britain. Toussaint had no yearning for royalty and doubted Britain's commitment or ability to protect an independent Saint Domingue from a France now increasingly victorious elsewhere. He did, however, want both an end to the British blockade and a major trading partner who would supply manufactured goods, including arms, in return for the products of an independent Saint Domingue. He made two conditions of his own. The treaty should be a secret one, so as to avoid provoking France, and the British were to leave behind as free the six thousand black slaves serving in their forces at the ports. Maitland agreed.

The treaty was eventually signed on June 13, 1799. In it, the United States was granted the same trading rights as Britain, and both countries were to have consular agents in Saint Domingue. Toussaint would have an agent in Jamaica and was pledged to undertake no expedition against any of Britain's Caribbean colonies or against the territory of the United States. The treaty was, however, no longer secret. Months before, the British press had published its main provisions, and this had come close to wrecking the whole agreement. Between Toussaint and France, little but distrust remained.

The Directory had already dispatched, as its Special Agent to the colony, General Hédouville, who had met Toussaint at Le Cap in May 1798. The talks had not gone well, and subsequent relations steadily deteriorated. Hédouville's policy was to set mulatto and black against each other, as part of the process directed at toppling Toussaint. His strategy was too transparent. In fact, Toussaint had no illusions about the readiness of most mulattoes to accept equality with blacks, yet he knew that conflict between the two would imperil his whole purpose of securing an independent state. He made repeated efforts to reassure mulattoes of his good will toward them. He even sent supplies to Rigaud in the south.

The division between Hédouville and Toussaint surfaced in two other issues. Hédouville objected to Toussaint's employment of royalists and other émigré opponents of France's republican regime. Toussaint, believing such whites to be all the more reliable for that reason, ignored the objection. In seeking to keep black cultivators at work on the plantations, Hédouville issued an edict requiring them to accept three-year labor contracts. Toussaint protested that this was widely seen as a partial return to slavery.

Hédouville and the Directory now sought to set a trap for Toussaint. They proposed that he undertake, with French naval help, an invasion of Jamaica and the South of the United States to liberate the slaves there. It was a design so ill-timed and dangerous that Toussaint would have rejected it, even had he not recognized this for the device that it was. Hédouville and the Directory then decided on direct confrontation. First, however, Toussaint had to be deprived of the means to offer serious resistance.

Hédouville set out to disband most of the army on the pretext that the British withdrawal had made such a large force unnecessary. He began with the 5th Negro Regiment garrisoned at Fort-Liberté to the east of Le Cap and meanwhile urged Rigaud to march his own forces northward as soon as possible. While Rigaud delayed, Toussaint acted. He sent a detachment of troops to isolate Fort-Liberté, where white and mulatto forces were now in control, and roused cultivators on the northern plain with the cry that Hédouville had, by his labor edict, revealed his intention to restore slavery. Arming themselves as best they could, the cultivators descended in their tens of thousands on Le Cap. Hédouville boarded a ship for France, after formally advising Rigaud that he need not recognize Toussaint as commander-in-chief and should assume overall military command throughout the south.

War between Toussaint and Rigaud was becoming unavoidable, and Rigaud struck first with a successful assault on the black garrison at Petit-Goâve. To the north and the west, mulattoes, black generals suborned by Rigaud, and maroons suspicious of any advance in centralized power, rebelled. Toussaint reacted with his usual determination and speed. Having sent his loyal generals, including the two most able, Dessalines and Christophe, to deal with the more menacing outbreaks elsewhere, he marched northward himself. The rebellion was over almost as soon as it had begun.

Immediately Toussaint turned his attention to the south. Traveling with little more than an escort across the mountains to Port-au-Prince, he narrowly escaped two assassination attempts. In a country where information spread rapidly by word of mouth, as it still does today, reports of his seemingly miraculous survival greatly increased his prestige.

The fighting that followed in the south was so ferocious that it came to be known as the War of the Knives, since blacks and mulattoes, in their very fury to get at each other, sometimes threw away their muskets to use their knives and even their teeth. Rigaud's forces were soon in retreat, but resistance was resolute. The port of Jacmel, blockaded by land and sea, held out for five months before succumbing. At last, when Toussaint's army had reached the edge of Les Cayes, Rigaud left for France. On the first day of August 1800, Toussaint entered Les Cayes, to the clarion of church bells and cannon, for a greeting from mulatto notables who temporarily transferred their homage from Rigaud to their new ruler. In Paris, Napoleon, who had recently taken power as First Consul, would listen to Rigaud's litany of misfortunes and then comment, "General, I have but one fault to find with you—you have lost."[18]

Concerned as ever to promote an understanding between black and mulatto, Toussaint granted a general amnesty. He also appointed as commander in the south, to conduct the policy of reconciliation, General Dessalines, whose attitude toward the defeated proved to be quite different from Toussaint's own. Many prominent mulattoes were executed, and this would come to fester in mulatto memory just as the incidents of mulatto contempt or betrayal would fester in the memory of blacks.

Having made himself effectively master of Saint Domingue, Toussaint advanced to realize his ambition of liberating the entire island. The Spanish colony had been ceded to France in 1795 but was still under a Spanish governor and garrisoned by Spanish troops. Not only did slavery survive there, but raiders were increasingly crossing the border to kidnap blacks in Saint Domingue, often for transport to Cuba and Puerto Rico. Toussaint sent his nephew, General Moyse, with a force of ten thousand men, to cross the border in the north, while he himself led a force of four thousand men along the southern coastal route. Any resistance was easily overcome.

On January 26, 1801, Toussaint arrived at the capital of Santo Domingo, to be handed the keys by the Governor. He at once abolished slavery throughout the colony and forced the slave ships in the harbor to surrender their slaves. He reorganized the administration and the judicial system. He ordered the cultivation of export crops, with land concessions as an inducement. He opened the ports to British and United States trade. He initiated a program of road building that soon enabled four-wheeled vehicles to be used for the first time ever in the colony. He cleared the mountains of marauders. It was a display of creative energy astonishing to all and disagreeable to some. With characteristic generosity, he gave those unwilling to accommodate themselves the right to leave and take their movable property with them.

He returned to a Saint Domingue scarcely less in need of his creative energy. After so many years of rebellion and war, little of the plantation economy was functioning. Of the thirty thousand whites who had been living in the colony at the start of the turmoil, only some ten thousand remained. Perhaps one in four among the free blacks and mulattoes had been killed. The number of former slaves who had been killed topped 100,000.[19] Their deaths involved the loss of much needed skills in agriculture, industry, commerce, and construction. In many of those still living, there were habits of hatred, mistrust, and violence with which to contend. The comments of contemporaries, not necessarily captivated by the concept of black government, testified to the extent of the recovery already initiated and now advanced by Toussaint's direction.

The countryside was made safe from marauding groups. The towns were restored and embellished, schools established, bridges built, roads repaired.

Above all, sustaining such progress was the rise in production. The English writer James Stephens remarked:

> So rapid was the progress of agriculture, that it was a fact, though not believed at the time in England, that the island already produced, or promised to yield in the next crop, one third part at least of as large return of sugar and coffee as it had ever given in its most prosperous years. This, considering all the ravages of a ten years' war, and the great scarcity of all necessary supplies from abroad, is very surprising, yet has since clearly appeared to be true.[20]

Even in this tribute, however, Stephens failed to do Toussaint's administration full justice. The crop in 1800 was two-thirds that of the record, and the crop in 1801 was larger than that in 1800. Moreover, this was accompanied, as Stephens observed, by "a large increase in the rising generation of Negroes, instead of that dreadful falling off which is always found in a colony of slaves." Malouet, a former Minister of Marine and himself a plantation owner, identified one reason: "All accounts agree that there is a decrease in mortality among Negro infants. This is ascribed to absolute rest enjoyed by pregnant women and to better working conditions."[21]

The recovery, it must be admitted, was not achieved by Toussaint's translation of purpose into voluntary mass commitment. On the contrary, most of the liberated slaves wanted nothing so much as to escape from the plantations to the independence of farming their own land. Toussaint prevented this by virtually militarizing agriculture on the two-thirds of the plantations that the death or flight of their owners had left to the state. There, as on the remaining, privately held plantations, workers were forbidden to leave without a "legal permit" to do so.

Such regimentation of labor, with a bondage to the land so like the Hédouville edict which Toussaint had condemned as a partial return to slavery, was relieved by a regulated reform of conditions that reached well beyond the care of pregnant women. The workday now began at five in the morning and ended at five in the afternoon, with three hours of rest in the middle of the day. Whipping was forbidden, and when Toussaint learned that Dessalines was resorting to it on the plantations under his control, he threatened to strip him of his command if the practice persisted. Furthermore, workers were to receive a quarter of the revenue produced by their respective plantations.

This paradox of the dictatorial liberator was the mark of the man. He was both tireless and austere. He had trained himself to do with only two hours of sleep a night and to live for days at a time on a diet of water and a few bananas. He worked with five secretaries, dictating letter after letter through the night and signing nothing that he had not read first. On his visits to inspect agricultural management, building programs, or the quality of the schools, he would, as in his military campaigns, travel with such speed as to arrive where he was least expected. He could also impose private prejudice on public policy. A devout Catholic himself, he set out to eradicate traditional black religious beliefs and practices. He ordered the military to destroy Voodoo altars and detain whoever persisted in conducting Voodoo ceremonies. In this policy, however, he had no more success than future rulers of like mind would have.

Toussaint's haste to rehabilitate the economy was soon invested with a particular concern. Napoleon had a mean-minded racism in his character. He persecuted the mulatto General Dumas,[22] whose abilities had raised him to command one of France's revolutionary armies, and in July 1802 even banned people of color from coming to France.[23] He was now determined to take control of France's maverick colony and restore slavery there. He saw this as necessary not only in itself but as part of his grand design for a North American empire. With a pacified and productive Saint Domingue as a strategically placed supply base, he might conquer the United States from the French colony of Louisiana.

Toussaint was almost certainly informed of some such design by his agents in Paris. In Napoleon's burgeoning police state, repression and secrecy excited the search for intelligence and the communication of confidences. Toussaint accordingly needed to prepare for the looming conflict. In fact, many millions of francs, earned from the recovery of agriculture, were spent to buy cannon, muskets, gunpowder, and swords from the United States.

The threat prompted Toussaint to a preemptive move. On July 7, 1801, at Le Cap, he proclaimed a Constitution. It abolished slavery forever and made all citizens, regardless of color, eligible to hold public office. Toussaint himself was to be Governor for life with the power to appoint his successor. Catholicism was made the state religion. There was no provision for a representative of France in the government. This was in effect, therefore, a declaration of independence.

Toussaint's nephew, General Moyse, who had been appointed Military Commander in the north, feared Napoleon, considered the Constitution needlessly provocative, and might well have had political ambitions of his own. Across the north he now fomented revolt with the promise of an end to compulsory labor and the distribution of plantation land to its cultivators. Toussaint was journeying toward the former Spanish colony when a courier brought him the news that in the north soldiers were joining cultivators in raiding plantations, killing whites, and occupying towns in the name of General Moyse.

Toussaint set out immediately for the affected area, took command of the loyal garrisons, and attacked the rebels, while Christophe moved from Le Cap against them, and Dessalines swept up from the south. Caught in the middle, the rebellion rapidly collapsed, but not before exacting a heavy cost.

Some thousand blacks and three hundred whites had been killed, and much property had been destroyed. Toussaint, in an exceptional recourse to exemplary punishment, had the hundreds of prisoners lined up and every tenth one among them shot. Moyse himself faced a firing squad.

Toussaint, evidently expecting Napoleon to be encouraged by reports of a serious if unsuccessful rebellion in Saint Domingue, intensified his preparations to meet an invasion. He ordered the strengthening of coastal fortifications, the movement of military supplies from the coastal towns to secret places in the interior, and the distribution of some 100,000 muskets among the cultivators. Mass training in the techniques of guerrilla warfare began. On one occasion, addressing a large gathering of cultivators, he held up a musket and proclaimed, "This is your liberty!"[24]

Meanwhile, many whites, responding to the prospect of invasion, began displaying some of their old arrogance. In 1797, when they had behaved in much the same way, Toussaint had written of them to the Directory in Paris: "Blind as they are! They cannot see how this odious conduct on their part can become the signal of new disasters and irreparable misfortunes, and that far from making them regain what in their eyes liberty for all has made them lose, they expose themselves to a total ruin and the colony to its inevitable destruction. Do they think that men who have been able to enjoy the blessing of liberty will calmly see it snatched away?"[25] Napoleon would have done well to ask himself the question.

In late September 1801 came the order from Napoleon for the invasion force to be prepared. A fleet of eighty-six warships and transports was as soon as possible to be assembled at French ports. Two successive armies of twenty thousand soldiers each were to be sent, with monthly reinforcements to follow. Spain and Holland agreed to help with the transport. Despite the treaty with Toussaint, Britain promised supplies from Jamaica. Napoleon's secret and confidential instructions contained a reference to the United States: "Jefferson has promised that the moment the French army sets foot in the colony all necessary measures will be taken to starve out Toussaint and to aid the army."[26] All differences were evidently being shelved in the cause of white solidarity against self-liberated slaves.

As commander of the invading force, Napoleon appointed General Leclerc, the husband of his favorite sister, Pauline, who accompanied the expedition with a large quantity of furniture, dresses, and attendants to sustain her in the style befitting her exalted relationship. Also accompanying the expedition were Rigaud and other prominent mulatto exiles, along with Toussaint's son and stepson, who had been sent, in a gesture of trust, to be educated in France.

The extent of Napoleon's planned deceits were of a piece with the disreputable purpose of the whole undertaking. In what he termed the first phase of the campaign, blacks would be assured that slavery was not to be restored, while Toussaint and his generals would be encouraged to believe themselves secure in their posts and powers. In the second, Toussaint and his generals would be stripped of all authority and their armies disbanded. In the third, Toussaint, his generals, and all other officials of his regime would be deported to France and the population disarmed. In the fourth and final phase, slavery would be restored; no public instruction of any kind would be allowed in the colony; and anyone, regardless of rank or record of service, found advocating the rights of blacks, would be deported to France. Allies were to be betrayed no less unscrupulously. Rigaud and other mulatto leaders participating in the expedition would be deported to Madagascar as soon as they had played the part assigned to them. In the first three phases, the United States would be permitted to trade with the colony; in the final one, the French trade monopoly would be restored.

The first strike of the expedition was at Fort-Liberté, which a French detachment under General Rochambeau captured, to massacre all those taken prisoner. It was an atrocity that was bound to affect the conduct of the war, and Dessalines would come to reply with the call, "War for war, crime for crime, atrocity for atrocity."[27]

The bulk of the fleet made for Le Cap, where Christophe was the general in command. The city had been not only restored but embellished since the fire of 1793, and Lebrun, the French emissary to Christophe, was impressed by what he saw. Christophe was less impressed by Lebrun's promise that he would be showered with honors and favors if he agreed to surrender the city before Toussaint arrived there. Visited by a deputation of municipal councillors who pleaded with him to deliver up the city rather than sacrifice it to bombardment from the fleet, Christophe replied, as Toussaint's determined policy required, that he would rather set fire to the city himself.

On the morning of February 4, 1802, Christophe's soldiers went through the city and warned the inhabitants to leave. Soon the road up the nearby slopes was filled with people and their movable possessions. At nightfall the first cannon sounded from the fleet. Led or directed by Christophe himself, squads of soldiers immediately began setting fire to the eighty-three public buildings. Shops and houses came next, including Christophe's own mansion, which he personally set on fire with all his accumulated possessions inside it. One massive explosion, which loosened rocks from the heights above the huddled refugees, spelled the end of the arsenal.

When Napoleon's sister at last ventured ashore, she found only the smoldering ruin of the elegant city that Lebrun had so invitingly described to her. Of the more than two thousand houses, only fifty-nine were still habitable. The streets were littered with debris and the corpses of people who had chosen to save themselves by staying. General Leclerc had not looked for this, or for the spectacle of the plantations on the northern plain ablaze behind Christophe's retreating army.

He now resorted to the duplicity he had been directed to employ. To Toussaint he sent a letter from Napoleon, along with Toussaint's son, stepson, and their tutor, charged to persuade Toussaint of Leclerc's good intentions toward him. Toussaint studied Napoleon's letter, replete with compliments, reassurances, promises of riches and honors, but was aware that Napoleon had other designs, for he pointedly demanded that Leclerc should reveal to him "the orders of which he is the bearer."[28] At last, he declared that he would agree only to an armistice, and to that only if Leclerc were to suspend all hostilities at once. He then turned to his son and stepson and asked them to choose between France and the cause of black freedom, assuring them that they would remain dear to him whatever they decided. His son Isaac refused to bear arms against France and returned with his tutor to Leclerc. His stepson Placide renounced France and stayed.

On February 17, two further French squadrons arrived at Le Cap. Leclerc proscribed by proclamation Toussaint, Christophe, and Dessalines, and five French armies set off to subdue the interior. The former Spanish colony, the south and much of the north were already under French control. Leclerc was satisfied that it would not be long before he controlled the rest of the colony, but he was to learn that his campaign had barely begun. The enemy offered fierce resistance and destroyed what they could not hold.

Toussaint himself hastened at the head of 5,500 men, of whom 2,400 were armed cultivators, to confront General Rochambeau and his 5,000 veteran soldiers at the mountain pass of Ravin-à-Couleuvre. He inflicted a defeat on a general who had announced in an address to his troops: "It is only slaves you have to fight today—men who dare not look you in the face and who will flee in every direction."[29] At the mountain fortress of Crête-à-Pierrot, some twelve thousand French soldiers under able generals laid siege to twelve hundred black troops. By the time the fortress finally fell, the French had lost two thousand men, and their wounded included four generals. Five hundred of the defenders were found dead or wounded, and the others had escaped. Napoleon was painfully affected by the news.

By the end of March, five thousand French soldiers had died and five thousand more were injured or ill, from among the seventeen thousand so far landed. In the north, under Toussaint's leadership, the resistance of black military detachments was augmented by cultivators trained in guerrilla techniques, who dropped rocks onto French troops marching below them, set traps along the route, and sniped from behind trees and boulders. However the map might be marked with French military advances, Leclerc's campaign was not going according to plan.

Yet it was now that Toussaint offered to negotiate. Perhaps he believed that some form of reconciliation should be explored before little was left but the dead. Perhaps he believed that the French, discovering the difficulties of their undertaking, might be disposed to settle for the shadow of sovereignty without the substance. Certainly he underestimated the extent of French duplicity. Leclerc, as relieved as he was surprised, responded to the approach with ready reassurances. To Christophe, sent by Toussaint to discuss terms, he gave his pledge that all black officers would be allowed to keep their commands. Christophe yielded, to bring with him twelve hundred soldiers and a hundred pieces of cannon. Toussaint himself received from Leclerc a threefold pledge: that all blacks were to remain free; that all officers were to retain their ranks and functions; and that he might keep his staff and retire wherever he wished in the colony. Once he had submitted, Dessalines and all the other generals followed suit, to join the French army.

Toussaint retired in confidence that he could always rouse the black population if the pledges he had been given were broken, and that meanwhile his generals were still in command of their troops. On June 7, 1802, the French general Brunet, in a letter laden with expressions of respect and assurances of good faith, requested Toussaint to visit his headquarters for a meeting. Accompanied by only two of his officers, Toussaint arrived, to be arrested, taken to the harbor at Le Cap, and put on board a frigate for France.

If Leclerc had calculated that Toussaint's departure would mark the end of the matter, he soon discovered his mistake. In the mountains, drums summoned the blacks to rebellion. From the north, resistance spread to the west and south, gathering strength as reports began to circulate in early July that slavery was being restored in some French colonies. Late in July, a frigate arrived at Le Cap, with blacks being transported from Guadeloupe on board. A number of these leapt into the sea and swam ashore, to spread the news that slavery had returned to their island. The rebellion was everywhere reinforced.

Meanwhile, the rainy season had brought yellow fever, which was killing the invaders in their thousands. Conventional graves could not be dug fast enough. The dead were thrown into huge holes, which were dug, filled, and covered with earth at night, so that the rate of loss would not become known to the enemy. Appealing in an anguished letter to the Minister of Marine on September 17 for more reinforcements, Leclerc wrote: "I lose 100 to 120 men a day. To hold these mountains when I shall have taken them, I shall be *obliged to destroy all the provisions there and a great part of the laborers. I shall have to wage a war of extermination and it will cost me many men. A great part of my colonial troops have deserted and passed over to the rebels.*"[30]

In October, Pétion, who had assumed the mulatto leadership when Rigaud was deported to France, rebelled with the mulatto troops he commanded near Le Cap. Dessalines, still serving with unease in the French army, only just managed to escape the soldiers sent preemptively to arrest him and joined the rebellion. On the night of November 2, Leclerc himself died, after confessing his distress at the whole enterprise. Of the thirty-four thousand soldiers brought to the colony so far, twenty-four thousand were dead, eight thousand were ill, and the rest were exhausted. The colony, whose legendary riches had so strongly recommended its repossession, was in ruins.

Leclerc's successor was General Rochambeau. He wrote urgently for more and yet more reinforcements from France. He would receive in all a further twenty thousand French troops. He seems to have become frantic with fury. While the rebellion now commanded all of the north and west but Le Cap and several towns, the south, largely controlled by the mulatto planters, was still loyal. Rochambeau struck at the mulattoes, shooting and drowning hundreds at a time and confiscating their properties. Within a few months, the south was as disaffected as the rest of the colony.

Toward the blacks, Rochambeau was violent on a larger scale and with a particular display of cruelty. He had so many of them drowned in the bay of Le Cap that blacks would not eat fish from there for some time. He had sixteen of Toussaint's former high-ranking officers chained to rocks on an uninhabited island and left to waste away. It took the last of them seventeen days to die. Maurepas had been one of Toussaint's most distinguished generals and had shared Toussaint's conciliatory attitude to whites. His wife and children were drowned in front of him, while sailors nailed epaulettes onto his bare shoulders.

In France, meanwhile, Toussaint was coming to the end of his agony. On August 24, 1802, he had been taken to the Fort-de-Joux high in the Jura. There he was subjected to an increasingly harsh regime. His jailers allowed him neither privacy nor peace. They searched his room at night as well as by day. He was given insufficient food and in the winter insufficient fuel for his fire. He began to complain of pains in his stomach, to vomit, to develop a swelling in his face, to cough continually. On April 3, 1803, the commandant left the fort for a visit to Neuchâtel and told his staff that during his absence Toussaint should not be disturbed. When he returned four days later, he found Toussaint dead. The recorded cause was apoplexy and pneumonia. The body was buried, with the grave unmarked, in the basement of the chapel.

Some years later, near the end of his own life and in exile on the island of St. Helena, Napoleon interrupted his complaints at his own ill-treatment to confess that his expedition against the blacks of that other island had been his greatest mistake and that he should have ruled them rather through Toussaint L'Ouverture. Even then he failed to understand the meaning of the freedom for which Toussaint had stood.

From the beginning of their war to retain that freedom, the rebel armies had fought under the flag of the French Republic. But on May 18, 1803, a new flag was unfurled, with the white removed from the tricolor and the words "Liberty or Death" put in place of the "RF" that stood for République Française. It was symbolic of the total commitment to independence that consummated a revolution.

War between Britain and France broke out again, to set British naval forces between Rochambeau and his supply base. In Saint Domingue, the revolutionaries, both black and mulatto, now effectively united under the leadership of Dessalines, drove the French from their remaining fortified positions in the interior to a few coastal towns. Dessalines's men then took to the rivers and the sea in specially built light boats to attack French ships and kill those on board. By the middle of November 1803, the revolution held all of the colony except for Le Cap, whose outlying fortified posts were under siege. In these last of the battles, the revolutionaries fought with such bravery as to elicit a tribute even from Rochambeau, who was soon reduced to treating with the British fleet outside the harbor on the terms for a French evacuation.

On November 28, the revolutionaries entered Le Cap. Napoleon's great expedition had cost over fifty thousand French lives and probably double that number of black ones. His vision of an American empire had vanished. Already in April, recognizing the extent of his failure, he had sold for $12 million France's vast Louisiana territory to the United States.

On New Year's Day 1804, the victory of the revolution culminated in a Declaration of Independence, proclaimed to a gathering of officers at Gonaïves. To symbolize the final break with France, Saint Domingue was renamed Haiti, after the indigenous name Ayti, meaning "mountainous land," for the island. In October, Dessalines was crowned emperor, with a crown presented by Philadelphia merchants and in robes brought by a British frigate.

Early in the following year, Dessalines set out to expel the French from the neighboring colony ceded to them by Spain. He was besieging the capital when a French squadron arrived, and there were rumors of another such squadron already in the harbor of Gonaïves. Dessalines raised the siege immediately and hurried home, there to order, against the advice of Christophe and other generals, a massacre of all French whites in Haiti. It may have been his judgment that once the French white community had been eliminated, all French interest in regaining the territory would evaporate.[31] Many blacks, roused by their fear that the French might be returning to restore slavery, and with past outrages still alive in their minds, took to the task with relish. After the first massacre, Dessalines, with a duplicity and cruelty he had learned from Europeans who were masters of both, promised a pardon to all French whites who had so far escaped by going into hiding. When they emerged, they were slaughtered as well.

The first Constitution of the new Haiti was promulgated in May 1805. It abolished slavery forever in the state. It declared that all Haitians were to be called black, whatever their color, so that the term now encompassed even those Germans and Poles who had fought for the black revolution and been accepted as citizens. One modern scholar, David Nicholls, suggests that this may have been the first time in history the word "black" came to be used in an ideological sense.[32] The Constitution further declared that no white man, regardless of nationality, might set foot in Haiti as an owner of slaves or acquire property there in the future.

The new Constitution set out to allay the anxieties of slave-owning powers abroad with the assurance that "the emperor will not undertake any enterprise with a view to making conquests or to troubling the peace and the internal regime of foreign colonies."[33] Dessalines seems to have been satisfied that the very meaning of Haiti would promote the liberation of slaves elsewhere, without his running the risk of foreign intervention by the provocation of a more militant engagement.

"Unfortunate Martiniquans," he declared on one occasion, "I am not able to fly to your assistance and break your chains . . . But perhaps a spark from the fire which we have kindled will spring forth in your soul."[34]

13 | UNQUIET ISLANDS

In 1623, the English invaded the island of St. Kitts. In 1625, the French did so as well. The two colonial powers then decided to partition the territory between them. In 1639, some sixty slaves in the French part fled to establish themselves on the summit of the central mountain range. Five hundred troops stormed the position and quartered or burned alive many of the rebels. The rebel leader escaped but was hunted down and shot. His body was then quartered and each of his limbs hung up for display in a different place where it might frequently be seen by passing slaves.

The French had early trouble in Guadeloupe as well, where slaves from Angola revolted in 1656 with the alleged purpose of killing all the whites and electing two of their number to rule as kings. They expected slaves elsewhere on the island to join in the rebellion, but these, apparently, had come from other parts of Africa and did not do so. The Angolan slaves fought on nonetheless for fifteen days before being subdued. The two prospective "kings" were quartered; the other rebels were torn to pieces alive, hanged, or flogged.[1]

The planters of Barbados, the richest of England's first sugar colonies in the Caribbean, suffered little from the problem of fugitive slaves. As intensive sugar production consumed the flat island's forest cover, there came to be no natural retreat in which slaves might hide. By the middle of the seventeenth century, however, the slave population had become so large that fear of an uprising preyed upon the minds of the planters.

"If any tumult or disorder be in the island," a contemporary historian wrote, "the next neighbour to it discharges a musquet, which gives the alarm to the whole island for on the report of that the next shoots and so the next, until it go through the island; upon which warning they make ready."[2]

The planters deliberately bought their slaves from different West African areas of origin, in the belief that tribal and language distinctions would provide barriers against collective revolt. Time undermined that precaution, as slaves began to communicate with one another in pidgin, and the deeper hatred of white mastery overwhelmed any animosities of African origin that there may have been.

In June 1675, a house slave named Fortuna informed her master of plans for a slave revolt, due to break out in a fortnight, which aimed at killing all the whites and making a very old slave called Cuffee king of Barbados. The Governor ordered the arrest of the alleged leaders and their secret interrogation by militia officers. Six slaves were sentenced to be burned alive and eleven others to be beheaded. One of those sentenced to be burned, a slave named Tony, replied defiantly: "If you roast me today, you cannot roast me tomorrow."[3] Fortuna was given her freedom, to reward her loyalty and encourage others to follow her example.

In 1686, a conspiracy was discovered that reportedly encompassed Irish indentured servants as well as black slaves. The eighteen Irish servants arrested were subsequently freed in the absence of evidence against them, but all Irish servants on the island were disarmed and prohibited from leaving their plantations without written permission. The twenty slaves arrested were all executed.

Another slave conspiracy discovered on Barbados in 1692 reportedly involved three months of planning toward a rebellion directed at seizing control of the island with a military force of six regiments, two of them mounted on horses taken from the stables of their owners. The Governor instructed a court-martial to investigate the "Devilish but cunningly managed Designes."[4] Two suspects were suspended in chains for four days until they confessed to details, true or fabricated, in fear or anguish. The slaves identified as leaders were mainly foremen, craftsmen, house servants, and "such others that have more favour showne them by their Masters, which adds aboundantly to their crimes."[5] Of the three alleged top leaders, one, named Sambo, was tortured and died before his trial. Another, named Ben, was tortured as well, and the third, named Hammon, confessed when promised that he would be reprieved if he did so. Both were executed, along with ninety-two others.

It would take well over a century before a substantial revolt actually emerged on the island. This started in St. Philip on April 14, 1816, and spread rapidly to most of the southern and central parishes together with one in the north. The leading figure was believed to be an African slave named Bussa. His main associates—Jackey, Davis, King Wiltshire, Dick Bailey, Johnny, and a woman known as Nanny Grigg—were all Creole slaves, while free persons of pure or part African descent were also involved. The rebels, with no alternative to engaging the troops and militia sent against them, surprisingly succeeded in holding out for four days. Moreover, the survivors who fled must have found haven or help, since pursuit of them continued into June. Official figures for the rebel dead were 214 executed under martial law or by sentence of the courts.

On St. Vincent, black resistance was long directed not at overthrowing slavery but at preventing its establishment. In 1719, a French force of four hundred men invaded the island, but were ambushed and put to flight by a force of Black Caribs, the descendants of escaped African slaves and the indigenous Carib population. A British expedition in 1723 met the same fate, and for some fifty years thereafter the island was avoided by the contending colonial powers.

In 1772–73, the Black Caribs, under their leader, Chatoyer, fought a five-month war against a second British invasion force. It was a resistance as hopeless as it was heroic, and the Black Caribs at last agreed to a peace treaty which recognized British sovereignty over the island but conceded to the Caribs a designated area of their own. It was, however, a concession with a hook. They were pledged to capture and restore any fugitives from among the slaves that the British proposed to import.

By 1779, the Black Caribs were at war with the British again, though now they were aided by the French. During the next four years the French became directly involved and eventually won control over the bulk of the island. In 1783, a peace treaty between Britain and France restored British sovereignty and returned the Black Caribs to their corresponding status. Twelve years later, war broke out yet again between the Black Caribs, still under Chatoyer's leadership, and British troops augmented by the local settlers' militia. Chatoyer was killed, and the defeated Black Caribs were deported to Central America, where their descendants today constitute some 8 percent of the population in Belize.[6]

In 1733, there were 208 whites and 1,087 black slaves on the small Danish-ruled island of St. John. On November 13 of that year, slaves who were delivering fuel to the fort of Coral Bay and who had hidden weapons in the bundles of wood took the soldiers by surprise and captured the fort. Together with their fellow slaves, whose rebellion had been set to coincide with this event, they seized control of the island and held it for six months, until Danish troops, supported by four hundred French soldiers from Martinique, reconquered it. All the whites had been killed except for a doctor, who had been spared to tend the blacks.[7] Many of the defeated rebels, facing reenslavement, preferred to kill themselves. Of those taken alive, twenty-seven were tried and executed.[8]

British settlement of Antigua was troubled from the first by the flight of its slaves, often to the dense forest cover of the hills in the southwest of the island. By 1684, the authorities were offering bounties to encourage the hunting down of fugitives. Three years later, there were still some fifty such fugitives operating from a fortified camp in the hills and visiting by stealth the plantations "to Excite and stirr up the Negroes to forsake their Masters, and . . . to make themselves masters of the Country." The bounties were doubled, and militia, adequately induced, attacked the camp and killed or captured most of the fugitives. A slave of the Governor was found to have been involved in inciting slave revolt. His tongue was cut out and one of his legs chopped off, to provide "a Living Example to the rest."[9]

In 1736, a general uprising of slaves on Antigua was frustrated after the disclosure of the design by one of the conspirators, who had been arrested for a minor offense and confessed in his panic. The plan had been to blow up with gunpowder the assembly rooms on a night when the leading whites were to be at a ball there, and this would have provided the signal for rebellion. The record of the subsequent trial noted that many of the arrested were able to read and write and had been baptized. It added that "they could none of them complain of the hardships of slavery, their lives being as easy as those of our white overseers and tradesmen, and their manner of living much more plentiful than that of our common whites." The convicted included twenty-three drivers, twelve carpenters, seven coopers, three waiting-men, two masons, two coachmen, two fiddlers, a sugar boiler, and a drummer. In all, five were broken on the wheel, five were gibbeted, and seventy-seven were burned alive.[10]

Much the most turbulent of Britain's Caribbean island possessions was Jamaica, whose very size, mountainous terrain, and rich forest cover afforded ample opportunity for fugitive slaves to find concealment and conduct guerrilla activities. The majority of the fifteen hundred slaves in what had been a Spanish colony had taken to the mountains when the English conquered the island in 1655. Within a year, Major General Sedgewick was complaining that these "gave no quarter to his men, but destroyed them whenever they found opportunity; scarce a week passing without their murdering one or more of them; and as the soldiers became more confident and careless, the negroes grew more enterprising and bloody-minded."[11]

Forty soldiers in all lost their lives when "carelessly rambling from their quarters." The English forces struck back and in 1656 recorded a notable success. A body of fugitive slaves, by now coming to be called Maroons, surrendered under their commander, Juan de Bolas, in return for a pardon and their freedom. In 1663, the authorities offered a full pardon, freedom from "all manner of slavery" and twenty acres of land to every Maroon who surrendered. None took up the offer, and Juan de Bolas, elevated to colonel of the Black Regiment, was sent to suppress the Maroons. His force was ambushed and cut to pieces. In this way, the Maroons "continued to distress the island for upward of forty years, during which time forty-four acts of Assembly were passed, and at least £240,000 expended for their suppression."[12]

As increasing numbers of slaves were brought to the island, mainly for the burgeoning sugar industry, they became a source of turbulence in themselves as well as potential recruits to the Maroons. In 1673, slaves on a plantation in the parish of St. Ann revolted, and some two hundred of them fled into the mountains, where it was reported that they "secured themselves in difficult places . . . from which they were never dislodged."[13] Two years later, a slave conspiracy discovered in the parish of St. Mary provoked a declaration of martial law, and thirty-five slaves were executed. In 1678, slaves from various plantations, brought together for the building of a fort, plotted a revolt. On one plantation, within five miles of Spanish Town, slaves killed their mistress and several other whites. While some were caught, thirty escaped to rouse slaves on other plantations. Ferocious punishments followed the suppression of the revolt.

In 1683, a conspiracy involving 180 slaves in Vere was betrayed, and the informer was rewarded with his freedom. In 1685, some 150 slaves revolted on four plantations at Guanaboa Vale. Seven of them were killed and many others arrested, but sixty-three escaped and may have formed the basis of the guerrilla band, led by a certain Kofi, which operated in St. Catherine and St. Thomas ye Vale during 1685–86. Then, on a night in March 1686, slaves on Madame Guy's plantation revolted and managed to seize arms "through the faults of the white servants, who were gotten drunk and therefore unable to Quell them."[14] Fifteen of the seventeen whites there were killed, though Madame Guy herself, hidden by a loyal slave, escaped. All the slaves subsequently captured were killed by being burned alive, torn by dogs, or drawn and quartered. Such punishments might have satisfied a white appetite for revenge, but did not make the whites any safer. In 1690, the largest slave revolt to date broke out at Suttons in Clarendon. The rebels, reportedly numbering five hundred, suffered heavy losses in their efforts to hold the plantation, until 150 survivors, with the guns they had seized, escaped to establish a mountain fastness in the center of the island.

By 1702, the Lieutenant Governor, himself a planter, was reporting that escaped slaves "have mightily increased in number these twelve months and have been so bold to come down armed and attack our out settlements to Windward and have destroyed one or two."[15] Increasingly, Maroons took to raiding plantations and seizing slaves. In 1718, planters at Plaintain Garden River, for instance, were "robbed by a great gang of rebellious negroes," who took away with them skilled craftsmen and women. The colonial authorities at last decided that a major military campaign had become necessary: the British government sent several regiments to assist, and in 1728 what would come to be known as the First Maroon War began.

The Maroons responded by combining into two large groups: the Leeward, or western, Maroons, under a leader called Cudjoe in alliance with an influential "Obeah woman" or sorceress known as Nanny, and the Windward, or eastern, Maroons under a leader called Quao. The authorities calculated on a protracted campaign but could scarcely have imagined that it might last for more than a decade and result in an acknowledgment that the Maroons could not be defeated, except by an excessive investment of men and money. The successful strategy of the Maroons is clear from the indignant account by Bryan Edwards, the eighteenth-century West Indian merchant and historian:

> By night they seized the favourable opportunity that darkness gave them, of stealing into the settlements, where they set fire to cane-fields and out-houses, killed all the cattle they could find, and carried the slaves into captivity. By this dastardly method of conducting the war, they did infinite mischief to the whites, without much exposing their own persons to danger, for they always cautiously avoided fighting, except with a number so disproportionately inferior to themselves as to afford them a pretty sure expectation of victory. They knew every secret avenue of the country; so that they could either conceal themselves from pursuit, or shift their ravages from place to place, as circumstances required. Such were the many disadvantages under which the English had to deal with those desultory foes; who were not reducible by any regular plan of attack; who possessed no plunder to allure or reward the assailants; nor had anything to lose, except life, and a wild and savage freedom. [16]

At the start of March 1738, the authorities signed a peace treaty with the Leeward Maroons and, on June 23, 1739, another with the Windward ones. These were followed on August 5, 1740, by a grant of five hundred acres to the Obeah woman Nanny and those residing with her. The Articles of Pacification granted the Maroons freedom and autonomy within designated lands which they might cultivate as they wished except for sugar and whose produce they might sell in towns according to prescribed rules. In return, the Maroons agreed to accept the jurisdiction of white courts in interracial disputes; inflict the death penalty in their own area only with white permission; and deliver up all future fugitive slaves who came to them. Not least, they pledged "their best endeavours to take, kill, suppress, or destroy either by themselves, or jointly with any other number of men, commanded on that service by his excellency, the Governor, or Commander in Chief for the time being, all rebels whatsoever they be, throughout this island, unless they submit to the same terms of accommodation . . ."[17]

The Maroons, evidently convinced that such terms were the best they could get and virtually conceded independence to them, began honoring their part of the bargain in the first of the rebellions which marked the notably turbulent year of 1760. On April 8, some four hundred slaves on a plantation in the parish of St. Mary revolted under the leadership of one among them called Tacky. They then moved stealthily on Fort Haldane, where they took the sentries by surprise, armed themselves, and proceeded to more protective terrain in the interior. Two army regiments and the militia, assisted by Maroon mercenaries, went in successful pursuit. Tacky himself was reportedly killed by a Maroon.

Almost immediately, another rebellion surfaced in St. Thomas, and though this was soon suppressed, a third, much larger, began on June 2 in the southwest of the island, on several plantations in Westmoreland. Some six hundred slaves were involved; and, although three army companies, a force of one hundred marines, and the militias of three parishes were sent against them, the last of the rebels were still being hunted down five months later. In addition, four separate conspiracies were discovered in the parishes of Clarendon, St. John, St. Dorothy, and St. Thomas in the east of the island.

In all, the various rebellions of that year resulted in the deaths of sixty whites and a thousand slaves, with a loss to planters, "in ruined buildings, cane pieces, cattle, slaves and disbursements," of at least £100,000. Their impact on Jamaican white planters was such that one modern historian has likened it to the impact which the Mutiny of 1857 would have on whites in India.[18] The treatment meted out to some captured rebels was hideously inventive. Employing a technique that would become in modern times standard practice for torturers, those in charge of the prisoners administered electric shocks to Obeah men, whose influence was adduced to explain the disaffection of slaves supposedly well treated by their masters. "Upon other *Obeah-men*, who were apprehended at that time, various experiments were made with electrical machines and magic lanterns, but with very little effect, except on one, who, after receiving some very severe shocks, acknowledged that 'this master's *Obi* exceeded his own.' "[19]

Maroons may well have been involved once more in helping the authorities to crush a slave uprising in the parishes of Westmoreland and Hanover during 1777, as a result of which thirty rebels were executed. If so, it was to prove the last manifestation of Maroon trust in the good faith of the British. In 1795, a war with the Maroons broke out whose conclusion would produce one of the most disreputable episodes in the record of Britain's Caribbean colonial government.

Since the First Maroon War, the Maroon population had more than doubled, to an estimated fourteen hundred by 1788. Their discontent had grown as well in the major Leeward Maroon settlement at Trelawney Town, whose inhabitants considered the land assigned to them inadequate, complained of the treatment meted out to them by whites, and objected to the new Superintendent-General appointed to reside among them. Their grievances were hardly alleviated when, in 1795, two of the Maroons were found guilty of stealing pigs in Montego Bay and flogged in punishment. "As the culprits went through the town and plantations, they were laughed at, hissed, and hooted by the slaves," and the flogging was inflicted "before the slaves in the common workhouse, by a runaway negro who had formerly been taken by them."[20] Given the antagonism between Maroons and slaves that the authorities had promoted, it was not strange that the slaves should have behaved as they did, nor that the Maroons should have interpreted such behavior as an officially sanctioned humiliation.

The Trelawney Maroons drove the new Superintendent-General from their town in the middle of July. This was subsequently held by the authorities to have been a "decided act" of rebellion. The Maroons would maintain that they had been forced to take measures of self-preservation, after becoming convinced, from the conduct of the whites, that their own destruction was planned. Certainly, the colony was in a mood of aggressive anxiety. It was seething with reports of turmoil in the nearby French colony of Saint Domingue, rumors of French agents operating among the Maroons, and fear of a general slave insurrection fired by the message of the French Revolution. Martial law was declared in Jamaica, and a frigate was summoned to land troops.

At this point, six Maroon captains, having duly obtained passports from General Palmer, "were proceeding on their way to Spanish Town, to make their submission." On the way, "they were stopped, notwithstanding their passports, and secured by the commanding officer of the militia, to wait the pleasure of the Governor." When Lord Balcarres arrived, on August 5, he had them placed in irons. Three days later, "he sent a message to the Maroons, in which, after upbraiding them for their conduct, and informing them that the passes to their town were all occupied by troops, and that they were surrounded by thousands, he told them that he had issued a proclamation offering a reward for their heads after the 12th of August, and advised and commanded every Maroon capable of bearing arms to appear before him at Montego Bay on that day, to submit themselves to his Majesty's mercy."[21]

On August 11, only thirty-seven Maroons, including "old Montague," the Chief at Trelawney Town, arrived and surrendered their arms to the Governor. They evidently expected to be welcomed and treated with respect. Instead, they were arrested, and all but one of them were confined. The exception was a Maroon who, "exasperated at his disappointment," had "put an end to his existence by ripping out his bowels."[22] Two of the prisoners, both Maroon captains, were then sent to Trelawney Town with the charge of getting the Maroons there to surrender. On hearing what had happened, however, the Maroons immediately set fire to their town and moved to the more defensible settlement of Schaw Castle. It was the start of the Second Maroon War.

The Maroons possessed, in one of their number named Johnson, a military commander of exceptional ability. Reinforced by fugitive slaves who were now made welcome, they moved as necessary from one mountain retreat to another and inflicted heavy casualties on the forces sent against them. Planters and officials alike came, as month followed month, increasingly to fear that if the war continued, many of the colony's slaves would be encouraged to revolt and join the Maroons. The authorities decided to import from Cuba its notorious hunting dogs and their handlers or chasseurs.

"No time . . . was lost in landing the chasseurs and their dogs: the wild and formidable appearance of both spread terror through the place; the streets were cleared, the doors of the houses shut, and the windows crouded. Not a negro ventured to stir out. The muzzled dogs with the heavy rattling chains ferociously making at every object, and forcibly dragging on the chasseurs, who could hardly restrain them, presented a scene of a tremendous nature, well calculated to give a most awful colouring to the report which would be conveyed to the Maroons."[23]

Major General Walpole, commander-in-chief of the government forces, had acquired much respect for the fighting qualities of the Maroons and was not convinced that dogs, however fierce, would defeat them. His own forces, no less than the Maroons, were suffering from the lack of water in the mountainous terrain of the conflict. There was growing pressure on him to finish the war before the Christmas festivities, when the plantation slaves were more than usually restless. He advanced his troops, along with the dogs, and offered the Maroons an opportunity to negotiate a treaty.

On December 21, 1795, agreement was reached. The Maroons pledged that "they would on their knees beg his Majesty's pardon"; that they would go to Trelawney, Montego Bay, "or any other place that might be pointed out, and would settle on whatever lands the Governor, Council, and Assembly might think proper to allot"; and that "they would give up all runaways." Conditional on all this, however, was another, secret article of the treaty, to which Walpole swore his personal oath, "promising that the Maroons should not be sent off the island."[24]

Lord Balcarres ratified the treaty, including the secret article. Then, after the Maroons had surrendered and been disarmed, Walpole came to learn that Lord Balcarres and the Colonial Assembly intended to ignore the secret article and proceed to the deportation of the Leeward Maroons. In a letter dated March 11, 1796, Walpole wrote in confidence to Lord Balcarres and expressed his "considerable uneasiness" at the report that had reached him:

> My lord, to be plain with you, it was through my means alone that the maroons were induced to surrender, from a reliance which they had in my word, from a conviction impressed upon them by me that the white people would never break their faith.
>
> All these things strongly call upon me, as the instrumental agent in this business, to see a due observance of the terms, or, in case of violation, to resign my command; and if that should not be accepted, to declare the facts to the world, and to leave them to judge how far I ought or ought not to be implicated in the guilt and infamy of such a proceeding.[25]

The Assembly voted not only thanks to Walpole for his services but a sum of 500 guineas to purchase a sword for him. Walpole wrote to decline the honor, "which he conceived he could not with credit to himself receive, as the House had thought fit not to accede to the agreement entered into by him and the Trelawney-Town Maroons, and as their opinion of that treaty stood on their minutes very different from his conception of it."[26] The Assembly ordered his letter to be excluded from the minutes.

The Leeward Maroons, with Johnson among them, were soon deported, first to Nova Scotia and subsequently to Sierra Leone, where they arrived in time to be employed in helping to suppress a rebellion.[27] Walpole, having resigned from the army, campaigned for the correction of the injustice done to the Maroons. His campaign generated much dispute but failed in its objective.

There was soon trouble for the white colonists from another source. In 1799, a conspiracy was discovered among some of the slaves recently brought to Jamaica by their owners from the upheaval in Saint Domingue. The Governor was so alarmed by this development that he ordered more than a thousand of these slaves to be deported. The impact of the events in Saint Domingue was not, however, to be neutralized merely by the deporting of slaves who had come from there.

In 1803, a conspiracy among slaves in Kingston was discovered, and two of the alleged conspirators were executed. In 1806, another conspiracy came to light in St. George; one alleged conspirator was executed, and five others were transported. Two years later, fifty slaves serving in the 2nd West India Regiment mutinied at Fort Augusta and killed two officers. In 1809, yet another conspiracy in Kingston was discovered; two of the alleged conspirators were hanged, and several others were transported. Then, in 1815, a considerable conspiracy, involving some 250 slaves, most of them reportedly Ibo in origin, surfaced in St. Elizabeth. The arraigned leaders, who had apparently been encouraged by the expectation of help from British abolitionists, were sentenced to be hanged. One of them had been offered his freedom if he agreed to give evidence against three others. He had refused.

The mounting impatience for an end to slavery from among militant Christian converts had been a feature of this frustrated rebellion. According to the contemporary writer Matthew Gregory "Monk" Lewis, who was also a Jamaican plantation owner, the rebels had elected "a King of the Eboes . . . and their intention was to effect a complete massacre of all the whites on the island."

"On their trial," Lewis noted, "they were perfectly cool and unconcerned, and did not even profess to deny the facts with which they were charged. Indeed, proofs were too strong to admit of denial; among others, a copy of the following song was found upon the King . . .

'Oh me good friend, Mr. Wilberforce, make we free!
God Almighty thank ye! God Almighty thank ye!
God Almighty, make we free!
Buckra in this country no make we free;
What Negro for to do? What Negro for to do?
Take force by force! Take force by force!
(Chorus)
To be sure! To be sure! To be sure!'

"The Eboe King said, that he certainly had made use of this song, and what harm was there in his doing so? He had sung no songs but such as his brown priest had assured him were approved of by John the Baptist."[28]

In 1823, six of the leaders were hanged and eight others were transported after a slave conspiracy in St. George was discovered. In 1824, another conspiracy, in Hanover, was discovered; eleven slaves were hanged and a number of others transported or flogged. Then, on the night of December 27, 1831, the greatest slave uprising in the history of the British Caribbean colonies broke out in the west of Jamaica. It would involve some twenty thousand slaves.[29]

This so-called Emancipation Rebellion was designed as a phased campaign, to start as a general strike against slavery and, if the demands of the strikers were not met, advance to widespread arson and military action. The surfacing of a conspiracy in which so many were engaged and which had nonetheless been kept so successfully secret shocked the authorities. They committed British military and naval forces as well as the mobilized militia in response. Yet for all this investment of force, it took until the first week of April 1832 and the reported killing of over two hundred rebels before a sullen peace was restored.

There was much to alarm planter society and the colonial government in all this, apart from the scale of the uprising. Unlike so many earlier rebellions, the leadership and much of the following in this one had been both Creole and Christian. Moreover, under abolitionist pressure, the treatment of slaves had been improving. The bewilderment of the authorities, for whom the longing of slaves to be free was not explanation enough, might have contributed to the ferocity of their response.

Some 750 slaves and 14 free persons of color were convicted of rebellion. Most of these were sentenced to death. The remainder were flogged, with from two hundred to five hundred strokes each, with or without subsequent imprisonment, and twenty-one were transported. The principal leader, Sam Sharpe, was a devout Christian. To the minister of religion who visited him in prison before his execution, he said, "I would rather die upon yonder gallows than live in slavery."[30]

~~~~~~

Slave resistance in the United States faced a peculiar combination of formidable factors. Elsewhere in the hemisphere, the leadership of such resistance, with most of its support, came mainly from African arrivals who retained the identity and outlook of their origins. Slaves of this sort were a dominant part of the slave population in North America only during the colonial period and not even for all of that. By the time that slavery was established as the distinctive and crucial institution across the South of the United States, the slave population was overwhelmingly native.

The psychical displacement involved certainly contributed to the readiness with which the slaves took to Christianity. This is not to suggest that Christianity was a religion of slave acquiescence, predictably the doctrine professed by slave owners and their clergy. Indeed, some of the most notable slave conspiracies and revolts were led by ardent adherents to Christianity, albeit at times with residual elements from traditional African beliefs and cultural expression. Yet in the very process of making Christianity their own, the slaves were particularly taken by those parts of the Bible, notably Exodus, which held out the promise of divine intervention to provide the deliverance from bondage. There must have been slaves who regarded revolt as preempting a design which time would duly disclose.

There were as well demographic, environmental, and military factors that discouraged resort to revolt. Taken together, the so-called slave states had roughly two whites for every slave; and taken separately, only South Carolina, with 57 percent, and Mississippi, with 55 percent, contained more slaves than whites. To be sure, there were various counties where slaves outnumbered whites by more than two to one, and a few, such as Issaquena in Mississippi, with a ratio of over ten to one.[1] Even there, however, slaves were well aware that any such local predominance existed alongside considerable concentrations of whites in other counties and the organized white resources of the South as a whole. It was no secret that "the white population constituted one great militia—fully and even extravagantly armed, tough and resourceful, and capable of all the savagery that racism can instill."[2]

On the smaller scale of the immediate environment, there were relatively few such concentrations of slaves as were common across much of the slave system elsewhere in the hemisphere. The average large plantation in the South had a score of slave laborers, compared to the corresponding average of between one and two hundred slaves in Brazil and on the Caribbean sugar islands. Slaves in the South, for all the size of their overall population, were physically and psychically contained to a peculiar degree.

This context was unfavorable not only to revolt but to the alternative resistance of flight to form or join maroon communities. The South certainly contained areas—swampy, mountainous, forested—which elsewhere in the hemisphere afforded opportunities for fugitives to conceal themselves or conduct guerrilla activities. Yet these were generally remote from the areas of slave concentration and correspondingly difficult to reach. The mobilizing of militia, let alone the summoning of troops, was rarely required. Rural whites were brought up to be practiced marksmen and responded quickly and enthusiastically to any appeal for the capture or killing of fugitive slaves.

There were a few countervailing factors. The very creation of the United States, with its revolutionary doctrines enshrined in the Declaration of Independence and regularly celebrated, constituted a moral indictment of the Southern slave system and a corresponding moral encouragement of resistance to injustice and oppression. The success of the slave revolution in Saint Domingue lit the lives of slaves who heard of it, and three decades later, the abolition of slavery throughout the British Empire raised slave expectations wherever in the hemisphere slavery survived. Within the United States itself, militant opponents of Southern slavery promoted one form of resistance by providing guides and safe houses along the escape routes to the North.

In reaction, however, a virtual totalitarianism to protect the slave system took command of white society in the South. Laws crowded the statute books to discourage and punish white as well as black dissent, tighten the surveillance and control the movement of slaves, impede or prevent the freeing of slaves, and restrict the rights or secure the departure of free blacks. All in all, it is surprising not that there were relatively so few slave conspiracies and revolts but that there were so many.

Though nowhere on the scale of some slave systems in the hemisphere, notably Saint Domingue, individual and collective resistance seems to have been responsible for poisonings. Certainly, there were enough, actual or suspected, to excite the enactment of special laws to deal with the phenomenon. Five slaves in Maryland, for instance, were convicted in 1755 for having plotted to poison four masters.[3] In 1804, slaves in three counties of

North Carolina were held to have conspired to poison their masters and to have caused the deaths of two "respectable men." Some twenty slaves were arrested, of whom one was burned alive; several were hanged; and one, having been pilloried and whipped, "had his ears nailed down and then cut off."[4] In 1830 two Virginia slaves were tried, convicted, and punished for the crime.

Producing more frequent and widespread alarm was the incidence of fires attributed to arson by slaves. According to one modern scholar, Kenneth Stampp, arson was "the most common 'slave' crime" next to theft and "a favourite means for aggrieved slaves to even the score with their master."[5] Another, Eugene Genovese, has argued for caution, since arson was difficult to detect: "Authorities and aggrieved parties . . . often simply assumed it and further assumed its perpetration by slaves."[6] Some fires attributed to slave arson may well have been started by owners in financial distress who sought to collect the insurance. Others, similarly attributed, may simply have broken out in frame buildings with little protection. Whatever the truth, skepticism could be as misleading as paranoia. The Southern soil chemist and authority on plantation agriculture Edmund Ruffin refused to credit the suspicion voiced by others that the repeated fires on his plantation had been started deliberately by his own slaves. Only after the fifth serious fire did he accept that the suspicion almost certainly suited the facts.

All that can be maintained with confidence is that some slaves were likely to have found in arson a tempting form of expressing rage or exacting revenge; that every fire attributed to arson fed the fear which made the slave system so repressive; and that the very repressiveness of the system served to strengthen the abolitionist cause elsewhere in the country.

The years 1829–30 were marked by especially large fires in various parts of the South. Among these, that in Augusta, Georgia, destroyed much of the state's arms store; that which swept through part of New Orleans in January 1830 "burst out almost simultaneously on all sides of the square,"[7] to cause an estimated $300,000 in damage. In all such instances, slave arson was blamed, and white public pressure for discovering and punishing those responsible required results. A visiting Englishman, writing of the Augusta fire, recorded: "One slave, a female, was convicted, executed, dissected, and exposed, but she died denying the crime. Another, now with child, is sentenced to be executed . . . but she still denies her guilt. I fear these unhappy creatures are convicted on what we should consider insufficient evidence."[8] By August 1831, a businessman in Richmond, Virginia, was writing to inform a New York supplier that "we should not, just at this time, care to have goods sent us on which we might have to make advances," since goods destroyed by fire "would not be paid for by insurers."[9]

Serious fires, blamed on slave arson, continued breaking out not only until the beginning of the Civil War but beyond. In July 1860, fires caused enormous damage in the cities of northern Texas. Some whites were arrested and executed along with a number of slaves, in a frantic repression that lasted for eight weeks. In December 1861, the greatest fire ever attributed to slave arson in the United States raged through Charleston, to destroy some six hundred buildings and cause damage valued at $7 million.

If the extent of arson as a form of slave defiance was open to question, other forms were not. Herbert Aptheker, in his pioneering study, *American Negro Slave Revolts*, limited his record to revolts and conspiracies which involved at least ten slaves, had the achievement of freedom as their apparent aim, and were cited in contemporary records as plots, insurrections, uprisings, or the like. He identified 250 of these within the territory of what became the continental United States.

The first occurred as early as 1526, when some of the one hundred black slaves brought by Spaniards in the process of establishing a small colony in what would become South Carolina revolted and sought refuge among the indigenous Indians of the area. The first relevant conspiracy in an English North American settlement involved white indentured servants as well as blacks. Discovered in Virginia in 1663, or three years after the authorities there had designated the blacks as slaves, it resulted in several executions, with heads displayed on chimney tops to discourage further attempts.

By 1672, various armed groups of fugitive slaves were troubling the peace of Virginia, and the use of force was authorized to deal with them. In 1687, a slave conspiracy, held to have been devised during the mass funerals that slaves were then allowed, was discovered in the colony. The alleged leaders were executed, and public slave funerals were banned. Nor were such troubles long limited to Virginia. By 1702, an "Act for Regulating of Slaves" was passed in distant New York to deal with "running away, or other ill practices."[10] In 1708, a group of slaves in Newton, Long Island, rebelled. Seven whites were killed, and four slaves were subsequently executed. In 1711, a slave called Sebastian led a group of armed runaway slaves in "robbing and plundering houses and plantations" in South Carolina, whose white inhabitants were reportedly "in great terror and fear."[11] He was eventually tracked down and killed.

In April 1712, the most serious uprising so far took place in New York City, where there were roughly a thousand slaves and five times as many whites. Nine white men were killed and others injured before the military intervened. Of the twenty-one slaves subsequently executed, the Governor reported to the British Lords of Trade, "some were burnt, others hanged, one broke on the wheele, and one hung a live in chains in the town, so that there has been the most exemplary punishment inflicted that could be possibly thought of . . ."[12] One important result of the uprising was mounting opposition in the North to any increase in the slave population there. An Act of August 1712 in Pennsylvania, for instance, placed a discouragingly high duty on fresh slave imports, and an Act of 1713 in Massachusetts banned the importation of slaves altogether.

In Virginia, slave conspiracies were discovered and crushed in 1722 and 1723. In 1729, a number of slaves escaped, with guns, ammunition, and agricultural tools, to establish a settlement in the Blue Ridge Mountains. There they were attacked by a substantial white force, and those who survived were returned to captivity. The following year yet another conspiracy, involving some two hundred slaves, was discovered, and four of these, convicted as leaders, were executed.

Such turbulence was much exceeded, however, by that in South Carolina. Already by 1720, the colony had twelve thousand slaves and nine thousand whites, and by 1740 the number of whites would fall to five thousand, while the number of slaves would rise to forty thousand. Major conspiracies were discovered in 1713, 1720, 1729, and 1730, to be followed during the 1730s by increasing unrest, encouraged in part by the promise of freedom for fugitives which the Spanish authorities in Florida had made.

On September 9, 1739, a score of slaves at Stono revolted under the leadership of a slave called Jemmy. They killed the two white guards at a storehouse and seized firearms there. Then they headed for Florida, setting fire to buildings and killing whites along the way. Joined by other slaves until they numbered seventy-five, they were encountered and attacked by a similar number of white militia. Fourteen of the slaves were killed in the battle and twenty-one others were killed by pursuers. The surviving forty were taken prisoner and subsequently executed. In June 1740, a conspiracy in Charleston was betrayed twenty-four hours before the revolt was due to begin, and fifty slaves were hanged, in groups of ten a day, "to intimidate the other negroes."[13]

In the following year, virtual panic gripped many whites in the city of New York. In 1740, there had been rumors of a slave conspiracy to poison the water supply. The exceptionally harsh winter of 1740–41 had produced much suffering among the poor, free as well as slave; and in March and April 1741 a series of suspicious fires involved not only private houses, but the Governor's residence, the King's Chapel, and the military barracks. Some 150 slaves and twenty-five whites were arrested on charges of conspiracy and arson. Four of the whites were executed; and of the slaves, thirteen were burned alive, eighteen hanged, and seventy banished.

For the next three decades, there was some decline in the rebellious activity of slaves, though conspiracies continued to be discovered, and South Carolina in particular was seldom altogether undisturbed. Then, in 1774, the American Revolution began. It was not intended to include the slaves in its assertion of equality and its commitment to liberty, but inevitably there were slaves who included themselves. In November, slaves in St. Andrew's Parish, Georgia, rebelled and killed four whites before being overpowered. Two of them were burned alive in punishment. In 1775, a major conspiracy involving slaves in three counties of North Carolina was discovered, and there were reports of rebelliousness in New York, Virginia, and South Carolina.

Not least, the revolutionary war provided peculiar opportunities for the development of maroon activities. In 1779, Savannah, Georgia, was being besieged by a combined French and colonial American force. The British armed the slaves, who fought in the belief that they would be rewarded with their freedom. Temporarily victorious, the British tried to disarm them and return them to slavery, but they rebelled and, after the British surrender, took to the Belle Isle Swamp some twenty miles north of Savannah. From there they conducted guerrilla warfare until 1786, when they were overwhelmed by a militia force from both Georgia and South Carolina. Maroon activity continued elsewhere, however, until well into the 1790s.

By the spring of 1800, preparations for a massive rebellion in Virginia had begun under the leadership of a slave named Gabriel, later described as "a fellow of courage and intellect above his rank in life."[14] His lieutenants were his wife, Nanny; his brothers, Solomon and Martin; and Jack Bowler, a slave who would declare, "We had as much right to fight for our liberty as any men."[15] While weapons and bullets were made, Gabriel visited Richmond on Sundays to fix in his mind the layout of the city, with particular reference to the location of armament stores. The time for the uprising had been fixed for the night of August 30, and secrecy was preserved until the very afternoon before. Then, two slaves named Tom and Pharaoh disclosed the conspiracy to their master. The Governor of Virginia, James Monroe, was immediately informed. More than 650 men were rapidly mobilized, and every militia commander in the state was alerted.

Nature now took the side of authority. In the early evening, a storm decanted so much rain as to make impassable the route between the rendezvous of the rebels and Richmond. When some one thousand slaves armed with crude weapons and a few guns assembled six miles from the city, they found their way blocked and decided to disperse. During the next few days, many were hunted down, and Gabriel was captured, to be taken in chains to Richmond. At least thirty-five were subsequently hanged, without one of them having agreed to confess or to supply information. Of Gabriel himself, James Monroe reported: "From what he said to me, he seemed to have made up his mind to die, and to have resolved to say but little on the subject of the conspiracy."[16]

In response to this and other disclosed conspiracies, states across the South passed new laws to tighten the control of slaves. The North took a different direction. By 1802, all the states there except for New Jersey had enacted measures toward the freeing of slaves, and New Jersey followed in 1804.

With the purchase by the United States in 1803 of the Louisiana Territory, which France had obtained from Spain, the South acquired not only a corresponding expansion of the slave system but a slave population with a record of rebelliousness. The new rulers were not left long in doubt over whether slaves there would continue to be troublesome. In the evening of January 8, 1811, several hundred slaves revolted in the parishes of St. Charles and St. John the Baptist, where at least two whites were killed and a few plantations destroyed. White refugees streamed into New Orleans, reporting their escape from "a miniature representation of the horrors of St. Domingo" and the involvement of "a free mulatto from St. Domingo," named Charles Deslondes, as one of the rebel leaders.[17]

A force of four hundred militiamen and sixty federal troops was sent from New Orleans, with a further two hundred soldiers summoned from Baton Rouge. The combined detachments attacked the rebels on the morning of January 10, killed sixty-six of them and dispatched seventeen captives to New Orleans, before proceeding to hunt down those who had fled. All those put on trial in New Orleans were convicted and executed. Whites in the affected areas, however, were bent on exacting their own revenge, to the point where a Louisiana paper delivered a public rebuke: "We are sorry to learn that a ferocious sanguinary disposition marked the character of some of the inhabitants; our laws are summary enough and let them govern."[18]

The South was not entirely without whites who had compassion for the slaves. George Boxley of Virginia went further, to instigate in late 1815 a conspiracy that reached across three counties of the state. Early in 1816 a slave woman betrayed the plans, and some thirty slaves were arrested. Boxley fled only to surrender himself, but then escaped from prison and was never caught. Six slaves were executed, and six more, condemned to be hanged, were reprieved under pressure from whites for clemency.

The leader in the largest slave conspiracy since Gabriel's in Virginia was a remarkable man named Denmark Vesey, who had reputedly been born in Africa, had managed to purchase his freedom in 1800, and was working as an artisan in Charleston, South Carolina. Resolute in resisting the various pressures exerted on free blacks to leave the South for assisted settlement in Africa, he declared on one occasion that "he had not the will, he wanted to stay and see what he could do for his fellow creatures."[19] Relevantly, these included his own slave children.

In December 1821, when he was in his late fifties, he set about recruiting associates in the leadership of his rebellious enterprise. He found some, such as Peter Poyas and Mingo Harth, among slave artisans, and others, such as Rolla, a slave owned by the Governor himself, in particularly useful positions. Literate as well as fluent in several foreign languages, he drew on various sources in making his appeal, citing not only the Bible but debates in the United States Congress on the issue of slavery, and the successful struggle of the slaves in Saint Domingue to seize and secure their freedom.

The leaders developed their plans in secrecy and enlisted others with care.

Recruiting agents were, for instance, specifically instructed to avoid domestic slaves. In the event, however, one agent did recruit a domestic slave who proceeded to inform his master. On May 30, 1822, Peter Poyas and Mingo Harth were arrested, but they conducted themselves with such "composure and coolness" that they were released on the very next day.[20]

The date for the uprising had been set for the second Sunday in July, when many whites would have retreated elsewhere from the close heat of the Charleston summer, and the presence of many blacks in the city might merely be ascribed to their customary Sabbath visits there. The preparations had been extensive. They involved conspirators up to eighty miles away from Charleston and perhaps as many as nine thousand in all. More than five hundred crude weapons had been especially made, along with wigs and whiskers to conceal the identities of the conspirators. Vesey had even written twice to Haiti, informing the government there of the intended rebellion and appealing for help.

Despite the release of his two associates, Vesey was apparently disturbed by the original betrayal. He advanced the date of the uprising by a month. The new date proved to be still too late. Perhaps alarmed by news of the arrests, a conspirator turned informer. Others were arrested, among them a slave who provided more damaging information. Of the 131 conspirators taken into custody, almost all followed the advice of Peter Poyas, to "die silent, as you shall see me do."[21] Thirty-seven of them, including Vesey, were hanged and twelve others were sentenced to death but then pardoned and transported.

The extent of the conspiracy and the character of its leadership had a considerable impact on the North, where much of the press was fired to publish articles attacking slavery. In the South, new laws were enacted to tighten still further the control over slaves. Various vigilante groups took their own action against free blacks, and Bishop Moses Brown, whose African Methodist Church in Charleston had some three thousand members, was forced to leave the state.

Manifestations of slave rebelliousness continued to disturb the South. In 1823, a band of fugitive slaves killed several whites in Norfolk County, Virginia, before succumbing to a substantial force of militia. Three years later, seventy-seven slaves being shipped down the Ohio River from Kentucky for sale in the Deep South killed the five whites on board, sank the boat, and made for Indiana, where they were eventually caught. Five of them were executed. In the same year, twenty-nine slaves being shipped from Maryland to Georgia killed two members of the crew and ordered the third to land them in Haiti. The boat was seized during its passage and taken to New York, where the rebels somehow succeeded in escaping. Only one of them was subsequently caught, to be duly executed.[22] In 1827, a fugitive slave settlement in Alabama was discovered, and in the battle that ensued the slaves were reported to have "fought like Spartans" so that "not one gave an inch of ground, but stood, was shot dead or wounded fell dead on the spot."[23]

In August 1829, a group of ninety slaves—men, women, and children shackled together—was being taken from Maryland for sale in the Deep South. While passing through Kentucky, the men, who had managed to file themselves free from their shackles, set upon their guards and killed two of them. The third guard, owner of the slaves, was attacked but escaped to summon help. Five of the men and one woman were subsequently sentenced to be hanged. The men were reported to have addressed with "the utmost firmness and resignation" the multitude that had collected to witness their execution. One of them simply declared, "Death—death at any time in preference to slavery."[24] The woman was found to be pregnant and was kept in prison until after her child was born. Then she was hanged.

In 1831 came the rebellion that more than any other traumatized the white South. Nat Turner had been born in 1800, the year of the Gabriel conspiracy, and had lived as a slave ever since in Southampton County, Virginia. He had learned how to read and had studied the Bible. According to his own subsequent confession, he was working in the fields during the spring of 1828 when he "heard a loud noise in the heavens, and the Spirit instantly appeared to me and said the Serpent was loosened, and Christ had laid down the yoke he had borne for the sins of men, and that I should take it on and fight against the Serpent, for the time was fast approaching when the first should be last and the last should be first."[25]

An eclipse of the sun on February 12, 1831, seemed to him the sign for which he had been waiting, and he disclosed his purpose to four other slaves. Together they fixed on the Fourth of July as an appropriate date for their rebellion, but Turner was ill on that day, and the conspirators decided to wait for another sign. This came on August 13, when the sun appeared to have a strange color. On August 14, a Sunday, Turner addressed a religious meeting of slaves at which some wore red bandannas round their necks as a sign of their commitment to the conspiracy. Then, on the following Sunday, Turner met with five other conspirators, and together they decided to start the rebellion that evening.

Turner killed not only his master but all the members of his master's family. The rebels seized whatever arms and horses they could find, killing whites, and joined by other slaves on the way to the county capital of Jerusalem, where they intended to raid an armory. They were three miles from the town and seventy in number when, despite Turner's opposition, the group insisted on stopping at a plantation to enlist the slaves there. While many of the rebels were diverted by the large wine cellar they discovered, the militia arrived. A short battle ensued, and the rebels fled.

By August 24, vigilantes, militia, and military forces were dispensing retribution more by massacre than by process of law. The Richmond *Whig* referred on September 3 to "the slaughter of many blacks without trial and under circumstances of great barbarity." Turner himself evaded capture until October 30. Sentenced to be hanged, he went calmly to his death. Sixteen other slaves and three free blacks had already been executed.

The unique impact of the Turner rebellion was due to the number of whites—at least fifty-seven men, women, and children—who had been killed in its course. Whites across the South were seized by hysteria, as rumors and reports of slave conspiracies and disturbances spread. A niece of George Washington wrote, in a letter to the Mayor of Boston: "It is like a smothered volcano—we know not when, or where, the flame will burst forth but we know that death in the most horrid forms threaten us. Some have died, others have become deranged from apprehension since the South Hampton affair."[26] The customary treatment was applied to restore morale. A new law was enacted in Virginia, with similar measures elsewhere in the South, that "no slave, free negro or mulatto, whether he shall have been ordained or licensed, or otherwise, shall hereafter undertake to preach, exhort, or conduct, or hold any assembly or meeting, for religious or other purposes, either in the day time or the night."[27]

It proved to be of no more avail in securing social peace than any of the other enactments. Not a single slave state escaped some form of slave disaffection in the following years. Among the major instances, widespread rebelliousness emerged in seven parishes of Louisiana during September and October 1840. In Iberville, some four hundred slaves revolted, and twenty of them were hanged. In the Avoyelles and Rapides, a conspiracy for the mass escape of slaves was betrayed by its own leader, and many slaves were taken in chains to Alexandria, where they were lynched. A regiment of soldiers had to be summoned to contain the white frenzy.

The last decade before the outbreak of the Civil War was marked by a considerable increase in slave escapes. More and more often now, former slaves who had fled the South would return to help others flee. One such, named Ben, returned repeatedly to encourage and guide the slaves of his former master, until he was caught and reenslaved. Harriet Tubman, who had been a slave for twenty-five years before escaping from her master in Maryland, served as a "conductor" on the Underground Railroad and returned to the South no fewer than nineteen times during the decade, to take parties of slaves northward to freedom. Texan slave owners suffered especially from mass escapes, since Mexico and freedom lay just the other side of the border. The slave owners mounted various expeditions to recover their property but returned with only a few wounds to show for their exertions.

In 1856, a conspiracy involving a large number of slaves was discovered in the Texas county of Colorado. Some two hundred were arrested and so severely whipped that two of them died in the process, while three alleged leaders were hanged. It was a year in which every slave state experienced some form of revolt. There was also evidence of increasingly sophisticated planning. In one instance, preparations to blow up bridges were discovered; in another, telegraph poles were damaged to cut communications.

The mass of slaves could scarcely have failed to support the Union in the Civil War. Some escaped to make for the camps of the Union armies, while others, unable or unwilling to flee, engaged in strikes, sabotage, conspiracy, and revolt, as conditions and opportunity prompted. The impatience for freedom became bolder with the growing belief in its imminence. Slaves were not the last to be aware that the odds which for so long had been stacked against them were coming increasingly to be stacked against a Southern society at war.

Before the outbreak of the Civil War, a slave leader named Scipio had assured James Gilmore, a wealthy merchant and close associate of Lincoln's, that the South would be defeated, " 'cause you see dey'll fight wid only one hand. When dey fight de Norf wid de right hand, dey'll hef to hold de nigga wid de leff."[28] A similar observation came early in the war from someone in New Orleans, part of whose letter to an English friend, dated May 30, 1861, was published in the London *Daily News*: "The agricultural population, which in other countries furnishes the fighting masses, is here, of course, ineligible for the purpose and ever requires armed power to keep it in order. There have been very alarming disturbances among the blacks; on more than one plantation, the assistance of the authorities has been called in to overcome the open resistance of slaves." If it was President Lincoln who signed the order emancipating them at last, the slaves of the South were coauthors.

15 | DISPERSED RESISTANCE

~~~~~~

In Brazil, settlements founded by runaway slaves were common enough for a word to be coined for them in Brazilian Portuguese: they came to be called *quilombos*; and their inhabitants, *quilombolas* or *quilombadas*. The earliest emerged in the second half of the sixteenth century, virtually with the first arrivals of African slaves, and they continued to emerge, even thrive, despite all the efforts of slave owners and the authorities to prevent and suppress them.

Preeminent was the quilombo of Palmares, named after its large forest of palm trees, in the eastern bulge of the territory, north of Bahia and south of Pernambuco. The date of its beginning is uncertain but is likely to have been 1612, and it grew rapidly, to become, according to one historian, the "largest independent American settlement of persons of African origin until Haitian sovereignty was recognized in 1804."[1] At the peak of its development, it probably contained upwards of twenty thousand people, and it certainly proved powerful enough to survive, between 1630 and 1695, at least twenty significant assaults from Dutch, Portuguese, or mobilized irregular forces.

Initially, the quilombo relied on raiding the plantation districts for supplies and indigenous Indian settlements for women. Increasingly, however, the inhabitants took to growing their own food and developing a more complex economy, with skilled craftsmen and mechanics. The society was essentially African in structure, and economic organization was based on the family unit. Slaves who voluntarily joined the quilombo were received as free and equal members; slaves seized in raids on plantations remained slaves, but even these were freed as soon as they volunteered to take part in plantation raids.

Religion seems to have been a form of Catholicism, unconnected with the Church and infused with African beliefs and rites. Political power was exercised by a small number of chiefs, including a supreme chief, called the *ganga-zumba,* and a war chief, called the *zumbí.* All this, but especially perhaps the evidence of a flourishing economy, may well have concentrated the minds of nearby planters on the advantages of peaceful relations. An understanding was reached which guaranteed the planters that their own estates would be safe from raids in return for their agreement to trade with Palmares. Yet, as long as the quilombo survived, it was an inducement for slaves far and wide to abscond from their masters and find a refuge in it. A more destructive way of dealing with Palmares was bound to be chosen. Indeed, the very extent and prosperity of Palmares invited attack, as planters and merchants looked to appropriate the territory.

In 1678, the Palmarinos were attacked by a formidable force and sustained such heavy losses in the protracted fighting which followed that the ganga-zumba sought to negotiate a peace. The Portuguese offered to recognize the freedom of the Palmarinos, confirm their right to much of the territory they held, and give the ganga-zumba the rank of a royal field commander. In return, they required the Palmarinos to surrender some territory, help in crushing slave or Indian revolts, and deliver up all future fugitive slaves who came to them.

The ganga-zumba agreed. There were many Palmarinos who did not. They may well have doubted the good faith of the Portuguese authorities or at least the ability of the authorities to control the whetted appetite of the planters. They may have considered the surrender of any territory a strategic blunder, given the distinct possibility of future invasions. Not least, they may simply have rejected a commitment to help in the crushing of slave revolts and to hand over such fugitives as they or those before them had been. They rose under the leadership of the zumbí, executed the ganga-zumba, and repudiated the agreement. In 1695, a very large force that included indigenous Indians invaded Palmares and overcame all resistance. The zumbí, described in a Portuguese document as a "Negro of singular courage, great spirit and constancy," was wounded, captured, and executed along with others. The survivors were duly enslaved. The territory of Palmares was shared out among the victors—except, of course, for the Indians.[2]

In Bahia, references to the existence of quilombos date back to the 1580s, and expeditions to eliminate them in 1663, 1692, 1697, and 1723 are evidence of how ultimately unsuccessful such efforts proved to be. The quilombos involved were not, however, substantial independent polities on the model of Palmares. They were relatively small communities in marshlands and woods close enough to plantations and towns to allow surprise raids on these for supplies, including arms, and for slave recruits. Their impact was nonetheless considerable, not only in undermining the security of white settlement but in providing slaves with a prospect of some refuge for runaways. The colonial society responded by conscripting the adult males of whole Indian villages to serve in expeditions against them.

In the mountains and forests near a number of the larger towns in Minas Gerais, an estimated total of some twenty thousand runaway slaves established their various quilombos, from which they emerged to kidnap or kill white settlers. They came to represent such a threat that a considerable campaign, financed from Lisbon, was undertaken to eliminate them. One expedition in 1757 returned with 3,900 pairs of ears as proof of how many had been summarily punished. The runaways generally defended their freedom with the more ferocity for knowing that defeat was almost certain to mean death. In Mato Grosso, where numerous quilombos existed as well, the one at Carlota succumbed to a Portuguese military assault in 1770 only after the most frenzied resistance.

By the nineteenth century, quilombos were able to survive only in sufficiently remote regions. The most renowned of these was that of Para, established in 1820 along the Amazon at Trombetas, northwest of Manaus, by runaways whose leader, a slave of mixed black and Indian parentage, was Atanasio. Within three years it had a population of some two thousand and was not only trading with whites and Indians in the vicinity but exporting cacao and other commercial crops to the Dutch colony in Guiana. Destroyed in 1823, it was reestablished by Atanasio and survived into the 1830s. Even then, its history was not at an end. A number of its members went further up the Amazon and established Cidade Maravilha, a quilombo which as late as the 1850s was sending children for baptism to the priests of the nearest white communities.

In Maranhão during the late 1830s, the larger quilombo of Campo Grande, under the leadership of another remarkable slave named Cosme Bento das Chagas, even provided an army of some three thousand to fight alongside the region's whites in the Liberal republican revolution. The forces of Brazil's imperial government, having crushed the revolution, then proceeded to crush as well the quilombo, whose leaders were subsequently executed.[3]

Revolt was the more immediate militant alternative to flight for the prospect of surviving in freedom to fight another day. Yet uniting in revolt was not always easy among slaves from different regions of Africa. In 1719 and again in 1724, slaves in Vila Ria de Ouro Prêto, the capital of Minas Gerais, planned an uprising but were, on both occasions, defeated by the divisions within their ranks. Some slaves were of Angolan origin, others from the Guinea Coast; and conflict developed over which of the groups would exercise ultimate control once they had overthrown white rule.

Of all the regions, Bahia came to be the most turbulent. The first slave revolt there took place as early as 1607, and among the more notable that followed was one at Ilhéus in 1789, when at least fifty slaves on the Santana plantation killed their overseer and then fled under the leadership of a mulatto, Gregório Luís. For two years the plantation was virtually idle, while successive expeditions were sent to hunt down the fugitives. These eventually offered to return as slaves but only on agreed terms, in a form of collective bargaining for better conditions. They demanded, for instance, reductions in work quotas; land of their own on which to grow food for themselves, with the right to market any surplus; the right to choose their own overseers; and the right "to play, relax and sing any time we wish without your hindrance nor will permission be needed." The plantation owner pretended to accept the terms and even promised to free Gregório Luís. When the slaves returned, they were all arrested. Luís himself was imprisoned, and other leaders, actual or supposed, were sold to new ownership in Maranhão.[4]

It was during the first half of the nineteenth century that slave revolts in Bahia threatened or broke out so often and sometimes on such a scale as to imperil the social order. The peculiarly harsh labor demands of sugar production, the predominant economic activity of the region, had long been accompanied by a high rate of mortality among the slaves involved. The rate now increased along with the demands on labor during the sugar boom that followed the revolution in Saint Domingue and the related loss of supplies to the world market. This led to an increasing volume of mainly male slave imports, to replenish and augment the labor force. The gender disproportion rose with each new shipload of arrivals. A survey of six sugar plantations in 1816 revealed an average ratio of 275 male slaves to every 100 female ones, and even the capital of Salvador had an average ratio of no better than 193 male slaves to 100 female ones in the periods 1805–6 and 1810–11.[5]

Nor was this the only source of heightened slave disaffection. While large numbers of Angolan-Congolese continued to be brought from the Portuguese areas of colonial control and influence, a rapidly rising proportion was being drawn from the Bight of Benin, where supplies were more readily available, from the turbulence spreading across much of West Africa. These slaves, mainly Hausa, Yoruba (or Nagôs, as they were called), and Ewe (Gêges), included many with experience of conflict and resistance.

Of special significance here was the Muslim affiliation not only of the Hausa but of many Yoruba converts. There was a strong Muslim tradition of political militancy, along with a commitment to religious study. While many slave owners in Bahia were illiterate, many of the newly arrived slaves were themselves literate and invested with corresponding influence over other slaves.

The first manifestation of a heightened militancy came with a conspiracy in the city of Salvador. In 1807, a number of Hausa slaves elected a "governor" who appointed as his "secretary" a free mulatto, with the charge of touring the adjacent sugar-rich Recôncavo area and recruiting plantation slaves for a general uprising on May 29. This date was chosen because it fell during the Corpus Christi festivities, when the authorities might be so preoccupied as to be taken unawares. The conspiracy was betrayed, however.

The Governor of Bahia ordered troops to guard the city's fountains against the reported plan to poison the drinking water. Arrests led to the discovery of weapon stores. The leaders were then put on trial for having violated the rights of their owners and having disrupted "the public tranquillity on which the conservation of states depends." A slave and a freedman—presumably the "governor" and his "secretary"—were sentenced to death, and eleven others were flogged.

In 1808, during the Christmas festivities, a few hundred slaves in the south of the Recôncavo revolted, set fire to cane fields, and then marched on the town of Nazare. In the battle with government forces that followed, the rebels suffered heavy losses and fled. A few days later, on January 4, 1809, some four hundred Hausa, Yoruba, and Ewe slaves, roused by reports of the rising, ran away to join it, burning and killing on the way. A detachment of government troops attacked them, killing some and capturing ninety-five. Others made their escape, and weeks afterward, São Cristóvão, in the subcaptaincy of Sergipe de El-Rey to the north, was reported to contain a number of the rebels.

On February 18, 1810, slaves revolted at the fishing and whaling stations north of Salvador, killed whites, and burned buildings. Then they set out for the town of Itapoam, setting fire to plantations along the way. A combined force of cavalry and infantry intercepted them, killed more than fifty and took captive many others. At the ensuing trial, four were sentenced to be shot, while others were given four to five hundred lashes each, followed by penal exile. The peace that ensued proved to be only a pause.

In March 1814, the militia were mobilized to deal with a slave revolt in the Iguape district. In December 1815, a planned slave uprising in the town of Alagoas was frustrated by discovery. Then, in 1816, a major rebellion broke out when slaves on seven plantations in the vicinity of Santo Amaro and São Francisco rose on their return to their quarters from Sunday festivities. They burned part of one plantation and attacked another before a force of local settlers and loyal slaves sent them retreating into the woods. From there they raided the town of Santo Amaro, killed some of the inhabitants, and produced such a panic among the rest that many fled. While the Governor hesitated, fearing that any public announcement in response might provoke a flight of citizens from Salvador or an uprising of slaves there, a leading planter, Colonel Barreto, took the military initiative and received for his success the title Savior of the Recôncavo. Hundreds of captured rebels were executed, flogged, or deported to penal colonies in Africa.

In the alarm produced by the succession of revolts and particularly the latest, slave owners came close to rebelling themselves. They demanded a ban on the *batuques*, or black dances often connected with traditional religious ceremonies, which they believed to be occasions for conspiracy. The more than forty thousand blacks in the Recôncavo were, they insisted, barbarous, capable of understanding only force, and encouraged to rebel by the leniency of the authorities. The slave owners required the right to deport any suspect rebels and hang any who were involved in rebellion. Governor Arcos, more rational, more humane, and accordingly derided by the planters, resisted their demands. He argued that the batuques provided a release from the "sad state" of captivity and, besides, promoted divisions among the slaves between Muslims and adherents of traditional African beliefs. He regarded the slave owners as unnecessarily fearful and repressive. He did, however, take precautionary and repressive measures himself. He instituted a system of patrols in various districts of the Recôncavo and sanctioned in Sergipe de El-Rey curfews and passes for slaves, along with the arbitrary arrest of any freedman or slave suspected of criminal conduct.

It may be that this accounted for the temporary decrease in slave resistance that followed, but there was another factor as well. Whites themselves were divided and fighting over whether to break away from Portuguese rule—an issue resolved only in September 1822, when the Portuguese king departed for Portugal, and his son, Pedro, was crowned emperor of an independent Brazil. In the past, to be sure, slaves had exploited the existence of white divisions. This conflict, however, militarized white society as never before, and it appeared that slave resistance would be met with more than usual rapidity and rigor.

Nonetheless, already in 1822, Bahia experienced three slave disturbances, the last of which led to the execution of fifty slaves. Then, in the second half of the decade, slave revolts became more frequent and formidable. In August 1826, there was one in Cachoeira. In December of that year, at Cabula on the outskirts of Salvador, government troops fought a pitched battle with Yoruba from a nearby quilombo, and the questioning of captives revealed that this had been designed to draw troops from the city, where a general uprising of slaves was planned. In March 1827, the slaves on three plantations near Cachoeira revolted. In September, apparently roused by rumors of revolt in the Recôncavo, slaves on ten plantations in Sergipe de El-Rey revolted, to kill not only their owners but any slaves who refused to join the uprising. A large military force was necessary to crush the spreading rebellion. In March 1828, Yoruba slaves in Pirajá attacked a number of plantations and were making for the fisheries at Itapoam when government troops arrived. On April 17, again, and yet again on April 22, slaves in the Cachoeira area revolted. In December there were slave revolts on various plantations in the vicinity of Santo Amaro.

The 1830s began tumultuously. Slave stevedores in Salvador seized arms from shops and marched to the slave markets, where they incited a hundred or so newly arrived slaves to join them. Together the rebels attacked a police station but were driven off and then confronted by troops from the city garrison. Some were killed by the soldiers, others were lynched by civilians, and forty-one were captured. A curfew was imposed, and various restrictions on the movement of slaves were introduced. The period of repression that followed did nothing, however, to prevent the most serious slave challenge, which came in January 1835.

Muslim slaves in Salvador planned a rebellion to coincide with a Catholic festival centered on a church at the northern edge of the city, where public and security attention was likely to be concentrated. The plan was betrayed, but the very move by police to arrest some of the conspirators simply ignited the insurrection. For two days, fighting raged across the city, as rebels attacked police and military quarters. Then, some three hundred rebels set off to rouse the plantation slaves in the Recôncavo and were intercepted by a large detachment of troops. Some fifty rebels were killed. Of the captured survivors, five were executed and dozens publicly flogged. The relatively few free blacks involved were deported.[6]

This was the last serious slave revolt in Bahia, but it was by no means the end of slave resistance in Brazil. In February 1848, for instance, a slave conspiracy to revolt at Pelotas in Rio Grande do Sul was discovered, and in July 1848 several such were discovered in the province of Rio de Janeiro. All these conspiracies and revolts, with their threatened or actual cost in lives and property, failed to achieve their prime objective, but they did, in their own way, contribute to Brazil's withdrawal from the slave trade.

Paradoxically, it was often the most fervent of white racists who confronted the trade on the basis that it was Africanizing a country they wanted to be white and was, as each new slave conspiracy or revolt demonstrated, "heaping barrels of gunpowder into the Brazilian mine."[7] Evaristo da Veiga, a leading opponent of the trade, protested on March 10, 1834, in the influential paper *Aurora Fluminense*, which he edited: "Our country is inundated without measure by a rude and stupid race, the number of whom already existing ought to alarm us."[8]

That this inundation of slaves, with their disturbing desire to be free, did not succeed in bringing about the abolition of slavery itself much sooner was largely due to a policy that effectively set one component of the black population against another. Free blacks were used to hunt down fugitive slaves or suppress slave revolts, while distinctions of trust and treatment promoted division among the slaves themselves between the *crioulos* or Brazilian-born and those brought from Africa.

Most effectual in this regard was the relatively liberal provision of opportunities for slaves to buy their freedom, along with the widespread practice among slave owners of freeing their own mulatto children, which led to a large free black, and much larger free mulatto, population. In Mato Grosso, for instance, 28 percent of blacks and 79 percent of mulattoes were free in 1803; in Minas Gerais, 27 percent of blacks and 87 percent of mulattoes in 1830.[9] Color prejudice continued to constitute barriers against advancement for the free, even those of lighter complexion and straighter hair. Yet the distinctions between crioulo and African, mulatto and black, free and slave, had their own formidable impact.

In 1798, stirred by reports of the revolutionary developments in France, a conspiracy that came to be known as the Tailors' Revolt revealed itself in Salvador. Posters appearing in the city called notably not for an end to slavery, but for independence, free trade, higher pay to soldiers, and an end to racial discrimination. Most of the conspirators were mulattoes, mainly skilled workers, including a number of tailors; there were five whites from the educated elite; three free blacks, only one of them African-born; and twelve slaves, all artisans or domestic servants, and almost all of them crioulos. It was a rare mixture, but one far from inclusive in its aims. One of the leaders, Lucas Dantas, repeatedly made it clear that the purpose was the dismantling of barriers between white and mulatto rather than between mulatto and black. "My friend," wrote another, Cipriano José Barata de Almeida, "caution with the African rabble."[10]

THREE

Chains of
Emancipation

The increasing pressure for an end to slavery within the British Empire involved a variety of factors. The humanitarian constituency, with an influential, largely Evangelical component, pursued the moral logic of Britain's formal withdrawal from the slave trade in 1807. A British working-class movement of mounting militancy assimilated abolitionism to its objectives. British commercial and industrial interests, devoted to the profitable virtues of free trade, opposed the costly preferential treatment accorded colonial sugar, whose production was sustained by slavery. Their political power was significantly augmented by the electoral changes that came with the Reform Act of 1832. Jamaica's Emancipation Rebellion of 1831–32 came as a timely reminder that the slaves were impatient for their freedom. In 1833, Parliament passed the Emancipation Act, which abolished slavery in all of Britain's colonies.

The legislation freed immediately only children under the age of six. Other emancipated slaves were to continue serving their former owners: field workers for an apprenticeship period of six years; the remainder, for one of four. They were to work without pay for three-quarters of the working week, though they might, by saving the wages received in the quarter left over, buy their release. The effect of these transitional terms varied from colony to colony, according to the way they were applied or misapplied, in the local economic and political context.

Barbados emerged with 501 apprentices per square mile, much the highest density in the British Caribbean. The abundance of labor in relation to land, moreover, reached beyond demographic statistics. The land was so contained by sugar estates or other freehold ownership that the prospect of finding an available piece for cultivation was as remote to the apprentice who contemplated absconding as the prospect of finding a hiding place had previously been to the slave. Nor was there room for any realistic hope that a British government which had freed the slaves would now exercise itself to protect and promote the interests of the apprentices in preparation for their release. While ultimately subject to the Colonial Office, the island's narrowly representative Assembly had long been generally left to its own lawmaking devices. The planters dominated the Assembly and ensured that it interfered with their interests only to advance them.

Confident in their power to do much as they pleased, they moved other workers to the fields so as to extend their apprenticeship from four to six years. They inflicted punishments for offenses that they would previously have ignored as trivial, to make it clear that the end of slavery involved no relaxation of authority or discipline. They rejected all responsibility for the children under six who had been freed. Given the meagerness of the food rations now provided to laboring parents, this led to a rise in the infant mortality rate, which had been falling during the last years of slavery.

When the British government ended the apprenticeship system in 1838, two years early, the planters were ready with laws to continue their control of labor by other means. The Masters and Servants Act passed by the Assembly in 1838 was so oppressive in its provisions that it was vetoed by the Colonial Office. The modified Act of 1840, which was allowed, still established a system of tenant labor that scarcely differed in its effects from serfdom. Employed on monthly contracts, laborers were supplied with housing and a plot of land which they lost on their departure or dismissal and for which they were meanwhile charged a rent equivalent to one-sixth of their wages. They became, in brief, free labor with the right to find alternative employment only at the cost of surrendering the land, food rations, and housing they had for themselves and their families.

It was a system that would in its essentials survive for almost a century. It helped to ensure that the laboring wage in Barbados was and remained the lowest in the British Caribbean. In the period 1846–50, for instance, the pay was on average 6 pence a day, compared to 15 in Jamaica, 20 in British Guiana, and 24 in Trinidad.[1] Such discrepancies, along with the readiness of other colonies to admit reliable laborers, could not be kept from Barbadians, some of whom were employed on the Caribbean shipping routes. Despite such measures to impede emigration as banning the activity of foreign recruitment agents on the island and requiring the equivalent of an exit visa, granted only to those who could prove that they were leaving no needy dependents behind, at least 16,000 had departed for work in other colonies by 1870.

Many of these, however, were not traditional emigrants, disposed to make new lives for themselves in new homelands, but essentially migrant workers. Some returned at Christmas and crop time, when the demand for labor in Barbados was at its peak. Others stayed away until they had saved enough to return home with some protection from the pressures of having to accept employment there on any terms. Besides, the vast majority of Barbadians were unable or unwilling to leave. The census of 1871 would record a black population of roughly 110,000, or an increase of a third since 1838. The planters continued to enjoy the benefit of an abundant labor supply.

The beneficiaries became no more generous in their social attitudes. An education commission had reported in 1838 the ardor of former slaves "to secure for their children the blessings of education."[2] The ardor of their former owners was more directed at preserving education for themselves. Only in response to mounting pressure from the Governor did the Assembly vote, in 1846, money for educating the "poor," and then no more than £750 in all to cover a period of three years. The Governor's recommendation for secular schooling was successfully resisted. Planters and Anglican clergy agreed that black children needed above all to be taught the values of hard work and the fear of God. It would take forty years from the end of apprenticeship for an Education Act to provide the basis for compulsory secular elementary schooling. Meanwhile, the very denials of such education sharpened a hunger for it which blacks used every means at their disposal to satisfy.

The planters had repeatedly warned that slaves would lose more than they would gain by being freed. They were clearly determined to demonstrate how right they had been. Not only did they generally abandon all responsibility for the welfare of infants, the elderly, and the infirm on their estates; they rejected the costs of transferring the responsibility to the government and used their domination of the vestries—the parish assemblies—to withhold poor relief from all but those whose labor records were deemed satisfactory.

This, together with indifference to issues of public health, promoted the spread of insanitary slum conditions in plantation-based villages and in Bridgetown itself, whose open sewers and polluted water supply contributed to its reputation as the most squalid capital in the West Indies. The planters and other powerful whites came to recognize, however, that disease was not sensitive to their racial prerogatives. A cholera epidemic in 1854 killed so many people of every complexion that a new Public Health Act two years later recognized at last the need for preventive medicine.

The nature of planter concerns was all too evident in the distribution of government expenditure. In the period 1838–50, for instance, a mere 10 percent was devoted to education, health, and poor relief combined, while more than half went on measures to secure the social order. A whole series of laws so abridged the freedom of blacks as to mock the very meaning of their emancipation. Police were empowered to arrest and imprison them on mere suspicion of vagrancy, and provisions against riotous assembly were so extensive that these were used to prohibit or disband black social or ceremonial gatherings virtually at will.

For all the formidable difficulties in the way, a number of former slaves did escape from dependence on plantation labor. There were those with marketable skills who saved enough from their earnings to buy freehold property. Others used their temporary holdings of land to raise foodstuffs or sugarcane for sale and accordingly acquired enough capital to establish themselves as traders. The more successful joined those, mainly of mixed race, who had been free for much longer and who had inherited or accumulated sufficient resources to constitute a colored middle class. This had its stronghold in Bridgetown, where enough in that class qualified for the franchise to become a decisive factor in elections there.

One free-born colored of means, Samuel Jackman Prescod, chose to promote the interests of the laboring blacks. Editor of *The Liberal*, a radical newspaper, and elected to the Assembly in 1843 for one of the two Bridgetown seats, he led intermittent attacks on the Masters and Servants Act. He opposed the measures against black emigration, to the point of defiantly becoming an agent for British Guiana's labor recruitment campaign. He agitated unremittingly against the infringement of black civil rights and for an extension of the franchise. When he died in 1871, there was more to show for his efforts in the mounting militancy among laboring blacks than in any changes to the law.

At last, encouraged by divisions within the white community over constitutional issues, black discontent erupted. On April 17, 1876, blacks took to attacking the police with whatever they could use as weapons, from their agricultural implements to stones. They destroyed plantation property. They seized food from storehouses and ships. By the night of April 20, disorder was so widespread that the Governor sent troops to help the police. Even so, it was not until the morning of April 26 that order was fully restored. Hundreds of blacks and eight policemen had been injured; eight people, all of them blacks, had been killed. Many whites had grown so alarmed by the extent of the revolt that they had taken refuge on ships anchored at a reassuring distance offshore. Such evidence of the dangers in rising black discontent increased Colonial Office impatience with white inflexibility.

Conrad Reeves, an eminent colored lawyer, was largely instrumental in the achievement of a constitutional compromise between Colonial Office demands for reform and local white reluctance to grant concessions. This effectively reduced the powers of the planter-dominated Assembly. He was rewarded by being made Chief Justice in 1882, and his influence was partly responsible for a Franchise Act two years later that lowered the property qualification for the vote. The result was scarcely remarkable. In 1849 there had been 1,322 voters. By 1900, there would still be less than 2,000, and with very few blacks among them.

Meanwhile, the planters had their own economic troubles. In the last two decades of the century, Caribbean sugar prices plummeted as Europe turned increasingly to domestic beet production for its supplies. In Barbados, where the major estates were owned by local planters rather than by absentee investors and where local merchant enterprise was exceptionally well established, the merchants came to the rescue of the planters, in mergers of their interests which were often fortified by marriages between members of the leading planter and merchant families. The sugar industry was made more efficient by the measures of modernization which the merchants promoted, and white dominion was tightened by the alliance. Excluded from the benefits were the black laborers, whose wages were slashed in the determination to reduce costs.

An opportunity to escape from plantation labor and poverty came in 1905, when the Panama Canal Agency, backed by pressure from the United States, was permitted to open a labor recruitment office in Bridgetown. By 1914, some twenty thousand black Barbadians had departed for work on the construction of the Canal. If those left behind believed that they would now be able to extract higher wages because the demand for labor was outstripping the supply, they were soon disillusioned. The sugar estates found more than enough black women in need to meet the demand. It proved to be the migrants themselves who had a significant impact on the economic contours of the black population.

In the period 1906–20, some £560,000 in postal remittances reached Barbados from the Canal Zone. Many returning migrants used their savings to buy land, to open shops, or to acquire a craft or education. By 1929, there were over 17,700 small-scale proprietors, more than double the 8,500 there had been in 1897.[3] As the ground rose for some, however, it sank further for others. Planters and merchants exploited the increase in available money to increase the price of provisions. The result was a resurgence of militancy among the poor, manifested in the so-called "potato raids," which involved the seizure of plantation food supplies.

"Panama money" fed a rapid growth in the Friendly Societies, which functioned more as savings than as insurance institutions. Much of their activity was concerned with collecting weekly subscriptions from their members for lump-sum repayments to meet the costs of Christmas. Alongside this, there developed the "landship" movement of voluntary neighborhood associations, which took their organizational vocabulary, along with their ceremonial drill and uniforms, from the British navy, and which collected the weekly dues of members or "crews" as insurance premiums against unemployment, illness, death, and the expense of a suitable funeral. Such served to cultivate in Barbadian society not only its distinctive preoccupation with thrift and discipline but that special adherence to Britain which took pride in the description of the island as Little England.

It appears to have been the very extent of white domination that promoted adherence rather than resistance to the imperial power. A BBC program, "Blacks in Britain," in 1991 included an interview with a black Barbadian who had come to Britain on a labor contract in the 1950s. "They say," he explained, in reminiscing about his decision to emigrate, "Barbados is Little England. And I think that is so, because the majority of everything that was run of any note in Barbados when I was a boy was run by white folks, so that you get the feel that England, where these people come from, was your mother, your father, the lot."[4]

The Colonial Office was not indifferent to the advantages that might be derived from this attachment. Police and teachers are the essential servants of empire: the first, to guard its security, and the second, its ideology. The people of Barbados increasingly provided both police and teachers for service in other British Caribbean colonies.[5]

This attachment to England did not, however, preclude manifestations of discontent. The census of 1891 had reported that the vast majority of black Barbadians were avowed Anglicans. In that very year, Baptist missionaries from the United States had brought their vigorous Revivalism to the island. They found ready converts among blacks who regarded the established Anglican Church as no more than the local white social ascendancy at prayer. By the end of the 1920s, the advance of Revivalist sects was evident in the many little wooden churches built by the black poor and with preachers chosen from among themselves.

In the 1920s, there emerged as well the first attempts at modern political organization to press for social reform. Clennell Wickham, whose experiences abroad as a black soldier in the First World War had imbued him with a hatred of racism and a passion for the socialist cause, used his editorship of the weekly *Barbados Herald* to assail the local white ascendancy of planter and merchant. Charles Duncan O'Neale, a black physician who had developed a similar outlook during his years of study and practice in Britain, and who was further influenced during a stay in Trinidad by Captain Cipriani's civil-rights movement there, preoccupied himself in Barbados with mobilizing the laboring poor. These two initiated a campaign of social arousal in 1924, first by publicly petitioning the Governor for an end to the use of child labor on the sugar estates and then by establishing the earliest Barbadian political party.

The Democratic League was attacked in the white-owned press as racist and bolshevik, but it attracted enough support from voters of the black and colored middle class to win a seat in the Assembly. This was followed in 1926 by the establishment of the Workingmen's Association, largely modeled on the labor movements of Trinidad and British Guiana. This was too much for the Governor, who ordered police surveillance of all opposition meetings. The organizers responded by interspersing the political discussion at their meetings with the singing of "God Save the King" and with prayers. Frustrated by such impediments to reprisal and infuriated by a dockworkers' strike in 1927, the upholders of the social order turned, as their counterparts elsewhere in the British Caribbean would increasingly do, to the law of libel. Ruinous damages and costs were awarded in 1930 against Wickham for having libeled a Bridgetown merchant in the *Barbados Herald*.

Counsel for the merchant in the case was Grantley Adams, who represented that liberal component of the black and colored middle class which had been initially drawn to the Democratic League but had then become alarmed at its radical drift. As the League lost support with the effective silencing of Wickham and its own failure to bring about change, Adams took possession of its less radical demands. From the seat in the Assembly that he won in 1934, he began campaigning for compulsory elementary schooling—still merely an official aspiration—together with the right of workers to combine in trade unions and the abolition of child labor.

Charles Duncan O'Neale died in 1936, and the radical movement was now without both its leaders. Then, in March 1937, Clement Payne, a young black born in Trinidad to Barbadian parents, arrived in Barbados to attract within weeks a considerable following, especially among the workers of Bridgetown, by his eloquence and militancy. Impatient to deport him but needing a legal pretext to do so, the authorities charged him with having falsely declared on entry that he had been born in Barbados. Thousands of his supporters gathered outside the courthouse during his trial; and though he was convicted on July 22, they were appeased by the lodging of an appeal. On July 26, the Court of Appeal quashed the conviction, on the grounds that Payne had spent much of his infancy in Barbados and might well not have known that he had been born elsewhere. Supporters were preparing to greet him on his release when they learned that he had already been deported. Rioting broke out in Bridgetown. This was quelled by armed police, but crowds returned, more enraged, on the following morning to target buildings in the commercial center. As reports of events in the capital spread across the island, so did the disturbances, with hungry laborers raiding plantation food stocks. Before control was restored, fourteen blacks had been killed, forty-seven had been injured, and more than five hundred had been arrested.

The official commission of inquiry issued a report unexpectedly critical of conditions in Barbados.

We have been impressed by the high dividends earned by many trading concerns in the island and the comfortable salaries and bonuses paid to the higher grades of employees in business and agriculture. If the whole community were prosperous and enjoyed a comfortable standard of living, high dividends might be defensible, but when these are only possible on the basis of low wages the time has clearly come for a consideration of the fundamental conditions and organisation of industry . . . A fundamental change in the division of earnings between the employer and his employees is essential if hatred and bitterness are to be removed from the minds of the majority of employees.[6]

Grantley Adams had represented Payne before the Court of Appeal. This enhanced his popular standing, while Payne's deportation left popular militancy leaderless again. Two months after the disturbances, Adams visited Britain and much impressed the Colonial Secretary. From then onward, he could count on an accommodating Colonial Office and local Governor. Recognizing the need for a political movement to reflect his views, he promoted the establishment in October 1938 of the Barbados Labor Party, soon to be renamed the Barbados Progressive League. While this grew rapidly, its leadership, much to his indignation, revealed a mind of its own. Herbert Seale in particular demonstrated a disturbing radicalism by instigating a general strike which attracted wide support from among workers in the sugar industry, at the docks, and on the buses.

Adams was one of those Caribbean leaders moderate in all but the exercise of his personal authority. He reacted by forcing first the departure of Seale himself from the movement's executive and then the resignation of the unmanageable executive itself. His influence with the Colonial Office and the Governor yielded its first results in the two laws of 1939 and 1940 which, with certain limitations, allowed the functioning of trade unions. Yet such measures did no more than point to the possibilities of serious social change. Once again a radical leader emerged in the Progressive League, and once again he was driven out by Adams. This time, though, the victim struck back with surprising force. Wynter Crawford, standing as an Independent, won a seat in the Assembly and went on to establish the West Indian National Congress Party, whose name was popularly truncated to its last two words.

Both Adams and Crawford were now publicly urging the introduction of full adult suffrage, though Adams, more mindful of the opposition from the Colonial Office to such a leap, was less vociferous. In 1943, the suffrage was extended to women and the income hurdle lowered, to produce an electorate five times its previous size. In the ensuing general election of that year, Crawford's Congress Party emerged with one seat more than the Progressive League and the same number as taken by the Electors' Association of the planter and merchant interest with its black and colored middle-class allies. Yet Adams continued to enjoy the backing of the Colonial Office, and the more openly so when labor discontent surfaced in increasing strikes and the firing of cane fields.

In 1946, further constitutional reforms introduced an embryonic form of self-government. The party leader able to command a majority in the House of Assembly would now be responsible for recommending the members of the Executive Committee, each of whom would preside over a sector of government business. During the campaign for the elections that followed later that year, the Governor made no secret of his view that a Congress Party success might lead to difficulties, while the Progressive League, returning to its original name of the Barbados Labor Party, praised him as personally committed to the island's development.

The prospect of a measured advance in step with the beat of the British government was apparently appealing to those who had the vote, and the Barbados Labor Party emerged as the largest party. As its leader, Adams was in a position to exploit the new possibilities of power and patronage. He first formed a coalition with the Congress Party to achieve control of the Assembly and then persuaded some of its members to join his own party. His prestige was much augmented by his appointment as a British delegate to the United Nations for a debate on decolonization in which, to the rage of radicals across the Caribbean, he defended British policies.

In April 1950, property or income requirements for the franchise were finally swept away, to provide an electorate of almost 100,000. In the elections of 1951, the Barbados Labor Party took 60 percent of the popular vote. Full adult suffrage had only enhanced the authority of Adams. It made him all the more impatient with any stirrings of independent judgment among his associates. In March 1954, Errol Barrow, lawyer and economist, more radical than his leader and with some regard for his own abilities, found the subservience required of him intolerable and left to establish the Democratic Labor Party, which Crawford and others joined from the graveside of the Congress Party. In the elections of 1956, the new party took four seats, with 20 percent of the popular vote, and the Barbados Labor Party romped home again, with a popular vote reduced to a little less than half, but a comfortable majority of seats.

Increasingly now the politics of Barbados, as of other Caribbean islands, came to be influenced by involvement in the West Indies Federation, initiated in 1956 as the price set by Britain for the grant of independence. Of the five Federal Assembly seats allocated to Barbados and contested in the elections of March 1958, the Barbados Labor Party took four. Adams, translated to Premier of Barbados with further constitutional advance there, became as well Prime Minister of the Federation, to spend much of his time at the Federal capital in Trinidad. In his absence, the Barbados Labor Party seemed to lose its bearings, while Errol Barrow and the Democratic Labor Party found theirs with attacks on the high unemployment rate on the island, the inadequate provision of social security, and the pursuit of economic policies set by white priorities.

The Federation was seeking to unite societies that had a colonial experience in common but had also been divided from one another by their competing sugar economies. As no less an authority than Eric Williams, historian of slavery and the Caribbean but also Chief Minister and then Premier of Trinidad during the period of Federation, would later write:

To the formidable contributions that sugar has made to contemporary Caribbean psychology must be added this one . . . that it engendered and nurtured an intercolonial rivalry, an isolationist outlook, a provincialism that is almost a disease, which are among the most striking characteristics, as they are among the most difficult to eradicate, of the twentieth-century West Indian mentality.[7]

Set on this fault line, the structure was at risk from every dispute that involved a major component. There were differences over the relative representation accorded particular constituents: Jamaica, much the most populous, wanted the share of total population to be the basis, while Trinidad, being richer, insisted that the extent of the contributions made to Federal revenues should be taken into account as well. There were differences over the degree of centralization to be determined. There were differences between moderates and radicals. Adams himself became a significant factor, since he was Prime Minister of the Federation, a leading moderate in the political demarcations of the British Caribbean, and an advocate of centralized control, not least through the power of taxation on income and profits. His statement in mid-1958 on the need for such power raised particular disquiet in Jamaica and was, in the judgment of an eminent Trinidadian political scientist, "the most damaging blow that had ever been delivered to the fledgling union."[8]

On September 19, 1961, the Jamaican electorate voted in a referendum by 54 percent to 46 percent against continued adherence to the Federation. Trinidad, not indifferent to the calculation that it would have 55 percent of the population but contribute 75 percent of the revenue in the Eastern Caribbean Federation which remained, withdrew from this, and at the beginning of June 1962 the Federation was legally dissolved. The long political career of Grantley Adams was over. Already, in the Barbadian elections of December 1961, the Democratic Labor Party had taken a majority of seats.

The government of Errol Barrow lost no time in securing substantial changes. It amended the labor laws to permit peaceful picketing and to require, albeit only in certain circumstances, severance pay and compensation for industrial injury. While dismissing the option of nationalization, it nonetheless set out to reduce the dominance of sugar in the economy. It encouraged the development of tourism, which had been loyal but languid since the twenties. The proliferation of hotels led directly to a large demand for labor and promoted as well a growth in agriculture, commerce, and industry. Tax holidays and duty-free raw material imports were among the incentives provided to attract foreign investment in local manufacturing. The rapid fall in the unemployment rate was accompanied by an expansion of the middle class. All this augmented government revenues, to pay for advances in the provision of social security and the extension of free schooling from the primary to the secondary level.

In 1966, the British government granted the island its independence, and the electorate granted Barrow's Democratic Labor Party a further five-year term, in new elections. The Barbados National Party, the last in the line of merchant- and planter-led parties, was buried with little distress. If any prospect of their exercising open political power had long since disappeared, the still substantially white combinations which dominated the economy must have recognized that their interest had been far better served by their supposed opponents than it was ever likely to have been by themselves. They could now safely leave elections to the two rival black parties, while their various agricultural, commercial, industrial, shipping, insurance, and banking companies minded their own profitable business.

Should they have needed any reassurance, it came during the surge of militant black consciousness which developed in the United States and swept across much of the Caribbean region. The Public Order Act of 1970 provided measures to suppress the Black Power movement in Barbados, and local radicals suspected of infection came under tight police surveillance. In the elections of 1971, Barrow and his Democratic Labor Party were elected yet again, with widespread support from within the white community.

It was the Barbados Labor Party that won the general election in 1975 and would win the next, in 1981, as well. But there was little to choose between the two parties, which had increasingly taken to dressing from the same wardrobe. The return of the Democratic Labor Party to power in 1986 was mainly due to the death of Tom Adams, son of Sir Grantley, which had plunged the Barbados Labor Party into a leadership struggle.

The economy had ridden the waves of world oil-price rises and falls, fluctuating but still relatively high rates of inflation and interest, with markedly more success than had most economies in the region. In 1973 the Caribbean Community and Common Market (CARICOM) had come into being, to afford the comparatively well developed sector of financial services in Barbados particular opportunities. As the nineties arrived, it remained for black Barbadians to consider not only how far they had traveled from the past but what they might have lost along the way.

17 | THE PALM TREES OF JAMAICA

~~~~~~

From the given number of men able to bear arms in any country, it is usual with political writers to estimate the inhabitants at large; but their rule of calculation does not apply to Jamaica, where the bulk of the people consists of men without families. Europeans who come to the island have seldom an idea of settling here for life. Their aim is generally to acquire fortunes to enable them to sit down comfortably in their native country; and, in the meanwhile, they consider a family as an incumbrance. Marriage, therefore, being held in but little estimation, the white women and children do not bear the same proportion to the males, as in European climates. For these, and other causes, I have found it difficult to ascertain with precision the number of the white inhabitants. [1]

So wrote Bryan Edwards in the last decade of the eighteenth century. He did, however, provide his rough estimates, which were 30,000 whites; 10,000 free blacks and "people of colour"; 1,400 Maroons; and 250,000 black slaves. The first official census in 1844 recorded a population of 15,776 whites, 68,549 colored, and 293,128 blacks. [2] The relatively small and diminishing number of whites in Jamaica would have made the containment of the colored in racial subjugation there a rash undertaking. The white planter ascendancy endeavored to do so, nonetheless, by imposing various limitations on colored social mobility. The British government was more humane or less shortsighted. In 1830, all free persons on the island were granted equality of basic rights. This promoted a process which the colored themselves had already initiated, by climbing over or going around the obstacles placed in their way.

Avoiding agricultural labor as associated with slavery, the colored settled in the towns and took advantage of the educational opportunities peculiarly available there. They pursued careers in trade, journalism, and the law.

They entered politics by way of electoral districts where enough of them had acquired the material means to meet the corresponding franchise requirements for electing members to the House of Assembly.

Their rising numbers reflected the relaxed sexual attitudes of a white population with a considerable disparity between the numbers of its women and the appetites of its men. Yet color discrimination remained a distinct social force, adapted by whites to their own purposes. In the towns, for instance, white men organized dances to which young colored women were invited while colored men were rigorously excluded. Although there was much colored resentment at such assertions of superiority by whites, the lighter in complexion among the colored were not beyond asserting their own superiority to the darker, as in their choice of marriage partners and social associates. Light or dark, however, most of the colored were at least united in an attitude of collective superiority to the black slave population.

There were even some who associated themselves with whites in resisting the approach of emancipation. These were, however, relatively few. The vast majority had no economic stake in slavery. Distrustful of local white intentions toward them, most clung the more closely to the protective British connection and were correspondingly loyal to whatever policies the British government chose to pursue. Not least, arguably in making for a harbor from their uncertainties, they were the most committedly Christian of the three racial groups and tended to reflect the views of the missionaries on the institution of slavery.

The compulsory period of apprenticeship for which the Emancipation Act of 1833 provided was imposed in outline, with details left for local legislation to determine, under the ultimate authority of the Colonial Office. In Jamaica, the planter-dominated Assembly had long been allowed a substantial measure of autonomy, which it exploited to concede the letter and confront the spirit of the Emancipation Act.

Field workers were to serve 40½ hours a week until the beginning of August 1840. On most of the sugar estates, they were now made to work five days of eight hours each instead of four and a half nine-hour ones. This involved a tiny cut in total weekly work time but also a loss of the free Friday afternoons which field workers had customarily devoted to their own "provision grounds" in preparation for the Saturday markets. Required allowances of food and clothing continued, but the so-called customary indulgences, such as the weekly distribution of salt fish, were often stopped. Flogging had been forbidden on the estates and replaced by a period in the parish workhouse as a form of labor discipline. Some planters simply ignored the law, but most resigned correction to the workhouses willingly enough, since these were run by the vestries, or parish councils, under planter dominance and soon included flogging in their disciplinary regimes. Special Magistrates, sent from Britain to ensure compliance with the law, came under such social pressure from the planters and met with such resistance in the pursuit of their responsibilities that most of them either took to collaborating with the planter class or resigned in despair to go home.

With the end of the apprenticeship system, planters turned to ways of controlling free labor. They initially set their sights on the long-term work contract, but the terms they offered were so oppressive that missionaries advised field workers to reject them, and blacks were themselves opposed to any arrangements that suggested slavery under another name. The fallback device was to serve field workers with notices of eviction from their shacks and provision grounds, while permitting them to remain as tenants at a high rent in cash or its equivalent in labor. Many blacks reacted by abandoning the estates and finding land on which to settle and farm.

In Jamaica, unlike Barbados, the plantation economy had, even at its height, taken less of the island than it left. Now, in its decline, there were estates largely or wholly uncultivated where blacks might settle and survive for years without being noticed. Beyond were unowned or at least unclaimed expanses. Getting legal title to these was a different matter, requiring much time and expense. Yet good land could be bought at between £5 and £10 an acre, sometimes for less, and could yield crops to a value of £30 an acre in a year. Many proprietors willing to sell their land were, however, disposed to do so only in large blocks. Missionaries solved the problem by buying such blocks, establishing "free villages," and reselling the land to black settlers in plots of an affordable size. The Baptists, who were the most active in this enterprise, settled more than three thousand blacks at free villages in the west of the island alone in the short period 1835–41. For those blacks unable to afford any purchase and unwilling to settle only as squatters, good mountain land might be rented for merely £1 an acre a year.

Some black settlers were soon engaged in more than subsistence production. They grew fruit, root vegetables, and sugar for the local market; ginger, pimento, and coffee for the export one. By 1865, there were an estimated fifty thousand small properties. Yet many did not produce sufficient for need, and their settlers were driven to make up the difference through seasonal labor on the sugar estates. The labor shortage there was accordingly seldom acute. It was, instead, chronic.

The planters had only themselves to blame, though they generally blamed everyone else. Their policies might have been deliberately designed to create the very difficulties of which they complained. Under slavery, for instance, they had provided their labor force with medical attention so as to preserve their own capital. Now that they used free labor, most planters dispensed with the cost of doctors, whose number on the island dwindled till, by the early 1860s, it was a quarter of what it had been at the time of emancipation. If the Assembly, under planter dominance, voted more funds for public health than for education, this was because it could scarcely have voted less.

Sanitary conditions were so bad and medical treatment so scarce that a cholera epidemic in 1850–51 took the lives of between twenty-five and thirty thousand in the laboring class, and further lives were lost in a smallpox epidemic that struck shortly afterward. A medical survey in the wake of the epidemics found that the laboring class in general suffered from malnutrition and hookworm.[3] The planters were given to lament the laziness of their laborers. It was more remarkable that they were able to find and employ so many who were able to work at all.

In British Guiana and Trinidad, where freed slaves were also denying the planters an adequate and stable labor force, large numbers of indentured laborers came to be imported, the vast majority of them from India. In Jamaica, this alternative was pursued with markedly less enthusiasm. The missionaries, concerned for the welfare of the blacks, objected that such immigration would be used to depress wages. The colored, the merchants, the small-scale planters who had enough indigenous labor because they were prepared to pay for it, agreed to support a program of immigration only if the estates that would chiefly benefit from it met the bulk of the cost.

When East Indians arrived after the Immigration Act of 1845, the leading planters grew uneasy at the costs in transport, housing, subsistence, medical care, and pay that they were required to meet. In British Guiana and Trinidad, where the daily wage for indigenous labor in 1848 was 20½ and 25 pence respectively, indentured labor proved relatively cheap. In Jamaica, where the corresponding daily wage was 15 pence, indentured labor, when all costs were taken into account, proved relatively expensive. The scheme was in due course abandoned, and the Jamaican population remained an overwhelmingly black one.

The very movement of so many freed slaves away from the estates to settlements in the countryside contributed to the retention of African cultural influences in folklore, music, and religion. Moreover, even in the towns, there was little available schooling for blacks to promote the spread of European culture among them. The part played by the missionaries in the pressure for emancipation, in protecting the rights of black laborers, and in promoting their settlement in free villages, was rewarded with mounting adherence to their denominations. The Baptists, the most vigorously engaged in the social advancement of blacks, found their membership correspondingly triple, from ten thousand in 1831 to thirty-four thousand in 1845. Yet alongside all this there developed black adaptations of Christianity and cults based on myalism, the practice of traditional magic, and the term was soon loosely applied to all cults based on traditional African religion.

The Native Baptist movement, introduced by a black freedman from Virginia who arrived at Kingston in 1783, came to spread so successfully that by 1846 its adherents in the sugar parish of Vere outnumbered the membership of all other Christian congregations there combined, and by

1860 constituted half the churchgoing population in Kingston. With the effective relaxation of the controls which the slave system had provided, myalism flourished as though fed by the very laws that were now passed against its practice.

Black resentment at such prohibitions erupted from time to time in active resistance. In 1841, for instance, a move by the secular authorities to suppress the emotive Christmas festivities of blacks in Kingston led to a riot in which two men were killed and which developed beyond the capacity of the police to contain it, so that the military were summoned to restore order. In September 1842, the press reported:

> Myalism has lately extended its ramifications over a section of country, including sixteen estates . . . This extraordinary superstition has evinced itself in fearful paroxysms, bordering on insanity, accompanied with acts of violence on those who attempt to restrain it. Lately a set of these people took possession of a meeting-house on Palmyra estate, and commenced their orgies by singing, or yelling, and dancing in the most frantic excitement. The overseer and bookkeeper, attempting to restrain them, were assaulted with stones and other missiles, with a degree of ferocity perfectly demoniacal.[4]

The missionaries discovered how useless and even counterproductive their own denunciations proved to be. They condemned drumming, dancing, breaking the Sabbath, and excessive festivities at Christmas: the very activities in which blacks engaged not only for entertainment but for artistic and spiritual expression. They condemned concubinage, when few blacks regarded the formality of marriage as important, and many young black women rejected marriage altogether as a form of bondage.

In 1860–61 an evangelical revival, which had started in the United States and spread to Britain, swept Jamaica. The missionaries were initially elated but then became aware that this was not so much a Christian development as one that mixed Christianity with myalism in a new Afro-Christian cult. Their congregations began to dwindle as blacks became disillusioned with a white missionary commitment that seemed to operate only on its own terms. It was part of a process in which racial attitudes were hardening.

The whites were becoming more apprehensive and correspondingly more aggressive as their numbers continued to diminish. By 1861, there were fewer than fourteen thousand of them, and many of these lived on remote plantations. Alarmed by the largely religious excitement among the blacks, whose drumming at revivalist meetings seemed so menacing, they increasingly carried guns about with them. Yet any alliance with the colored community was not to be contemplated. The gender disproportion among whites was rapidly narrowing,[5] and many more of the women were in Jamaica to stay. As elsewhere in the empire, such women tended to be the guardians of racial standards, not least against the sexual threat from women of color. There can have been few colored who did not resent the discrimination to which they were subjected, even as most of them kept their own disdainful distance from blacks.

Some of them, more rational, recognized the demographic realities of Jamaica. One such was Robert Osborn, a colored member of the Assembly. In November 1865, he warned his fellow legislators that they might make what laws they liked but that these would prove to be of no avail, since the very community in whose interests they were made was wasting away. The government of the colonies, he predicted, would eventually fall into the hands of blacks.

Financial requirements of various kinds had continued to maintain an electorate to which few blacks belonged and an Assembly from whose membership blacks were wholly excluded, while restricting the colored to a manageable minority. The Assembly of 1865, representative of less than fifteen hundred voters, had thirty-seven white members and ten colored ones. Even more than the character of the legislature and its laws, however, it was the conduct of the courts, by local—predominantly planter—magistrates, that stirred black resentment. Such was the distrust they commanded, indeed, that blacks simply stopped approaching them for redress. In the parish of St. Thomas-in-the-East, for instance, the defendant in no less than 250 of the 256 cases recorded for 1864 was a black settler or laborer, and in only two was a planter the defendant.

It was in the same parish, on October 11, 1865, that some four hundred black settlers from the hills around collected in the square before the courthouse at Morant Bay to protest against a particular decision of the magistrates. The protesters were met by the militia; some threw stones, and the militia responded with gunfire. The infuriated crowd drove the militia into the courthouse, set the building on fire, and attacked the fleeing occupants. Fifteen of these, including the magistrates, were killed, and thirty-one were injured. In the following few days, bands of black settlers roamed the parish, looting several plantation houses and killing three white men against whom there were special grievances.

The disorder was serious, but never spread beyond the parish. It might have been quelled with little force or none at all, if the authorities had announced some commitment to address the causes. What followed instead, by the will of Governor Eyre, was a military campaign of the fiercest repression. One thousand black homes were burned, six hundred people were flogged, and 439 were killed. Among these last was George Gordon, a colored landowner of wealth and evangelical fervor, who had been elected from the parish to the Assembly. He was taken to Morant Bay for military trial, convicted with dispatch, and hanged in front of the burned courthouse. In Britain, a raging controversy would result over whether Governor Eyre should be prosecuted or praised for his conduct. In Jamaica itself, the planter class at last recognized the extent of its isolation and vulnerability. The Assembly, which had for so long asserted its relative independence, resigned itself to control by the Crown.

The decline in the power of the sugar interest accelerated with the investment of United States capital in banana plantations, mainly by a Boston businessman whose United Fruit Company would extend its operations and influence across much of Central America as well as the Caribbean. Bananas, not needing the considerable labor engagement and capital for machinery that sugar demanded, provided an export crop which peasants could raise on their small holdings. In 1850, peasants had produced only 10 percent of the island's exports. Fifty years later, with their numbers much increased, peasants were producing 40 percent. By then, however, population growth and the spread of the banana estates had reached the limit of available land, and labor was necessarily moving into other sectors. Between 1861 and 1921, the share of the labor force engaged in agriculture fell from almost 70 percent to just over 55 percent, while that in commerce, including market trading, more than doubled, to almost 6 percent, and that in domestic service rose from 10 percent to almost 18 percent or slightly more than all those engaged in industry and construction.[6]

Some surplus labor had, from the 1850s onward, migrated to employment abroad, in the construction of the Panama Canal and Costa Rican railroads, for instance, or on plantations in Cuba and the United States. During the Great Depression of the 1930s, such opportunities all but vanished, while in Jamaica the demand for labor declined, and wage rates were cut. Economic and racial grievances merged. "Colored persons and negroes are found in all professions and occupations," a former Governor of Jamaica wrote at the time, "but leadership and initiative still remain predominantly with the white and lighter-skinned citizens. Most of the elementary school teachers of both sexes are black."[7] So, too, were the vast majorities of peasants, laborers, servants, and the unemployed.

One Jamaican black addressed the plight of blacks not only on the island but throughout the Diaspora, with lasting impact. Marcus Garvey, born in 1887, left in 1916 for the United States, where his Universal Negro Improvement Association attracted a mass following with the message that blacks should take pride in themselves and unite in confronting their oppression. Imprisoned after a dubious conviction for fraud, he was deported in 1927 to Jamaica and there founded the People's Political Party. This included among its objectives "a law to impeach and imprison Judges who, with disregard for British justice and Constitutional rights, dealt unfairly."[8] This reflected the grievance which had sparked the Morant Bay uprising of 1865 and whose expression now led to his imprisonment. In 1935 he left to spend his last years in Britain, with black disaffection in Jamaica made more militant by his example and teachings. There was a further influence. In 1930 the publicity attendant on the crowning of Haile Selassie I as Emperor of Ethiopia spread the knowledge of an African kingdom not yet conquered by European power and of a royal dynasty that claimed descent from Solomon and the Queen of Sheba. A Rastafarian movement emerged on the island, combining religious fervor, based on Haile Selassie's supposed divinity, with an assertive black consciousness.

Labor unrest which started on a single sugar estate in the spring of 1938 spread to become a general strike. Confronted by a massive defiance which paralyzed plantations, transport, docks, factories, offices, and which was proof against the usual methods of dissuasion, the authorities decided that an orderly retreat was advisable. Wage increases were conceded, along with agreement to a minimum wage for sugar workers. Trade unions were recognized as a new force that needed to be accommodated. The perception that political reform was becoming unavoidable initiated a process that would culminate in 1962 with the grant of independence to Jamaica.

The virtual revolt of the blacks, manifested in their massive engagement to the general strike, was directed less at colonial rule—rallies often concluded with the singing of "God Save the King"—than at a domestic social ascendancy of colored as well as white. Yet the organized labor movement had been brought into being in 1936 by Alexander Bustamante, a colored moneylender whose charismatic personality and oratorical skill were matched by such self-regard that the movement was named the Bustamante Industrial Trade Union (BITU). His cousin, Norman Manley, a colored lawyer who mediated the settlement of the general strike, was also the leading figure in the founding of the People's National Party (PNP) in September 1938.

It would be tidy to identify in this a hijacking of emergent black militancy by a sector of the colored elite to promote its political dominance. The motivations and processes were, however, more complex and less engineered. Manley, like his closest colleagues in the PNP, was influenced in particular by the British Labor Party, whose policies shaped the PNP program for extensive public ownership, industrial development, mass education, and social welfare. Bustamante was more conservative in outlook, but with a more personal dynamic that was shrewd in its pragmatism.

It was the PNP that initially took and held the political foreground with a campaign for full adult suffrage and the grant of responsible government. Then, in 1942, Bustamante founded the Jamaica Labor Party (JLP). This inaugurated the two-party system which still survives and whose contending partisanship has come to be described as tribal politics. The launch of a PNP-aligned trade union movement brought the partisanship into organized labor as well. In 1944, the first elections based on full adult suffrage were held for a legislature of enhanced authority. The PNP now campaigned for independence as well as social reform. The JLP countered with the slogan

"Self-government means slavery." Bustamante spelled it out more precisely. Self-government, he proclaimed, would "replace a white man with a brown man on the backs of black men."[9] The sweeping victory gained by the JLP might well have owed much to the appeal of this message, as well as to Bustamante's known personal following in the provincial towns and countryside.

The two parties drew closer in policies, as the PNP retreated from its relative radicalism, and the JLP became more radical to blunt its rival's edge. The JLP was returned at the next election, to be succeeded in 1955 by the PNP, which would also win reelection, in what came to be a pattern of alternating two-term governments. Both parties engaged in patronage on a wide scale, which reinforced partisanship with a material stake in the outcome of the polls. This expanded to involve large companies, whose financial assistance to one or other party would be rewarded after electoral success with contracts and appointments to regulatory boards. After 1970, when the PNP spread through the countryside, each party had a base among the peasantry as well as organized labor. Each could count on an estimated 20 percent of the electorate as active in its interest. Each continued to have a middle-class colored face; Norman Manley gave way to his son, Michael, and Edward Seaga succeeded Bustamante. It would take until 1992, thirty years after the island's independence, for the PNP at last to have a black leader and Jamaica a black prime minister.

The one break in the pattern of similar policies came in the years 1972–80, with the relatively radical government of Michael Manley. It emerged from a mood of mounting impatience with the pace of social change, reinforced by the recurrent disillusionment with the corruption of the party in power. One factor was clearly the spread of the Black Power movement through the Diaspora. This had found a ready adherence in Jamaica but not in its JLP government, whose decision to ban from the island Walter Rodney, the Guyanese black revolutionary and renowned historian, had detonated two days of demonstrations by students and rioting by street youth in October 1968. By the time of the election campaign in 1972, the PNP had come to invest its program of reform with elements of populist and Black Power rhetoric.

Such was the reach of disaffection that the PNP triumph at the polls apparently owed less to the revolt of the deprived than to the shift in allegiance among the relatively privileged. The party was estimated by the island's leading pollster to have taken 75 percent of the white-collar worker vote and 60 percent of the vote in the high-income category of business and the professions, while winning a bare majority of the vote among the poorest. What might have happened had the international economic climate now been congenial is the merest speculation. In the event, the new PNP government was overtaken by the storm of soaring oil prices and inflationary pressures.

To discourage the import of more costly manufactures and promote exports, the government devalued the currency. In 1974, domestic inflation topped 27 percent. The government was undeterred from its commitment to raise the living standards of the poor. It subsidized food staples, encouraged or imposed increases in real wages, and inaugurated a job creation program. To increase government revenues and deliver on its promise to reduce the foreign profits from exploiting the island's resources, in 1974 it confronted the multinationals in control of the bauxite industry and wrested a levy from them which multiplied the state's related income sevenfold. The multinationals began switching production to countries with more docile regimes.

Economic assertiveness was accompanied by the adoption of a less subservient foreign policy. This involved closer relations with Cuba, the island's nearest neighbor. Such a policy did not commend itself to the United States or to those in Jamaica who were led to believe that the new relationship with Cuba portended an adoption of Cuba's domestic regime. In addition to large legal outflows of foreign capital, not altogether unrelated to the displeasure of the United States, large illegal ones of local capital made their way abroad. Despite tightening controls, the net foreign exchange reserves of Jamaica rapidly dwindled until, by 1976, the figures were being entered in red ink.

The introduction of a national minimum wage and of equal pay for equal work was chiefly responsible for a rise in real wages, of almost 14 percent for men and over 35 percent for women, in the period 1974–76. Sugar cooperatives were established. A "land lease" program released state and privately owned idle land for peasant farming. Such measures bore little resemblance to the claims of incipient revolution with which opposition politicians and press greeted them. The alarm spread nonetheless by such claims was evident in the mounting emigration of skilled workers, managers, and those in the professions.

Political violence, promoted by partisan passions, had long been a feature of Jamaican society. Now, however, it entered a new dimension, with the design of the opposition to destabilize the government. In early January 1976, the JLP organized a series of demonstrations, which soon became riots, to coincide with a conference of the International Monetary Fund (IMF) in Jamaica. Armed attacks on PNP supporters and meeting places followed until, in June, the government declared a state of emergency. Soon afterward, a bomb factory was discovered at Montego Bay with enough dynamite to wreck the island's power stations and water supply system.

The government won the elections of December 1976 with a popular vote of almost 57 percent, but this encompassed shifts in allegiances which pointed to an increasing division along class lines. Estimates based on public opinion polls suggested that support for the PNP from those in the high-income groups had plummeted while that among the poorest workers, such as domestics, the unemployed, or others at the economic edges, had soared.

Support was stronger, too, among farm laborers, but had fallen among farmers apparently influenced by JLP charges that the PNP was Communist.

In the euphoria of its reelection, the government seemed to be signaling a quickened pace of reform, with an Emergency Production Plan directed at agricultural development and eventual economic self-sufficiency. In fact, the plight of the economy, most acute in the shortage of foreign exchange, had already provoked an approach to the IMF for rescue credits. The second of two Standby Agreements on loans was especially exacting. The government was required to acquiesce in hefty devaluations of the currency; new taxes on consumer goods; a large reduction in state expenditure, which led to a virtual doubling of bus fares, for instance; an end to many price controls so as to encourage the growth of the private sector; and a limit of 15 percent a year on wage rises for a two-year period, despite an inflation rate bound to be much higher than that.

The living standards of the working population fell sharply, as real wages declined by more than a quarter for men and well over a third for women in 1976–77.[10] Labor unrest spread throughout the economy. Huge price hikes in basic commodities led to mounting public protests. Inflation, the shortage of imported goods, and price controls on some commodities combined to promote hoarding and the practice among shopkeepers and higglers, or market traders, of selling scarce items only to customers who also bought other items at exceptionally high prices. Voluntary Price Inspectors, charged with monitoring trade practices, often discovered and proceeded to "liberate" hoarded stocks, but this merely lapped at the cliff of the problem. The government was warned that women, however supportive of reform, would not simply watch their children starve, and that fear of hunger was turning many in the working class against the PNP.

The year 1980 started ominously with a two-day strike by power supervisors that switched off most of the island's electricity. New negotiations with the IMF were accompanied by such protests from among the radical ranks of the PNP that the government decided to do without further credits, but only by effectively pursuing IMF prescriptions. Social and medical services continued to deteriorate. Half the buses ceased running for lack of maintenance and spare parts. Power cuts became common. Shortages of food and household goods persisted. Real wages fell still further and the gross national product contracted by over 5 percent. Violence, which had claimed 383 lives in 1978 and 336 in 1979, reached new records in 1980, when 933 people were killed, 236 of them by members of the security forces. Meanwhile, in the elections of October 30, the JLP had swept into government with almost 60 percent of the votes. Even among the poorest voters, only 40 percent had supported the PNP, though the party had kept the loyalty of almost half the manual workers.[11]

Various surveys and statistics for these years of PNP government revealed, for all the measures of reform, the daunting scale of Jamaican deprivation. In 1980, out of a labor force of a little more than one million, 269,000 were unemployed, while large numbers of others were underemployed. In 1977, some 84 percent of small-scale farmers had earnings below the estimated defining line of poverty for peasants; while 50 percent of the working class as a whole and 94 percent of those defined as lower working class had earnings below the poverty line for the population outside the farming sector. A survey a few years earlier had found that the poorest 70 percent of Jamaicans had a daily intake of protein below the recommended allowance and that almost half of all pregnant or lactating women were anemic.[12]

One autopsy on the body of that PNP government, conducted by the Jamaican political scientist Dr. Trevor Monroe, identified as a major cause of death the failure of the party to take account of the racial factor in the development of its policies. "The 1972 electoral campaign," he wrote, "saw Michael Manley making dramatic use of all the symbols, personalities and groups associated with the struggle against racism—both white and brown . . . It is not easy to explain therefore, except on grounds of electoral opportunism, how the paraphernalia of the black struggle could so dominate an election campaign and yet the race question be so absent from a fundamental programmatic document which began to be elaborated little more than three years after by some of the very same personalities."[13] Dr. Monroe, himself a Marxist, placed part of the blame on the "ideological deficiencies" of Marxist groups, and on influences which submerged the racial issue in that of class.

The belief or pretense that because there was a correlation between race and class, the two were the same, and that to deal with the issue of the second was to deal with the issue of the first, did not so much mislead mass mobilization as miss mobilizing much of the mass altogether. The echoing slogans of working-class struggle had little impact on the peasantry, the unemployed, the higglers, the hustlers—the varied multitude of those who scraped some sort of survival from the land, the markets, the streets.

The PNP avoided the racial factor not because it avoided racism; the two are very far from the same. It avoided the racial factor because it avoided the issue of white and colored social ascendancy, which might have cut too close to the quick of the political leadership. In the process, it avoided, despite all its proclaimed commitment to "Power for the People," promoting any real popular participation in the making of decisions. Populism is a thin and dry layer of soil in which only weeds tend to thrive. The PNP government of rectitude and reform came to be seen as rank with its own patronage and corruption.

. Only a democracy that reaches deep below the surface can promote that change in popular attitudes without which no sustained social transformation is possible. Centuries of social and psychical distortion in Jamaica were not to be waved away by instituting a minimum wage or leasing idle land for peasant agriculture. The victims needed to begin taking control over their lives by processes which invested them with the confidence and purpose to do so. For all the benefits it sought to confer, the PNP government of 1972– 80 left the mass of Jamaicans much as it found them, the captives of their past.

The JLP government of 1980–89, under the prime ministership of Edward Seaga, provided a shift in foreign policy, including a diplomatic break with Cuba, that was as substantial as even the new Republican administration of Ronald Reagan in Washington could reasonably have wished. In economic policy, Seaga was content to follow the prescriptions for development favored by the IMF, and Jamaica duly received financial transfusions from the Fund, the World Bank, and the United States. Yet the promised success, except for the exultant groups who could take advantage of the new possibilities, proved elusive.

The trade deficit widened alarmingly as the government opened the sluice gates for the import of consumer goods to meet accumulated demand. This led to a massive devaluation with its corresponding inflationary pressures. By October 1982, the unemployment rate had reached almost 28 percent of the labor force, and underemployment, defined as employment for less than 33 hours a week, over 20 percent. Reports of mounting corruption targeted various government Ministers. A snap election, called at the end of 1983 on the 1980 electoral register, in breach of an interparty agreement for updating it, provoked the PNP to call a boycott, and the JLP was reelected by default. It did little to counter widespread disillusionment and political violence.[14]

By the election of another PNP government in 1989, Jamaica had heaped up a foreign debt of over US$4 billion, whose servicing consumed almost half of all foreign exchange earnings. In the period 1980–88, the gross national product, as valued in United States dollars, had fallen by an average of just over 2 percent a year, or a figure disreputably identical with that for stricken Haiti. Given the social priorities of the JLP government, this did not reflect the extent of the fall in living standards among the mass of Jamaicans.

The new PNP government, under the leadership first of Michael Manley and then, after Manley retired for reasons of ill health in 1992, P. J. Patterson, was now devoted to the virtues of the free market with all the ardor of the convert. Indeed, such was the extent of its devotion to deregulating the economy that the JLP attacked it as going too far and too fast. A sharply depreciating currency fueled inflation, while the government sought to deal with the budget deficit and the pressure on the exchange rate by cuts in health, education, and other social expenditure. Yet in part due to squabbling within the JLP over its leadership and in part to Patterson's emergence as the island's first-ever black prime minister, the PNP won reelection in April 1993 by a landslide that gave it 55 of the 60 seats. Its government faced a number of formidable problems, from a decaying infrastructure and persistent pressure on the exchange rate to a popular deprivation all the more dangerous for the expectations raised by the promises in the election campaign.[15]

The end of slavery had been followed by the constraints of colonial rule, and the end of colonial rule had been followed by a democracy of floating disillusionment.

"The British sprayed the island about fifty years ago. They got rid of the mosquito, but what nobody knew, and still nobody can actually prove, was that the mosquito was the natural enemy of a mysterious insect vector that attacks the tops of palm trees. So that now, all along the coast, there are those weird landscapes, a panorama of headless palm trees, the very swaying palms of paradise standing there bereft like lost telegraph poles."[16]

Blacks in British Guiana had a vigorous tradition of resistance to slavery. They were not disposed to welcome the emancipation of 1833 on its own terms. They bargained with plantation owners over the level of wages. They moved from one plantation to another in search of the best returns available for their labor. They turned their backs on the plantations altogether, for subsistence agriculture on abandoned land or, by uniting their resources, bought Crown tracts for collaborative ventures. The peasant village population rose steeply, from fewer than sixteen thousand in 1842 to more than forty thousand by the end of 1848, and this excluded the numbers who took to the creeks and rivers for the too often deceptive promise of productive settlements in the vast interior.

Looming labor shortages had early provoked the planters to look elsewhere, mainly to India, for supplies. In May 1838, the first group of East Indians, some four hundred, arrived. They were treated so badly that twenty of the survivors were reported a year or so later to be cutting through the bush eastward in the hope of reaching Bengal.[1] Meanwhile, in November 1838, the Governor-General of India, learning of conditions in Guiana, had banned further shipments. Various schemes to attract other immigrant labor, from within the West Indies, from Madeira, and from Africa, proved unsuccessful. West Indian planters were reluctant to suffer labor shortages for the sake of their counterparts in British Guiana and promoted measures against such recruitment. The Madeirans died in frustrating numbers. The means by which Africa had supplied so much reliable labor in the past were no longer acceptable. The British government, under pressure from the colonial lobby, reopened the route from India; up to 1918, British Guiana received some 341,000 immigrants, of whom India supplied some 236,000.[2] The laborers were indentured for a period of ten years, or five if they were able to find the $35 required toward the cost of their return passage.

The treatment of these workers on the sugar estates was in general no better than was to be expected from planters whose social dominance was indifferent to rebuke. Nor were blacks, after their initially expansive exercise of freedom, more fortunate. Those settled in the towns found few opportunities for employment. The power of the planter interest was, moreover, increasingly directed against the development of an independent peasantry. Successive ordinances raised the price of Crown land and the minimum size of tracts for sale, lowered the maximum number of those allowed to collaborate in purchases, and in 1856 not only ended such collaboration altogether but began the partitioning of established joint holdings.

The coastal strip, to which village agriculture had effectively been limited, was very fertile but in constant need of drainage from the encroaching sea. Without the capital to invest in the steam-driven pumps used on the large estates, the independent villagers grew careless and even suspicious of cooperative efforts at drainage and irrigation that might benefit some of them more than others. Neglect led to declining yields, and declining yields to a disillusionment or despair which led in turn to the abandonment of holdings.

In these conditions only disease, mainly cholera and malaria, thrived. In 1872, the Registrar General reported that the high rate of child mortality, especially among blacks, resulted from "insufficient and innutritious food, unwholesome lodging, insufficient clothing, bad water and want of timely medical aid."[3] It was common for whites in the colony to lament the widespread apathy among blacks. It was not apathy that they were soon lamenting.

Portuguese immigrants had early taken a grip on shopkeeping and tightened it by developing connections with importers and wholesalers to command a virtual monopoly. This enabled them not only to raise the prices of basic commodities as they pleased but even to sell one commodity on condition that another was bought as well. "It is a constant complaint among the poor," the *Colonist* reported, "that whenever they send to a Portuguese shop for cheese, they cannot get it without buying at the same time an equal amount of bread."[4]

In February 1856, a black preacher, John Sayers Orr, took to inveighing against the Catholic Portuguese. He was arrested on a charge of unlawful assembly, and on the evening of February 18 the so-called Angel Gabriel riots began. Every Portuguese-owned shop in Georgetown was burned to the ground, and the rioting then spread from the capital to involve most of the settled areas. Indentured immigrants joined with black villagers in a fury that demonstrated its economic cause by targeting property and only the property of the Portuguese. When the last of the fires had died, it was because there was no further material on which they could feed.

Meanwhile, the treatment of indentured East Indian labor on the estates was such as to leave in doubt only the time and extent of some protest reaction. In August 1869, rioting broke out on one estate, to be followed by demonstrations and strikes on many others. From the early 1870s, as their particular indentures ended, many East Indians simply left the estates. The census of 1881 found some 2,500 settled in towns and some 25,000 in villages, settlements, and farms. Of importance in loosening the Portuguese commercial grip, 540 were found to have become shopkeepers. Few were at first able to buy land in the coastal strip on the terms available. Most became squatters on abandoned estate land or rented plots from black villagers or moved into areas beyond the practical reach of regulations.

The movement away from the estates continued with the lapsing of indentures and accelerated markedly in the 1890s, when a slump in sugar prices excited the customary planter reaction of wage cuts. The number of East Indians living outside the estates soon doubled, to some fifty-eight thousand. Lower prices and less harsh conditions of purchase enabled many more than before to buy land with savings or loans. Some made a success of cattle breeding or the cultivation of rice.

Blacks were learning to exercise pressures of their own. They took to exploiting the need for a steady supply of cane in the grinding season by choosing that time to move in cane-cutting gangs from estate to estate in search of the highest rates or by going on strike when they noted the supply of cane to the mill running short. Some planters responded by offering three-month contracts with bonuses attached. They found few black takers. Labor contracts were associated with the compulsions of slavery.

There remained large numbers of blacks and East Indians for whom employment on the sugar estates was the sole source of income or provided a necessary supplement to small-scale farming. United militancy among these might well have wrested concessions from the planters. Instead, the two racial groups were divided by cultural—including religious—differences, and the planters promoted the division by racially segregating them from each other on the estates. In consequence, when workers from one group went on strike, those from the other continued working, which in turn reinforced the racial division.

Yet for all their success in securing a sufficiently tractable labor force, the local planters found themselves in increasing difficulties. The high recurrent costs of drainage and the capital expenditure required for technical advances to keep the sugar of the colony competitive in price exhausted their resources. With each slump in the sugar market, more of them were unable to meet their mortgage or other loan commitments and sold their estates to merchant houses, local and British, or to the absentee estate ownership of British trading companies. Already by 1870, a Commission of Enquiry recorded that only fourteen or fifteen of the 135 estates were wholly or partly in the hands of resident proprietors. The rest were in absentee ownership, or owned by local estate attorneys or merchants. The most successful of all owners were those who combined productive with mercantile operations; and from among these, the British company of Booker Brothers emerged predominant. By 1904, it would own directly or control through a combination of ownership and agencies 44 percent of all sugar estates. By the 1950s, only one independent sugar estate would survive; and of the nineteen giants in existence, Booker Brothers, McConnell & Co. would own fifteen.[5]

Meanwhile, constitutional change moved at a pace that might well have raised the question of why it was moving at all. It was only in 1891 that direct voting for the elected members in the Court of Policy was introduced, and the electorate of 1892 numbered little more than two thousand. The power of the sugar interest was most crudely demonstrated in the composition of the Executive Council, whose three Governor-appointed unofficial members were all local representatives of leading sugar companies. Only in 1896 did a new Governor take the step of appointing as an unofficial member a colored barrister to represent the interests of middle-class coloreds and blacks. And the authorities, perhaps attentive to the rebellious past of the colony, took no chances. British Guiana was the most heavily policed of Britain's Caribbean colonies, and its police force was organized along military lines.[6]

By 1900, East Indian peasants were increasingly taking to the cultivation of rice, which required much less capital investment than did sugar. The outbreak of the First World War gave a fillip to such production, as imported supplies dwindled fast. Yet rice agriculture was no economic match for sugar. The productivity gap between the two was so vast that by 1957, for instance, sugar workers would be producing a crop worth $58 million from 81,000 acres of cane, while rice cultivators were producing a crop worth $17 million from 137,000 acres of paddy. For a while around the turn of the century, El Dorado gleamed once more, from gold mining conducted mainly by small groups of black workers, but the discovered deposits were soon exhausted. Substantial mining of bauxite for the North American aluminum industry began in 1914 and came to be of increasing importance to the economy. From the outset it was the preserve of one North American company and was extended only by becoming the preserve of another as well.

The largely black and colored middle class grew slowly but with disproportionate consequences for the character of the electorate. By 1915, of the 4,300 who met the property or income requirements for the vote, more than 60 percent were wholly or partly of African descent, some 20 percent were British, some 11 percent Portuguese, and 6 percent East Indian. In 1928, under the influence of the sugar interests, the British government imposed a Crown Colony control with correspondingly augmented powers for the Governor. Britain's Caribbean subjects, however, became less easy to coerce during the economic depression and social militancy of the 1930s. In 1938–39 a Royal Commission visited the region. In response to its recommendations, British Guiana was provided with a more liberal constitution in 1943. That was also the year when a young East Indian Guianese returned from the United States.

Cheddi Jagan, whose father was a "driver," in command of cane-cutting gangs on a sugar estate, was lifted above the expectations of all but a very few local East Indians by the efforts of his parents. Sent to Queen's College in Georgetown, the leading secondary school, he left in 1936 for further education in the United States, where he worked his way first through Howard University in Washington, D.C., and then through the Northwestern University Dental School in Chicago.

By 1942, when he received his degree in dentistry, he had come to regard himself as something of a Marxist and was involved with Janet Rosenberg, whose own more determined opinions were closer to the line of the Communist Party. In the summer of 1943 they married, and Janet followed her husband to Georgetown, where she soon won over his parents to the strangeness of having a white daughter-in-law. Her training as a nurse was useful to him in the dental practice he established, but dentistry was not the preoccupation of either. Along with others, they formed the Political Affairs Committee in 1946, to prepare for the launch of a political party that, equipped with the theory of "scientific socialism," would unite black and East Indian workers in confronting colonial rule.

For the elections of 1947, the first since 1935 and with a much less restrictive franchise than had then applied, the Committee fielded three candidates. Of these, only Cheddi Jagan was successful, in a constituency where support from the large East Indian component of the electorate was augmented with a black vote mobilized by the black schoolteacher Sydney King. Using his platform in the legislature to assail the dominance of the sugar and bauxite companies in the colony, Jagan attracted a mounting popular following. In April 1948, discontent among the sugar workers surfaced in a widespread and protracted strike. In June, five workers were shot dead by police during a demonstration on the Enmore estate. The Jagans led a huge protest march the sixteen miles from the estate to Georgetown. The time was fast approaching for the launch of a political party, and the prevailing view in the Political Affairs Committee was that a suitable black should be found to hold a high position in it as confirmation of its interracial commitment.

Linden Forbes Sampson Burnham, whose father was headmaster of a Methodist primary school, had gone to Queen's College and won the sole government scholarship for university education in Britain, where he had received his law degree from the University of London in 1947. Much affected by the racism he encountered in Britain, as Jagan had been by his own experiences in the United States, he had become a political activist, serving as president of the West Indian Student Union in 1947 and indicating a loosely socialist affiliation.[7]

In 1949, Burnham returned to British Guiana and was invited to become chairman of the prospective People's Progressive Party (PPP), with Cheddi Jagan as leader, Janet as general secretary, and Sydney King as assistant secretary. In the following year the party was at last launched, to campaign for immediate social reforms, full adult suffrage, and independence as soon as possible. Attacks from an alarmed colonial establishment and censorship measures from the authorities only served to promote the popular appeal of the party, whose young activists spread its message through the urban slums and villages.

The British government opted for inaction until this became too evidently counterproductive, when it conceded adult suffrage and a new constitution for the colony. Elections by direct voting for all but a few of the twenty-seven seats in the Legislative Assembly were set for April 17, 1953. Its leadership expected the PPP to win eight seats at most. Instead, it won eighteen, with 51 percent of the popular vote. The PPP took all five predominantly black seats in Georgetown and all eight predominantly East Indian ones in the sugar belt. One of its black candidates was elected in a predominantly East Indian constituency; Janet Jagan, in another. It looked like the dawn of interracial popular government. It proved to be the dusk.

Even before the elections, Burnham had sought to challenge Jagan for the leadership but been frustrated by the support that Jagan enjoyed from influential blacks. The election victory produced differences between them over the distribution of offices. There was, however, no rift in policy. The party had made specific promises during the campaign. It proposed to keep them. Such consistency was unexpected.

As one writer subsequently put it, "there was at that time a sort of unwritten code of behaviour expected of colonial politicians; it was assumed that they would take a radical, nationalist, and usually left-wing line, be swept into power under new constitutions and then, realizing the responsibility of office, become moderates in a partnership with British officials and foreign business men . . . In British Guiana the leaders of the People's Progressive Party did not accept, perhaps did not even understand, these unwritten clauses in the Colonial Office-drafted contract."[8]

Even so, the disposition to deliver on promised progressive policies might in the end have had to be tolerated, if the Jagans had not come to be considered agents of the Soviet Union or so close to its ideological line as made no difference. The United States communicated its disquiet at developments in British Guiana to a British government disquieted already.

If the PPP was given to an often extravagant rhetoric, in reality there was little that it could constitutionally do by using its control of the Legislative Assembly. Regarded as one of its most provocative proposals, for instance, was that to make landlords responsible for providing proper drainage facilities on the holdings of their tenants. This was rushed through the Assembly and then defeated in the State Council. Moreover, behind the State Council there stood at readiness the reserve powers of the Governor. The fear which the party generated was related rather to the very ease with which its democratic mandate could be legally denied. For this was likely sooner or later to rouse such a popular rage as might make the colony well-nigh ungovernable, if not deliver it to the very revolution that the Jagans were believed to have designed.

The sugar workers were in a ferment of discontent. Since 1939, their bargaining agent had been the Man-Power Citizens Association. This had come to be widely viewed as a mere creature of the estate owners, who repeatedly refused to recognize the radical Guiana Industrial Workers Union (GIWU) founded in 1946. Strikes, with outbreaks of violence, spread across the estates in August and September 1953. On September 24, the PPP introduced a Labor Relations Bill to establish free collective bargaining procedures and provide in particular for the right of workers to change one bargaining agent for another by a vote of 65 percent in favor.

The Governor, Sir Alfred Savage, had arrived in early 1953 from four years in Barbados. Nothing in his experience there had prepared him for the situation in British Guiana. As hysteria mounted among opponents of the PPP, he advised the British government of the need to take urgent and decisive action. On October 6, the BBC reported that Communist activities in British Guiana had led the British government to dispatch military and naval units to the colony. Three days later, the constitution was suspended. The Governor assumed emergency powers, dismissed the six PPP ministers from office, and banned all political meetings. Police raided the home of the Jagans to carry off piles of papers.

Jagan and Burnham, still in uneasy alliance, prepared to leave for Britain and present their case to public opinion there. Trinidad, Barbados, Jamaica, and the United States refused them transit. British, French, and United States airlines refused to sell them tickets. If it was the values of freedom and democracy that Britain and its allies were determined to protect, this seemed a curious way of demonstrating it. In the end, by chartering at considerable cost a private plane so as to catch a Dutch airline flight to London, Jagan and Burnham arrived in time for the relevant debate in the House of Commons.

The British government's White Paper accused the PPP of having spread racial hatred; of having flooded the colony with Communist literature; of having conspired to set on fire business premises and the homes of prominent Europeans; and having done all this in the cause of establishing a totalitarian control of the state. During the Commons debate, the Colonial Secretary denied the existence of any pressure from the government of the United States to influence the British decision. The Labor Opposition deplored the conduct of the PPP leadership but questioned the need to suspend the constitution when the Governor's use of his reserve powers might have sufficed.

The crucial claim of a conspiracy to burn down parts of Georgetown seems to have been custom-made for the occasion, since it subsequently emerged that this had been added as a reason only several days after the decision had been taken to suspend the constitution. Embarrassingly, too, despite Labor demands, the British government failed to prosecute those supposedly responsible for the criminal acts cited in the White Paper. Finally, whatever else might have been held against the PPP, the spreading of racial hatred was hardly a charge that could survive serious examination. The party had brought together blacks and East Indians as never before in the colony's history. Indeed, it was this very achievement which British conduct, wittingly or not, increasingly imperiled.

Jagan and Burnham returned in February 1954 to a British Guiana where other PPP leaders had only just been released from detention. The emergency regulations, however, remained in force. The PPP was all but paralyzed by restrictions and bans. First Cheddi and then Janet Jagan were given prison sentences of six months for infringing the emergency regulations. An interim government, nominated by the Crown from among the politically reliable, provided the front for direct rule by the Governor.

A Royal Commission under the chairmanship of a Colonial Office mandarin had been appointed to investigate the whole troublesome affair and to no one's surprise endorsed the British government's conduct. In the process, while distinguishing between such so-called Communists as Jagan and such so-called moderate democratic socialists as Burnham, it asserted that the differences between Jagan and Burnham had been more personal and "racial" than political. Indeed, the use that the Commission made of the racial issue cast doubt on its judgment, if not its motives:

> Education is now eagerly sought by Indian parents for their children; many Indians have important shares in the economic and commercial life of the Colony; the rice trade is largely in their hands from production to marketing. Their very success in these spheres has begun to awaken the fears of the African section of the population, and it cannot be denied that since India received her independence in 1947 there has been a marked self-assertiveness among Indians in British Guiana. Guianese of African extraction were not afraid to tell us that many Indians in British Guiana looked forward to the day when British Guiana would not be a part of the British Commonwealth but of an East Indian Empire. The result has been a tendency for racial tension to increase . . . We do not altogether share the confidence . . . that a comprehensive loyalty to British Guiana can be stimulated among peoples of such diverse origins.[9]

Such official signals did not go unremarked by those with an interest in promoting racial divisions. By February 1955, conflict between Burnham and Jagan over the leadership of the PPP had led the authorities to allow only those meetings that served to advance it. The party soon split into two rival ones, each clinging to the name; but if Burnham's following was overwhelmingly black, influential black activists continued to support Jagan. It was by his own misjudgments that Jagan undermined this support. He blamed "deviation to the left" for the excesses of the PPP's period in office and, in a somersault of policy, came out against British Guiana's membership in the projected West Indies Federation. Sydney King and the poet Martin Carter, among other black activists, resented the apparent attempt to blame them for policies which had been Jagan's also and interpreted his new policy toward the Federation as a racial rejection of the overwhelming black majority this would have. They abandoned him.

Marking the start of a measured return to democracy, a new Governor was appointed in the autumn of 1955. For elections in August 1957, the 1947 design of fourteen constituencies was restored, and this, with full adult suffrage conceded, resulted in anomalies that were almost certainly premeditated. The predominantly East Indian constituency of Eastern Berbice, for instance, had more than three times the number of voters as there were in the predominantly black constituency of Georgetown North. The crucial contest was clearly going to be between the two PPPs, and there were those in both who proceeded to insinuate racial appeals into the campaign. The Jagan party emerged with nine of the fourteen seats. The Burnham one took three, all of them in Georgetown. This command of the capital would come to be increasingly important.

Burnham reacted by yielding to the Jagan party the PPP name and calling his own party the People's National Congress (PNC). The Governor accommodated himself to the election result and used his reserve powers to block uncongenial measures. By 1961, the Jagan government had achieved much. The village health centers, established under Janet's powers as Minister of Labor, Health, and Housing, had been widely welcomed. Drainage and irrigation schemes had expanded agriculture on the coastal plain. New government-funded housing had replaced the barracks on many sugar estates. Working conditions had been improved by extending the protection of the labor laws. With hefty compensation, the notoriously inefficient private electricity company had been nationalized. What had not been achieved was substantial support among blacks for a government viewed increasingly as an East Indian one.

Both the PPP and the PNC began demanding the grant of independence. Burnham, however, pressed for prerequisite elections on the basis of proportional representation. Britain rejected an electoral system to which its own two major parties were understandably opposed and resisted a grant of independence as premature, but conceded elections on a more democratic constituency system as the prelude to self-government in all but defense and foreign affairs. Jagan introduced into the 1961 election campaign a pledge to secularize all education. Burnham himself had, when Minister of Education in 1953, committed himself to precisely this course, but now responded by backing the religious denominations and black teachers in furiously attacking it. The PPP took twenty of the thirty-five seats with close to 43 percent of the popular vote; the PNC, eleven seats, with 41 percent. The United Force led by Peter d'Aguiar, the party of the Portuguese community and the conservative middle class, took the rest.

Burnham might convincingly claim that popular support for the PPP was substantially short of a majority, but Jagan had an overall majority of seats and duly became Premier. He proceeded to visit the United States in search of economic aid. Intensively questioned on the television program "Meet the Press" in October, he emerged as a rather muddled admirer of the Soviet system. A meeting with President Kennedy shortly afterward did little to repair the damage. Already confronting the Castro regime in Cuba, the Kennedy administration was disturbed by the prospect of a self-governing British Guiana under Jagan.

The PPP budget introduced at the end of January 1962 was directed at raising resources for economic development. It imposed new taxes and increases in old ones, along with a compulsory savings scheme and higher duties on inessential imports. The Georgetown press assailed it as both Marxist and hostile to the interests of labor. While Burnham excited his black following against it, and d'Aguiar mobilized the middle class for resistance, Guianese trade unions, in particular the strategically based and largely black civil service ones, joined the attack, with funds and advice from anti-Communist unions in the United States.

On February 15, Burnham and d'Aguiar defied a ban on demonstrations in the vicinity of the Assembly and led their followers there. Faced by what looked like a rebellion in the capital, Jagan appealed to the Governor for the use of troops. By the time that these arrived, during the afternoon of February 16, five people had been killed and fifty injured, while much of the central shopping area had been looted and burned. Jagan modified the budget proposals, conceding in particular the demands of the civil service unions. Burnham derided him for depending on British troops to sustain his government.

In late March 1963, Jagan resurrected the ill-fated Labor Relations Bill of ten years before. It was a misjudged attempt to seize the initiative and rally the ranks of organized labor behind him. The Trades Union Council opposed the Bill, and so did Burnham, despite the support he had given its predecessor. On April 5, rioting struck Georgetown again. The TUC called a general strike, and the Civil Service Association backed the call. With close to a million dollars in aid for the strikers arriving from the United States, the strike lasted eighty days. Virtually throughout the civil service, it was blacks who stopped working, and East Indians who continued. East Indian sugar workers were given no choice; they were locked out by the estate owners.

Shortages of food and oil became critical. At Jagan's request, the Governor declared a state of emergency, but this did little more than acknowledge the obvious. As the incidence of violence increased, Jagan requested the use of British troops to maintain order. He was rebuffed. By the end of the strike on July 8, after the government had announced that it would consult with employers and the TUC before proceeding with the Bill, nine people had been killed.

The British and United States governments agreed that Jagan and the PPP should be ousted from power. How this was to be done acceptably was less certain. Jagan himself would soon provide them with the means. On October 22, 1963, a Constitutional Conference on the future of British Guiana opened in London under the chairmanship of the Colonial Secretary. Unable to reach any compromise with Burnham and d'Aguiar for joint presentation, and in an act of faith inconsistent with his view and experience of British policy, Jagan suggested to his rivals that the Colonial Secretary be left to impose a solution. At the end of October, the Colonial Secretary announced new elections in 1964 on the basis of proportional representation, with the colony's electorate contained in a single constituency.

Returning home in dismay, Jagan sought to reassert his strength by mo-bilizing the sugar workers for a display of support. A labor dispute at a plantation in February 1964 spread rapidly to most of the estates. Blacks from Georgetown were recruited to take the place of East Indian strikers. By July some 150 people had been killed and some 800 had been injured in interracial violence. In October, a Labor government was elected in Britain. Jagan now hoped for a change in British policy. He should have known better.

In the crucial elections of December 7, strangely quiet after a fiercely fought campaign with intermittent acts of violence, the turnout of voters topped 95 percent. Apart from some middle-class blacks and East Indians who supported d'Aguiar's UF, the voting reflected the racial division between the two major communities. The PPP polled 46 percent, to take twenty-four of the fifty-three seats; the PNC, 40.5 percent, to take twenty-two; and the UF took the remainder.[10]

Jagan offered Burnham the Premiership in a grand coalition. Burnham would have none of this. He had the backing of the UF and formed a corresponding government on December 13. He proclaimed his commitment to promoting racial harmony and received a substantial sum in supposed development aid from the United States. Jagan decided to boycott the in-dependence talks in November 1965. It seemed a petulant gesture and proved to be a profitless one. It disposed of the outside chance that he might have wrested some concessions. Independence arrived on May 26, 1966.

As Minister of Finance, d'Aguiar piloted a businessman's budget through parliament. It was the high point of an influence that now ebbed. The PNC

packed the civil service and in particular the judiciary with its own appointments. Despite his previous pledges to enlarge the East Indian component
in the Guyana Defense Force and the police, Burnham was determined to
ensure a massive black predominance in both. A National Security Act
empowered the government to suspend habeas corpus and detain anyone
regarded as a threat to security. The coalition partners had agreed to the
holding of new elections by the end of 1968. It was widely believed that by
then the higher East Indian birth rate might lead to an overall majority of
PPP voters in the country. Burnham was apparently taking steps to deal with
such an eventuality, but in ways that posed a potential danger not only to
the PPP.

Reports of a rift between the two party leaders in the coalition were confirmed in September 1967, when d'Aguiar resigned from the Cabinet, though
without withdrawing UF support from the government. In the Assembly,
two members from the PPP and one from the UF saw the Burnhamite future
and abandoned their affiliations so as to greet it. Then, in October 1968,
with elections due soon, Burnham introduced legislation which permitted
the inclusion of votes cast by Guyanese living abroad and extended the use
of proxy voting. The opportunities accordingly provided for electoral rigging
were obvious. Belatedly, d'Aguiar withdrew his party from the coalition. But
another UF member had decided where the future led his loyalty. With the
Speaker already secured to his side, Burnham had his majority.

The Elections Commission, whose independence was constitutionally
guaranteed, had been suborned and marginalized. The PPP and UF together
applied to the courts for a stay of the elections, but Burnham had by now
made the courts his own. It was the PNC, with the Minister of Home Affairs
as overseer, that effectively conducted the elections of December 16. Opposition party agents were sometimes simply excluded from the count, which
was conducted at only three places instead of the thirty provided in 1964.
The transport of ballot boxes allowed ample opportunity for tampering with
the contents.

The declared results within Guyana itself gave the PNC a bare majority
of votes and seats. When the overseas votes were included, the PNC had 56
percent of the popular vote and a working majority in parliament. There
was clear evidence of fraud on a considerable scale.[11] The number of voters
in certain predominantly black areas had risen beyond any natural explanation. A check of five hundred overseas voters in London found only one
hundred genuine ones. Half of three hundred addresses cited in Manchester
did not exist. Of the thirty thousand Guyanese registered as living abroad,
the votes of thirty-six thousand had been recorded.

The government had already designated one of the eighteenth-century
slave rebel leaders Guyana's national hero. Burnham was, in his own way,
committed to promoting the dignity of blacks through encouraging a sense

of pride in their history and culture. The tragic irony was that the way he chose to maintain himself in power was likely to promote not dignity but doubt. On February 23, 1970, Guyana was declared a Cooperative Republic within the Commonwealth. It was a republic with a Caesar and cooperatives that were little more than the parade grounds of his party.

The more hollow the socialist container, the louder resounded the socialist commitment of the regime. In 1971, Burnham announced that the Demerara Bauxite Company, owned by Alcan (Aluminum Company of Canada), was to be nationalized. Even as talks over compensation were taking place, the company's militant black workers were first demonstrating and then striking for higher wages and guaranteed pension benefits. Arrests failed to subdue them, and peace was only made by concessions. Mackenzie and Wismar-Christianburg, the twin company towns, together became Linden, after one of Burnham's names, and the nationalized enterprise became the Guyana Bauxite Company. The workers were to find that such changes were not accompanied by any acceptable change in their own conditions.[12]

For all the flow of aid from the United States, the economy, under a management as inept as it was corrupt, was in decline. The regime was coming under fire from a few, but nonetheless influential, black activists. Among these, Sydney King commanded considerable respect, for the austerity of his private life and his consistent identification with the cause of the poor. In 1968, he had been persuaded by Burnham that it was his duty to accept an appointment as the head of the Guyana Marketing Corporation. Three years later he had denounced government corruption and resigned. Having renamed himself Eusi Kwayane, to assert his black Guyanese heritage and identity, he now urged the landless poor to seize the unused land of the sugar estates and himself led groups that did so. Burnham ordered police to eject the squatters but then set out to appropriate the cause, by threatening to confiscate the unused land and so securing the acquiescence of the estate owners in its loss.

The elections of July 1973 were different from those of 1968 only in the enfranchisement of 18-year-olds, an engagement to electoral fraud both more blatant and more reliant on recourse to violence, and Burnham's order for the delivery of the two-thirds majority needed to change the constitution. Over 70 percent of the vote was accordingly delivered.

Leading black opponents of Burnham had approached Jagan to join them in calling for a boycott of the elections. He had refused. Now, instead, he chose to boycott parliament. This did little more than relieve the government of the need to defend itself in debates there. A more serious initiative was taken in November 1974 when Eusi Kwayana, with a number of both black and East Indian radicals, founded the Working People's Alliance, which called for the unity of all working people against the dictatorship of Burnham and for the attainment of democratic socialism. Among those involved was

Walter Rodney, a Guyanese black with a doctorate in history from the University of London in 1966, who had taught at the University of the West Indies in Jamaica, until dismissed for his views and banned from the island in 1968. After teaching at the University of Tanzania, he had been offered a post at the University of Guyana, only to have his appointment vetoed by the government. He was already a figure of influence far beyond Guyana, where he looked likely to provide a formidable force of opposition to Burnham.

Burnham himself went on a takeover spree. He nationalized the Reynolds Bauxite Company, the sugar estates of Britain's Jessel Securities, and then those of the giant, Booker Brothers, McConnell, itself. Jagan brought the PPP members back to parliament in celebration of this last measure. The return rather blunted the point of the previous departure. In 1977, he proposed to Burnham that they share power in a National Patriotic Front government. His only condition was that there should be free elections first. Burnham predictably refused. Jagan called the sugar workers out on strike. The government dispatched black strikebreakers, and this brought other workers, including blacks at the bauxite mines, to take strike action in protest. After 135 days the sugar workers surrendered, many of them only to find that their jobs had been permanently given to strikebreakers.

With elections due in 1978, Burnham decided instead to hold a referendum that would effectively empower him to alter or replace the constitution as he pleased. The opposition parties, along with such independent groups as the Committee of Medical Practitioners, called for a boycott. The voter turnout on referendum day, July 10, 1978, was certainly low—if probably not quite the mere 15 percent claimed by the opposition—but the government simply declared that 71.45 percent of the electorate had voted and that 97.4 percent of these had voted in favor. Leading churchmen responded by issuing a statement that the use of fraud and force to keep the government in power had become intolerable. Parliament postponed elections for fifteen months while a new constitution was drafted. None of this made much of a stir in the outside world. Then, suddenly, Guyana was news.

On November 18, more than nine hundred members of the Jonestown sect, a multiracial group of evangelical Christians from the United States who had settled under Burnham's patronage in the interior, committed suicide or were killed on the orders of their leader, Jim Jones.[13] Foreign journalists descended on Guyana, many of them to include in their dispatches reports on conditions in the country. Attracting attention was the existence of another sect under the apparent patronage of Burnham: the House of Israel, led by a fugitive from the United States who held that blacks were the real Children of Israel, but whose most evident view of their destiny was the provision of hooligans to disrupt meetings of Burnham's opponents.

In February 1979, various opposition groups united to form a Council of

National Safety, which demanded a return to constitutional government. As the first anniversary of the referendum approached, the Council decided to mark the occasion with a protest week of remembrance. On July 11, Georgetown awoke to find in flames the building that contained the Ministry of National Development and the office of the PNC's general secretary. Police arrested three leading members of the Working People's Alliance, including Walter Rodney, and charged them with arson. During a demonstration of support for the three, a Jesuit priest who was photographing the scene was stabbed by a House of Israel activist and died soon after.

The government secured a further postponement of elections. Yet if Burnham could do what he liked with parliament, the economy was a different matter. Production per head had been plummeting for five years. In 1975, some 7,500 Guyanese had emigrated; in 1978, the number had been 13,000, or almost 2 percent of the total population. Inflation was now running at almost 20 percent a year, while the unemployment rate was 30 percent and underemployment was widespread. The electricity and water supply systems, the drainage and irrigation works had long been neglected. Well over a third of government expenditure went on servicing or repayment of debt and almost a third on state salaries and allowances. This left little enough for everything else.

On June 13, 1980, Walter Rodney, still to be tried, was killed by a bomb. According to his brother, with him and wounded at the time, they had been offered a walkie-talkie by an electronics specialist in the Guyana Defense Force who professed opposition to the regime, and they had been testing the device as instructed when it exploded. The avowed specialist was helicoptered into the interior on the day following and from there flown out of the country, subsequently to surface in Suriname. How far Burnham was personally implicated remains uncertain. The assassination itself produced outrage throughout the region. Rodney's funeral procession attracted more than twenty-five thousand Guyanese of all races.

With Burnham as Prime Minister, the President of the Republic had been a ceremonial symbol, at least when Burnham did not choose to appropriate both ceremony and symbolism himself. Under a new constitution, Burnham became on October 6 Executive President with virtually limitless powers. Elections were at last set for December 13, and Jagan again rejected the call from opponents of Burnham for a boycott of the polls. Burnham himself, in a misguided gamble or in sheer disdain, announced that international observers were free to attend, and opponents secured a distinguished team. It made no difference to the conduct of the elections, except for some attempts to intimidate the observers. Britain's Lord Avebury, for instance, who headed the team, was twice arrested. The team was unanimous in subsequently reporting that the elections had been massively and flagrantly rigged. The turnout had been low; Avebury estimated that the poll in Georgetown had been no higher than 15 percent; but the government decided instead that 82 percent of the electorate had voted, and that the PNC had taken more than three-quarters of the votes.

In May 1981, the arson case against the surviving two accused collapsed, since the only evidence presented came from security guards who so contradicted one another under cross-examination that not even a subservient court could take it seriously. The government was more successful when, in February 1982, it brought to trial Walter Rodney's brother, Donald, on a charge of having been in illegal possession of an explosive device. The magistrate sentenced him to prison for eighteen months and was subsequently promoted.

The economy remained less tractable. By 1982, debt was preempting three-quarters of current revenues, and the government was forced to begin cutting into the very trunk of its support, by dismissing some six thousand state employees. A steep decline in agricultural production, without the resources to pay for imports, was leading to unprecedented food shortages. The army and police were loyal, however, and able to intimidate or repress a great deal of discontent.

During his last years, Burnham was an ill and lonely man, isolated from any of his old associates and friends. When he died in August 1985, there can be few who mourned him, outside of those who owed their employment and privileges to his tyranny. And perhaps not all of these mourned someone who had provided them with protection and fear together.

His successor, Desmond Hoyte, who had been his Vice-President in charge of economic planning and finance, was in no doubt of how parlous was the condition of both. The election of 1985, which confirmed him as President, was conducted as its predecessors had been. Yet Hoyte was well aware that such contrivances would not reverse or even arrest the decline in popular morale and productive effort. He began by gradually emancipating the press. While twice postponing elections, he sanctioned a registration of voters that restored some semblance of reality to the lists, and at last, on October 5, 1992, reasonably free elections were held.

At the age of 74, Cheddi Jagan emerged as President, with a PPP parliamentary majority of a single seat. The support registered for minor parties, in particular the Working People's Alliance, suggested an incipient disposition to cross the main racial divide. Yet politics remained dominated by racial demography. While blacks generally held little property but composed so much of the civil service and some 95 percent of the armed forces, it would take an exceptionally skillful and generous political leadership to cultivate the conditions for a creative interracial democracy. Yet nothing less would serve the real interests of Guyana's black minority.

19 | THE HEMORRHAGE OF HAITI

~~~~~~

The Haitian revolution had done away with slavery and white rule. It had not brought any closer together the blacks and the mulattoes, who were divided by cultural and social differences that reinforced the old obsessive discriminations of color. The mulattoes in general identified themselves with the European component in their ancestry. Some had been freed before the revolution and had acquired, by inheritance or enterprise, considerable property. To others had fallen, during the upheaval, the family holdings of departed whites. Those who were less fortunate found solace in the supposed superiority of their complexion. Few, whatever their circumstances, regarded the mass of blacks, culturally closer to Africa, without a mixture of fear and disdain.

The black general Jean-Jacques Dessalines, scourge of the whites and the proclaimed Emperor, declared: "We have all fought against the whites; the properties which we have conquered by the spilling of our blood belong to us all; I intend that they be divided with equity."[1] He did not extend this principle to the expropriated colonial estates. These were leased to officers in his army and cultivated by labor tied to particular plantations, in what amounted to a form of feudalism. Many of the laborers, not happy with this interpretation of their freedom, deserted to the mountains, where they joined former runaway slaves already settled as peasants on the slopes. The mass of blacks and mulattoes in the north were subjected to a regime both authoritarian and militarist.

In the south, mulattoes were more numerous and better organized. Headed by General Alexandre Pétion, their leaders looked for a regime that would limit centralized authority and protect mulatto prerogatives. A revolt against Dessalines's sovereignty broke out in the region. On October 17, 1806, Dessalines, having hastened south, was killed by a group of mulatto officers in an ambush outside Port-au-Prince. The different color of the murdered and the murderers made the murder itself one of the seminally symbolic events in Haitian history. Blacks would see Dessalines as the father of Haitian independence and black power, assassinated by mulattoes in the cause of promoting their own dominion. Alone among the black revolutionary leaders, he would come to be accommodated in the Voodoo pantheon.[2] In such histories and polemical writings as those of Beaubrun Ardouin and Joseph Saint-Rémy, mulattoes would treat the assassination as that of a tyrant in the cause of liberty.

Another of Toussaint's black generals, Henri Christophe, succeeded Dessalines in control of the north, while Alexandre Pétion presided over mulatto rule in the south. For fourteen years, with intermittent conflict, Haiti was to be accordingly divided.

In 1811, Christophe had himself crowned as King Henri I and created titles which he distributed to those whose interests were further bound to him by the grant of substantial landholdings. He was well aware, however, that the security of his regime required a wider engagement. Measures for the provision of state land to commoners were early announced. Though long delayed, these did eventually come into effect and significantly expanded the class of peasant proprietors. Christophe instituted as well a code of laws and courts to enforce it. W. W. Harvey, a contemporary British observer who lived in the kingdom during its last days, found defects in the officers appointed to an undertaking for which they had not been trained, but his verdict on the courts themselves was such as to suggest, by the standards of what Haiti would come to suffer, a veritable Golden Age:

> By their means it was that due punishment was afflicted on those guilty of evident injustice and oppression: that as far as the fear of suffering and disgrace operated, so far were unprincipled and turbulent men restrained from the commission of crimes: that open dishonesty seldom failed to be detected, and never escaped its just punishment: that injuries of the person wantonly afflicted always met with their desert: that the unhappy effects of private revenge were prevented: and that crimes affecting the general safety were rendered less frequent.[3]

The same observer was moved, after visiting one of the schools which Christophe had established with the help of teachers supplied by the British and Foreign School Society, at the contrast between the sight of so many children at their books and what he had seen of their condition under slavery. Above all, he was impressed by the spirit of freedom and equality which blacks at every level of society revealed:

> Hence, the labourer addressed his employer, the soldier his officer, and an attendant a man of authority, with that freedom which a mutual opinion of

equality could alone dictate or suffer. On the other hand, the officers of the army, when not on duty, frequently associated with the common soldiers; the nobles sometimes selected their companions from among the people; and the secretary of state was occasionally seen in a tailor's shop, sitting on the board with the workmen, engaged in close and familiar conversation.[4]

Christophe encouraged peasants to cultivate crops for the internal market, while maintaining the plantation system to provide commodities for export, on the basis that a quarter of the revenue should be paid in wages and a further quarter in taxes to the Treasury. The result was a sharp economic revival, as local trade thrived, and sugar, coffee, indigo were sold to markets abroad. Le Cap became again a bustling port and commercial center. Splendid silver coins were issued, and millions of dollars' worth were still in the Treasury at the time of Christophe's death.

The strength of the economy must, indeed, have been considerable, since such reserves had been accumulated despite the expenditure of the state on two great public constructions. In the mountains some twelve miles from Le Cap, there rose the palace of Sans Souci, beautiful as well as grand, with gardens to match, and, on the peak of the range behind it, the massive Citadelle. Both would survive, if the palace only in ruin, as reminders to black Haitians of past glory.

In the republic to the south, a mulatto oligarchy governed under the leadership of Pétion, who was elevated in 1816 to the office of president-for-life. Like Christophe, he established a number of schools, one of them for girls, and even proclaimed the principle of free primary education. The economy, however, was in no such prospering condition as that in Christophe's kingdom. The small parcels of land, distributed mainly to officers and soldiers, were devoted by their new proprietors to subsistence agriculture, while the production of export commodities declined.

In 1820, Christophe suffered a stroke, and while recovering at Sans Souci, he received reports of an advancing army revolt. Deserted by the very nobles he had raised to their distinction and riches, he put a bullet through his head. General Jean-Pierre Boyer, the mulatto who had succeeded to the presidency of the republic on the death of Pétion in 1818, marched his forces northward and reunited the country under his rule, before marching eastward in 1822 to conquer Santo Domingo.

On the map, independent Haiti might now have seemed stronger than it had ever been, but this itself promoted its isolation. Governments with interests in the maintenance of slavery and colonial control regarded its survival as more than ever setting a dangerous example. France refused to recognize it, and no other great power would risk antagonizing France by doing so first. Boyer, yearning for an end to such quarantine, was ready to pay a heavy price for it.

In 1825, the French government concluded an agreement with his regime. In return for French recognition of its independence, Haiti undertook to pay an indemnity of 150 million francs and reduce customs charges on trade with France to half of those imposed on trade with other states. It was to prove a calamitous deal. The customs concession to France impeded the development of a diversified trade. The commitment to pay such an enormous indemnity could not be met by taxation, and any attempt to raise even appreciable amounts in this way seemed all but certain to raise a revolt instead. The regime accordingly had recourse to foreign loans. These not only added servicing costs to the capital burden, but would come to provide, with the predictable failure to satisfy creditors on time, the pretext for foreign intervention.

Boyer's period in power, which lasted a quarter of a century, was marked by a steep economic decline. The policy employed to promote the production of commodities for export could hardly have been more of a disaster if it had been devised as sabotage. The Rural Code of 1826 was virtually an attempt to revive serfdom. It assigned badly paid labor to particular plantations and imposed harsh punishments for vagrancy. The new serfs labored badly or took to their heels. The precipitous fall in sugar exports revealed the extent of the damage. From some 2,500,000 pounds in 1820, the total in 1842 was a mere 6,000. Without the coffee which peasants cultivated along with such subsistence crops as bananas, yams, and corn, on their small land-holdings, there would have been very little of an export trade left.

Such an economy was required to meet pressing foreign obligations, sustain the mulatto elite in the style to which it was accustomed, and pay not only for a regular army of 32,000 men but also a national guard of 40,000—from a total population of less than 800,000. It is scarcely astonishing that public works and services came to be so neglected. One foreign visitor observed that "there seems to be a disposition on the part of the government to efface every vestige of the former roads."[5] Another remarked, over a decade later: "Port-au-Prince, with all its advantages of situation, with every inherent capability of being made and kept delightfully clean, is perhaps the filthiest capital in the world."[6]

The widening distance between the overwhelmingly mulatto rulers and the overwhelmingly black ruled extended far beyond the composition of the government. In the army, the vast majority of soldiers were black, while mulattoes dominated the higher ranks. Despite intermittent attempts since the time of Toussaint to counteract it, Voodoo persisted as the popular religion. The Boyer regime made Roman Catholicism the established religion and appointed priests to spread the faith through the country. Many of these priests had no religious training, and some were soon revealed as racketeers. While the capital itself was provided with a variety of weekly newspapers and monthly reviews mainly for the tastes of the mulatto elite, public education was starved of resources. In Christophe's northern kingdom, there had been 2,000 pupils in well-stocked and well-staffed primary schools. In Boyer's Haiti, by 1843, there were only 1,000 primary school pupils, each school had a single teacher, and no school had any writing materials or books.

Blacks who were persuaded that it was deliberate policy to keep them in poverty and ignorance expressed such opinions at their peril. Felix Darfour, African-born and exceptional enough to be publishing his own periodical, addressed to the legislature in 1822 a petition which suggested that the government was not altogether innocent of color prejudice. This was held to be "offensive and seditious." Darfour was arrested, tried, and executed, while Boyer seized the occasion to order the rounding up of other critics.[7]

Within the mulatto elite itself, a serious challenge began to develop. Attacks were made on the diversion of public money into private pockets and on the conduct of elections, which had increasingly become an exercise in altering the contents of ballot boxes and intimidating opponents. The very degradation of Haiti was a target. Spirited young intellectuals argued for an economic nationalism to reverse the long decline and for a reassumption of Haitian leadership in advancing the cause of color everywhere. There was an abundance of combustible material. In 1843, a revolt broke out, and Boyer boarded a British ship bound for Jamaica.

There is a Creole saying rooted in Haitian political experience: "The fever is not in the sheets, it is in the blood."[8] The new mulatto President, Charles Hérard, was pledged to cure Haiti of injustice, oppression, and color prejudice. It was soon clear that only the sheets had changed.

Not all blacks were peasants or soldiers. Prominent within the black elite of the south was the Salomon family, which now fomented for its own purposes a peasant revolt in the region. The government imposed martial law and arrested members of the family. This only promoted the disaffection. Rebellious black peasants, who came to be known as *piquets* from the pikes with which they armed themselves, demanded an end to mulatto dominance, the election of a black President, and the confiscation of land from the rich for distribution to the laboring poor.

The east of the island had exploited Haitian turmoil to declare its independence as the Dominican Republic. The Hérard government's attempt at reconquest was a humiliating failure. The decisive blow at the staggering regime was struck from within the army. Philippe Guerrier, an elderly black general, commanded the garrison at Cap-Haïtien, as Le Cap had come to be called. He moved south with his forces and was proclaimed President in May 1844. The real power in his regime was, however, wielded by mulattoes who dominated the council of state. It was the beginning of what would become a feature of successive regimes and be known as *la politique de doublure*: the politics of the stand-in or understudy.[9]

Guerrier died in 1845 and was succeeded by another elderly black general,

Louis Pierrot, who was a northerner and a nationalist with a commitment to the cause of black power. He even moved the capital to Cap-Haïtien, to distance the government from the strongholds of the mulatto elite in Port-au-Prince and elsewhere in the south. He also attacked French intervention in Haitian politics, denouncing "the enemies of the African race" who continued to work against "the complete emancipation of the blacks and of their descendants."[10] In the following year, he, too, was toppled by an army revolt. A new black President was succeeded by yet another, who was at least chosen at the ballot box, though he proceeded to declare himself Emperor Faustin I two years later.

In 1859, yet another army revolt brought to power General Fabre Nicolas Geffrard, a dark mulatto from an elite family. Within a year an agreement had been concluded with the Vatican and a policy inaugurated to confront Voodoo and eradicate "these last vestiges of barbarism and slavery, superstition and its scandalous practices."[11] The new investment in education consigned many schools to control by Catholic orders, and the employment of mainly French teachers fortified the attachment of the elite to French culture. The British minister to Haiti, Sir Spenser St. John, remarked on the evident extent of color distinctions in the social life of the capital. The three preoccupations of the mulatto elite—color, culture, and religion—were being relentlessly pursued.

In 1865, Silvain Salnave, a mulatto general, led a revolt in Cap-Haïtien. It was crushed, with the assistance of a British warship. Foreign powers would now come increasingly to intervene, as opportunities arose for them to pursue their own interests. Salnave fled to refuge in the Dominican Republic and returned in 1867, after Geffrard's overthrow, to become President.

Here at least was a ruler who made some attempt to reach, rather than merely send messages, across the social divide. So light-skinned himself that his opponents claimed he was not Haitian at all, he acquired a significant personal following among the black poor in the capital and the towns of the north. In the manipulative color politics of Haiti, however, this did him little good. For almost the whole period of his rule, he had to contend with a peasant guerrilla movement as well as with the usual manifestations of discontent from among those who regarded their influence as inadequately prized. With his authority shaken, he was driven from Port-au-Prince in 1869, then hunted down and executed.

His successor, Nissage Saget, came from the mulatto elite. He proved exceptional in serving his full term of office and then retiring gracefully in 1874. Less edifyingly, he offered Britain the territorial bribe of Môle St. Nicolas at the northwest tip of Haiti in return for British financial support; but the British government was not interested, perhaps because it considered the returns inadequate to the outlay. His successor, another black general, only lasted until 1876, though long enough to propose a virtual British protectorate over the southern province and meanwhile raise a massive loan from France. A mulatto general succeeded him but was defeated at elections in 1879, and L. E. L. F. Salomon, of the rich and influential black family, returned from exile to become President.

Like black Presidents before him, he formed an administration dominated by mulattoes. By now, however, color attitudes had so hardened that a mulatto minister was upbraided by another mulatto in revealing terms: "You are an undisguised scoundrel, because you, as a mulatto, serve a negro government . . . Being a mulatto, I am sure that you have a horror of negroes, *just as I have*."[12] Salomon's own persistent calls for national unity, reinforced by his reminder that his own children were mulattoes, were of little avail. It was a situation that beckoned foreign interference.

In 1883, a party of exiles led by a prominent mulatto politician invaded the country from Jamaica, an enterprise likely to have required at least the connivance of the island's British authorities. Sympathetic revolts broke out in several southern towns. These were soon crushed, but the invasion force itself, established at Miragoâne, withstood a siege for many months, until the last mulatto defender had fallen, and only after much loss of life among the black forces of investment.

Salomon went further than any of his predecessors in an apparent willingness to concede encroachments on Haitian independence in exchange for foreign protection. He offered territory to the United States in return for diplomatic and military aid. He even opened negotiations for the establishment of a French protectorate over Haiti. Nothing came of these initiatives, and they might well have been devised to divert a British interest that was perceived as the primary threat. All the same, they were admissions of weakness that were bound to whet the interventionist appetite. Furthermore, Salomon did launch two changes that were loaded with dangerous cargoes. He amended the law that had lasted since the time of Dessalines, so that foreign companies could now own property in Haiti, and he established the Banque Nationale with French capital.

An uprising in the north put an end to his rule in 1888. After a brief period of disorder, the black general Florvil Hyppolite took power. It was during his Presidency that a Ministry of Public Works was inaugurated, a comment in itself on the extent of previous neglect. Associated with this was a development program which introduced a telephone and telegraph system along with the construction of iron bridges and market buildings. Hyppolite also successfully resisted mounting pressure from an imperially assertive United States for a grant of territory. In 1896, he was confronted by a mulatto-led revolt in the important southern port town of Jacmel. He dealt successfully with it, but, even as he was entering the town, he fell dead from his horse. It was the close of a relatively benign and productive period in Haitian government.

While six Presidents in succession took office during a period of intense social instability, foreign enterprise took increasing advantage of Salomon's concession. In 1910, one black general raised to the Presidency signed the McDonald Contract, which gave a United States company the right not only to build a railroad but to cultivate the land alongside it. A substantial German business community established itself in Haiti, while Syrio-Lebanese merchants moved into the retail trade under the protection of British and United States citizenship papers. Nationalist demands to restrict such intrusions made little headway against the evident readiness of foreign governments to send a gunboat every now and then as a reminder of Haiti's vulnerability. Nor was this the only form of intervention. Foreign, mainly German, merchants in Haiti came to finance rebellions as an investment, with interest of 100 percent or more to be paid along with the return of all capital advanced in the event of success.[13]

In 1911, German troops actually entered Port-au-Prince to protect the property of German nationals. Indeed, as Europe moved toward the outbreak of the First World War, the commercial importance of the German community in Haiti seemed likely to become the pretext for an attempt at outright annexation of the country. If this agitated Britain and France, it scarcely left indifferent a United States whose expansionist interpretation of its undertaking to preserve the independence of its hemisphere had already led it to invade Puerto Rico and Cuba in 1898, Panama in 1903, and Nicaragua in 1909. Economic interests here, as elsewhere, played a part in the protective design. In addition to the McDonald Contract, the United States had an important investment: the French had yielded their control of Haiti's Banque Nationale to United States bankers.

"If I am not to eat the soup," goes an old Creole saying, "I shall spit in the soup."[14] There were those in the mulatto elite who, for all its representative predominance in both the indigenous commercial community and successive black-led governments, yearned for the open political supremacy that mulattoes had once so enjoyed. Many of them initially welcomed the United States occupation, and some might well have secretly encouraged it.

On July 27, 1915, President Vilbrun Guillaume Sam, confronted by a revolt in the north and the threat of another in the capital, ordered the slaughter of 167 political opponents held in the city jail. Reports of the slaughter fired rioting, and the President fled to the French Embassy. An enraged mob, led by relatives and friends of the slaughtered, stormed the embassy, seized the President and tore him into pieces, which were then paraded through the streets. Some 300 United States marines landed from a waiting cruiser, as the first contingent in a force of occupation.

From the outset, the United States authorities made it clear that they did not intend to rule the country directly, but that theirs were the policies to be pursued. A succession of three mulatto Presidents accepted such guidance, during an occupation that would last for almost twenty years, with fiscal control for a further thirteen. The pretext for this protracted engagement was the promotion of a stable democracy, through the development of a productive class based on technical and vocational training. Suitable schools were established. Roads were built and other public works undertaken. Sanitation and medical services, for so long neglected, were provided or improved. Haitian nationalists were unimpressed. They regarded the occupation as an injury all the more intolerable for the added insult of making Haiti pay for it. The increase in revenues from a 50 percent rise in exports was more than offset by subtractions to meet the salaries of United States personnel (most of such money was repatriated) and to service or repay, sometimes early, foreign (mainly United States) loans. From total receipts in 1927, for instance, 40 percent went on debt and 20 percent on maintaining the army.[15]

Outraged nationalism apart, the occupation soon produced mounting hostility. Many United States citizens, in the army or the civilian administration, brought with them an attitude of racial superiority, and related practices of discrimination became more marked with the arrival of white women from 1916 onward. "Military personnel made a fetish of segregation, while businessmen were more relaxed; but Americans of any persuasion who persisted in fraternizing openly with Haitians were ostracized and vilified."[16] Initially acquiescent and even approving members of the mulatto elite had expected the occupation to give their white ancestry its due. They did not take kindly to being regarded and treated as "niggers."

Nor were peasants disposed to welcome the corvée system, by which they were required to labor on the laying of roads, or an agricultural development by foreign companies that threatened to turn them into a rural proletariat. A guerrilla movement emerged in 1917, with an attack on the home of a United States military officer, and the Cacos War,[17] as it came to be called, would end only in May 1920, with the killing of the last guerrilla leader. At the height of the conflict, some three thousand United States marines were active in the Central Plateau, and some six hundred Haitians would lose their lives in the various campaigns. The chief guerrilla leader, Charlemagne Pérault, who was ambushed, killed, and then tied to a door for public exhibition in November 1919, would become a major figure in Haitian heroic history.

Resurgent nationalism stirred a reassessment of the African heritage among Haitian intellectuals. Dr. Arthur Holly, for instance, son of the first Anglican bishop in Haiti, argued that Haitians should stop adapting themselves to the standards of European civilization and revalue all that they owed to Africa, including the creativity of Voodoo.[18] Dr. Jean Price Mars, born to a Protestant father and a Catholic mother, had assailed Voodoo as "African idolatry," but now acclaimed it as traditional African belief in a spiritual power which manifested itself in material forms. He lauded the vivid expressiveness of Creole, a language which had preserved popular traditions and might be the means of drawing together the peasant masses and the elite. He drew attention to the growing interest abroad in the achievements of African music and sculpture, and to the new black literary movement in the United States.[19]

A number of young intellectuals from the mulatto elite founded or contributed to various venturesome magazines. Among the leading figures in this literary revival were several gifted poets, who denounced the obeisance to European culture in their own background and exulted in Haiti's African heritage. Among them, Carl Brouard became devoted to Voodoo, and Jacques Roumain, who was also a novelist, expressed his hostility to the occupation with such force that he was twice arrested and once imprisoned.

By 1928, little was left of the moral pretensions with which the United States had begun the occupation. Censorship of the press was blatant but so inadequate to the purpose of silencing dissent that it was rare for the jails not to be accommodating at least one editor. National elections were avoided, and local ones were conducted on the basis of ballot rigging. In 1929, a demonstration by students at an agricultural college triggered widespread strikes against the occupation. In the national election allowed in 1930, all contenders for the Presidency called for an end to the occupation. Sténio Vincent, the victorious candidate, immediately opened negotiations for the withdrawal of United States troops. These finally left in 1934, though a United States fiscal agent stayed behind to control customs revenues until all of Haiti's foreign debts had been cleared. Neither Haiti nor the United States would prove willing to preserve such an arrangement for so long.

An avowed nationalist, President Vincent enjoyed a popular support that reached from the largely mulatto movement of socialists, whether Marxist or technocratic, to proponents of black power. His version of democracy, however, had an authoritarian strain, and his patience with radical ideas was fragile. In 1934, Jacques Roumain founded the Haitian Communist Party to propagate revolutionary principles, albeit in their misshapen Stalinist form. He was soon in exile. The nationalist alliance between mulatto and black frayed and then snapped as the old mulatto preoccupation with dominance reasserted itself and the mulatto President did little to restrain it. The mulatto elite at the time encompassed some thirty thousand family heads, representing with their dependents roughly 5 percent of the population. Of these, however, one modern scholar, Robert Rotberg, has estimated, "fewer than 2,000, and perhaps as few as 300, actually ran Haiti."[20] For the mass of black Haitians, not much had changed.

To the neighboring Dominican Republic, under the dictatorship of Rafael Trujillo, many had fled from destitution at home to find employment as cane cutters on the sugar plantations. In 1937, Trujillo's professed commitment to European culture and Catholic values took the form of ordering an estimated twenty thousand of these migrants to be driven into stockades and slaughtered with carbines and machetes. In the outcry that followed, Vincent accepted an indemnity of $750,000 for the families of the victims; and though most of the indemnity was never paid, he left unchanged the name of Avenue Trujillo, a major road in the capital, so distinguished in tribute to the dictator.

This inadequate response to the massacre did nothing to sustain Vincent's claim that he was "Haiti's Second Liberator." Yet Elie Lescot, another mulatto elected to succeed him as President in 1941, pursued policies that made Vincent's departure from office seem regrettable in retrospect. The advance of mulatto dominance drove almost all blacks from command posts in the army and the civil administration, while the Roman Catholic Church was backed by the state in waging a campaign against Voodoo.

By the end of 1945, Lescot had excited a formidable alliance of interests against him. It involved mulatto liberals in revolt against an increasingly repressive rule, radicals in revolt against policies directed by the priorities of United States investment, a black elite in revolt against its exclusion from authority, and a populace whose poverty looked everywhere except to the government for relief. In January 1946, student demonstrations triggered strikes and rioting, market women in the capital stormed the home of the hated Interior Minister, and Lescot flew off with his family to Canada.

A medley of political parties emerged, with no less than four associations of trade unions representing perhaps ten thousand members in all.[21] Equipped with its own periodical was a group of black power proponents, among them François Duvalier. He had qualified as a physician in 1934 and then worked in various hospitals and clinics before attaching himself to a United States army medical mission from 1943 to 1946. His preoccupation with black power was neither new nor superficial. Early in his career he had belonged to a group of black intellectuals who called themselves Les Griots, from the West African griot—tribal poet, storyteller, healer, and guardian of customs and myths.

By August 1946, there were eight candidates for the presidency left in the field, seven of whom were black. Of the seven, Dumarsais Estimé was a moderate with the broadest backing, and he was elected after a contest notable for a surfacing of the color issue in a more feverish form than at any time since before the occupation. Duvalier himself had supported a different contender but was offered and accepted a post in the new government as Secretary of State for Labor and Public Health.

Estimé's administration was responsible for various social and economic reforms. It introduced a minimum wage, with maternity and child welfare services in rural areas, undertook irrigation projects and improvements to the water supply, encouraged industrialization, and inaugurated a major urban reconstruction program in the capital. If the absence of sufficient resources made some of these measures more significant for their symbolism than for their substance, it was at least a symbolism of some commitment to alleviate the popular lot. The administration also aroused mounting hostility: from a mulatto elite that attacked it for pursuing a policy of black dominance, from a business community alarmed by such revolutionary initiatives as the introduction of income tax, and from the hierarchy of a Roman Catholic Church alienated by official support for the movement to revive African values. Unhappily, Estimé chose to secure himself not by establishing an organized base of democratic support but by resorting instead to repressive measures. He banned political parties, student associations, newspapers. His attempt to amend the constitution so as to permit himself more than one term in office did not even have the virtue of success. It was blocked by a hostile Senate.

In May 1950, he was ousted by a military coup, which entrusted provisional power to a junta of three. Among the early decrees of the interim regime was one that outlawed Voodoo ceremonies. Paul Magloire, a member of the junta, was then elected President. He was no less impatient of opposition than his predecessor had been, while essentially concerned with the diversion of public money, including United States aid for specific projects, to himself, his relatives, and his associates. Contemporary estimates of his personal plunder, much of it dispatched abroad, ranged from $12 million to $28 million.[22] In December 1956, he followed his predecessor into exile, leaving an empty Treasury behind.

After a period of mounting instability in which numerous parties and candidates emerged to contend for power, Duvalier was elected President in September 1957. He had campaigned on a pledge of allegiance to the policies of Estimé, though with reassurances for all those groups that the policies of Estimé had antagonized. He was to rule for fourteen years, in pursuit of no policies but his own and eventually by a use of terror beyond anything that independent Haiti had yet seen. He reacted to early dissent by having opponents arrested or assaulted by soldiers, police, or members of his private force, the *cagoulards* or hooded men. This strategy of preemptive violence might itself well have promoted an expedition of exiles in July 1958 which succeeded in seizing the capital's Dessalines Barracks. The attempt was crushed, but promoted an extension of the violence employed by the regime.

Duvalier needed no lessons in his country's political history to recognize the threat of a military coup represented. He set out to tame the army. He dismissed suspect officers, many of them mulattoes, and appointed others, mainly black and young, who were likely to associate their further advancement with loyalty to him alone. Then, in a demonstration that no one, however highly placed, was beyond his reach, he dismissed in December 1958 the entire general staff (two generals, ten colonels, and forty lieutenant colonels), to reconstitute it with appointments of his own. Yet changing the command of the army was not enough. He wanted a force that owed its very existence to him, and created this in a civilian militia that came to be known as the Tontons Macoutes.

The name was borrowed from the bogeyman (*tonton* means "uncle" in Creole) who comes at night to take away naughty children in his *macoute* (the straw satchel of the peasant). And these real-life versions of the folklore figure were to carry out a program of surveillance, control, and terror that reached from the capital into the most remote villages. Their way of dealing with protest strikes by members of the mainly mulatto business community was straightforward: Macoutes would break open the doors of all closed businesses and leave the contents to be looted. They dealt with recalcitrant newspapers by raiding their plants and destroying their machinery. They dealt with real or suspected opponents by killing them, sometimes along with their families, and ordering that the bodies be left a full day in the street.

It would be a mistake, however, to infer that the Macoutes were all merely licensed hoodlums, though many undoubtedly were, and some were unbridled sadists. There was more than coincidence in the blue denims, red scarves, and peasant hats worn in the countryside both by the Macoutes and by many Voodoo priests (Macoutes in the capital were given to sporting dark glasses as their own insignia). The Macoutes and the Voodoo priests were sometimes the same people, loyal to a regime that afforded rare protection and respect for the practices of Voodoo. Local notables, too, became Macoutes to secure their authority, as Macoutes in turn exercised their own authority to become local notables. Government in Haiti had long been remote from the people. Duvalier brought it among them, but essentially for his own repressive purposes.

The inherent risk for the most tightly organized autocracy lies in its reliance on the loyalty of whoever commands the forces of repression. Clément Barbot had been put in charge of the Macoutes from the start. He came to wonder why he should control them for the sake of Duvalier rather than for his own. Had he been more reticent, he might have succeeded in the assassination of Duvalier that he planned for the Carnival period in 1960. Instead, he consorted with foreign diplomats and even criticized a speech in which Duvalier had attacked the inadequacy of United States aid to Haiti. He was arrested, then released. For a while, he lay low, before going underground and conducting a terrorist campaign in 1963 which included an attempt to kidnap Duvalier's children. He was hunted down and killed. Duvalier, who had taken personal control of the Macoutes, would never again yield it to anyone else. This was not, however, the only effect of the affair. His appreciation of the danger to which he and his family had been exposed seems to have promoted a distinct paranoia, as his escape from it promoted his assumption of a special destiny.

He had already taken on with marked success the Roman Catholic Church.

In August 1959, he banned the teachers' union backed by the Church, and he expelled from the country two priests, one of whom was secretary of the union. The Archbishop protested to no avail, and a prayer meeting of protest in the cathedral was dispersed by police. In November 1960, a student strike received support from the Church and its mouthpiece, *La Phalange.* Duvalier expelled the Archbishop and sent the apostolic administrator after him. The Pope excommunicated all those connected with the expulsions. This only confirmed Duvalier in his determination to end Church dominance over education. He placed the university under state control and made parents responsible for the attendance of their children at the university and schools. When *La Phalange* protested, it was banned. A purge of teachers was ordered. Various priests and nuns were arrested.

A third confrontation followed in November 1962, when the Bishop of Gonaïves was expelled from Haiti for his campaign against Voodoo practices. The Pope once more excommunicated all those responsible, and also recalled the papal nuncio. This proved no more effective than previous sanctions had been. By April 1964, Duvalier had come to seem so unassailable that he was able to command expressions of loyalty and support first from an assembly of Catholic priests and then from one representing the clergy of other denominations. In October 1966, the Vatican settled its differences with the Haitian regime. Monseigneur François Ligonde was enthroned as the first Haitian-born Archbishop of Port-au-Prince and would subsequently write to Duvalier: "I can assure you of our entire collaboration in the political, economic, and social domain."[23]

Of scarcely less moment, Duvalier challenged the United States with comparable success. After an initial period of moderately good relations, the United States government became increasingly critical of the regime, not least over the conduct of the Macoutes. In June 1960, Duvalier responded with a speech in which he blamed the United States for Haiti's low level of development and suggested that Haiti might be driven to reconsider its Western alignment. As relations continued to deteriorate, the regime rejected successive United States ambassadors, invited trade delegations from Eastern Europe to visit Haiti, and encouraged the publication of articles in the Haitian press that criticized United States policies. In 1963, the Kennedy administration reportedly went so far as to consult with Juan Bosch, President of the Dominican Republic, over ways to oust Duvalier from power. In the event, it was Bosch himself who was toppled, and Kennedy's assassination came shortly afterward. New administrations in Washington proved to be increasingly accommodating, on the principle that governments were to be accepted for what they were, provided that they were not aligned with the Soviet Union. Duvalier became the recipient of United States aid.

How far he came really to believe in his messianic destiny, it is impossible to know. He certainly made it clear that he expected others to believe it.

Followers or those seeking favor or safety took to expressing adulation in ever
more extravagant forms. Pictures of him were widely displayed with the
inscription "Ecce Homo," traditionally applied to Christ. A Catechism of
the Revolution was published in 1964 which contained a new version of the
Lord's Prayer addressed to Papa Doc, as he was commonly called in Haiti.

> Our Doc, who art in the National Palace for life,
>   hallowed be thy name by generations present and future,
> thy will be done in Port-au-Prince and in the provinces . . .[24]

Of more relevance to many Haitians, he also claimed supernatural powers
within the Voodoo context and got rid of those *hougans*—Voodoo priests—
who were known to be questioning these. More and more frequently, he
invested official occasions with Voodoo signs and ceremonies and came to
be regarded by some adherents of Voodoo as the very incarnation of Baron
Samedi, the Voodoo *loa* or spirit who is Lord of the Dead.

What his regime signally failed to do was alleviate the plight of the
populace. In fact, it increased its exactions through indirect taxes that
were disguised in the price of the commodities provided by the various
state monopolies. The business community, including those mulattoes who
showed themselves to be sufficiently subservient, acquired immensely profitable licenses and franchises, in return for providing kickbacks to the government or influential officials. There was certainly some darkening of the
rich, from the political assault on the mulatto elite and from the possibilities
of profit afforded members of the black middle class, partly by appointment
to places in the bureaucracy, but the enormous disparities between rich and
poor survived and even widened.

The rates of illiteracy and unemployment rose. In 1963, the palace guard
received new uniforms at a cost of $150 each and high leather boots at a
cost of $40 a pair, but public expenditure per head on education was sixty-
one cents a year and that on health, sixty-five. A random sample survey of
three hundred Haitians found an average intake per person of less than 1,600
calories, and an average expenditure on food of eight cents a day. Another
survey found that over half the adults studied were more than 5 percent
underweight in relation to their height.[25]

What Duvalier provided instead was not only a successful assertion of
nationalism but an assertion, albeit more symbolic than real, of black dignity.
Much was made of such occasions as the unveiling of a powerful monument
to the *marron inconnu*—the Maroon equivalent of the unknown soldier—
in Port-au-Prince, the visit to Haiti of Haile Selassie, and the official mourn-
ing that followed Martin Luther King's assassination. The very repressions
of the regime mattered less to black Haitians who saw the mulattoes as the
most conspicuous victims, while the apparent end to mulatto dominance of

the state was seen as evidence that they themselves were at last coming into their own. That the despotism of Duvalier should have been seen at all as serving rather than exploiting the cause of black dignity demonstrated how profoundly that dignity had for so long been affronted and denied.

In April 1971, Duvalier died after naming his nineteen-year-old son, Jean-Claude, "Baby Doc," to succeed him as President-for-Life. A change to the constitution lowered the age of eligibility for the Presidency from forty to eighteen, and a referendum produced an official result of 2,391,916 votes in favor with none against, in an exercise that sacrificed credibility to zeal. The United States reacted by promising an increase in aid. The Nixon administration in Washington preferred the assurance of continuity and order in Haiti to the risk of upheaval. At the ceremony to celebrate the succession of the overweight young man whom schoolfellows had nicknamed *Tête-Panier* (Basket-Head), the Catholic Archbishop informed him, "Your authority is a participation in divine authority."[26] Baby Doc was to rule for fifteen years, one year longer than his father.

If the prestige of the father was an implicit factor in the son's survival, the existence of the Macoutes was an explicit one. Indeed, their numbers would grow to an estimated range of 100,000–200,000 by 1986, when they included government officials, businessmen, office and factory supervisors, priests, teachers, and neighborhood or community leaders. Even at the lower limit of 100,000, this would, with families, have represented some 10 percent of the population, and, with clients, an even larger proportion.[27] Such a force was formidable enough and would have been more formidable still if some were not there less from a Duvalierist loyalty than from the sense that it was safer to be inside than out.

Foreign, mainly United States, financial aid to the regime rose steeply, to top $100 million in 1981, when Haiti's total operating budget was $150 million. In return, the regime pursued acceptable policies that included the promotion of an assembly-line economy based on cheap labor. Industrial parks sprouted at the edges of the capital for the processing of imported components into radios, baseballs, brassieres. As many as sixty thousand workers came to be employed in the parks; for a time, they supported with their earnings perhaps a quarter of the capital's population.[28] Yet, arguably less oppressive than his father's had been, Baby Doc's regime was more corrupt and would become outrageously so.

In 1980, Baby Doc married Michèle Bennett, a dashing divorcée of mulatto family, in defiance of the leading Duvalierists who stood guard over his father's memory and policies. The wedding, with food, finery, and fireworks flown in from Paris, reportedly cost $7 million and prefigured the spree that was to follow. The father of the bride, Ernest Bennett, hitherto a businessman of unremarkable accomplishments, rose so rapidly in resourcefulness that by 1983, apart from his numerous other profitable enterprises, he had become the leading coffee exporter outside of the state sector. Far from attempting to disguise the high cost of the pleasures pursued at the palace, the first family flaunted it. Fancy dress parties were held at which jewels were given as prizes to arriving guests, while the populace was invited to watch part of the proceedings, either live from the immediate vicinity or on the television screens installed in the public parks for the occasion.

In part to stanch the bleeding of support, the government much increased the number of its employees, many of whom came no closer to actual employment than collecting the regular payments that they received for it. Other superfluous personnel were placed in the business sector, where the so-called national industries heaped up losses equal to almost 4 percent of the gross national product in 1982–85. Baby Doc himself drew $2.4 million a year for his expenses, along with various recorded supplemental amounts, from public funds. This, however, represented only a small part of the plunder. An estimated $30 million was skimmed from the state tobacco monopoly, while $20 million of the $22 million supplied by the International Monetary Fund in budgetary assistance went astray.

The United States government and the international lending agencies pressed upon Baby Doc the necessity of appointing to head the Finance Ministry Marc Bazin, a Haitian who had been a respected official of the World Bank. After a short while in his new post, Bazin reported that at least 36 percent of Haitian government funds were being stolen. He also refused to sanction a government purchase of sugar from Ernest Bennett at a price that was roughly double the one then prevailing on the world market. Baby Doc sacked him, and he returned to exile. The United States government was disturbed, and became even more so with reports of a Haitian connection to the traffic in cocaine.[29]

During the six years from 1980, the Haitian economy contracted by some 15 percent. The favored rich, however, grew still richer by distributing the quotas for imported commodities among themselves so as to permit monopoly pricing practices. In the period from March 1984 to February 1985, for instance, one importer had over 90 percent of the quota for metal household utensils; another, over 90 percent of the quota for slippers, as well as even more of the quota for paper and plastic bags; a third, over 60 percent of the quota for toothpaste.[30] One consequence was a trade in smuggled goods that flourished the more safely with the involvement of officials and that accordingly alienated from the regime members of the legitimate business community. Meanwhile, conditions in the countryside continued to deteriorate, and peasants were further antagonized by a United States-sponsored program to deal with an outbreak of swine fever by killing the pigs, which were a traditional form of savings account.

Alongside an accelerating internal migration to the urban slums, especially those of the swollen capital, large numbers left the country altogether, for legal or illegal settlement abroad, in a much augmented process that had begun in the era of Papa Doc's rule. By 1985, there were an estimated 750,000 Haitians living in the United States, with other, much smaller communities in Canada, France, and various islands in the Caribbean. The Haitian government was undismayed that this emigration included disproportionately many of the skilled—doctors, nurses, teachers, engineers—since these were also the most likely to prove troublesome in their disaffection at home. Besides, legal remittances from emigrants to their families in Haiti provided a growing source of foreign exchange. By 1980, they were equivalent to more than a quarter of the country's total income from exports.

For many of those left behind, life became an increasing struggle merely to survive. The World Bank, using its own measure of $13.50 per adult per month as the level below which there existed a condition of "absolute poverty," estimated that 40 percent of the population in the capital were absolutely poor. The unremitting migration from the countryside was evidence of how much worse the conditions there must have been.

In November 1985, during a peaceful demonstration against food shortages in the town of Gonaïves, security forces shot dead four schoolchildren. All at once the whole country seemed to be heaving towards revolution. Students went on strike. Protest marches took command of the streets. Radio Soleil, the Roman Catholic broadcasting station, transmitted its support of reform. The Macoutes would have killed many more demonstrators than they did had they been accordingly ordered. Baby Doc, however, was not his father. He wavered. The pressure increased. At last he asked the United States government to put a plane at his disposal and agreed in return to place the Macoutes under the control of the army. On February 7, 1986, the plane took him, his family, and a much reduced retinue to exile in France.

The Haitians have a word—*parenthèse* or parenthesis—for the period of upheaval that follows the fall of one ruler and the establishment in power of another. What followed the departure of the second Duvalier was to prove a protracted parenthesis. General Henri Namphy, at the head of a military junta, took command and promised "a firm, just and good transition to democracy."[31] The source of the promise did little to promote a peaceful and patient expectancy. Besides, there was too much accumulated rage that required release.

Déchouke is the Creole word for "uproot," and the cry to *déchouke* those closely associated with so many years of deprivation and distress produced a response that an uncertain army seemed unable to contain. Macoutes were a prime target. The majority went into hiding. A few of the most prominent fled the country, with the evident connivance of the authorities. Those who were caught found as little mercy from the mobs as they in their time had shown to their prey. Where leading Duvalierists were personally beyond reach, vengeance was visited on their property instead. Yet the commanders of the army had themselves been loyal servants of the Duvalier regime. Soon the cry of *déchoukay* was being directed against Namphy.

Eminent exiles began returning to Haiti. Among them was Leslie Manigat, who had pursued a distinguished academic career abroad. On the day of his return, a demonstration outside Fort Dimanche, the prison where so many political opponents had been tortured, was dispersed by gunfire which left six dead and a hundred or so wounded. The army had indicated its determination to keep control.

Sustained by it, a makeshift government now presided over the corrupt bureaucracy, with support from an increasingly alarmed business community. The potentially formidable force of Duvalierist functionaries and Macoutes, many of them the same people, had been immobilized by fear. Reassurances from the army brought this force into the open for the pursuit of its former practices.

Confronting it was a radical popular opposition, surfacing in sometimes massive protest demonstrations through the streets. Yet this involved a large number of small groups which could or would not combine to develop a coherent strategy. Moreover, it was an urban movement, unconnected with the peasantry whose early passion for change was giving way to apathy as the old controls were reasserted.

Somewhere in between was a plethora of political parties and politicians —no fewer than two hundred candidates for the Presidency emerged— preoccupied with the prospect of elections for which no date had been set. Meanwhile, these oscillated between soliciting popular support by aligning themselves with protest, and avoiding such conduct as might provoke the army to intervene. In consequence, they tended both to promote and to demoralize the movement for change.

Under pressure from the United States for progress to elections, a Constituent Assembly was appointed, most of whose members were supposedly safe nominees. The result was startling. The Assembly produced a constitution which provided for an independent Electoral Council to organize and supervise elections and which prohibited, for a period of ten years, "notorious" and "zealous" Duvalierists from standing for election to public office. Walls were soon painted with the slogan *Aba Konstitisyon Kominis* or "Down with the Communist Constitution." This campaign of officially arranged protest, however, only commended its target to popular support. On March 29, 1987, more than 99 percent of those who defied intimidation and went to the polls voted in favor of the new constitution.[32]

In June, Namphy set out to recapture control of events by announcing that only the government, or in effect the army, had the authority to supervise elections. Mass demonstrations of protest erupted, in which scores of people were shot. Namphy retreated, but this only encouraged popular militancy, which now called for the overthrow of the government. More people were shot. In early November, the Electoral Council, having disqualified twelve others as associates of the Duvalier dictatorship, published a list of twenty-three "acceptable" candidates for the Presidency. A matter of hours later, armed men drove up to the building where the Council was lodged, ransacked it, and then set it on fire. No one from either the police station or army headquarters, both a short distance away, intervened.[33] The Macoutes were back on the streets. The message was unmistakable. The army had been asked to keep clear of elections. It would do so. Any violence or disorder would not be its responsibility.

On election day, November 29, the main independent radio stations were no longer broadcasting. Armed men had arrived the night before and smashed the transmitters. Attacks were made on polling stations across the country. People were shot on their way to vote. In the capital, Macoutes rampaged through the streets. A band of them arrived at a small school where polling was in progress. Few there or in the immediate vicinity survived the assault that followed. The Electoral Council used one of the radio stations still left broadcasting to announce that the election was canceled. The United States government cut off all but humanitarian aid. An embassy spokesman, asked by journalists whether there had been no warning of the widespread attacks, replied, "Today—today was a surprise."[34]

General Namphy appointed his own Electoral Council to supervise a new election. The four leading candidates in the first refused to take part in the second and called for a general strike. By now, though, the prevailing popular mood was a mixture of disillusionment and fear, so that there was a poor response. On election day, January 17, 1988, polling was light, and despite the stuffing of ballot boxes, the claim of the government was that 35 percent of the electorate had voted. Leslie Manigat, the returned exile, had previously declared that the army was an institution "without which—still less against which—no workable political solution can be found."[35] The favored candidate of the army, he reportedly polled just over 50 percent of the vote.

He was to last for a mere few months. Presuming that the instrument could dispense with the hand which had wielded it, he removed General Namphy as head of the army and Colonel Prosper Avril—like Namphy a former Duvalierist—as commander of the Presidential Guard. Two days later, on June 19, 1988, a coup mounted by the Presidential Guard took Namphy to the Palace as President and Manigat to the airport for a flight to the Dominican Republic. The constitution, approved so massively at the polls little more than a year before, was revoked. Colonel Avril became a general. Corpses began appearing in the streets for no more evident reason than to concentrate the minds of the living on the realities of power. Since manifestations of discontent continued, a more emphatic warning was deemed desirable. On Sunday, September 11, several hundred men, armed with a variety of weapons, marched on a Catholic church where the officiating priest was Father Jean-Bertrand Aristide, a passionately outspoken opponent of the regime. They killed thirteen people, wounded more than seventy-five, and then set fire to the church.[36]

On September 17, there was another coup. Namphy was driven to the airport, and General Avril announced that, at the request of the Presidential Guard, he found himself "forced to accept the Presidency of the military government."[37] Within a month, he had ordered the arrest of some non-commissioned officers who had helped hoist him to power but revealed destabilizing tendencies to serious reform. The United States government released some $30 million in aid to Haiti. "We are encouraged by what the Avril government is doing," a spokesman declared.

Few Haitians were similarly encouraged. During the almost eighteen months this government lasted, popular disaffection mounted, as did the disorder in the state's finances. On March 12, 1990, Avril left Haiti on a U.S. Air Force jet for the United States. After a protracted parenthesis, the first passably free elections to be held in Haiti for several decades swept Father Aristide into the Presidency, with 67 percent of the popular vote, in June 1991.

A radical with a consistent concern for the plight of the poor, Aristide began his term by spooning soup into the mouths of cripples and beggars on the Palace lawns, cutting his own pay from $25,000 to $4,500 a month and donating that to successive worthy causes, and turning Fort Dimanche into a museum.[38] Those rather more accustomed to spooning soup from the tureen of the state into their own mouths grew increasingly alarmed. Many in the mainly Catholic mulatto elite, which had seen much of its old ascendancy restored since the end of the Papa Doc era, made a distinction between the messages conveyed in church and the duties they owed to themselves. The Macoutes and the army had little but grief to expect from a priest more militant than meek. On September 30, General Raoul Cédras, head of the army, mounted a coup that dispatched the new President into exile.

In June 1992, Marc Bazin, the very candidate whom Aristide had so overwhelmingly defeated a year before, was made Prime Minister by the military regime. A trade embargo, imposed by the Organization of American States but without a blockade to enforce it, opened profitable opportunities for businessmen, government officials, and army officers to dispose of acquired imports with value added for themselves in the supposed national interest. Cocaine in transit, of which only an estimated 15 percent was seized, for symbolic purposes, afforded financial transfusions, as did continued remittances from emigrants reluctant to let their relatives starve. The new Clinton administration in Washington, just before taking office, reportedly offered the Haitian military leaders a $50 million inducement to restore democracy.[39] Those responsible for the proposal clearly had little idea of how much such rulers could loot for themselves through corruption and terror.

Within a year of the coup, at least three thousand people—political opponents or simply those attacked at random to prove a point—had been killed in Haiti. Tens of thousands more were taking to virtually anything that floated in the hope of making their way to safety in the United States. The United States Coast Guard, with a naval blockade that flouted international law as well as endlessly professed principles of humanitarianism, stopped the Haitian vessels on the high seas, arrested refugees, and returned them to Haiti. This was not how the United States had treated and continued to treat refugees from Cuba.

The embarrassment that all this caused the Clinton administration might well have contributed to the hardening of United States policy toward the Haitian military regime. The United Nations moved to impose an embargo on oil and arms shipments and a freezing of Haiti's official financial assets, such as they were. A few days later, on July 3, 1993, Aristide and Cédras signed an agreement, drawn up by U.N. and U.S. negotiators, for Aristide's return as President to Haiti, the retirement of Cédras as head of the army, and a political amnesty for those involved in the coup of 1991. U.S. assistance to the island's stricken economy was reportedly expected to exceed $1 billion over the following five years.[40] By the end of July 1994, the army had not yet permitted Aristide to return and the U.S. government had secured a U.N. resolution authorizing the use of force to remove the Haitian military regime. A deal with the regime brokered by former U.S. President Jimmy Carter, in September, ensured that the arrival of some 12,000 U.S. troops met no resistance. Cédras, along with some of his associates, soon departed, and Aristide returned, to much popular rejoicing, in mid-October. The Haitian people have had occasion to rejoice before. They deserve better than to find this one turn into merely another parenthesis.

The movement in Cuba for an end to Spanish colonial rule engaged a range of different interests, from that of native planters, who looked for a more assured way of prolonging slavery, to that of radicals, whose clamor for civil rights encompassed the freeing of the slaves. In 1868, rebellion broke out, accompanied by a manifesto which echoed the American Declaration of Independence in its first principle ("We believe that all men were created equal") but qualified the application of this ("We desire the gradual, indemnified emancipation of slaves").

It was the beginning of what would come to be known as the Ten Years' War, which would cost in its course some 200,000 lives and $700 million in the value of property lost.[1] The Spanish army, backed by the bulk of the substantial Spanish population on the island, was favored by the odds. In fact, the rebellion would not have lasted nearly as long as it did without two exceptional military commanders, the Dominican-born Máximo Gómez and the mulatto Antonio Maceo, initially marginalized because of his color and then reluctantly advanced in response to his achievements. Together they conducted a guerrilla war directed mainly at spreading devastation and disorder. Both would have had the rebellion commit itself to freeing the slaves. Maceo, in the absence of such a commitment, led raids on plantations to free the slaves himself. Arguably, the rebellion might even have succeeded if it had adjusted its sights to the view of its most effective military commanders and accordingly sharpened its appeal to the population of color. Its political leadership, however, would have none of this.

In 1877, the rebellion suffered a series of serious setbacks, and its political leadership communicated a readiness to negotiate the terms of a settlement. The government of Spain offered an amnesty, some measure of political reform, and the freeing of slaves who had fought on the rebel side. When an armistice was signed in February 1878, Maceo repudiated it. Peace, he insisted, was inseparable from the abolition of slavery and the grant of independence. With 1,500 followers in Oriente, he continued the war, but, without wider rebel support, capitulated in May and went into exile.

The Spanish negotiator of the settlement had expressed himself sympathetic to the abolitionist cause in his discussions with Maceo. In 1879, he became Prime Minister of Spain and announced that slavery in Cuba would end in 1888. No compensation would be provided to slave owners, but slaves would be required to serve an eight-year period of paid apprenticeship, the *patronato*, out of which they would buy their freedom at the rate of $30–50 a year. Between 1880 and 1886, the number of slaves in Cuba plummeted from some 200,000 to scarcely 26,000, and the *patronato* was abolished two years early. The planters, after raging for so long against the very idea of abolition, had found contract wage labor more productive and cheaper; indeed, the move from the one form of labor to the other is estimated to have saved the average planter at least 50 percent in overall costs.[2] Rather than continuing to pay the apprenticeship fee and meet the costs of upkeep, the planters had simply proceeded to free their slaves.

In its new frame of mind, the Spanish government took measures to promote racial integration. It banned the exclusion of anyone from public employment solely on racial grounds, outlawed discrimination against blacks or mulattoes in theaters, cafés, and bars, and ordered that state schools should admit black and mulatto children on the same basis as white ones. Yet the law was not always obeyed and, besides, dealt only with certain racist practices. Cubans of color were, for instance, still segregated at swimming pools along the coast. Not least, economic differences effected their own forms of segregation. There were few state schools, while other ones discriminated, by fees, locality, or social attitudes, against children of color.

The new dispensation soon proved little more acceptable than the old. The Spanish party in Cuba dominated elections on a restricted franchise. The captain-general retained the power to ban public meetings and to exile critics. Spanish rule had been and remained shamelessly corrupt. It was also bad for business. The island's main market for exports of sugar and tobacco was the United States. Spain imposed various taxes and restrictions to increase its share of Cuban trade.

The independence movement needed only an inspirational leader. It found one in José Martí. Born of Spanish parents in Havana in 1853, he was drawn to the cause of independence while still at school, where the rebellion of 1868 enjoyed widespread support among his fellow students. Outspoken in his views, he was imprisoned at the age of sixteen and was subsequently twice deported to Spain. In 1879, he established his base in New York, where he worked as a journalist and headed the Cuban revolutionary committee. He found little to allure him in the culture of the United States and much to alarm him in that nation's imperial longings.

Tirelessly, in his writings, at public meetings, and by clandestine planning, he prepared for an attempt to wrest Cuban independence from Spain through a popular rebellion. By 1892, he had succeeded in engaging in his design both Gómez and Maceo. In March 1895, with groups of armed revolutionaries ready to leave for Cuba, the two issued a manifesto which was primarily the work of Martí himself. This promised a free republic and a new economic system able to provide work for all, called specifically on blacks to join in the struggle, and declared that those who spoke of the Negro race as a threat to a free Cuba were committed to maintaining Spanish rule indefinitely.

The expeditionary forces landed in April. On May 19, Martí was killed in a skirmish. The revolutionary cause lost its leader and gained a martyr. Gathering recruits, the revolutionaries numbered by June somewhere between six and eight thousand, to confront fifty-two thousand Spanish troops backed by nineteen warships. The revolution, however, enjoyed spreading support, especially among blacks, who came to constitute over 80 percent of the fighting force by the end of the year. Gómez and Maceo, employing their developed skills in guerrilla warfare and concentrating on the selective destruction of property, made much of the countryside unsafe for the movement of government troops.

A troubled Madrid sent to Cuba a general of formidable repute, Valeriano Weyler. Acting promptly and ruthlessly, he organized the population into military districts and recruited groups of counterinsurgents to protect or pillage the countryside. Reports of atrocities were fed by representatives of the revolutionary cause to United States newspapers captivated by the vision of their country's "manifest destiny" in the hemisphere. By the end of 1896, Weyler's strategy was showing signs of success; Maceo had been killed in battle, and the less highly motivated in the revolutionary forces were beginning to desert. The war dragged on, however, at great cost to Spain in men and money, while increasing the likelihood of military intervention by the United States. In November 1897, Madrid summoned Weyler home and offered Cuba a form of home rule. The command of the revolutionary forces rejected the offer.

In February 1898, the warship U.S.S. *Maine*, anchored in Havana harbor ostensibly to evacuate citizens of the United States if necessary, exploded with the loss of 266 lives. Urged on by a bellicose press and ignoring the communicated readiness of a now dismayed Spanish government to accept virtually any terms for a peaceful settlement, the United States declared war on Spain in April and speedily seized the Spanish possessions of Puerto Rico and the Philippines as well as Cuba.

More than ever alive to the danger that the United States might come to annex Cuba, supporters of Cuban independence had shortly before, with the help of $2 million distributed among certain senators,[3] succeeded in steering through the United States Congress the so-called Teller Amendment on Cuba. This required the United States government to disclaim "any disposition or interest to exercise sovereignty, jurisdiction or control over the said island except for the pacification thereof and assert its determination, when that is accomplished, to leave the government and the control of the island to its people."

Capable only of hope that the Teller Amendment meant what it said, the revolutionary forces submitted to the United States occupation. The new rulers proved to be more efficient and less corrupt than the old. They restored the stricken economy, reorganized local government and the courts, dredged harbors and built highways and railroads, much increased the number of state schools, and virtually eliminated the scourge of yellow fever which had been taking an average of 750 lives a year in Havana alone. They also, however, paraded an insensate racial arrogance. Even the officials who undertook the census in 1899 abandoned science for bigotry. Having found a decline in the black and mulatto share of the population, they identified this as "doubtless but another illustration of the inability of an inferior race to hold its own in competition with a superior one."[4]

There had, indeed, been such a decline, but one that had been due to rather different factors. While white immigration had increased, the importation of blacks had all but ceased with the approach of an end to slavery. Furthermore, as the census findings themselves demonstrated, there was a close correlation between color and social deprivation, with all the effects of this in malnutrition, disease, and early death. Blacks and mulattoes owned only 5 percent of the farms, and almost all of these were small (less than twenty-five acres). They outnumbered whites in such low-paid occupations as laundering, shoemaking, woodcutting, and, of course, domestic service. They accounted for only 3 of the island's 1,406 lawyers; 10 of its 1,223 physicians; 17 of its 473 government officials; 17 of its 245 journalists; 102 of its 1,708 teachers; and 3,453 of its 47,265 merchants.[5]

By 1900, partly in response to mounting popular Cuban pressure for an end to the occupation, the United States was moving toward compliance with the Teller Amendment, but only by rewriting the script of ascendancy. A Cuban Constitutional Convention was presented with the conditions, which came to be known collectively as the Platt Amendment. This limited the powers of a Cuban government to contract foreign debt and conclude treaties with foreign countries, conceded certain naval facilities to the United States, and invested the United States with the right to intervene for the preservation of Cuban independence and the maintenance of orderly government. Recognizing no alternative, the Convention acquiesced.

Cuba became a protectorate in all but name. Spanish rule had been characterized by a disregard of civil rights, a view of government as an opportunity for private plunder, and a racial prejudice rather more relaxed than in the country which was now the island's guardian. The United States would accommodate itself with little difficulty to two-thirds of the Spanish colonial legacy, as long as sufficient order was maintained. In racial matters, its influence would be mainly malign.

Tomás Estrada Palma, respected for his long service to the cause of independence, was elected President and took office on the departure of the United States Governor in May 1902. An able administrator of personal probity, he enriched the Treasury but was less attentive or competent in his command of political developments. The elections to the national Congress in February 1904 were corruptly conducted by both contending parties. In its aftermath, preoccupation with the spoils of power promoted an increasing readiness to threaten or employ violence in the interest of maintaining or achieving access.

Palma was reelected in December 1905, and by September 1906, some twenty-four thousand armed rebels of the Liberal opposition confronted a government without an army. On September 29, 2,000 United States marines landed, and Cuba soon had a United States Governor again. Charles Magoon reorganized the civil service, laid the basis for a standing army that he hoped would secure the authority of government, and introduced electoral reforms. José Miguel Gómez, the Liberal leader, won the relatively clean presidential election of November 1908. The intervention by the United States ended in February 1909, to mark the start of corrupt government on a massive scale.

From the President down to the lowest local official, power was employed for pillage. Anything that could be bought, from a building contract to a pardon, was sold. A national lottery was instituted, to become, through control over the sale of tickets, a prime channel for the transmission of patronage and kickbacks. Any interference by the United States was somewhat inhibited by the large local involvement of United States economic interests in their exploitation of corrupt practices.

Such was scarcely the new social system which Martí and other leaders of the 1895 revolutionary engagement had envisaged and which blacks especially had been given to expect. One disillusioned black, Evaristo Estenoz, had already in 1907 founded the Independent Party of Color, protesting that blacks, so disproportionately represented in the ranks of those who had fought for independence, had been "robbed . . . of all the fruits of victory."[6] Arrested in 1910, he was soon freed, but a new law banned political parties based on color. In May 1912, a black rebellion began, to the accompaniment of demonstrations and strikes across the island. The government, alerted and prompt in its response, rapidly crushed the rising everywhere except in Oriente. There, United States marines landed at the end of May, ostensibly "to protect sugar estates."[7] They were not needed. Government troops defeated some four thousand black rebels commanded by Estenoz and then hunted down surviving small bands of black guerrillas.

Blacks continued to be generally excluded from the political and cultural life of the country, except for the Afro-Cuban rhythms to which whites increasingly danced. They retained, however, a cultural life of their own, notably in Afro-Cuban cults which the government viewed with indifference.

In 1912, after the crushing of the black rebellion, the United States-owned United Fruit Company sought permission to import 1,400 Haitian laborers for its plantations in Oriente, and President Gómez lifted the ban on black immigration which had been imposed in 1898. During the next ten years, more than 150,000 blacks, mainly from Haiti and Jamaica, where wages were low and unemployment high, arrived. Although required to leave at the end of their contracts, many stayed on illegally, with most of these settling in the cities. Government connivance at their presence would seem to suggest that they were viewed as a labor supply whose submissiveness could be the more easily secured by the threat of deportation hanging over them.

Elected in 1912 to the Presidency was the Conservative candidate, General Mario García Menocal, a man so devoted to corruption that he would eventually leave office, in 1921, with a personal fortune estimated at $40 million. The discontent of the opposition Liberals erupted in rebellion after his blatantly rigged reelection in 1916. The government of the United States condemned the rebellion and sold Menocal a quantity of arms. The regime soon crushed the rebellion, and Menocal proceeded to govern largely by decree.

His chosen successor, Alfredo Zayas, won a presidential election marked by widespread violence and fraud in November 1920. He appealed to the United States for financial help, and Cuba was provided with a loan on pledges of fiscal prudence and political reform. After the arrival of the money, Zayas ignored the pledges and concentrated on more profitable concerns. By January 1923, the University of Havana was in a ferment of disaffection, led by the newly formed Students' Federation (FEU). Other protest groups surfaced, notably the Cuban Committee of National and Civil Renovation, whose manifesto was composed by Fernando Ortiz, the Cuban anthropologist renowned for his writings on Afro-Cuban culture. Corruption rather than the plight of blacks was the concern. Against a background of threatening rebellion, Gerardo Machado won the presidential election of 1924 for the Liberals.

One plunderer, it soon became clear, had merely been replaced by another. In August 1925, the Cuban Communist Party was founded. During the flurry of strikes that followed, a number of labor leaders lost their lives. While diverting to himself and his friends a flow of funds each year equivalent to a fifth of Cuba's gross national product, Machado kept the army loyal by expanding its resources and appointing to key positions officers he regarded as reliable. Then, as the date of the next presidential election approached, he postponed it by getting his term extended from four to six years. The assent of Congress was assured by the expedient of extending its term as well. Thomas Lamont of the influential New York bank J. P. Morgan expressed the hope that Cubans would find a way of keeping Machado in power indefinitely.[8]

With such a prospect in mind, Machado arranged for a constitutional convention in April 1928, effectively to prolong still further his stay in office. Even many in the middle class who had so far remained indifferent found this intolerable. The United States government seemed unmoved. The Chase National Bank in New York supplied the Machado regime with a succession of loans. In early 1932, a secret society, calling itself ABC and drawn from among the youth of the middle class, launched a campaign of violence directed in particular at the more notorious police chiefs. It was now, paradoxically, the Communist Party that came to the aid of the regime. Having promoted a widespread strike of sugar workers, it became apprehensive of United States intervention and concluded a deal with Machado. In return for his agreement to adopt a more nationalist posture toward the United States, it condemned ABC as "fascist" and called off the sugar strike.

In all this turmoil blacks played such an insignificant part that reports, almost certainly emanating from the regime itself, were rife of mass black support for Machado. This would not have been altogether incomprehensible. Many of Machado's police were mulattoes. Machado himself was known to be providing the Afro-Cuban cults with money. His middle-class opponents were also the main source of racist opinions and practices. Yet it is likely that blacks were not so much loyal as they were indifferent. They had been politically marginalized for so long that they may well have regarded the conflict as merely a domestic quarrel among whites.

The new Roosevelt administration in the United States sought a suitable settlement in Cuba, sent an ambassador there to mediate, and encouraged the process with financial pressures. Meanwhile, labor militancy mounted in Cuba. The Communist Party itself shifted position again, in the belief that United States intervention would become inevitable if Machado stayed in power. In early August 1933, the call for a general strike was so widely observed in Havana that, for the first time in Cuban history, even the cafés and bars all put up their shutters. Senior officers in the army began to change sides. On the night of August 12–13, Machado left Cuba by plane with five bags of gold.

Popular rejoicing turned into a riot of revenge which claimed more than a thousand lives. An interim government, whose membership owed much to the preferences of the United States ambassador, proved unable to deal with a disintegrating civil order and spreading strikes for higher wages. Fulgencio Batista, an army-sergeant stenographer with a reputation for charm and quick wits, mounted a successful coup from a base camp on the discontent of noncommissioned officers, elevated himself to the rank of colonel, and took command of the army. The United States government ignored its own ambassador's pleas for intervention and in January 1934 formally recognized a Cuban government headed by Colonel Carlos Mendieta. Many blacks, as well as others in the sunken sector of the population, saw some reason for hope. Batista himself was a mulatto; he and most of his associates in control of the army had come from a background of labor and poverty.

The Platt Amendment was at last abrogated in a treaty signed in March 1934, though United States possession of the Guantánamo base was confirmed. It made no difference to the economic overlordship of the United States. In the aftermath of the 1920 sugar-price collapse and the related financial crisis, United States interests had come to control well over half of all the island's sugar production. The preferential treatment given to Cuban sugar and tobacco in the United States market was crucial to the island's economy. An agreement signed in August 1934 increased Cuban dependence even further. By providing preferential treatment for manufactured goods from the United States, it not only established a virtually captive market for them in Cuba but impeded the development of a substantial manufacturing sector there.

As civil disorder continued, the regime increasingly relied on violence to sustain itself. It suspended constitutional guarantees, made such disruptive acts as the burning of sugarcane a capital offense, outlawed troublesome trade unions, and confiscated their funds. Social reforms were meant to sweeten the repression. A minimum wage was introduced; employees were protected against dismissal without due cause; women were given the vote. When elections were allowed in January 1936, Miguel Mariano Gómez was elected President. He did not last long. He defied Batista by opposing military control of rural schools. He was impeached and, before the year was up, gave way to his more tractable Vice-President.

New social measures, associated with Batista's control of the Congress, included paid holidays for workers and a guarantee of tenure to the *colonos* or smallholders who leased their land. The Constitution of 1940 entitled all children to eight years of primary education and outlawed racial segregation. In the presidential election of the same year, the least corruptly conducted since that of 1912, Batista polled almost 60 percent of the votes.

With the entry of the United States and Cuba into the Second World War, the two governments drew still closer together. Cuba provided the United States with military facilities and got in return improved trade agreements and fresh flows of credit. The war also brought to Cuba, along with a high price for sugar, shortages of all sorts and an inflation that eroded the purchasing power of wages. Corruption flourished. Batista himself made much of being the protector of the poor. He was so concerned to preserve himself from joining their number that he would leave office with a huge private fortune, estimated by a cabinet colleague at $20 million.[9] He did not stand for reelection in 1944. He may have wished to project the image of a genuine democrat, uneasy at perpetuating his own power. Certainly, he seems to have believed that his chosen candidate would be successful. He was mistaken and departed for Florida, where he was reported to have investments in real estate.

The onetime academic and new President, Dr. Ramón Grau San Martín, was expected to provide prosperity with probity and order without violence. He presided instead over a period of mounting corruption, disorder, and gangsterism. Even the pension and social security funds, entrusted to the Treasury and so far safe, were relentlessly pillaged. Proliferating political factions took to shooting out their differences. Lectures at the University of Havana were frequently interrupted by gunfire. By the arrival of the next presidential election, won by Dr. Grau's protégé and Minister of Labor, Carlos Prío, on a minority vote, disillusionment with the political system was gathering pace. It continued to do so under the new President, who attacked his predecessor for corruption but, on an annual salary of $25,000, spent between two and three million on the building of his private home.[10]

In 1948, elected to serve as a senator in the Cuban Congress, Batista returned from Florida. Four years later, he announced that he would be a candidate in the forthcoming presidential election. Then, apparently doubtful of the result, he once again mounted a successful coup. On March 10 he suspended constitutional guarantees for forty-five days and promised free elections to follow. The United States did not wait. It formally recognized the new regime within a fortnight. The elections would be a long time in coming. And when they came, they would be far from free. Meanwhile, a younger Cuban was already engaged in preparing for a revolutionary challenge.

In 1945, Fidel Castro Ruz, son of a successful Spanish-born farmer in Oriente, had arrived at the University of Havana. Soon a leading student activist, particularly impassioned in opposing United States domination of the hemisphere, he graduated as a lawyer in 1950, but then devoted himself more to politics than to any pursuit of his profession. He gathered around him a group of the like-minded, some 90 percent of whom were, by his own account, workers and farmers. Few, however, were black, and the racial issue did not feature among Castro's concerns.

Two armed attacks, planned for July 26, 1953, the main one on the Moncada military barracks in Santiago and the other on the barracks in Bayamo, were directed at seizing arms and igniting a popular rebellion for liberty and social reform. They ended in disaster. The few blacks and mulattoes among the hundred prisoners taken were taunted by black soldiers for having followed a white revolutionary against such a friend of color as Batista had shown himself to be. "You a revolutionary, you?" one black soldier rebuked a black bricklayer. "You don't know that Negroes can't be revolutionaries? Negroes are either thieves or partisans of Batista, not revolutionaries."[11]

Castro, his standing enhanced by the eloquent speech he made at his trial, was sentenced to fifteen years' imprisonment. Neither the speech nor its elaborated version in the pamphlet "History Will Absolve Me," which emerged for clandestine circulation in June 1954, referred anywhere to the racial issue. There was a prescient mournfulness in the song of the mulatto Carlos Puebla, then performing at a restaurant in Havana:

Los caminos de mi Cuba
Nunca van a donde deben.

The roads of my Cuba
Never lead where they should.[12]

By the time that the promised elections were at last allowed to be held, in November 1954, Batista had so packed the election boards that his rival had withdrawn in protest, and he was returned unopposed, with only half of the electorate reported as voting. Moved to make a magnanimous gesture, he declared a general amnesty in April 1955, which led to the release of Castro and other surviving prisoners from the July 26 venture. In the aftermath, Batista seemed to have some cause for confidence. The opposition was disunited. Student riots were easily contained with the exercise of a brutality that by now had become common. Capital was flowing in from the United States, much of it connected with the Mafia, for new casinos to prey on the increasing number of tourists. Representing the views of the local United States business community, the *Havana Post*, in an editorial of March 19, 1956, declared: "All in all, the Batista regime has much to commend it."

In fact, the regime was rotten and required only a sufficient push to send it crashing. Castro provided this with a guerrilla war, planned from a base in Mexico. Overcoming the initial disaster of the landing in late November 1956, a force reduced to only fifteen fighters established itself in the Sierra Maestra mountain range. Gathering and training recruits from the rebellious in the cities, as well as from a protective peasantry, it proceeded to spread disruption over an ever wider area of eastern Cuba.

In May 1958, Batista launched a belated major military offensive. In June, a whole battalion of his army was ambushed and defeated in battle. The capture of radio equipment and the army code book now enabled the guerrilla forces to know in advance the pattern of army movements. In July, after other defeats, a demoralized army withdrew in such disorder that large quantities of arms were left behind for the guerrilla forces to use. A new presidential election in November, won by Batista's candidate on a reported poll of only

30 percent, was no more than a sideshow. Across the island, town after town was falling to the advance of the revolution. On New Year's Day 1959, Batista departed for the Dominican Republic.

The black component of the total population had long been increasing. Walterio Carbonell, a black Cuban who served the Castro regime for a while as one of its more influential diplomats, has estimated that the proportion had reached at least 50 percent by the time of the revolution. There is, however, no acceptable official evidence of what the racial ratio then was or would later come to be, with the exodus mainly of whites. The racial details identified in the 1970 census were never published, and the published details of the census in 1981, which left racial classification to the enumerators, were widely distrusted. Demography proved simply too sensitive a subject for the regime. What remains are more or less well-informed estimates. In 1983, *Quid*, the French yearbook, reported the ethnic proportions as "blacks 55 percent, whites 30 percent, mulattoes 15 percent, orientals 1 percent." In the same year, Jean Ziegler, a Swiss sociologist, cited a consensus among foreign specialists that Afro-Cubans probably exceeded 65 percent of a total population then roughly ten million.[13]

The silence of the revolutionary leadership on the racial issue was finally broken on March 22, 1959, in response to a public challenge from several prominent blacks. In the course of a televised speech, Castro proclaimed that the revolution would confront racial discrimination in employment, education, and recreation. "We all have lighter or darker skin color," he said. "Lighter skin implies descent from Spaniards who themselves were colonized by Moors that came from Africa. Those who are more or less dark-skinned came directly from Africa. Moreover, nobody can consider himself as being of pure, much less superior, race."[14]

The uproar which followed from among Cubans of lighter skin was such that, only three days later, Castro devoted a televised press conference to the issue. In condemning racial prejudice, he cited the instance of "a young lady" who had objected to his speech and had in particular complained that ever since its delivery, "Negroes have been walking around all over Havana getting fresh." He proceeded to reassure her and others in revealing terms. "I am perfectly sure that more than ever—precisely because with greater honesty than ever before their call for justice is being defended—Cuban Negroes will be even more respectful than ever. They are conscious that not to be so would give the enemies of the Revolution cause to attack them."[15]

His attitude toward blacks had advanced a long way from that of his father, who had hated them. It had not, however, moved beyond the Hispanic American ideal of a paternalism that did not consult blacks on what they wanted, but determined what was best for them and expected respect in return. This would not have mattered so much if only the revolutionary leadership had developed a democratic structure by which blacks might have promoted their own priorities. Instead, from the start and increasingly as the revolution ran into foreign and domestic difficulties, Castro's personal ascendancy determined policies, and these essentially reflected his own view that blacks needed only to recognize the benefits which the regime conferred on them.

All the same, many blacks responded to the new dispensation with gratitude and allegiance. Some exulted in the belief that they were now effectively whites. One army sentry rejoiced in his membership at a country club from which blacks had previously been barred. "It's hard to say to myself: Pablito, all that's finished. You're not a nigger anymore. Ever since Fidel said, 'Negroes and white folk are all the same, all just men,' I look myself in the mirror every morning. 'Pablito,' I say, 'Pablito, you're not a nigger anymore. You've become a white man. Fidel said so and Fidel's always right.' "[16]

Others were more critical. In April 1959, during a televised discussion on the declared commitment to racial integration, Dr. Eudaldo Gutiérrez Paula, formerly a distinguished black opponent of the Batista regime and now national chairman of the Association of Cuban Journalists, broke ranks. He pointed out that revolutionary blacks were conspicuously absent from Castro's cabinet and argued that integration should have started at the top. He was denounced by his fellow panelists and soon enough subjected to the displeasure of the regime.

Repression was not restricted to only such embarrassing criticism. It was extended, avowedly in the cause of integration, to the very assertiveness of a black consciousness and its claims. The mutual-aid *Sociedades de Color* (Societies of Color) had long been channels for the expression of Afro-Cuban cultural and social concerns. In short order, their functions were limited to weekend parties, the proceeds of their festivities were confiscated, and their national headquarters and provincial offices were closed. All 526 societies ceased to exist, and their national president, the sociologist Juán René Betancourt Bencomo, went into exile.

Disillusioned blacks were still, however, far outnumbered by those loyal to a revolution which was dismantling segregationist barriers and providing new opportunities for employment: Not least, as relations between the regime and the United States government deteriorated, Castro exploited the contrast between the way blacks were being treated in the United States and their treatment in Cuba. Castro was soon afforded the means to amplify this message.

In September 1960, he arrived in New York to attend a meeting of the United Nations General Assembly. The management of the Manhattan hotel where visiting Cuban diplomats had often stayed in the past now affrontingly demanded payment in advance, and reports, ridiculing the conduct of the Cuban delegation in its rooms, appeared in the press. The Cuban party moved to the Hotel Theresa in Harlem, where a crowd of blacks gathered to greet Castro, while huge rallies in Cuba denounced racism in the United States.

At the prompting of Walterio Carbonell, moreover, Castro was already engaged in promoting close relations with the independent states of Africa, for an influence that could offset Cuba's increasing military and economic dependence on the Soviet Union. When in October, President Sékou Touré of Guinea paid a state visit to Cuba, blacks from across the island poured into Havana and demonstrated their enthusiasm.

Carbonell made the mistake of supposing that such alliances might well promote a more tolerant attitude from the regime toward the expression of the black identity in Cuba. During Touré's visit, in an essay published by *Revolución*, Carbonell wrote that the policy of the government toward Afro-Cuban culture would be the test of its sincerity in developing a commitment to black Africa. Some months later, in his published book on Cuban culture, he ascribed to "African religions" the success of Afro-Cubans in preventing Spanish colonialism from destroying their rich ancestral heritage:

> Thanks to the vitality of these religions, black music could survive: the rhythms and music that gave birth to Cuban music, the highest expression of our culture. I have said that these religious organizations have played a politically and culturally progressive role in the forging of our nationality. This statement may surprise many, because up till now the contrary thesis has prevailed, that is, that black religions are a manifestation of savagery . . . As a matter of fact, the silence of certain revolutionary writers concerning the political and cultural role of these cults of African origin is becoming highly suspect. [17]

Within three months of its publication, the book was withdrawn from sale and was subsequently banned by Castro's personal order. Carbonell himself was sacked from the Cuban Foreign Ministry. In December 1961, a National Institute of Ethnology and Folklore was established, to conduct continuous research into "religious sects of African origin." It made no secret, however, of its primary purpose. "Studies will be centered," it declared, "on those sects which have come into conflict with the Revolution."[18] The regime also looked, to be sure, with distinct disfavor on organized Christianity. Yet generally it did not prevent the churches from functioning or persecute their priests. Its treatment of the Afro-Cuban cults was more aggressively hostile. Increasingly, restrictions were placed on their functioning; their leaders were often arrested and sometimes imprisoned; their adherents encountered discrimination in employment. Such activities and affiliations, it was clear, were intolerable to a regime which required a national uniformity behind Castro's view of the socialist commitment.

What was involved here also, however, was the regime's peculiar rage at such behavior by blacks as smacked of ingratitude for all the benefits conferred on them by the revolution. In mid-April 1961, a force of some thirteen hundred exiles, materially backed by the CIA, landed at Cuba's Bay of Pigs in what proved to be a disastrous enterprise in initiating a counterrevolution. Some fifty blacks in the invasion force were taken prisoner, and Castro personally visited two of them in custody. Furiously he berated them for having betrayed not only their country but, in an echo of the rebuke from Batista's black soldiers to black captives from the Moncada barracks assault some eight years before, their race. When all the prisoners were brought to the sports arena in Havana for an examination which he personally conducted, Castro became suddenly enraged by the sight of the black Tomás Cruz among them. "You, Negro, what are you doing here?" he asked and then proceeded to cite the benefits "given" to blacks by the revolution, including the right to go swimming with whites. "I don't have any complex about my color or my race," Cruz replied. "And I did not come here to go swimming."[19]

Sékou Touré's visit was followed, at the invitation of the Cuban government, by the arrival of nineteen Guinean students in October 1961. By their own subsequent accounts, they became bitterly disillusioned by what they found: "We arrived believing the Revolution was homogeneous, for all and with all. But little by little we discovered the racial cleavage. It was Black and white, subtly divided in a thousand different ways and with the latter having the upper hand." Cuban officialdom resented their attempts to establish personal relations with black Cubans and placed every obstacle in the way. Their particular wish to attend Afro-Cuban cult ceremonies was continually frustrated. Nor did they have "any real contact" with white Cubans, especially the women, "who would flee from us."[20]

The objective of an alliance with black Africa was scarcely better served during the so-called missile crisis of October 1962, when evidence that the Soviet Union was installing nuclear missiles on Cuba led the United States government to demand their withdrawal, and the Cuban populace was mobilized to meet the possibility of a United States military invasion.[21] Castro, in the course of addressing the Cuban nation, drew an invidious contrast between the capacity of Cuba to resist aggression and that of Africa to resist Western intervention. "Cuba is not the Congo," he declared, and huge posters, bearing this message, soon appeared across the island. African diplomats and students in Cuba were indignant. Yet Castro, it is certain, had no intention of offending them. Indeed, it was his very failure to realize that he would be doing so which said much about his attitude toward blacks both in Africa and in Cuba itself.

After the Soviet Union decided, without even consulting Castro, to withdraw its missiles from Cuba, the regime sought to reassert itself by a more vigorous commitment to promoting alliances in Africa. While blacks remained rare within the political leadership at home, they came to be prominent as representatives of that leadership in missions to African capitals. The embassy in Algiers was soon second only to Moscow as a center of the regime's diplomatic activity. When war broke out between Algeria and Morocco in October 1963, Cuba was quick to supply its Algerian ally with substantial military assistance, including ships, tanks, fighter planes, and two thousand troops.

This was the precursor of a wider military engagement, announced by the President of Cuba, Osvaldo Dorticós Torrado, when attending the summit of nonaligned states at Cairo in October 1964. Cuba, he declared, would provide "solidarity and backing for the liberation movements of the peoples of Angola, Mozambique, so-called Portuguese Guinea . . . and all other African peoples engaged in the liberation struggle."[22] It did not take long for this commitment to be tested. In November, Belgium and the United States intervened in the Congo civil war to sustain a government subservient to Western interests.

Some weeks later, "Che" Guevara, on a visit to Algiers, stressed the racial linkage between Africa and Cuba. The advance guard of what would be two Cuban battalions was already in the Congo. This was part of a design for a Black Diaspora force which would include blacks from the United States. There, the crucial figure was Malcolm X, and his assassination in February 1965 effectively ended the possibility of that involvement, but Guevara did not abandon the rest of the design. He recruited to the Cuban force Dominican and Haitian blacks who had been receiving guerrilla warfare instruction in Cuba, and all others in the force were Cuban blacks, except for the commander, Guevara himself.

Even before "Operation Congo" got going, it suffered a serious setback. On June 20, 1965, a military coup removed from power in Algeria Cuba's paramount African ally, Ahmed Ben Bella. The new regime withdrew all support from the enterprise, and complex logistical arrangements fell away, along with the promise of token forces from several African states. Guevara pressed ahead, however, to set out for the Congo in July.

The whole venture met with increasing problems, from the rivalry of three separate rebel movements, each with its own war zone, to dwindling African support from among even radical African regimes for the Cuban engagement. On November 25, Colonel Joseph Mobutu came to power in the Congo by a coup and launched a military campaign, guided by counterinsurgency experts from the United States, in the area where the Cubans were operating. In January 1966, Guevara withdrew his forces to the former French colony of Congo (Brazzaville), with the intention of continuing the war in the neighboring western part of the Congo. By now, however, African support for the enterprise had virtually evaporated, and in March, by direct order from Castro himself, Guevara reluctantly left for Cuba, to be killed in the following year while conducting a guerrilla warfare campaign in Bolivia.

The heightened commitment to Africa did little to change the climate for blacks in Cuba. By 1966, there were five hundred students from various African countries on the island.[23] Complaints from among them that they were subject to racial prejudice were all too frequent and scarcely lessened by the occasional expulsion of some students for being "racially divisive." Ninety Congolese ones themselves insisted on being sent home, after a fight with Cuban soldiers who, they maintained, had made racist remarks. The regime took the course of isolating foreign students on the Island of Youth rather than confronting the cause of their discontent.

Still worse, prominent black radicals from abroad, welcomed with much publicity as visitors or exiles, did not always find the revolution as racially agreeable as they had been led to expect. Robert Williams arrived from the United States in 1961, left in 1966 for China, and from there, in a newsletter, assailed the subtle racism in Cuba. In August 1967, Stokely Carmichael, the Black Power radical, arrived to attend, as a special guest, a meeting of the newly formed Organization for Latin American Solidarity and was presented by Castro to a rally with the assurance, "Stokely, this is your house!"[24] Shortly afterward, in Paris, he expressed his doubts about the extent of the "racial democracy" trumpeted to him by Cuban officials during his stay, since his own impression had been that Cuba's top leadership was all white and that blacks were in no positions of real power.[25] Castro's interest in the black radicals of the United States shifted to the Black Panthers, whose doctrines of class struggle were closer to his own. On December 25, 1968, their leading intellectual, Eldridge Cleaver, arrived secretly in Cuba but was soon complaining of racism there and, after a few months, left for Algeria.

Certainly, while ready to applaud manifestations of black militancy in the United States, the Castro regime continued to regard and treat black assertiveness in any form at home as an altogether different matter. From 1967 onward, black Cubans who adopted "Afro" hairstyles or clothes were summoned for rebuke to the nearest police station or the more menacing Ministry of the Interior. An important review, Casa, published an essay by Alberto Pedro, which warned against "falling prey to the fetishistic belief that the world's racial problems can be solved by the mere fact of donning African tribal garments—regardless of their beauty—or by importing a traditional god, like Shango, from Bahia or the Guinea Coast." The essay concluded:

The problem is even more serious since oppression has practically emptied the Negro's head; where there ought to be a clear understanding of the most complex problems of the contemporary world, we are instead faced with an idiotic, puerile and inconsistent reasoning. We have noticed with alarm that all too frequently such a narrow reasoning affects not only the mass of Blacks, but their leaders and intellectuals as well. It is useless to adopt an ostrich-like

attitude when what is at stake is the very dignity of the Negro. Black intellectuals must be cautioned: no one has the right to replenish the empty brains
of the Negro masses with new imbecilities.[26]

Such cautioning clearly did not suffice. In 1969, there emerged a *Mo-
vimiento Black Power* among Afro-Cuban intellectuals who adopted "Afro"
hairstyles and met to discuss the works of foreign black writers, in particular
Frantz Fanon. Subjected to the usual surveillance, almost all of them were
arrested in 1971. Some recanted and were provided with employment that
might be of use to the regime. Others conformed until at various times they
left to live abroad.

In early May 1972, Castro visited black Africa for the first time. After a
day in Guinea, he expressed his excitement. "Everything is so beautiful here,
so united and homogeneous. It is just as if everything was endowed with a
soul . . . But what strikes me most is to discover that a Guinean culture,
an African culture, does exist. You can feel it everywhere: in the music, the
dances and songs . . . Guineans even speak with their drums, with their
hands, their gestures, dances and smiles."[27] It was surprising enough that
someone so intelligent, educated, and in command of a modern state should
up till then have been unaware that a Guinean culture, an African culture,
existed. That Castro himself came from a country where much of that culture
survived, in drums, music, dances, songs, gestures, spoke volumes for his
remoteness from black Cuba. Now, at least, he might have been expected
on his return home to explore and encourage the Cuban black heritage of
the culture which had so elated him in Guinea. Yet for all the impact of
this elation on the policy of his regime towards Cuban blacks, he might
never have visited Africa at all.

In 1974, the surface of Cuban conformity was disturbed again by the
emergence of various Afro-Cuban study groups, though they avoided giving
themselves any such provocative description. They met at first to hear music
together, to dance and to chat, but soon took to talking about African culture
and what black movements in other parts of the Diaspora were doing. As
one of the founding members, Reinaldo Barroso, later explained, "the black
dignity and self-knowledge we were acquiring was worth the risk of the
inevitable knock on the door."[28] The members were generally young, between eighteen and twenty-five, and in no doubt of the risks they were
running. In 1975, the authorities struck. Police, in deliberately intimidating
numbers, raided homes and detained so-called conspirators for questioning,
at least one hundred of them in Havana alone. Some of these were released,
watched, and rearrested; others were imprisoned for illegal association, an-
tisocial behavior, or divisive activities; still others were sent to "reeducation"
work camps.

In 1970, the regime had dispatched its first military force to fight alongside revolutionaries of the MPLA (Movimento Popular de Libertaçao de Angola—Popular Movement for the Liberation of Angola) against Portuguese rule. In April 1974, a group of officers successfully mounted a military coup in Portugal and announced the readiness of the new regime to grant Portugal's African colonies their independence. The subsequent MPLA government of Angola was confronted by a rebellion with military backing from South Africa. In "Operation Carlota," named after a black woman who had led a nineteenth century slave revolt in Cuba, a Cuban military force that would come to number fifty thousand troops, some 75 percent of them blacks, was dispatched to neutralize the South African intervention. It was a commitment widely approved not only in Africa but among black Cubans.

Less acceptable was the Cuban intervention, with twenty-five thousand troops, that began in December 1977, to defend the military Marxist regime in Ethiopia against an avowedly socialist Somalia and the separatist Eritrean Marxist-led movement, some of whose members had received their military training in Cuba. For here it was not the hated apartheid regime of South Africa that was the enemy, and the Cuban engagement was motivated not by support for black liberation, but by what Cuba and the Soviet Union together took to be in their state interests.

In 1980, some 125,000 Cubans, of whom an estimated one in five was black, left the island by sea before the escape route was blocked in September. Among the blacks, there were certainly those who, assured of refuge in the United States, looked for economic advancement there, and those who wished to escape being called up for military service somewhere in Africa. But there were also those who, by their own account, were adherents of Afro-Cuban cults, seeking a place where they might pursue their beliefs in freedom, and others, outside of any such adherence, who had simply abandoned all hope of being allowed to express their black identity in Cuba. In 1981, the regime lost even its leading black apologist in René Depestre, who slipped away for exile in France.

It is idle to consider what might have happened had there been no "Operation Carlota." What did happen is history. Cuban intervention in Angola, with the related supply of sophisticated Soviet equipment, neutralized South African military power. The withdrawal of Cuban forces from Angola, completed in 1991, took place on condition that South African and United States assistance be withdrawn from the rebellion. Not least, the cost of the war in Angola was an element in the compound of pressures on the South African regime which led to independence for Namibia and the phased retreat from apartheid in South Africa itself.

Nor can there be any doubt that the Cuban revolution in its course did materially improve the lot of the island's poor and accordingly that of the blacks who constituted the majority of these. Cuban society became a substantially more egalitarian one, beyond the privileged treatment which the bureaucrats secured for themselves.[29] Between 1958 and 1978 the per capita income of the poorest 40 percent of the population increased more than fourfold, from $182 to $865, while that of the richest 5 percent declined by virtually half, to just over $3,000.

Moreover, shifts in income distribution were merely part of the process. Advances in education and health care, now free to everyone, were immense. In 1958, almost half of all children aged six to fourteen had received no schooling at all. By 1986, almost all children from six to twelve years old and an estimated 86 percent of those aged from thirteen to sixteen were enrolled in schools. Before the revolution, health care had been largely limited to Cubans with means, especially those living in Havana and the provincial cities. There were only some six thousand physicians, and more than three thousand of these subsequently emigrated. By 1984, the number of physicians had increased to over twenty thousand, and an annual average of eleven hundred were graduating from Cuban medical schools. New hospitals and polyclinics spread health care across the countryside.

Malnutrition, so common among the poor before the revolution, was effectively eliminated. In the early eighties, the U.N. Food and Agricultural Organization estimated the daily per capita intake of calories at just over 2,700, or well above the recommended minimum of 2,500. The effect of this and of improved health care led to a rise in average life expectancy from fifty-seven years during the fifties to seventy-four by the mid-eighties.

No less striking was the extent to which women, traditionally tethered to the home, were incorporated into the economy. Their numbers in employment increased from some 256,000 in 1953 to more than a million in 1985, when they constituted 64 percent of all those in public health—including 38 percent of all physicians—60 percent of those in education, 41 percent of those in light industry, and 37 percent of those in commerce.[30]

Sustaining the whole economy and, accordingly, the costs of social welfare, however, was the connection with the Soviet Union and its satellites. Trade with these accounted for 80 percent of the island's annual total and involved considerable financial subsidies. The collapse of the Soviet system proved correspondingly calamitous for Cuba. Factories closed for lack of raw materials and markets. The local currency rapidly lost its purchasing power. Particularly mortifying for the regime, the United States dollar increasingly became the main medium of exchange for scarce commodities. Women teachers turned their backs on peso-paying jobs to queue or scramble for household necessities. Routine hospital operations were canceled because light bulbs in operating theaters had been stolen for use in the home. Rationing of basic foods was inadequate to avert hunger.[31] Diseases related to malnutrition reemerged.

If the extent of the dependence on the Soviet Union and its satellites could be blamed on the United States trade embargo against Cuba, the shifting, bureaucratically driven economic policies of the Castro regime could scarcely escape blame for the extent of the impact, in particular on food supplies, which the enforced end to that dependence produced. Nor could anything excuse or extenuate a repressiveness which had bled from the revolution so much of its moral meaning.

The regime came to practice and even institutionalize the abuses against human rights, all in the name of socialism, that characterized the Soviet system. The increasing persecution of dissent mocked the prime promise of the revolution to provide democracy. Without a judiciary of any independence, the law was whatever officials chose to make it. So-called deviants, from political dissidents to homosexuals and those who simply dressed or wore their hair unacceptably, risked intimidating interrogation, loss of employment, imprisonment, detention in camps for "rehabilitation," and even in particular cases the imposition of psychiatric treatment. Workers whose revolutionary enthusiasm was suspect might find themselves charged and punished for laziness, social parasitism or economic sabotage, a crime of vague definition but nonetheless invested with the death penalty.

In this context, any initiatives by blacks to express their own identity were bound to attract a ruthless reaction. Such activities were doubly offensive: they confronted the paternalism of an overwhelmingly white, culturally Hispanic political leadership which regarded its revolution as the panacea for all racial ills; and they were in conflict with a Communism of Stalinist principles traditionally given to treating the racial issue only on its own selective terms.

Such Communism had long internationally targeted white racism as one of the oppressive and manipulative manifestations of capitalism, while regarding the racial issue itself as essentially subservient to the class struggle. In obedience to this, the Communist Party of the United States had at one time campaigned for the ultimate in segregation, the establishment of a Negro national home in the black belt of the country; while, at another, the French Communist Party responded to the rise in racism among French workers fearful of unemployment by joining in the campaign against colored immigration.

Castro's Communism was of the kind that used blacks as counters in a doctrinal class conflict rather than as people with a plight and corresponding sense of identity all their own. A revolution that had begun in the commitment to freedom ended by denying the blacks of Cuba the right to be themselves.

~~~~~~

On the first day of 1863, Lincoln signed the proclamation that freed the slaves in the territory controlled by the Confederate South. In March, anti-black rioting broke out in Detroit and then spread to several other Northern cities. The mounting casualties of the Civil War had been made no more acceptable by the developing association of the Unionist cause with that of black freedom. Nor did the enthusiasm of free white labor for an end to the rival system of slavery extend to accommodating racial equality in competition for jobs.

Consistency and common sense combined with idealism in securing the Thirteenth Amendment to the Constitution, ratified in December 1866, which outlawed slavery throughout the United States. That black freedom should not mean black equality with whites was, however, widely agreed. Even such a significant figure in the history of abolitionism as William Lloyd Garrison of the *Liberator* had declared in 1864: "When was it ever known that liberation from bondage was accompanied by a recognition of political equality? . . . According to the laws of development and progress, it is not practicable."[1] In 1865, Connecticut, Minnesota, and Wisconsin had resolved to retain a franchise restricted to whites. They were followed by New Jersey and Ohio in 1867 and by Michigan and Pennsylvania in 1868.

It was the cavalry of political self-interest that rode to the rescue of racial equality in the franchise. The return of an overwhelmingly Democratic white South to the political institutions of the Union threatened an end to Republican control of them. The return was accordingly made conditional on the acceptance by the Southern states of racial equality in the right of adult males to vote, and military rule under the Acts of Reconstruction ensured compliance. The Fifteenth Amendment, ratified in March 1870, outlawed the denial or abridgment of the right to vote "by the United States or by any State on account of race, color, or previous condition of servitude."

The new Southern state legislatures, produced by electorates with variously large black components, were far from being models of moral deportment. It was not an era famous for probity in political life. The idealism invested in the Unionist cause had not precluded the War Department itself from involvement in considerable corruption during the Civil War. Afterward, state and municipal governments across the North sold themselves to the highest bidders, while several major financial scandals snapped at the heels of the federal government. "Corruption was confined to no class, no party and no section: the corruption and extravagance of the Tweed Ring in New York City and the Gas Ring in Philadelphia made the Southern Radicals look like the feckless amateurs that most of them were."[2]

Feckless or amateurish as some of their administrations might have been, the Southern Radicals were largely directed by the need for economic regeneration and social reform. Some two-thirds of the notorious $131 million in debt contracted by the eleven former Confederate states went in guarantees to attract railroads and industries. Much revenue was devoted to enlightened measures, notably in providing free public schools and relief for the poor. Nor were these black administrations. In fact, for all their electoral weight, blacks were never in control of a single Southern state. Only in South Carolina, and then but briefly, did they even constitute a majority in the legislature. The newly enfranchised blacks revealed a remarkable readiness to vote for sympathetic whites in the interest of an interracial alliance.

The collapse of Southern Reconstruction had little to do with the supposed financial irresponsibility of black rule. There was a more traditional factor involved. The culture of individualism in American society vaunted the values of liberty, enterprise, and self-reliance, but not the violence that was so often the vehicle for conveying them. Yet there had been violence in the beginnings and growth of colonial settlement, the relentless extension of the frontier, and the very genesis of the United States in revolution. It was in this tradition that violence spread across the South.

In the very dust of the Confederate defeat, white supremacists established secret associations, of which the Ku Klux Klan became the most important, to advance their values and confront Reconstruction. Their campaigns to intimidate blacks from exercising the right to vote or to serve in the militia employed threat, assault, and murder, along with not a little looting for private purposes. An investigation of the KKK reported the murder of 153 blacks in a single Florida county and of over three hundred in the parishes outside New Orleans during 1871. Whites identified with Reconstruction were treated with the relative deference their color required. They were subjected to the pressures of economic boycott and social ostracism. Increasingly they retreated from their radical allegiance or from the South altogether.

An appeal by state governments to Washington brought back military rule, with measures to suppress the violence of the secret associations. This response, however, required resolve and time to be effective. Both were running short. Liberalism seemed to have exhausted its moral reserves on the racial issue. The captains of industrial capitalism looked to an alliance with a conservative white leadership in the South for profitable investment there. The bulk of public opinion in the rest of the country wanted an end to the whole Southern mess. By 1875, all but the three state governments of Louisiana, Mississippi, and South Carolina had fallen to a conservative ascendancy. By the beginning of 1878, those three had fallen as well. The new, so-called Redeemer regimes hastened to repeal much social legislation, cut the spending on schools, and engage in corruption on a scale consistent with reintegration into the institutions of the Union.

The Republican Party paid the price of cynicism without consistency or courage. In the Congressional elections of 1878, the South sent 101 Democrats and four Republicans to the House of Representatives. All the same, Democratic domination of the region, though dedicated to white supremacy, was not yet synonymous with black exclusion. Confident in its power to ensure black subservience, it accommodated black participation in the political processes, even as members of state legislatures. Paradoxically, indeed, relations between the races were such as to provoke much comment from Northern visitors, some of whom were repelled by the absence of segregation in restaurants or on trains; the sight of black women suckling white babies, and of white and black children playing together; the cohabitation of white men and black women without outraging propriety.

None of this would last. The alliance of Southern conservatives with Northern business interests generated more financial scandal than prosperity. In no fewer than seven Southern states during the 1880s, the state treasurers absconded with, or were indicted for having misappropriated, public funds. An agricultural depression fed a Populist movement against the rule of the rich. Conservatives responded by deploying the black vote, with or without the collaboration of the blacks themselves. In 1896, for instance, conservatives carried only one in five of the Louisiana parishes which had a registered majority of white voters, but they captured the state with ballots cast either by blacks or on their behalf.

Some Populist leaders had been drawn for a while to the prospect of an alliance between the black and the white poor against the dominion of capital. This, though, demanded a long-term investment in political education for which populism had neither the passion nor the patience. Racism clearly provided a quicker and easier way of winning over those whites fearful of economic competition from blacks and longing for a return to the days when a white skin was sufficient to secure respect. Soon conservatives and Populists were rivals in rallying whites behind the commitment to deprive blacks of their rights and otherwise degrade them.

The Supreme Court, reflecting a disposition of power more concerned to protect the rights of property than those of people, countenanced a series of contrivances by which blacks in the South were effectively stripped of the vote. It countenanced, too, statutes which imposed racial segregation in a multitude of forms. Blacks came to be separated from whites in factories and schools; on trains and streetcars and steamboats; in restaurants and theaters and parks; in prisons and hospitals and asylums; in institutions for the aged, the poor, the deaf, the dumb, and the blind.

All this was accompanied by what amounted to a racial license for whites to use violence against blacks on virtually any pretext or no pretext at all. Planned or impromptu raids by whites on black districts, to intimidate the residents or for mere entertainment, came to be undertaken with impunity. Blacks were assaulted for proceeding along the same pavement toward a white instead of moving aside into the gutter. More serious infractions of the racial code were summarily punished with lynching. In the three decades from 1890, some four thousand blacks were killed by whites in the South, outside the processes of the law. None of those responsible for such killings was ever brought to trial and punished.

If many blacks were intimidated, there were others who were not. Some of these, indeed, paid for this at the end of a rope. In March 1892, three black men in Memphis were lynched because their People's Grocery store was taking black business away from the white-owned store which had previously monopolized it. Two black women, who knew well one of the victims, became impassioned campaigners against such lawless violence.

Mary Church Terrell, whose father had made himself reputedly the South's first black millionaire by investing in property, would devote her mind, time, and money to working for a federal antilynching law, as well as for women's suffrage. Ida B. Wells, co-owner of the black Memphis newspaper *Free Speech*, had already challenged in the courts, though with ultimately no success, the encroachments of segregation. After the Memphis lynchings, she bought herself a pistol with which to defend herself, called on blacks to leave a city where their rights were denied and their lives were at risk, and undertook a study of the circumstances in which 728 lynchings had taken place during the previous decade.

She reported that many lynchings, which included children among the victims, had been due to such declared crimes as "race prejudice" and "quarreling with whites." Her evidence that, in a number of alleged rapes for which black men had been lynched, white women had taken the sexual initiative produced a storm of fury in the South. While she was away in New York, a mob in Memphis burned down the office of her newspaper, and scouts were posted at the railroad station to await her return, so that she might be hanged from a lamppost at once. She assented to the advice that she stay in the North and continue her struggle in "exile."[3]

Yet the white South was not comfortable with the thought that its regime relied so largely on violence. Nor was it wholly indifferent to the criticism its violence provoked. It turned facts into fantasy, for its own reassurance no less than for its reinforcement against enmity abroad. *The Clansman: An Historical Romance of the Ku Klux Klan*, by Thomas Dixon, which was first published in 1905, was the most influential of the early attempts to revise history by transforming hooligans into heroes. The subsequent translation of the novel onto the screen in *The Birth of a Nation* by D. W. Griffith, himself a Southerner, was released in 1915 and had all the impact that the power of this director's talent as well as the force of the new form could command. A whole school of fiction and film, culminating in *Gone with the Wind* during the thirties, would come to romanticize the Old South and by implication the racism of its posterity.

Meanwhile, in the real South, where nine out of every ten American blacks lived at the turn of the century, the economic condition of the now virtually voteless black population was grim. Some 80 percent resided in rural areas, and some 60 percent subsisted on agriculture. Of these, only one in four owned even a little land. The remainder were tenants, most of them sharecroppers. For those outside of agriculture, the only jobs generally available were those as unskilled laborers or domestic servants. The rare openings for higher employment were in the few black businesses or as teachers in black schools and colleges.

The most eminent of such teachers was slave-born Booker T. Washington, who established in 1881, at Tuskegee, Alabama, the Normal and Industrial School for Negroes, to give blacks vocational training, together with habits of work and thrift. In what was effectively a working relationship with segregation, he would famously declare during a speech at the Atlanta Cotton Exposition of 1895: "In all things that are purely social, we can be as separate as the fingers, yet one as the hand in all things essential to mutual progress."[4] With this approach, he attracted honors and finance from institutions and industrialists ready to encourage a black investment in patient and serviceable effort rather than in racial agitation.

There were blacks who took a different view. Outstanding among these was a sociologist, William Edward Burghardt Du Bois, educated at Harvard and Berlin, before teaching at Atlanta University. His *Souls of Black Folk*, published in 1903, included a frontal assault on Washington's policy of gradualism. Two years later he founded the Niagara Movement, essentially to confront racism through the courts. This led in turn to the establishment in 1910 of the National Association for the Advancement of Colored People, the NAACP.

Its headquarters were in New York, and apart from Du Bois himself, who was director of publications and research, all its first officers were white. This reflected the growing unease among white liberals, in particular Jews, at the treatment of blacks and at the implications of advancing racism for American society. Yet for all its reliance on white finance and influence, the NAACP was soon attracting black support, mainly through its monthly publication *Crisis*, which Du Bois himself edited and which by 1913 was selling some thirty thousand copies, three-quarters of them to blacks. Ignoring protests from the NAACP's white board members and backers, Du Bois used *Crisis* to attack the white Churches as citadels of racial prejudice and black preachers for their hypocrisy and cowardice; to promote an interest in African history, culture, and art; and to stress the connection between the black struggle for racial equality in the United States and the struggle of blacks elsewhere against European colonial rule.

During the First World War, blacks in the United States began that mass migration from the South which would, within less than half a century, leave fewer of them there than lived outside the region. With immigration from Europe interrupted by the war, industry in the North boomed with the demand for goods. Short of labor, Northern businesses sent recruiters to the South. Those blacks who responded were soon writing home to their families and friends about the better economic and social conditions available in the North. In May 1917, the *Chicago Defender*, the leading black newspaper of the time and one with a large black readership in the South, launched its own "Great Northern Drive," which it promoted with such highly charged slogans as "The Flight Out of Egypt" and "Bound for the Promised Land." In Chicago itself, the black population would leap from 44,000 in 1910 to 109,000 in 1920 and 234,000 in 1930.[5]

When the United States entered the war, the propaganda of a belligerence based on the commitment to freedom and democracy seemed to promise a peace which would reflect such values in the treatment of blacks. Du Bois was sufficiently persuaded of the possibility to call for a moratorium on the expression of grievances and even to support the establishment of a segregated training school for black officers in the armed forces. He was angrily attacked by more militant blacks.

The *Messenger*, a new black radical paper cofounded by A. Philip Randolph, assailed Du Bois for his "superlative sureness" that black contributions to the war effort would be rewarded by a retreat from racism.[6] Marcus Garvey derided the NAACP as the National Association for the Advancement of (Certain) Colored People and attacked Du Bois himself, with his light skin and rich white backers, as "more of a white man than a Negro."[7]

It was the militants who proved to be justified in their dissent. In the summer of 1919, the first since peace had arrived, antiblack rioting broke out in twenty-six cities, most of them in the North and the worst of them all in Chicago. Blacks revealed a new readiness to defend themselves, but this only fed the fury of the mobs. The end of the wartime boom was followed by a rise in unemployment that fired white labor resentment at black competition for jobs. Pressure from white labor proceeded to secure the exclusion of blacks from trade unions and from employment in institutions such as the police and the postal service which shortages during the war had opened to them. One result was that family need drove more black women to find jobs among those peculiarly available to them, mainly in domestic service. By 1920, for instance, close to 40 percent of black women, well over double the proportion of white ones, had joined the workforce.[8]

If blacks continued moving to the North, however, it was less because they now believed that this was the Promised Land than because conditions were still worse in the South. Marcus Garvey, thundering from his paper *The Negro World*, drew an increasing number of followers with his summons to black militancy. "Two hundred and fifty years," he proclaimed, "we have been a race of slaves; for fifty years we have been a race of parasites. Now we propose to end all that. No more fear, no more cringing, no more sycophantic begging and pleading; the Negro must strike straight from the shoulder for manhood rights and for full liberty."[9]

In 1924, Garvey founded the Negro Political Union to mobilize the black vote. The Union issued a list of approved candidates in that year's elections and dispatched teams of canvassers who had a marked impact on returns from the black districts in Chicago and New York. Indeed, it was Garvey rather than Du Bois who pioneered in this way a constitutional form of pressure that would become an increasingly potent component in the struggle for civil rights. Yet more important even than that was his assertion of black dignity, after the many decades of white contempt and black humiliation that followed the end of slavery itself.

The arrival of the Great Depression led to a Democratic federal government whose New Deal was freighted with old discrimination. Social security initiatives excluded farmers and domestics, groups that accounted for 65 percent of black workers. The Department of Agriculture supplied relief on the basis that black families needed less than white ones to sustain themselves. The Federal Housing Administration refused guaranteed mortgages to blacks for any purchase of property in white neighborhoods. All the New Deal agencies, by entrusting to officials in the South the distribution of federal funds there, accordingly sanctioned the related display of racial discrimination.

This last was largely responsible for a further surge in black migration to cities in the North. Some 400,000 went there from the South during the thirties, to augment the force of the black vote in an increasingly urban-dominated politics. As the elections of 1936 drew near, this was recognized by the Democrats, whose wooing of blacks played some part in winning for Roosevelt over three-quarters of their votes. The conventional bargain of benefits for ballots argued the need now to offer some return for such substantial support, but this was not the only prod. Blacks had begun to show their growing impatience by boycotts and demonstrations—even, in Harlem in 1935, by rioting. Though much of the press hastened to blame this riot on Communist agitators, the *New York Post* acknowledged that "it would have been impossible to inflame Harlem residents if there had not been discrimination in employment and on relief, and justifiable complaints of high rents and evil living conditions."[10]

Since 1934, Eleanor Roosevelt had become increasingly concerned at the denial of black civil rights; and though her influence on her husband's policies was nowhere near as considerable as was then generally supposed, her public indications of concern may well have encouraged the more liberal members of the Administration to urge arguments for action. Blacks were appointed to a number of posts in the New Deal federal agencies, among them the National Youth Administration (NYA), created to promote the employment of sixteen- to twenty-year-olds, by work relief, through vocational training, and in private industry. Chosen to be director of its Negro Division was Mary McLeod Bethune, a black educationalist who proudly proclaimed her unmixed African descent, and who had founded in 1935 the National Council of Negro Women.

From her new post, and with her influence reinforced by the high regard in which Eleanor Roosevelt held her, she soon brought together the initially squabbling black advisers and administrators into the Federal Council on Negro Affairs. Within the sphere of her own responsibilities, she wrested unprecedented funding for black education out of the NYA's resources and secured the appointment of blacks to state commissions, even in the South, on the basis that blacks were best qualified to judge how money should be productively spent in their interests. Moreover, roaming often beyond her official sphere, she was largely responsible for such integrationist advances as the admission of black journalists to White House press conferences and of black doctors to the staff of the leading Johns Hopkins Hospital.[11]

The slow, limping progress of liberalism could not keep pace with an increasingly militant black impatience. In the booming defense industries, as the country provided armaments for export and prepared for the possibility of being drawn into the Second World War, blacks found themselves effectively barred from employment. In June 1941, A. Philip Randolph threatened to lead a protest march of at least 100,000 blacks on Washington. Roosevelt was prepared neither to permit such a massive demonstration against racism nor to risk the consequences of prohibiting it. He issued an Executive Order to "encourage full participation in the national defense programme by all citizens . . . regardless of race" and established a Commission on Fair Employment Practices to promote compliance. The victory proved, however, to be more moral than material. Defense industries complied mainly by employing black women for the most menial tasks.

Racism was not shelved for the duration of the war. Nor was the response to it. In 1943, a black riot erupted in Harlem when a white policeman, roughly arresting a black woman on a charge of disorderly conduct, wounded a black soldier who confronted him.[12] The United States not only maintained segregation in its armed forces at home but took it abroad. In Britain, however, where many of them were stationed, and subsequently in liberated Europe, blacks encountered societies with more relaxed racial attitudes and less overt racist practices. Returning home after the war, they saw the world rather differently from the way they had before. In racial matters, they found the United States little changed.

The wartime industrial boom had brought swelling numbers of new black immigrants from the South and black immigrants from the Caribbean to the jobs available in the North, where they moved into the already crowded urban black neighborhoods. What happened in Chicago was part of a pattern. In December 1946, the Chicago Housing Authority assigned a few carefully selected black families to a new housing project in a white neighborhood on the city's Southwest Side. A mob of more than a thousand whites collected to stone the intruders, and white rioting followed until, after two weeks, the black families withdrew. In August 1947, a further attempt to move blacks into the neighborhood failed after sustained white rioting again. Despite a decision from the Supreme Court in 1948 that racially restrictive covenants were unenforceable, housing policy in Chicago changed, to concentrate on building all-black projects within existing black neighborhoods.[13]

The organized black response to institutionalized racism remained, in general, recourse to the courts and the mobilization of the Northern black vote. There was, however, a particular pressure that had come to be used as well. In October 1947, the NAACP filed formal charges at the United Nations that the United States was engaged in practices of racial discrimination. The influence of the United States there ensured the defeat of a Soviet proposal that the charges be investigated, but the charges themselves were embarrassing enough. They were bound to become more so, in the developing conflict of the Cold War and the retreat of European empires that was creating new sovereign states of color.

President Truman ordered in July 1948 the desegregation of the armed forces and made civil rights an issue in the elections of that year. His unexpected success at the polls suggested a shift in public opinion on the issue. This would come to have an impact on the judiciary. In its *Plessy* v. *Ferguson* judgment of 1896, the Supreme Court had upheld racially segregated schooling on the principle of "separate but equal," and by extension other racially segregated facilities. In the case of *Brown* v. *Board of Education of Topeka*, it ruled on May 17, 1954, that "separate educational facilities are inherently unequal," and it subsequently ordered that the Southern states proceed to desegregate education "with all deliberate speed."[14]

Having found racially segregated schools to be unconstitutional, the Court could scarcely fail to deal similarly with other racially segregated facilities. Across the South, state governments sought to escape compliance by one contrivance after another. Then, on December 1, 1955, an incident in Montgomery, Alabama, triggered a momentous black commitment to direct action that would ultimately lead to the transformation of the South.

Mrs. Rosa Parks, a black woman who earned her living as a seamstress and was active in the local NAACP, was asked to give up her seat on the bus to a white man. Tired and angry, she refused and was arrested. There were other black women in Montgomery who were by now tired and angry. They urged a protest boycott of the buses. Local black ministers, including Martin Luther King, Jr., agreed to lend support, provided that they might do so anonymously. E. D. Nixon, president of the local NAACP and a black trade unionist, threatened to call off the boycott because, he would explain to the community, the ministers were "too scared." The ministers agreed to associate themselves publicly with the boycott and join in forming, with King as its president, the Montgomery Improvement Association to promote black demands. On Monday, December 5, no blacks boarded the buses. So exultant was the mood at such success that a boycott called for a single day was indefinitely extended.

It would last for over a year, while the case of Rosa Parks made its slow and costly way through the judicial process. Private cars provided regular transport, but most of the fifty thousand boycotters were forced to walk, day after day. Some whites took to attacking the boycotters. It served only to confirm the boycotters in their resolve. The confrontation came to command increasing coverage in the press and on television, across the country and well beyond. Funds flowed to the boycotters from the North, where solidarity meetings spread the message of nonviolent militancy. On November 13, 1956, the Supreme Court ruled against the constitutional validity of the segregation ordinance under which Rosa Parks had been required to give up her seat. On December 20, the court order arrived in Montgomery to desegregate the buses.

The triumphant conclusion to this single-issue local campaign might easily have been followed by mere rejoicing or a debilitating dispute over what to do next. Instead, during January 1957, black ministers from various Southern cities formed the Southern Christian Leadership Conference, the SCLC, with King at its head and a black woman, Ella Baker of the NAACP, as its coordinator, to develop the strategy of nonviolent resistance in the South. In May, the "Prayer Pilgrimage" to the nation's capital became the largest demonstration for civil rights so far held by blacks and their white supporters in the United States. Three months later, Congress passed the Civil Rights Act of 1957, the first such law since Reconstruction, though only with a provision, to allow trial by jury, which made it most unlikely that any prosecution for infringement would succeed in a Southern court.

With the beginning of the new school year, the battle moved to Little Rock, Arkansas, where blacks had won a court order for the desegregation

of the Central High School. Orval Faubus, the Governor of Arkansas, defied
the order, first by using the National Guard to keep any black child from
entering the school and then, required by the courts to end his defiance, by
inviting local whites to provide it instead. The televised violence of the white
mob that collected in response was watched by many millions round the
world. On September 24, 1957, President Eisenhower dispatched federal
troops to Little Rock. "Mob rule," he declared, "cannot be allowed to override
the decisions of our courts."[15] The Governor closed the schools and leased
them to a private company, but the courts ruled against this contrivance,
and in the autumn of 1959 the schools of Little Rock were opened to racial
integration.

A few months later, on February 1, 1960, four black college students in
Greensboro, North Carolina, sat down at the whites-only lunch counter in
the local store of a national chain and initiated a new phase in the development of nonviolent direct action. Within a week, there were sit-ins in
fifteen cities across five states of the South. By the end of the month, four
national chains had conceded desegregation of their lunch counters. The
campaign, whose young black activists were increasingly joined by white
students, moved across the country and against other segregationist practices,
to include stand-ins at cinemas, kneel-ins at churches, wade-ins at beaches.
Within eighteen months, well over fifty thousand had participated in the
spreading defiance, and some thirty-six hundred of them had been arrested.

Such a massive engagement was spontaneous only in part. Ella Baker had
been quick to size up the potential of the student movement and promote
a meeting of representatives from the various independently acting campus
groups. In April 1960, more than three hundred students from fifty-six
campuses in the South and nineteen in the North met at Shaw University
in Raleigh, North Carolina, and agreed to establish the Student Nonviolent
Coordinating Committee, the SNCC. It was to prove the most radical force
in the civil rights movement and would exercise an influence beyond it. A
number of those who engaged in its campaigns subsequently played leading
parts in the protest movement against United States involvement in the
Vietnam War.

The Congress of Racial Equality, CORE, founded in 1942 with an emphasis on direct action but relatively listless for some time, made James
Farmer its national director in early 1961, and he set out to challenge
Southern disregard of a recent Supreme Court ruling against segregation in
interstate transport facilities. On May 4, 1961, seven blacks and six whites
boarded buses in Washington, D.C., for the first of the Freedom Rides
through the South. In Alabama, white mobs met the buses and attacked the
Riders. While CORE was reportedly considering whether to call off the
Rides, a group of SNCC activists boarded a bus in Nashville, Tennessee.
They made their way to Birmingham, Alabama, where they were arrested

and then released. They proceeded to Montgomery, where a white mob attacked them, along with attendant journalists and President Kennedy's special emissary. They then boarded a bus bound for Jackson, Mississippi, where they were arrested and jailed.

All through the summer, despite Attorney General Robert Kennedy's plea for a "cooling-off period" and Martin Luther King's promise of a "temporary lull," SNCC activists, pursuing a policy that CORE had initiated of "jail, no bail," continued the Rides and were joined on the buses by both black and white clergymen. At last, in September 1961, the Interstate Commerce Commission banned racial discrimination from all interstate buses and related facilities. On November 1, a group of students from the Albany State College for Negroes decided to test the force of the ban at the bus station in Albany, Georgia. They were promptly ordered out of the whites-only waiting room by police. The Department of Justice, duly informed, declined to intervene. SNCC activists, who had opened an office in the town a month before, joined with local black church and social groups to establish the Albany Movement. It came to be known as the "singing movement," from the songs that accompanied its meetings, its demonstrations, and the arrests of its members, more than seven hundred of whom had been imprisoned by the middle of December. It would continue until, in 1964, the town abandoned the last vestige of imposed segregation.

In August 1961, the SNCC had set up, in Pike County, Mississippi, its first voter registration school, to inform blacks of their right to vote and encourage them to insist on exercising it. A number of Freedom Schools were soon conducting registration drives in small rural communities of the South, where no television camera crews traveled to record the quiet courage of those who registered or to inhibit the frequent ferocity of the retribution. Each act of hospitality to a civil rights worker, each attendance at a Freedom School, as well as each application to register, was a protest demonstration in itself, and there were countless such demonstrations.

Fannie Lou Hamer, a sharecropper in Sunflower County, Mississippi, was forty-four years old when in 1962 she discovered from civil rights workers that blacks actually had a right to register for the vote. She decided to do so, whatever the consequences. "The only thing they could do to me was kill me," she later explained, "and it seemed like they'd been trying to do that a little bit at a time ever since I could remember."[16] When she returned from registering, the proprietor of her holding told her to withdraw her name from the register or leave. She left to stay with a friend, whose home was raked with bullets that evening. Subsequently becoming an instructor herself in the voter registration program, she was arrested at Winona in 1963 and beaten horribly. It did not stop her.

Meanwhile, the Southern Christian Leadership Conference had been preparing to confront segregation in Birmingham, Alabama, one of its chief

Southern citadels. Beginning on April 12, 1963, and continuing for more than four weeks, mass demonstrations of protest were led by Martin Luther King and his colleagues. They were a crucial test of the nonviolent strategy. The police used dogs, clubs, cattle prods, and fire hoses against the demonstrators and arrested thousands of them. Press and television coverage excited widespread revulsion across the country. Then, after a white campaign of bombings, the city's black community erupted in rioting, on May 11 and 12, to burn white-owned stores and give battle against police and state troopers. Black urban rioting had occurred before—more than once in Harlem, New York, for instance—but not on this relative scale, and not at a time of such heightened black militancy as the nonviolent resistance movement had itself promoted. The Birmingham riot now suggested that black militancy could be provoked beyond the capacity of the nonviolent commitment to contain it. For one black leader in the North, Malcolm X, this marked a turning point in black American history.

Malcolm Little was six years old when his militant father, much influenced by the views of Marcus Garvey, was lynched in Lansing, Michigan. As a young man, he drifted into Harlem's hustler culture of robbery, prostitution, and drugs. He was arrested for robbery in 1946 and sentenced to seven years in jail. There he became a convert to the Black Muslim movement, founded in Detroit in 1930 and since 1933 led by a certain Robert Poole who had taken the name of Elijah Muhammad. The Nation of Islam, as the movement called itself, represented the extreme of black separatism, aspiring ultimately to an independent black republic and meanwhile urging blacks to focus on their own schools and newspapers and business enterprises. On his release from jail, Malcolm, in conformity with Nation of Islam practice, discarded a surname owed to the owner of some slave ancestor and called himself Malcolm X. With his eloquence and rage, he soon became a leading figure in the movement and was largely responsible for a rapid growth in its Northern ghetto following.

"If I go home and my child has blood running down her leg and someone tells me a snake bit her," he said in one of the parables to which he was given, "I'm going out and kill snakes, and when I find a snake I'm not going to look and see if he has blood on his jaws."[17] Such views brought him into conflict with King and other leaders of the demonstrations in Birmingham, whose commitment to nonviolence was not merely political principle but religious doctrine. They blocked his proposal to join them in the Birmingham challenge. His furious response—"Martin Luther King is a chump, not a champ!"—made evident the existence and extent of the divergence in outlook and strategy developing within the black protest movement.

At long last, in June 1963, President Kennedy sent a new civil rights bill to Congress. The recognition of the difficulties likely to lie in its way, along with rising black impatience at the pace of change in the South, prompted the various organizations in the civil rights movement to combine in calling for a march that would end with a huge rally in the nation's capital. A quarter of a million attended the rally in August, to hear King give his renowned "I Have a Dream" speech, and John Lewis, Chairman of the SNCC, attack the federal government for its inadequate commitment to civil rights.

The following month, a bomb exploded in a Birmingham black church during a Sunday School class and killed four children. In November, President Kennedy was assassinated. Malcolm X called this a case of "chickens coming home to roost." In the storm raised by this remark, he was suspended by Elijah Muhammad. In March 1964, he broke with the movement altogether and established an independent mosque in New York.

One year after President Kennedy had submitted it to Congress, the Civil Rights Act of 1964 was signed by Lyndon Johnson, his successor. Its main provisions prohibited racial discrimination in places of public resort. It offered no prospect of change for those blacks less concerned with remote restaurants and beaches than with conditions in the overcrowded urban ghettos. In July, black rioting struck New York City, to be followed by rioting in the upstate city of Rochester, the supposedly well-managed domain of the Eastman Kodak corporation. By September black anger had struck five more cities.

Nor did the new Act provide effectual means for securing the right of blacks to vote in the refractory South. In 1963, as part of its voter registration campaign, the SNCC had promoted an unofficial election for Governor of Mississippi, and some eighty thousand blacks, or four times the number registered to vote in the state, had braved threats, assaults, and arrests to take part. Having demonstrated how far their rights were denied, Mississippi blacks had then proceeded to establish the Freedom Democratic Party, the FDP. This sent its own delegates, among them Fanny Lou Hamer, to the Democratic Convention in August 1964, where they challenged the legitimacy of the all-white Mississippi delegation. The embarrassed managers of the convention, after consulting with President Johnson, offered as a compromise to seat the official delegation and grant the FDP two delegates-at-large. The official delegation rejected this and withdrew. The FDP, despite the urgings of King to accept the compromise, staged a sit-down on the official Mississippi seats and were forcibly removed.

Aware of the shifting emphasis within the civil rights movement, King, with his prestige much enhanced by the award to him of the Nobel Peace Prize, launched in January 1965 a voter registration drive in Selma, Alabama. Within a fortnight, some three thousand of those involved in the drive, including King himself, had been arrested. Malcolm X had visited the town in early February 1964 at the invitation of the SNCC and had warned at a church rally that "whites had better deal with Reverend King before they had to deal with him."[16]

After his break with the Nation of Islam, Malcolm X traveled abroad, visiting Mecca and West Africa, and returned to take a more international view of black struggle. His experience of meeting in Mecca white, blue-eyed Muslims had affected his racial vocabulary but not converted him to King's doctrine of nonviolence. As late in his life as December 16, 1964, speaking at Harvard, he declared: "We don't believe that Afro-Americans should be victims any longer . . . We believe that bloodshed is a two-way street, that dying is a two-way street, that killing is a two-way street."[19] He had himself been threatened by Black Muslims with death and seemed now increasingly to be expecting it. On February 21, 1965, he was shot dead by gunmen at a meeting he was addressing in Harlem. Nation of Islam members were the most obvious suspects, but the motives of the gunmen remain uncertain.[20]

On March 7, 1965, several hundred of the civil rights activists in Selma, led by King, began a march of protest to the state capital, Montgomery, but were beaten back by brutal attacks from police under the command of the local sheriff. Successive subsequent attempts met with the same treatment. On March 17, President Johnson submitted to Congress new draft legislation which would empower federal officers to register voters in states where the right to vote was demonstrably being denied. Four days later, the march from Selma was allowed to proceed and, swollen to twenty thousand along the way, reached Montgomery on February 25 to protest in peace. The Voting Rights Act, passed in the summer, was to prove decisive in bringing the six strayed states of the South into constitutional line.

President Johnson had, in May 1964, proclaimed his commitment to a Great Society from which poverty and deprivation would be banished. In August 1965, the very month when the Voting Rights Act was signed, Los Angeles was swept by five days of black rioting that left at least thirty-four people killed and thirty-eight hundred arrested, the overwhelming majority of them blacks, with property damage valued at some $175 million. This was evidence enough that if a start on creating the Great Society was needed anywhere, it was in the urban ghettos of black America. Trapped in his other commitment to winning the Vietnam War, however, Johnson was confronted by the soaring costs of military escalation.

The war not only diverted both resources and will from the Great Society undertaking. It radicalized the young, but effectively along divergent racial lines. White students had played no small part in the civil rights movement. Many had confronted white brutality in the South. It was from among these that much of the militant leadership came in the movement of opposition to the war. It was not that they had ceased to concern themselves with the plight of blacks, though that plight seemed less pressing as the South began to change. It was simply that the war had become their preoccupation. Young blacks in the civil rights movement reacted differently. For them, the war was a manifestation of an imperial white racism in the United States, and the developing preoccupation of young whites with opposing the war rather than confronting the racism behind it was evidence of the need for blacks to rely only on themselves.

In 1962, James Meredith had been the black applicant whose acceptance marked the University of Mississippi's reluctant racial integration. On June 5, 1966, he set out on the 225-mile march from Memphis, Tennessee, to Jackson, the capital of Mississippi, in the belief that his lone brave demonstration would encourage Mississippi blacks to exercise their voting rights. On the second day of his march, when he was a mere ten miles into Mississippi, a white man shot and seriously wounded him. Though King agreed that the Southern Christian Leadership Conference should join with the young activists of the SNCC and CORE in immediately continuing the "March against Fear," it was the young activists who came to dominate the mood of the march. Increasingly, it seemed as though two contending marches were involved, as King's followers would sing "We Shall Overcome," only to be submerged in the singing of the new SNCC version, "We Shall Overrun."

Stokely Carmichael, chairman of the SNCC, was arrested during the march and, going straight to a protest rally after his release, raised the cry of "Black Power" that would resound through the Black Diaspora.[21] Yet this was not a cause that commended itself to the mass of Americans. Many of these distinguished between the struggle of blacks for full civil rights, which involved Southern acquiescence in the rule of law as well as in the decencies of democracy, and the struggle against racism, which threatened the right of individual citizens in the United States to be as racist as they pleased. With the evidence that the South was coming to accept the judgments of the courts—between 1966 and 1968, the number of Southern black voters increased from one million to more than three million—and with the course of the Vietnam War dominating the headlines, the racial issue moved in general to the back pages.

The Black Panther Party, founded in November 1965 by SNCC members in Lowndes County, Alabama, sought to establish itself in the major urban ghettos. It was crushed by arrests, imprisonments, and raids that on occasions included what looked suspiciously like assassinations. "America won't come around," H. Rap Brown, who succeeded Carmichael as Chairman of the SNCC in July 1967, declared, "so we're going to burn America down."[22] Rioting could be contained by troops, and it was black neighborhoods rather than the protected white business centers and suburbs that burned.

Yet rioting did stir a still dominant American liberalism which provided, through affirmative action programs and equal opportunity enactments, enhanced black access to higher education, with employment in the professions and the expanding service industries. The result was an accelerating social divergence, as some moved upward, within or into the middle class, and others downward, to the edge of poverty or beyond, among the multitude already there. Black America itself came to be more deeply divided into psychically as well as physically different worlds.

This was not an exclusively black phenomenon, though one the more emphatic both because it was more extreme and because of the unity, if often more apparent than real, that had marked the civil rights movement. American society had long accommodated large economic inequalities, and these were becoming ever larger. In 1949, the poorest 20 percent of families had 4.5 percent of total family income, while the richest 20 percent had 42.7 percent. In 1986, the respective figures were 4.6 percent and 43.7 percent. This might have suggested that little had changed in thirty-seven years. In fact, the numbers of people in the lowest group had risen disproportionately, as many farming families abandoned agriculture, and elderly families were rescued from poverty by selective social security entitlements. The lowest group of family income came more and more to consist of female-headed families with children and of families headed by men whose earnings had relatively declined. As measured in constant (1987) dollar value, one in nine children had lived in a family with an income below the poverty line or less than $10,000 a year during the late seventies. During the late eighties, the figure was one in six.[23]

Some of this was due to a change in the nature of the economy and a reduction in the rate of growth overall which together produced rising unemployment. With increasing industrial competition, especially from Japan, there was a relative contraction in precisely that sector of manufacturing which had historically been the main source of jobs for the less educated and skilled. This hit the blacks hardest, and not only directly. Economic difficulties fed a successful revolt predominantly of the suburban middle class, at the extent of taxation to fund social welfare and other measures for dealing with the blight of poverty in the inner cities. A liberal era that reached back to the arrival of the New Deal came to an end in widespread white impatience with what was perceived as an essentially black problem.

By the nineties, the extent of this problem was plain enough in the statistics. In September 1992, the Census Bureau reported that while one in seven Americans lived in poverty, for blacks the figure was almost one in three.[24] Some 13 percent of white children were living below the defined poverty line. The figure for black children was 46 percent, close to half.[25] The rate of black unemployment was well over twice the rate of unemployment among whites. While blacks were some 12 percent of the population and just over 10 percent of the total labor force, they made up over 31 percent of nursing aides, nearly 30 percent of domestic servants, nearly 28 percent of postal clerks, over 26 percent of laundry and dry-cleaning workers, and 21 percent of janitors but only 2.9 percent of designers, 2.6 percent of lawyers, 2.1 percent of architects and cabinetmakers, 1.5 percent of dentists and commercial pilots.[26] Black poverty and unemployment, with the alienation and despair that they promoted, were major factors in an internal hemorrhaging of black America. Among youths from fifteen to nineteen years old, the white death rate from homicide was roughly 8 per 100,000, while the black rate, at 77 per 100,000, was almost ten times as high.[27] Across the country, almost one in four blacks in their twenties was, at any given time, in prison, on probation, or on parole. In California, the figure was closer to one in three; in Nevada and Washington, D.C., two in five.[28]

Blacks had historically been at the moral center of the American experience. The Civil War itself was fought over the issue of Southern secession, and the South seceded essentially to preserve slavery. Subsequently, whatever the other social preoccupations, the treatment of blacks was the ultimate test of those values—liberty, equality of opportunity, democracy—for which the United States, in its distinctive genesis and character, claimed to stand. At last whites came to believe that they had really done all that might reasonably be expected of them, in securing for the blacks their constitutional due. Whites were confirmed in their belief by the very success of particular blacks not merely in scaling the heights of their professions but, in such dominant forms of popular culture as film and television, acceptably asserting their identity and deriding the black stereotypes of white racism. With a sigh of relief, whites could put blacks to one side, as just another of America's ethnic minorities that have to make their own way and take the knocks which life delivers. Yet whites had not treated and still did not treat blacks as just another ethnic minority.

On April 29, 1992, four white Los Angeles police, on trial for having brutally beaten a black man and with the beatings recorded on video by a white amateur cameraman, were acquitted by an all-white jury. Three days of rioting in the city left 53 dead, more than 2,000 injured, and some 1,100 buildings damaged or destroyed at an estimated property loss of $1 billion. It was the worst single race riot in the United States during the century. Yet, if this suggested that there might be an unresolved, peculiarly black problem, which revealed in its folds the deformity of America itself, this was not evident in the moral and political concerns of the presidential election that followed. That came to be the first, for almost half a century, in which the Democratic platform made no reference to the redressing of racial injustice and in which the campaign avoided any promises to blacks. The lessons of Republican success in wooing whites with support for their racial preoccupations had been well learned.

Martin Luther King had himself come to see how much more than the achievement of civil rights the black struggle involved. He was engaged in support of a strike by sanitation workers in Memphis when he was assassinated there on April 5, 1968. He spoke for those blacks who believed with him in the American dream, addressing other Americans—or, rather, America itself—with the demand that it deliver the reality.

Malcolm X spoke not to other Americans but to other blacks, and not of the American dream but of the American nightmare which so many of them, in their deprivation and humiliation, their vulnerability and violence, experienced. If he had no such clear strategy of struggle as King developed, he offered a strategy of survival, in self-respect, self-reliance, self-determination, self-defense.

If it is to Malcolm X rather than to Martin Luther King that increasing numbers of young blacks are drawn, it is not because that strategy has proved its success, except in saving many of them from repudiating themselves as society seems to repudiate them. It is because theirs is the rage that Malcolm X expressed. Despite the rejoicing among those blacks who have made it to the other side, and perhaps even for those, the deep river has yet to be crossed.

~~~~~~

There were blacks in Britain more than a thousand years before the beginning of the transatlantic slave trade. Africans arrived as soldiers in the Roman army of occupation, and one of them is recorded as having been bold enough to make fun of an emperor, Lucius Septimius Severus, in the year 210 or thereabouts, near what is now Carlisle. The emperor was so troubled by the man's "ominous" color that he ordered appeasing sacrifices to be performed at once. There is such further evidence of an early black presence as the skull of an African girl found at a tenth-century Anglo-Saxon burial ground in Norfolk.

By the sixteenth century, there were black women, of so elevated a condition that they had their own maidservants, at the Court in Scotland, and two of them received New Year's gifts from the King in 1513. In England, a black musician was employed to play the trumpet at the Court of Henry VII, and by the late sixteenth century blacks were in the country not only as entertainers and sexual companions but more commonly as domestic servants, in a growing fashion among the rich for adorning their establishments with such examples of the exotic as symbolized their ability to afford them.

By 1596, indeed, Queen Elizabeth I was so disturbed by the numbers of "divers blackmoores" brought into her realm that she addressed a letter to mayors, expressing "Her Majesty's pleasure . . . that those kinde of people should be sent forth of the lande."[1] Her pleasure was evidently an inadequate inducement, for in 1601 she issued a proclamation that required the expulsion of blacks as infidels and an economic burden. Never one to neglect an opportunity for profit, she secured a suitable payment from the German slave trader commissioned to arrest and deport them.

Whether by design or dereliction, the purge was incomplete. A scattering of blacks remained to survive her own departure. Then, from the middle of the seventeenth century, with England's colonial commitment to sugar production and accordingly to the slave trade, blacks in increasing numbers arrived in Britain. They came in the retinues of visiting or settling West Indian planters and of their young sent to acquire an education, social polish, and well-connected spouses. They were brought by officers and even ordinary seamen engaged in the slave trade. They were imported as merchandise for a developing domestic market.

Slaves were publicly on sale, especially in those port cities connected with the trade. One street in Liverpool, for instance, was nicknamed Negro Street or Negro Row from the concentration of such sales there. In London, slave children featured prominently in the advertisements of the time. They were particularly sought as companions or toys for their rich white counterparts and as embellishments for the salon or boudoir. When bought for these purposes, they were often relieved of those harsher domestic tasks which were left for the numerous white servants to perform. Yet the indulgence extended to a black child who entertained a white one or who completed the fashionable furnishings of a salon might not be enjoyed by the slaves who had inevitably outgrown such functions or who had been bought with more menial employment in mind.

Newspaper advertisements for the return of runaways indicate the cruelties to which slaves were subjected and which they sought to escape. They were generally described as wearing metal collars around their necks, and numerous references to scars suggest that brutal punishment was common and acceptable enough to be revealed in such details without risk of embarrassment.[2]

If slaves were peculiarly vulnerable to physical abuse, free blacks had difficulties of their own. From 1731, when blacks were barred there from being taken on as apprentices, London effectively operated a color bar in employment. Inevitably there were those who were reduced to begging, while women became prostitutes, as a way of surviving and supporting the family, until taken from street to prison for their activities. Others left London for work in the provincial towns or the countryside, the men as artisans or agricultural laborers, the women as laundresses, seamstresses, or children's nurses. Musical aptitude enabled some to secure employment as entertainers at great houses or as bandsmen in the army, while others survived by busking in the city streets.

Racial stereotypes were not slow in developing. The eighteenth-century artist William Hogarth, who included blacks in several of his works, was notable in using such stereotypes in scorn not of the blacks but of the culture into which they had been thrust. In his painting "The Countess's Morning Levée," from his series "Marriage à la Mode" of the 1740s, the countess converses with her lover in the company of assorted entertainers, visitors, and attendants. A black manservant is engaged in handing round sugared chocolate, symbolic of the connection between so much wealth and colonial slavery, while grinning at the neutered tenor in full voice. The contrast between his mocking savage virility and a culture effeminate and effete is elaborated by the inclusion of a sumptuously costumed black boy, presiding over various art objects, at one of which, a horned figure, he laughingly points, to represent the cuckolding of the Earl.[3]

Estimates of the number of blacks in eighteenth-century Britain vary widely. The *Gentleman's Magazine* in 1764 claimed that there were 20,000 in London alone. A modern scholar has argued that ill-treatment, poverty, and disease kept the numbers down to a probable maximum of 10,000 for the whole country at any one time.[4] Few and scattered as they were, however, blacks in Britain and particularly those in London were active in promoting their fellowship. They gathered to mark such occasions as christenings, weddings, and funerals, or merely to meet at taverns, often with music and dancing. They readily responded to the plight of any among them. In 1773, when two of them were imprisoned in Bridewell for begging, these were visited by more than three hundred fellow blacks and sustained during their stay by contributions from the black community. Not least, blacks pursued the cause of freedom for those who were still slaves. The militancy of some provoked Sir John Fielding, magistrate and half-brother of the novelist Henry Fielding. He complained that it was their practice "to enter into Societies, and make it their Business to corrupt and dissatisfy the mind of every fresh black servant that comes to England." Moreover, they had so managed to get "the Mob on their Side" that it was "not only difficult but dangerous" for owners to recover slaves "when once they are spirited away."[5]

In 1722, Lord Chief Justice Mansfield ruled that slaves might not be shipped from England against their will. Representatives of the black community had attended the court proceedings, and some two hundred blacks, "with their ladies," celebrated the result at a public house. The judgment had an immediate impact on the number of slaves imported, since visiting owners were disinclined to bring in such capital at the risk of having to leave it behind when they departed.

Free blacks who arrived were not correspondingly welcome. During the American War of Independence, many colonial blacks associated themselves with the British cause, either as free already but doubtful of their fate in an emergent United States, or as slaves promised their freedom in return for their loyalty. With the British defeat, thousands of blacks escaped to Canada, and a substantial number came to London. The reception afforded them was strikingly lacking in gratitude or generosity. Of some five thousand white loyalists who submitted claims for compensation from the British government, few failed to receive lump sums of at least £25 each. Twenty black applicants were paid between £5 and £20 each, while the rest got nothing, and some did not even get the back pay owed to them. By the middle of

1786, most of the more than eleven hundred black loyalists living in London were destitute.

A dole of sixpence a day came to be provided, from funds raised by public appeal with a grudging contribution from the government. Even this turned out to be bait rather than charity. The administering Committee for the Relief of the Black Poor saw the solution to its problem in dispatching its charges to Sierra Leone, a part of West Africa notorious as a catchment area for the slave trade. Payment of the dole became conditional on the agreement of recipients to such resettlement. Few blacks could be found to swallow this. The Vagrancy Act was then applied, to jail some of the destitute for the encouragement of the others.

When this failed also, further pressure was applied. A new treaty with France provided the occasion for calls in the British press to follow the French example, expel all blacks, and impose a total ban on the entry of any others. A meeting of blacks to protest against such proposals provoked the *Morning Post* to a discharge of racist rage and biological muddle. "Are we to be told what articles in a treaty should be adopted or rejected, by a crew of reptiles, manifestly only a single link in the great chain of existence above the *monkey*? Should a sooty tribe of Negroes be permitted to arraign, with impunity, the measures of Government? A few constables to disperse their meetings, and a law, prohibiting *blacks* from entering our country, would be the proper mode of treating those creatures, whose intercourse with the inferior orders of our women, is not less a shocking violation of female delicacy, than disgraceful to the state."[6]

Hundreds of the black poor were eventually bribed, intimidated, or otherwise pressed to take part in the resettlement scheme. Even while they waited on board the ships provided by the government, 50 of them died of cold and disease, while others came to reconsider the future that had been assigned to them and rejected it for flight. When the voyage began, there were only 350 black settlers, 41 of them women, and 59 white wives, some of them widowed by the recent deaths, still aboard. A further 35 died on the way. Within four years of their arrival, the remaining 374 were reduced, by hardship, disease, and enslavement, to 60.[7]

The first great victory, since the Mansfield judgment of 1722, in the campaign to abolish slavery came in 1807, with the end of Britain's engagement to the slave trade. It was a campaign to which British blacks made a notable contribution. Their readiness to emancipate themselves, by running away or by refusing to work without wages, gnawed away at the institution from within. In particular, it provided the material for the court cases in which the property rights sustaining slavery were confronted by the established safeguards, in tradition and law, of personal liberty. Not least, blacks spoke, with the authority of their own experience and to corresponding effect, against the horrors of slavery.

Most illustrious among these spokesmen was Olaudah Equiano, first brought to Britain at the age of twelve in 1757. Subsequently sold and taken to Monserrat, he there earned and saved enough by petty trading to buy his freedom and return to Britain. This was to remain his base, from which he then traveled widely abroad to educate himself. Drawn into the ill-fated Sierra Leone resettlement scheme in November 1786 as commissary of provisions and stores, he soon encountered cases of corruption and proceeded to report them. The Navy Board found that he had "acted with great propriety." He was dismissed from his post all the same.

He had already formed a close working relationship with Granville Sharp, the leading abolitionist in the mounting of legal challenges to slavery. Indeed, it was he who had drawn Sharp's attention to the murder of 132 slaves, thrown alive into the sea from the Liverpool slave ship Zong. Sharp's campaign to secure the punishment of the murderers failed in its immediate objective, but the case so aroused public opinion as significantly to promote the enactment in 1788 of a law to regulate the slave trade. Meanwhile, Equiano was increasingly active in campaigning against slavery. He wrote letters to the press, addressed meetings across the country, and coordinated the work of black militants with other components of the abolitionist movement. In the process, he came to identify himself with the working-class campaign for radical reform and in 1792 joined its organizational thrust, the London Corresponding Society.

By then, he had produced what was to prove his most influential contribution to the abolitionist cause, the publication in 1789 of his autobiography, The Interesting Narrative of the Life of Olaudah Equiano, or Gustavus Vassa, the African. The simple power of its prose, with the stark details of his personal sufferings, secured such success for the book that it exhausted eight editions in Britain alone during the eight years that remained of his life.

Another such influential former slave was Ottobah Cugoano, brought to Britain by his owner in 1772 and freed there. He came to be one of the main black militants in London, worked closely with Equiano and Granville Sharp, and in 1787, with some assistance from Equiano in the writing of it, produced his Thoughts and sentiments on the evil and wicked traffic of the slavery and commerce of the human species.

This was an indictment not only of those who personally engaged in the slave trade but of those who profited from it at a comfortable distance. He went still further, to hold "every man in Great-Britain responsible, in some degree" for the oppressions of slavery, "unless he speedily riseth up with abhorrence of it in his own judgement, and, to avert evil, declare himself against it."[8] He argued the economic case for an emancipation that would make black labor on the sugar islands far more productive and allow Africa to develop a prosperous trade which "would soon bring more revenue in a righteous way to the British nation, than ten times its share in all the profits that slavery can produce."[9] It was an argument that found a ready reception among the British commercial and industrial interests pressing for free trade and against the costly tariff protection given to slave-produced British colonial sugar.

There were other British blacks who made their mark mainly through their association with the wider movement for radical change. William Davidson, an active trade unionist, eventually became involved with a group of extreme militants who decided, at the promptings of a police spy, to assassinate cabinet ministers. Five of the conspirators, including Davidson, were convicted of high treason, hanged, and then beheaded in 1820. Robert Wedderburn was directly engaged in the struggle against slavery and produced a series of pamphlets, copies of which he succeeded in getting to Jamaica, where their surreptitious circulation much agitated the planters. It was his speeches and writings in support of the British working-class movement, however, that caused him to be arrested in 1819 on charges of sedition and blasphemous libel. Though the first of these was dropped, he was tried and convicted on the second, to be imprisoned for two years.[10]

It was not only ill-treatment, poverty, and disease that restricted the growth in the numbers of British blacks, despite such additions as those brought by the development of steamship lines to West Africa and the Caribbean. Most of the blacks who came to Britain were male, and many of them married white women. Nor is there any evidence that black women found it more difficult to find white husbands. If not the immediate progeny, then those that succeeded them often merged into the rest of the population.

In Britain, there was no such popular preoccupation with race as in the United States, where anyone with a trace of African ancestry was regarded as black. The very importance of slavery in the United States promoted a widespread view that whatever the Declaration of Independence might have said about all men being created equal, this applied in practice only to whites. In Britain, the black community was so small that for most of the population it represented no more than people of another color. But higher up the social scale, and especially from among those in the middle class, an increasingly vocal racism came to be expressed, not least in outrage at the apparent popular indifference to color in sexual relations. The expression of such outrage extended far beyond the reactionary press. William Cobbett, the distinguished fighter for the rights of rural laborers and then for the working-class program of social reform, vented his abhorrence in the pages of his own periodical.

Who, that has any sense of decency, can help being shocked at the familiar intercourse, which has gradually been gaining ground, and which has, at last, got a complete footing between the Negroes and the women of England? No black swain need, in this loving country, hang himself in despair . . . Amongst white women, this disregard of decency, this defiance of the dictates of nature, this foul, this beastly propensity, is, I say it with sorrow and with shame, *peculiar to the English.*[11]

The connection between class and racism was not coincidental. The minds of the educated had long been infected by the association of color with the slave trade, whose importance to the economy promoted the rationalization of an inherent black inferiority. Furthermore, such inferiority came in turn to be associated with the physical and particularly sexual side of human nature. This last was alarming to a middle class distinguished from the classes above and below by a sexual repressiveness that may have owed something to the Puritan strain in its ancestry.

Articles, tracts, and books from the slave-trading and colonial planter interests had their cumulative effect but might be dismissed as self-interested. More reputable was the influence of the most renowned thinkers. No less a figure than the philosopher John Locke, the intellectual father of the political commitment to the inalienable rights of man, delivered himself of a curious argument in his *Essay Concerning Human Understanding* of 1690:

> A Child having framed the *Idea* of a *Man*, it is probable, that his *Idea* is just like that picture, which the Painter makes of the visible Appearances joyned together; and such a Complication of *Ideas* together in his Understanding, makes up the single complex *Idea* which he calls *Man*, whereof White or Flesh-colour in England being one, the Child can demonstrate to you, that a *Negro is not a Man*, because White-colour was one of the constant simple *Ideas* of the complex *Idea* he calls *Man*: And therefore he can demonstrate by the Principle, *It is impossible for the same Thing to be, and not to be*, that a *Negro is not a Man.*[12]

In a land of black people, a child would presumably reach the rather different conclusion that a white is not a man. The selectiveness of Locke's example reflected a racial prejudice that might have been not altogether unconnected with his personal investment of £600, a considerable sum of money for those days, in the slave-trading Royal African Company.[13]

Racial prejudice was soon so rooted, however, that it needed no personal investment in its exploitation to advance it. David Hume, the great eighteenth-century philosopher of empiricism, took the search for infallible proof so far as to demonstrate the impossibility of knowing anything for certain. This did not, however, preclude him from arguing for a natural white superiority.

> I am apt to suspect the negroes, and in general all the other species of men (for there are four or five different kinds) to be naturally inferior to the whites. There never was a civilised nation of any other complexion than white, nor

even any individual eminent either in action or speculation. No ingenious manufacture amongst them, no arts, no sciences . . . In JAMAICA indeed they talk of one negroe as a man of parts and learning; but 'tis likely he is admired for very slender accomplishments, like a parrot, who speaks a few words plainly.[14]

By the time that slavery itself was outlawed, this sort of racism had become the conventional wisdom which provided the rationalization for the dynamic of an expanding empire. Respectable scientists, along with not a few pseudo-scientists, supplied their specious justifications for a commitment essentially concerned with the control of raw materials and markets, but paraded in all the meretricious morality of a mission to civilize the savage. The Anthropological Society, of which Richard Burton, explorer and writer, was vice-president, became a very center for the propagation of racist theories.

Among its members was Edward Eyre, the Governor of Jamaica who dealt so ferociously with a black rural rebellion on the island in 1865 that several hundred blacks, including children and pregnant women, were slaughtered. A Jamaica Committee, which included John Stuart Mill and Thomas Huxley among its members, with support from Charles Darwin, demanded a full investigation and the recall of the Governor. When a Royal Commission effectively exonerated Eyre, the Committee sought his prosecution for murder. It was no match, however, for the Eyre Defense Committee, which represented the dominant values of the age and counted among its supporters not only such rampant racists as Thomas Carlyle and Charles Kingsley, but Matthew Arnold, Charles Dickens, John Ruskin, and Alfred Tennyson. The case against Eyre was dismissed "because," as the *Spectator* commented, "his error of judgement involves only negro blood."[15]

It was against this ascendant racism that blacks born in Britain or arriving there had to make their way as best they could. Among those who rose to prominence nonetheless was William Cuffay, born at Chatham in 1788, who became a tailor and in 1839 joined the massive Chartist movement for the radical reform of Britain's political system. By 1842, he was president of its Metropolitan Delegate Council, and *The Times* characteristically took to sneering at the London Chartists as "the Black man and his Party." Six years later, the national convention of the movement appointed Cuffay chairman of the committee to manage the immense procession which, it was planned, would present to the House of Commons a Chartist petition bearing almost two million signatures.

The commissioner of police banned the procession, and Parliament rejected the Charter. Arrested in August 1848 as a member of the "Ulterior Committee" which was held to have planned an uprising in London, Cuffay was tried with others in September. He declared his innocence and defended himself with dignity, but was convicted of levying war against the Queen and sentenced to exile in a penal colony for the rest of his life. Transported to Tasmania, he worked at his trade into his eighties, and died in 1870 at a workhouse whose superintendent described him as "a quiet man, and an inveterate reader."

Mary Seacole, born at Kingston, Jamaica, around 1805, learned traditional medicine from her mother and became a nurse, to do valued service during a cholera epidemic in Panama and subsequently during a yellow fever epidemic in Jamaica. She was visiting London in 1854, when reports arrived of the inadequate nursing available to the wounded of the British army in the Crimean War. She volunteered her skills and experience, with authoritative testimonials as evidence of both. She was rejected by one department or agency after another until, convinced that her only disqualification was her color, she gave way to tears in the street.

She was not to give way again. She made her own way to the Crimea, where she was soon running the British Hotel, a combination of store, dispensary, and hospital. She also visited the military hospital daily to do any service allowed her, if only the repair of uniforms, and often visited the battlefield as well, to treat the wounded even under fire. Reports of her activities reached London, and when she returned there after the war, ill and virtually penniless, it seemed that an appreciative nation had been waiting to honor and help her. She was accorded a four-day musical benefit, an official dinner by the Guards, and an appeal on her behalf in the pages of *Punch*. She chose to remain in Britain, where she died, in obscurity though financial comfort, in 1881.

Ira Aldridge, born at New York in 1807, took early to the stage and emigrated to Britain, where his first appearance, at a London theater in 1825, was derided by *The Times*, in a review which claimed that he was unable to pronounce English properly, "owing to the shape of his lips."[16] Driven by such hostility to make his way in the provinces, he gathered experience and success before returning to try London again in 1833, with what he must have supposed to be the safe choice of Othello. The *Athenaeum*, excited by racist rage to the absurd, protested "in the name of propriety and decency" that "an interesting actress and ladylike girl, like Miss Ellen Tree" should be "pawed about on the stage by a black man."[17] While he played to crowded houses in the provinces, the capital of culture remained effectively closed to him, and in 1852 he set out on the first in a series of Continental tours. The public and critical acclaim he received abroad for his performances in Shakespearean roles, not least that of Othello, led even London at last to accept him. By 1867, when he died during a tour of Poland, he was celebrated as few other actors of his time.

Born at London in 1875, Samuel Coleridge-Taylor soon showed such musical promise that in 1890, after initial hesitancy at accommodating his color, the Royal College of Music admitted him as a student. Eight years later, his work for orchestra and chorus, *Hiawatha's Wedding Feast*, established him as a leading young composer, whose subsequent rich output, much of it influenced by traditional African music, was cut short only by his death at the age of thirty-seven. His three visits to the United States were virtually ceremonial triumphs. He was acclaimed both for his compositions and for his conducting. Yet of far more importance to him, he was greeted in one city after another by large crowds of blacks, for whom he was a source of pride in their identity and a symbol of their own creative possibilities. Indeed, rather than seeking, as many blacks did, to blur or block out the connection with Africa, he proclaimed it. He called himself an Anglo-African and associated himself with the emergent Pan-African movement.

Though the line of that movement's progenitors reaches back in Britain to Equiano and Cugoano, it was Sylvester Williams, a Trinidadian living in London to qualify for a career in the law, who was the immediate one. In 1898, he took the initiative, as secretary of the recently formed African Association, in calling for a world conference of black people. This met in London two years later and established a Pan-African Association, with Williams himself as general secretary and Samuel Coleridge-Taylor as a member of the executive. The conference adopted an "Address to the Nations of the World" which contained the soon celebrated statement: "The problem of the Twentieth Century is the problem of the colour-line."

Williams visited Trinidad, Jamaica, and the United States, to plant the Pan-African Association there. In Britain's own black community, however, it had little nourishment. Most of its merely fifty active members were sojourning students. It shriveled away in 1901, and the political paper founded by Williams, *The Pan-African*, came and went in one issue. Williams himself was called to the bar, the first black barrister ever to practice in Britain, and in 1906 became a councillor in the London borough of Marylebone, one of the two first blacks elected in Britain to public office. Two years later he returned to Trinidad, where he died in 1911.

Yet there was always someone else ready to take on the tasks. Duse Mohamed Ali was black, born of Egypto-Sudanese parentage in 1866 or 1867 and sent to Britain for his education at the age of nine or ten. He grew up to scrape a living as a journalist and actor, until, in 1912, with help from a Sierra Leonean businessman, he founded the *African Times and Orient Review*. It was the first political paper produced by and for blacks in Britain to survive beyond its initial appearance. In fact, it kept going until 1920, was read by blacks in both Africa and the Diaspora, included Marcus Garvey among its various contributors, and was so outspoken that on August 4, 1916, it welcomed the First World War as likely to exhaust the combatants: "Watch and wait! It may be that the non-European races will profit by European disaster." In 1921, Ali left for the United States and ten years later settled in Nigeria, where his weekly *Comet* would become a force in the movement for colonial freedom.

John Robert Archer, born at Liverpool in 1863, moved in his late twenties to London, where he earned a living as a photographer in Battersea. This was the most radical London borough of the time, and Archer won a seat on the local council in 1906. Then, in 1913, he was elected mayor, an achievement so momentous for a black in Britain that it made an impact across the Diaspora and especially in the United States. Having joined the Labour Party, Archer became its Battersea secretary and constituency agent, breaking through yet another barrier to office in the British political system. An ardent advocate of the Pan-African cause as well, he was elected president of the African Progress Union when this was founded at London in 1918, and was a delegate from Britain to the first Pan-African Congress, held at Paris in 1919. He died in 1932, while still serving on the Battersea borough council, as deputy leader of the Labour group.

On the rockface of racism in Britain, however, such were no more than markers of where some combination of special gifts, courage, and persistence, in special conditions, had reached. Indeed, for all the long alliance of black struggle and white working-class militancy, there were white workers who came to be contaminated by color prejudice. In part this was doubtless the influence of dominant middle-class racial attitudes, sustained by an imperial pride in which the poorest of whites might share. Mainly, however, white workers in particular occupations or areas saw, or were led to see, a potential threat to their jobs from black competition. Black seamen, for instance, laid off at ports such as Cardiff and Liverpool, found it all but impossible to get work on other ships or ashore, since white seamen and dockers refused to work alongside them. Only with the start of the First World War did jobs suddenly become available to blacks, in munitions and chemical factories, the merchant navy and the army. Yet such service at home, at sea, or on the battlefield was not proof against a prejudice that, as in the United States, emerged all the more sharply in a peace beset by economic difficulties.

The two labor unions of seamen were increasingly hostile to the employment of blacks, hundreds of whom were dismissed from their ships, and similar hostility from white workers at factories led to the dismissal of black ones, many of whom had been in their jobs for years. Nor was white prejudice, fed by fear and frustration, satisfied merely by securing black unemployment and hardship. In Liverpool, during May and June 1919, violence against blacks grew in incidence and intensity, from individual assaults to riot. White mobs fired homes and wrecked boarding houses and hostels where blacks were staying. By June 10, when such rioting was at its height, close to one thousand blacks were forced to take refuge in fire stations and prisons. On June 11, the *Liverpool Courier* commented: "One of the chief reasons of popular anger behind the present disturbances lies in the fact that the average negro is nearer the animal than is the average white man, and that there are women in Liverpool who have no self-respect."

By then, race rioting had broken out in Cardiff as well, where some three thousand blacks, of whom roughly twelve hundred were unemployed seamen, came under siege from white mobs, often led by ex-servicemen themselves unemployed. On June 13, a procession of black seamen, accompanied by police and followed by a jeering crowd, left the city. Most blacks, however, refused to be driven out and defended themselves as best they could. The *Manchester Guardian* commented from its moral height: "The quiet, apparently inoffensive, nigger becomes a demon when armed with revolver or razor."[18] The insults added to injuries culminated in the official decision to exclude black troops from the Peace March in London on July 19 to celebrate victory in the war.

Lord Milner, Britain's Colonial Secretary, was sensible enough to recognize the implications of all this. He warned that blacks from the colonies who had served in the armed forces and merchant navy only to find themselves targets of racial attack in Britain might well on their return home be a source of hostility to whites. So it was to prove. Trinidadians who had experienced the Cardiff riots and returned to the island were soon fighting against white British sailors in the streets. In Jamaica, the Acting Governor ascribed a like outbreak of fighting in Kingston to "the treatment which had been received by coloured sailors at Cardiff and Liverpool."[19]

Claude McKay, the black Jamaican socialist, poet, and future novelist, was in the United States during the antiblack rioting there in 1919 and came to Britain at the end of the year with illusions of receiving better treatment in that mother country of widespread Caribbean fantasy. He was not to keep his illusions for long. In 1920, E. D. Morel, a member of the Independent Labour Party, wrote in the *Daily Herald*, the newspaper of the British left, an article that inveighed against the use by France of black troops in occupied Germany. Luridly this depicted the indiscriminate rape of German women, girls, and boys by syphilitic black savages of insatiable sexual appetite.

It provoked an outraged reply from McKay, which was rejected by the *Daily Herald* on the pretext that it was too long, and which found space only in the small-circulation *Workers Dreadnought*. Not content with the publicity for his views that he had already received, Morel expanded his article and published it as a pamphlet entitled *The Horror on the Rhine*. Copies were distributed free to all delegates at the Trades Union Congress of 1920, where it made a deplorable impact, and by April 1921 eight editions of the pamphlet had spewed from the presses. By then, McKay had left Britain, convinced that antiblack prejudice was "almost congenital" among the English.[20]

The evidence that racism in Britain infected even those in organized labor could hardly have failed to heighten the commitment among blacks against the colonial system. London was the site for some sessions of the 2nd Pan-African Congress in 1921 and all of the 3rd Congress in 1923. The West African Students' Union was established in London on August 7, 1925, and from among its members would come many of those subsequently prominent in the African engagement against imperial rule.

Influential as well in its own way was the League of Colored Peoples, founded at London in March 1931. Its prime mover and president until his death in 1947 was Dr. Harold Moody, a Jamaican born in 1882, who came to London in 1904 to study medicine. Qualified as a doctor, he applied for various posts but was rejected because of his color, and so set up his own practice. His personal experience of racial rebuffs directed much of the League's work in helping blacks find accommodation and employment, but this did not preclude public campaigns on other racial issues, from police harassment of blacks in Cardiff to the repression of labor unrest in the West Indies. *The Keys*, a quarterly published by the League, counted among its contributors the black settler from Trinidad C. L. R. James.

Born in 1901, James came to Britain in 1932 and within a space of three years brought to publication as many major books: *Minty Alley*, a novel largely based on his Trinidadian childhood, in 1936; *World Revolution 1917–1936*, a Trotskyist study of the Communist International, in 1937; and a seminal history of the great Haitian slave revolution, *The Black Jacobins*, in 1938. In that year, he left for the United States on a lecture tour and stayed on as an illegal immigrant for fifteen years. Then, for the remainder of his life, except for four and a half years in the West Indies, mainly Trinidad, he used Britain as his base and died there at the age of 88, long a major influence on West Indian and British black intellectuals.

The invasion of Abyssinia by Fascist Italy in 1936 inflamed black consciousness across the Diaspora. When Emperor Haile Selassie arrived in London, he was welcomed at Waterloo Station by representatives of the recently formed International African Friends of Abyssinia movement, whose chairman was James and whose secretary was Jomo Kenyatta, one day to become leader of an independent Kenya. Britain increasingly became an organizational center of Pan-African political activity, some of it financed by an immigrant from British Guiana, who had been born George Thomas Nathaniel Griffith, but who changed his name to Ras Tefari Makonnen after the Italian invasion.

Beginning from the Ethiopian Teashop in Manchester, Makonnen established a chain of restaurants that proved most profitably popular with black servicemen stationed in the north of England during the Second World War. His liberality and local contacts, which enabled him to secure suitable lodgings and halls, supported his view that Manchester, with the historical connection between its cotton mills and the slave trade, would be the right site for the projected 5th Pan-African Congress in 1945.

Delegates came not only from political organizations but from trade unions in Africa and the Diaspora, to make this Congress less of an airing cupboard for intellectuals than any of its predecessors had been. Kwame Nkrumah, who would become the first Prime Minister of the Gold Coast in 1952 and in 1957 lead the colony to independence as Ghana, drafted the declaration which summoned colonial workers to use boycotts and strikes as weapons against imperial rule. Nor was the Congress concerned only with the colonies. It devoted the whole of its first day to "The Colour Problem in Britain," and a resolution, carried with others on the subject, demanded the use of the criminal law against discrimination based on race, color, or creed.

There had always been whites in Britain who had confronted racism, and it is arguable that there had been many more who rejected it in silence than those, disproportionately vocal, who had espoused it. The Second World War created the very conditions in which an essential decency might well have asserted itself against the racism of the imperial tradition and the anxious graduated snobberies of the British class system. The unity of an imperiled people, the association of racism with the Nazi enemy, and the demands of war which removed the factor of unemployment, provided a course in moral antibiotics that needed only official support to make it generally effective. In fact, there was a ready widespread response of personal welcome to black servicemen from the colonies and then the many more of those from the United States who began arriving in the spring of 1942.

The United States armed forces, however, were rife with segregationist practices, and white servicemen, especially those from the South, reacted aggressively to incidents of social mixing across the color line. Inevitably, among the victims of attack were not only blacks from the United States but those from the colonies and from Britain itself. This last alone should have prompted the British government to take firm action in confronting racism. Instead, insofar as the government acted at all, it did so only to collaborate with the United States military authorities. It sanctioned an article in *Current Affairs*, a periodical for circulation among its own armed forces, which advised that "the average American attitude" should be respected, since Americans needed to "exercise a certain measure of control to prevent the mixture of blood which would, at the present stage, benefit neither side."[21] Either ashamed of this effective instruction or uncertain of the wider domestic reception, it asked the British press to avoid any reference to the article or its contents.

This furtive commitment to accommodating racism was bad enough. Worse, because it reached further, was the official indifference to racist practices in the civilian sector, promoted by prejudice or the presumption that such prejudice was widespread. Blacks came increasingly to be barred, on some pretext or other, from hotels, restaurants, dance halls. This suddenly surfaced as an issue in the case of Learie Constantine, the great cricketer from Trinidad, who was being employed by the Ministry of Labor welfare department to help with the problems of recruited West Indian technicians in the Liverpool area.

Granted leave during the summer of 1943 to captain the West Indies team in a cricket match against England in London, he had reserved rooms for himself and his family at the Imperial Hotel. On his arrival, he was informed that he might stay for that night but no longer. A senior official from the Ministry of Labor asked why Constantine was being required to leave. "Because of the Americans," the manageress said. The official argued that Constantine was a British subject and civil servant. The manageress was unimpressed. "He is a nigger," she retorted.

Forced to find another hotel, Constantine proceeded to sue the Imperial for breach of contract. When the case came to court, the judge dismissed in severe terms the evidence given by the defendants and, with the highest praise for the dignity and modesty that had marked Constantine's performance in the witness box, awarded him token damages of £5. The verdict, reinforced by the wide publicity that the case attracted, did more to discourage such practices of discrimination than a national government, for all the Labour Party's participation, had so far done.

In 1948, with the unifying moral dynamic of the war succeeded by the different difficulties of peace, antiblack rioting broke out in Liverpool during the summer. Blacks, determined to defend themselves, were attacked by the police for doing so. In June, 492 Jamaicans had arrived in Britain, and those among them who had served there during the war were greeted by the London *Evening Standard* with the headline WELCOME HOME.[22] They might well have wondered what sort of welcome the events in Liverpool signified.

The boatload of Jamaicans marked only the beginning of the postwar black immigration from a West Indies of high unemployment to a Britain short of labor for the recovering economy. The Nationality Act of 1948 invested with British citizenship the citizens of British colonies, who were accordingly entitled to enter Britain without any restriction and stay there for as long as they pleased. Many of the early immigrants did not come on their own initiative. London Transport was the first major employer actively to recruit black workers and even advance the cost of fares for subsequent repayment out of wages. The British Hotels and Restaurants Association followed suit, as did the National Health Service. By the end of 1958, postwar immigrants from the West Indies would reach a total of some 125,000.

Along with smaller numbers of black immigrants from Africa, they had more than the shock of the climate to overcome. Even when no slight was intended, let alone hostility expressed, the contrast between traditional British reticence and the easy friendliness to which they were accustomed in their homelands was disconcerting. One immigrant from Dominica would later recall, "You go to a place and you say good morning, as you always did in the West Indies, and people look at you and say, you're crazy—what did she say? . . . and you walk in the street and say, hello, I mean you always did that at home, and people just stand there and look at you, you know, they think you're crazy, because you're talking to yourself . . . It's completely different."[23]

In fact, however, the experience of black immigrants was also one of increasing discrimination, especially in employment and housing. Generally they were given jobs that whites were unwilling to take, such as cleaning or night work. Not all of them were grateful for anything they could get. One Jamaican woman, refusing work as a cleaner in a café, explained, "I didn't borrow and save and come all this way just to scrub and clean. I can do that back at home."[24] A man from Barbados, recruited by London Transport with the promise of work as a guard, found himself instead assigned to cleaning and sweeping. "It was humiliating, honestly," he would recall, many years afterward.[25] By the late fifties, over half the male West Indians in London were employed at levels below those for which their skills and experience qualified them.

There was soon developing pressure from among white workers and their local trade union representatives for limits on the numbers of blacks and Asians employed in particular workplaces or companies or services. White bus crews were notably militant on the issue. Employers became reluctant to take on "colored" staff. Officials at the Employment Exchange on Tyneside, for instance, disclosed that most local employers, including the nationalized public utilities, refused to consider "colonials" even for unskilled work. In consequence, the unemployment rate among blacks and Asians was far higher than that in the working population at large. The Nottingham Labor Exchange, which unofficially kept separate records of "colored" unemployment, reported in 1958 a related rate of 14.5 percent alongside a general rate of local unemployment below 1 percent.

During the war, close to a quarter of a million dwellings had been destroyed in bombing raids, and the demobilized young, marrying and wishing to acquire homes of their own, augmented the pressures on available accommodation. One result was highlighted by the Institute of Race Relations:

> Coloured migrants on arrival are naturally at the end of the queue for housing of any kind and they have to take accommodation where they can. Not only is there the general shortage but there is unwillingness in the country among white landladies and landlords to take in coloured tenants—whether they are workers, students or professional men. The coloured population, therefore, swell the numbers of those inadequately housed. They add to the problem but did not cause it; it would still be bad if they had never come.[26]

In effect, while blacks found it disproportionately difficult to get jobs suitable to their qualifications or any jobs at all, they were blamed for taking or threatening the jobs of whites; and when, finding it disproportionately difficult to get decent housing, they crowded into whatever accommodation they could get, they were blamed for taking scarce housing away from whites and turning such enclaves into slums. The Suez crisis of 1956 led to rising oil prices and an economic recession with a rising rate of white unemployment. Given the apparent official obliviousness to gathering evidence of racial tension, a major outbreak of violence became virtually inevitable.

After months of increasingly frequent individual attacks on blacks, rioting struck Nottingham in August 1958. Coverage by the press and television seemed to encourage the racist excitement, and at the height of the rioting, thousands of whites collected in the streets, led by shouts of "Let's get the blacks." In the event, blacks kept to their homes, and the rage blew itself out with little physical damage. More serious were the developments in London's north Kensington area, where gangs of young whites, including members of a neo-Nazi group, had taken to arming themselves with iron bars and knives to go "nigger-hunting."

Many years later, one black recalled the evening of August 25, 1958: "I heard like a swarm of bees coming along the road. I opened the door and saw the crowd coming."[27] On the following day, the rioting began. As their casualties mounted, the blacks attacked with petrol bombs the local head-quarters of the neo-Nazi group and a club where whites were known to be planning their raids. At the beginning of September, white rioting climaxed in a rampage of attacks on blacks and their property. The police, ordered to clear the streets, displayed particular enthusiasm in dispersing small groups of blacks, however innocently employed.

Subsequently, in the most notable action from someone in authority, a judge sentenced nine white youths to four years of imprisonment each. Their behavior, he declared, had "filled the whole nation with horror, indignation and disgust."[28] If this was plainly an exaggeration, it was true that a majority in Britain remained opposed to racism. In a Gallup Poll of March 1955, no less than 79 percent of respondents had said that it was wrong to refuse work alongside a black man or woman; only 12 percent had said it was right; and 9 percent had said that they did not know. Three years later, at the height of the north Kensington rioting, a poll in London was distinctly less encouraging but—given the timing, the form of the question, and the purely urban basis of the survey—not altogether without comfort. Half the respondents said that "coloured people from the Commonwealth" should be allowed to compete for jobs on equal terms with the native British, 36 percent said they should not, and 14 percent said that they did not know.[29] The danger was that it was racism which was setting the pace.

Led by a pack of its parliamentary members from the Birmingham area who were baying for immigration controls, a Conservative government was manifestly moving toward such measures. The result was predictable. Reports that the door was likely soon to be shut promoted a rush to get through the opening, and the rise in arrivals promoted the clamor for controls. In 1959, some 16,000 West Indians and 3,860 Asians had arrived. In 1960 the respective figures were roughly 50,000 and 8,500, rising again in 1961 to 66,000 and 49,000.[30]

Social conditions, without remedial measures, concentrated the stresses. Blacks did not disperse across the country but were drawn to urban areas where jobs were most likely to be available, other blacks were already settled in reassuring numbers, and initial accommodation might be found with relatives or friends. Of an estimated 300,000 West Indians in Britain by the middle of 1962, some 135,000 were in London, 67,000 in Birmingham, 9,500 in Nottingham, 7,100 in Wolverhampton, and 7,000 in Manchester. Predictably, such settlements were essentially in the districts of existing social deprivation, such as Brixton in London and Moss Side in Manchester.[31]

In 1962, the Conservative government propelled through Parliament the first-ever Commonwealth Immigrants Bill, restricting the entry of Commonwealth immigrants with British passports to those specifically provided with employment vouchers, and making even these immigrants liable to deportation if convicted of any offense within five years of their arrival. Hugh Gaitskill, leader of the Labour Party, described the bill as "miserable, shameful, shabby." His death soon afterward led to a weakening in the principled opposition of his party.

In the general election of 1964, the Conservative candidate in the Smethwick constituency of the Birmingham area based his campaign on the demand for a program of "coloured repatriation" and on the slogan "If you want a nigger neighbour, vote Labour." The Labour candidate, a former cabinet minister, chose not to confront this overt racism but to try turning its edge against the Conservatives themselves. "The whole wave of immigration," he stated, "has occurred since 1951 while the Conservatives have been in power. It is false and unfair to blame the Labour Party for immigration."[32]

In a race of rivals for the racist prize, it is the front runner at the start who usually draws strength from the pressure of those behind. The Conservative took the formerly safe Labour seat despite a national swing to Labour, and this result could not have failed to impress the new Labour government of that devoted pragmatist, Harold Wilson. New restrictions on Commonwealth immigrants now provided a ceiling on the number of required labor vouchers, at 8,500 a year. The 1966 Race Relations Act was passed as a reassurance of Labour's opposition to racism. The first prosecution under this law was that of a black immigrant, for a speech held to have contained incitement to racial hatred.

So far, the laws restricting immigration from the Commonwealth had effectively been directed against those of color while being masked as indifferent to race. In 1968, the mask was at last discarded, when a special Commonwealth Immigrants Act restricted the entry of Kenyans with British passports but exempted whites. Among the Labour members of Parliament who protested, Andrew Faulds declared: "This Measure makes racialism respectable . . . that a Socialist Government should be responsible fills me with shame and despair."[33]

In April of that year, Enoch Powell, academic turned politician and now a member of the Conservative shadow cabinet, delivered a speech in Birmingham that depicted a nation whose whole way of life was under threat from the invasion of color. White Britons were finding "their wives unable to obtain hospital beds in childbirth, their children unable to obtain school places, their homes and neighbourhoods changed beyond recognition, their plans and prospects for the future defeated." After an erudite reference to "the River Tiber foaming with much blood," he looked to a less dated source of foreboding. "The tragic and intractable phenomenon which we watch with horror on the other side of the Atlantic, but which there is interwoven with the history and existence of the States itself, is coming upon us here by our own volition and our own neglect."[34]

In the furor that followed, the leader of the Conservative Party, Edward Heath, sacked Powell from the shadow cabinet. Yet the Conservative government elected in 1970 was quick to proceed along the route of racial restrictiveness. Fresh legislation related citizenship rights of entry and residence to British ancestry, with the effect of narrowing still further the space through which immigrants of color might pass, while leaving wide the way for potential millions of white immigrants. Moreover, police and immigration officers were given powers to arrest without warrant suspected illegal immigrants and deport, at the Home Secretary's discretion, any immigrant worker if this was considered "conducive to the public good." These provisions would intrude into the lives of many black and Asian Britons, required to account for themselves and provide evidence of their status.

The Labour government of 1974–79 did at least recognize the need for further legislative action to confront racism. The Race Relations Act of 1976 outlawed not only direct but also "indirect discrimination," such as job requirements with which members of one race could more easily comply than could those of another, and established a Commission for Racial Equality to monitor the functioning of the Act and promote its purposes. Over a decade later, in its annual report of 1987, this Commission would declare that levels of discrimination in employment, housing, and other social sectors remained alarmingly high, with the government unwilling to strengthen the relevant legislation so as to make it effective.[35]

The reality was that the Labour government had no stomach for the necessary fight, and the Conservative government which followed no mind for it. When Margaret Thatcher displaced Edward Heath as leader of the party in 1975, it signaled primarily a harder economic policy, but this came to be followed by a rhetoric on race that, given the existing restrictions on colored immigration, had more to do with mood than with measures. In an interview on television in February 1978, Mrs. Thatcher cited the prediction of some committee that "if we went on as we are, then by the end of the century there'd be four million people of the New Commonwealth or Pakistan here." She continued, "Now that's an awful lot, and I think it means that people are really rather afraid that this country might be swamped by people of a different culture. And you know, the British character has done so much for democracy, for law, and has done so much throughout the world that if there is any fear that it might be swamped, people are going to react and be rather hostile to those coming in."[36]

She pressed the same panic button one year later, a few months before the general election that would bring her to power, saying, "Some people have been swamped by immigrants. They've seen the whole character of their neighbourhood change . . . Of course people can feel that they are being swamped. Small minorities can be absorbed—they can be assets to the majority community—but once a minority in a neighbourhood gets very large, people do feel swamped. They feel their whole way of life has been changed."[37]

This seemed to blame blacks and other immigrants of color for their very concentration in "neighbourhoods" to which discrimination effectively confined them. Moreover, while references to "swamping" implied the victimization of whites, it was the "swampers" who were the primary victims, of a society which had once welcomed, even invited them, and then increasingly come to treat them as invaders. Nowhere was this more evident than in the conduct of the police.

If the ghetto, with its inferior schools and social amenities, its inadequate housing and disproportionate numbers of unemployed, fostered a recourse to crime, it was not altogether surprising. Yet statistics which reflected a relatively high rate of black crime had to be qualified by the disposition among police to believe this was so and to act accordingly. A targeting of blacks in making arrests and securing convictions did not provide the most reliable basis for establishing racial differentials in crime rates. Nor was such targeted zeal in catching criminals the only source of a disquiet which extended well beyond the black community. Increasing complaints from blacks of police violence and abuse were supported by published evidence of widespread racism in the police force.[38]

An authoritative account of such racism came in 1979, with the submission from the Institute of Race Relations to the Royal Commission on Criminal Procedure.[39] On the basis of numerous case histories and interviews, this criticized the police for gratuitous raids on black youth clubs; the repeated arrest of individual blacks on frivolous pretexts; the refusal to provide blacks with protection against racially motivated violence and the treatment of victims as though they were responsible for the attacks upon them; the arrest of blacks for insisting upon their rights; the intimidation of witnesses to police abuses; the entry of black homes and premises at will; the use of unnecessary violence in arresting blacks and of brutality in seeking to obtain confessions from black suspects.

The effect of such treatment was to make many blacks feel that the police represented racism in uniform, and there were those, especially among the young, who reacted accordingly. Clashes between young blacks and police at successive Notting Hill Carnivals in the late seventies were signs of an increasing racial turbulence which the mood of the new Conservative government, elected in May 1979 under Margaret Thatcher, did little to avert.

In April 1980, blacks in the St. Paul's district of Bristol resisted with such force a raid on one of their few meeting places that the police deemed it prudent to retreat. It was a warning all the more ominous for sounding from a city with a reputation for relatively harmonious race relations. It was nonetheless disregarded. Racist attacks on individual blacks, incited when not executed by members of such extremist groups as the National Front, increased while the police continued to display less interest in preventing them or pursuing those responsible than in sieving black communities for suspected criminals.

In the Deptford district of London, a number of black homes and a black community center had already been burned in a campaign of arson when, in January 1981, thirteen young blacks died in a fire. The bereaved families and the black community in general were convinced that the fire had been started deliberately. The police, in what had become a stock response, discounted this. Subsequently, in the largest demonstration ever mounted by blacks in Britain, some fifteen thousand marched the ten miles to central London from Deptford to protest against a police inquiry they considered more concerned with burying than with investigating the case.

In what many blacks saw as a response to the march, police in the substantially black London district of Brixton launched "Swamp 81"—not the happiest choice of word—as an exercise in saturation policing. Well over a hundred plainclothes police stopped almost a thousand people in the street, arrested 118 of them, and later charged 75 of these. Shortly afterward, Brixton was swept by rioting. In the subsequent account of Lord Scarman, a senior judge appointed by the Home Secretary to inquire and report:

> During the week-end of 10–12 April (Friday, Saturday and Sunday) the British people watched with horror and incredulity an instant audio-visual presentation on their television sets of scenes of violence and disorder in their capital city, the like of which had not previously been seen in this century in Britain. In the centre of Brixton, a few hundred young people—most, but not all of them, black—attacked the police on the streets with stones, bricks, iron bars and petrol bombs, demonstrating to millions of their fellow citizens the fragile basis of the Queen's peace.[40]

It was to prove no more than a prelude. In July, having begun in the London district of Southall, rioting spread within a few days to some thirty cities across the country. In Manchester's Moss Side district, a thousand youths besieged the police station. In the Toxteth district of Liverpool, four days of rioting left some 150 buildings burned and some 780 police put out of action. So serious did the rioting become there that at its height, the Chief Constable woke the Home Secretary at three in the morning to seek and get permission for the first ever use in Britain of CS gas. * Though blacks were generally in the forefront of this virtual revolt, many young Asians were also involved, as were, notably in Toxteth and Moss Side, young whites. These had reason enough of their own for protest in a period of soaring unemployment, urban decay, and a government, apparently indifferent, whose repressive edge the police represented.

The Prime Minister's view was that nothing justified the rioting. If parents could not control the actions of their children, she said, what could the government do to stop them from engaging in "hooliganism" and "a spree of naked greed"? The government was reported to be considering plans for involving parents in "the consequences of offences committed by their children."[41]

In November 1981, the Scarman Report on the Brixton riots was released, to provide a more rational view of the social causes behind the rioting. "The evidence," Scarman wrote, "leaves no doubt in my mind that racial disadvantage is a fact of current British life," and "urgent action is needed if it is not to become an endemic, ineradicable disease threatening the very survival of our society." He praised the police for the way they had dealt with the rioting, but implied in his recommendations their share in the responsibility for it. He called for more recruits from ethnic minorities; the dismissal of any police officer found guilty of racially prejudiced behavior; a review of policing methods in inner-city areas; and a commitment to procedures of consultation with local communities. He went further, to characterize the riots as "essentially an outburst of anger and resentment by young black people against the police."[42]

The Home Secretary announced that he accepted many of Scarman's recommendations on the police, along with the need to take action on the issue of racial disadvantage. Yet it was the preoccupation with public order and the priorities of the Prime Minister herself that determined the extent to which Scarman's warnings were heeded. When serious outbreaks of black disaffection struck cities again, during September and October 1985, one notable site was the Handsworth district of Birmingham, up till then claimed

---

* CS is a gas producing severe nausea that had been used in the Vietnam War and been stockpiled in Britain for military purposes rather than with any employment against civil disorder in mind.

to be a prime example of the success achieved in transforming relations between the police and the local community. On this occasion, it was significantly not a senior judge but a senior policeman who was asked to conduct an inquiry. The Chief Constable of the West Midlands attributed responsibility for the local disturbances to the violence of a criminal element:

> The majority of rioters who took part in these unhappy events were young, black and of Afro-Caribbean origin. Let there be no doubt, these young criminals are not in any way representative of the vast majority of the Afro-Caribbean community whose life has contributed to the life and culture of the West Midlands over many years and whose hopes and aspirations are at one with those of every other law abiding citizen.[43]

The Home Secretary adopted the same approach in a speech to police chiefs:

> Poor housing and other social ills provide no kind of reason for riot, arson and killing. One interviewer asked me whether the riot was not a cry for help by the rioters. The sound which law-abiding people heard at Handsworth was not a cry for help but a cry for loot. That is why the first priority, once public order is secure, must be a thorough and relentless investigation into the crimes which were committed.[44]

In April 1991, the BBC devoted a special program to reviewing the riots of ten years before and the extent of the changes that had taken place since then. One of those interviewed, Margaret Sidey, had chaired the Merseyside Police Committee at the time. She had, she declared, warned years before the rioting had broken out that there would be civil war on the streets, and "the ferocity came because after years of suppression the lid had blown." Since then, it seemed, the wrong lessons had been learned. "The style that the police have adopted, and this is national since '81, is, we are not having rioting in our streets, and they will use their best techniques to have instant control over any evidence of disorder. Now that's all very well after disorder has broken out, but it's the wrong style if you want to prevent disorder ever developing."[45]

Several blacks who recalled the riots of 1981 gave their versions of subsequent developments: hard policing, with a cosmetic exercise in community relations; helicopter surveillance and more police vans in the streets; a growth in the race relations industry, with some handouts to local communities; a few upwardly mobile blacks who had done well, while nothing had changed for the mass. "We are living," said one, somewhat overstating his case, "in a concentration camp with fringe benefits."

Yet it would be difficult to overstate the danger presented by the enormous rise in racially motivated violence against blacks and Asians. Home Office figures disclosed that there had been 7,793 such attacks in 1992, an increase of 78 percent from the number four years before.[46] The Anti-Racist Alliance among others argued that only one in ten of such attacks was ever reported to the police—a comment in itself—so that the real figure was close to 80,000. This estimate also, however, it soon emerged, fell far short of reality. In July 1993, Peter Lloyd, Minister of State at the Home Office, told a House of Commons select committee that the findings of the British Crime Survey suggested racial attacks in Britain could be running at a rate of between 130,000 and 140,000 a year, though "only a minority are serious acts of violence."[47]

Furthermore, if nowhere near to the appalling extent in the ghettos of the United States, there was rising violence within the black community itself. In part, as there, this was related to the traffic in narcotics. More marginal, but significant for the source from which it fed, was the emergence of a homophobic strain. The phenomenon surfaced to concern with the release in August 1992 of a reggae song, "Boom By By," which called in its lyrics for the shooting of gay men or "battyboys."

Oscar Watson, who organized a Black, Queer, and Fierce arts festival in London, commented: "In order to understand what is going on, you have to understand immigrant culture. Having your culture continually threatened by the wider culture is a very frightening experience. For a lot of black men, the only power they have in society is the power of the stereotype of being powerful and masculine. A black gay man is seen as a threat to that self-image, so he is attacked." In order to combat racism effectively, Watson added, the black community needed to stand together, "and I don't really see how they can hope to do that when they're losing an active percentage of their own people as a direct result of their own prejudices."[48]

FOUR

Travels in the Historic Present

23 | THE BAJAN CAGE

~~~~~~

Barbados, the most easterly of the Caribbean islands, is one of the most crowded countries on earth. It has more than a quarter of a million people crammed into its small space, for a density of over fifteen hundred per square mile. The flatness of the island, created by coral, makes it seem even smaller than it is, as the mountains of other, volcanically created, Caribbean islands make them seem rather larger than they are. The very sea surrounding it, far from stretching, seems instead to shrink the sense of space, as though the island were enclosed by glass.

Barbadians—or Bajans, as they commonly call themselves—take pride in a culture that seems to have developed in isolation from its regional environment. One of them described his island to me as the slipped disc of the Caribbean. It is more popularly known as "Little England," because of its celebrated loyalty and supposed likeness to the big one. It is said to have signaled the extent of its allegiance at the outbreak of the South African or Boer War in 1899 by sending to London the telegram: "Go ahead! Barbados is behind you!" Apocryphal or not, the story says something of how seriously Bajans take themselves.

Their vaunted qualities of discipline, diligence, thrift, and rectitude are not correspondingly admired by other Caribbeans, who tend to take a larger, more exuberant view of life. Yet Barbados is not without its foreign defenders. A publisher, striving to survive against the odds of political repression and economic decay in Guyana, declared over lunch with me: "Whatever else may be said about Barbados, it is an open and thriving society, with a free press and a freely elected government that changes without any fuss. These are not attributes I lightly dismiss." Nor should they be lightly dismissed by anyone.

Small societies are not necessarily less complex than large ones or more secure from contradictions. In such a free and open society as Barbados, the local campus of the University of the West Indies might reasonably be expected to contain numerous young rebels. The contrary is the case. A professor there lamented to me that he could not get his Bajan students to question any statement he made: "They seem to regard it as, at the very least, impolite to disagree with their teacher."

This is not because education is the preserve of a relative few whose families can afford it and who are accordingly complacent in their prerogatives: free education for all was an early achievement of independence and is a prime source of Bajan pride. It is rather that education has long been highly valued, not only as the route to social advancement, but, in alliance with the home, as a means of promoting respect and obedience. Those Bajans with the aptitude to reach university arrive in general with a training in deference and docility.

In other parts of the Caribbean, women are increasingly rebelling against the traditional exercise of male authority. In Barbados they are widely held to feel more comfortable in acquiescence. There is some hard evidence to support the anecdotal. The University of the West Indies has, among its extramural activities, a Women and Development unit. Barbados is host to the headquarters. Yet it is in Barbados that there has been the most disappointing relative response by women to the services that the unit affords. The concept of development evidently smacks too much of revolt.

Economic statistics place Barbados in that category of "middle income" countries above the plight of most others in the Caribbean and the wider Third World. At the end of the 1980s, its gross national product per head, at US$6,370, was more than twice that of Trinidad and Tobago, more than five times that of Jamaica, and more than twenty times that of Guyana. Such statistics, however, are the bluntest of instruments. By dealing in averages, they divert attention from the existence of the extremes. The "middle income" status of Barbados encompasses the very rich and the very poor, with a respective racial correlation that elsewhere in the Caribbean would have proved less acceptable.

The lines are not altogether straight. A few poor whites survive as reminders of the once more substantial population of white poor. There is a flourishing black middle class, much of it rooted in the government under undisputed black control, and with suckers throughout the economy. Below, through class and subclass to the bottom, the society is overwhelmingly black. Above, in command of the sugar estates, banking and insurance, manufacturing and marketing, shipping and tourism, it is overwhelmingly white. On this small island, the homes of the white rich are no more difficult to find than are the huddles of black wretchedness for those in subsistence agriculture, casual labor, or no labor at all, in a population where more than one in five are unemployed.

Despite the reputation of Barbados for interracial accommodation, the reality is bizarre. Representative of this reality is the so-called 6 p.m. factor. The working day brings black and white together and ends at 6 o'clock with their departure for effectively segregated residential areas. Social crossing of the border at private functions, such as parties at home, is said by some Bajans to be increasing but admitted by the same Bajans to be still rare. At least two white clubs are widely known to bar Bajan blacks. A small group of visiting Jamaican blacks succeeded in gaining entry to one of them, but only after providing proof of their foreign identity. My informant, a prominent Jamaican journalist who was one of the group, was even more startled when she subsequently broached the issue with black Bajans. "Why should we mind?" they responded. "We don't want to mix with them."

In 1934, a Bajan teacher and journalist named Gordon Bell assumed the pseudonym of George Bernard to produce for publication a small book, *Wayside Sketches: Pen Pictures of Barbadian Life.* He identified four social categories above the "masses": the elite, an upper middle class, a middle class, and a lower middle class. "The middle class," he wrote, "is the largest of the four groups mentioned and I would add the most conservative if they had anything more material to conserve than an unfortunate misconception of dignity . . . Standing upon their dignity at all times and keeping up appearances are their besetting sins.

"The difference between the lower middle classes and the masses," he continued, "is largely a difference in occupation, and it is edifying to know how many kinds of occupations are considered too menial for contemplation by the members of the lower middle classes. There is a great gulf fixed between the office messenger and the grocer's delivery boy; between the night-watchman of a large department store and the hand-cart man; even between the road-mender and the road-sweeper."

Further, he wrote: "Mention must be made of the strong religious feeling of the masses because it is one of the important components of their makeup. It is largely responsible for the fact that the Barbadian at home is one of the best-behaved and most tractable citizens on the face of the earth. The average Barbadian (of the masses) is deeply religious, and even without wishing to endorse Karl Marx's famous dictum, it is impossible to separate their spiritual complacency from their material subjection."[1]

In his introduction to the second edition of the book, published more than half a century after the first, the Bajan journalist John Wickham disclosed the real name of the author and commented: "The fact that this deep dark secret . . . can now be revealed is a measure of the distance we have travelled in the years since 1934. Gordon Bell was still a teacher until his death in December, 1982, but it is now inconceivable that any of his present day successors in the profession would feel compelled to mask his identity in a nom-de-plume because he dared to author some pen pictures of Barbadian life."

The measure of the distance that Bajans have traveled is a matter of opinion. In 1990, Dr. Hilary Beckles, a teacher in the Department of History at the University of the West Indies in Barbados, became the target of attack for his book A *History of Barbados*, regarded as inflammatory. I could find nothing in this essentially academic study that remotely justified such a reaction, though Dr. Beckles did write that the government since 1966 had seemed "unprepared to tackle the manipulative might of the commercial elite" and that the "development of a black professional middle class" had filled only "part of the vast socio-economic gulf which hitherto separated the white elite from the black labouring masses."[2]

Certainly, much has changed since Gordon Bell penned his pictures. The middle class, for instance, now has a great deal more material to conserve than a misconception of dignity. Yet much has stayed the same. The preoccupation with status.and appearances had made manual labor unacceptable to many Bajans. It was becoming increasingly difficult, one businesswoman wailed, to get gardeners or masons, and field workers were having to be imported.

During my stay on the island in February 1991, the local press gave due prominence to an assault on Bajan attitudes, including a reluctance to take risks and assume debt, from no less startling a source than Dr. Kurleigh King, the governor of the central bank. Bajans, he declared, had a propensity to save, were critical of one another, concerned about what other people believed. They were "apprehensive and fearful." They "preferred an autocratic style of management" and "liked to be told what to do." Indeed, "attempts to give them more freedom and flexibility made many Barbadians uncomfortable." This "tendency to be so cautious and reserved" might explain, he added, why Barbados lagged behind other islands, notably Jamaica and Trinidad, in developing an indigenous music.[3]

That this fusillade should have drawn no counterfire was doubtless due in part to the rank of the assailant. What would not have been countenanced from someone of subordinate station was permissible to established authority. No one suspected the governor of the central bank of any design to subvert the social order. Besides, most of the characteristics which Dr. King had criticized were widely held in high regard. He seemed accordingly to be blaming Bajans not so much for vice as for excessive virtue.

The description of Barbados as "Little England" is not wholly misconceived. It is simply more an anachronism than an analogy. If the preoccupation with class, deference, discipline, diligence, thrift, and rectitude owes little resemblance to England today, it bears a certain resemblance to the dominant values of England in the Victorian Age. It is rather as though Barbados were a colonial conservatory, to which those values had been brought, there to thrive within the protective panes of the sea. And just as in Victorian England, they thrive in an environment of emotional repression that sends out its own strange shoots.

There is, for instance, a remarkable measure of serious, even solemn, press attention given to occasional incidents of bestiality. The case of the violated cow was provided with front-page coverage that included a photograph of the victim being raised to its hooves. The case of the violated dog was accorded similar coverage, which included a photograph not only of the victim but of the alleged offender. A Guyanese now settled in Barbados, whose many charms for him include civility and safety, commented to me: "Nowhere else in the Caribbean would an editor dream of giving so much space, if any at all, to such cases. Readers there would only have fallen about, laughing."

Sometimes a sudden excitement disturbs Bajan reserve. My arrival on the island coincided with such an occasion. A magistrate had just decided to order the use of the cat-o'-nine-tails on certain young offenders, a punishment which had long been part of the law but had not been imposed since the 1930s. By the time I left, the sentence had not yet been executed, but was pleasurably expected to be.

When Walter Rodney, the Guyanese radical and historian, was banned from Jamaica, protesters in Kingston set fire to much of the downtown commercial district. When Ricky Singh, a Guyanese journalist, fled from the increasing terrorism of his government to refuge in Barbados, he encountered much public abuse there, along with threats to the safety of his family as well as himself.

In a speech to undergraduates at the University of the West Indies in Barbados, the distinguished Bajan novelist and critic, George Lamming, declared that this reaction had "given us a glimpse of that aggressive and demonic force which lurks behind the cautious and deceiving surface of Barbadian respectability. I have always known that this beast was there." He denounced those "political illiterates" who sought to hunt down all so-called subversives, and reminded his audience that "the word subversive glitters with the names of men who have laid the only foundation of liberty and dignity that Black people have known."

He went on: "It is a very ominous moment when a man like Mr. Sandiford, a supreme example of loyalty and universally known to be decent, has, nervously, to remind his country, and I quote: 'Do not fall into the trap that you are unpatriotic because you do not agree with the Prime Minister.' Who would have thought that a country which has so carefully cultivated for itself a reputation of independent and free public expression, would have required such a reminder?"[4]

The passion for conformity is not one which is generally associated with Caribbean blacks. Its particular presence in Barbados can scarcely be satisfactorily explained by the peculiar flatness of the natural environment. There seems to be a widespread fear of dissent for which the incidence of such dissent can scarcely account. This raises the suspicion that Bajans may, in their very passion for conformity, be less concerned with stamping out any supposed individual subversives than with stamping out the subversive in themselves.

Theirs is, after all, a society whose values are elsewhere more conspicuous in the literature of the past than in life today. And Bajan rectitude itself is no longer so protected by the sea. If narcotics are increasingly making their way onto the island, this is no more than part of an international consumer culture that ceaselessly arrives in foreign television programs and magazines, in visits from Bajans settled abroad, and in each new planeload of tourists. The rising incidence of crime will not be reversed by recourse to the cat-o'-nine-tails.

Subversive ideas may be slow in having an impact, but it does not follow that the impact must be light. The Black Power movement, for instance, that once swept through so much of the Diaspora, did little but rustle across the island until recently. Then, having abated elsewhere, it began blowing in Barbados against the emplacements of white business dominance. If this spirit of protest, still mainly confined to the intelligentsia, should increase and become more widespread, it will severely test the strength of the conservatory frame.

A high wind is especially dangerous to a flat island, whose inhabitants are accordingly more wary of it. Yet there is in Bajans a force that may yet overwhelm wariness. The last impression I expected to bring back from Barbados was one of rage. Yet it was a repressed rage that I found myself so often encountering, not least behind the tight smiles and recited expressions of pleasure at the opportunity to be of service. "Tourism is our business" directs the government in its campaign of advertisements to promote the welcoming of visitors, "Lets [sic] play our part." The script is well-rehearsed, but the members of the cast clearly have other matters on their minds.

I suspect that it is rage which informs the "aggressive and demonic force" of which George Lamming spoke. It is a rage that goes back to the very beginnings of a black Barbados and that has, ever since, been sustained by the very repressions of "respectability" developed to contain it. The more that the Bajan conservatory is examined, the more it takes on the character of a cage; and the same human spirit that has sought the protection provided by the panes of the one may well sooner or later hurl itself at the bars it finds in the other.

~~~~~~

In Barbados I met a black Guyanese woman who had been born Sandra Williams and had changed her name to Andaiye in assertion of her black identity. She had cancer and spoke freely of her fight against it. She had been fighting far longer against Guyana's repressive black regime, and speculated that her cancer might well have emerged as a form of internalized rage or grief. It was easy enough in Guyana to find an abundance of reason for both.

Unlike Haiti, which it has come to rival as the poorest country in the hemisphere, Guyana has natural resources whose sensible exploitation might easily support a population many times its present size. Some 83,000 square miles in extent, it contains, by most current estimates, fewer than 700,000 inhabitants. I was told that international aid agencies do their calculations on the basis of 690,000; but no one can know. The last census was conducted in 1980, and the results, of dubious validity, were suppressed. The regime was determined to conceal what had long been common knowledge: that the community of East Indian extraction accounted for roughly half the total population, while blacks ruled the country on the basis of roughly 35 percent. The surviving indigenous people and the whites, mainly of Portuguese origin, were marginal to the basic ethnic division.

Probably 90 percent of the Guyanese live within a ribbon of land along the coast, where the staple crops of sugar and rice are grown. Inland, there stretches a rich expanse of rain forest, preserved less by any ecological concern than by economic disorder and decay. The principal economic activity there is bauxite mining. Gold and diamonds are sifted from the material of riverbeds by individual prospectors or small independent groups. There is enough promise of oil to have engaged exploration by a large Texas company. Four major rivers course through the interior to the coast. They are navigable in their lower reaches but otherwise formidable with rapids and waterfalls. In the mouth of one, the Essequibo, there are islands as large as Barbados.[1]

Yet out of all this, a combination of repression, corruption, and incompetence has managed to reduce what was relatively little to very much less. In the early 1970s, the sugar yield of Guyana was approximately the same as that of Fiji. As Fiji's rose, Guyana's fell, till in 1990 the first was some four times as great as the second. A Guyanese yield of just over 300,000 tons in 1981 dwindled to just under 130,000 in 1990, when the condition of the industry was so dire that the government concluded a management contract with the same British company (Booker Brothers, McConnell) whose interests it had nationalized in 1975.[2]

The record of the bauxite industry has been no less calamitous. Frequent strikes for decent wages by the mainly black workforce, combined with the absence of investment in the repair and replacement of machinery, have sent production figures plummeting. Guyana is rich in calcined bauxite, the highest grade of the mineral. Processing this into alumina for export can generate significantly more profit than simply exporting the raw material. In 1981, the country exported 165,000 tons of alumina; in 1982, it exported 65,000. Then the sole refinery ceased functioning altogether.[3]

In a country whose rivers seem custom-made for the production of plentiful hydroelectric power, the provision of electricity was so inadequate and defective that cuts, some of them lasting many hours, occurred with increasing frequency during my stay, not only plunging streets and homes into darkness at night, but stopping the supply of water then or at any time in the working day. Those businesses with the necessary funds, such as foreign-owned hotels, had long ago installed their own generators and pumps.

The decay of the infrastructure was nowhere more alarmingly evident than in the encroachments of flooding. Most of the coastal plain is below sea level. The seawall was crumbling; the dikes went unrepaired; sluice gates were clogged. Clean spring water was available in Georgetown only in bottles sold at a price that very few could afford. The liquid that came out of the taps looked as though it needed to be strained. I was warned unnecessarily by almost every Guyanese I met to avoid drinking it.

A few days before I arrived in Georgetown, the Guyanese dollar had been devalued to just over 100 from 45 to the U.S. dollar. By the time I left, it was being traded on the free market at a rate of 120. On this basis, the average worker's wage was worth little more than one U.S. dollar a day. The monthly wage of the worst paid was as little as 3,000 Guyanese dollars, or the equivalent of US$25.[4] Exchange rates are not, to be sure, the most reliable guides to the purchasing power of a local currency. They were, however, reliable enough in a Guyana under International Monetary Fund tutelage, where currency trading had been largely unclamped, devaluations were rapidly translated into rising prices, and wage demands were contained both by a repressive regime and by the pressures of so many who were without any work at all.

The popular plight was in part relieved, if at wider and longer-term cost, by two factors: the thriving illicit economy and the constant drain of people from the country. Smuggling of goods and currencies, overland and overseas, was so rife that the amount of U.S. dollars economically active in Guyana during 1990 was estimated to be three times the officially traded total, and virtually anything could be bought in the country for a high enough price. If this provided a multitude of "mules" and other minions with some small income, it mainly enriched still further the few with the resources to manage the traffic or with the power to permit it in return for sizable bribes. Such smuggling, of course, further undermined the structured economy and deprived the state of revenue from the levies on licit trade, at least some of which might have escaped the clutch of corruption.

There were no official figures for the scale of emigration, and unofficial estimates agreed only in maintaining that it was relatively huge. Of three knowledgeable Guyanese, one claimed that without the loss of so many emigrants, the population would have been nearly twice its current size; another, that half the population had departed since 1979; a third, that 300,000 had, legally or not, made their way to the United States alone. This last informant put the phenomenon into vivid perspective. The closest parallel in the past, he believed, had been the massive emigration from Ireland during the potato blight famine of the 1840s.

Remittances from Guyanese emigrants certainly helped to sustain a substantial number of relatives who had remained behind. The cost to Guyanese society, however, was much greater, not least because it was those with the training and skills most needed at home who found it easiest to leave, in the confidence that they could obtain legal entry to other countries and subsequent employment there. In Antigua, for instance, many of the teachers and even more of the nurses were Guyanese, while in Guyana the educational and medical services were starved of qualified staff. In 1990, some four hundred teachers left Guyana to work in other Caribbean countries.

The number of the manifestly ill, physically or mentally, who wandered through the streets of the capital seemed so extraordinary to me that I checked my impression with various Guyanese. All expressed only surprise that I might have expected anything else. The incidence of illness, especially mental, was bound to be high and getting higher in a society so traumatized by racial conflict and political repression, where the only economic growth was in poverty, and nothing functioned but the institutions of corruption and violence. The facilities for treating the ill were simply falling ever further behind the increasing need for them. The most haunting memory I have of Guyana came near the end of my stay. As a tall black man, gaunt and in rags, with the top of his trousers slit open in front so that he could support with a hand his monstrously swollen testicles, walked muttering to himself along the pavement, not a head turned, and no eyes but my own moved to remark him.

The lassitude with which so many Guyanese went about their business was dismaying. An eminent civil servant described this to me as an internal migration to match the external one. "They are so exhausted by worry over how they can survive that they spend their days at work in merely waiting for them to end." A businessman said much the same: "The only reason that people are not marching through the streets or rioting in protest is that they have opted out altogether. You can rig the elections, but you cannot rig production."

This was not apparently a lesson that the government had learned. The record of the state-owned Bauxite Industry Development Corporation (BIDCO) was bad enough, but would very probably have been much worse without its secretary, Leon Rockcliffe, who had the rare reputation of being an honest and efficient public servant. It was a tribute to this reputation that he had been chosen by the Georgetown Chamber of Commerce and Industry to serve as its representative on a Civic Committee to report on the workings of the country's Election Commission. The report that he coauthored with a leading lawyer made measured recommendations. Shortly afterward, while I was in Guyana, Rockcliffe was summarily dismissed from BIDCO, after nineteen years of service.

Guyana's solitary independent newspaper, *Stabroek News*, launched in 1986 as the darkness of Forbes Burnham's twenty-one years of despotic rule seemed to be lifting under Desmond Hoyte, his successor, expressed its outrage in an editorial: "The dismissal is inexcusable and disgraceful. It strikes at the root of a free society and freedom of expression. It is precisely the kind of vindictiveness that devastated the civil service and more generally the public sector under Burnham and chased most of the competent, independent people out of it . . . Incidents like this make one despair."[5]

Despair, indeed, was the prevailing Guyanese mood, and it was most evident in the readiness of blacks, whose racial ascendancy the regime represented, to devalue themselves. This was not a new attitude. A quarter of a century before, Guyana's leading poet, Martin Carter, had contributed a short essay, entitled "A Question of Self-Contempt," to the special Guyana Independence issue of a distinguished Caribbean quarterly. In this, he told a story from the late 1940s, when he had been involved in a radical discussion group that met once a week:

"Among those who came on the Sunday nights of our desperation, was a talkative middle-aged black gentleman I knew as Bovell. Stoop of a tired tree. Face of a face. One of the best of us all. So strange and disheartening therefore to discover that he came no longer to meet with us on Sunday. I could not understand."

One day, catching sight of him by the side of a road cutting grass for his donkey, Carter went up to him and sought an explanation.

" 'Week after week I come to you meeting. I hear you talk about exploitation. I hear you talk about how poor people must rise up. About socialism. About revolution.'

"I stared at his hopeless hands as he spoke. Eyes and hands.

"He leaned forward. A new intensity informed his very eye.

" 'Tell me,' he said suddenly, and I responded to the fury in his voice and heart.

" 'Just tell me something,' and I knew I had no answer.

" 'You and your friends really believe you can fight white people? Rass!'

"Spat, shook his head . . . By the side of the road his donkey stood yoked. The iron tyres of the two wheeled cart were shining in spots. No rust anywhere. And I looked at Bovell's skull and saw a bump.

"I wondered whether an owner had turned homuncule and taken up residence. My own head I rubbed. He was wondering why. Incapable of explanation, I remained silent."[6]

More than forty years since that encounter, I spent an evening with Martin Carter at his home in Georgetown. As we talked, interrupted only by the usual power failure that plunged us into darkness until his wife lit a lamp, it seemed to me that this major black Caribbean poet, whose urge toward the best kept him working intermittently for years at a lyric, was still, in much of what he said to me, rubbing an invisible bump on his head. It was not that he had ever been fearful. No one familiar with his political record or his poems would have supposed this for a moment. He had fought the white colonial regime, which had detained him during a state of emergency, and he had fought the black regime of repression. Yet more formidable than either opponent was the suspicion which he shared with so many other blacks, that there was, had to be, some unfightable fault in themselves.

Despair may become the natural condition when hope is repeatedly crushed. Burnham's death had no sooner stirred some hope of change than this was being crushed by the regime. All that remained was the extent of the social debris he had left behind. There were once-disaffected blacks who were now saying that Burnham had not, after all, been so bad. He had won for blacks a sense of dignity by securing their political power to confront the demographic and economic power of the East Indians. If this political power had demonstrated in its failings some black inadequacy, this was all the more reason for grimly holding on to it, as the sole alternative to black subordination.

Dr. Denis Williams, the distinguished black anthropologist who heads the Museum of Anthropology in Georgetown, seemed somewhat more sanguine during the interview I had with him. No such sense of being "embattled," he said, existed in Guyana as it did in the United States or in the rest of the Caribbean, "where everything is owned by the white man." Here, the white man had been confronted for a quarter of a century, and this, with an assertion of black culture, had been Burnham's undertaking and achievement. It was the Hindus, among the most conservative peoples in the world, who constituted the majority of Guyana's East Indians and who were psychically insecure, in their remoteness from their home base. The blacks possessed the culture of the country. If they were to lose political power, they would still have that culture in their keeping. Theirs was the unquenchable spirit of the Black Diaspora, which was not Africa—"When I am in Africa, I find myself a stranger"—but an African sense of an organic nature, with a place for magic, in a Creole world that the blacks have made their own.

"I know about culture. You cannot remove the traits of culture that have come to us genetically. My wife, who collaborates with me, will say, for instance, 'This door does not want to open.'" (His wife, who was sitting with us, nodded her head vigorously.) "Black people are not rationalist. They do not make good scientists. Those of us who perform successfully in the rationalist world are simply good pupils. That is why I left Britain at the age of forty. I did not want to be just a good pupil and get the answer right and be written about in the newspapers. The black person is only a tenant in the world of reason. He brings instead a tremendous capacity for feeling and for freedom. The steel band, for instance, with its discovery of how to make music out of the dustbin, is a metaphor for Caribbean man. We have only just begun to explore English as an instrument of thought. Yet already we can bend that language to express our feeling."

I am still wondering how far all of this was merely another way of rubbing that bump on the head. I am not persuaded that the black mind is formed for feeling rather than for thought. What is the creative mind, black or white, if not one capable of both? The whole concept of a genetically communicated culture has distressing associations. It is certainly questionable. Less so is the likelihood that those who come to believe in the concept will adapt their own minds, along with the minds of others they can influence, to reflect it.

Perhaps, in some such view as that of the anthropologist's wife, the door to an escape from Guyana's social predicament does not want to open. Or, on a rationalist view, the door can only be opened inward, and there is a mob of animosities, fears, and doubts pressing against it, to keep it closed.

The extent of a particular Guyanese black's despair was revealed to me in his approving reference to the last resort, which he defined as the racial partitioning of Guyana. Such a prospect is not appalling because there is something sacrosanct about the particular products of the past that parade as sovereign states. It is appalling because it would rend apart two interdependent communities, and without even bringing peace. How often in history has such a solution done so? Indeed, aside from the inevitable conflict that would accompany and then pursue it, partition would only excite the appetites of neighboring states. Venezuela in particular has long been claiming a large part of Guyanese territory.

It was easy to take away from Guyana only forebodings. There was so much evidence to justify them. But I found instead that far more forceful were my recollections of those Guyanese for whom the commitment to their blackness was a dynamic dimension of the commitment to their humanity. Such a one was Eusi Kwayana, a strong and gentle guide of the interracial Working People's Alliance, who had discovered that the children in a certain village did not know the meaning of the calendar and who had begun their joyous education by arranging for them to celebrate one another's birthdays. There was Andaiye, confronting the cancer inside her and yet with enough hope and courage left over to confront as well the cancer of subjugation suffered by so many Caribbean women, and in Guyana, which remained her home, the cancer of racism. There was Martin Carter, who, for all his gloom, could not but light a way with the lyrics he wrote. They, along with other individual blacks, and individual East Indians and whites whom I met in Guyana, continued to represent and convey, among so much else that was dying there, the illumination of life.

25 | THE MASK OF TRINIDAD

~~~~~~

On July 27, 1990, some 120 Black Muslims, members of a group that called itself the Jamaat al Muslimeen, stormed the Red House, where the Parliament of Trinidad and Tobago[1] conducts its business, and held hostage a large number of parliamentarians, including the Prime Minister. In another part of the Caribbean, delegates to a regional conference were at a reception when someone burst into the exchange of pleasantries and political gossip with the news that there had been a coup. "Where? Where?" came the shocked question from all sides. "Trinidad," came the reply. "Ah," sighed a civil servant with relief to a journalist, "then it can't be serious. Perhaps it's a practical joke."[2]

It was not a joke. As the price of oil had fallen sharply on the world market, so had the fortunes of a country where oil in various forms accounts for around a quarter of the gross national product, two-thirds of government revenue, and four-fifths of exports. In the period 1980–88, the gross national product per head of population had fallen by an annual average of more than three times the rate in Haiti or Guyana and well above the rate in beleaguered Nicaragua. The existing poor were the hardest hit and were joined by a multitude of the new, from among those who had clambered into relative prosperity during the boom years. Increasingly, government ministers, themselves not notably austere in their own lives, preached austerity to those whose lives were all too austere already. Early in 1990, a Value Added Tax, essentially a levy on consumption, was introduced at a rate of 15 percent. Its catchment included food, a category which even the hard-line Thatcher government in Britain had considered it necessary to exempt. Economic hardship and political disillusionment were widespread.

The Black Muslim rebels hog-tied the Prime Minister and issued three demands: the resignation of the Prime Minister; the formation of an interim government that would include the rebel leader, Abu Bakr; and a general election within ninety days. One member of Parliament became an unintended fatality: he was hit in the ankle by a ricocheting bullet and died on the operating table four days later. The army shelled the television station, which rebels had also occupied. On July 29, an incipient engagement by police and troops to recapture the Red House was halted by order of the Prime Minister, who signed a document agreeing to the rebel demands and was then released. The occupation continued while argument outside the Red House raged between those willing to grant the rebels the amnesty they required and those who pressed for the building to be stormed. On August 1, with an amnesty signed by the Acting President, the rebels surrendered, and the Prime Minister repudiated the document he had agreed to sign only under duress.* In five days of violence, thirty people had reportedly been killed.

Further details, some of them peculiarly Trinidadian, emerged from people I interviewed during my stay on the island in early 1991. Though the Black Muslim movement had barely two thousand members, its attempted coup was apparently part of a grandiose design to Islamize Trinidad. Its leader himself was a former policeman, Lennox Phillips, who had taken the name of Abu Bakr with his conversion to Islam. He was described to me by someone who knew him as a man gentle in manner, especially to women and children. "He saw his coup attempt," I was told, "as a sort of Caesarian operation. He seems to have expected the mass of the population, with steel bands playing, to rise in support. In fact, the most marked reaction was the looting of shops." The rebels, once established in occupation of the Red House, watched movies pulled from the satellite dish. One night, they mimed politically radical calypsos being played on the radio station, NBS.

The video camera installed in the Parliament chamber recorded the first ten minutes or so of the rebel irruption. Subsequently shown on television to excite outrage at the treatment meted out to the elected representatives of the people, this footage seems instead to have been relished by a people who had been looking for their elected representatives to get their comeuppance. What was termed "the video effect" invoked a connection with calypso and its essential spirit of "the little man answering back." There were soon calypsos being composed and sung that came close to reveling in the humiliation of the Prime Minister and others in authority.

Paradoxically, the assault on Parliament, for all the evident absence of public outrage at it, pointed not to the weakness but to the strength of the hold which parliamentary government has in Trinidad. As one Trinidadian

* Britain's Privy Council, still the ultimate judicial authority for Trinidad, as for some other former colonies, was asked to rule on whether the amnesty granted to the members of the Jamaat al Muslimeen was binding in law or might be ignored as having been granted under duress. By the middle of 1994, the Privy Council had not yet announced its ruling, and Abu Bakr remained at liberty.

expressed it to me: "No one in Jamaica would have thought of mounting a coup by an assault on Parliament there, because Parliament there is not the source and focus of power that it is here. Jamaica has so many other sources and focuses: the political parties, the trade unions, the big boardrooms, the drug barons. Jamaica seems always on the point of flying apart. And Barbados, well, Barbados is the one place where apartheid works. Trinidad is so much more fluid than either."

Trinidadians are given to asserting their particular aptitudes, and it says something for their style and discrimination that they do not seem boastful or pompous in the process. Indeed, one aptitude is a highly developed sense of fun, which includes their ability to laugh not only at others but at themselves. My most cherished encounter with this occurred with a taxi driver whose services I would repeatedly employ, as he proved to be both unusually punctual and unusually prudent in negotiating traffic. At the start of our association, he identified himself as a Jehovah's Witness, and I immediately made it clear that the services for which I was paying did not include an effort to convert me. The subject did not arise again until he was driving me to the airport for my departure. Somehow we slid into a discussion on the acceptability of a blood transfusion to save a life. As I found myself becoming incensed at his own dogmatic attitude, I said sharply, "We really must put an end to this. You haven't the slightest chance of converting me." He laughed richly, with obvious enjoyment. "There you are. I'm just no good at it. I've been trying to convert people for seventeen years. Seventeen years! And I haven't converted anyone yet."

Not altogether unconnected with this aptitude, perhaps, is their adaptability, apparent above all in the relative success claimed by Trinidadians in integrating the different racial components of their society. The claim even has its celebrated symbol in callaloo, the popular soup or stew of many merged ingredients. Certainly, the symbol overstates the case. Yet Trinidad has no such color-based class structure as exists in Jamaica, let alone an accepted white ascendancy that sustains itself, behind a sort of social privet hedge, as in Barbados. The strains intrinsic to the existence of gross economic inequalities are evident enough, but the society is that much looser for being less strapped by the significance of complexion.

Nowhere has Trinidad demonstrated this adaptability better than in its response to a demographic development of profoundly disruptive potential: the growth in the population of East Indian origin to parity with the black one, in a country which blacks had come to consider unchallengeably their own. Some politically prominent blacks have sought to exploit this racial factor. It was Tubal Uriah Butler, the labor leader whose activities triggered the widespread rioting of 1937, who first proclaimed that oil and sugar did not mix: euphemisms for blacks, predominant in the petroleum industry, and East Indians, predominant in the sugar one. More dangerously, Eric

Williams himself, Prime Minister for more than two decades and with all the influence of his intellectual renown besides, made the same remark.

There is little doubt that such oblique appeals worked for some time in rallying blacks behind the People's National Movement (PNM), which Williams led, while East Indians rallied to the opposition. Yet this was never enough to dig a permanent trench between the two major racial communities. The gathering unpopularity of the PNM government promoted the formation in 1985 of the National Alliance for Reconstruction (NAR), on the basis of a joint commitment by blacks and East Indians to provide a new direction. In the general election of the following year, the NAR campaigned on the theme of "one party, one leader, one nation, one love," while George Chambers, leader of the PNM and Prime Minister since the death of Eric Williams in 1981, raised the racial issue more blatantly than his predecessor had done. He publicly claimed that the formation of the NAR was "all part of a grand design to wrest political power from a certain section of the community."[3] Yet the social climate was such that pronouncements of this sort were recognized as risky. As Selwyn Ryan, Trinidad's leading political scientist, recorded: "Much of the racial rhetoric was whispered rather than shouted over the megaphones."[4]

The yield of such rhetoric was poor. Doubtless it helped that A. N. R. Robinson, himself black, headed the NAR. Yet many of his closest colleagues were East Indians, chief among them Basdeo Panday, who began by campaigning mainly in East Indian-dominated areas but soon found, in testing the temperature, that his warmest reception came in areas where blacks were numerically dominant. In the event, over two-thirds of the voters, including roughly four out of ten black ones, supported the NAR. Disillusionment soon set in, yet this, too, was significantly interracial. A public opinion survey in June 1988 revealed that 66 percent of East Indian and 61 percent of black respondents were "dissatisfied" or "very dissatisfied" with the NAR.[5] Scarcely less significant in its own way was the presence of ten young East Indians among the 120 Black Muslims who seized the Red House in 1990.

This is in sharp contrast with developments in Guyana, which is the only other Caribbean country with a large East Indian population. To be sure, Trinidad did not suffer from the racial mischief made or countenanced by the British colonial government in Guyana. The East Indian community in Guyana is proportionately still larger than it is in Trinidad, where, according to the 1980 census, blacks composed 41 percent of the total population; East Indians, 40.8 percent; a "mixed" population, 16.4 percent; and "others," including whites, 1.8 percent. The very size of the "mixed" population provides some reassurance against demographic polarization. Yet with all such factors taken into account, there is, simply, a different spirit in Trinidad. The very existence of such a substantial "mixed" component testifies to the much greater ease with which racial "mixing" has taken place there.

An opinion poll in 1987, a quarter-century after the achievement of independence, revealed a level of racial prejudice in Trinidad startlingly low by Caribbean or most other standards. When asked whether they preferred to work under a black manager, a white, or an East Indian one, 56 percent of black respondents, 57 percent of East Indian ones, and 75 percent of the "mixed" said that it made no difference. More impressive still, 85 percent of blacks stated that they had no objections to intermarriage with East Indians, while 55 percent of East Indians said that they had no objections to intermarriage with blacks.[6]

Trinidad is beyond question the most cosmopolitan country in the Caribbean, not only in the variety of races, nationalities, religions, and cultures from which its population has been drawn, but also in the degree to which such components have combined to create a composite identity without denying the identities of its participating peoples. Spanish and French cultures, with their shared Roman Catholic element, continued to exercise an influence throughout the long period of British colonial rule, whose own character they affected. Slavery itself promoted an enriching cultural interaction, as new arrivals from Africa to the British colony merged with those who had arrived under Spanish rule, some of them brought by French owners in flight from the slave revolution in Saint Domingue. With the emancipation of the slaves came large numbers of East Indians and some Chinese, to provide indentured labor. Moreover, a relatively liberal immigration policy, with a record of religious tolerance and a reputation for relatively relaxed racial attitudes on the island, attracted an inflow of blacks from the United States and the Caribbean, as well as Germans, Swiss, and other continental Europeans, to join the whites who immigrated from Britain.

If Trinidad's particular expression of song in the calypso derives essentially, in both its rhythm and the strain of mockery in its lyrics, from African culture, it has also absorbed Spanish, French, British, and East Indian influences. If Carnival itself is rooted in a European and particularly Roman Catholic cultural tradition, it has flourished in Trinidad as a predominantly black cultural engagement. "Pan"—the instrument of the steel band—is, like calypso, a peculiar product of Trinidadian culture and essentially its black component, but it is not only blacks who play pans.

Peter Minshall is white. He was born in Georgetown, Guyana, brought up in Port of Spain, Trinidad, and trained in London as a theater designer. He has done more than anyone else in recent years to extend the artistic possibilities of Carnival in Trinidad, not only by the introduction of new themes and even new forms, but by combining music, dance, costume, decor, and lighting for a new dramatic dimension rather than for mere display. His work is controversial; it disturbs those who feel comfortable only with old formulas; but it enjoys popular approval and has had a wide creative impact. Musicians, painters, sculptors, dress and textile designers have responded richly and rapidly to the new impulses and opportunities he has provided. There has, too, been remarkably little racial resistance to the exercise of so much influence by a white over a Carnival which blacks have traditionally identified with themselves; but then blacks in Trinidad have been confident enough in their own relationship with Carnival, calypso, and pan to have welcomed the increasing involvement by whites, East Indians, and those of "mixed" ancestry in these performing arts.

A comparison with the development of Carnival and the samba schools in Brazil is instructive. There, white racial disdain, bent on evicting a black identity from the national consciousness, finds little room for black cultural expression. The result is not only an erosion of the black relationship with these forms but a degradation of the forms themselves. Carnival, particularly in its capital at Rio, is increasingly directed at avoiding any real content of social criticism, and provides instead the titillating, the extravagant, and the exotic, with a corresponding effect on the samba schools for which Carnival is the culmination of their efforts. There is no evidence that any of this stimulates and extends other art forms.

Instructive also is the comparison with Martinique, where so much money and political patronage is devoted to promoting black cultural expression and achieves so little. But then it could scarcely be otherwise there, on an island preoccupied with the conspicuous consumption that the acceptance of a French identity sustains. The culture of Trinidad is infused by a black identity and experience. It is richly productive with scarcely more political patronage and financial investment than supports the "Best Village" competition, to encourage small communities in the pursuit of music, dance, drama, and crafts. Indeed, those who dominate politics and the economy are disposed to dismiss or belittle the value of cultural activities.

Pat Bishop is a remarkable black Trinidadian who describes herself as a "facilitator" but who is, in fact, a combination of musician, painter, designer, and historian. She put the case against this dismissal or belittlement when opening an exhibition of student work from the University of the West Indies Creative Arts Center in 1990:

> It is utterly beyond the comprehension of our newly landed robber barons that playing a pan IS work. That standing for eight hours on one's feet in search of excellence is about personal discipline, a perception of standards and a willingness, in that pursuit, to postpone gratification.. . .
>
> Equally we must with sorrow acknowledge that nothing offends the "serious" people in our society more than the so-called Carnival mentality—a mentality which has to do with meeting deadlines, with productivity, and all the rest of the very things which they enjoin us in all sorts of ways to take seriously.[7]

It is not only, however, the attitude of those who manage society that consigns culture and art to the margin; it is also the acquiescence of the culturally creative in being marginalized. Carnival itself is essentially masquerade; it is generally known in Trinidad as Mas'. The participant "plays" Mas' by masking the face or assuming, in costume and action, another identity in order to enjoy a corresponding exercise of freedom. This exercise of freedom, by special license on a set occasion, derives from different sources to the same effect: the Catholic festivities preceding Ash Wednesday and the self-denials of Lent; the practice of permitting slaves the periodic therapy of music, song, and dance, to relieve the oppressions of labor and so reduce the impulse to rebellion; the West African custom of sanctioning social criticism, at particular times and in particular contexts, through songs and stories that blamed and even ridiculed those in authority. It is this last which Gordon Rohlehr, a Trinidadian scholar, believes to have been the prime source of the political calypso.

"An understanding of this wise West African convention," he has written, "might help us to understand the mixture of astringency and ineffectuality which exists even today in Trinidad's calypso tents, where political calypsos annually perform a cathartic function similar to what must have obtained in the satirical songs of various West African societies."[8]

Calypso composition and performance reach an annual climax at Carnival time, in the contest of steel bands and singers. The political calypso is accordingly, at its moment of maximum impact, contained within an occasion of conceded license. In fact, only once in recent times has this containment been significantly breached, with the Black Power challenge of 1970. This was, however, a challenge that had begun months before and that had involved careful planning to exploit the occasion of the coming Carnival. When this arrived, Carnival troops and steel bands displayed Black Power symbols, which fueled the demonstrations that followed. In short, Carnival was hijacked by a political movement rather than being integral to a cultural movement for social transformation. For all the success of the hijacking, the experiment has not been repeated.

Is it, then, only for a short time each year, during Carnival, that Trinidad feels free to express itself—only when it is wearing a mask that it reveals what it otherwise conceals? Is it, in this sense, the mask that is really the face, and the face that is only a mask?

In 1955, Eric Williams, reviewing the five years of the preceding Gomes government, declared that this had found a nation "swimming in oil and sucking sugarcane" and left it a nation "swimming in oil and sucking sugarcane." Reviewing the record of Eric Williams himself, Dr. Trevor Farrell, Senior Lecturer in Economics at the University of the West Indies and Chairman of the Trinidad and Tobago Petroleum Corporation, wrote: "When he died in 1981 he too left a nation swimming in oil and sucking sugarcane." Dr. Farrell continued: "In 1987 we are struggling to balance our books. In 1987 we are back to where we were in 1967. The problems and the crises are the same."[9]

Reviewing the first twenty-five years of Trinidad's independence, one of its leading novelists, Earl Lovelace, began with an account of a recent visit he had paid to the village of Upper Morvant, where a local group was performing a play set in the era of slavery. The leading roles were those of the slave master and his wife, both whites, and the next in importance was that of the black overseer. Lovelace commented:

> In this history, they see the Africans as objects. I really cannot blame the group. I am sure that the members want to be stars in their own history . . . But, the history that had come down to that group, that has come down to us, has been one that depicts Africans as slaves, the brutalised objects of European power and mischief. I cannot blame the group. The play they produced is based on that history that had been taught and continues to be taught from primary school to university. The chief thing wrong with it is that Africans do not star in such a history, for it presents a history concerned with what the Europeans did and that is geared, it seems true, to cultivate in Africans a sense of inferiority.[10]

V. S. Naipaul, the most famous living writer to have emerged from Trinidad, has provided his own explanation for the difficulties of dealing with the West Indian past: "The history of the islands can never be satisfactorily told. Brutality is not the only difficulty. History is built around achievement and creation; and nothing was created in the West Indies."[11]

Those with a different view of achievement and creation in the West Indies may well wonder whether the history that is taught goes any more unquestioned than does the integrity of politicians. Eric Williams told Trinidadians, "Massa Day Done." It is not, however, the master's day that is over, their subsequent experience has told them; it is only the day of the white master. For blacks in particular, therefore, the subjection of the past, with the implication of inferiority, informs the present in a different guise. Democracy itself must seem a masquerade, in which their new overseers play at serving the people only to use them. It is no wonder that so many of the used hide behind their faces, as they hid what they thought and felt from the overseers of old; and only in the celebration of their culture, in song and dance, in costume and mask, do they joyously reveal themselves.

Rex Nettleford, Jamaican writer, educationalist, political analyst, and choreographer, has warned Trinidadians against being merely "minstrels." Certainly, there is in Trinidad no such militant black consciousness as has in Jamaica confronted the past of slavery: to assert not its subservience but its resistance, not the inferiority but the dignity of the victim. Yet Trinidad has achieved something different. It has shown how a basically black culture can promote a cosmopolitan creativity, without denying itself or abandoning a sense of black identity. This is no small contribution to life for minstrels in masquerade to have made. "Play mas' " is an exhortation which others in the Black Diaspora and beyond would do well to heed, so as to discover, through the liberation of the mask, what the face of humanity should be.

~~~~~~

The taxi driver was commenting furiously on the latest details disclosed in the so-called furniture scandal: "It is a shame and a disgrace. This island is corrupt from head to foot, from head to foot, I tell you." He had taken me to Spanish Town the day before, and I had found him to be, for a Jamaican taxi driver, exceptionally reticent and even shy. Now he was, almost alarmingly, beside himself.

A 250 percent increase in parliamentary salaries and the appointment of an unprecedentedly swollen government had been among the scandalous harbingers. As the *Jamaica Record* reported: "Prime Minister Michael Manley presides over a governing party of 58 parliamentarians, 45 MPs and 13 senators. Four members are functionaries, namely the speaker and deputy speaker, president and deputy president. Some 40 members of the remaining 54, or 74%, are part of the government (executive). This must certainly be a world record.

"The 40 members of the government include 18 cabinet ministers (14 MPs and 4 senators) and 22 junior ministers and parliamentary secretaries . . . The provision of offices, houses, furniture, cars, maids, and drivers for this group was obviously not considered by Manley as an important factor."[1]

The impact made by particular instances of reported corruption is often reduced by their sheer remoteness from the realities of popular comprehension. The waylaying of J$500 million worth of zinc supplies acquired for the relief of hurricane victims or the award of a J$1,500 million contract, without competitive tendering, for a housing project, involved sums beyond the grasp of Jamaican workers, many of whom earn less than J$300 a week.[2] What made the furniture scandal so explosive was the disclosure of the particular items bought and the particular prices paid, with public money, for furnishing the homes of particular junior ministers and parliamentary secretaries.

The goods supplied to only five of the ten parliamentarians and by only one of the three commercial companies that were involved cost a total of J$831,395. They included a "Fisher component set comprised of turntable, compact disc, equalizer tape deck, stand and two speakers" for J$3,000; a "chandelier (brass) for dining room" at J$12,000; the supply and installation of "drapes and rods" at one home, for J$68,000, and the supply and installation of carpeting, at the same home, for J$44,122; a "Castro convertible sofa (Queen size)" for J$14,000; and a 60-piece set of "Mikasa crystalware including champagne flutes, wine goblets, water goblets, hi-ball tumblers" for J$9,000. The 48-piece set of unnamed "crystalware consisting of 48 glasses for water, wine, champagne, scotch," supplied to a mere parliamentary secretary at a cost of J$4,200 seemed relatively austere.[3]

A certain David Nunes of Kingston wrote to the editor of the *Daily Gleaner*: "Why were brass lamps at J$3,600 each supplied . . . when a locally produced mahogany lamp at J$200 would have sufficed? Further, according to sales catalogues, a first class brass lamp costs about US$50 in Miami. Based on the then exchange rate of J$7 to a US dollar and even allowing a 50 per cent mark-up on cost price, J$3,600 is more than five times a fair selling price, in my opinion! Similar margins were charged off chandeliers. I've visited the showroom of CMP Electrical Ltd. and have seen most beautiful chandeliers for J$750–1,000. Prices of around J$10,000 by suppliers are preposterous. In my view, the excess over fair market values must be refunded! I stand ready to help the Auditor General unravel this mess."[4]

The drift of the letter, whose elaborations certainly served to fuel the public outrage, reflected a primary concern with repairing the damage to public funds. The taxi driver's comment was likely to have been more representative of the popular reaction. Estrangement from the way that society functions both politically and economically is extensive, and this can scarcely be ignored in any consideration of that violence which, for other Caribbeans as for many Jamaicans themselves, so distinguishes Jamaica.

The capital of the chandelier, drapery, and crystal political class is New Kingston, where much of the business leadership conveniently resides as well. Two large hotels there provide the bar and other catering facilities in air-conditioned spaciousness for business conferences and the more sumptuous wedding receptions. Close to a cluster of banks, a shopping mall offers the range of imported consumer goods unavailable in Kingston itself, as are the conditions of comparative safety the mall provides. Safety is, indeed, a conspicuous preoccupation. The homes of the New Kingston rich are remarkable not only for their size and lavish gardens, but for the protective devices on their doors and windows, often augmented by guards.

A mere two miles away is Kingston, with its three-quarters of a million inhabitants, or almost a third of the island's 2,400,000. There, a different Jamaica seethes, not only in the sprawling slums but through the streets of offices and shops, to make its way in various forms of labor, in begging, and in crime. There, violence seems to hang in the air, as sunshine always does in the photographs of Jamaican holiday brochures.

While I was visiting Jamaica, some two hundred convicted murderers were awaiting a decision by the government on how many, if any, should be executed in accordance with their sentences. An evident fear informed the attitude of otherwise thoughtful people to the death penalty. One white woman, for instance, an art historian who had come from a country in Europe where capital punishment had long since been abolished, said to me: "I know no one—and I mean that, no one—who has not been held up and robbed at least once. I have already been held up and robbed three times. I just don't know whether I am against the death penalty anymore."

A Jamaican black woman, successful in journalism and in business, had no doubt whatsoever. "I have watched one man die on my bed, and two other men have been killed in my back yard. There are too many honest people suffering badly, for me to worry about gangsters." I suggested that the recent release in Britain from life imprisonment of supposed terrorists, who were found to have been wrongfully convicted and who would have been hanged years before if the death penalty had still been in force, might recommend a little worry. "I can't help that," she replied. "Conviction by due process is good enough for me."

Women are especially aware and fearful of violence in Jamaica because they are so commonly the victims of it. On the phone-in radio programs, one after another calls to recount some recent experience of domestic violence and seek help or advice. They are the more anguished because the police, overwhelmingly male, are themselves widely regarded as violent and likely enough to answer a complaint from a woman by taking the side of the male culprit or even by assaulting the victim. One prominent black lawyer ascribed the extent of this domestic violence to the conflict between the role and the status of women in Jamaican society:

"It is the women who are so often the functional heads of the homes. They are responsible for raising the children and keeping the family together. It is mainly they who run the schools and set the standards. Yet the society is by tradition strongly patriarchal. Deep down the Jamaican male is very resentful at a functional authority that confronts the traditional one."

If there is such a deep male resentment at the unsubservient female, it may move easily enough from the home into the streets, against women in general or generally into violent behavior. This can hardly, however, be held wholly responsible for the scale of violence outside the home. There are other factors. Jamaican history is turbulent with resistance to slavery, to colonial rule, to the very presumptions of white racial supremacy. It was no mere coincidence that Jamaica was the homeland of Marcus Garvey, the father of the black-consciousness movement in the Diaspora. If black militancy has involved or promoted recourse to violence, this was, after all, a lesson taught by masters.

The new political class exploits where it does not encourage the influence of old lessons. Conflict between the two rival political parties is intense, not least for control of the patronage that attracts and rewards allegiance. It is a conflict both represented and reinforced by territorial division. Kingston itself is divided into areas controlled in the interest of one or other party by its associated gangs. Battles between these were, until the middle sixties, conducted with machetes, knives, and stones. Then, guns came increasingly to be used until, by the middle seventies, they were the common weapon. Virtual commando raids, by a gang of one party into the territory of the other, with reprisals and counterreprisals, have on occasions ended in an armistice of temporary exhaustion only after hundreds of casualties.

Political violence, however, no more encompasses all the activity of gangs than the activity of gangs encompasses all political violence. Gangsterism of the conventional kind is rife, much of it connected with a drug traffic that now deals in the big business of cocaine as well as the traditional *ganja*, or marijuana. A Jamaican journalist who has cautiously explored the subject told me: "There is a great deal of drug money here. Bits of Montego Bay and Ocho Rios have been built with it." Whatever the extent, it is not the gangsters of Kingston who get to keep much of this money, but the men behind them.

An apparently uncontrollable or at least uncontrolled access to guns combines with the cult of macho assertiveness to produce frequent shoot-outs, not only between rival gangs but between gangs and police, soldiers, or both. In fact, these shoot-outs are so frequent that I was advised by more than one Jamaican to worry less about being mugged than about being hit by a bullet from the cross fire. As with those road signs that warn motorists about low-flying aircraft, I was left to wonder what precautionary measures I was expected to take.

The recruitment centers for public violence of every kind are the urban ghettos, from which there are so few possibilities of escape.

"For a poor youth—uneducated, lacking the social and job skills required to get ahead, with an accent and a bearing that bear witness to his life—there are only three ways out of the ghetto. The most improbable is to make it as a reggae star, the theme of the Jamaican movie, 'The Harder They Come,' and the life story of singers such as Bob Marley. The second way is to be 'a ranking.' To be ranking means being either a gunman (with or without the political connections) or an assistant to local politicians—either in a legitimate or a violent role . . . As a ranking, you made it materially, if not physically out of the ghetto. The final way out of the ghetto (by now it should be obvious) is in a coffin."[5]

This summary, by a Canadian academic, says little for legitimate social mobility in Jamaica. Certainly, there is little enough to be said. A still relevant statistical assessment of social levels in Jamaica was provided by a market research agency in 1975. It identified an "AB" category of "top managerial and occupational persons," such as doctors, dentists, lawyers, company directors, head teachers, architects, and qualified accountants, amounting to 3 percent of the adult population. Next came a "C1" category of "supervisory and highly skilled personnel," such as qualified engineers and technicians, shop managers, senior secretaries, nursing sisters, and police inspectors, amounting to 12 percent. This was followed by the "C2" category of "semi-skilled and other clerical workers," such as trained carpenters, telephone operators, plumbers, police constables, and bus drivers, who amounted to a further 17 percent. Then came the largest category, "D," of the "unskilled and manual fully employed," such as domestic helpers, unskilled workers in factories, laborers, delivery men, junior shop assistants and garbage collectors, together accounting for 35 percent. Last and almost as large came the "E" category, of "casual workers and the unemployed," who constituted 33 percent of the adult population.[6]

Without an updated study of the same kind, it is not possible to establish how far this distribution has changed. The direction of change, however, is less of a mystery. It is generally accepted in Jamaica that the few at the top have been growing still richer, while the numbers of those at or near the bottom have substantially increased. This is supported by evidence of a sort commonly associated with such developments: a marked decline in average annual income, as measured in United States dollars, and an irregular but high rate of price inflation.

Whatever the extent of change, one characteristic of Jamaican society stays the same. Virtually all the poor are black, the middle class is mainly light in complexion, and the heights are occupied disproportionately by whites. This does not mean that there is rampant racial discrimination, though advertising agencies, for instance, are conspicuously biased towards the use of light-skinned models for television and billboards. The correlation between color and class simply perpetuates itself, in the functioning of the economy as well as in the attitudes of Jamaicans to themselves and one another.

The whites, Creole and expatriate alike, sustain their economic presence not by separating themselves but by an identity of interest and outlook. It is from the brown or "colored" that most of the political leadership, of the civil servants, of those in the professions and at the managerial level of business, come. The mass of blacks are separated from white and brown by the poverty and powerlessness of their lives, along with a culture and consciousness of their own.

Olive Lewin, a Jamaican woman who has probably done more than anyone else to rescue from indifference or contempt the rich heritage of Jamaica's traditional music, said to me: "I have had the greatest difficulty in getting the schools at all interested. The sort of parents who run these schools regard such music as 'common.' And they are themselves so remote from the lives of most Jamaicans. I remember once, when I had arranged a school concert which included a corn-shelling song, one of the parents, a political activist no less, asked me afterward, 'Do people still eat corn meal?' In some respects, you know, Jamaica is like pre-Revolutionary France."

Yet, for all the unyielding structure of Jamaican society, the deepening mass poverty, and the increasing disillusionment with alternating governments that are indistinguishably corrupt, there is no sign of a revolutionary movement or even of such a development in thought as looks likely to promote one. What remains is violence, by the individual or the group—violence which, beyond the particular motive or victim, is the revolt against captivity itself.

Of all the press reports that dealt day after day, during my stay in Jamaica, with instances of violence, the one that made the most forceful impact described an act of lynching in a small rural community:

> Cecil Thomas, 40, of no fixed address, lay bleeding to death in a tomato patch on a farm in Cowans district, St. Catherine. On hearing his uncle's voice, he slowly lifted his head and looked up at the man who had raised him from age three.
>
> "Uncle Lennie . . . Uncle Lennie . . . help me . . . ," he begged.
>
> His uncle looked at him disdainfully.
>
> "You have brought shame to the family. Look at you. You have shamed the family."
>
> Thomas' eyes were still pleading, but he got no help. A few minutes later he rolled over and died.
>
> He had multiple wounds inflicted all over his body and head. His two hands had been severed and one of his legs broken, near the knee . . .
>
> Thomas, said to be a praedial larcenist, had been chased and caught, beaten, chopped and later killed by about 100 residents of Cowan, on Friday, March 15.[7]

In fiction, such an account might well read as luridly unreal. In fact, this report reflects much of the Jamaican reality. The theft of food crops is itself an act of violence not against the distant and dominant rich, but against the deprived, and the more outrageously so for being committed by one of their number. There is no trusted recourse to the forces of a social order that is concerned only with protecting itself. The community looks for protection to its own sustaining values and sanctions. If these sanctions are sometimes so ferocious, it is because the experience of deprivation and despair is not an ennobling one. There had been repeated thefts of food crops—yam, melon, tomato—in the district. Thomas had been caught stealing such crops before and had been beaten. The thefts had continued. The community now summarily determined the guilt and inflicted punishment. It was an ugly incident in an ugly situation.

Nowhere else in the Black Diaspora did I have such a sense of the slave past as in Jamaica. It was in Trinidad that a black economist, much taken with the need to promote a militant black consciousness there, said to me: "The central problem of blacks in the Caribbean is their total inability to accept the slave experience." This is largely true, but less so in Jamaica than anywhere else. For in Jamaica, along with a social order that seems to bear the tracks of the slave past, as fossilized rocks retain the prints of some extinct species in its passage, there is the counterculture of a consciousness that reaches back to an old resistance and in doing so, accepts the experience of the slave, not as servile but as defiant.

It was in Trinidad, too, that a black woman who designed textiles, in talking of the island's music, remarked to me, "There is simply no way that Jamaican reggae, with its heavy, oppressive beat, can be confused with our own calypso." It is this beat which informs much Jamaican writing as well as reggae. And if it relates to the heavy, oppressive black experience of Jamaican society, it does so as the music of the slave quarters related to the experience of slavery. It is no accident that the most influential figure in the development of reggae was the Rastafarian musician Bob Marley. For Rastafarianism does reach back in order to reach out, from so much suffering to a particular vision of identity and meaning for the Black Diaspora.

Realization is another matter. Religious movements that have begun with messages of liberation have all too often ended in denying it for purposes of their own. Whether Messiahs of any kind are reliable guides to a creative realization of identity and meaning for the Black Diaspora must be doubted. Certainly, acceptance of the slave experience cannot in itself achieve such a realization. But certainly, too, such a realization cannot be achieved without it. Insofar as the Jamaican beat expresses this acceptance, it comes from the Diaspora's heart.

27 | THE DILEMMA OF IDENTITY IN MARTINIQUE AND GUADELOUPE

~~~~~~

Volcanically created in the middle of the Caribbean are islands constitutionally designated as components of Overseas France and accordingly as much a part of Europe as any Department of the French mainland. Martinique and Guadeloupe have certain similarities to Haiti. Their populations are overwhelmingly black, and while French is the official language, there is another, widely spoken, that is the Creole of a largely West African syntax grafted onto a French vocabulary, much of it from an earlier age.

The similarities end there. Martinique, named by its long vanished Carib inhabitants Madinina or the island of flowers, is lush and gorgeous with colors. Flourishing plantations of banana and pineapple as well as of sugarcane cover the *mornes* or hills of which so much of the landscape is composed. Gleaming wide roads reach out from the capital of Fort-de-France, which contains some 177,000 people, or more than half of the island's total. The center of the city is clogged with cars, an astonishing proportion of which are Mercedes-Benz. Astonishing also is the number of shops specializing in gold jewelry, of an assortment to shame the stocks of a similarly sized Swiss city.

The cult of collecting and wearing gold ornaments goes back to the days of slavery, when they were a distinguishing display of property by those who were not—or were saving to escape being—property themselves. It is not, however, merely the survival of the cult but the arrival of the means, in cash or credit, to practice it that accounts for so much gold jewelry, as it does for so many costly cars.

The resources to support all this lavish consumption come not from a local modern economy with a thriving manufacturing base and advanced services sector, but mainly from the subsidies supplied by France to sustain the constitutional connection. Transfer payments for administration and other public sector employment, for social welfare and investment in infrastructure, account for some 70 percent of the island's gross national income. This is reflected in the composition of the so-called economically active, of whom 4 percent are engaged in agriculture, 5 percent in construction, 7 percent in agriculture and fishing, 23 percent in government and other public sector employment, and 26 percent in services, including tourism. The remaining 35 percent are unemployed.[1]

Among the employed themselves, incomes differ sharply. While the minimum wage, for instance, is 16 percent lower than that in metropolitan France, those in the public service receive not only the salaries paid to their metropolitan counterparts but an additional 40 percent. This bonus, introduced decades ago partly as an inducement to overseas service and partly as compensation for the higher cost of living on the islands, is now a conspicuous anachronism. French recruits to public service in the Caribbean no longer require such a financial inducement, and the cost of living on the islands is at most 20 percent higher than the overall rate in France.

The inflated salaries provided to a large component of the workforce contribute substantially to fueling the consumption of imports, in an island economy which produces so little of its own to consume. The result is a trade imbalance so prodigious as to be sustainable only by the readiness of metropolitan France to accommodate any deficit. The value of Martinique's annual imports in the late eighties was some seven times that of exports.[2]

All this constitutes a case study in the paradox of impoverishment through prosperity. The more that Martinique may call on French subsidies to support its lavish consumption, the less it is disposed to develop its own productive economy. One effect is the very high and rising rate of unemployment, which consigns so many to the economic waste and social degradation of subsistence on welfare payments; another, the propensity of the rich to invest their surplus resources in more productive economies abroad or in such unproductive, price-inflating instruments at home as real estate. Meanwhile, a multitude of various functionaries, existing to administer the dependence on France, has an interest in preserving this dependence as the source of their own prerogatives.

It is difficult to believe that this was the Martinique of Frantz Fanon, who so passionately assailed the violence of the rich white West against the wretched of the earth, or of Aimé Césaire, who advanced so passionately the cause of Negritude—a creative black consciousness with which to confront the materialist dominion of white culture. Fanon died in 1961, having thrown in his lot with the Algerian war of independence from France. Aimé Césaire has for many years now been the prime figure in Martinique's allegiance to the constitutional connection with France.

Much has changed since Césaire wrote his celebrated long poem of protest, Cahier d'un retour au pays natal (Notebook of a Return to My Native Land), fragments of which were first published in 1938, with the whole in 1956.[3]

Martinique is not the sullen colonial slum it was. Negritude has been institutionalized in a cultural commitment which commands large financial resources, mainly channeled through SERMAC (Service municipal d'action culturelle), itself established and supported by the Municipal Council of Fort-de-France. Since Aimé Césaire is the long-serving mayor of Fort-de-France, and his son, Jean-Paul, is director of SERMAC, while other children hold posts in the cultural edifice, there is an identity of interests between the encouragement of culture and the dominant political force on the island.

SERMAC provides an enviable range of facilities, including a studio for artists, in the main park of the capital (Parc Floral et Culturel). It also cosponsors, with the Municipal, Regional, and General Councils, the Festival of Fort-de-France, which brings theater, dance, music, painting, sculpture, film, photography, and textile design, from the rest of the Caribbean and from Africa, for a cultural celebration every year. Another cultural organization, Corps musical de Martinique, is developing its own complex of facilities for musicians and artists, with an auditorium, studios, and exhibition space.

And yet, there is something moribund in all this display of commitment, rather like a comatose patient attached to the elaborate equipment of a life-support system in a costly clinic. In the art shops that seek to divert some of the local and tourist consumption from the abundance of gold jewelry, the paintings on sale are mainly Haitian ones and all too often only the most commonplace of these. There is no such exciting indigenous textile design as now engages a number of young artists in Trinidad, for instance. Indeed, there is no indigenous design or manufacture of textiles in Martinique at all. Nor is there any such continuing musical inventiveness as distinguishes Trinidad, Jamaica, or Cuba, though it existed in Martinique once upon a time, without the facilities and financial nourishment available today.

An official at SERMAC itself lamented to me: "Standards are in general not high. Artists here tend to be artists only with a capital A. When I was a boy, there used to be beautifully colored hand-painted signs outside barber shops and other places. We celebrated the different seasons. We had a mango season and a shrimp season and a season for flying our kites. Now kites are forbidden because they get caught in the wires. In all this metropolitan conformity, we have a sense of loss."

A painter, now spending much of his time behind a desk in the building devoted to the promotion of the visual arts, implied in his own lament a scarcely less scathing indictment of Martinique's cultural impotence: "It was only when I went to Africa that I began to discover myself. It was a sort of second birth. But Africans did not accept me as one of themselves. We have a different past. We emerge from a different experience. We must develop our own particularity, if we are to engage creatively in universal art."

In his anguished poem, Césaire wrote of a return to Martinique:

Once more this limping life before me, no not this life, this death, this death without sense or piety, this death where there is no majesty, this death which limps from pettiness to pettiness; little greeds heaped on top of the conquistador; little flunkeys heaped on top of the great savage; little souls shovelled on top of the three-souled Caribbean.[4]

The greeds, the flunkies, and the souls seem not much bigger now than they were then. French financial feeding has served only to lengthen their shadows. The resources so lavishly committed to Martinique's creative expression by the political and cultural institutions of the island have had such a paltry yield as to suggest that they disappeared into the space between two identities. Departmental Negritude may well be a contradiction in terms. In getting and spending the material benefits of the French constitutional connection, Martinique has lost its own identity without gaining a French one to replace it.

The issue is most challengingly raised in the massive migration to metropolitan France. Césaire himself once denounced French government measures to encourage this as "genocide by substitution."[5] A radical Martiniquan lawyer described the phenomenon to me as one of "demographic deflation." Estimates for the total number of French Caribbean immigrants in France vary widely but agree in confirming that it is huge in relation to the size of its source. One recent scholarly book claims that by 1990 the total had reached some 400,000, to make a "third island . . . in the very heart of France."[6]

Most of such immigrants arrived in the expectation that they would be received for what they believed themselves to be, acceptably French. Instead, many found themselves the target of a racial discrimination, especially in such socially sensitive sectors as employment and housing, not always so fastidious as to differentiate between "foreign" blacks from Africa and "French" ones from the Caribbean. The flow of people between overseas and mainland France is rather less directed one way than it once was. Those returning to the islands, on visits or for good, often bring back with them their disillusionment. A popular Creole "Song of an Antillean Emigrant" has disseminated the message that poverty in France may be more uncomfortable than it is in the Caribbean:

I had understood that life in Paris
Was Pigalle, was Barbès.
When I arrived in Paris,
I slept outside, I slept outside,
I slept in the mouth of the Metro.
Ai! It was cold, cold as a refrigerator.
I did not even have a decrepit pullover.

I came here and met up with misery.
What a folkloric situation![7]

Since 1981, when Césaire mobilized widespread support behind his call
for a moratorium on the issue of independence while the priorities of economic and cultural development were pursued, concern with the costs of
the constitutional connection has grown, to surface even among its main
beneficiaries in the public sector. As a university lecturer expressed the rising
disquiet to me:

"There is a new generation that does not feel French but that wants French
money. And this, especially for the intellectuals, is a humiliating position.
Increasingly as well, we have a sense of exile, even of claustrophobia, in the
isolation of Martinique and Guadeloupe from the other islands, except for
Haiti. The access that the French language gives us to Europe and to parts
of Africa is no substitute for communication with our Caribbean context."

Another view of the predicament came from a rich businessman: "I don't
want us to have a history of impoverishment like Haiti's. But I ask myself,
is the money worth our having no seat in the United Nations, no flag, no
identity of our own? We know who we really are, how our color defines us.
In my heart, I am for self-government now, as a step towards independence."

However strong this stirring may be in Martinique, it is manifestly stronger
in Guadeloupe. The two islands resemble each other so much in the ascendancy of French culture, their economic dependence on France, and
their isolation from their Caribbean context that the differences between
them seem all the sharper. Guadeloupe has, at a little more than 340,000,
a marginally larger population than has Martinique. Yet Pointe-à-Pitre, its
single city, has only some 80,000 inhabitants. Guadeloupe is, in fact, not
one island but two, separated by a narrow strait. The administrative capital,
Basse-Terre, is on the island of that name, while Pointe-à-Pitre, the commercial capital, is on the other, Grande-Terre. Guadeloupe is, accordingly,
nowhere near as centralized, let alone urbanized, as Martinique. It is, too,
economically more dependent. While its imports are roughly the same in
value as Martinique's, it exports much less; the value of its imports is some
eleven times that of its exports. Not surprisingly, the unemployment rate is
even higher. It was 38 percent of the labor force at the end of the eighties.

In short, Guadeloupe is poorer than Martinique, and the signs of squalor
are more conspicuous. In Pointe-à-Pitre itself, a city that seems to have been
built expressly to counteract the charm of its natural setting, tower blocks
for mass housing close in on the center, while rusting shanty settlements
collect at the edge. Then, abruptly, the city disappears into a countryside
less lush and less cultivated than Martinique's.

Here, too, however, are the copious, if selective, dividends of the French
connection. Some years ago, a study of the economy, published by the Pop-

ular Movement for the Independence of Guadeloupe (Mouvement pour le Guadeloupe Independent: MPGI), pointed out that while the working population numbered some 92,400, there were some 130,000 motorcars. It cited, among other instances of the frenzy to consume, the huge imports of airfreighted flowers from Europe and, more remarkable still, the arrival in one year alone of one million bottles of champagne or twice the quantity imported in the same year by richer Martinique. Indeed, as one advertising agency in Pointe-à-Pitre chose to proclaim: *"Acheter n'est pas la satisfaction d'un besoin en Guadeloupe, mais une FÊTE"* ("Shopping in Guadeloupe is not for satisfying need but a CELEBRATION").[8]

If so, it is a celebration in which rather fewer are able to join than in Martinique. The middle class is smaller, and the slope between poverty and riches is correspondingly steeper. Moreover, it involves a starker racial contrast. The population is more extensively black of unmixed ancestry than it is in Martinique, and the top posts in the public service are more commonly held by whites. This is certainly a factor in the growth of a more widely based movement, and within it a more militant strain, for separation from France. And it is a factor the more forceful for being related to a past that is still so alive in the consciousness of the present. In one interview after another, I was advised to take account of a history different in important respects from that of Martinique.

The regime of slavery was far harsher in Guadeloupe, and the French Revolutionary Terror reached here, to guillotine a nobility which comprised much of the slave-owning planter class. The Place de la Victoire, where the guillotine was raised, remains today the heart of Pointe-à-Pitre. The Terror never reached Martinique, which was under British occupation from 1794 to 1802. There, the slave-owning planter class, already engaged in exploring a more secure supremacy with the help of miscegenation, and with minds concentrated by the course of events in Haiti, survived to pursue its own interpretation of the obligations on nobility.

After slavery was abolished in 1848, differences in the character of dominion continued. To Martinique, as the headquarters of the French Caribbean empire, came high imperial officials more urbane in their outlook and more concerned to promote the allegiance of the mulattoes. In Guadeloupe, relations between white and black were rougher. Minor French officials were the more arrogant in exercising an authority to which they were elsewhere unaccustomed, and there was no such mulatto component in the population as might have exercised a mediating influence.

Yet if each river followed a different course, both merged at the mouth, in the postcolonial acceptance of a constitutional absorption by France. In Martinique, this had been prepared by a policy of cultural assimilation which admitted Negritude only to absorb it. In Guadeloupe, it had been prepared instead by what a leading lawyer described to me as "cultural occlusion."

Either way, acquiescence in a French identity became the route of least resistance. Such acquiescence is, however, not what it was. And if the movement for separation from France is stronger in Guadeloupe, this is partly because indigenous culture has proved more resilient there. It survives in the jazz of particular groups; in the music and theater of the countryside; in the hawkers of brooms who sing the attractions of their wares along the pavements of Pointe-à-Pitre.

Even the most sanguine among the leaders of the independence movement, in Guadeloupe as well as Martinique, admit that in the referendum for which they call, a majority at present would vote to continue the constitutional connection with France. Their call is immediately directed at advancing rather than achieving their objective. They recognize the strength of the popular perception that the economic effect of a break would be, at least for a while, devastating.

The predicament of the populist politician was made clear to me at the opening of a sumptuous new school in Pointe-à-Pitre, a very symbol of what French money could provide. As various functionaries and guests waited with mounting impatience outside, the dignitary I had come to see allowed me to interview him in the hall where the formalities were due to be conducted.

"Yes," he said, reciting old arguments, "our dependence, psychical as well as material, our ever-growing commitment to consumption and our ever-widening trade deficit, all this presents us with formidable problems. But what are we to do? We are so much richer than the other islands, even Trinidad, with its petroleum. We are a democracy. We must give the people the consumer goods they demand. In time, perhaps, there will be popular support for independence, and we will be strong enough to seize it.

"Meanwhile," he added, in a sudden flare of passion, "why should we feel any guilt or shame about taking all that we can get from France? How much has France taken from us, in centuries of slavery and colonial rule? We are only getting back what is our own." On this high note, a functionary arrived to whisper urgently in his ear, and he closed the interview with practiced courtesy.

It is difficult to understand how the ever-growing commitment to consumption and the ever-widening trade deficit can develop the sort of strength capable of seizing independence. Beyond this, however, I found profoundly repugnant the attempt to offset, as in a moral ledger, the entries of so many privileged public service salaries, so many motorcars and gold necklaces, so many bottles of champagne, against the accumulated horrors of several centuries—and by this process, to wipe out the guilt and shame of dependence. In fact, of course, the very suggestion that this should be done reveals that it cannot be. The guilt and shame were demonstrated in the dignitary's very effort to repudiate them.

There is, to be sure, no safe and simple way of resolving the dilemma of identity for either Martinique or Guadeloupe or both together. One way, neither safe nor simple, lies in the very distraction of the Caribbean context, where so many other islands, whatever their formal status, have their own problems of identity, isolation, dependence, and vulnerability. A Martiniquan with a distinguished record in international negotiations dismissed CARICOM, or the still essentially incipient Caribbean Community based on the English-speaking islands and Guyana, as a "smokescreen," but then declared that some part of the answer to the problem of dependence lay in regional cooperation. "Politics," he added with a sigh, "is full of nuances."

Identity, however, is not a nuance. In Martinique and Guadeloupe, it is, as elsewhere in the Caribbean but especially so for them in their peculiar predicament, the essence of politics. For if politics is about the body, it is also about the spirit or the soul, and the conflict between the profit to the one and the loss to the other can as little be resolved without anguish as by pretending that it does not exist.

28 | A HAITIAN SPACE

≈≈≈≈≈≈≈≈≈≈≈≈≈≈≈≈≈≈≈≈≈≈≈≈≈≈≈≈≈≈≈≈≈≈≈≈≈≈

The praise from Christopher Columbus for the island he had found and decided to name Hispaniola was lyrical. The rivers could scarcely be counted, the trees reached to the stars, and the nightingales were always singing. No one coming upon Haiti today would recognize it from that description. It is the open sewers that can scarcely be counted. There are few trees left, and these look as though they require all their strength merely to stand. If there are nightingales still singing, it is a lucky listener who can catch the song.

From the air, the largely mountainous land beyond the enormous sprawl of the capital and away from the liquid beauty of the towns along the coast appears to have been stricken over wide areas by some terminal blight. Along the border with the Dominican Republic, the contrast between the barren stretch on one side and the succulent green on the other seems as stark if not as straight as that which separates the surrounding desert in Egypt from the reach of the Nile. What has overtaken Haiti is little short of an ecological disaster. Barely more than 1 percent of the tree cover that existed at the time of the Spanish arrival remains, and this continues to be reduced by the demand for timber or for charcoal, the common cooking fuel. The disappearance of the trees has had a predictable impact on areas that were once productive from visiting rains and are now barren from drought.

Once the richest of colonies, Haiti has long been considered the poorest country in the hemisphere. According to the World Bank, its gross national product per capita was a mere $400 in 1989. Dire as this figure is, it disguises a mass poverty far worse, in a country where disparities of income must be among the widest in the world. The extent of such poverty is paradoxically less conspicuous in the countryside, for there the very space conceals the evidence, than it is in the closely packed capital that represents a relative refuge of hope. Port-au-Prince, with roughly 15 percent of Haiti's 6,380,000 people, accounts for 80 percent of all salaries, subsidies, and budgetary commitments. It is difficult to believe this, except on the basis that four-fifths of very little is still not much.

When I visited Haiti in January 1990, General Avril was still in power at the head of a military regime. I had reserved a room at the Hotel Oloffson in Port-au-Prince—called the Hotel Trianon in Graham Greene's novel *The Comedians*, which is set in Haiti under the rule of Papa Doc. In my ignorance, I had expected such a celebrated hotel, in the Caribbean warmth of the Northern winter, to be full. Yet for all the charm of its nineteenth-century structure, a stretched white cuckoo clock of a building, it was almost empty, except in the evenings, when locals came to chat in the lounge or cluster at the bar.

Reports of political repression and civil disorder attract few visitors, except those with a professional interest who arrive to record the course of the latest emergency and leave when this appears to be no more than a heightening of the normal unrest. Haiti has failed to provide those elaborate facilities available elsewhere in the Caribbean for enjoying the sun and the sea in sealed-off ease. As though this were not enough, Haiti came in 1982 to be widely if absurdly held to be the source of AIDS. Then, four years later, as the belief was receding, Haiti's Minister of Health stated, to fresh unfavorable publicity, that perhaps 10 percent of all Haitians were now carriers of the disease.

In the streets of the capital, the visitor encounters numerous souvenir sellers, offering baskets, mats, carvings, paintings, for a tourism that has all but disappeared. Some of them stand forlornly beside their stocks. Others vivaciously invite interest. None of them pesters. They accept rejection with dignity. This is true, too, of the many beggars. They approach or simply sit, often with such deformities as reproach any resistance, expressing their need in a look or a gesture, never a whine.

Everywhere are signs of neglect and decay, in the crumbling main roads, the mounds of uncollected refuse, the suppurating sewers. Yet there is no mockery in the reminders of heroic Haitian history and of foreign black achievements provided by monuments and street names. For there is in the demeanor of these people a courage, a resilience, a striking vitality that is a kind of triumph.

One manifestation of this vitality is the common form of public transport, the privately owned "tap-tap," closer to a small lorry than to a bus, which carries up to sixteen seated passengers, eight squeezed together along either side, and others sometimes clinging to the extremities. With few exceptions, each is decorated with brightly painted pictures and its particular name, such as *L'Eternal Devant* (The Eternal Ahead), *Tous est Vanité* (All is Vanity), and *Kris Kapab* (Christ, I can do it). Given the way that Haitians drive, the names are chosen with wry humor as well as piety.

My first interview was with Jean Dominique, a mulatto of slight figure,

who owned a broadcasting station called Radio Haiti-Inter with a large following across the country. After the fall of Jean-Claude (Baby Doc) Duvalier
in 1986, he had returned from exile in the United States to be met by a
crowd of the poor and to collect, mainly in donations of one-gourd (25-cent)
notes, over $90,000 toward the cost of setting up his new station. This had
come, he made it clear in case the meaning should have escaped me, not
from the mulatto rich but from the black poor, and was surely evidence of
a new alliance for change across the color divide. He told me of the peasant
woman who had come to see him, all the way from the northwest:

"It took her two days to get here. She said that she had had a dream in
which I came and held her hand, as a son holds his mother's hand. As we
sat in her dream, there had come floating downward balloons of different
colors with words on them. She had turned to me in her dream and said,
you know I cannot read, tell me what the words say, and I had told her,
that word is Guinea, and that word is Congo, and so on. Now, sitting in
my office here, she said to me that the dream was a message for me, and
the message was this. In 1957 (the year Papa Doc Duvalier became President),
when the devils took over Haiti, the Good Ones had gone away, and the
balloons were to tell me that the Good Ones were now coming back from
heaven to help us."

Certainly, Jean Dominique needed all the help he could get. At 5:30 in
the afternoon of April 6, 1989, a detachment of helmeted men in plain
clothes arrived in several trucks at the radio station, leapt out and fired
repeatedly at the building before storming inside and smashing the transmitters. "On your way out," he said to me, "look up at the face of the
building and see where the bullets went. Our logo is high up on the left. It
is based on a Voodoo sign."

When I left the building, I stopped to stare up at the front. On the left
where the logo was, there was not a single bullet mark; on the right, the
wall was all but covered in such marks, from what looked like a very fury
of gunfire. I shook off the unsettling sense that the Voodoo sign had somehow
protected itself. There remained something unsettling about that scrupulous
avoidance of a symbol, so close to the marks of so much violence.

Near the end of my stay in Haiti, I went to visit Dr. Max Beauvoir, a
black man of imposing presence and smooth manner, who is a biochemist,
a Voodoo priest and a traditional healer. He is reputed to have been one of
Papa Doc's Voodoo intimates and though never close to Baby Doc, was a
target of attack in the campaign of vengeance that followed Baby Doc's fall.
He did not flee the country or go into hiding. It seems he had forces enough
at his disposal to defend his home and temple, on his extensive walled site
south of the capital.

The estate was still well-guarded at the time of my visit, as I found before
being ushered onto the patio of the house. There, at the table with him,

were his wife, a sturdy blonde Frenchwoman of a startlingly white complexion, and a statuesque black woman, introduced to me as Carole Lawouze,
who wore large enameled earrings in the shape of Africa. Madame Lawouze,
Dr. Beauvoir informed me, was a Voodoo priestess who had spent fifteen
years in the United States, where more Voodoo ceremonies took place than
in Haiti itself. Madame Beauvoir took part in the talk, usually to confirm
her husband's remarks. Madame Lawouze occasionally nodded her head
and otherwise glowered.

Dr. Beauvoir was passionate in denouncing the long persecution of Voodoo
and the part played by the Churches in this. Since 1806, he declared, there
had been twelve separate Church-promoted "pogroms" against adherents of
Voodoo, and some two thousand had been killed in the six months from
the fall of Jean-Claude Duvalier in February 1986 to the end of the vengeance
campaign in August. Christian priests had been conspicuous in the hunting
down of such prey. He assailed the Churches also for their long domination
of the educational system which had ensured adequate schooling only for
those from Christian families. Was it surprising that illiteracy was so widespread in Haiti?

When I succeeded at last in directing the talk to the ecological disaster
whose evidence had so struck me, he argued that it was not the peasants
who had been responsible for this. It was not they who had felled whole
forests for the export of timber. In fact, it had been the persecution of Voodoo
which had led to the cutting down of so many *mapous*, the trees regarded
as resting places for the spirits. Of the enormous sums provided by aid agencies
of every sort, he continued indignantly, so much went to the Churches.
Had any of this led to the planting of a single tree? The day that such money
came the way of Voodoo, reforestation would follow fast. Madame Beauvoir
expressed her agreement with vigor. Madame Lawouze glowered.

As I was leaving, Dr. Beauvoir presented me with a cassette that had a
photograph of Madame Lawouze on the front of the sleeve. "You may," he
said with a smile, "find this interesting." When I had climbed into the taxi,
I asked the driver if he had a cassette player in the car, since I had traveled
in several Haitian taxis where cassettes had served to divert my attention from
displays of driver bravado. He took the cassette from me, and I sat back
expecting to hear the drumming and prayer of Voodoo ceremony. Instead,
the car was suddenly filled with song from a voice so joyous and backing of
such rhythmic richness that I sighed with pleasure. The driver turned his
head in disregard of the road and said with a wide smile, "Carole!"

According to the sleeve of the cassette, Carole herself had written the
music or lyrics or both for some of the songs. The music of one and the
lyrics of another had been written by Tiga, whose art school I had already
visited. It was a school for children, encouraged to paint, draw, and sculpt
to the accompaniment of music, played on drum or guitar by Tiga himself,

by one of his assistants, or by any of the children who cared to try. Tiga's own infusing theory, as he expounded it to me, was that authentic Haitian art expresses not the external object but the interior vision and even the anterior one, from far back in the Haitian past or beyond.

The importance of painting in Haiti has, for several decades now, been a phenomenon. There is no other country in the hemisphere, perhaps in the world, where it is so dominant an expression of popular culture and relatively so prominent a form of economic activity. Beyond the licit or illicit activities of the military, bureaucratic, and business elites, painting offers a rare source of escape from destitution—and even of wealth for a few. One leading dealer estimated the number of professional painters as somewhere between one and two thousand, along with countless others who painted and occasionally sold their work, but who were not to be considered professionals in his terms.

Within the multitude of paintings on view at galleries, shops and hotels, in the stocks held by dealers or on display in the streets, there are inevitably the commonplace and incompetent. More than one dealer informed me scornfully that there was a ready market in North America and Europe even for such inferior work, which was bought by the crate, in part to supply the needs of interior decorators. There were as well, however, numerous paintings of the manifest originality and quality for which discerning dealers and collectors abroad are prepared to pay high sums, at least by Haitian standards. The walls of the Hotel Oloffson itself displayed a few of these.

In a gallery at Cap-Haïtien, which specialized in contemporary paintings, I saw some that had as their subject the recent campaign of vengeance against the Duvalierists. It was art as reportage, in a society where so many are unable to read or write in Creole, let alone in the French which is the language of books, magazines, and newspapers. Philomé Obin, one of the early masters, devoted a number of his now most famous pictures to recording events and social scenes from the Haitian past, in the use of art as history.

Yet beyond all this, there is, simply, an abundant love of color. It is conspicuous throughout Cap-Haïtien, in the greens and blues, yellows and reds, with which so many houses and shacks are painted. There is certainly little else, apart from its natural setting, remarkable in a city which had been the most embelished of the French colony, but then been so extensively burned in the wars of the slave revolution that virtually nothing remains of its dubious glory.

It was in Cap-Haïtien that I had arranged to meet up with Patrick de la Tour, a distinguished mulatto architectural historian involved in the restoration of Sans Souci and the Citadelle, the two great monuments from the early years of Haitian independence, some distance from the city. He exulted in both, as applications of Haitian technology to the best in the European architecture of the time. Yet these and later public buildings, from churches and barracks to the Presidential Palace in Port-au-Prince, have little to do with popular architecture in Haiti today.

Between the ornate homes of the rich and the slum shacks which scarcely qualify as architecture at all people build their houses or have them built in phases that accord with their financial resources. A room is added here, another there, sometimes to be let as a source of subsidiary income. Yet even in evidently unfinished structures, sometimes scarcely more than a single room, there would be a square of figured concrete, a sort of arabesque window, that held my passing attention. Nothing more tellingly testified for me the widespread Haitian love of form.

It was Patrick de la Tour who took me to a party in Pétionville, the capital of the Haitian mulatto elite, pleasantly situated above the crowded heat in Port-au-Prince. Along the Avenue John Brown that joins the two, cars and tap-taps pass at night the market women plodding upward, with their burdens of vegetables and fruit, or downward during the day, with their empty baskets. As the road rises, larger houses and residents of lighter complexion come into view, until Pétionville itself provides the culmination. Here, the walled gardens, the quiet cypress-lined square, the galleries and boutiques seem an immeasurable distance rather than a few miles away from the tumultuous slums below.

At the party, the men were all mulattoes except for a black official from the United States Embassy and myself. The women, all mulattoes except for the embassy official's white wife, were exquisitely dressed. The conversation, which drifted faultlessly between English and French, with an occasional shift into Creole quickly translated for my benefit, was much about the plight of Haiti and how much longer the disreputable military regime was likely to last. A high official at the central bank informed us that there was at anchor outside the harbor an oil tanker, whose captain would not permit any further progress until he had been instructed by the owners that payment had been made for two previous deliveries. The state of the foreign currency reserves was not such as to yield even an appeasing down payment.

General Avril had recently taken off for Taiwan, with a jet load of family, advisers, and other functionaries, reportedly in expectation of getting up to $60 million in aid. Perhaps, one of the women suggested, the trip might be the cover for a more extensive stay abroad. No such luck, another sighed. Throughout, the talk was taut, rather as though they were all waiting for a guest suddenly to arrive whose conduct was wholly unpredictable and sometimes violent. At no point in the evening did anyone indicate an outlook beyond the fall, somehow, of the military regime. No one expressed faith, however faint, in a lasting democratic dispensation to follow. Given the apparent apprehension of what might yet precede or accompany that fall, and the apparent absence of any confidence in the consequences, the force of the desire for an end to the regime spoke volumes about its character.

No more optimistic, if involving a more courageous commitment than that made by anyone else at the party, was the view of Bobby Duval, with whom I had several talks during my stay in Haiti. Even among the leading families of the mulatto elite, his own was particularly distinguished. One ancestor had been a slave owner who had led his slaves into the revolution. Later ancestors had scaled the heights of Haitian commerce, where the family was still prominent. Bobby himself headed an organization for political prisoners, a type of post not commonly associated with a scion of the mulatto elite, but one for which he had unimpeachable credentials. He had spent two years as a political prisoner, and his remark to me that he had emerged weighing ninety pounds—a large man, he looked as though he now weighed three times as much—was no less eloquent than his other, that he had watched 180 prisoners die during his detention. He would almost certainly have joined them, he allowed, without the influence that his family had exercised in Washington.

His was the doctrine of class struggle, but based on a social analysis that provided a less than uplifting prognosis. The middle class was divided. One part, of liberal disposition, was in conflict with what he termed "the feudal state." The other prospered on the principle of what he called the three C's: Corruption, Contacts, and Contraband. He had had particular experience of the last; his attempts at setting up an indigenous manufacturing plant had been thwarted by those with profitable investments in smuggling from abroad the goods he intended to produce. The workers, he admitted bleakly, were largely a restless lumpen proletariat, without an institutional structure. Furthermore, there was the factor of the United States, which dominated Haiti. Avril did only what Washington wanted.

This assertion was becoming increasingly doubtful. On January 15, 1990, Avril returned from Taiwan with the reported assurance of one million dollars in aid, or scarcely more than his trip, with so many attendants and such possibilities of shopping, was likely to have cost. Five days later, soldiers were dispatched to deposit piles of human excrement outside the homes of prominent political opponents. It was the snarl before the leap. Shortly afterward, Avril declared a state of siege—a stage beyond a mere state of emergency— and dispatched his soldiers again, this time to beat up and arrest the selected victims. From my hotel, sporadic gunfire could be heard. Some of those I had come to know or with whom I had arranged interviews were no longer reachable on the telephone.

Bobby Duval and a few others, who had fortuitously been away from home during the raids or been alerted before the soldiers arrived, went into hiding. A few opponents were seized only to be expelled from the country. Most were taken into indefinite detention. Among these was Serges Gilles, leader of a socialist party, who happened to have established warm personal relations with François Mitterrand, President of France, and his wife. According to the Haitian word-of-mouth news service, which communicates on such occasions more rapidly than the radio and more reliably than the press, a phone call from President Mitterrand to the Presidential Palace in Port-au-Prince conveyed so forceful a message that Avril promised both the immediate release of Gilles from detention and a personal apology to him. Gilles was duly brought to the Palace but was unable to appreciate the expression of Avril's regret. He had been so badly beaten about the head that he was deaf.

A small flock of foreign correspondents—Haiti had long since ceased to be considered important enough for a large one—flew in, all but a few of them to perch at the Hotel Oloffson, where they were joined by representatives of various United States and international aid agencies, fluttering over the fate of projects and protégés. It all brought a glint to the eyes of Aubelin Jolicoeur, the model for Graham Greene's mulatto information gatherer, Petit Pierre, in *The Comedians*. He was still haunting the hotel in fact, as he had been doing in fiction for a quarter of a century; still dapper, with his gold-topped walking stick; still a gossip columnist by profession, though now dealing in paintings on the side and styling himself on his proffered visiting-card "Ambassador-at-Large."

He was in quite a different class from the bulky, baldheaded mulatto in a navy beret who took to appearing, occasionally with a woman on his arm, at the bar or in the lounge of the hotel, and glaring balefully around him. A number of different people warned me to beware of him. He was, they whispered, a particularly dangerous member of the security forces. At first I wondered what purpose was being served by the presence of a secret agent who was so widely identified as such. Then I realized that this was the whole point. He was not there to find out anything, but merely to remind everyone, by his very presence, of the menace he represented.

The unease at the possibility of yet uglier reactions from a regime that seemed both frightened and enraged soon gave place to a prevalent view that nothing much was likely to happen for some time. There were no reports of rioting or massacre. A shooting here or there was only normal. In the capital, the tap-taps made their frantic way through traffic that was as congested as ever; and outside the schools, the children fortunate enough to have places there collected in their neat uniforms. The foreign correspondents and the roving representatives of foreign aid agencies began leaving, in the expectation of having to return when the military regime at last yielded to the tightening financial squeeze. The word was out that the United States, which had sustained one corrupt and repressive regime after another, had lost all patience with the latest and would not provide it with any further transfusions.

As I packed my bags, I remembered one of the talks I had had with Roger Desire, a black Anglican priest who had been Dean of the Cathedral before resigning in protest at Papa Doc's interventions. The whole social structure of Haiti, he had told me, is based on domination. You are either one of the "eaters" or one of the "eaten," and if you cannot make yourself one of the first, which so few can do, you have to learn how to live with your lot. The "eaten" are by definition always in the wrong. Their only recourse is to the mercy of the "eaters." It is a relationship expressed in the Creole plea *fè pa-m:* literally, "make my part," which means, "do it for me; although I am innocent, I beg your pardon, and ask you to be kind." It is the way to survive.

Michel-Rolph Trouillot, a Haitian emigrant who teaches in the Department of Anthropology at Johns Hopkins University, wrote in 1985 a short historical analysis of Haitian society. It contained the grisly story of 250 Haitians who set off for the United States in July 1981 on a small boat, the *Jézula* (Jesus There). During the three-week voyage to the Florida Keys, the two Haitian masters of the boat killed 96 of the passengers, by beating, strangling, hacking them with machetes or pushing them overboard. The failure of the 250 to overwhelm the two with their sheer numbers epitomized for Trouillot "the fate of an inattentive majority whose last resort of security is the habit of obedience." The two masters were subsequently absolved of murder "on procedural grounds" by a United States court. Trouillot commented that in this "tale of horror," there was a "vignette of the Haitian situation, with its connections of hope and despair, its toll of deaths with impunity, its continuing presence within the international sphere defined by North American notions of peace, power and justice."[1]

Yet there is another strain in Haitian history that belongs to its very birth. It is the spirit of the runaway slave and the revolutionary. "The Haitians," Patrick de la Tour said to me, "are the freest of people. They piss when they want where they want. They negotiate on their own terms. That is why there are so many political parties." How, then, does this passion for freedom survive within the society of domination? The answer is that it has made its own space.

It has made this in painting and sculpture. Here, indeed, may be the ultimate explanation for why there has been such a creative commitment to art in Haiti. Those compositions of line and color, those metal, wood, and ceramic forms, express in their own way the rejoicing in an order of freedom beyond the grasp of the greedy and the tyrannies of the state.

Freedom has made its own space in Voodoo, to hold it against not only persecutions from without but assaults from within. The important Voodoo center of Nan Souvenans in the northwest, founded by some four hundred Dahomeans who had been bought from a slave ship by Christophe in the early years of independence, withstood the various attempts by Papa Doc Duvalier to control it and emerged with its influence enhanced. Increasingly now, there are even Christian priests in Haiti who are coming to recognize that Voodoo has something positive and timely to offer. "Its doctrine of creation," Roger Desire said to me, "is ecologically more relevant today than the Christian doctrine being taught in the seminaries. Man must learn to be reconciled not only with God but with Nature."

Freedom has made its own space in Creole, a language which the dominating French culture might exclude from serious study but could not extinguish. Roger Desire is himself engaged in producing the first-ever Creole dictionary. It is a language which, while possessing different words for such nouns as "man" and "woman," "father" and "mother," has, unlike French, no gender in its syntax. In this, as Desire pointed out to me, it is like Voodoo, which has no gender discrimination in its rites. Furthermore, time and space are intertwined in the structure of the language, so that, for instance, the same word, *kote*, is used for both "when" and "where," according to the context.

Significantly, the movement to promote Creole is stronger among Haitian intellectuals abroad than among their counterparts at home. One such intellectual is Carole Charles, a black woman who teaches sociology at a college in Manhattan. She defined to me the very nature of the Haitian diaspora as a sense of transnational continuity instead of the rupture which marks the settlement of so many other immigrant communities in the United States. That is why, she elaborated, Haitians abroad refer to themselves as a diaspora and why so many of them do not apply for naturalization or, if they do, disguise the fact.

The Haitian diaspora adheres to its homeland and history in its particular intertwining of space and time. In the process, it is freer than are those in Haiti to explore what the Haitian identity has become or what, in being true to itself, it should be. If Haiti has, indeed, become a society of the "eaters" and the "eaten," this is not the society which the slaves envisaged in the making of their revolution, or for which Haitians of every generation since have craved. It would be appropriate if part of the reach toward a different Haitian society should come from the Haitian diaspora within the United States, the avowed protector of freedom in the hemisphere which has often done so much damage with the worst of intentions, and with the best of them, even more.

It may be that the time for Haiti to make of itself a space for freedom has arrived. Trouillot attributes the increasing migration of Haitians abroad to their being "intuitively conscious of a fundamental crisis in their society, one for which no easy solution can be foreseen. They are somehow aware that the economic organization upon which the nation has established the use and distribution of its resources—for the unequal yet sustained livelihood of its majority—now faces an impasse. They are aware that passivity and obedience may never again provide the fragile veil of security that even the humblest could hope for in better days. They are aware that the norms of social behavior, evolved in struggle during nearly two centuries of ongoing, short-term compromises, are now drastically changing in ways that will eventually leave the bulk of the population only acknowledging its impotence."[2]

Yet impotence can never be an end for a Haitian people that owes its beginning to the single successful slave revolution in modern history. If some sort of tolerable survival is no longer possible for a system of passivity and obedience, nothing is left but the last commitment that was also the first, in the very identity of Haitians with freedom. There is a saying in Creole that refers to much of the Haitian past as well as the Haitian landscape: *dèyè mòn gên mòn*—"Beyond the mountains are more mountains." The mountains have been climbed and crossed before.

29 | BRAZIL AND THE COLOR OF INVISIBILITY

≈≈≈≈≈≈≈≈≈≈≈≈≈≈≈≈≈≈≈≈≈≈≈≈≈≈≈≈≈≈≈

The Metro in São Paulo is being extended, and a new underground line is taking its name from the Avenida Paulista, the "supreme symbol of São Paulo's present and future as a major financial and economic centre of Latin America."[1] While I was visiting the city in 1990, there was on display in a mall off the avenue a model of the immediate area, adapted to suggest the changes that the new line would bring. Hundreds of small figures were positioned on the model, among buildings, at cafés and restaurants, on sidewalks and escalators. I looked cursorily and then carefully at each of the figures. Not one of them was black. I found this all the more astonishing since I had recently been given an estimate that not far short of half the city's population was black.[2]

The *Jornal do Brasil*, a venerable Rio newspaper not renowned for its radicalism but never reluctant to score a point in the rivalry between Rio and São Paulo, carried in its gossip column a curtly critical reference to the model. Under the heading "Curiosity," it wondered whether the omission of blacks should be ascribed to "racism or forgetfulness."[3] The sole examples of the race, it reported, appeared dressed in feathers and brilliants to represent the mulattas of Ôba Ôba, a well-known cabaret troupe.

Abdias do Nascimento has devoted much of his life to promoting black cultural and political consciousness in Brazil. In 1944, he founded the Black Experimental Theatre, and in 1950 organized the First Congress of Brazilian Blacks. He took to painting as well, much influenced by African traditional religious symbolism. At his apartment in Rio, I spoke to him about a problem that had been worrying me. In various Brazilian cities and towns that I had visited, I had seen paintings which depicted blacks with blobs or blurs instead of faces. This had struck me all the more forcefully for the contrast with the paintings I had seen before in Haiti, none of which I could remember as having depicted blacks in this way. Nascimento looked at me in surprise. He had never seen such Brazilian paintings.

Sitting with us was a black woman from the United States, staying with Nascimento while working on a doctoral thesis about the Black Experimental Theatre. She told us about two women she had recently met in Rio. "One of them was black, and in the course of our talk, she said to me, 'There are no blacks in Brazil.' I was so startled that I burst out with, 'What do you mean? You are black yourself.' She got rather angry and told me that she had, after years of effort, succeeded in getting the word 'black' in her birth certificate changed to 'brown.' The other woman was a mulatta. She paints, and I have two of her paintings. I think that they have black figures in them. They are in one of my suitcases. Let me get them, and we can see if the figures have faces." She left the room and returned with two rolls of canvas, which she proceeded to unroll in front of us. The paintings had black figures, and the figures had no faces.

Some two weeks later, I visited the Museum of Contemporary Art in São Paulo and interviewed Ana Mae Barbosa, its director. She had caused a considerable scandal by holding an exhibition at the Museum on "The Ecstasy of Candomblé." What passes for the cultural establishment of the city had been disturbed by the idea that anything associated with black religious rites and beliefs should be regarded as art or at least as art at a level qualifying for display in the Museum.

I mentioned to Professor Barbosa my puzzlement over the faceless blacks in Brazilian paintings. She could not recollect, she replied, ever having noticed this, but she would make it her business to look out for black figures without faces. She did not have far or long to look. At the end of the interview, she proposed that I visit the exhibition of Brazilian painting that was to be opened formally that evening and she offered to accompany me. The part with which we started was a retrospective of work by Nône de Andrade, a white painter from much earlier in the century. "How very strange," she remarked, as we arrived at a painting with blacks as its subject, "no features on the faces." She must have looked at the painting before, but purely as a painting, without seeing the subject.

If the practice in Brazil of painting blacks without faces is not invariable, it is clearly common enough to require explanation. I increasingly pestered people for one. Some replied that it was probably a convention; but this only begged the question of why the convention had ever begun or become so acceptable. Others suggested that painters in Brazil must suppose potential buyers expected blacks to be depicted in this way; but that begged the question of why painters in Brazil should suppose anything of the sort. It might be, still others allowed, that the depiction of facial features was beyond the competence of some Brazilian painters. Yet this was plainly not the case, since the same painters who depicted blacks without faces were competent enough in depicting the intricate details of landscape, plants, animals, and even, like Nône de Andrade, the facial features of whites.

It is difficult to escape the conclusion that the cause is a complex one, related to a kind of Brazilian psychical censorship; and if this seems bizarre, it is surely no more bizarre than the practice of painting blacks without faces or the claim by a black woman that there are no blacks in Brazil. Is the depiction of blacks without faces a way of admitting the presence of blackness in Brazil but not the presence of blacks? Is this symbolic of the way that blacks are used by the society?

Television is as devotedly watched in Brazil as anywhere on earth, and the soaps, which compose much of the fare, are devotedly followed in the favelas or slums, where the inhabitants are disproportionately blacks. These soaps in general affect to deal with the lives and the preoccupations of people in the upper reaches of society, and the casts could scarcely be whiter if they had been designed to illustrate the celebrated effect of detergents on the domestic wash. Should blacks make any appearance, they do so either un- avoidably in street scenes or as servants, though most servants in the soaps that I watched were as white as their employers. The basis of one popular soap was a book by José Lins do Rego entitled *Riacho doce*, whose two main characters, a grandmother and grandson, are black. The title was kept for the soap, but the two main characters were turned into whites.

This concentration on whiteness is by no means limited to soaps. It may well be that somewhere, on one of Brazilian television's local channels, there is a black prominent enough to report the news or the weather forecast or to host a chat show. I never saw one in the viewing that my travels in Brazil encompassed, and no one I asked seemed able to tell me where to look.

All this would, for anyone from abroad who is acquainted even vaguely with the racial composition of Brazil, be remarkable enough. It is made more remarkable by the contrast with television in such other multiracial societies as the United States and Britain. In the United States, the black population is proportionately smaller than it is in Brazil, yet television there includes blacks across the full range of programs, from newscasting to soaps, sitcoms and talk shows. In Britain, where the black population is propor- tionately smaller still, blacks also appear in many programs and are prominent among high-profile newscasters as well.

The virtual invisibility of blacks on Brazilian television is accompanied by the concealment of so many in an effectively segregated poverty. With notable exceptions, such as Salvador, where their relative numbers provide a prominent presence, blacks in urban Brazil are largely contained in the favelas, out of sight. This is true even of Rio, where most favelas have established themselves conspicuously on hills. For slums disappear with distance. Far enough away, the squalid becomes the picturesque, as people are lost to view, and the shacks in which they live merge into landscape.

These hill favelas accommodate a minority of whites among the blacks and reveal the impact of racial discrimination within poverty itself. The older, lower reaches of such settlements are held predominantly by whites. There the structures are in general concrete or brick, with a more secure footing against the force of the rains. The higher they are up the hill, the more makeshift these structures are, and the darker is the skin of those who live in them. From time to time, heavy rains produce a landslide. Television and the press, provided that there are sufficient casualties, report it. The camera records a sudden sight of stricken blacks, which lasts until different news commands attention.

Elsewhere, more commonly than in Rio, favelas are scattered on the outskirts of cities or otherwise hidden, behind the walls made by the sides of their own shacks or by strategically placed high hoardings. Some blacks remain there, invisible. Others, fortunate enough to have some form of paid labor, join in the daily migrations to and from factories, offices, shops, and other people's homes. Still others emerge to engage in whatever activity holds out some prospect of making enough to help them and their families stay alive.

They hawk small packets of peanuts to the customers of bars, cafés, and restaurants, or chocolate and fruit to the occupants of cars in arrested traffic. They hawk themselves from an early age in a prostitution that recalls the accounts of foreign visitors in previous centuries who expressed such astonishment at its extent. They scavenge. They beg. They steal. There are those who do not even have a place in the favelas and who live in the city streets, sleeping huddled in doorways or prostrate on sidewalks. Many are children. Here they are offensively visible and become in increasing numbers the victims of those who would have them otherwise.

In September 1989, the Brazilian Institute of Social and Economic Analysis (IBASE) published a report, "Children and Adolescents in Brazil: The Silenced Life," on the killing of the young. Relying on such official sources as forensic medical records and on cases reported by television and the press, the Institute considered 1,397 cases. In 95 of these, the victims had been children aged ten and under; in 156, those aged from eleven to fourteen. In 80 percent of the cases, the victims had been males aged from fifteen to eighteen. There had been no information available on the ages of 113 victims. In the first six months of 1989, more than half of such killings in the state of Pernambuco had been attributed to death squads. In those cases where ethnic origin had been noted, 82 percent of the victims had been recorded as black or "of mixed race."[4]

It is bad enough that there are such practices to report, and all too likely that more killings of this kind occur than are recorded. What is worse is that the report of them is met with such indifference from the society at large. This raises the question of whether the society is so perverse as to approve such killings or whether it is simply accepted that society is out of all moral control.

In Rio, I discussed the issue with Joel Rufino dos Santos, a black Brazilian who is a distinguished historian and who also writes stories for children. His view is that the development of the Brazilian nation is still incomplete and continues to be largely based on a Portuguese preoccupation with hierarchy. Most of the children and adolescents killed as an exercise in street cleaning or—the usual explanation offered—crime prevention have been abandoned by their families. They belong to no one and so have no place in the hierarchy. They are not regarded as people and are not, therefore, children at all.

"You mean," I asked aghast, "that they are regarded in much the same way as stray dogs, to be put down as a social nuisance?"

"Yes," he replied grimly. "I suppose that they are."

Support for such a contention is provided in a report from Amnesty International. In June 1989, a television crew from the Brazilian Amazonian Network (RBA) filmed for inclusion in the evening news the beating of a young black suspect by police in Belém, the state capital of Pará. Subsequently questioned by the press, the governor of Pará responded: "Why is there all this fuss about the beating of a down and out?"[5]

All this makes some grotesque sense out of black invisibility in Brazil. In this nation of "incomplete development," the very poor are a people apart or, rather, not people at all, for they repudiate the image that Brazilians have of themselves. That is why abandoned and destitute white children can also be killed with impunity. Blacks, however, suffer a form of double jeopardy. They are disproportionately numbered among the very poor, and as blacks, their visibility in the streets is a disconcerting reminder of a presence that no bleaching of the television output and no hoardings, however high, around the favelas can remove.

The black Brazilian woman who says that there are no blacks in Brazil is pursuing the national logic. The myth of a Brazilian "racial democracy" tells her that all Brazilians are treated alike, while her experience tells her that blacks are treated differently. She is led accordingly to conclude that a black cannot be Brazilian; and since she believes herself to be a Brazilian, she cannot believe that she is black.

Nor is it altogether extravagant to suppose that this may help to explain the reported targeting of black victims by those in the military and civil police who are themselves black. I offer no more than my personal suspicion that in killing blacks, black killers may be set on killing the blackness in themselves.

It is widely accepted that the narrow victory of Fernando Collor de Mello in the presidential election of 1989, against Luis Inacio "Lula" da Silva of the Workers' Party (PT), was due to the large number of blacks who voted for him. In this Brazilian reverse of United States voting patterns, blacks supported Collor precisely because he was a rich white who represented the rich white ascendancy. They chose to identify themselves with him in much the same way as they identify themselves with the rich whites in the soaps which they watch on television. It was a way of believing that they belonged to the people of Brazil.

Their identification with Collor was made all the easier because Lula, along with the trade unions and political parties which supported him, no more questioned the myth of Brazil's racial democracy than did Collor, who had the coalition of landowning, financial, and industrial interests behind him. The official line of the left has long been that the essential conflict in Brazil is between classes, and that insofar as there is a racial problem to be recognized, it can only be solved by the triumph of labor and the eradication of the poverty on which the racial problem is based.

What the traditional left will not accept is the reality that racism has a life of its own. Middle-class blacks in Brazil on visits to apartment blocks all too often find themselves directed to use the service lifts. In restaurants, they are refused accommodation, despite the display of available tables, because there are blacks already accommodated, and discreet managements accept only enough blacks at a time to defend themselves against any complaint of racial discrimination. Too many blacks, it seems, give an establishment a bad name.

Dr. Milton Santos, a black Brazilian and a geographer whose teachings and books have made him widely known beyond the borders of Brazil, returned from a post abroad to take up a professorship at the University of São Paulo. On his first visit to the faculty restaurant, he was accosted by the manager and asked to provide evidence that he was a faculty member.

"Are you sure," I asked, "that it was because you are black, and that it wasn't standard procedure or a random check?"

He is such a gentle-mannered man that the vehemence of his denial was all the more telling. "Quite sure," he replied. "I made inquiries, of course, and no white member of staff had ever been asked to show his credentials. Besides, it was the tone of voice in which I was addressed. He simply could not believe that there was a black on the staff."

Dr. Kabengele Munanga, a professor of anthropology at the same university, had come from Zaire. Any illusions that he might have had about the absence of racism in Brazil had not survived for long. His son had been repeatedly stopped and interrogated by police for no better reason than that he was black and yet driving a car. In fact, Dr. Munanga maintained, any social advancement by individual blacks, far from blunting discrimination, seemed only to sharpen it, as competition for the better-paid jobs stirred a resentment at successful black applicants which then led to the raising of racial barriers. Where highly educated blacks continued to get jobs, they did so only by accepting lower rates of pay. He knew of black engineers who were earning between ten and thirty percent less than their white counterparts.

It is doubtful that highly educated blacks encounter peculiarly sharp discrimination. It is more probable that they respond more sharply to the experience. Those lower down the social scale are more accustomed to rejection. They are too often confronted by it before they get to the door. Advertisements make no reference to race, since the law forbids it, but the reference is no less real for being obliquely communicated. The phrase *boa aparência*, or "good appearance," is a euphemism ubiquitously understood.

How does a Brazil so persistent in proclaiming racial indifference and yet so pervasively racist in its practices get away with this? For the extent of its success is undeniable, not only in the readiness abroad to accept the pretensions at their face value, but in the existence of so marginal an expression of protest at home. There is no mass movement of organized opposition, let alone any such fire and rioting as that with which racial rage has swept through cities in Britain and the United States.

The explanation I often had offered to me by black intellectuals and activists I met is that the "system" is so sophisticated, its functioning so subtle and manipulative, that the victims are scarcely aware of their victimization. In consequence, no strategy of struggle has yet been developed to deal with it; without such a strategy, struggle itself seems hopeless; and hopelessness only promotes an acquiescence among blacks in the role that is assigned to them.

Yet I doubt that the "system" is any more subtle or manipulative than it is in Britain or the United States. Nor should a strategy of struggle be more difficult to develop in Brazil. The black community there is larger, both absolutely and relatively, than it is in Britain and the United States, where blacks have nonetheless asserted their identity and their rights.

There must be special factors involved to account for the absence of a militancy that the plight of blacks should long since have aroused. One such factor may be found in Brazil's linguistic isolation. For Portuguese connects Brazil only with countries in other continents, and countries, moreover, in which few Brazilians have much interest. Portugal itself is rather patronizingly regarded, Portuguese-speaking Africa hardly regarded at all. Even among intellectuals, surprisingly few know French, historically in Brazil the language of high culture; roughly half of those I met, and my introductions were mainly to those who supposedly knew the language, could not communicate in English; and I met only one who knew Spanish. This was also the case among those in business, including publishers, a number of whom I met at a major book fair. Without the occasional interpreter or such Portuguese as I had acquired in preparation for my visit, I should from time to time have been linguistically isolated myself.

In consequence, Brazil is largely cut off from developments and ideas in, or more accessible to, the rest of the hemisphere. It is this which may help to account both for the preoccupation of so many in the left with a rather narrow view of social conflict, and for the widespread apparent unawareness among blacks in Brazil of influences and movements elsewhere in the Diaspora. The mass of such blacks are confined not only by language but by illiteracy or the lack of adequate, if any, access to schooling.

There is another factor. Linguistic isolation has combined with the vastness and diversity of Brazil to promote among its people a sense of inhabiting not so much a country as a world of their own. This has been reflected and reinforced by political developments. Every regime—colonial, imperial, republican—has sought to centralize power, only to find itself confronted by regional or even more localized challenges. Within the present federal system, the component states possess substantial authority, supported by corresponding sentiments of identification and allegiance. One consequence has been to divide black communities from one another.

In short, the largest single component in the Black Diaspora is itself a collection of components. Moreover, these components have been, and still are, far from static. Internal black migration, from climatically or economically stricken rural areas to the towns, and from the north to the glitter of the cities in the south, has long been considerable. Adrift between their old allegiances and the problem of acquiring new ones in a more complex environment, many blacks lose any sense of identity.

A further factor may help to explain the very contrast between the extent of resistance among blacks to slavery and their apparent acquiescence in their different plight today. Blacks in Brazil did not, like their counterparts elsewhere, emerge from slavery into another form of overt oppression. In the United States, slavery was succeeded by the denial to blacks of virtually all civil rights in the South and by persisting, even spreading, segregationist commitments in the North. In the Caribbean outside of Haiti, freedom from slavery was circumscribed by the colonial condition. In Brazil, however, abolition released the slaves to survive as they might, along with many of the previously freed, in economic distress, but with no such institutional subjugation as provided both provocation and target.

Not least, blacks in Brazil have, since the last slave ship arrived, been denied such black immigration as has elsewhere in the Diaspora spread ideas and solidarity. A commitment to the whitening of Brazil emerged, indeed, even before the end of slavery. The leading abolitionist, Joaquim Nabuco, wrote in 1883, five years before abolition, that he looked for a Brazil "where European immigration, attracted by the generosity of our institutions and the liberality of our regime, may constantly bring to the tropics a flow of lively, energetic, and healthy Caucasian blood, which we may absorb without danger . . ."[6] Three years later, prominent planters in São Paulo founded the Society for the Promotion of Immigration, to recruit white immigrants from Europe, pay their passage, and provide them with plantation work contracts. The Society, whose activities came to be centered on Italy, received a substantial subsidy from the São Paulo Treasury.

Soon after abolition, the Minister of Finance, Rui Barbosa, issued Circular No. 29 of May 13, 1891, which ordered the destruction by fire of all historical documents and files that related to the slave trade and to slavery.[7] If this was an attempt to remove from the Brazilian past the details of a shameful engagement, it was also a symbol of the resolve to remove, at some stage in the future, the black presence from the population.

In an age when white imperial rule around the world sought its moral rationalization in some supposed hierarchy of races, and even enjoyed some specious scientific support for this view, varieties of racial discrimination required no further excuse. For Brazil itself, racial purity was an option long since denied. Instead, Brazilian nationalism laid claim to a unique racial amalgam, which the very absence of racial discrimination had fostered and would continue fostering still. Yet what was claimed was not necessarily practiced. Racial discrimination had always existed in Brazil and came to be more extensively practiced in the international climate of the times.

By 1904, for instance, blacks were being excluded from employment as guards at Rio's renowned Teatro Lírico. By 1906, blacks and even mulattoes were no longer welcome as recruits to the Guarda Cívica, or state militia, of São Paulo. In 1907, blacks were barred from a naval mission to the United States.[8] Significantly, however, such instances of discrimination were assailed by the press in the process of reporting them. The contrast between racial discrimination in the United States and its absence in Brazil was a persistent theme of Brazilian politicians and publicists.

The established doctrine was that the United States would, by its legal and implicit pressures against various forms of racial mingling, inevitably perpetuate its black problem, while in Brazil, the freedom of races to mingle, combined with the influx of white settlers, would eventually lead to the total disappearance of blacks. It was this doctrine which gave rise to the myth of Brazil as a "racial democracy," in distinction from a multiracial one. The meaning of the term is elusive, except for Brazilians devoted to its use, for whom it seems to mean a society of total integration. Whether this in turn means a society of only one race or a society without races at all is not clear.

That the commitment to a whitening of Brazil was itself a form of racial discrimination was always obvious and soon became explicitly so. As early as June 1890, the government issued a decree which provided for the free entry of all healthy and able-bodied immigrants, "except natives of Asia or Africa, who can be admitted only by authorization of the National Congress and in accordance with the stipulated conditions." This was reinforced by a subsequent article which authorized the provision of special incentives to any landowner wishing to "settle European immigrants on his property." The decree was signed not only by the President, but by the Minister of Agriculture, who was himself a mulatto.

In 1907, a new decree on immigration omitted any reference to the continent of origin, since this qualification looked too provocative in print. Public policy, however, remained unchanged and was pursued with zeal by Baron Rio Branco, Foreign Minister from 1902 to 1912, who employed all the powers of his office to promote white immigration and packed the diplomatic service with whites to project the image of a white Brazil.

In fact, the commitment to whitening Brazil through immigration was so widely accepted that it was rarely discussed. Then, in 1921, the state of Mato Grasso provided certain developers with a land concession, and it emerged that these developers were associated with a group in the United States which was recruiting blacks there for immigration to Brazil. The Catholic Bishop who was President of Mato Grosso canceled the concession at once. This did nothing to quiet a rising clamor of alarm.

In the national Chamber of Deputies, a bill was introduced to prohibit from entering Brazil "human beings of the black race." One prominent opponent, Joaquim Osório, argued that this would amount to a "new black code, a policy of race prejudice which fortunately has never existed in our country." The bill wasted away in committee, only for a successor to be introduced in 1923. Again it was unsuccessful, but less because of its racist sentiments than because their expression was at odds with the dominant doctrine that the very absence of racial prejudice would itself promote the disappearance of the black population. As one of the opponents, Carvalho Neto, confidently declared, "in Brazil the Negro will disappear in seventy years, while in the United States he constitutes a permanent danger."[9]

From the early thirties, there developed a new interest in the history and cultural impact of this supposedly disappearing component of the population. In 1933, Gilberto Freyre published his influential *Casa-Grande e Senzala*.[10] If it rather romanticized the paternalist engagement of the plantocracy, it did much to rescue the African slave from the prevailing perception of a primitiveness that had contributed nothing of value to the civilization of Brazil.

Freyre himself was a major figure in the organization of the first Afro-Brazilian Congress at Recife in 1934, which was followed by another in Bahia three years later. The papers delivered at these Congresses and subsequently published dealt with a wide range of Afro-Brazilian cultural expressions and influences, from folklore and linguistics to costume and cuisine. Among others exploring this territory was the eminent writer Mário de Andrade, who studied folk festivals and that seminal black contribution to the distinctive music of Brazil, the samba.

Yet the more information that was gathered and communicated about the black contribution to Brazilian culture, the more dedicated the social leadership became to the vision of a white Brazil. It was as though the recognition of the cultural richness blacks had brought to the national identity excused the pursuit of their disappearance; as though the record of their contribution, safely stored away on the shelves of history and social anthropology, made their survival less desirable or necessary. There is a certain symbolism in the coincidence that Nône de Andrade, who painted the picture of blacks without faces, was Mário de Andrade's son.

In 1930, Getulio Vargas failed to win the presidential election and registered his protest with a march on Rio de Janeiro which put him in power for a quarter of a century. His increasingly authoritarian rule, culminating in a totalitarian constitution for his so called *Estado Novo* (New State), effectively came to involve government by decree. Shortly before popular revolt brought an end to the regime in 1945, Decree No. 7967 was issued. It laid down that immigrants were henceforth to be admitted only in conformity with "the necessity to preserve and develop, in the ethnic composition of the population, the more desirable characteristics of its European ancestry." The subsequent Constitution of 1946 for the restored democracy declared simply in Article 162 that immigration was to be regulated by law. Since the racist decree of Vargas remained the law until revoked, it continued in force, throughout the period of democracy and then the period of military rule which began in 1964 and lasted well into the eighties.

If there was, in all this time, no militant mass black challenge to the essentially racist policies of a whitening Brazil, this does not mean that blacks failed to make any challenge at all. The rapid growth of Candomblé, the Afro-Brazilian religion with similarities to Haitian Voodoo, was one response.

Muniz Sodré, a Brazilian sociologist who writes and talks vividly about the distinction between territory and space, attributes such growth, in the era that followed the abolition of slavery, to a conquest of space without territory.[11] The *quilombo*, or independent community of runaway slaves on their own area of land, however small, had been a way of restoring a physical piece of the Africa that had been lost. With the end of slavery, this ceased to be a credible option, even as the commitment of the state to bleaching the population was becoming clear. A few blacks of cultural leadership and material means, such as Aninha, a learned woman who wrote a book on Afro-Brazilian cuisine in Bahia, established a neo-African space in the Candomblé *terreiros* or temples.

For all the Brazilian pretensions to religious tolerance and racial indifference, these quilombos of the spirit were subjected to various pressures that intermittently amounted to open persecution. Virtually from the first, the terreiros were required to register with the police and report the date and time of their ceremonies in advance. During the thirties, they were frequently raided and their religious objects seized. The Police Museum in Rio came to possess a notable collection of Candomblé art and artifacts.

The Catholic Church itself, more pragmatic in Brazil than in most of Latin America, decided to concede a measure of syncretism and in due course even permitted Candomblé priests to attend Mass. There were bounds to this tolerance, however. In 1977 a special Mass was proposed by adherents of Candomblé to commemorate, at the traditionally black Church of the Rosary in São Paulo, the inauguration of the largest terreiro in Brazil. This symbolic celebration of syncretism was forbidden by the supreme Catholic authority in the São Paulo metropolitan area. The organizers then planned a street procession instead, and the police intervened to ban black priests and priestesses from singing religious songs in it. [12]

Another form of black resistance was artistic expression, and this, too, encountered a hostile reaction. When in 1955, for instance, the Black Experimental Theatre sponsored a competition in the visual arts on the theme of the Black Christ, this raised a secular as well as religious outcry. An editorial in Rio's *Jornal do Brasil* demanded that the "exhibition should be prohibited as highly subversive" and continued, "We register here our shout of alarm. The ecclesiastical authorities must, as soon as possible, take measures to prevent the realization of this attack on Religion and the Arts." [13]

Even the musical expression of black creativity came under early fire. In 1901, an editorial in the *Jornal de Notícias* called for police intervention to stop the black musical and dance celebrations, the *batuques*, which were spreading the traditional samba through the streets, "for all this is incompatible with the state of our civilization." [14]

By the early thirties, however, the samba had become so integral to Carnival, with the competition of the samba schools such an institutionalized feature of the festivities, that the black cultural element in the parades was generally accepted as indispensable. For what was the alternative? As the lyrics of a renowned Rio samba declared: "If the people of the hill were to strike and not descend, the city would be sad; Carnival would die; the whole city would be a cry for help . . . If the samba schools are denied freedom, Carnival should stay on the hill; no one should go to the city." [15]

Any black challenge through overt political organization and activity was treated otherwise. In 1931, the Brazilian Negro Front was founded, only to fall an early victim of the repression pursued during the period of the authoritarian New State. In 1969, during the period of military rule, General Jaime Portelo identified, as a prime target for the General Commission of Military-Police Investigation, the "campaign conducted through the press and television in connection with foreign organs of the press and of international studies on racial discrimination, with the vision of creating new areas of friction and dissatisfaction with the regime and the constituted authorities." [16]

A repressive reaction to any significant raising of the racial issue has outlasted the end of the military regime. Movements committed to advancing black consciousness or militancy are seen as subversive, and such demonstrations or marches of protest or celebration as take place seldom escape containment or dispersal by police. Yet ultimately more formidable than physical repression, for the small groups of militants that continually arise, has been the psychical one which has deprived them of a mass political responsiveness. The very spaces occupied by the black identity for its preservation have been besieged, infiltrated, and bribed into becoming peripheral or dependent.

Candomblé itself has come to be partly incorporated. Prominent priests and priestesses are accorded every respect that can yield a suitable return in service to a social ascendancy more concerned with corruption than with culture. There is much exchange of favors for votes in the communication between the spiritual black and political white worlds. Whatever the spiritual black world may have gained from the exchange, it has not advanced the cause of black identity in Brazil. This is not to suggest that Candomblé has altogether ceased to be a space for the survival and transmission of black culture, but the space has been shrinking.

More spectacular has been the shrinkage of the space provided by Carnival and the samba schools, from the expanding pressure of white entrepreneurial involvement. Increasingly and most markedly in Rio, the traditional capital of Carnival, spontaneity has given place to calculation, creativity to commercialism, the celebration of sexuality to titillation. Symbolically, Carnival itself has shifted in Rio from the freedom of the streets to enclosures where the rich may watch from high-priced seats and the cameras televise the parade in controlled conditions.

This has involved a cumulative process of intervention which dates back at least to 1935, when regulations formalized the competitive aspect of the parade. Participation was limited to those in the Union of Samba Schools; the powers of the *Comissão Julgadora*, or Committee of Adjudicators, were defined; and certain restrictions were placed on musical performance, such as the banning of wind instruments.

By the sixties, a new element was establishing itself, which might have proved creative in different conditions, but which proved otherwise in Brazil's. This was the *carnavalesco* or designer who chose the theme of the particular entry, the props, the material and colors of the costumes, and who would come even to intervene in the lyrics of the sambas.[17] Not surprisingly, the most influential of such designers were those with experience and skill in the fine arts and in cinema. They tended to be whites more representative of dominant consumerist social values than of Afro-Brazilian culture. The result was a preoccupation with spectacle, at a commensurate cost, and this led in turn to mounting dependence on sponsorship money that favored the gigantic, the ostentatious, and the exotic.

In the middle of 1990, the reputed idol of Brazil was appropriately a particular package of singer, movie star, and children's show hostess on television known as Xuxa. Her four recordings had sold twelve million copies; four million people had so far been to see the latest of her eight movies; and tens of millions, adults as well as children, watched her morning television show. Sandals and shampoo, yoghurt and bicycles, schoolbooks and lunch boxes were among the forty products she endorsed.

Not only was she herself flaxen-haired and blue-eyed, but she performed with a group of seven others, similar to her in appearance, called the Paquitas. Asked about this chromatic monotony, she was reported as replying that it was a response to the children's own choice. "Children like Snow White, Cinderella, Barbie. When they see me close to them, it's as if the mythical person has become reality."

"Our culture," commented Herbert de Souza, a sociologist in Rio, "is profoundly racist."[18]

In 1988, a congress was held at the University of São Paulo to mark the centenary of the abolition of slavery in Brazil. At the formal opening, there was not a single black to be seen on the platform. The particular occasion would seem to have required one, if only as a symbol. Instead, the absence of any provided a different symbol: for the translation of blacks, in the dominant consciousness of Brazil, from indispensability in the past to invisibility today.

"Racial democracy" is not the only Brazilian illusion that reality refutes. The traditional expansionist optimism, infused by the belief that resources are limitless and that the solution to any problem will be found one further step across the frontier into the future, has become less tenable with the intimations of environmental mortality, the economic mayhem of so much debt and inflation, and the gulf between rich and poor that grows ever wider.

During my travels in Brazil, I saw, painted or scrawled on a number of walls, the slogan *Saudade do Futuro*. The Portuguese word *saudade* means both "longing" or "desire" and "homesickness" or "nostalgia." What the slogan reveals is the yearning for a return to faith in the promise of the future. It is a comment on the disillusionment which the present promotes.

It is not the rich who paint or scrawl on walls. If they no longer have faith in the future of Brazil, they send their money abroad, to a more reliable home. The poor have no resources but faith, and can get no return for investing this abroad. If the blacks of Brazil may at last be losing faith in any promise of a future that demands their disappearance, they may find a different faith, in a future that belongs to the recognition and assertion of their own identity.

~~~~~~

In 1964, while traveling in the United States for a book I was writing, I spent some time in Mississippi and visited McComb, a small city in Pike County near the Louisiana state line. Civil rights militancy, reinforced by Supreme Court decisions, was confronting an institutional white supremacy in arguably the most recalcitrant state in the Deep South. Whites in McComb had taken to burning black churches and bombing the local voter registration school. When the local newspaper, representing the views of a less frantic white social leadership, expressed opposition to such violence, shots were fired at its offices, and a cross was burned on the lawn outside the home of the editor.

Returning to McComb in 1991 and walking from the bus station, I watched a patrol car cruise by with two policemen, one white and one black, sitting together inside. In the fast food restaurant where I had lunch, attendants both white and black served customers both white and black with indiscriminate Southern civility. In the offices of the Southwest Legal Services, white and black waited patiently to discuss their particular problems with whichever white or black member of staff was next available. It all seemed so smooth and quiet compared to the turbulence I remembered that I might have been sleepwalking through the American dream. Before I left McComb, I would buy a pair of slippers as a souvenir.

I went to the home of a black man who had been a civil rights militant and a target of violence twenty-seven years before. It was wresting the vote for blacks, he remarked, that had led to such changes. The state schools in McComb were now largely integrated. There was a black superintendent in control of the system. "Of course," he added, "those whites with enough money send their children to private schools. Racism functions at the level of economic differentials."

In the city of Jackson, the state capital, much also had changed since

1964. At the busy bus station, blacks and whites mingled with an ease that I suspect was remarked only by me. At a demonstration in a shopping center, representatives of various black groups protested against the dismissal of a black police chief. There was not a policeman in sight. The State Historical Museum had on exhibition a record of the civil rights struggle by "Afro-Americans" in Mississippi.

What had it all been for, that era of investment in racism, whose violence had taken so many black lives and blighted so many more? It had corrupted and degraded its supposed beneficiaries, kept the region backward and poor. It seemed crazy to me at the time, as it seems crazy to me today that racism should be continuing to spread its moral and material blight elsewhere in the United States, and is even changing the changed South as well.

The more temperate racial climate in the South has promoted a reversal in the long historical migration of blacks to the Northern cities. Yet those escaping from the North arrive to find that the North has arrived before them. I met one who was working at two jobs in Jackson and living in the small town of Carthage some fifty miles away. He had left Mississippi as a child, when his family had migrated to Detroit. "I came back in 1982. Almost all those who had graduated with me from school in 1977 were either dead or in jail. I had been mugged so many times that I had stopped counting. They took your shoes from you, and your hat. To this day, I don't wear a hat. Now the gangs are here, and so is the crack. I went to Carthage for some peace of mind. I have a family. But there are no jobs in Carthage."

What is happening in metropolitan America reaches beyond even the forebodings which I recorded from my travels in the North two years or so after my travels in the South. I had written then: "The American city itself, as traditionally known, seems to be dying under the assaults of racial tension and a constant battery of fears. Negro ghettos are advancing steadily towards the centre, while whites flee in panic to the suburbs; New York City, Chicago, Detroit, Philadelphia are increasingly assuming the design of archery targets, with a business bull's-eye overwhelmingly white, an inner congested ring of black slums, and an outer one of spacious white suburbs escaping ever further into the countryside. (Whether, indeed, the business centre will itself survive, with the flight of commerce also to the suburbs in pursuit of the white purse, and the advance of Negro control over city government, is already a reasonable speculation. It is hideous but no longer fantastic to suppose a society of white swollen suburbs lavish with services, and cities sinking into abandoned black decay.)"[1]

The statistics now are dismaying. An analysis published by USA Today[2] and based on the 1990 census returns provided a segregation index for 219 major metropolitan areas. This measured the percentage of a resident ethnic minority—black, Hispanic, or Asian—which would need to move out of effectively segregated neighborhoods for full integration to be achieved. An index figure of 60 was adjudged the entry point for a highly segregated area. On the specifically black segregation index, the top ten were led by Gary–Hammond, Indiana, with a figure of 91, followed by Detroit, with 89; Chicago, with 87; New York, with 83; Philadelphia, with 81; Nassau–Suffolk on Long Island, with 80; Los Angeles, with 74; Boston, with 72; Atlanta and Houston, with 71 each; and Washington, D.C., with 67.

The article found that Hispanics and Asians were surmounting those barriers raised in practice despite the law of 1968 which banned racial discrimination in housing, and "were moving into white neighborhoods where blacks have never found a welcome, no matter what their wealth." In fact, it concluded, "the majority of the nation's 30 million black people are as segregated now as they were at the height of the civil rights movement in the '60s." The reality, however, is worse than any such historical parallel implies.

Nowhere is this more appallingly revealed than in Detroit. In the fifties, the city was fast becoming the epitome of the country's economic might, as the capital of an automobile industry in a consumer culture dominated by the automobile. Some two million people lived there, of whom roughly 75 percent were whites and the rest blacks. Race relations were far from harmonious. In 1943, racial rioting had taken thirty-four lives. Yet such rioting also struck other Northern cities from time to time, if rarely on this scale.

By 1962, when the magazine *Look* described it as "a city on the go,"[3] Detroit was pursuing new policies in search of social concord. Under the command of technocrats, and encouraged by a like-minded state administration in Michigan, corporate management in the automobile industry was moving toward some measure of collaboration with the trade unions, after decades of intermittent industrial strife. The mayor of Detroit, himself close to the leadership of the United Automobile Workers, was bringing blacks into the city government and had appointed a progressive chief of police. When Martin Luther King came there in 1963, Detroit gave him an official welcome in accordance with its claim to be taking the initiative in promoting a liberal urban commitment.

Yet, all the time, a movement of whites from the city to the spaciousness, seclusion, and security of the suburbs was gathering pace. Predictably, commerce pursued the migrating money wherever it settled, and new, high-tech industry sited itself near the congenial neighborhoods and suitable schools sought by its white employees and their families. It was a self-promoting process which simultaneously reduced the population of the city and increased the black component. Detroit's tax base contracted, its facilities deteriorated, its schools decayed, and growth was confined to unemployment, poverty, and crime. It was a vicious circle which, however otherwise depicted, essentially reflected and reinforced the functioning of racism.

Other cities were similarly afflicted. The very success of the civil rights movement in confronting institutional white supremacy across the South fired a fury of frustration in the effectively segregated and economically deprived urban black communities elsewhere in the country. In 1967, rioting erupted in dozens of cities, and the worst of it raged in Detroit. Whole blocks of shops and homes were swallowed by flames. Forty-three people were killed, most of them blacks shot by police or by soldiers of the National Guard. What had been a white migration to the suburbs became a stampede. Soon it was not only whites who were leaving. In the early seventies, Berry Gordy, Jr., the black songwriter turned entrepreneur whose Motown Record Corporation had made the city celebrated as a center of popular music, took his business operations, along with many of the leading musicians involved, to the West Coast. For black Detroit, it was equivalent to the diagnosis of an incurable wasting disease.

Today the metropolitan area of Detroit encompasses seven counties and some 4,400,000 people, of whom roughly 75 percent are whites and 21.5 percent are blacks, with Hispanics and Asians accounting for all but a few of the rest. These conglomerate statistics conceal, however, a sharply different demographic pattern on either side of the frontier that is the Eight Mile Road. In the self-governing suburban communities, some of them among the richest in the country, live more than three million people, of whom barely 5 percent are blacks. In the city, little more than one million people, or virtually half the number once living there, are left, among whom blacks compose almost 80 percent.

It is a city without a single large store. Hudson's, its once nationally renowned, block-sized department store, made an early, influential departure to the suburbs. There is now no downtown shopping area at all. Some skyscrapers accommodate public-sector bureaucracy and such private-sector services as banking which feed on it. Others stand empty and like monolithic gravestones to the death of a city. High above the eerily silent streets, cylindrical walkways connect one skyscraper with another; constructed for convenience, protection from the weather, and security, they look like enormous, motionless worms. There is no bustling along the pavements to and from subway stations. There is no subway system. The proposal for one was blocked by the very suburbs it would have served, because they saw it as a conveyor belt for black intrusion and crime. I never saw a bus in the streets.

Luxury waterside apartment blocks were built as part of a belated effort at urban renewal. They might, however, compose some vertical suburb, for all the organic relation they have with the city. Hamtramck is a small incorporated municipality surrounded by Detroit. With fewer than 25,000 people, the majority of Polish extraction, it has the restaurants, bars, delicatessens, even a local weekly, that suggest what much of Detroit must once have been. Now it merely emphasizes the surrounding desolation.

Some of this desolation is the result of an exercise in socially blind industrial renewal. Part of Hamtramck and part of Detroit were demolished to make way for a highly automated General Motors plant. Called Poletown after the name of the neighborhood that disappeared under the bulldozers, this created its required flat space out of some fifteen hundred homes, six hundred businesses, and two hospitals. The promised benefit was six thousand jobs, though fewer than half that number were delivered.

Elsewhere in the city, whole neighborhoods look as though they have been blitzed. Homes stand among plots of weeds or the blackened skeletons of buildings. Setting fire to piles of garbage had once been a way of celebrating Halloween. Then, in 1983, abandoned houses, shops, and factories went up in flames, along with homes caught by the spreading blaze, in three days and nights of a Halloween that had turned into a kind of celebratory rage. In the years that followed, Devil's Night became a renowned spectator event, as thousands of people, some of them arriving in contingents of cars from the suburbs, collected to watch still more of the city burn.

By the time of my visit in 1991, Halloween had passed with no more fires than were usual for any night of the year. I was told that this had been due to intensive policing, reinforced by community groups and individual residents standing guard over what remained of their neighborhoods. It may also have been that the rage had for a while slaked itself on its own flames.

This is still a city of more than a million people, if only just. Neighborhoods, or at least areas of settlement, survive in it. Here and there, shops survive, selling groceries, liquor, cheap clothing. Many of them are owned by Iraqi Christians, known as Chaldeans, who protect their property and persons with small arsenals. They are the target of crime and also of resentment for those who strike at them in striking at their own plight. Today an estimated half of all young blacks in Detroit have never had a job, however brief. Few whites, even among those of liberal disposition, seem able to comprehend the nature and extent of the black predicament.

While I was staying in Detroit, the hard-line state administration was withdrawing general welfare assistance from many thousands of single adults without dependents, and these were being evicted from public housing onto the streets because they could no longer pay the rent. Essentially directed at cutting the state budgetary deficit, this policy was proclaimed to be an exercise in "tough love," to cure a supposed addictive reliance on welfare by effectively forcing recipients onto the job market. It was already becoming a national issue, and I caught a televised discussion of it in a talk show from Washington.

Defenders of the policy cited the numerous advertisements in the Detroit metropolitan press for jobs in supermarkets and fast food outlets. Opponents attacked not only the policy's total lack of compassion, but also its failure to comprehend that many of those from whom welfare was being withdrawn might be unfit, through drug abuse or mental illness, to compete in the job market. Even the opponents, however, ignored certain relevant connections. Many of those being deprived of welfare were blacks living in Detroit. The jobs being advertised were in the suburbs. Given the prevailing attitude in the suburbs toward blacks, especially those without an employment record and corresponding references, it was unlikely that such jobs were available to them. Moreover, even if they were, the costs of commuting in the absence of a mass transit system would have been an obstacle.

For black America, education has traditionally been the main gateway to economic opportunity and social advancement. In Detroit this gateway is all but closed. Social disadvantage would argue for relatively more expenditure on schooling there. Instead, roughly twice as much is spent per pupil in the suburbs than in the city. Nor does the city provide the sort of environment that attracts the best teachers or encourages the most attentive classes. The results are appalling. Some 70 percent of teenagers in Detroit never make it to the end of high school. Of the twenty thousand who enter the first grade in the city's school system every year, only some five hundred (no more than one hundred of them males) leave school with the qualifications for proceeding to further education.[4]

Joblessness and truncated schooling interact to promote a culture of poverty and despair associated with other problems, too. Drug addiction, mainly to cocaine in the form of crack, is epidemic in black urban communities. In Detroit I met one of the very few black young men who had made it through the city's school system to university and who was currently writing his doctoral thesis. His own account of growing up in the poverty and violence of the ghetto—at the age of ten, he had been woken one night with a gun held to his head by a policeman—led me to wonder how he had survived at all. Errol Henderson seemed to me an obviously street-smart source of information. "What proportion of young blacks in Detroit," I asked him, "would you say is irredeemably on crack?" He thought for a few moments and then replied, "Between the ages of, say, eighteen and thirty, I would guess around 30 percent." I have no way of knowing how exaggerated, if at all, this estimate was. Since drug-taking is a serious crime, its extent is bound to be hidden. It is enough, perhaps, that the scale of the problem is generally conceded to be huge.

The traffic in drugs battens easily on the poor, so many of whom turn to drugs as a form of escape from the negation of their lives, only to develop a need that they then feed from the proceeds of crime and prostitution. The poor are also peculiarly drawn into becoming dealers or "mules" for a traffic whose financial rewards are beyond anything available elsewhere. "If I were poor and without any prospect of a job," a distinguished black woman historian remarked to me in Atlanta, "and I were offered $350 to take a package from one place to another, I do not know that I would refuse."

The traffic is connected to young black gangs, whose organization can so readily provide surveillance, protection, and delivery. Yet not all young black gangs are connected to the traffic. Such gangs are a form of bonding that has long been part of American history among the socially deprived, and that has often been associated with crime and violence. They were a feature of such white immigrant urban communities as the Irish and Italian, as they still are today of Hispanic communities. What distinguishes the young black gangs is the extent of their numbers in their neighborhoods and the scale of the violence involved.

In a community where the sense of being demeaned and repudiated by society is so widespread, the gang becomes a collective means to demand and achieve respect. This contemporary need for respect is given a paradoxical and dangerous twist by a long tradition in black America of verbal battering, whose principal form came to be called the dozens. This is in part an exercise in verbal dexterity, which has its most creative current expression in "rap." It is in part also, however, a ritual of challenge to test emotional control— the word itself perhaps derives from the test of a dozen insults, though "dozen" is also a way of saying "a lot"—so that the participant who first gives way to rage loses the contest.[5] It may well have been that such cultivation of self-control was, under slavery or the subsequent aggressions of white supremacy, required survival training. In the setting of the ghetto, it is more likely to produce injury or death.

There are so many occasions for violence, where humiliation looks everywhere for a slight, and an expensive pair of sneakers on someone else's feet becomes a boast that is a reproach. Conflict between one gang and another need not arise from a dispute over control of territory. A mere difference of opinion between two young blacks from separate gangs may bring the associates of each into confrontation. Yet violence is far from limited to the activities of gangs. It is often an explosion of rage in an individual life, detonated by a word or gesture or look. John Singleton's film, *Boyz N the Hood*, is set in a black Los Angeles neighborhood where violence makes anyone a victim, even at the very point of escaping into the promise of a different life.

Killing is the leading cause of death among young black men and women. Suicide comes third. A young black man has one chance in twenty-one of dying violently, more often than not at the hands of another black man. Some 12 percent of Americans are black, yet blacks make up more than 40 percent of all murder victims. An investigation undertaken by the Center for Social Policy found that between 1986 and 1991, violent deaths of black teenagers rose by 78 percent, or at a rate almost eight times that of the increase among their white counterparts.[6]

There is another source of premature death. Blacks represent 29 percent of all AIDS cases reported in the United States, or almost two and a half times the rate for which their share of population would account. The injecting of drugs with shared needles, poor access to health care and its advice, sheer ignorance of how the disease is spread provide the likely explanations. Yet it is at least possible that the ever-present peril in which blacks find themselves and the spreading despair make the prudence of "safe sex" seem relatively irrelevant. I was discussing with Errol Henderson in Detroit the waste of so much creative potential among the young in the ghettos. "Young blacks," he replied, "feel that they don't have the time. They have to act immediately. If they only had the time, you would see what they are capable of creating."

All this is not new to black America. In a recent book, Nicholas Lemann cited a striking parallel with the South's "black sharecropper society on the eve of the introduction of the mechanical cotton picker" in the mid-forties. "It was the national center of illegitimate childbearing and of the female-headed family. It had the worst public education system in the country, the one whose students were most likely to leave school before finishing and most likely to be illiterate even if they did finish. It had an extremely high rate of violent crime: in 1933, the six states with the highest murder rates were all in the South, and most of the murders were black-on-black. Sexually transmitted disease and substance abuse were nationally known as special problems of the black rural South."[7]

Then, however, there had been places for blacks, full of hope, to go, such as Detroit. Many would have arrived at that grand railroad terminal building which still stands there. Only now this is a shell, from which the weed-lined multiple tracks mockingly emerge. The ticket office and the waiting room are in a shed next to the solitary platform. And those who leave from there to go South do so less in hope than in despair. Nor is this only a territorial end to promise. The last constitutional frontier seems to have been reached in the settlements of the law.

These settlements have afforded some blacks enlarged opportunities of upward mobility. They have widened the way to office, elected or appointed, in the many mansions of government and the annexes of the public sector, including the administration of welfare. Measures to promote equal opportunity have reduced the bias of business to exclude blacks from management. Affirmative-action programs have increased black admissions to the universities and employment in the professions. The old openings in sports, entertainment, and the arts have expanded and been augmented by new ones in advertising and mass communications, with the recognition by business of the market to be exploited in the black community.

The growth of the black middle class has, however, only sharpened the plight of the other black America. The flight of so many to a more congenial environment has put a physical distance between them and the life of the ghetto, whose degradation is advanced by their departure. For those left behind, the escape route is so difficult that it permits dreaming only at the cost of a more painful awakening. For the middle class itself, the distance from the ghetto is as much psychical as it is physical. America looks different according to the height above the street from which it is seen.

In an article entitled "Race, Gender and Liberal Fallacies," Orlando Patterson, a black professor of sociology at Harvard, wrote:

> The sociological truths are that America, while still flawed in its race relations and its stubborn refusal to institute a rational, universal welfare system, is now the least racist white-majority society in the world; has a better record of legal protection of minorities than any other society, white or black; offers more opportunities to a greater number of black persons than any other society, including all those of Africa; and has gone through a dramatic change in its attitude toward miscegenation over the past 25 years.[8]

The mass of ghetto blacks do not need to dispute the relevance of a comparison between the number of opportunities available to the number of blacks in the world's richest society and equivalents in the stricken economies of Africa, or draw a distinction between what the law lays down and how the society functions, or question whether America is really less racist than, say, Canada or Spain. They simply would not recognize the America of their experience in the America that Professor Patterson describes.

Nor is it only their own experience that provides evidence for the view that racism in America, for all its formal retreats, has in fact formidably advanced. The significance of the Republican Party's "Willie Horton" television commercial in the 1988 Presidential election campaign was not that George Bush, a candidate of frail rather than reprehensible convictions, was himself a racist. It was that the commercial made race an issue, by focusing on a black rapist to support the claim that the Democratic candidate was soft on crime. The commercial was meant to do so; and in doing so, was then widely held to have served its electoral purpose.

The advance in this kind of racism is camouflaged not so much to conceal racist appeals as to make them more acceptable and even, under pressure, deniable. Ronald Reagan in the Presidential election campaign of 1980 used such camouflage to considerable effect in his references to "welfare queens," with the implication that it was black women, disproportionately dependent on these payments, who were living high on the substance of the state. President Bush, in condemning "quota bills," played to a gallery of white resentment at supposed preferential employment opportunities for blacks.

It was no coincidence that David Duke, with a record of leadership in the Ku Klux Klan, should have run in 1991 as the Republican candidate for governor of Louisiana on the issues of "welfare" and "quotas." By then, no more explicit references to race were necessary. He was defeated, but he did receive some 55 percent of the white vote.

In an editorial entitled "The Many David Dukes," *The New York Times* commented:

> There are many David Dukes across the nation. There always have been. The difference now is that their bigotry is encouraged, even fanned, by the tone of mainstream political discourse. And the alarming success of political appeals to racism suggests a deeper malady.
>
> All too many voters, alas, share Mr. Duke's prejudices. As economic times got worse, white Americans became ever more susceptible to the lie that black welfare cheats and affirmative action were the source of their discomfort.
>
> It makes little difference that racist political messages are delivered in political "code" rather than ethnic slurs. The code has actually given racism a new respectability.[9]

A worsening economic time has not been the only source of mounting white disquiet. The American melting-pot was acceptable enough while the pot itself was assumed to be permanently white. This is no longer seen to be a safe assumption. The rapid growth in communities of color now projects the real possibility of an America in which the whites themselves have become a minority, in a people of minorities. History may suggest that this is a consummation devoutly to be wished. History, however, also suggests that those who feel themselves trapped or victimized by social developments beyond their control may all too easily seize on a racial scapegoat or be led to find one.

It may seem strange that blacks, who have for so long been trapped or victimized themselves, should be chosen in America for this role. Yet this is not as strange as is the anti-Semitism still surviving in Eastern Europe, for instance, though so few Jews are left there. The reason is that Jews have historically been the racial scapegoat for those who need one, and tradition dies hard. Indeed, precisely because blacks in America have been traditional victims, they are the prime target of racial scapegoating, and one all the more necessary in representing a social problem for which whites bear so much of the responsibility. Their very plight becomes their fault. They are peculiarly identified with the drain of social welfare payments on the state and its tax revenues, along with other provisions of a now popularly repudiated liberal commitment.

Liberalism has successfully been given a bad name by its opponents, whose own record in power would seem to make them better qualified for such disrepute. Yet, for all its concessions and condescensions, liberalism represents the politics of that confident generosity in the lifeblood of the American creed. The repudiation of liberalism has at least in part reflected a loss of that confident generosity and its replacement by the uncertainty, defensiveness, and fear on which racism battens.

One casualty has been the celebrated alliance between blacks and Jews.[10] In fact, the alliance was never as substantial or direct as it is presently supposed to have been. Certainly, among whites involved in the long development of the civil rights movement, Jews seem to have been disproportionately represented. They were perhaps most prominently so among the militant white students who went South in the sixties. Given the historical Jewish experience of racial persecution, such individual identifications were scarcely surprising. The mass of American Jews, however, identified themselves less with blacks than with a liberal commitment on which the traditional strategy of black struggle also relied.

Other factors have been adduced to explain the subsequent apparent rupture between blacks and Jews—among them, differing attitudes to Israel and the Palestinian cause. These remain, if relevant at all, subsidiary to the main one. What essentially happened was not that Jews abandoned blacks, but that so many Jews abandoned the liberal commitment. This may not make their estrangement from the cause of black America any more admirable, but does help to explain it. Whatever the case, this estrangement, in being perceived as the rupture of an old alliance, also highlights the predicament of the traditional black strategy for change.

Indeed, this strategy is caught in a pincer movement, of which the decline in the liberal commitment constitutes only one force. The other is the decline in the underlying cohesion of black America itself. Old ties are snapped or fraying; among them, even the one which may historically have been the strongest of all, that of blacks to their Churches. In Detroit I met a black woman who had come North as a young girl from a Mississippi sharecropper family. She had lost a teenage son to the violence of the ghetto, and was now prominently involved in a movement against such violence. SOSAD, an acronym for Save Our Sons And Daughters, is essentially a counseling service that provides emotional reassurance and moral direction to the young of the city. Years ago she would have been the local stalwart of some black Church. Today she dismisses these Churches as a "moral void."

Above all, while many in the black middle class still share the dream of Martin Luther King in an American deliverance, there is little of such dreaming in the ghetto. America itself, like some railroad company whose resources have been squandered or embezzled by its management, no longer offers transport to a land of any promise. There have been too many false prospectuses, too many timetables with misleading information, too many visits to the station where trains never appear or pass through without stopping.

What does survive of the old ties is the one of a different dream, of an African deliverance by a return there. Few ever actually returned, and few seem any more dedicated to doing so today. It remains what it has been, a psychical rather than a physical return, to a source of strength in the affinity with the black multitudes of Africa and a source of cultural pride in the achievements of the African past. Afrocentrism, as it has come to be called, is the current form of an established engagement, to revise the evaluations of a history long written and taught by whites to reflect their own dominance. What is new is the scale of the engagement, mainly in the ghettos but also among those in the black middle class who are uneasy in their very distance from so many of their fellow blacks.

The Afrocentrism that ascribes an African genesis to virtually anything of value in white Western culture is merely the black mirror image of a white Western culture that ascribes virtually everything of value to itself. And if any evidence were needed of the effect produced on blacks by the white distortion, this may be found in the beneficial effect that the black revision of history has so often had. Black children who have attended Afrocentric schools or classes proceed to perform disproportionately well in the state system, and there is no reason to dispute the sincerity of young people in the ghetto who claim that Afrocentrism saved them from crack and from crime.

Cornel West, a leading black intellectual who is a professor of religion in the Afro-American Studies Program at Harvard University, gave a talk which I went to hear at Spelman College in Atlanta.[11] "If black folk cannot love themselves," he said at one point, "there will be no black freedom." It was clear from the context that Professor West saw black freedom as the essential objective of black struggle. There was nothing startling in this, since it has been the peculiar power of that struggle to have sung and spoken always in such a voice. It was the prerequisite he cited, that blacks must love themselves, which startled me, in putting so simply what I had come so elaborately in my travels to believe.

The question this raises in turn is not whether Afrocentrism, by teaching blacks a new valuation of themselves, helps them to do well at school or escape the traps of crack and crime, though these are scarcely accomplishments to be belittled. It is whether Afrocentrism teaches blacks to love an idealized past instead of themselves. For that would not be a way to freedom but a way into a new captivity.

Idealizing the past, like certain drugs, alters the perception of reality rather than reality itself. It all too easily ends in an addictive escape from reality, or an attempt to make reality correspond with perception. On a collective level, this can have calamitous consequences. One prominent Afrocentrist, Leonard Jeffries, contends that the skin pigment melanin determines collective personality and distinguishes the generous black Sun People from the rapacious white Northern Ice People. It is a contention whose closest relatives in this century have nothing to recommend them; though the danger here, given the realities of power in America, would come not from a futile fanaticism but from the white racism it would feed.

For black folk to love themselves, they must value their past for what it is. Their African heritage needs no artificial light, to detract from its natural luster. Nor does the past stop there. Indeed, perhaps the principal cost of idealizing the African past is that it diminishes, when it does not altogether deny, the value of the black American past—still more, the past of the whole Black Diaspora. That past is less remote, and it has an epic quality all its own.

It is this epic quality, of the commitment to endure and resist, surmount and create, and above all else to be free, that has informed the culture of the Black Diaspora. And it is the failure of so many blacks to value this culture in its integrity that in large measure keeps the Black Diaspora, and black America in particular, psychically so divided and subverted.

Many years ago I wrote a book on America which had as its central theme the personal lovelessness which the American materialist culture promotes.[12] In all the time since, I have found no reason to revise my view and every reason for disquiet in the speed with which that culture has spread. Its desolation is no different because the systems which have challenged it have been so disreputable in their own assaults on freedom.

Americans talk often about love, if more often in movie or television dialogue than in life, but the real love that their culture promotes is that between the consumer and the commodity. Where personality itself is packaged, love is another name for a marketing exercise. In the hollow solitudes made of so many lives by this culture, all the talk becomes no more than an echo communicating with itself.

It is from this, the new slavery, that black America may be driven, by its very disillusionment with the American promise, to a new struggle for freedom. For, in this sense, Cornel West's remark is no less true the other way round. If black folk cannot free themselves, there will be no black love. Either way, freedom and love are inseparable, and it is necessary to look for them together, if they are to be found. In recognizing and asserting this, black America may yet prompt America itself to question its own different, desolating quest.

31 | A SEAT ON THE CANADIAN TRAIN

"How full the train was. It was not until the third or fourth carriage that she found an empty seat. She was surprised, really shocked at all the white faces on the train. Ridiculous of course. It was amazing, given all this time, how alarmed she still was at the sight of white faces. In the city, she hardly looked. She moved quickly along noticing only what was there, only what concerned her. Oh God, she thought, she had not noticed a single black face to sit with. She anticipated all the other seats, except the one beside her, filling up; the furtive eyes at her, their longing for her removal, then someone without a choice sitting next to her, 'Christ!' "[1]

This passage from a short story by Dionne Brand, a black Canadian writer, reveals the stain beneath the gloss with which Canada has long painted its race relations. It is true that the country was the terminus of the Underground Railroad to freedom for slaves escaping from the South. It is true, too, that after the end of slavery, prevailing racial attitudes and practices were, as they continue to be, more relaxed in Canada than in the United States. To be better, though, was not the same as to be good.

In 1785, sheriffs in St. John were instructed to deny blacks the vote, and in 1795 the city council rejected a petition from local blacks for fishing rights. By the 1830s, many churches in Canada consigned black worshippers to a back gallery known as Nigger Heaven. In the 1850s, blacks were refused admission to hotels in towns such as Chatham, Hamilton, and Windsor, and could not buy tickets on the Chatham steamer or bid at local land auctions. In 1860, the main theater in Victoria banned blacks from the dress circle and orchestra seats.

The Separate School Act of 1850 enabled whites to require the relegation of blacks to their own schools, with only black teachers teaching black children. The Teachers' Association of Canada West in Toronto condemned segregated schooling in a resolution of 1864, but it was not until the end of the century that the practice began withering, and even as late as 1960, an all-black school was functioning in Alberta, at Amber Valley.

The present century, indeed, proved at times even worse. During the twenties, blacks in Victoria and Edmonton, for instance, could not find a single barber willing to cut their hair. Canada soon acquired its own Ku Klux Klan, founded in 1925, and some eight thousand people attended its inaugural meeting in Saskatchewan. Other bases were established in Alberta, British Columbia, Manitoba, and Ontario, till there were 119 local Klaverns in the country.

In 1924, the City Commissioner in Edmonton banned blacks from the public parks and swimming pools. Black delegates to the World Baptist Conference of 1929 in Toronto found no local hotels which would accommodate them. McGill University in Montreal had racial restrictions not only during the two decades before the Second World War but even afterward for a time. At Calgary in 1940, a mob of three hundred white soldiers stormed the home of a black bandleader and attacked as "nigger-lovers" the whites encountered there. In 1954, a white teacher married to a black Jamaican woman was dismissed from a school near Victoria, for no other evident reason than the marriage, and three years later a black schoolteacher was prohibited from teaching white children at Breton in Alberta.[2]

As the spread of the Ku Klux Klan across the border would suggest, white attitudes and conduct may well have been influenced by those in the United States. Yet racism was already part of domestic culture. It came to Canada in the minds of its white settlers and in the literature—histories and tracts, novels and newspapers—which informed teaching at school and discussions at home. It flourished, moreover, without even a substantial black presence to feed it. As late as 1986, there were officially fewer than 175,000 blacks in the country, or not quite 0.7 percent of the total population.

In fact, racism itself ensured the smallness of the black presence. Immigration policies were racially so restrictive that married white male applicants from the Caribbean were required to provide photographs of their wives and children so as to prevent a "chain migration" of black dependents. This did not mean that blacks were altogether barred. Canada found room for a few blacks who would take jobs that whites refused to do, though only those blacks who were also willing to leave their dependents behind or had no dependents to leave. Black women from the Caribbean, for instance, were admitted for domestic service provided that they were young (aged twenty-one to thirty-five), single, and without children. In all, only 2,363 Caribbean blacks were allowed entry, mainly as domestics or laborers, in the period 1904–31, and such immigration virtually ceased during the Depression.[3]

It was Canada's increasing investments in mining, insurance, and banking over much of the Caribbean region that led to a self-interested shift in immigration policy toward blacks. In 1951, the Cabinet decided to admit a small number of Caribbean immigrants "of exceptional merit"—a euphemism for those of high professional qualifications or skills—on humanitarian grounds.[4] Government policy was also relaxed in response to the mounting demand for domestics, as the postwar industrial boom drew unprecedented numbers of Canadian women into the paid labor force.

The so-called Domestic Scheme, negotiated by Canada with Barbados and Jamaica through the British Colonial Office, was not to the liking of Canada's Director of Immigration, who argued vehemently against it in January 1955:

> It is from experience, generally speaking, that coloured people in the present state of the white man's thinking are not a tangible asset, and as a result are more or less ostracised. They do not assimilate readily and pretty much vegetate to a low standard of living . . . To enter into an agreement which would have the effect of increasing coloured immigration in this country would be an act of misguided generosity since it would not have the effect of bringing about a worthwhile solution to the problem of coloured people and would quite likely intensify our own social and economic problems.[5]

Such vehemence rather implied that the government envisaged admitting vast numbers. Yet, between 1955 and 1966, fewer than three thousand Caribbean black women arrived in Canada under the scheme. Many found their conditions of employment more oppressive than they had expected. They worked such hours as the convenience of their employers required. They certainly had little enough time to vegetate. Nor were they disposed to do so. They soon developed networks of their own to support one another and greet new arrivals with advice and help. Many attended night schools or took correspondence courses to acquire skills that enabled them to find better employment. In fact, less than a quarter of each successive group stayed in domestic service for more than three years. Most of the rest escaped to become nurses or nursing aides or secretaries, or work in restaurants, laundries, hairdressing salons, or textile factories.

Whatever their immediate or eventual occupations, black women had particular problems. Since only single ones without children were admitted through the scheme, those not listing on their application forms the children they had left behind subsequently found it dangerous as well as difficult to sponsor their entry. Seven such women from Jamaica were deported in 1977 after seeking the sponsored admission of their children. Moreover, the very immigration policies toward blacks that favored single women led to a corresponding black gender imbalance. As though this did not present difficulties enough, many of the black men admitted from the Caribbean were university students who brought their class discriminations with them. One black student organization, for instance, chose to disband its choir for lack of sufficient singers rather than admit domestic servants to it.[6]

From 1962 onward, racial restrictiveness came to be somewhat relaxed. The adoption of a "points system" widened the way for blacks with valued skills. In addition, the rise of separatist sentiment in Quebec encouraged politicians there to press for a more welcoming policy toward French-speaking Caribbean blacks, whose cultural contribution to confronting the force of English-speaking Canada outweighed for the while the defect of their color.

The Canadian authorities made efforts to direct the settlement of new black immigrants on the principle that the more widely they were dispersed, the more acceptable the intrusion of color would be. They were not notably successful. According to the findings of the 1986 census, just under 52 percent of all blacks in Canada settled in Toronto and just over 20 percent in Montreal. The census also found a still significant gender imbalance among blacks, of whom roughly 47 percent were male and 53 percent female.

A census is concerned only with those who legally exist. The numbers of illegal black immigrants are believed to be substantial, and their continued presence in Canada depends upon their evading detection. The economic benefits derived from such evaders dissuade the authorities from pursuing detection with too much zeal. Illegal immigrants who are gainfully employed pay taxes through their wage packets, but since they do not legally exist, they have no claim on the various social services. Furthermore, there are substantial numbers of legal black immigrants who refuse to identify themselves as black, a phenomenon that may well be associated with the perceived disadvantages of being black in Canadian society. Evidently almost 10 percent of Canadian blacks born in Haiti, more than 25 percent of those born in Senegal, and 58 percent of those born in Guadeloupe gave French as their ethnic origin.[7]

With every allowance made for such additions, blacks still constitute a small component of the total population in Canada, a much smaller one than blacks constitute in Britain, let alone the United States. Yet, for all this and despite the degree to which they are concentrated in two cities, Canadian blacks are arguably the most compartmentalized in the Diaspora.

The most obvious divide is linguistic, between blacks in the English-speaking provinces and those in French-speaking Quebec. This divide exists even within Quebec, where English-speaking blacks tend to mix with one another rather than with French-speaking ones. Origin also divides. Among French-speaking blacks in Montreal, there is little cohesion between those from Haiti and those from Martinique or Guadeloupe, let alone between those from the Caribbean and those from Africa. Within English-speaking Canada, the 12,000 blacks of Nova Scotia, descended from a settlement that goes back to early colonial days, seem separated by history as well as space from blacks elsewhere. Among blacks in Toronto, there were, in 1985, more than 130 sport, cultural, and business organizations representing the distinctive interests of groups from different parts of the Caribbean alone.

One explanation may lie in the relatively recent arrival of so many blacks. According to the findings of the 1986 census, 64 percent or close to two out of every three blacks in Canada were born elsewhere. A majority of these come from the Caribbean, where some have left children behind, for economic if not legal reasons, and few are without some family. It is cheap enough to fly back for visits and a reinvigorating connection with what many still regard as their homes. Certainly, there are far more who intend to go back for good one day than are ever likely to do so. Meanwhile, however, their sense of a merely temporary stay in Canada conditions their attitude not only to the host society but to blacks within it whose Caribbean homes are different from their own. And if Caribbeans can retain such distance from one another, it would not be surprising if the distance were still greater between them and black immigrants from Africa or the United States.

Another possible explanation is that Canadian society has accommodated a relatively large measure of black mobility, horizontal as well as vertical. Even in Toronto and Montreal, blacks share with whites the same neighborhoods rather than being compressed into the ghettos produced by functional segregation in the United States and even Britain. This may be due to what are still proportionately small numbers in these large urban populations, though it is arguably due as well to a time lag. In Nova Scotia, there are small towns that are virtually all black. Yet it is in the cities that the state of race relations is most relevantly to be assessed, and conditions there suggest no such degree of black social deprivation as exists elsewhere. In Canada, there are relatively more blacks who have made it into the middle class, and relatively fewer who have sunk to the social depths. Economic circumstances define and divide blacks more diversely, by such distinctions as dress, housing, and the particular schools which their children attend.

Conceding a more moderate character and impact to racism in Canada nonetheless implies that racism exists. And there is more than enough evidence to support this. In 1985, the *Toronto Star* published the results of a three-month inquiry into how each of the city's seven largest ethnic minorities viewed its treatment by Canadian society.[8] Almost two out of every three blacks who were surveyed believed that they had less opportunity for job promotion or election to public office than other Canadians. Some 55 percent held that they had more difficulty in finding jobs.

The survey also found fewer respondents among the blacks than in any other of the ethnic groups who believed that prejudice was decreasing. Indeed, almost as many blacks held that it was increasing as held the opposite view; they were the only group with such a "pessimistic" response. More comforting to Canadian assumptions, only 34 percent of black respondents regarded their treatment on the street, 26 percent their treatment in shops, and 25 percent their treatment by the courts, as reflecting less courtesy and respect, while only 10 percent believed that their opportunity to acquire a good education was inferior.

Some six years later, every black I met maintained that there had been a marked increase in racism, with a particular rise in the incidence of violence against blacks and in their harassment by police. A Haitian settler in Montreal told me of eight young blacks, most of them university students, who arrived at a bus stop to wait for a bus. Within a few minutes, an equal number of police cars had arrived as well, decanting police who quickly surrounded the blacks. The Haitian, eminent in the black community and beyond, watched this from a window and rushed from his home to intervene. Such incidents, he claimed, were becoming more common in Quebec, where the rise in racism reflected the rise in France and for much the same reasons—mounting economic difficulties and a high rate of unemployment.

An English-speaking black in Montreal, who had immigrated to Canada from Britain in 1962, agreed that racism had become more widespread and overt in Quebec, where "the political establishment is now hostage to a petit bourgeois nationalism." He, too, identified the deteriorating relations between blacks and police as particularly indicative and cited the killing a few months before, in July 1991, of a black man from the island of St. Lucia, shot by police who had allegedly mistaken him for a suspect significantly taller. Even before the coroner's inquest, the authorities had announced that no action would be taken against the police.

Quebec is, to be sure, a special case. Under pressure from an occasionally violent separatist militancy, the provincial government has instituted linguistic and cultural controls that increasingly combine the absurd with the oppressive. An official force of police with corresponding responsibilities descends on businesses whose French-language signs are deemed not dominant enough, by size or position or vividness of color, in relation to English-language ones, while groups of vigilantes act with apparent impunity where they believe the authorities to have been remiss in prosecuting.[9] In such a social climate, it is hardly surprising that racism thrives and that a prejudice against blacks outweighs for many whites the contribution made by French-speaking black immigrants to reinforcing French culture.

Yet blacks themselves are by no means persuaded that the rise in racism is restricted to special cases. In May 1990, some four dozen black organizations submitted a brief on "The Precarious Situation of Blacks in Ontario" to the premier of the province. This protested against the "iniquitous practice of streaming Black students into low-level dead-end programs in schools"— a grievance that had manifestly grown since the survey of 1985—and against "institutional practices which guarantee that black families will be over-represented in the ranks of those last hired, first fired, and slowest promoted." It complained of "conditions that put inordinately high numbers of our youth in the correctional system" and cited in support the finding from the Ontario Human Rights Commission that a "young Black first time offender . . . has a 23 percent higher possibility of going to prison than a white youth similarly charged."

The main thrust of the brief, however, was directed at "police racism . . . manifested in such aspects as humiliating and antagonizing name-calling, unnecessary harassment, unlawful arrests, multiple charges, beatings and shootings." The brief argued for an independent civilian investigative body to address particular abuses:

> Black youths continually complain of intimidation and harassment in their communities, particularly low-income neighbourhoods. They are often charged with loitering for standing on sidewalks and in community centres . . . Many are refused entry to shopping malls, as police have warned storekeepers that Black youths are most likely to shoplift.
>
> In communities like Jamestown and Flemingdon Park where Black families are concentrated, police have terrorized and brutalized innocent Black children, youths, mothers and fathers under the guise of conducting drug sweeps. These drug raids often result in little or no drugs being found.

There had been, the brief asserted, a particular increase in police brutality toward black women, and five shootings of black men and women, two of these by traffic officers, in the previous two years: "In all these shootings the charges laid have been inappropriate as they do not reflect the severity of the acts of these officers. Further, no police officer has been convicted for shooting or killing a Black person."

It is difficult to believe that all this was a product of black paranoia and accordingly to dismiss the brief's crucial contention: "Racism is not maintained by the poor, the powerless, and the uneducated. It continues to thrive and to hurt Afro-Canadians as long as those in power fail to see it as primarily their problem, and not so much the problem of those who are its victims."

Were further evidence needed of increasing white racism, it may be inferred from the very coming together of many organizations, previously so indicative of a compartmentalized black community, for protest and pressure. It was just such an increase, albeit with the additional factor of antiblack rioting, that stirred among black Caribbean immigrants in Britain during the late fifties an awareness of their collective identity. The eye does not differentiate between a Haitian and a Senegalese, a British and a Jamaican immigrant, when they are the same color, and the blacks in Canada are increasingly coming to find themselves regarded and treated, even officially defined, as a "visible" minority.

Moreover, while there is still a majority of blacks in Canada who were born elsewhere, those blacks born in Canada constitute a minority that is not only large but growing. Except in the unlikely event of Canada's substantially relaxing its immigration policy toward blacks, the majority will soon be composed of those who consider Canada the homeland where blacks should assert their rights and of a youth less disposed than the generation of their parents to meet prejudice with discretion rather than resistance. Young blacks in Canada seem to be especially drawn to Jamaican culture, arguably the most militant in the Black Diaspora.

Meanwhile, here on the northern edge of the Diaspora, the community is one of striking creative energy, not least in literature. During the single year of 1991, merely among the Haitian immigrants settled in Montreal, seven black writers produced for publication three novels, three books of poetry, and one collection of children's stories. In English-language Canada, black writing is remarkable for both the extent and quality of its output.

"Black people and women," the writer Dionne Brand declared in an interview carried by *Books in Canada*, "have to make their humanity every goddamned day, because every day we are faced with the unmaking of us. Sometimes any words I throw at this feel like pebbles. But the purpose in throwing them is to keep, to save, my humanity, and that is my responsibility . . . I don't consider myself on any 'margin,' on the margin of Canadian literature. I'm sitting right in the middle of Black literature, because that's who I read, that's who I respond to."[10]

FIVE

Selections from an Anatomy of Achievement

"There is without doubt, no people on the earth more naturally affected to the sound of musicke than these people: which the principall persons do hold as an ornament of their state, so as when wee come to see them their musicke will seldom be wanting."[1]

So reported Richard Jobson, an English sea captain, sent in 1620 to explore the prospects of trade in Africa. Similar comments came from subsequent European visitors, struck by the variety of occasions on which music was played, and by the variety of indigenous musical instruments, from drums of different kinds to bells, gong-gongs, rattles, xylophones, hand or thumb pianos, harps, horns, flutes, lutes, fiddles.[2]

One visitor whose observations were of particular value, since he was himself an amateur musician and took copious notes, was Edward Bowdich, sent in 1817 by the African Committee of London to establish commercial relations with the Ashanti in the region of what is now Ghana. He transcribed melodies, described individual instruments, and remarked on the complex rhythms and melodic improvisation that he found so characteristic of the music.[3] There were other features generally reported as common: the call-and-response form, in which a lead singer and a chorus sang alternately; the harmony achieved by the simultaneous singing of different voices at various intervals from the basic melody; and the abundance of dances, often accompanied by the rhythms of hand-clapping from the onlookers.

Whatever else Africans lost in being transported as slaves, it was not their musical attachment and aptitude, which came to be valued especially in providing entertainment at the parties and dances that were the main source of colonial diversion. The market reflected this value in such advertisements as that carried by the *Virginia Gazette* of March 1766: "TO BE SOLD. A young healthy Negro fellow who has been used to wait on a Gentleman and plays extremely well on the French horn."

Nor was entertainment the only sanctioned channel of black musical expression. In the fields, singing was widely encouraged, since it seemed to sustain the slaves in their exertions. Many planters appointed special song leaders, sometimes even excusing these from labor, to excite greater effort from fellow slaves. "Field hollers," or calls from laboring slaves to one another, were often musically conveyed. Not least, the slaves took to music in such leisure as they were allowed.

Clergymen intent on converting the slaves to Christianity soon discovered that the singing of psalms constituted a powerful appeal. As the missionary Samuel Davies wrote in 1755: "The Negroes above all the Human Species that I ever knew have an Ear for Musick and a kind of extatic Delight in *Psalmody*; and there are no Books they learn so soon or take so much pleasure in, as those used in that heavenly Part of divine Worship."[4]

In the new United States, it was the establishment of separate black churches, in revolt against the white control of existing ones, that provided a major impulse to musical development. An Englishman, William Faux, who attended the service at one such church in 1820, recorded:

> After sermon they began singing merrily, and continued, without stopping, one hour, till they became exhausted and breathless. "Oh! come to Zion, come!" "Hallelujah, &c." And then, "O won't you have my lovely bleeding *Jasus*," a thousand times repeated in full thundering chorus to the tune of "Fol de rol." While all the time they were clapping hands, shouting and jumping, and exclaiming, "Ah Lord! Good Lord! Give me *Jasus*! Amen."[5]

The black churches did more than provide occasion and space for blacks to make their own religious music. They sponsored schools where children and adults could learn singing, promoted concerts, and raised funds for the most gifted to pursue their musical studies.

Whites were increasingly receptive to the richness of black musical expression but sought to separate it from its source. The minstrel show emerged, to present black song and dance without the socially unsettling implications of employing black performers for the purpose. Furthermore, lest the relevance of the white face beneath the blackface makeup should still be lost, minstrel performances came to involve the crudest ridicule of blacks, as in the two caricature figures of Zip Coon, the black city slicker, and Jim Crow, the stupid slave.

Meanwhile, a new black musical form was developing in such slum areas of the Northern cities as the Five Points district of Manhattan in New York, where free blacks and fugitives from slavery lived alongside working-class whites. There, in black-owned assembly rooms, shows were given on Saturday nights, and midway in the nineteenth century a journalist named George Foster went to one. He heard music "of no ordinary kind," from one instrumentalist whose sounds "pierce through and through your brain without remorse" and from a bass drummer who "sweats and deals his blows on every side, in all violation of the laws of rhythm."[6] It is difficult to believe that this was not an incipient form of jazz, a half-century or so before its supposed beginning.

Improvisation, the very lifeblood of jazz, belonged to another uniquely black form of musical expression known as the spiritual. It marked, for instance, a whole series of spirituals on the theme of Judgment Day, such as "In That Great Getting-Up Morning" and "Steal Away, Steal Away," whose very titles suggest that they had more than a merely religious purpose and may have been sung to signal the arrival of guides along the escape routes.

Vital elements of black song, which would continue to inform the development of black music, were remarked, along with the formidable problem of transcribing them, by contemporary researchers. Lucy McKim Garrison, who edited *Slave Songs of the United States*, wrote in 1862: "It is difficult to express the entire character of these negro ballads by mere musical notes and signs. The odd turns made in the throat, and the curious rhythmic effect produced by single voices chiming in at different irregular intervals, seem almost as impossible to place in the score as the singing of birds or the tones of an Aeolian Harp."[7]

These odd turns were the flatted or "bent" notes that shifted the key from major to minor and gave so many of the songs their mournful or melancholy quality. The curious rhythmic effect was the result of that rhythmic complexity in which the basic pulse of two beats to the bar, conveyed by the clapping of hands or the tapping of feet, was accompanied by one or more different rhythms from one or more singers. Along with these rhythmic crosscurrents came harmonic ones, as singers wandered from the prime melodic line for the stressing of particular words or for variety of expression. The involvement of musical instruments enhanced the possibilities of rhythmic and harmonic complexity. And improvisation made whatever song was transcribed, insofar as adequate transcription was possible, no more than the record of a particular performance.

The end of slavery in the United States led to a much greater measure of black economic and geographical mobility, further promoted by the postwar expansion in industry and transport. With the related experiences came new songs, mainly of suffering and sorrow, from blacks who labored on laying the railroads or who landed, for one reason or another, in jail. Songs of suffering and sorrow were, to be sure, as old as slavery. What was new was now the form of such songs, derived partly from spirituals, that came to be known as the blues. They were songs about loss, mainly of a lover but also of money or a job, and often with an ironic or mocking twist. It was rather as though these echoed the disillusionment that freedom had brought, but expressing at the same time the resilience of a new realism.

The classic twelve-bar three-line stanza of the blues, uncommon in European and related white American folk song, was common enough in traditional African music. It was peculiarly suited to the form of statement, repetition, and twist which the blues adopted, as in:

When a woman gets the blues she hangs her head and cries,
When a woman gets the blues she hangs her head and cries,
When a man gets the blues, he grabs a train and flies.[8]

The end of each vocal line provided a break in which the instrumental accompaniment, from a guitar, piano, or ensemble, might improvise, while the vocalist interjected with asides such as "Oh, Lordy" or "Oh, play it," in the call-and-response pattern of African music. In between, the vocalist might "scoop" or "swoop" or "slur," to produce the "bent" or "blue" notes, and use other devices, such as shouting, moaning, or falsetto, to express pain.

Another black musical form that exercised its own influence emerged in the last decade of the nineteenth century. This was a syncopated melodic line with regularly accented accompaniment, played mainly on the piano, that came to be known as ragtime. Its success was considerable and swift. In 1899 the first rag pieces written by Scott Joplin (1868–1917), the greatest of the ragtime composers, were published, and soon the impact of ragtime had spread beyond black musicians and the United States to influence the composition of classical music in Europe, as in the "Golliwog's Cakewalk" in Debussy's piano suite *Children's Corner*, of 1905, and the ragtime movement in Stravinsky's *The Soldier's Tale* of 1918.

It was in New Orleans that jazz itself now emerged as a recognized new and major form of music. That it should have been New Orleans was no mere coincidence. Blacks constituted a third of the population, or the largest such component of any city in the United States at the time. It was often black orchestras that provided the music at white dances and often the same musicians who played horns and trumpets in the brass bands that paraded in the streets by day. In 1897, the city had set aside a district, which came to be known as Storyville,[9] for brothels and gambling, and it was there, in dance halls and saloons, that pianists and other instrumentalists made innovative music together.

Sometime around the turn of the century, the so-called hot band of Charles Bolden (1877–1931) incorporated blues and ragtime in performances with a large element of improvisation. By 1913, the Original Creole Band of Bill Johnson, the first black dance band to do so, was touring the country and spreading its own version of New Orleans jazz. Already, however, jazz was flourishing in New York City, where Harlem had become a magnet for black musicians. Its nightclubs and dance halls resounded with the blues, made all the more popular by the contributions to the form from W. C. Handy (1873–1958), in particular his "Memphis Blues" of 1912 and "St. Louis

Blues" of 1914. There, jazz was generally played on combinations of three instruments: piano, drum, and banjo or harmonica. Soon Chicago, too, drawing large numbers of black migrants from the South, was a center of the new music and especially renowned for its black bands. With the entry of the United States into the First World War, such bands were sent to Europe, where they went beyond entertaining the troops to give public performances that stirred much excitement.

The very origin of the word "jazz" remains a mystery. It has been traced to an itinerant black musician named Jazbo Brown. Yet it was spelled "jass" in its early days, and its New Orleans background would suggest that it may have come from the French word *jaser* (to chatter or gossip). Another possibility exists in the sexual connotations of the word, to which song titles such as "Jazz Me Blues" and "Jazzin' Babies Blues" themselves point. The slang word for semen was "jism" or "jizz,"[10] and "jazz" was used as equivalent to "fuck."

The association of jazz with the excitement and climax of the sexual act is not far-fetched. There is, however, another significant association. Sexual slang is also used to express dismissal or defiance, and jazz, from the first, dismissed and defied the conventions and confinements of white music. It did so essentially as a music of improvisation, where composer and performer became one and the same in spontaneous creativity. There had been notable examples of this in classical music. Mozart, who would surely have delighted in jazz, composed on occasions in performance at the keyboard. Yet this was a particular musician, not a new form of music, and Mozart did it on his own, while jazz often involved three or more performers in interacting composition.

Here, jazz owed much to the traditional African music which the slaves had brought with them. Yet its spirit of revolt and resilience owed at least as much to the spirit of the Black Diaspora itself, whose own revolt and resilience had begun with the first slave ship to land its cargo. It was this spirit which was crucial not only to generating the creativity of jazz but to reinvigorating it continually, so that an innovation needed only to be established for another to be introduced in response to it.

By 1915, the name of jazz was so widely known that a white band in Chicago was advertising itself as "Brown's Dixieland Jass Band, Direct from New Orleans," and in 1918 W. C. Handy staged a "jass and blues" concert in New York. The connection between the two forms of new music was, indeed, exceedingly close. As Eileen Southern writes in her book *The Music of Black Americans*:

> The most salient features of jazz derive directly from the blues. Jazz is a vocally oriented music; its players replace the voice with their instruments, but try to recreate its singing style and blue notes by using scooping, sliding,

whining, growling and falsetto effects. Like the blues, jazz emphasizes individualism . . . A traditional melody or harmonic framework may serve as the takeoff point for improvisation, but it is the personality of the player and the way he improvises that produces the music . . . Finally, jazz uses the call-and-response style of the blues, by employing an antiphonal relationship between two solo instruments or between solo and ensemble."[11]

Jazz also developed its own effects, with a vocabulary to describe them. The break, for instance, was a short series of notes played by a soloist while the rest of the ensemble stayed silent; the riff was the frequent repetition of a short phrase; and the term scat singing applied to the wordless sounds made by a vocalist.

The essential element of improvisation in both blues and jazz long limited them to live performance. It was only in 1915 that the great jazz pianist, Jelly Roll Morton (born Ferdinand Joseph Lemott, 1890–1941) transcribed his own "Jelly Roll Blues" for the first ever published jazz arrangement. But it was the development of the gramophone that permitted the perpetuation of immediate performance. In 1920, the blues singer Mamie Smith was recorded, and the market for black music that the release of this recording revealed led to the recording of others, including Bessie Smith (1894–1937), widely regarded as having been the greatest of all blues singers.

By 1922, the recording industry had turned to jazz as well, and in the following year it recorded Louis Armstrong (1901–71), playing second cornet in the six-piece Creole Jazz Band. This Chicago group was led by Joe "King" Oliver (1885–1938), one of whose own contributions to the development of jazz was to incorporate the technique of blues singers by vocalizing the horn, in particular by the use of various mutes. Soon to become the most celebrated of jazz soloists, Armstrong himself came to exercise a major influence, both by his prodigious ability to improvise, which extended the musical possibilities of the instruments he played, and by his style of scat singing.

In 1923 Fletcher Henderson (1897–1952) started, with a ten-piece jazz group, the big-band movement in New York. Four years later, at the Cotton Club in Harlem, Duke (Edward Kennedy) Ellington (1899–1974) opened a season with his own ten-piece group, which grew to thirteen by 1932, the year in which he wrote "It Don't Mean a Thing If It Ain't Got That Swing." It was this that popularized the word "swing" for a jazz of flowing rhythm, though Armstrong had already developed the style, by placing a note just before or behind the beat, or by stretching phrases or notes across it. Ellington himself invested the style with the complex harmonies and contrasts that were the mark of his band. It was, however, as a composer that he made his supreme contribution, producing some two thousand compositions, from musicals and symphonic suites to such jazz classics as "Mood Indigo."

By the mid-thirties, Kansas City was a jazz center that attracted black musicians from all over the United States to meet and match their skills against one another. Out of such "cutting" contests a new style developed. Using the basic structure and material of the blues, the musicians would play together and then in turn improvise on the chorus before coming together again in the close. Count (William Allen) Basie (1904–84), pianist and bandleader, provided an innovation of his own, by playing the first chorus on the piano, to set the tempo and mood.

Fats (Thomas Wright) Waller (1904–43) was a master of the New York stride piano style and a composer who added such works to the jazz repertoire as "Honeysuckle Rose" and "Ain't Misbehaving." It was he who announced at a club where Art Tatum was present: "Ladies and gentlemen, I play piano, but tonight God is in the house."[12] For Art Tatum (1909–56), though virtually blind from birth, came to be widely regarded as the greatest pianist in the history of jazz. He had a dazzling technique, as well as seemingly limitless resources of rhythmic and harmonic inventiveness for his improvisations. Among the black musicians he influenced was Coleman Hawkins (1904–69), who was the first to use the tenor saxophone as a major instrument in jazz.

By 1926, *Melody Maker* in London was carrying articles on jazz, and in 1934 a magazine called *Downbeat*, concerned wholly with jazz, began publication in the United States. While generally recognized to be an essential black creation, jazz was increasingly drawing white practitioners, whose big bands were in general the more prominent and popular. Some of these employed black arrangers, but were more cautious about employing black singers and instrumentalists on the stage. Jazz was also influencing white composers, notably George Gershwin in the United States and even "classical" composers such as Ravel, Stravinsky, and Walton in Europe.

The testimonials by whites to the genius of jazz did little, however, to affect the practices of racial discrimination in the United States. This led some black musicians to settle in Europe, where Paris became a favored refuge. Others, partly protected by fame, stayed in the States, while touring Europe from time to time. The vast majority never got to playing before a racially mixed audience in a racially mixed area. But then, exclusion was the experience to which they were born. It belonged to the music that welled up within them.

"There was always," the black poet LeRoi Jones, who changed his name to Amiri Baraka, has written, "a border beyond which the Negro could not go, whether musically or socially . . . The Negro could not ever become white and that was his strength; at some point, always, he could not participate in the dominant tenor of the white man's culture . . . And it was this boundary, this no man's land, that provided the logic and beauty of his music."[13]

The vitality of jazz was nowhere more evident than in the emergence of radical new styles improvised by creative performers. One such performer was the trumpeter Dizzy (John Birks) Gillespie (1917–93), whose quintet at the Onyx Club in New York initiated in 1944 the bebop style. He was subsequently to describe how the term came to be used:

> We played a lot of original tunes that didn't have titles. We just wrote an introduction and a first chorus. I'd say, "Dee-da-pa-da-n-de-bop . . ." and we'd go into it. People, when they'd wanna ask for one of those numbers and didn't know the name, would ask for bebop. And the press picked it up and started calling it bebop.[14]

It was a style characterized by complex rhythms and intermittently dissonant harmonies, steady but subtle beats and irregular phrases, with improvisation on chords instead of melody. "When we borrowed from a standard," Gillespie recollected, "we added and substituted so many chords that most people didn't know what song we really were playing."[15]

One of Gillespie's collaborators was the saxophonist Charlie "Bird" Parker (1920–55). He had a style of his own, derived from the blues, and he influenced the development of what was virtually a chamber music version of jazz. Influential, too, was the pianist Thelonious Monk (1917–82) whose playing explored for new notes between those already known, and whose tunes have, since his death, reportedly been used by more jazz musicians than anyone else's except Ellington's.[16]

Such innovations gave rise to complaints that jazz was no longer a music to which you could dance. One result was the development of cool jazz, associated mainly with the trumpeter and composer Miles Davis (1926–91), whose soft, lyrical style relied more on tonal beauty than on speed. Some of those involved in bop were moved to develop hard bop as a return to the primacy of rhythm and the blues in black music. This became a major source of innovation from the mid-fifties, to coincide with the new black political assertiveness that was surfacing in the civil rights movement. Indeed, there came to be an explicit connection between black music and politics, with compositions such as *The Freedom Suite* of tenor saxophonist and composer Sonny (Theodore Walter) Rollins (born 1929).

Making his own musical statement on the course of the civil rights struggle with his *Alabama* was tenor saxophonist and composer John Coltrane (1926–67). A member of the quintet formed by Miles Davis, he began in 1959 to lead small groups himself and became, by exploring new rhythms and styles, with influences from African, Arab, and Indian music, one of the great innovators.

By the sixties, too, black popular music began to include soul music, which incorporated "gospel" idioms. Some black churches had continued the practice developed during slavery of celebrating the faith with hand-clapping, feet-stomping, ring shouts of repeated chanting that rose in intensity, the call-and-response pattern, and a singing characterized by rhythmic richness and melodic improvisation. Increasingly, musical instruments from the pump organ to the tambourine had been introduced as full partners in the making of music.

By the twenties, such music was becoming a sacred counterpart of the blues, to the extent of employing "bent" notes. Thomas A. Dorsey himself, known as the Father of Gospel Music, who composed numerous gospel songs from 1921 onward, was also a blues pianist, guitarist, and composer. Two sorts of gospel-singing groups emerged: the male group of four or five singers (indiscriminately called a quartet) who harmonized to a rhythmic accompaniment that they themselves supplied by snapping their fingers or slapping their thighs; and a female group which sang with piano accompaniment and the rhythmic clapping of hands. Slow-tempo songs involved the more elaborate melodies; fast-tempo ones, the more syncopated rhythms.

The new form established its own market. Leading gospel soloists were paid by churches and church groups. In 1938, "Sister" Rosetta Tharpe became the first gospel singer to record for a major commercial company; and in the forties, gospel singing became secular live entertainment when Tharpe performed at the Apollo Theatre in Harlem. As the market expanded, the form developed. Gospel groups ceased to be separated by gender. Appropriate recognition of the music as a major new force came in 1957, when the Newport Jazz Festival included gospel singers, and gospel took its place alongside jazz and the blues. Mahalia Jackson (1911–72), the greatest of the gospel singers, performed at Newport in 1958.

In the fifties, the electric organ as well as amplified guitars and drums joined gospel music's traditional instruments of accompaniment, and by the seventies, strings, brass, and bongo and conga drums were being added. The vocal embellishments were those of black musical tradition and included growls, falsetto, humming, moaning, and transgender shifts, by which male singers emphasized their falsetto and female singers their low register. Rhythmic improvisation involved stressing accents between the strong and weak pulses of the music, so as to produce a subtle syncopation, and interjections, such as "Hallelujah" and "Yes, Lord," were common. Bodily rhythmic accompaniment was essential, with swaying as well as clapping and tapping, from audience as well as performers. All this had an influence on the development of other black musical forms, notably rhythm and blues, or R & B for short.

In the heyday of black music-making at Kansas City during the thirties, so-called shout blues singers, such as Big Joe Turner (1911–85), began the rise in importance of the vocalist over the rhythm section. Muddy Waters (born McKinley Morganfield, 1915–83), blues singer, guitarist, and composer, enriched what was essentially a version of the blues, with its urgent sexuality and its pain, from his deep knowledge of their early form and adopted the electric guitar as his instrument. Louis Jordan (1908–75) and his Tympany Five extended the market for the developing form with nineteen hits in the period 1946–49.

In June 1949, the arrival of rhythm and blues was recognized by the trade magazine *Billboard*, which began to publish a list of the top records in R & B that was separate from the list of pop hits. R & B drew on gospel music as well as the blues for improvisation, expressive vocal effects, and the call-and-response communication between singer or singers and instrument or instrumental group, but emphasized the duple meter and, heavily, the strong beats. Its lyrics were often more humorous or down-to-earth than those in the music of white pop, and it soon attracted growing numbers of young whites.

In 1959, Berry Gordy, a songwriter who owned a record shop, founded Motown Records in Detroit, and the swift success of the company was largely due to its developing the new Detroit or Motown sound, which combined characteristics of R & B, gospel, pop, and big-band effects. Its recordings, notably those of the Supremes (later, Diana Ross and the Supremes) and Stevie Wonder (born Stevland Judkins or Morris in 1950), soon began to make their way onto the weekly listings of the top hits. It was with rock 'n' roll—rock, for short—however, that black music, if mainly through its adoption by white musicians, took and long held possession of the popular music market not only in the United States but across much of the world.

In 1954, the Chords, a black male group specializing in R & B, provided in "Sh-Boom" the first rock record. Its distinctive rhythmic intensity and unromantic lyrics took it into the Top Ten of the pop charts. A blander recording of the same song from a white Canadian group called the Crew Cuts finished the year among the Top Five. Similarly, Joe Turner's "Shake, Rattle and Roll" was followed by the more successful version from the white group, Bill Haley and his Comets.

Elvis Presley, more than anyone else responsible for the rapid popularization of rock, was first commercially recorded by a Memphis company, Sun Records, whose proprietor was looking for a white who could sing like a black.[17] Presley's style, which came to be called rockabilly, was a fusion of country (American folk) music and R & B, with an urgent beat, so that it did, indeed, have an unblanched, unbland black element.

In Britain during the early sixties, two white groups, the Beatles and the Rolling Stones, each developing its own style within the wider realm of rock, achieved enormous popularity, which they spread by their tours in the United States. Both groups readily acknowledged their debt to black music, though the Rolling Stones drew more faithfully on the tradition of such music—taking their very name, in tribute to Muddy Waters, from a hit of his in 1950—and so contributed to a revival of interest in R & B and in classic blues as well.

Assisted in its dissemination by an assertive youth culture, the new pop effectively introduced black musical forms, albeit adapted ones, to new parts of the world—even, against more or less resolute state resistance, countries in what was then the Soviet bloc. Meanwhile, black music itself was moving beyond rock to other innovations. The blind pianist, organist, singer, and composer Ray Charles (born 1930) brought to R & B the vocal techniques of gospel music, in particular melisma (singing a group of notes to a single syllable). He became the first major figure in the development of soul music, which not only involved a more severe and driving style of musical expression but increasingly turned in its lyrics to protests against racism and social injustice, with the assertion of a militant black consciousness.

Singer, drummer, and composer James Brown (born 1928), who came to be called the Godfather of Soul or Soul Brother No. 1, made his own notable statement in his song "Black Is Beautiful: Say It Loud: I'm Black and I'm Proud." He was influential, too, in the development of funk, which roughened the smoothed texture of mass-marketed R & B and soul music, but was also characterized in performance by extravagant costume and staging. Yet another development came during the seventies with the proliferation of discos for dancing.

"Disco" was music of more regular rhythms and of dramatic effects such as the Syndrum, or drum synthesizer, produced. Stevie Wonder, among singer-composers in the form, recorded ballads of distinction for the market. Increasingly, however, the musical material provided little more than a relatively simple rhythmic emphasis. Moreover, black teenagers were generally unable to afford the price of visiting discos and, besides, looked for music more relevant to their lives than that which the disco market promoted.

They took the disco beat, played about with various styles from which disco was derived, and accompanied their musical explorations with a competitive agility of movement that was called break dancing. This gave place to a chanted accompaniment of improvised street poetry, and so arose rap, which subordinated melody to rhythmic lyrics of increasingly sharp social or political content. Rap became the main musical expression of protest in the black ghettos during the eighties and soon spread from the United States to other parts of the Diaspora.

Jazz itself was not indifferent to changes in black popular music, and certainly its own impulse to innovation was as vital as ever. Alto saxophonist Cannonball (Julian Edward) Adderley (1928–75) was prominent among those who developed soul jazz. By the end of the sixties, Miles Davis and his group were incorporating rock drums, along with electric guitar and piano, into jazz, and jazz rock or fusion came to be an important new style in the seventies. In that decade, too, Ornette Coleman and his group, Prime Time, took to rock-related rhythms and the use of electric bass for a style called "harmelodic," or harmonic improvisation.

Jazz was also continuing to explore new sources. Don Byron, a young black clarinetist, drew on klezmer, Jewish folk dance music from Eastern Europe, in his jazz. Pianist-composer Abdullah Ibrahim (born Adolph Johannes Brand in Cape Town) brought to his jazz elements of South African black township music. Like Ellington, he distrusted the label of jazz. "We simply call it," he once remarked, "the music of the people."[18]

If the whole huge musical achievement of blacks in the United States must be regarded as the richest and most influential, it has by no means been the only rich and influential music of the Diaspora. Indeed, black music in the United States has itself been enriched by Caribbean and South American black musical influences. In particular, the distinctive music of Brazil, mainly black in its sources and development, has had its own global impact.

Oneyda Alvarenga, the Brazilian musicologist, has identified a number of major African elements in Brazilian music. These include the frequency of the six-note scale with a flatted seventh "blue" note; the call-and-response style of singing, with a generally improvised solo line and short unvarying chorus; the fracture of the typically European neat melodic framework; the *umbigada* or belly bounce in dance; and the many musical instruments of African origin, especially the various drums or *atabaque*. The basic melancholy of the Portuguese melodic line is certainly characteristic of much Brazilian music but is often so syncopated and combined with complex rhythms that the African influence is equally evident there.[19]

A seminal musical form, brought by Angolan slaves to Brazil and first noted in 1780 for its lasciviousness, was *lundu*, a song and circle dance which included the navel-to-navel touch or belly bounce. Purged of such suggestive contact and with the refined harmonies of a guitar or piano accompaniment, the form made its way even to the height of the Portuguese court in Brazil. Then in Rio around 1880, black Brazilian musicians took the syncopation and flatted seventh note of lundu, the rhythm of the Cuban habanera, and the movement of the European polka, to develop a dance of quick jumpy pace called the maxixe. Both lundu and maxixe were in turn to influence the development of the samba, which came to be the predominant musical form.[20]

The very word is believed to have been brought from Angola, where *semba* was the term for the belly-bounce invitation to the dance. There are some scholars who hold that the samba itself, in its basic form, was brought by slaves to Bahia and subsequently taken to Rio by Bahian blacks who moved there. Supporting this has been the connection adduced between the samba beat and the rhythmic drumming and hand-clapping in the rites of the Bahian Candomblé religion. Certainly, there is one historical figure in whose life the three elements of Bahia, Candomblé, and the samba came together.

Born at Salvador in Bahia, Hilaria Batista de Almeida (1854–1924), better known as Tia Ciata, moved to Rio and settled in a district favored by Bahian

black migrants to the city. A successful confectioner, she made of her home
a center for Candomblé and visiting black musicians. It was there that the
first known samba, "Pelo Telefone" (On the Phone) was collectively composed, though emerging in 1917 as the work of "Donga" or Ernesto Joaquim
Maria dos Santos (1891–1974). A hit song at the Carnival that year, it created
immediate and widespread excitement.

It is classified today by many musicologists as a samba-maxixe rather than
pure samba. Yet it nonetheless began the rapid development to the samba
form, which discarded the restrictive maxixe elements for a 2/4 meter, with
heavy emphasis on the second beat; a stanza-and-refrain structure, based on
call-and-response; connected syncopated lines; and a main rhythm accompanied by complex cross-rhythms from drums and other percussion. So vital
was the form that it became, like jazz, an abundant source of innovation
and variety. For it was also, like jazz, creatively and expressively, sometimes
mockingly, sometimes defiantly, "the music of the people."

The standard samba emerged during the twenties in Rio's Estácio district,
where the black poor frequented its small bars to drink and talk and make
music together. It was here, too, in 1928, that the first *escola de samba* came
into being. There were soon many of these schools, which came increasingly
to involve composers, instrumentalists, singers, dancers, directors, conduc-
tors, choreographers, costume and set designers, all working toward an annual
competitive performance at the Carnival.

In acknowledgment of the source for so much of its vitality, the standard
form came by the forties to be called the *samba de morro* (hill samba), in
reference to the favelas, the largely black slums on the city's hills, where so
much of the music originated. Then, by the late fifties, the description was
dropped, in part because the standard form had spread across the country
and in part because the favela connotation was no longer deemed acceptable.
The term "standard" should not, however, suggest that the form was static.
It continued to develop elaborate rhythms and complex instrumentation. It
explored new styles of singing, as in the *samba de breque*, initiated by Moreira
da Silva (born 1902), who would interrupt his song to improvise dialogues
or otherwise dramatize the theme of the lyric during a "break." It extended
its range of themes to explicit social protest, as in the celebrated samba
"Acender as Velas" (Light the Candles), composed by Zé Keti (José Flores
de Jesus, born 1921).

> When there's no samba
> There's disillusion
> It's one more heart
> That stopped beating
> One more angel that goes to heaven
> May God forgive me

But I'll say it
The doctor arrived too late
Because on the hill
There are no cars to drive
No telephones to call
No beauty to be seen
And we die without wanting to die.[21]

Already by the thirties, under the influence of white middle-class taste, there were composers, most of them whites, who were developing a slower and softer version of the standard in the *samba-canção* or samba song that shifted the musical emphasis from rhythm to melody and the lyrical content from wide-ranging to generally romantic themes. This in turn gave rise to such forms as the *sambolero* and eventually the bossa nova.

The white musician João Gilberto (born 1932), with his individual, highly syncopated plucking of guitar chords, developed a cooler, slower variant of the samba rhythm, and others were quick to explore and extend the possibilities of the variant form. In 1959, the film *Orfeo Negro* (Black Orpheus) spread the new bossa nova sound beyond Brazil. In the United States, the guitarist Charlie Byrd (born 1925) and the tenor saxophonist Stan Getz (1927–91) assimilated this promising material to their jazz.

Associated with Gilberto in the early days of bossa nova was the Brazilian white composer "Tom" (Antônio Carlos) Jobim (born 1927). With the poet Vinícius de Moraes as lyricist, he wrote "The Girl from Ipanema," and this song, released in 1964, just when the interest in bossa nova seemed to be ebbing, produced an even stronger flow of popularity for the new form. He became Brazil's leading composer of popular music, but one who drew readily from black musical sources.

Black musical creativity reasserted itself even as a hostile regime sought to repress it. The military dictatorship that lasted from 1964 to 1985 regarded the eclectic movement of MPB (*música popular brasileira*) as culturally and, therefore, politically subversive. Guitarist and composer Gilberto Gill (born 1942), who merged samba and Brazilian folk music with rock, was detained without charge for a while in 1969, went into exile until 1972, and after his return added African music and Jamaican reggae to the influences on his individual amalgams. Singer, guitarist, and composer Jorge Ben (later, Jorge Benjor; born Jorge Duílio Menezes in 1940) combined elements of samba, maracatu, rock and *baião*, a song style from the northeast of Brazil, with African ones, to develop a personal style of emphatic rhythm that came to be called rhythm and samba.

Singer and composer Milton Nascimento (born in 1942) became as celebrated for the extraordinary range and expressive power of his voice, much admired by jazz musicians, as for the variety of the songs he wrote, with their moving melodies and their innovative rhythmic and chord patterns. For these he drew not only on traditional black Brazilian forms and regional folk songs but on Iberian styles, Andean flute music, jazz, rock, classical music, and even Gregorian chants. His increasing devotion to social as well as romantic themes provoked the military regime, which in 1973 banned most of the lyrics in his album *Milagre dos Peixes* (Miracle of the Fishes).

If the samba continues to be the predominant form of Brazilian music, it has not been the only significant black Brazilian musical influence. Predating the known development not only of the samba but of jazz in the United States was an instrumental form of African-derived elements and an emphasis on both improvisation and syncopation called *choro*. The word itself means "weeping" in Portuguese, but since melancholy was only one of the music's moods, it is at least as likely that it derived from *xolo*, an early Afro-Brazilian word for a party or dance, especially since the first choro groups, which proliferated in Rio from 1870 onward, went the rounds of homes to play at parties.

These groups used only three instruments: the flute, which was the melodic soloist; the guitar, which provided the low tones on its bass strings; and the *cavaquinho*, a four-stringed type of ukulele, which was mainly responsible for maintaining the medium to fast tempo. With certain similarities to jazz, choro provided its distinctive challenge in the charge on the soloist to explore the melody in such improvisations as reached a *derrubada* or "drop," at which the accompanists could no longer follow the riffs.

A seminal figure in the development of the form was Joaquim Antônio da Silva Calado (1848–80), whose flute solos were renowned for their octave leaps and quicksilver key changes. Pixinguinha (Alfredo da Rocha Vianna, Jr., 1898–1973), another black virtuoso flutist and among the earliest composers of samba, was still more influential. He changed the character of choro by extending its instrumental range to include such percussion as the *ganzá* (a metal box with pebbles in it), the *pandeiro* (a type of tambourine), the *reco-reco* (a notched piece of bamboo or metal scraped with a stick) and, after a successful visit with his band to Paris in 1922, the saxophone, clarinet, and trumpet.

After a decline in its popularity, choro returned to favor in the forties, and then again in the seventies, as successive generations of musicians reinvigorated the form. Along the way, the clarinet took the place of the flute as solo instrument, and the voice then took the place of the clarinet. The samba influence increased, and there was even a merger of the two forms in samba-choro. Paulo Moura (born in 1945), a black classical clarinetist, took to the saxophone, used it for the solo role in choro, and produced a fusion of choro, samba, and jazz. The black percussionist Naná Vasconcelos (born in 1945) introduced the *berimbau*, an instrument composed of a wooden bow, a metal string, and a gourd resonator, used in Bahia to accompany *copoeira*, the gracefully acrobatic martial arts dance that slaves from Angola had brought to Brazil.

Spanish influence has been dominant in the development of music elsewhere on the mainland of South and Central America. Yet there are musical forms in these regions which also bear distinct African influences.

The *pasillo*, a dance in both Colombia and Venezuela, is a sort of syncopated waltz, with heavy first and last beats, and an evident example of black influence on a European form. The Colombian *cumbia*, a popular form played by city bands, has still stronger black musical elements. Its emphasis on drum and rattle percussion involves improvised variations from the lead drummer, and a repetitive melodic line often provided by fiddle or accordion. The *currulao* of Colombia's Pacific coast has a fiery rhythm for both dance and song; and the singing is characterized not only by its call-and-response pattern but by lyrics of an oblique or fragmented kind that also echo an African connection.

Venezuela has numerous musical forms that are collectively called *golpe*, which means "beat," and originally referred to a black pattern of drumming. Features of African drumming still persist, notably in the Barlovento coastal region where a player may use a stick in one hand and mute the drumhead with the other, so as to widen the range of notes, while a second player beats a counterrhythm with a pair of sticks on the side of the same drum. The *galeron*, a popular dance form in the country, is played by string orchestra and owes its rhythmic techniques to such Spanish instruments as the guitar and the mandolin, yet even here there is an African musical influence in the call-and-response pattern often used for the development of the melody.

Most Panamanian music is clearly related to the music of Colombia, but one distinctively Panamanian form has a direct African derivation. The *tamborito* has a lead drummer who guides the other musicians, the dancers, singers, and spectators, in what is a collective, essentially cathartic experience. Whether in the style of call-and-response or short rhyming couplets, the lyrics, sometimes ribald, are repeated again and again, while the singing, dancing, and hand-clapping accompany the drums in mounting excitement. At last, when the tension seems to be no longer tolerable, the lead drummer signals a sudden shift from one rhythm to another, for an intermediate release.[22]

In countries of Hispanic South America with supposedly all-white populations, such as Argentina and Chile, or those with varyingly large indigenous Indian components, such as Bolivia and Paraguay, the extent or even existence of black musical influences is a matter of much dispute. Yet it would be astonishing if the music of these areas had been altogether unaffected by the black slaves who had lived there or subsequently by black musical forms or influences elsewhere in the region. Music is not easily seized by customs officials or arrested by border guards. Certain Argentinian dances, such as the *milonga*, the *malambo*, and the *zamba*, have names of evident African origin. There are indigenous Indians who not only play an African instrument, the marimba, but who use black drumming techniques.[23]

Few parts of the world can have produced, proportionate to their populations, such a richness of musical forms as the Caribbean has done. Cuban music has been especially rich and extensively influential. The most famous of its forms, the rumba, began as a black festival dance and involved improvisations by a lead drummer over rhythmic patterns from other percussive instruments: drums of distinctive tones, spoons, rattles, and claves (two sticks tapped together). As with the samba in Brazil, the rumba gave rise to variant forms, of which the *guaguancó*, with its fluid melodic line and relatively fast rhythm, was adopted by the popular theater and cabaret, to become eventually favored material for processing by Latin jazz groups. Meanwhile, the stylized rhythmic base of rumba spread across North America and Europe from the twenties onward, to establish itself as a staple of Latin American dance.

The *son* derived from the eighteenth-century Spanish *estrebillo* but came under early black musical influence, to acquire percussive cross-rhythms and syncopation. By 1918, a *son* style had developed that involved a vocal trio, bass, trumpet, guitar, *tres* (a type of guitar with six or nine strings), bongo drums, maracas, and claves. Then, under pressure from middle-class taste, it assumed a "whiter" character in the late twenties, with emphasis on melody at the cost of rhythmic improvisation and complexity, a quickened tempo, and more reliance on the trumpet for embellishment. Then one great black musician invigorated the form and changed its direction.

Called *El Ciego Maravilloso* (The Marvelous Blind Man), Arsenio Rodríguez (1911–70) was a virtuoso player of the *tres*, bass, conga drum and other percussion instruments, as well as a vocalist, bandleader, composer, and arranger. During the thirties, he strengthened the black elements in *son* by restoring the rhythmic emphasis and adding such instruments as the cowbell and the conga drum. He has also been widely credited with having introduced the mambo to the Cuban dance halls in 1937. This new musical form was based on a rhythm developed by Afro-Cuban cults of Congolese derivation (*mambo* or *mambe*, meaning "song," is a Congolese word). Making its way to the United States, where jazz bands began playing it with the forceful backing of Cuban rhythm sections, it became fashionable during the fifties.[24]

Meanwhile, mainly in response to middle-class white taste, the Cuban violinist Enrique Jorrin developed in 1948 the *cha-cha-cha*. This sweeter, softer form of the local *danzón* took its name from the shuffling sound made by the feet of the dancers. Recorded in 1953, it spread to the United States, where it soon displaced the mambo as the popular Latin American dance.

Afro-Cuban music had a considerable impact on the development of musical forms elsewhere in the Caribbean. In Puerto Rico, for instance, most popular music containing African elements acquired these from Cuba. Even the indigenous *bomba*, once danced by black slaves there, took directly from African musical tradition the call-and-response pattern of singing, the dialogue between male dancer and solo drummer, and the rhythmic improvisation of one drummer across the basic rhythm provided by another, but owed to Cuba the inclusion of the maracas, and the bongo and conga drums.

In New York City during the early seventies, there emerged a "hot and uptempo Latin music"[25] called *salsa*, a word meaning "sauce" in Spanish but used by Cuban musicians in the sense of "spice." This was mainly based on Cuban forms—the rumba, *guaguancó*, mambo, *son*, cha-cha-cha—and on Cuban percussion instruments and *conjunto* or band combinations. It encompassed as well such other forms, more or less influenced by black music, as the Colombian *cumbia*, the Puerto Rican *bomba*, and the Dominican merengue, a dance rhythm in 2/4 time. The salsa excitement ebbed later in the decade, to be succeeded in the early eighties by a preoccupation with merengue, until there was a resurgence of interest in salsa and its profusion of influences.

The calypso, though played and sung on other Caribbean islands, is most closely associated with Trinidad and was almost certainly born there. The lineage is largely African, not only in important musical elements but in the use of song to express social discontent and in particular to administer publicly a personal rebuke. In 1859, William Moore, an ornithologist from the United States on a visit to the island, claimed that calypso was merely a variant of the British ballad. A crowd, led by a singer called Surisma (or Sirisma) the Carib, collected outside the visitor's hotel to sing, in call-and-response style, its reprimand.

Surisma: Moore, you monkey—
Crowd: Tell me what you know about we cariso! . . .[26]

In 1943, using an old folk melody, the calypsonian Lord Invader (Rupert Grant) protested at the increase in prostitution from the presence of wartime United States military personnel on the island, in such verses as:

Since the Yankees came to Trinidad
They have the young girls going mad
The young girls say they treat them nice
And they give them a better price

They buy rum and Coca-Cola
Go down Point Cumana
Both mother and daughter
Working for the Yankee dollar . . .[27]

The calypso form had already been introduced in the United States by commercial recordings of it. A version of "Rum and Coca-Cola," recorded by the Andrews Sisters in 1944, became the most popular song in the country; in part, perhaps, because it was banned by the four major networks on various counts, from providing Coca-Cola with free advertising to portraying unfavorably the role of the armed forces in the Caribbean.

The early calypso was played mainly with drums, a scraper, rattles, and, in a local version of the West African gong, a bottle struck by a spoon. Then the guitar was introduced, along with Venezuelan-derived dance tunes, and subsequently the calypso has drawn from time to time on Cuban music, jazz, and rhythm and blues. The basic rhythm remains Afro-Spanish, with a markedly original ingredient in the vocal line, which varies widely as it stretches or shrinks its way to a rhyme of often challenging ingenuity. Melodies may come from Spanish, British, French, or black folk sources. The double-tone calypso has a relatively long melodic line likely to have been European in origin; the single-tone one, a shorter line, of call-and-response song form and with such other black musical features as a more marked measure of improvisation and rhythmic excitement.

Of indisputable Trinidadian origin is the steel band, whose instruments, called pans, are made from the heads of oil drums, each with bumps produced by heating and hammering the surface to afford various notes. Those with more notes are responsible for the melody, while those with fewer ones provide the bass part, and the result is closer to an orchestra of xylophones than of drums. If it is scarcely an instrumental form that lends itself to the exploration of textures, it presents instead the challenge of extending rhythmic inventiveness and virtuosity. Both the calypso and the steel band are, indeed, vehicles for the exercise of competitive musical skills, in composition and performance, which climax at the annual Carnival.

Jamaica had long been rich in folk music, such as digging songs, some of which became dance tunes, and ring games that became dances. It was only in the late fifties of this century, however, that a modern, distinctively Jamaican music emerged and soon came to exercise an international influence. It began as ska, a "shuffling hybrid" of rhythm and blues, whose recordings from the United States were very popular, and *mento*, the island's "raggedy calypso style."[28] This new form, whose name came from the chopped guitar or piano sound on the second or fourth beats of the music, took its energy and mood from the restive young black poor of Kingston, who defiantly accepted the dismissive term of Rude Boys applied to them.

Under the influence of rock, a slower and more sensual form then developed that came to be known as *rock steady*, from the title of an early hit, "Get Ready to Rock Steady." This in turn gave place by the early seventies to reggae, characterized by its forceful bass-dominated sound in conjunction with the ska chop on the offbeat. Three versions exist of how it acquired its name: from the English word "regular," descriptive of the beat; from the Creole word *streggae*, meaning rudeness; and from the Creole word *regge-regge*, meaning quarrel. Whatever its derivation, the new word became part of the world's musical vocabulary, as the form swept through the Black Diaspora and beyond, with one musician at the crest.

Guitarist, singer, and songwriter Bob Marley (1945–81) began his career with a Kingston group called The Wailers whose first ska recording in 1962 had some local success. Moving into rock steady later in the sixties and increasingly committed to the beliefs and values of Rastafarianism, Marley dominated the shift to reggae, which he developed not only as a new musical form but as a vehicle of political, religious, and racial protest. He and his group, renamed Bob Marley and the Wailers, had its first international success with its album *Catch a Fire*, of late 1972, and in the following year, the group began a series of tours abroad that did much to spread the appeal of reggae.

Marley himself was not satisfied simply to consolidate such success and found in African music a way of further developing the form. His 1979 album *Survival* was the first to reveal the effect of such influence, and in *Uprising*, of 1980, the last before his early death from cancer, the horns and rock sound gave place to a more markedly African musical treatment.

Haitian music is rich with African tradition, not only in forms associated with Voodoo, but in such secular ones as work, play, story, protest, and ridicule songs. The *rara* or *Ra-Ra* is a street dance that is connected in particular with the celebration of Carnival. Some *rara* bands use whistles, drums, and conventional trumpets; others mainly, or even solely, varieties of the *vaccine*, an African-derived bamboo trumpet whose single note depends on the size of the instrument and which may be tapped with sticks as well as being blown.

A European influence is evident in the Haitian dance form of the *méringue*, related to the merengue of the neighboring Dominican Republic. It has two versions, both of them with French melodic elements, but with black musical elements as well. The salon version has traces of ragtime and a pattern of syncopated triplets, while the street version is more robustly rhythmical. Haitian conditions and circumstances have scarcely been congenial to the assimilation of musical innovations from elsewhere in the Black Diaspora. Yet there is what is locally called *mini-jazz*, which combines elements of other Diaspora rhythms and styles.

Both Martinique and Guadeloupe have engendered distinctive black musical forms. Martinique was the birthplace of the *biguine*—called the beguine in its Anglicized version. This became popular in Paris, where it was first recorded by an Antillean orchestra in 1929, and was then more widely popularized by Cole Porter's whitened treatment in his song of 1935, "Begin the Beguine." The black form has a rhythm of rapid triplets and has been described as a calypso-rumba.[29] In both islands, the nineteenth-century mazurka survives, but is often played with a basic beguine beat. In Guadeloupe, the waltz survives with an additional, different beat, provided by percussive instruments, to produce a more complex rhythmic effect.

During the seventies, there developed in both islands a new dance form in 2/4, played on electric instruments and called the *cadence*. Derived from the beguine, but with elements of calypso, *soca* (an amalgam of calypso and soul), merengue, and Zairean influence in the use of guitar and cymbal, it was soon enriched by individual musicians or groups.

Blacks in Britain have made their own musical contributions, notably in jazz, reggae, and rap. Courtney Pine (born in 1964), composer, bandleader, and instrumentalist (on the tenor and soprano saxophones and on the bass clarinet) took the initiative in combining the talents of black musicians for a 21-piece big band, Jazz Warriors, in 1985 and a smaller group, The World's First Saxophone Posse.

Any study, however ambitious, of the Black Diaspora's musical achievements is bound to omit much of value. A survey which is merely part of a work such as this can provide no more than a series of signposts. And any treatment of music that is limited to words must deal only with the body while leaving the life behind. This is a limitation especially frustrating in a work on the Diaspora, so much of whose life has been that of the music it has made. Indeed, of no other people may it be said that music has been so essential to its very existence, as none has given, in creativity and love, more to the life of music in return.

33 | THE INNOCENT EYE

～～～～～～～～～～～～～～～～～～～～～～～～～～～～

At various times and places within the reaches of the Diaspora, blacks have been central to creative developments in the fine arts of painting, sculpture, and architecture. They brought their individual insights and aptitudes to the sophisticated tradition of Western art. In the selective studies here, however, it is perhaps more relevant to concentrate on that distinctive force which blacks came to contribute in a form of artistic expression once commonly and often patronizingly called primitive. For the term was long applied to African art, however technically accomplished particular examples might be, as the art of supposedly primitive peoples.

It was in late-nineteenth-century France, at the advance posts of the sophisticated Western tradition, that so-called primitive art came to be considered not as the art of a people at a particular cultural level, but as a particular kind of art and one, moreover, which offered a creative alternative to a sophistication that seemed to have exhausted its possibilities. This is how E. H. Gombrich, the distinguished art historian, puts it in *The Story of Art*:

> In one of his letters from Tahiti, Gauguin had written that he felt he had to go back beyond the horses of the Parthenon, back to the rocking-horse of his childhood . . . Many artists feel that the museums and exhibitions are full of works of such amazing facility and skill that nothing is gained by continuing along these lines; that they are in danger of losing their souls and becoming slick manufacturers of paintings or sculptures unless they become as little children . . . Henri Rousseau (1844–1910) proved to them that far from being a way to salvation, the training of the professional painter may spoil his chances. For Rousseau knew nothing of correct draughtsmanship, nothing of the tricks of Impressionism. He painted with simple, pure colours and clear outlines, every single leaf of a tree and every blade of grass on a

lawn. And yet there is in his pictures, however awkward they may seem to the sophisticated mind, something so vigorous, simple and forthright that one must acknowledge him as a master.[1]

The wish of adult artists to become as little children does not mean that they can do so. Indeed, the very wish involves something of a contradiction in terms. "A complete lack of self-consciousness might be said to be the essential quality of primitive art."[2] Here, again, Henri Rousseau provides a perfect example. He believed that he was painting in the style of the academic artist Bouguereau, whose work he much admired. Instead, he was painting as his innocent eye told him to do.

However essential, the lack of self-consciousness is not, to be sure, enough. If it were, countless little children would be not only engaging but important artists. Other qualities—of natural skill, judgment, control, a sense of harmony and rhythm—provide the means by which a simplicity of vision is translated into art. In the United States, for instance, three black artists, born during the 1880s, possessed the vision and, without training, found their own way to express it.

William Edmondson (1882–1951) lived in Nashville, Tennessee, and at the age of fifty took to stonecutting. His sculpture *Eve*, a limestone figure 32 inches high, has the directness and charm of an artist who believes in his own miracles. As he said of his work: "This here stone and all those out there in the yard come from God. It's the work in Jesus speaking His mind in my mind. I must be one of His disciples. These here is miracles I can do. Can't nobody do these but me. I can't help carving. I just does it."[3]

Clementine Hunter, born in 1883 at Natchitoches, Louisiana, spent much of her life as a cotton picker and cook on the Melrose plantation. It was a place frequented by artists, and at some time during the 1930s she herself began painting. *The Funeral on Cane River*, a painting of hers from 1948, provides an impressive example of her style. The human figures and other shapes, in their broad, basic treatment, have the immediacy of childlike transmission, but there is nothing childlike in her muted and harmonious use of color or the processional rhythm of the total composition in which the animals and even the seemingly attentive church are made to share.

Horace Pippin (1888–1946) was already forty-three years old when he finished his first painting. Working until his death in his native West Chester, Pennsylvania, he took increasingly to depicting domestic scenes. Two of these, *Saturday Night Bath* and *Christmas Morning Breakfast*, both of them painted in 1945, have black subjects, in rooms with patterned areas, from floorboards and rugs and cloths, set off by the tinted white of the walls. They are so integrally composed that they seem to have leapt as they are from the vision of the artist; indeed, as Pippin himself once explained, "Pictures just come to my mind, and I tell my heart to go ahead."[4]

Such art ought not to be described as primitive at all, a term which begs more questions than it pretends to answer. Increasingly, indeed, it has come to be described instead as intuitive or naïve art. Yet perhaps the term "innocent" is closer to its spirit, as that of the eye which looks at life directly and with wonder, rather than through the glasses that society grinds in its cultural and, not least, its artistic discriminations. It is in this sense that the innocent way of seeing was created by the very exclusion of Diaspora blacks from the way of seeing which white racial dominance secured for itself.

In early 1943, there arrived in Haiti from the United States a watercolorist on a wartime assignment to promote the teaching of English. DeWitt Peters was puzzled to find little evidence of art "in a country of very great natural beauty, with a clarity of atmosphere comparable to that of southern Italy, inhabited by a charming people rich in folklore and tradition."[5] In the autumn, he was driving through the coastal village of Mont Rouis when he saw a painting of birds and flowers on the door of a bar. A nearby sign announced: ICI LE-RENAISSANCE (Here is the Rebirth).

Provided by the President of Haiti with a building, he established in the capital the Centre d'Art, which came to be a combination of art school, exhibition space, and sales facility. For the inaugural exhibition in May 1944, numerous paintings were collected. They had been brought or sent to Peters as reports rapidly spread that there was an American willing to pay, by the standards of Haitian poverty, large sums for such work. Peters remembered the painted door of the village bar. He tracked down the artist and invited him to the Centre.

Hector Hyppolite, born at St. Marc in 1894, was a *houngan*, a Voodoo priest, who had been painting for many years, mainly by decorating furniture, with brushes of chicken feathers and enamels of various colors. He duly came to the capital and established himself not at the Centre but in a hut near the waterfront. In January 1947 a UNESCO exhibition, which included some pictures of his, opened in Paris. Suddenly his painting and the existence of Haitian art were celebrated. He died in the following year, one of two masters in the first phase of a phenomenon.

His are visionary pictures, with an originality of style and an integrity of form which make supposed technical inadequacies irrelevant. *Ogoun and His Charger*, for instance, painted c. 1948, depicts the deity or spirit of war in such red ferocity that his horse, more behind than beneath him, seems a mere emanation.[6] In *Maîtresse Sirène*, painted c. 1946, the consort of the sea god is depicted in a simple, peasant-style red dress. She is seated in a boat which has flowers not only painted on its side but growing in profusion from each end, and which in turn is borne on the back of a bird-headed whale. The whole suggests a kind of maritime garden which is infused by the pleasure of her presence.

Not all his pictures are devoted to religious subjects, and few painters have combined to such effect the visionary with delight in the voluptuousness of the female form. In *une famme nur* (a nude woman), as the title is written on the picture, the subject, painted with remarkable economy of line, lies invitingly on a couch. Her two clothed attendants, the very carpet of flowers behind her, the three circular pictures above her head, and the decorative top corners of the painting that look like triangular curtains, all emphasize in different but harmonizing ways the curved rhythm of her naked form.[7]

Philomé Obin, the other master, painted his first picture in 1908 at the age of seventeen. During the thirty-six years that followed, he painted in his spare time from such employment as cutting hair or selling small packets of coffee, but rarely found a buyer for any of his pictures and never sold one for more than a dollar. When report of the new art center reached him in his northern hometown of Cap-Haïtien, he wrote, devout Protestant that he was, on his blackboard: "Dear God, the year 1944 was a bad one for Philomé Obin. Please try and make the year 1945 a better one for him." And he sent a painting to Peters.

His prayer was soon answered, as it deserved to be. For he had, of all the Haitian painters, a magic closest to that of Henri Rousseau, with a meticulousness intrinsic to his innocence. In his painting of 1961, *Les Bourgeois du Cap-Haïtien avant L'Occupation de 1915*, on the middle class of his hometown before the United States seized command of Haiti, every tile or corrugated iron ripple on the roofs of the houses lining the street, each distinguishing detail in the faces and fashionable dress of the mulattoes on their horses or in their carriages, is depicted. Color and line combine in a composition dominated by the triple-arched structure which serves here to symbolize the ascendancy of the mulattoes in front of it. The horses seem as proud as their mulatto owners, while the laden donkey, led by a peasant black woman with a basket on her head, has its head disconsolately dipped.[8]

Obin's output was considerable, as though recognition was all he had needed to release a long accumulation of artistic energy. He painted great events of the past. His picture of 1954, *Battle between the Cacos and the American Marines, 5 September 1915*, succeeds in conveying the ferocity of the conflict by the very contrast of the lush green setting depicted with Obin's customary precision of detail. He painted religious pictures, such as his 1949 *Crucifixion* for the Protestant Episcopal Cathedral of Ste. Trinité in Port-au-Prince, a mural dominated not only by Christ but by a large disembodied eye—the Eye of God—watching from the top left corner. He painted himself: as in 1959, sitting in his bedroom. He painted landscapes that glow with pleasure in the play of different colors, as in his picture of 1950, *Centenary of the Bridge at Haut du Cap*, with the red of the bridge, the green of the trees, the brown bodies of the boys swimming in the river, the blues of the water and the sky.

Philomé, it soon emerged, was not the only painter in the Obin family.

Senêque, his younger brother, was a less meticulous and graceful artist, but one with a forceful forthrightness of his own. His *1905*, for instance, a rural landscape painted c. 1953, is vibrant with color and vigorous with movement; the very clouds and houses appear to roll in harmony with the wood-laden cart.[9] Télémâque, Philomé's eldest son, painted delicate landscapes; Henri-Claude, his youngest, street scenes and narrative pictures; Antoine, in between, tender pictures of his father and himself at work together in the studio; and a nephew, Michel, pictures of urban life and historical battles.

The Haitian "Renaissance" was, however, much more than a matter of two masters and one gifted family. From the outset, there were other painters of unquestionable quality and individual vision. Rigaud Benoit, born at Port-au-Prince in 1911, worked as a shoemaker and taxi driver before being employed by Peters as a chauffeur at the arts center and becoming a painter himself. Recognition of his exceptional talent enabled him to command substantial sums for his pictures, yet he painted only a few of these each year until his death in 1986.[10] One of his earliest paintings, done in 1947, is the portrait of a woman, in a red dress and a green jacket, whose tiny hands and feet appear at first glance to be the product of misjudged perspective but are imaginatively subordinated to the dominance of her large face. This and the use of color, not only in the figure but around it, in the furniture and flowers, the floor and background wall, together make for an integral harmony that seems to have painted itself.

Castera Bazile, born at Jacmel in 1923, found work as a houseboy for Peters and was excited by what he saw at the arts center to become in 1945 a painter himself. In his relatively short life as an artist—he died in 1964 —he produced some remarkable pictures. His painting of 1963, *Peasant Family*, has a tiny male, depicted as a naked adult instead of as a baby, suckling at the breast of the mother, from whose knee hangs a tiny girl in a shift, while the father, his eyes closed, rests his head hopelessly in one of his hands. It has its own intuitive logic which reveals, as no amount of mere technical competence could have done, the essence of Haitian poverty.

Wilson Bigaud, born in 1931 to a poor family in Port-au-Prince, was fifteen years old when Hyppolite saw some of his work and invited him to become an apprentice. In 1950, he painted *Murder in the Jungle*, a picture bought in the following year by the New York Museum of Modern Art. It is the product of an artist who has already reached a high level of technical skill yet conveys a sense of horror that is "primitive" only in its directness. There is a similar quality in *La Ronde* (The Circle), painted in 1953, where young girls move in a ring among their shadows and seem to be clinging rather than joined with clasped hands to one another and to be fleeing rather than dancing together.[11] In 1958, while still in his twenties, he suffered a series of nervous breakdowns, from which he emerged, during the sixties, to continue painting, but with a clouded vision and a hand that seemed to have lost its certainty. The innocent eye is not necessarily a joyful one.

Nor was painting the only form that flourished. Happening to visit the local cemetery at Croix-des-Bouquets, a village some fifteen miles from Port-au-Prince, DeWitt Peters was struck by the artistry of various iron crosses based on the Voodoo *vévérs*, the ceremonial designs traced in flour on the floor. Inquiry led him to the maker, Georges Liautaud, who had been born in 1899 and was working as a blacksmith in the village.

Encouraged by Peters to extend his range, Liautaud was soon making two-dimensional figures, marvelous with movement, from the flattened steel of old oil drums. They came in their metal immediacy from the same sort of eye that saw elsewhere in the colors of paint. He was soon selling his pieces to European and American museums, and his sculptures influenced other Haitians toward exploring the possibilities of the form. One artist, Murat Briérre, took to joining the flat figures for dramatic compositions in a style wholly his own.

It is not misleading to speak of successive generations in Haitian art, since generations overlap. Indeed, there has been no interruption to the continuity of such art from the initial quickening, and some of those who were part of this first impulse were still creatively engaged decades later, after a broadly classifiable second generation of artists and even a third had emerged.

Notable among those of the second was Gérard Valcin, born in the forties and a tile setter by trade, who brought to his paintings a corresponding sense of design along with a lush use of color. His *Coumbite* of 1971, whose subject is a communal planting rite conducted to the accompaniment of Voodoo music, lovingly depicts every leaf in receding rows of gradually lightening greens, which surround the rhythmic lines of musicians and laborers.

Probably the most celebrated of this generation has been André Pierre, who was working as a *la-place*, an assistant to a Voodoo priest, in Croix-des-Missions, near Port-au-Prince, when his painted half-gourds for use in certain ceremonies attracted interest and then patronage from a researcher into Voodoo. He became a painter of Voodoo subjects and in particular the deities, whom he has said he always consults in his work and depicts only when they have expressed a wish for him to do so.[12] His pictures are, according to the knowledgeable, complex with Voodoo lore, but certainly do not require such knowledge to be appreciated as visions in artistic form. They glow with rich colors—violet, gold, various greens and blues—along with a dramatic use of pure black and pure white, and have a flowing line in their composition, as in the painting of c. 1964, *Maîtresse la Sirène of the Sweet Waters*.

He was one evident heir to Hyppolite among the visionaries to whose art Voodoo was central. He came to be joined by another, of the third generation. Lafortune Félix began painting only in the late seventies, yet his *Mambo with Flowers and Sacramental Offerings* of 1980 already reveals a natural artistry in the command of its material. Employing acrylic paints, he juxtaposes soft and strong colors, to achieve a remarkable sense of depth (as in

Houngan with Black Pig) or an impression of emanating light (as in *Houngan with Centaur*).

Haitian art, phenomenal for both the number and the quality of the artists involved, is scarcely to be altogether explained by the existence of an international market for it, since such is as much a consequence as a cause. More significantly, the isolation of literature from the popular language, as of music from the facilities and transmissions available elsewhere in the Diaspora, has contributed to making the visual arts the predominant form of artistic creativity and communication. Yet there does also seem to be a further factor, a subterranean flow of insights and sensibilities that draws from a distant source. In African sculpture, as has been noted earlier, the ratio of head to body is traditionally 1:3 or 1:4, rather than the naturalistic ratio of 1:6 or 1:7 which is accordingly employed in the sophisticated European tradition.[13] This concern with expressionist rather than representational form is one to which the Benoit portrait of a woman seems to point.

The flowering of the visual arts in Jamaica has certain parallels with that in Haiti. It was in Jamaica, too, that the arrival and intervention of a particular person served to quicken a virtually barren expanse, arid with colonial culture. Having married a Jamaican, Edna Manley, a British sculptor, arrived expecting to encounter vital forms of indigenous art. She was soon declaring her disappointment:

> Who are the creative painters, sculptors and engravers, and where is the work which should be expressions of its country's existence and growth? A few anaemic imitators of European traditions, a few charming parlour tricks, and then practically silence. Nothing virile, nor original, nor in any sense creative, and nothing, above all, that is an expression of the deep-rooted, hidden pulse of the country—that thing which gives it its unique life.[14]

As in Haiti, it was not that there were no practicing artists, but that they needed to be discovered and encouraged, for their own creativity to become more confident, and for the stimulation of others. The first significant figure to surface was a "primitive" or, in the term which Jamaicans prefer, an intuitive painter and sculptor.

John Dunkley (1891–1947) had been painting in his spare time for seven years when a visitor to his barber's shop, impressed by the painted screens there, brought them to Edna Manley's attention. At her prompting and with her help, Dunkley successfully submitted pictures for exhibition abroad as well as in Jamaica, but he remained poor, since he painted few and usually refused to sell them, in the hope that they would one day form the basis of an art museum for the people.[15]

At his death, he left only forty-five pictures, some of them unfinished. All but a very few are infused with a disturbing force. Greens and grays predominate, along with the black of shadow or night and the use of white mainly for such light as seems to come from the moon. Plants, insects, birds, people are depicted as somehow menacing or menaced. In *The Tennis Player*, for instance, the subject seems almost under siege from the encroaching dark and the huge plants reaching over the tubelike palings of the fence. In *Path*, the subject leads from foliage and the gaping ends of lopped trunks or branches through the dark into the darker distance. Among the exceptions is a picture that suggests a distant African influence. Inscribed *Diamond Wedding*, it depicts the huge heads of an evidently embracing couple, in a heart-shaped setting of foliage above a wall.

Over the years that followed, a number of artists emerged and, often with help from Edna Manley, acquired the technical skill necessary to develop their own styles within the sophisticated tradition. Others were true intuitives. Amongst these was Mallica Reynolds (born in 1911), or Kapo as he came to call himself, a Christian Revivalist who brought to many of his carvings a devotional intensity. Then, during the sixties, he turned increasingly to painting, the form in which he had begun. Selden Rodman, the historian of Haitian art, while dismissing Kapo's sculptures, held him to be "as a painter . . . probably equal to the late Hector Hyppolite of Haiti."[16]

Certainly, Kapo shares with Hyppolite a mastery of line that can convey both the forceful and the serene, with a corresponding use of color. *Kubalee*, painted in 1972, is expressive of revivalist excitement, with its central circular rhythm. His *Silent Night* of 1979 puts the manger and its immediate attendants in the bottom right-hand corner of the painting, while the remainder is devoted to a flower-decked hillside township of houses all seemingly rapt in awe.

Gaston Tabois (born 1931) was only in his twenties when he made his mark with his intuitive paintings, such as his *Road Menders* of 1956, in which every stone laid on the road is there, along with every leaf in the succulent countryside, behind the dominant steamroller. Sidney McLaren (born 1895) worked as a coach builder, was already in his sixties before he taught himself to paint, and then produced pictures of street scenes in which cars and buses are depicted in cherishing detail. Clinton Brown (born 1954), a Rastafarian, brought an explosive force to his intuitive paintings, as in his *Morant Bay Rebellion* of 1975.

Among the intuitive sculptors, William Joseph (born 1919) might have sprung directly from the tradition of African carving, with his simplified emphatic forms, such as his *Figure* of 1980 and his *Babu* of 1981, where the apparently distorted proportions are essential to their aesthetic authority. In some of his work, such as his *Bob Jones* of 1983, he seems, indeed, to have arrived naturally at the traditional African sculptural ratio of head to body.

Most Brazilian black artists worked within the sophisticated tradition of

Western art, which some of them enriched with their own aptitudes. There were also those, however, who were either "primitives" or who brought to their art "primitive" elements of immediacy and innocence. One such borderline case, as long ago as the eighteenth century, was Leandro Joaquim, who was born in Rio de Janeiro, recorded as being "short, fat and brown-skinned,"[17] and died in 1798. Little else is known about him, except for the name of his teacher; that he assisted in the design and painting of backdrops and sets for the theater, presented an unexecuted architectural project for a midwives' home; and painted a number of pictures. These include the earliest landscapes and seascapes done by a Brazilian professional painter. They bear a certain resemblance to the paintings of Canaletto with their pleasure in light and the many little figures set against buildings and monuments or crowded in boats. Yet there is also a special quality, part playfulness, part wide-eyed wonder, in such pictures of Joaquim's as his *Vista do Aqueduta de Santa Teresa* (View of the St. Teresa Aqueduct) and *Pesca de baleia na Baía de Guanabara* (Whaling in Guanabara Bay).

Antônio Francisco Lisboa (1738–1814), who came to be known as Aleijadinho (Little Cripple) from his deformities, was born in Minas Gerais to a Portuguese father and a black mother. Effectively self-taught, he developed into an architect and sculptor of striking originality and power, all in the service of religious art. His most famous building, the Church of St. Francis of Assisi at Ouro Prêto, combines the traditional Portuguese rectangular style with carved wall sections, cylindrical bulb-topped towers, and ornamental stone reliefs on the façade, for a particular complex harmony like no other in colonial Brazilian or, indeed, European religious architecture of the age. This was the art of innocence in building, careless of convention and creative with an integrity all its own.

The central medallion at the front, of St. Francis, has an affinity with that European primitivism that preceded the Renaissance and informs the stone decorative carvings of Gothic architecture. There is a similar Gothic quality in the wooden carving of the medallion on the sufferings of the prophet Jeremiah, at the altar of St. John the Baptist in the Church of Our Lady of Carmo in Ouro Prêto. Yet there is also in Lisboa's work here a forcefulness of expression that has an affinity with African sculpture.

The end of the slave trade did not cut the living connection with African art. Bahia, the region with the highest proportion of blacks in Brazil, sustained an extensive trade with Africa, especially the West Coast, long after the last slave had been landed. The corresponding availability of African carvings and metalwork in the region inhibited the development of local artistic production there. By the beginning of this century, however, as the trade with Africa diminished and the Afro-Brazilian Candomblé religion thrived, it was local artists who supplied the market. In the Museum of Anthropology and Ethnology at the University of São Paulo are cult and other objects of

Bahian provenance which have an evident African artistic derivation but with a distinctive workmanship and beauty.

A specific popular art in the region was the carving of the *carranca* or figurehead to adorn the bows of boats which plied the São Francisco River from roughly 1880 until the 1950s. One Bahian artist came to dominate the form, Francisco Biquiba de Lafuente Guarany, who was born in 1882 of mixed black, white, and indigenous Indian ancestry. He was still working in his 97th year, and died, aged 103, in 1985. Many of his shapes are of animals, some of them fantastic, from the neck upward; others are of humans, upward from the waist; and each has an integrity that derives not from the real world but from Guarany's imagination.

Another Bahian sculptor, the black Agnaldo Manoel dos Santos, was born in 1926 on the island of Itaparica and died, at the age of 35, in 1962. Taken up by Guarany, who taught him how to select the most suitable wood for carving and whose figureheads excited him to carve some of his own, he was more directly influenced by African sculptural forms and by the cult of Candomblé. Some of his best pieces, indeed, are sculptures of cult deities; but these, no less than his secular works, such as his variations on the theme of *Mulher Acocorada* (Squatting Woman), are vigorous with his own innocent vision.

In Minas Gerais, Artur Pereira, born there in 1920, has specialized in complex carvings, such as his rhythmic *Sem Título* (Without Title), a hollow cylinder of crouching, prowling, climbing, sitting animals, and in his *Presépio* (Nativity), which has the sure innocent touch in the inclusion of animals with angels on the wooden cloud. In Minas Gerais, too, José de Pádua Lisboa, known as Zézinho Julião, with seven of his nine sons and his brother comprise a collective of carvers celebrated as the Julião Family. From them have come numerous wood sculptures of individual animals, such as the captivatingly contemplative lion (*Leão*), or groups, such as *A Montanha* (The Mountain), which is a cylindrical composition in wood of animals on a stylized tree, only eighty-two centimeters (thirty-two inches) in real height but seeming to be hugely higher through the magic of giving the animals' heads a downward tilt.

Gabriel Joaquim dos Santos, born in 1892 at São Pedro in the state of Rio de Janeiro, merged sculpture and architecture in creating a house and garden mainly from a multitude of discarded objects, as unlikely as car headlights and soft-drink bottles. Flowers, made from bits of white and blue plates, tile and seashells, line the steps in the garden and decorate the walls of what he called his *Casa da Flor* (Flower House), which is set in the slope of a hill and merges into the natural environment. The doors face east, to greet the sunrise; the single window faces west, to watch the sunset; and the bed is so situated as to escape at all times of the day the shafts of the sun. The whole is a work of art unique in its concept, though one related to the integral view of humanity and nature in the African culture with which the artist identified himself.[18]

The Flower House is a world away from those palatial shopping centers that are the pride of Brazilian urban progress and from a public architecture which even at its most impressive, as in the government buildings of Brasília, proclaims the isolation of power from people. Among all that the dominant culture of Brazil is discarding, in its commitment to keep up with the rich white world in manic materialism and environmental mayhem, the innocent eye is simply dismissed as blind. Yet where so much life and beauty has been turned into detritus, it is only such supposed blindness that may be capable of turning detritus into beauty and life.

Some form of communication was needed between master and slave, if only to convey commands or to elicit information. As at other times and in other circumstances, this need was met by what is called pidgin, a makeshift new language derived from an existing one, whose syntax is simplified and whose basic vocabulary is adapted to the purpose.

Derived from one or other language of mastery, English or French, Spanish or Portuguese or Dutch, and sometimes from a mingling as one imperialism gave place to another, the various pidgins of slavery were also used by slaves from different African speech communities to communicate among themselves. In the process, these pidgins incorporated words and constructions from African languages, to develop a more complex character. Yet they initially remained merely acquired second languages, with corresponding limits to their development. It was when the slaves bore children that these, speaking a particular pidgin as their first or only language, began more substantially to expand its possibilities of expression. In Louisiana and the French West Indies, this language of the slaves came to be called *créole*, from the French word meaning "indigenous." Stripped of the accent, it is the term now applied in English as well to a pidgin that has developed into "the first language of a speech-community."[1]

Such creoles are still today the first languages of many blacks in the Diaspora. Each has developed along its own lines. Yet those derived from the same European language, however distant geographically these may be, resemble one another more closely than they do the standard language of their derivation. The creole known as Gombo, for instance, still spoken in Louisiana today by the descendants of the slaves, is so different from the two forms of French spoken there that speakers of either form[2] and speakers of Gombo are unintelligible to each other, while speakers of Gombo and of other French-derived creoles in the hemisphere, such as those of Haiti,

Guadeloupe, and French Guiana, understand one another easily enough. The same holds true for the family of English-derived creoles, such as those of Barbados, Jamaica, and Guyana.

Surinam has two of these, with a difference from others and between them. One, called Taki-Taki, Nengre Tongo (Negro Language) or Sranan Tongo (Surinamese Language), has numerous words in it taken from the Dutch of the imperial power which took control of the territory in 1667. The other, known as Saramacca, is spoken by the people of that name, otherwise known as "Bush Negroes," descended from the slaves who absconded from their English-speaking masters and took their English-based pidgin into the interior with them. Both creoles retain certain words, such as *grandi* (large) and *pasá* (pass), from an earlier Portuguese-based pidgin. On the islands of Aruba, Bonaire, and Curaçao, the creole called Papiamentu is descended from two different pidgins or earlier creoles, one based on Portuguese and the other mainly on Spanish, with later borrowings from Dutch.

The linguistic changes involved in the development first of pidgins and then of creoles were not haphazard but informed by the functioning of certain rules whose fundamental dynamic was one of simplification. This included the facility of pronunciation. One or more consonants in a cluster might accordingly be dropped: as in the Haitian creole *zòt*, for the standard French *vous autres* (you others); or, in Jamaican creole, with the discarding of the initial consonant, as in *plít* for "split" or *kwíiz* for "squeeze."

Simplification was most marked in grammar. Haitian creole, for instance, abandoned all differences of number, person, and tense within the verb itself—a delight for those who have struggled with standard French conjugations, especially of the abundant irregular verbs. Thus, *bivè* for the standard French *boire* (to drink) and its various forms (*boi-*, *boiv-*, *bu-*) with all their various endings (*je bois*, "I drink"; *nous boirons*, "we will drink") stays the same, whatever the subject who drinks or the time of the drinking. Instead, there is the use of prefixes to indicate person and the particular aspect of action, whether continuing or completed. So, *n-* indicates the first person plural and *fèk* the completed process in *n-fèk-bivè* (we drank). Other prefixes may indicate tense by being placed somewhere in the predicate: *t(e)* for past; *a-*, *ava-*, or *va* for future; and a combination for the conditional. "He would be able" may be translated into Haitian creole as *li t-a-kapab*; *li* (he) *t-* (has) *a-* (will or will be) *kapab* (able).

What is involved here is a remarkable marriage of structure and word from different language families. The usage of aspectual prefixes for verbs derives from West African languages, though the forms of the prefixes derive from French elements. In Yoruba, *mo ti waa* is the equivalent of "I have come." The Haitian creole prefix *t(e)* to indicate action in the past comes, however, not from the Yoruba *ti* but from the French *était* for "was" or *été* for "been."

Similarly, the prefix *fèk*, for the aspect of completion, derives from the French *ne fait que* ("does only") and its variant, *fèk-rēk*,[3] from the French *ne fait rien que* ("does nothing but"), while the prefix for the continuing aspect, *ap(r)(e)*, comes from the French *après* ("after"). This last usage has an interesting parallel in the Anglo-Irish construction, as in "he's after eating" (he is engaged in eating). The prefix *a-*, *ava-*, or *va-* to indicate the future also has a West African linguistic equivalent in the Ewe *(a)va*, but again is actually derived from the French *va* for "is going (to)."[4]

Creoles also simplified syntax by dispensing with the prepositions essential in the standard European languages. A mere series of nouns and pronouns, for instance, may express possession without the use of a special word to indicate this, as in the Haitian creole *pòt kaj māmā li* (door house mother he) which means "the door of his mother's house." A verb, too, can be used in such simplified constructions, as in the Haitian creole *tā ašte tol* (time buy iron), whose equivalent in standard French would be *des temps pour acheter de tôle ondulée*, "time to buy corrugated iron."

One word order which is common to creoles but which has no basis in the European languages from which they were derived is similar to constructions in West African languages such as Ewe and Wolof. This positions the definite article (English "the") or demonstrative one (English "this" or "that") after the noun or even after a long series of nouns along with a verb. In Haitian creole, for instance, the equivalent of "the three pairs of black shoes which my father bought for me at Port-au-Prince" would be *twa* (three) *pè* (pair) *sulje* (shoe) *nwa* (black) *pap-m* (father-I) *te-ašte-m* (prefix for the completed aspect-buy-I) *Pòt-o-Prēs a* (the) *jo* (pluralizing word). In Jamaican creole, the phrase "his teeth" would be *hím tíit dem*, with the pluralizing demonstrative at the end.

Another word order probably derived from West African languages, which have similar constructions, involves successive verbs of motion to express an act, as in the Sranan Tongo (Surinamese Language) *ju mu tjári ju gón kóm* (you must carry your gun come—i.e., you must bring your gun) or in the Jamaican creole *I will carry you go* (I will bring you). Yet another is the use, as in West African languages, of a verb meaning "pass" or "surpass" to express a comparison, instead of the "more . . . than" in English or the *plus . . . que* in French. "She is uglier than you" becomes in Haitian creole *li lèd pase u* (she ugly surpass you); "my boy is older than my girl" becomes in the creole of Martinique *gasō mwē grā pas fi mwē* (in standard French, *mon garçon est plus grand que ma fille*).[5]

These examples merely touch on the differences in syntax of richly independent languages from that of the standard languages to which they are related. Similarly, a few examples of the difference in vocabulary can be no more than suggestive of languages which have grown from others to lead productive lives of their own.

Some words have been imported unchanged from West African languages. In Jamaican creole, for instance, *fufu* (mashed starch vegetables), *nyam-nyam* (food), and *kas-kas* (quarrel) come directly from Twi. The duplication of words, often to qualify or alter their meaning, is itself a usage taken from West African languages and may be directed into making new words from standard European ones. Jamaican creole has such examples as *was-was* for "wasp" and *mata-mata* for "pus." In Haitian creole, *tire-tire*, meaning "shoot repeatedly," comes from the standard French root in *tirer*, "to shoot."

Other words, brought from West African languages, have acquired new forms and meanings from the Diaspora experience, to enter the standard European languages with new forms and meanings again. The Haitian creole word *zōbi* (zombi), for instance, may have come from *nsumbi*, the word for "devil" in one of the Congo area languages,[6] or from *zumbi*, a West African word for "fetish."[7] Either way, it developed its creole meaning from Voodoo belief in the existence of a human soul, neither alive nor dead, subjected to the power of a sorcerer. As symbolic of the slave condition, this could scarcely be bettered. Its subsequent entry into standard English as "a corpse revived by witchcraft" and, colloquially, "a dull or apathetic person"[8] has lost in the process the particular power of the historical charge. Another example of such transition began with the West African Wolof word *jug*, which meant "to lead a disorderly life." This emerged in Gullah, the creole spoken by blacks in parts of Georgia and South Carolina, with the word *juk-haws*, juke house, for a disorderly house or brothel, and thence to enter American and subsequently all standard English in the word "jukebox."

Creoles have, however, done more than borrow words, sometimes to alter their meanings. They have invented them, by sound or sight associations and as metaphors. In Jamaican creole, for instance, a *chi-chi bus* is one whose doors hiss when operated by compressed air; *tufe* or *tefe* is a word for spitting; *heng-'pon-nail* is the word for ready-made clothes, often displayed like this in shops; *fingle* means to handle or fondle; a *sabbat-foot* is a lame or deformed foot that can do no work, as on the Sabbath; and *chew-water* is the word for thin soup.[9]

Yet for all their vitality, creole languages tend to be despised and dismissed by many in their very homelands, as the speech of the poor and uneducated. Those who are socially elevated, or at least wish to be thought so, avoid speaking creole except to people who would otherwise not understand them; they themselves expect to be addressed wherever possible in the standard language. A bus conductor in Kingston, Jamaica, for instance, will greet a passenger of apparently appropriate class by the invitation "Please step up," with "sir," "madam," or "miss" appropriately added, while instructing a passenger of apparently lower degree, *Me tell unu say step up.*[10]

Nowhere is the social degradation of creole more evident than in Haiti, where French has for so long been the language of culture and control, though commonly spoken by little more than 10 percent of the population, and where scarcely 15 percent of the rest have a working knowledge of the language. Indeed, though virtually the entire population knows creole— those born into the elite generally learn it in childhood from those employed to look after them—the language does not have a written form in widespread use among the highly educated, let alone the populace. One Haitian poet, Leon Laleau, has voiced the deprivation involved:

> This obsessed Heart, which does not correspond
> To my language and my clothing,
> And upon which bite, like a clamp,
> Borrowed emotions and customs
> From Europe—do you feel the suffering
> And the despair, equal to none other,
> Of taming, with words from France,
> This heart which came to me from Senegal?[11]

The scorn of creole by French-speakers in Haiti is answered by creole-speakers with a corresponding scorn of French. For them, creole is the vehicle of truth and honorable dealings, and French is the vehicle of deviousness and duplicity. *Se kreol m-ap-pale ave-u, wi?* (I am speaking creole to you, yes?) means "I am speaking directly and honestly to you, am I not?" *Pale frāse* (to speak French) means "to offer money as a bribe." *L-ap-māde šarite ā-frāse* (he is asking for charity in French) means "he is borrowing money with the promise but not the intention of repaying it." In Jamaica, Louise Bennett, better known as "Miss Lou," took her own stand in asserting the dignity of creole by writing her popular poetry in it.

More influential in making its mark on literature has been what may be described as a creolized form of the standard language. Such is Black English, spoken most widely by blacks in the United States, which is closer to English than to creole but has creole words and grammatical constructions, so that it bears a certain family resemblance to the English-based creoles of the Caribbean. Two examples may suffice to indicate both the differences and the resemblances. The standard-English question "where is he?" would be *where he is?* in Black English and *we-i de?* in Jamaican creole; the question "what does he do?" would be *what he do?* in Black English and *wa im do?* in Jamaican creole.[12]

The very closeness to standard form produces difficulties which the more distant creole, recognizably a different language, does not. J. L. Dillard provides in his book *Black English* a factual illustration of the misunderstandings that may develop from the different meaning attached to a word by a speaker of Black English and a speaker of the standard language. Told that he was being served with a restraining order by police in Dallas, a black man ran away. "They's goin' to strain me," he subsequently explained. Since the initial unstressed syllable in "restrain" was not part of his language, he assumed that the word was "strain," which, in Black English, means "beat."

Black children may score badly in linguistically based IQ tests at school, not because they are unintelligent but because they are intelligent in their own form of the standard language. Such a child may, for instance, fail to identify as incomplete the sentence, "He riding a horse," since this is the usual way of making the statement in Black English. As Dillard comments: "It is no more a disgrace to make a low score on the other man's test than it is to lose money playing poker with the other fellow's deck of cards."[13]

An acquaintance with one or other creole affords an easy passage to some of the patterns in Black English usage. There is the same simplification of the verb by the abandonment of variant endings, as in "he run" and "he go yesterday." There is the use of "done" to express the completed action, as in "I done go." There are verbal aspects which convey differences of meaning that can be expressed only more laboriously in standard English. "He workin' when de boss come in," for instance, means that he was working, perhaps to pretend that he had been doing so all the time, just when the boss arrived; while "he be workin' when de boss come in" means that he had been working before and, when the boss arrived, was still doing so.[14]

Relative pronouns may be omitted altogether. Dillard cites the sentence he overheard in Greenwich Village: "That's the chick I keep tellin' you about got all that money." Where they are not omitted, the all-purpose "what" may serve for the various forms in the standard language. Black English also has a more complex negative structure than either the standard language or associated creoles. There are three negators—dit'n, don' and ain'—as well as the use of double negatives, as in "it ain' no use me workin' so hard"; "you don' get no more from me"; and "he dit'n give me no money." More haphazard is the factor of "over-correction" or "fancifying" under the misapplied influence of the standard language. The wrong form of "to be" may come to be used, as in "he am sleeping" and "I wants"; or a superfluous ending added to any verb, as in "a li'l cullud chu'ch what de massas an' missuses in San 'Tone done builted."[15]

Black writers in the United States have used Black English in the context of the standard language to dramatic effect.

Zora Neale Hurston's novel *Their Eyes Were Watching God* was first published in 1937. Near the beginning, the protagonist, Janie, newly returned to her home village, walks past a group of spectators who constitute a kind of Chorus.

"What she doin' coming back here in dem overalls? Can't she find no dress to put on?—Where's dat blue satin dress she left here in?—Where all dat money her husband took and died and left her?—What dat ole forty year ole

'oman doin' wid her hair swingin' down her back lak some young girl?—
Where she left dat young lad of a boy she went off here wid?—Thought she
was going to marry?—Where he left her?—What he done wid all her
money?—Betcha he off wid some gal so young she ain't even got no hairs—
Why she don't stay in her class?"[16]

The novel, which then goes back in time to the events and the experiences
behind the answers to such questions, is about a woman's discovery and
assertion of her sexuality. This was daring enough, in theme and treatment,
for a woman writer in the 1930s; but the novel is also about a woman's right
to control her own life and in particular a black woman's right to do so, in
a society where the black woman is at the bottom of the heap. Janie's
grandmother, who raised her, raised in the process the young girl's sights.

"Ah raked and scraped and bought dis lil piece uh land so you wouldn't
have to stay in de white folks' yard and tuck yo' head befo' other chillun at
school. Dat was all right when you was little. But when you got big enough
to understand things, Ah wanted you to look upon yo'self. Ah don't want yo'
feathers always crumpled by folks throwin' up things in yo' face. And Ah can't
die easy thinkin' maybe de menfolks white or black is makin' a spit cup outa
you: Have some sympathy fuh me. Put me down easy, Janie, Ah'm a cracked
plate."[17]

Both cited passages are in Black English. Both are in markedly rhythmic
prose, and the second is vivid with metaphor. The words are Hurston's, but
she owes much to the welling of rhythm and metaphor in black speech.
What she owes only to herself, though perhaps with some influence from
novelists such as Jane Austen, George Eliot, and Henry James, is the dramatic
development of her theme through the consciousness of her protagonist.
The disaster of Janie's marriage to the propertied Joe Starks is correspondingly
explored. When he is elected mayor of the local black community, one of
those gathered to celebrate the occasion invites "uh few words uh encouragement from Mrs. Mayor Starks."

The burst of applause was cut short by Joe taking the floor himself.
"Thank yuh fuh yo' compliments, but mah wife don't know nothin' 'bout
no speech-makin'. Ah never married her for nothin' lak dat. She's uh woman
and her place is in de home."
Janie made her face laugh after a short pause, but it wasn't too easy. She
had never thought of making a speech, and didn't know if she cared to make
one at all. It must have been the way Joe spoke out without giving her a
chance to say anything one way or another that took the bloom off of things.
But anyway, she went down the road behind him that night feeling cold.[18]

His demand for her submission and her refusal to concede it wear away
what remains of their relationship. "The spirit of the marriage left the bedroom and took to living in the parlor. It was there to shake hands whenever
company came to visit, but it never went back inside the bedroom again."[19]

The culmination comes one day when Joe, in front of the Chorus-like
visitors to the store he owns, provokes Janie with a remark on her age and
looks. She responds defiantly, and he continues in kind, till she decisively
humiliates him.

> "Naw, Ah ain't no young gal no mo' but den Ah ain't no old woman
> neither. Ah reckon Ah looks mah age too. But Ah'm uh woman every inch
> of me, and Ah know it. Dat's a whole lot more'n *you* kin say. You big-bellies
> round here and put out a lot of brag, but 'tain't nothin' to it but yo' big voice.
> Humph! Talkin' 'bout *me* lookin' old! When you pull down yo' britches, you
> look lak de change uh life."
>
> "Great God from Zion!" Sam Watson gasped. "Y'all really playin' de dozens
> tuhnight."
>
> "Wha—whut's dat you said?" Joe challenged, hoping his ears had fooled
> him.
>
> "You heard her, you ain't blind," Walter taunted.
>
> "Ah ruther be shot with tacks than tuh hear dat 'bout mahself," Lige Moss
> commiserated.
>
> Then Joe Starks realized all the meanings and his vanity bled like a flood.[20]

Joe dies soon afterwards—Janie had noted before that there was "something
dead about him"—and Janie, a rich widow now, finds her fulfillment with
Tea Cake, a much younger man, whose own death provides the second
climax of the plot. The novel returns to its beginning and ends rhapsodically.

> The kiss of his memory made pictures of love and light against the wall.
> Here was peace. She pulled in her horizon like a great fish-net. Pulled it from
> around the waist of the world and draped it over her shoulder. So much of
> life in its meshes! She called in her soul to come and see.[21]

Like Hurston before her, Paule Marshall has drawn with her imagination
on the black and especially the black woman's experience in the United
States. But, born in Barbados and taken to the United States as a child by
her immigrant parents, she draws as well on the Caribbean black experience.

Her first novel, *Brown Girl, Brownstones*, published in 1959, concerns a
Bajan family, along with the wider Bajan community, settled in New York
City. The protagonist is the young girl Selina, whose mother Silla, strong-
willed and forceful, upholds the Bajan values of hard work, thrift, respectability, and whose father, Deighton, is errant, feckless, drifting with dreams.

Early in the novel, Silla and Deighton have one of their quarrels, in the Bajan Black English that Marshall uses to such dramatic effect.

"Wait!" Her voice impaled him. "You put aside anything this week toward the down payment of the house?"

"Not penny one!" he cried and wanted to wind his arms tight around his head to shut out her voice, wanted suddenly to strike her into silence.

Silla's wrath broke and she whirled from the sink, her voice flailing across the kitchen. "You mean it all gone on fancy silk shirt and shoes and cater-wauling with your concubine."

He shrugged at the old accusation. "You's God; you must know."

Suddenly her anger was tempered by bewilderment. "But be-Jesus Christ, what kind of man is yuh, nuh?" She jerked her head away and seemed to address someone else in the room. "But what kind of man he is, nuh? Here every Bajan is saving if it's only a dollar a week and buying house and he wun save a penny. He ain got nothing and ain looking to get nothing."[22]

It is Ina, Silla's other daughter and so unlike her, who takes the Bajan route to security and respect through marriage. Selina wonders at her sister's joylessness:

Wasn't Edgar Innis what she wanted: neat, cautious, Barbadian, light-skinned, so that the women at the wedding couldn't accuse her of not trying to lighten up the family? Why this apathy, when marrying Edgar would mean a mild happiness and a retreat? Did Ina glimpse the sad tinge to that happiness—in the sanctioned embrace two nights a week, the burgeoning stomach, the neat dark children, the modest home on Long Island, the piano lessons to the neighbors' children and church each Sunday—the slow blurring of the self, the steady attrition of the soul over all those long complacent years?[23]

Selina, who resists all that her mother wants for her and who turns down a scholarship to study medicine funded by the Bajan community, is finally reconciled to her, as they recognize their likeness to each other:

"Everybody used to call me Deighton's Selina but they were wrong. Because you see I'm truly your child. Remember how you used to talk about how you left home as a girl of eighteen and was your own woman? I used to love hearing that. And that's what I want. I want it!"

Silla's pained eyes searched her adamant face, and after a long time a wistfulness softened her mouth . . .

"G'long," she said finally with a brusque motion. "G'long! You was always too much woman for me anyway, soul. And my own mother did say two head-bulls can't reign in a flock. G'long!" Her hand sketched a sign that was both a dismissal and a benediction. "If I din dead yet, you and your foolishness can't kill muh now!"[24]

Invisible Man, Ralph Ellison's novel published in 1952, explores with a cutlass of comedy the racial experience, and uses Black English to particular effect in his ironic contrast with those, black as well as white, who speak the standard language. Early on, the young protagonist, ensconced at a Southern black college, is required to take its visiting white benefactor, the elderly Mr. Norton, for a drive. Sighting the log cabin of a black sharecropper, Jim Trueblood, he tries to blunt the benefactor's interest in it by disclosing that Trueblood has committed incest with his daughter. This only, however, incites the benefactor to insist that he hear the story from Trueblood himself. Trueblood duly obliges and ends his account:

> "Things got to happenin' right off. The nigguhs up at the school come down to chase me off and that made me mad. I went to see the white folks then and they gave me help. That's what I don't understand. I done the worse thing a man could ever do in his family and instead of chasin' me out of the county, they gimme more help than they ever give any other colored man, no matter how good a nigguh he was. Except that my wife an' daughter won't speak to me, I'm better off than I ever been before. And even if Kate won't speak to me she took the new clothes I brought her from up in town and now she's gettin' some eyeglasses made what she been needin' for so long. But what I don't understand is how I done the worse thing a man can do in his own family and 'stead of things gittin' bad, they got better. The nigguhs up at the school don't like me, but the white folks treats me fine."[25]

The benefactor, long obsessed with his own daughter, then proves the point by presenting Trueblood with a hundred-dollar bill. The need of whites to believe in the perversity of blacks in order to excuse their own has nowhere been more craftily put. *Invisible Man* has about it those qualities which James Baldwin attributes to jazz and especially the blues: "something tart and ironic, authoritative and double edged."[26]

Edward Brathwaite from Barbados employs English, standard and in various Diaspora black forms, with African languages, the rhythms of black music and the imagery of black culture, from Africa as well as the Diaspora, for poetry that ranges across the historical and contemporary black experience. Three cycles of poems—*Rights of Passage* (1967), *Masks* (1968), and *Islands* (1969)—were then published together, as *The Arrivants*, for an integral work as rich as it is complex in its synchronizations of imagery with various rhythms. Here is part of the poem "Tizzic" near the end of *Islands*:

An' then there was Tizzic.
He prefer the booze
an' women

it shame muh heart to think
how many t'ings he had wid chile:
Shirley, Bots, Phosphorine

all in the same month alone
not to mention big-bubbie Babs an' that
Queenie, who, as he say,

goin' have to look 'bout them good good good
if they tryin' to fine a chile father.
He a-rather

sit in the carpenter shop
pushin' draughts; plankin' down
dem domino dots till both he eyes

like they seein' white spots an' he foot
gone to sleep when de conch shell
bawlin' fuh work.

Yet you know, mister man, Hick Tizzic
was one o' de few hard back
man they got livin' down hey

you could trust (except wid yuh daughter).
All dat rum soakin' up in he liver,
into he bile an' he blood stream

like it ringin' a bell to tell
what we half-acre mean:
what it mean to a man to squeeze dirt

in 'e han' widdout killin' de soil;
what it feel like when you look up one day, see
de cane flags flyin' an' know dat you ownin' that green;

that you int shame no more
into beggin' the manager dollar;
that you free free man; that you fist

an' you back, an' the sole o' you foot
that you got pon the ground, is you own,
though you got to work like a mule;

an' Hick Tizzic know this while he ruckin'
the women, for Tizzic isn't no fool.[27]

These are but four of the many Diaspora black writers who have so enriched world literature. They have been selected specifically to illustrate further the Diaspora's linguistic creativity. Any more extensive treatment of Diaspora literature must be defeated by its very abundance, which puts it beyond the scope of this book and the competence of this writer. Indeed, all attempts at making a suitable selection, with illustrated excerpts, have simply buried the theme that was the initial function of the chapter. In the end, the only recourse seemed to be essentially a list of names additional to those cited earlier, here or elsewhere in the book. It is bound to be idiosyncratic and invidious, and especially so since literature, unlike music, comes with the mute of its own language.

This is most evidently true of poetry, and much of the art in the work of French-speaking Diaspora poets such as Jacques Roumain of Haiti (a novelist as well) and Léon-Gontran Damas of French Guiana (whose rhythms and imagery draw on both Créole and standard French) must be taken largely on trust by those who make their way with dictionaries or translations. This is less though still true of novelists, such as Martinique's René Maran, who was a major influence on subsequent black novelists in French, and the Marcellin brothers of Haiti. Perhaps easiest of all to reach are books mainly of insights and ideas, and few of these can have been as widely influential as those of Martinique's Frantz Fanon, psychiatrist and revolutionary, who wrote so profoundly and fiercely on the traumatizations of racism and colonialism.

He has no real equivalent in the English-language Diaspora, but James Baldwin, more widely known perhaps as a novelist, brought to his essays on racism an insight and an elegance of expression all his own. Black literature in the United States was long dominated by men. If Richard Wright requires particular mention here, it is because Bigger Thomas, the protagonist of his novel *Native Son* (1940), has become with time only more relevant, as the black male product of the urban ghetto who is drawn by fear and rage and frustration to the violence that ends by destroying him. Among many others, three may be cited for having brought to literature the spirit of jazz.

Langston Hughes did so in poetry, with his cycle *Montage of a Dream Deferred* (1951), which, in his own description, "like bebop, is marked by conflicting changes, sudden nuances, sharp and impudent interjections, broken rhythms, and passages sometimes in the manner of the jam-session, sometimes the popular song, punctuated by the riffs, runs, breaks, and disc-tortions of the music of a community in transition."[28] Chester Himes did much of this in his series of mordantly comic detective novels set in Harlem, which are excellent examples of the detective form itself but also infused with the exuberance and excitement of jazz. Ishmael Reed in his novel *Mumbo Jumbo* (1972) has gone furthest—indeed, arguably as far as it is possible to go—in the direction of jazz, playing not only with literary forms but with graphics, photography, typography, bibliography, as well as nu-merous subjects from anthropology and history to economics and religion.[29]

Nothing short of phenomenal has been the emergence in the United States of black women writers, since the pioneering novels of Zora Neale Hurston. In her autobiography, *Incidents in the Life of a Slave Girl* (1861), Linda Brent wrote: "Slavery is terrible for men; but it is far more terrible for women. Superadded to the burden common to all, *they* have wrongs and sufferings and mortifications peculiarly their own."[30] Adjusted to the survival of racism after slavery, the statement has lost none of its validity.

Black women have found their voices in literature. And what voices they are! Toni Morrison has received the Nobel Prize for Literature. Since *The Bluest Eye* in 1970, her novels have become more complex and richer, but none has surpassed the intensity of pain so penetratingly communicated in her first. Maya Angelou, whose first volume of autobiography, *I Know Why the Caged Bird Sings*, was published in the same year, has done that rare thing of elevating this form into art. In her novel *The Color Purple* (1982), Alice Walker has, through the letters that its protagonist, Celie, writes to God, drawn from the rich river of Southern Black English speech, and done so dramatically by providing the contrast of correct standard English in which Celie's sister, Nettie, writes to her. Among a number of black poets, Sonia Sanchez has written lyrics of extraordinary force and inventiveness.

Claude McKay of Jamaica, poet and novelist, produced in his novel *Banana Bottom* (1933) what one historian and critic of West Indian fiction has called "the first classic of West Indian prose."[31] From Jamaica, too, have come novels of Roger Mais and Andrew Salkey. *Brother Man* (1954) by Mais and Salkey's *A Quality of Violence* (1959) make particularly vivid use of Jamaican popular speech. Brathwaite, who challenged the West Indian nov-elist to improvise not only with words and rhythm, images and motifs, but with characterization, welcomed both novels as demonstrating this core ele-ment of the jazz novel.[32]

From Barbados has come not only Brathwaite himself but George Lam-ming, a major novelist of the Diaspora whose sheer skill in using different forms of Caribbean speech was most impressively demonstrated in *The Em-igrants* (1954), where black West Indians on their way by boat to Britain speak in their distinctive voices. It is a skill differently used in arguably his highest achievement, the mythic *Natives of My Person* (1971) on the theme of slavery and colonialism, in which he makes both the gender and the racial leap, to portray the white women of the colonizers and the black enslaved as different but equally victims. Here the movement is mainly between two historical forms of standard English, the sixteenth-century prose of the diarist on board the ship and the modern, muscularly descriptive language of the narrative.

Derek Walcott of St. Lucia, the second literary Nobel laureate from the Diaspora, draws extensively on European culture, not least the English poetic tradition, but is essentially, in his themes and imagery, a Diaspora poet and playwright. And from Guyana comes not only the poet Martin Carter but Wilson Harris, who has produced, from his first, mythic *Palace of the Peacock* (1960), a series of wonderfully woven short novels whose texture and colors gain the more in meaning the more closely and more often they are examined.

"If anything I do," Toni Morrison has written, "in the way of writing novels (or whatever I write) isn't about the village or the community or about you, then it is not about anything. I am not interested in indulging myself in some private, closed exercise of my imagination that fulfills only the obligation of my personal dreams—which is to say yes, the work must be political. It must have that as its thrust. That's a pejorative term in critical circles now: if a work of art has any political influence in it, somehow it's tainted.

"The problem comes in when you find harangue passing off as art. It seems to me that the best art is political and you ought to be able to make it unquestionably political and irrevocably beautiful at the same time."[33]

So many of these and other Diaspora writers are not only political in this sense. Particularly, in their various ways, they have recoiled from the kind of society and culture that has victimized blacks in one way or another for so long, and have turned instead to search for a direction and purpose in their history and their heritage.

Paule Marshall's novel of 1983, *Praisesong for the Widow*, moves from the United States into the Caribbean and from the present toward the past of slavery. It has as its protagonist Avey Johnson, a black American woman of such material means and respectability as Silla of *Brown Girl, Brownstones* wanted to be. Widowed and on a Caribbean cruise, she suddenly decides to leave the ship at Grenada.

She is tormented by the memory of her marriage to a man who had worked so hard in making his way through the white-dominated world that "finally the confusion, contradiction and rage of it all sent the blood flooding his brain one night as he slept in the bed next to hers."[34] And she has another, insistent memory, of her great-aunt at Tatem Island, on the South Carolina Tidewater, who used to tell her as a child of what her own grandmother had seen when the Ibo slaves had been landed there from a "big ol' ship with sails." They had looked about them, turned, and then, in their iron collars and chains, walked away on the river and past the ship.

"They feets was gonna take 'em wherever they was going that day. And they was singing by then, so my gran' said. When they realized there wasn't nothing between them and home but some water and that wasn't giving 'em no trouble they got so tickled they started in to singing. You could hear 'em clear across Tatem 'cording to her. They sounded like they was having such a good time my gran' declared she just picked herself up and took off after 'em. In her mind. Her body she always usta say might be in Tatem but her mind, her mind was long gone with the Ibos."[35]

In her search for the source of her deep discontent with a way of life that so many other black women desired, Avey is drawn to visit the little island of Carriacou, whose traditional festivities attract each year such numbers from Grenada. There she watches a dance and finds herself joining it.

"Her feet of their own accord began to glide forward, but in such a way they scarcely left the ground. Only the broad heels of her low-heeled shoes rose slightly and then fell at each step. She moved cautiously at first, each foot edging forward as if the ground under her was really water—muddy river water—and she was testing it to see if it would hold her weight."[36]

In the end she decides that she will sell her house in North White Plains and live part of the year in Tatem, where her grandchildren and others would visit her, and she would take them to Ibo Landing. " 'It was here that they brought them,' she would begin—as had been ordained. 'They took them out of the boats right here where we're standing . . .' "[37]

Did the Ibos walk on the water? Over the mud into the sea and suicide? Or was this magic? Or mirage? What matters is simply that the mind of the great-aunt's grandmother took off after them, and the mind of the widow herself is now following, to recognize and recount the history from which she came.

Beyond magic or mirage, it is metaphor, and one peculiarly apt in this context. For voices can, surely, walk on water, not only in literature but in life. And in doing so, they can become—already are—formidable forces in identifying the Diaspora to itself.

~~~~~~

In the intensifying ideological struggle of the thirties, the Olympic Games at Berlin in 1936 took on a special meaning for Hitler, who looked for them to display the racial superiority of "Aryans" in general and Germans in particular. "He himself followed the athletic contests with great excitement," Albert Speer, one of the top Nazis, would write in his memoirs. "Each of the German victories—and there were a surprising number of these—made him happy, but he was highly annoyed by the series of triumphs by the marvelous colored American runner, Jesse Owens."

Indeed, Jesse Owens was the star of the Games. He won four gold medals, including one for the long jump with a new world record. Moreover, three other black athletes won gold medals. "People whose antecedents came from the jungle were primitive, Hitler said with a shrug; their physiques were stronger than those of civilized whites. They represented unfair competition and hence must be excluded from future games."[1]

This vicious wish to have it both ways was by no means limited to Hitler and his Reich. There were other societies, professedly democratic, in which the popular elevation of the excellent in sport was accompanied by the arrangements of racism to exclude blacks from the opportunity of excelling. Indeed, even where blacks had once been permitted to compete, their very success led to the withdrawal of their right to do so.

The premier horse race in the United States, the Kentucky Derby, was inaugurated in 1875. Of the fifteen jockeys taking part, fourteen were black, and one of these rode the winner. In the next twenty-seven Derby races, fourteen of the winners were ridden by black jockeys, one of whom, Isaac Murphy, rode to victory in almost half of all the races in which he took part, a record which no jockey, black or white, has since surpassed.

This early black predominance in horse racing doubtless owed much to the knowledge and skill acquired by blacks who were employed in looking after horses. But blacks also had exceptional motivation. It was not only that horse racing provided them with a unique opportunity to compete against whites at the highest level. The financial rewards attached to their success were nowhere else so available to them. Top jockeys were able to earn from $25,000 to $30,000 a year, huge sums for that time.

Such possibilities of black enrichment were socially as offensive and unsettling as were the implications for white supremacy of black predominance in freely competitive sport. In the late 1880s, the Jockey Club took command over the renewal of licenses to jockeys. One by one, as licenses came up for review, the Jockey Club refused to renew those of blacks. The Kentucky Derby of 1911 was the last in which a black jockey took part for decades to come, and horse racing joined other forms of sport already segregated by race.

Among these was boxing, widely regarded as the supreme test of masculine strength and courage, in which the greatest prize was the heavyweight championship of the world. The commonly held view among whites in the United States that blacks were too weak and cowardly for success in such a contest clearly lacked conviction, since the boxing authorities ensured that they were given no opportunity to compete. One black changed all that.

Jack (John Arthur) Johnson was born, the son of a janitor, in Galveston, Texas, in 1878. Having developed his skills in street fights, he took to boxing with such success as credibly to challenge the Canadian, Tommy Burns, who had taken the world heavyweight title in 1906. Burns ignored the challenge, confident that the boxing authorities would not strip him of his title in consequence. Johnson's recourse was to taunt Burns publicly wherever he went. At last Burns agreed to a match, the two men met in December 1908, and by the fourteenth round, Burns was being so battered that police stopped the fight. Johnson's right to the title could not be denied.

In baseball, the national sport of the United States, playing in the major leagues had long been restricted to whites, and blacks were driven to establish leagues of their own. These leagues attracted a large black following for the game and enabled the development of such outstanding players as Hank Aaron, who would come to be the greatest home-run hitter of all time. Convinced that the future of his team lay in attracting both the best of players and the gate receipts of black spectators, the president of the major league Brooklyn Dodgers signed the black player, Jackie Robinson, in 1945.

The impact that Robinson made was immediate. In his very first season, in 1947, he became the leading player on the team and was voted "Rookie of the Year" by his peers. In the wake of his success, other black players were welcomed into major league baseball, and today roughly 30 percent of all professional baseball players in the United States are blacks, or more than twice the black share of the population.

Racial barriers in tennis were the next to go. There, too, blacks had been excluded from the U.S. Open Championships by the requirement that competitors had to win a qualifying tournament at a country club, and no black player was ever invited to take part in such a tournament. Blacks had organized their own American Tennis Association, from which Althea Gibson had emerged as a manifestly gifted player, and increasing pressure was brought on the white U.S. Lawn Tennis Association to make the U.S. Open precisely that. In 1950, Gibson became the first black player allowed to compete at Forest Hills, and in 1957 and 1958 she won both the U.S. Open and Wimbledon women's singles titles.

Yet, even as racial barriers to entry into competitive sport were dismantled, reservations survived. In American football, for instance, where blacks proved so successful that today they compose some 60 percent of all professional players, the strategic position of quarterback long remained effectively reserved for whites, on the racist presumption that blacks lacked the requisite "intellectual" qualities of leadership, including the ability to make sound and quick judgments under pressure. Even blacks who had excelled at college level by playing in the quarterback position were offered contracts by teams in the National Football League only to be assigned other positions.

It would take until 1984 before a black player, Warren Moon, who refused any other position, was assigned to play quarterback for the Houston Oilers. Four years later, Doug Williams, another black allowed to play in the quarterback position, led the Washington Redskins to victory in the Super Bowl.

Racism in sport was far from being restricted to the United States. The British Boxing Board of Control, for instance, long excluded from competition for the British titles black boxers, who were left to contend only for the less highly regarded and less rewarding Empire ones. Larry Gains, the black boxer who held the heavyweight Empire title from 1931 to 1934, was repeatedly refused the right to fight for the British championship. It was only after the Second World War that increasing public pressure, promoted in part by the persistence and popularity of the young black boxers in the Turpin family, secured the lifting of the ban. In 1948, Dick Turpin became the first black to qualify for a British title fight. He was successful, and held both the British and Empire middleweight titles from 1948 to 1950. His achievement opened the way for his brother, Randolph, who fought Sugar Ray Robinson in July 1951 to become, if only for a little while, Britain's first black world middleweight champion.

Within the Caribbean colonies, one racial barrier in the paramount popular sport of cricket remained insurmountable. The administrators of the game, most of whom were whites, repeatedly appointed whites to captain the West Indies team, in disregard of such great black cricketers as Learie Constantine and George Headley. It would take until 1960 for Frank Worrell to become the first black chosen as captain for a full test series, against Australia.[2]

In the 1991 World Athletics Championships at Tokyo, all eight finalists in the 100 meters sprint, traditionally regarded as the supreme athletic event, were black. Of these, six ran the race in under 10 seconds, the first time in history this had happened. It symbolized the mounting dominance of blacks, mainly from the Diaspora, in sports which whites had tried to reserve for themselves.

Sport should essentially be a measure of individual human striving and achievement. Yet it is not altogether irrelevant to consider what it is that accounts for the disproportionate dominance by Diaspora blacks. The question is certainly asked. One answer, which does not descend to Hitler's explanation of a "primitive" and "jungle" ancestry, nonetheless argues that there is a decisive genetic element involved: that slaves were selected from the physically strongest Africans, and that it was mainly the strongest of slaves who survived the tribulations of the ocean crossing and the subsequent ill-treatment and excessive labor demands.

Yet even were all this to have been so, sport is about much more than physical strength. There are other explanations. One of these may be found in Frantz Fanon's exploration of the rebellious psyche in colonial society.

"The first thing which the native learns," he wrote, "is to stay in his place, and not to go beyond certain limits. That is why the dreams of the native are always of muscular prowess; his dreams are of action and aggression. I dream I am jumping, swimming, running, climbing; I dream that I burst out laughing, that I span a river in one stride, or that I am followed by a flood of motor-cars which never catch up with me. During the period of colonisation, the native never stops achieving his freedom from nine in the evening until six in the morning."[3]

For so many blacks in the Diaspora today, whether they are citizens of states with white or with black majorities—as well as for many African blacks who enter international competition—theirs is still an essentially colonial world, in which white power sets the limits to their lives. Sport affords an opportunity outside of dreams to test and exceed those limits and the white power that sets them. Linford Christie, the black British 1992 Olympic gold medalist and 1993 World Champion in the 100 meters, put this in his own way when he said that there were no racial barriers for him in a race; it was only himself against the clock.[4]

There is yet another reason, which says much about the continuing plight of the Diaspora. It lies in the belief among blacks themselves that sport provides the prime route of escape from racial confinement and deprivation into the supposed freedom of fame and fortune. Certainly, for the very few who make it to the top, the material rewards can be enormous, as fame in sports of particular popular appeal commands not only high playing fees but still higher returns from being marketed to sell everything from soft drinks to shoes.

One last explanation comes from the very heritage of the Diaspora, where physical agility and rhythmic movement, as in dance, have long been held in special regard. Few black parents fail to admire and encourage any display of such ability in their children, who tend, therefore, to devote time and effort from an early age in practicing their skills. The most successful blacks in sport know all too well that ability, however derived, can achieve very little without a great deal of hard work. As one leading basketball player in the United States, Isiah Thomas of the Detroit Pistons, has put it, "I do it naturally because I spent so many hours doing it over and over again."[5]

Yet none of these attempts at explanation make the achievements of the Black Diaspora in sport any less extraordinary. For this is more than a disproportionate numerical dominance. Diaspora blacks have explored in sport new realms of expression, with an impact on the wider culture. One example has been basketball in the United States, where 60 percent of all professional players are blacks, and where these have brought to the game an element of improvisation that has been likened to jazz in its creative tension between the individual and the group. The resultant popular appeal of the game has reached far beyond the black community, to influence the vocabulary of business and fashion design as well as ordinary speech with such basketball expressions as "in your face," "one on one," "take it to the hoop," "down the lane," "jam it," "dunk it."

The contemporary image of sport has certainly been impaired by the increasing encroachments of commercialization; illicit invasions such as kickbacks and the use of physically enhancing drugs; the exploitation of it by divisive nationalisms. Beyond all this, however, sport at its highest is about the perpetual testing and exceeding of set limits which is the nature of human endeavor. It is about the very attributes—courage, fortitude, devotion, comradeship, grace—which inform the mythology of heroism. It is about something else, too.

C.L.R. James, one of the most influential Diaspora writers, wrote with his *Beyond a Boundary* of 1963 a book about cricket that is also about history and heroism; class and culture; colonialism and race; aesthetics and art:

Cricket was fortunate in that for their own purposes the British ruling classes took it over and endowed it with money and prestige. On it men of gifts which would have been remarkable in any sphere expended their powers—the late C. B. Fry was a notable example. Yet even he submitted to the prevailing aesthetic categories and circumscribed cricket as a "physical" fine art. There is no need so to limit it. It is limited in variety of range, of subject matter. It cannot express the emotions of an age on the nature of the last judgement or the wiping out of a population by bombing. It must repeat. But what it repeats is the original stuff out of which everything visually or otherwise aesthetic is quarried. The popular democracy of Greece, sitting for days in the sun watching *The Oresteia*; the popular democracy of our day, sitting similarly, watching Miller and Lindwall bowl to Hutton and Compton—each in its own way grasps at a more complete human existence. We may some day be able to answer Trotsky's exasperated and exasperating question: What is art?—but only when we learn to integrate our vision of Walcott on the back foot through the covers with the outstretched arm of the Olympic Apollo.[6]

The ancient Greeks had, in their ideals, some such integrated vision. It was no accident that athletes were so often the subjects of sculpture and so celebrated in literature, or that the statues of victorious athletes at the Olympian Games were placed in the Altis, the walled sanctuary which enclosed the temple to Zeus at Olympia. The athlete who brought back to his city the chaplet of wild olive that was the victor's only prize was as much a source of pride as peaceful rivalry could provide.

The ideals of ancient Greece were, to be sure, rather far from the realities of rival city states which spent, from greed and envy and fear, their achievements in the conflicts which led to their ruin and subjugation. Some of them were tyrannies, and even the culture of the citizen democracies depended on the wealth and leisure which the population of slaves supplied. Yet the ideals survive, and there is a long delayed but finally satisfying justice that these should be so largely sustained today by the descendants of slaves.

~~~~~~

The vast majority of slaves came from societies which adhered to variants of black African indigenous or "traditional" religion. This was not a religion with sacred texts that laid down details of doctrine, though the existence of such texts in other religions has scarcely precluded disputes, all too often attended by persecutions and wars, on differences of interpretation. What was, however, generally believed and practiced can be established from the survival of the beliefs and practices in Africa today.

The art of sculpture is itself a source, since this was a major form of religious expression. So was and is music in all its forms. "Even the secular dance cannot be separated from the religious, for both embody the life force or vital energy which is the supreme value of life, and the separation of sacred and profane cannot be made as it is in Europe."[1]

In the universe of traditional belief, everything has its own power and is related to everything else, so that the individual human interacts with everything in nature as well as with other humans. Infusing this universe is the Supreme Being, the first and final principle, omnipresent and mysterious. Most African traditional cultures envisage this Being as male. In some, such as that of the Fon people, the Being is both male and female. There are others, such as that of the southern Nuba, with a system of matrilineal descent, who envisage the Being as the Great Mother.

It was from cultures with a male Supreme Being that most slaves were drawn, and this certainly facilitated in the Diaspora the association of the Supreme Being with the God of Christianity. There were other bridges of belief. Among some African peoples, notably the Yoruba, morality was reinforced by the prospect of judgment after death, when the righteous would be rewarded with a heaven of cool breezes, while the wicked would be consigned to a kind of cosmic garbage dump.[2]

Significantly, the Supreme Being is not depicted in sculpture. There are various gods which are. These have been seen as particular manifestations of the Supreme Being, representing one or another of that Being's more prominent powers. They also perform the function of intermediaries—not an incompatible concept—in which aspect they came the more easily to be associated in the Diaspora with certain Christian saints and the Virgin Mary.

Given the force of a storm in the African environment, it is only to be expected that there is, identified with this phenomenon, an appropriately important god whose principal weapons are thunderbolts. Among the Yoruba he is called Shango and is believed to have been a king who ascended to heaven. Among the Ibo, another major people in the region of present-day Nigeria, the most important deity after the Supreme Being is Ala, the earth mother, who is the spirit of fertility both for the land and for the family.

Though all things in nature have power, some have more power than others. Mount Cameroon and Mount Kilimanjaro, for instance, have spirits with powers beyond those attached to hills and even particular rock formations. Certain trees have special spiritual power, as have all waters, wells and springs, and rivers. Snakes, especially those in the vicinity of waters, are widely revered, and among them, pythons in particular. In some places, dead pythons are buried, like dead people, in white cloth. In Whydah, on the West African coast, long a leading site for the embarkation of slaves, a celebrated snake temple beside a sacred tree contains pythons which are fed by priests. At the temple, too, are women who go into trances and convey messages from the spirits.

In this world so dominated by gods and spirits, it would be surprising if there were not ways to communicate with them. Divination is a crucial element of traditional religion and is employed for a variety of purposes, from a final recourse in arbitrating disputes to a way of identifying the causes of such personal troubles as infertility, illness, and strange dreams. The most famous oracle in West Africa, sited among the Yoruba at their supposed ancestral city of Ile-Ife, involves the use of sixteen palm nuts and a divining board. What has come to be known as the Ifa divination system has traveled far and wide. It is practiced, for instance, in New York today among adherents of the Afro-Cuban Santería religion.

The Ifa Oracle has its divine messenger in Legba, who conveys the prayers and sacrifices of humans to heaven and the predictions or will of heaven back to humans. In this function, he is not merely an Ifa deity. His counterpart is to be found under other names, in many traditional African cultures; he is, for instance, called Eshu among the peoples of Dahomey. Nor is he simply a conduit. He is a god that must be given his due, all the more so since he is commonly held to have a jealous, even mischievous bent and, if offended, may distort or block the messages.

Traditional religion takes the existence of evil, including human malice, thoroughly into account. Sorcerers and witches have power to do harm, from inflicting sterility and mysterious diseases to producing social tension and conflict. Against them, discovery and punishment are not enough, since these may come too late, and there is a widespread reliance on the protection offered by magicians, medicine, and charms. Such measures are, however, adjuncts to prayer and not a substitute. The prime force in defeating the power of evil is the power of good in the universe.

Ancestors themselves dispose of spiritual power and are capable of inflicting harm as well as providing help. "My spirit grandfathers," the Ashanti of Ghana pray, "come and receive this mashed plantain and eat; let this town prosper; and permit the bearers of children to bear children; and may all the people of this town get riches."

Yet, paradoxically, the dead, even as they remain spiritual beings, may also be reborn, in one or more descendants. Among the Yoruba, for instance, *Babatunde* (Father Returns) and *Yetunde* (Mother Returns) are popular names for children, and the Ifa Oracle is often consulted to establish which ancestor has "turned to be a child."[3] Manifestly, the spirit or "soul" of an ancestor is not an indivisible entity but one which may, in a particular traditional formulation, be "the spirit which comes back to see the world," while simultaneously existing elsewhere to hear and answer the prayer of a descendant. Those who do evil have a different fate. They become ghosts and are not reborn.

The possibility of dying to be reborn back in Africa might well have been a factor in the high rate of suicide among slaves. Certainly, slave owners believed this to be so, since they took to beheading slave suicides, in the hope of discouraging others with the fear of being reborn mutilated or not being reborn at all. It is likely, though, that the practice said rather more about the Christian slave owners' view of resurrection than it did about the nature of the soul and rebirth in traditional African religion. In certain parts of Africa, such as southeast Dahomey, for instance, the head of a dead person is removed some time after burial and placed in a box or bag for the annual ceremonies of commemoration.

The traditional religion of black Africa was essentially the product of the interaction between people and their environment. Indeed, not the least among the horrors of the slave trade was that it snatched people from places invested for them with a peculiar spiritual meaning. Yet, if the slaves were forced to leave the places behind, they took with them their beliefs, for the development of a more or less adapted spiritual geometry in the Diaspora.

Some simply transported their traditional religion to a new home. After all, the Supreme Being was omnipotent and omnipresent. Subsidiary deities and spirits, even if Africa was where they lived, could surely travel wherever they wished. If trees and rivers and stones had spiritual power in Africa, there was every reason to suppose that their counterparts elsewhere were similarly possessed.

For other slaves, conversion to Christianity, the socially dominant religion in their new environment, was an appealing alternative. This was not only because it brought with it certain real or apparent advantages, nor even that much in Christianity reflected, if in a glass darkly, traditional religious beliefs. Here at last was a sacred text parts of which spoke of enslavement, exile, suffering, promise, and redemption in the very language of the Diaspora experience.

For many, it was not a matter of wholly one or the other. Between traditional religion and Christianity was an uncharted expanse which blacks, both slave and free, explored to establish various compromises, while some individual worshippers accommodated in their beliefs supposedly incompatible extremes. In the Diaspora today, most notably perhaps in Haiti and Brazil, there are those who regularly attend church services as well as the rites of religions derived from the traditional source.

Few of such religions are without some element of Christianity, if no more than the association of traditional deities with specific saints, while there are Christian denominations which have in their services such elements of traditional religious worship as strongly rhythmic song, dance, handclapping, trances, and spiritual possession. One Diaspora religion illustrates, in its development and character, the essential longevity of tradition along with the motivation of its adaptability.

Cuban blacks were encouraged by the Roman Catholic Church to form *cabildos* or societies, in the hope that these would promote among their members the spread of Christianity. Most cabildos were apparently more concerned with measures of welfare. They provided help to their old and their ill, arranged funerals for their dead, and devoted a portion of their membership dues to a fund for purchasing the freedom of those among them who were still slaves. They did, however, celebrate with their own drum rhythms and dances the main Christian festivals and in particular Epiphany—*el día de reyes*—which provided, in the black Melchior among the Magi, a figure with whom they could readily identify themselves.

The cabildos were organized along "national" lines, to associate those extracted or descended from a particular African people. Since this would have required the compliance of the authorities, it is difficult to escape the inference that it was official policy, pursued by both Church and State, to promote disunity in a black population with reason enough to unite in revolt. Whatever the case, the consequence was to promote the cohesion of each such entity and its adherence to the form of traditional religion in its heritage.

The largest component of the black population was that of the Yoruba, who came to be known as the Lucumi, from their greeting of one another with the words *oluku mi* (my friend). Their own religion was known as Santería—worship of the saints—from their association of saints with the traditional *orishas* or spirits. We have a remarkable record of Lucumi beliefs and practices in the era of slavery from the recollections of Esteban Montejo, in his *Autobiography of a Runaway Slave*. It is a record which reveals not only the African roots of the religion at an early stage in its growth but the element of disguise in the very association of the spirits with saints.

> The Lucumi liked rising early with the strength of the morning and looking up into the sky and saying prayers and sprinkling water on the ground. The Lucumi were at it when you least expected it. I have seen old Negroes kneel on the ground for more than three hours at a time, speaking in their own tongue and prophesying . . . This they did with *dillogunes*, which are round white shells from Africa with mystery inside. The god Elegguá's eyes are made from this shell . . .
>
> The old Lucumis liked to have their wooden figures of the gods with them in the barracoon (slave quarters). All these figures had big heads and were called *oché*. Elegguá was made of cement, but Changó and Yemaya were of wood, made by the carpenters themselves.
>
> They made the saints' marks on the walls of their homes with charcoal and white chalk, long lines and circles, each one standing for a saint, but they said that they were secrets. These blacks made a secret of everything. They have changed a lot now, but in those days the hardest thing you could do was to try to win the confidence of one of them.[4]

There was clearly need for secrecy and for subterfuge.

> The fiestas in the Casas de Santo were good ones. Only Negroes went to them, the Spanish didn't approve of *santería*. But with time this changed, and now you can see white high priests with red cheeks. *Santería* used to be a religion for Africans, and even the Civil Guards, the pure-blooded ones, would have nothing to do with it. They would make some remark in passing like, "What's going on here?", and the Negroes would say, "We're celebrating San Juan." But of course it was not San Juan but Oggún, the god of war . . . the most famous god in the whole region then.[5]

Santería did, indeed, become more acceptable and its celebration more open with Cuban independence and the disestablishment of the Church. The revolutionary regime of Castro, however, became increasingly repressive in its view of the religion as socially deviant and divisive. Among those leaving the island, from one or other cause of disaffection, were priests and practitioners of Santería, who took their religion with them, mainly to the United States and in particular to Miami and New York. In the Hispanic neighborhoods of New York City alone, there are now more than a hundred *botánicas*, small specialty shops which stock ritual objects, including pictures and statues of the Catholic saints as versions or *caminos* (ways) of the *orishas* (spirits).

On sale are the various necklaces of beads, in the respective colors of the favored *orishas*: yellow or gold for Oshun (or Ochún), the goddess of sweet or river waters; blue and white for Yemaya, mother of the seas; red and white for the thunder god Shango (Changó). There are the *soperas* or large lidded bowls to contain the stones—river pebbles for Oshun, ocean stones for Yemaya, meteorites for Shango—which are alive with the respective spirits. "As embodiments of the *orishas*, the stones must be treated as the living things that they are, and so they are lovingly bathed in cooling herbs, cleaned and oiled, and fed with the blood of animals."[6] For believers, the voices of the *orishas* may be heard by the use of a divining board and cowrie shells or palm nuts, according to the code of the Ifa Oracle.

Herbs are powerful medicines, against spiritual and physical illnesses. Indeed, Santería does not distinguish between the two, since it regards illness, like health, as both a spiritual and a physical condition. Herbs may also be combined with symbolic objects to make charms against evil. The efficacy of such charms is not recognized by Western medicine, though it is arguable that they may have some psychosomatic effect. It is less easy to dismiss the botanical knowledge of the Santería priests and priestesses. Western science is no longer as contemptuous as it used to be of the traditional medicine practiced in other cultures.

Nor are the beliefs of African traditional religion, and of the Diaspora religions derived from it, altogether foreign to the development of what is called Western civilization. The very culture of ancient Greece, to which that development owes so much in literature, the fine arts, philosophy, politics, and science, was one whose polytheism bears a striking resemblance to the African religious view of Nature. Even the very movement in modern European thought which promoted the various revolutions for the Rights of Man gave rise to a literature, as in the poetry of Coleridge and Wordsworth, that invested Nature with a spiritual dimension akin to the animism in black Africa's traditional religion.

Animism is common to early religious beliefs across the world, and traces of it apparently survive in the behavior of the "civilized" and even the avowedly rationalist. Soon after finishing the first draft of this chapter, I was having dinner at the home of a friend. In the course of the meal, he made some remark and quickly tapped the wooden table twice with his fingertips. I announced that I did much the same on occasions, without knowing why, beyond the superstition that it warded off bad luck. Since he confessed to not knowing why either, I made further inquiries. The weight of informed opinion seems to be that in doing this, we are repeating an animist practice of touching a tree to acknowledge or appease its spirit.

The relevance of Africa's traditional religion is not, however, merely a vestigial one. The exploitation of the environment in the pursuit of what is held to be material progress has reached a point where the costs have become alarmingly evident. This is having an increasing influence on scientific thought, whose long-ascendant, essentially physical, concept of our planet as rotating through space in obedience to immutable laws is giving place to an essentially biological one, of our world as a living, sensitive, and vulnerable organism. At the frontiers of biochemistry, the relation between the genetic material of humans and that of other living forms is coming closer into focus. A belief in the spirits of rivers and trees, in oracles and charms, is not a prerequisite for recognizing the validity and value of the insights basic to the veneration of Nature in Africa's traditional religion and the related religions of the Diaspora.

Clearly, such religions have something to offer those who consider themselves neither black nor poor. In Haiti, members of the mulatto elite, who otherwise pay scant or no regard to their African ancestry, visit Voodoo priests for help with personal problems. In Brazil, there are mulattoes of "good appearance" and whites among the adherents of Candomblé. In the United States, Santería is attracting converts from among whites with no Cuban, let alone African, connection. Yet, across the Diaspora, it is from among blacks and especially the black poor that such religions draw most of their following and life. This is unlikely to be merely a matter of residual belief. Adhesion to such religions has historically been a form or expression of racial and social revolt, against the disdain of the dominant white culture and the discriminations of class.

It has been, too, a channel for the transmission of more than religious beliefs and rites. Voodoo in Haiti has translated various African peoples, such as the Bambara and the Ibo, into divinities, though the dominant cultural influence on the religion has been that of the Fon. In Cuba, Trinidad, and much of Brazil, it is Yoruba culture which has been the principal influence on the religions. Fanti-Ashanti culture, from the region of what is now Ghana, may be found in its purest American form among the so-called Bush Negroes of Surinam and their religion. In Jamaica, it is the culture of the Kromantis, also from the region of Ghana, that is dominant.[7] These religions accordingly convey a heritage that reaches beyond beliefs and rites, into history, folklore, and traditions of artistic expression.

There are other religions, whose adherents come mainly from among the blacks and especially the poor, which have also been and still are forms or expressions of revolt, but which are to be distinguished as Afro-Christian ones. One such, in Jamaica, is Revivalism, which emerged from within the Native Baptist Church there. The supernatural beings in whom Revivalists believe and who may communicate with them or possess them are drawn from the Bible. Yet there are important elements, too, drawn from traditional religion. Such African ritual objects as sacred stones, invested with power and used to invoke particular spirits, may be found in the homes of Revivalist leaders and on Revivalist altars. Songs which derive their melodies and words from Protestant hymns are accompanied by such African features as poly-rhythmic drumming, hand-clapping, and dancing. Along with the power of healing is the power of obeah or sorcery, which may be used for good or evil purposes and which encompasses the summoning of "duppies," the spirits of the dead.

Religion as the revolt of the black and poor has taken yet another form in Jamaica, to spread, mainly among emigrant Jamaicans, elsewhere in the Diaspora. Influenced by the ideas of Marcus Garvey, who maintained that blacks are the chosen people of God, the Rastafarian movement emerged in 1930, to proclaim Ras Tafari, enthroned as Haile Selassie I, Emperor of Ethiopia, in that year, the Living God. A political as well as religious move-ment of challenge to the "Babylon" of white power and materialism, it encompassed both pacifists who withdrew into lives of devout simplicity and those who advocated violence as a vehicle of deliverance. The dethronement of Haile Selassie in 1974 and his death in the following year led to a cor-responding theological shift among some adherents, while others refused to believe the reports. The crucial repudiation of "Babylon" and its works remained unaffected, with new converts made by the spread of the Rastafarian message through reggae.

That the major Christian denominations were failing to hold the allegiance of blacks in Jamaica was evident also in the rise of Pentecostalism, whose two Churches, the Pentecostal Church and the Church of God, increased their combined following from 4 percent of the population in 1963 to 20 percent in 1970. The reason is not difficult to find. A form of Christian fundamentalism, centered on the Holy Spirit, Pentecostalism offers dignity to the deprived and despised who accept it, since its teaching is that each of them has an individual value and, "by receiving the Spirit," comes to be invested with supernatural gifts. For blacks, this appeal is enhanced by beliefs and practices that are in harmony with their own heritage, from the invo-cation of the Holy Spirit, healing rites, and the dancing and rhythmic stamp-ing in the course of worship to the inclusion of hair-straightening among the activities forbidden the faithful.

Jamaica mirrored developments elsewhere in the Diaspora. By the early sixties, Pentecostalism was an emerging force in Britain among Caribbean immigrants, some 5 percent of whom were members of such churches and a further 10 percent of whom attended Pentecostal services from time to time. A decade later, one-fifth of the 55,000 Caribbean and African im-migrants in the city of Birmingham belonged to independent black churches, many of which were Pentecostal. In Brazil, by the early seventies, roughly one thousand a day were converting to Protestantism, almost all of them to Pentecostal sects.[8]

The European theologian W. J. Hollenweger has argued that "the growth of the Pentecostal movement throughout the Third World thus far has depended more upon its ability to use the American Negro's capacities of understanding and communicating by means of enthusiastic spiritual manifestations—hymns, speaking in tongues, and spontaneous forms of worship—than upon the 'baptism of the spirit.' "[9] Indeed, this influence was original, for the movement was actually born in 1906 among blacks in the United States, where it emerged and spread as an expression of revolt. In the view of one historian, John Nichol, himself raised in the Pentecostal faith, some blacks came increasingly to see themselves out of place in Christian denominations which "had accumulated wealth, built enormous churches, appointed them handsomely, eliminated the 'praise and prayer' service from the program of worship, and in some instances even provided little or no room for the people of the labouring class in the sanctuary itself. The result was that multitudes severed their affiliation with the so-called 'middle-class' denominations like the Methodist and the Baptist."[10]

Revolt was nothing new to black Christianity in the United States. It was inherent in the very conversion of slaves to a religion whose message of redemption might be held to include deliverance from bondage in this world, too. Significantly, all three major slave conspiracies in the South during the nineteenth century were led by professing Christians, who found in Biblical figures or texts the sanction for insurgency. It was revolt as well, against white supervision and control, that informed the establishment by blacks of their own denominations.

The related black churches were not only religious entities distinguished from their white counterparts by aspects of worship derived from African forms. They encompassed other community functions, such as the provision of welfare, the encouragement of education, and the expression of racial solidarity. Some of them came to be substantial institutions, especially in the Northern cities whose black populations grew rapidly with the swelling numbers of migrants from the South. By the 1920s, the Olivet Baptist Church in Chicago, for instance, pursued community programs with a pastor, five assistant pastors, and 512 officers, twenty-four of them paid.

Such institutions were little disposed to foster, let alone instigate, racial or social insurgency. In fact, except for their break with Churches under white control, the black clergy themselves had never been notable for a commitment to revolt. They had not been peculiarly prominent in the struggle against slavery, nor were they so in the subsequent struggle against racism, until the late fifties of this century. A wariness of militancy did not, to be sure, imply indifference. Secular protest organizations, such as the National Association for the Advancement of Colored People, were sustained in part by funds from collections in the black churches. Increasingly, too, in the Northern cities, the black churches became active in mobilizing the black vote, though not all the black clergy seemed able or willing to distinguish the interests of the black electorate from their own. Some black churches even lent their support to particular campaigns, such as the one for equality of economic opportunity in which Baptists were the most active.

All too often, however, the mass of black churches represented the view of the developing black middle class to which their clergy themselves belonged and which had its own perspectives of progress, pressure, and pace, not necessarily relevant to the plight of the impatient poor. Many blacks accordingly turned elsewhere: some to Pentecostalism; some to a variety of small storefront Christian churches that drew more or less heavily on elements of traditional worship; while some abandoned Christianity altogether for other religions.

In the period following the First World War, there were those in Harlem who took to claiming descent from the Falashes, or Ethiopian Jews, and to practicing a modified form of Judaism. Others, in various cities, were attracted to Islamic sects, among which the Nation of Islam, or the Black Muslim movement, emerged as the most influential, especially after one of its converts, Malcolm X, roused the ghetto poor with the eloquent militancy of his message.

Islam was not new to the Diaspora. Numerous slaves brought from Africa, mainly to Brazil, were Muslim already and converted others. Yet the contemporary spread of Islam owes little to any related descent, which came largely to be submerged. It results from the appeal that Islamic doctrine and practice have had. Muhammad himself, who had spent his early life in poverty as an orphan, provided in the Koran social ordinances that were of an advanced benevolence for the times, in particular toward the slaves, the poor, and the oppressed. The freeing of slaves was declared most pleasing to God and a way of expiating many sins. If the history of slavery in Islam suggests that the pleasing of God in this regard was not always a prime consideration, the message was powerful and remains so.

Moreover, the crucial kinship of all Muslims could scarcely have been more forcefully expressed than it was by the Prophet: "O ye men! harken unto my words and take ye them to heart! Know ye that every Muslim is a brother to every other Muslim, and that ye are now one brotherhood. It is not legitimate for any of you, therefore, to appropriate unto himself anything that belongs to his brother, unless it is willingly given him by that brother." As one scholar has assessed the consequences: "Of all world religions Islam seems to have attained the largest measure of success in demolishing the barriers of race, color and nationality—at least within the confines of its own community. The line is drawn only between believers and the rest of mankind."[11] Nonetheless, within the Black Diaspora, while the Islamic community continues to attract new members, it remains small in comparison to the various Christian communities.

The civil rights movement that began in the late fifties to confront the obduracy of institutionalized racism in the South propelled a significant number of the black Christian clergy in the United States at last into the forefront of revolt. Even so, Martin Luther King, who was primarily responsible for projecting "a new image of the Black church and a new awareness of the radical possibilities inherent in Black religion," received "only token support from many among the most prestigious Black ministers."[12] King himself was coming to accept the need for militancy on economic issues—he was personally committed to a strike by sanitation workers in Memphis—at the time of his assassination in April 1968. How far he would have gone had he lived, and how many of the black clergy he might have drawn along with him, is idle speculation.

What is now clear is that the civil rights movement, beyond its defeat of institutionalized white supremacy in the South, achieved mainly the advance of the black middle class, with equal opportunity enactments that provided new openings in the universities, business management, communications, and the civil service. Even the Black Power movement, for all the radicalism of its rhetoric, in practice promoted concessions more productive of gains for that class than any alleviation in the plight of the black poor.

By the seventies, black Christianity in the United States had come to represent a racial cohesion which concealed more than it revealed. Of the estimated twenty-two million black church members, little more than 800,000 belonged to the interracial Catholic Church and about 400,000 to interracial Protestant churches, while the three black Baptist organizations alone accounted for more than nine and a half million members.[13] Yet even in the crust of this racial containment, cracks were appearing, as the more militant among black Christians reached for a Christianity more relevant to the racial experience of blacks and in particular to the socially rejected of the ghettos.

One such militant, James Cone, argued that "black rebellion is a manifestation of God himself actively involved in the present day affairs of men for the purpose of liberating a people" and extended the concept of blackness to "all victims of repression who realize that their humanity is inseparable from man's liberation from whiteness."[14] Another, Joseph Washington, wrote of the Black Power movement that it involved not only the "embracing of Black identity" and the "unity of blacks" but "the renouncing of the "American Christ" insofar as his followers are paternalistic, condescending, engaged in keeping blacks separate, poor, illiterate, intimidated, and restricted. The call to humility by white Christians and their attempts to put down the responsive rage of black youth in the name of love, as well as sending them off to war without providing them with equal employment at home leads to a rejection of Jesus by these black youth."[15]

. To arguments and appeals of this sort, however, the black churches were in general impervious. They remained so, even as successive Republican administrations pursued policies which widened the divide between rich and poor, not least within the black population. This was all the more damaging to the moral leadership of the black churches, since the Republican ascendancy drew much of its most forceful support from white Christian fundamentalism and was itself given to invoking God at every step in the parade of its materialist exaltation.

In the Caribbean states of recent decolonization, a Christianity that had from time to time been a channel of revolt came to be clogged with the material and moral silt of the new rulers. Only in Guyana were the Catholic and Protestant Churches driven, by the increasing repressiveness of the regime, to a notable expression of resistance in the cause of civil liberties. Elsewhere they represented, by their very silence, their accommodation to the dominance of a middle class thriving on the revenues of government and its relations with business.

Beyond, in Brazil, institutionalized Christianity was no more insurgent. Even in Pentecostalism, the resort of much disaffection, converts were encouraged to concentrate on those "moral qualities" which would "permit them to ascend the social scale,"[16] rather than question the scale itself. No Church set its face against a repudiation of blackness by a society for which whiteness, visible or acquired by sufficient material means, had become a virtually sacred value.

What, then, is left, when the hold of the old gods has gone? If religion was the soul of the societies from which the Black Diaspora derived, it is not now, nor ever was, the soul of the Diaspora itself. Far from being a permeating and cohesive force, it has reflected and promoted divisions: among those adhering to different religions; among those adhering to different forms of the same religion; between those of some religion and those of none. Yet, surely, five centuries of distinctive experience cannot be without some underlying meaning, some redeeming force, a very principle of identity that may be called the soul.

This soul is freedom. It was in slavery that the Diaspora was born, together with the longing and struggle for freedom. When slavery ended, there were other kinds of racial confinement that stayed or were put in its place, to generate simultaneously related longings and struggles for freedom. If the Diaspora has expressed the essence of itself in one preeminent form, this has been music; and if the music of the Diaspora has had one preeminent feature, this has been the impulse to explore and celebrate freedom.

This does not mean that all those in the Black Diaspora have been similarly devoted. Some have failed in devotion even to their own freedom; the contented slave was not altogether a figment of white fantasy. Some were indifferent to the freedom of others; colonialism in the Caribbean had no difficulty in finding recruits to sustain its rule from among the ruled. Some today, besieged in the very exclusions of their own supposed freedom, pursue social priorities which confine other blacks in lives of deprivation and despair.

The Diaspora, indeed, has still to free itself. And to do so, it has to accept its past, as a source not of degradation, but of dignity; to assume its proper identity, as one of victimization and suffering but also one of courage and resilience and creativity; and, above all, to recognize here a heritage which belongs to all its people and asserts for each of them an equal claim to freedom.

Only then can the Black Diaspora proceed to a great purpose, for which its history has prepared it: to speak not only for its own freedom but for the cause of freedom itself, against all those who, in the name of the state, the nation, the race, this god or that god, would deny it. This is a purpose which becomes more urgent each day as the practice of "ethnic cleansing" spreads, and without humanity rising in horror to end it.

Rabbi Hillel, the Jewish sage whose lifetime encompassed the birth of the Christian Era, asked three questions: "If I am not for myself, who is for me? But if I am only for myself, what am I? And if not now, when?" In giving its own answers, the Black Diaspora need only respond to the insistent message of its soul.

NOTES

1: PEOPLE

1. R. de Roover, "The Organization of Trade," in *The Cambridge Economic History of Europe*, vol. 3 (London: Cambridge Univ. Press, 1971), p. 63.
2. St. Clair Drake, *Black Folk Here and There*, vol. 2 (Los Angeles: Center for Afro-American Studies, Univ. of California, 1990), pp. 228–36.
3. Philip D. Curtin, *The Atlantic Slave Trade: A Census* (Madison: Univ. of Wisconsin Press, 1969), p. 268, table 77.
4. Paul E. Lovejoy, "The Impact of the Atlantic Slave Trade on Africa: A Review of the Literature," in *Journal of African History* 30 (1989), p. 368.
5. Ibid., p. 381.
6. Ibid., pp. 384–85.
7. Joseph C. Miller, *Way of Death* (London: James Currey, 1988), p. 153.
8. Lovejoy, "Impact of Atlantic Slave Trade," p. 388.
9. Ibid., p. 392.
10. From the writings of Ibn Fadl Allah al Omari, who visited Cairo twelve years later and drew on the recollections of a court official who had been responsible for greeting the Emperor at the gates of Cairo. Basil Davidson, *The African Past* (Harmondsworth: Penguin, 1966), pp. 83–85.
11. Ibid., pp. 90–91.
12. Thomas Hodgkin, "Kingdoms of the Western Sudan," in *The Dawn of African History*, ed. Roland Oliver (London: Oxford Univ. Press, 1961), p. 41.
13. Ibid., p. 43.
14. Werner Gillon, *A Short History of African Art* (Harmondsworth: Penguin, 1986), pp. 82–84.
15. Cited in Roland Oliver and J. D. Fage, *A Short History of Africa* (Harmondsworth: Penguin, 1962), pp. 106–7.
16. W. E. F. Ward, *A History of the Gold Coast* (London: Allen & Unwin, 1948), p. 112. A twentieth-century photograph, reproduced opposite p. 113, shows the Golden Stool on a throne of its own higher than the adjacent one on which the Asantehene or traditional ruler is sitting.
17. Jan Vansina, *Paths in the Rainforest* (London: James Currey, 1990).
18. Ibid., p. 73.

19. Ibid., p. 81.
20. Ibid., p. 94.
21. Ibid., p. 253.
22. Miller, *Way of Death*, pp. 71–72.
23. Vansina, *Paths in Rainforest*, pp. 200–201.

3: MERCHANTS AND MARKETS

1. Robert Louis Stein, *The French Slave Trade in the Eighteenth Century* (Madison: Univ. of Wisconsin Press, 1979), p. 209, appendix table A1; p. 211, appendix table A10.
2. Ibid., pp. 61–72.
3. J. H. Rose, *William Pitt and the Great War* (London, 1911), p. 370.
4. Stein, *French Slave Trade*, pp. 180–81.
5. Curtin, *Atlantic Slave Trade*, p. 211, table 63.
6. Eric Williams, *Capitalism and Slavery* (Chapel Hill: Univ. of North Carolina Press, 1944), pp. 32–36.
7. Ibid., p. 51.
8. Ibid., pp. 68–73.
9. R. Muir, *A History of Liverpool* (London, 1907), p. 197.
10. Williams, *Capitalism and Slavery*, pp. 124–36.
11. Landeg White, *Magomero* (London: Cambridge Univ. Press, 1987), p. 11.
12. Curtin, *Atlantic Slave Trade*, p. 266, figure 26.
13. Ibid., p. 268, table 77.
14. Joseph C. Miller, "A marginal institution on the margin of the Atlantic system: The Portuguese southern Atlantic slave trade in the eighteenth century," in *Slavery and the Rise of the Atlantic System*, ed. Barbara L. Solow (Cambridge: Cambridge Univ. Press, 1991), pp. 120–34.
15. Hugh Thomas, *Cuba* (London: Eyre & Spottiswoode, 1971), p. 96.
16. David Turnbull, *Travels in the West* (London, 1840), p. 60.

4: TO THE BURNING IRON

1. William Bosman, *A New and Accurate Description of Guinea*, translated (London, 1705), quoted in Davidson, *African Past*, pp. 219–21.
2. Gustavus Vassa, *The Interesting Narrative of the Life of Olaudah Equiano or Gustavus Vassa, the African* (London, 1794).
3. Quoted in Basil Davidson, *Black Mother* (London: Gollancz, 1961), p. 107.
4. Michael Craton, *Sinews of Empire* (London: Temple Smith, 1974), pp. 73–74. The quotation is from a late-seventeenth-century trader.
5. Curtin, *Atlantic Slave Trade*, p. 160, table 46.
6. C. Duncan Rice, *The Rise and Fall of Black Slavery* (London: Macmillan, 1975), p. 117.
7. Stein, *French Slave Trade*, p. 86.
8. Miller, *Way of Death*, pp. 390–92.

5: THE CROSSING

1. Vassa, *Interesting Narrative*.
2. Miller, *Way of Death*, pp. 4–5.

3. Evidence given to Lords of Trade and Plantations, July 27, 1788. *Board of Trade Report*, part 2.
4. Miller, *Way of Death*, p. 412.
5. Ibid., pp. 422–24.
6. Report in the *Boston Post Boy*, June 25, 1750, in E. Donnan, *Documents Illustrative of the History of the Slave Trade to America*, vol. 2 (Washington, D.C.: Carnegie Institution, 1931), p. 485.
7. Lovejoy, "Impact of Atlantic Slave Trade," p. 368.

6: THE WEALTH OF THE INDIES

1. Eric Williams, *From Columbus to Castro: The History of the Caribbean, 1492–1969* (London: André Deutsch, 1970), p. 25.
2. Richard S. Dunn, *Sugar and Slaves* (London: Jonathan Cape, 1973), p. 16.
3. Ibid., pp. 53, 59.
4. George Downing to John Winthrop, Jr., August 26, 1645. Quoted in ibid., p. 68.
5. Curtin, *Atlantic Slave Trade*, p. 55, table 13.
6. Dunn, *Sugar and Slaves*, p. 87.
7. Ibid., pp. 96, 99.
8. Williams, *Columbus to Castro*, p. 104.
9. Curtin, *Atlantic Slave Trade*, pp. 59, 63.
10. Ibid., p. 59, table 14; p. 62, table 15.
11. Ibid., p. 65, table 16.
12. *An Inquiry into the Nature & Causes of the Wealth of Nations* (New York, 1937 Cannan edition), p. 366.
13. Craton, *Sinews of Empire*, pp. 139–40.
14. R. Cumberland, *The West Indian: A Comedy*, act I, scene 3 (London, 1775). Quoted in Williams, *Capitalism and Slavery*, p. 85.
15. Williams, *Columbus to Castro*, p. 119.
16. Admittedly, the modern cane used in the exercise was of a better strain. Michael Craton and James Walvin, *A Jamaican Plantation: The History of Worthy Park, 1670–1970* (Toronto: Univ. of Toronto Press, 1970), pp. 103–4.
17. F. W. Pitman, *The Development of the British West Indies, 1700–1763* (New Haven: Yale Univ. Press, 1917), pp. 59–60.
18. H. A. Wyndham, *The Atlantic and Slavery* (Oxford: Oxford Univ. Press, 1935), p. 284; Edward Brathwaite, *The Development of Creole Society in Jamaica, 1770–1820* (Oxford: Clarendon Press, 1971), p. 168. Cited in Craton, *Sinews of Empire*, p. 181.
19. The word was probably a corruption of the Spanish *cimarrón*, meaning "wild" or "untamed," which entered French as *marron* and English as "maron" and increasingly "maroon."
20. Craton, *Sinews of Empire*, p. 189.
21. Curtin, *Atlantic Slave Trade*, p. 78, table 19.
22. Ralph Korngold, *Citizen Toussaint* (London: Gollancz, 1946), p. 21.
23. Robert I. Rotberg with Christopher K. Clague, *Haiti: The Politics of Squalor* (Boston: Houghton Mifflin, 1971), p. 29.
24. Quoted in Korngold, *Citizen Toussaint*, p. 23.
25. Ibid.
26. Ibid.

27. Bryan Edwards, *An Historical Survey of the French Colony in the Island of St. Domingo: . . .* (London, 1797), p. 9.
28. Quoted in Pierre de Vassière, *Saint-Domingue (1629–1789)* (Paris, 1909), p. 222.
29. Martinique possessed 2,892 free persons of color in 1776; Guadeloupe, 1,382 in 1779.
30. C. L. R. James, *The Black Jacobins* (London: Secker & Warburg, 1938), p. 5.

7: ALIENABLE RIGHTS

1. Figures from Kenneth M. Stampp, *The Peculiar Institution* (London; Eyre & Spottiswoode, 1964), pp. 39–41.
2. Frederick Law Olmsted, *A Journey in the Back Country* (New York, 1860), pp. 444–45.
3. *Texas State Gazette*, Austin, October 10, 1857.
4. Hammond Diary, entries for April 29 and June 22, 1844. Quoted in Stampp, *Peculiar Institution*, p. 310.
5. Frederick Law Olmsted, *A Journey in the Seaboard Slave States* (New York, 1850), pp. 17–18.
6. Compendium of the Seventh Census (Washington, 1854), p. 94.
7. *Southern Cultivator* 7 (1849), p. 69.
8. Stampp, *Peculiar Institution*, pp. 228–29.
9. William B. Hesseltine and David L. Smiley, *The South in American History*, 2nd ed. (Englewood Cliffs, N.J.: Prentice-Hall, 1960), p. 189.
10. Curtin, *Atlantic Slave Trade*, p. 268; Stampp, *Peculiar Institution*, p. 39.
11. John W. Blassingame, *The Slave Community* (New York: Oxford Univ. Press, 1974), p. 78.
12. Olmsted, *Journey in Seaboard Slave States*, p. 57.
13. Francis A. Kemble, *Journal of a Residence on a Georgian Plantation in 1838–1839* (New York, 1863), pp. 59–61.
14. Stampp, *Peculiar Institution*, p. 243.
15. Ibid., p. 203. Stampp cites as his source Caterall, ed., *Judicial Cases*, vol. 2, p. 168.
16. Ibid., p. 205.
17. John R. Lyons to William W. Renwick, April 4, 1854. William R. Renwick Papers in Duke University Library. Quoted in ibid., p. 130.
18. Frederick Douglass, *My Bondage and My Freedom* (New York, 1855), pp. 250–51.
19. Harden E. Taliaferro, *Fisher's River (North Carolina) Scenes and Characters* (New York, 1859), pp. 188–89.
20. Lawrence W. Levine, *Black Culture and Black Consciousness* (New York: Oxford Univ. Press, 1977), pp. 99–101.
21. Works Progress Administration manuscripts, Mississippi File, Archive of Folk Song. Cited in ibid., pp. 107–8.
22. Frederick Douglass, *Narrative of the Life of Frederick Douglass*, ed. Benjamin Quarles (Cambridge: Harvard Univ. Press, 1960), p. 39.
23. Charles C. Jones, Jr., *Negro Myths from the Georgia Coast* (Boston, 1888), pp. 228–29.
24. Levine, *Black Culture*, pp. 118–19.
25. Cited in Blassingame, *Slave Community*, p. 54.
26. Cited in Eugene D. Genovese, *Roll, Jordan, Roll* (London: André Deutsch, 1975), pp. 285–86.

27. Ibid., p. 582.
28. Frederick Douglass, *Narrative of the Life*, p. 38.
29. William F. Allen, *Slave Songs of the United States* (1867), p. 46.
30. Maria Chapman, ed., *The Liberty Bell* (Boston, 1839), pp. 42–43.

8: THE MAKING OF BRAZIL

1. Hubert Herring, *A History of Latin America* (London: Jonathan Cape, n.d.), p. 222.
2. Curtin, *Atlantic Slave Trade*, p. 234, table 62; p. 268, table 77.
3. Herring, *History of Latin America*, p. 235.
4. F. A. Brandão, Júnior, *A escravatura no Brasil precidada d'um artigo sobre a agricultura e colonização no Maranhão* (Brussels: H. Thiry-Vern Buggenhoudt, 1865), cited in Robert Edgar Conrad, *Children of God's Fire: A Documentary History of Black Slavery in Brazil* (Princeton, N.J.: Princeton Univ. Press, 1983), p. 97.
5. Gilberto Freyre, *The Masters and the Slaves* (New York: Knopf, 1963), pp. 75–77.
6. Curtin, *Atlantic Slave Trade*, p. 234, table 67.
7. Robert Walsh, *Notices of Brazil in 1828 and 1829*, vol. 2 (London: Frederick Westley and A. H. Davis, 1830), pp. 323–28.
8. Correspondence cited by Conrad, *Children of God's Fire*, pp. 72–76.
9. David Gomes Jardim, *Algumas considerações sobre a higiene dos escravos* (Rio de Janeiro, 1847), pp. 7–12. Cited in ibid., pp. 95–96.
10. Ibid., pp. 99–100.
11. Cited in A. J. R. Russell-Wood, *The Black Man in Slavery and Freedom in Colonial Brazil* (London: Macmillan, 1982), p. 118.
12. For a number of such notices, see Conrad, *Children of God's Fire*, pp. 110–15, 133–34.
13. Russell-Wood, *Black Man in Slavery*, p. 37.
14. Ibid., p. 43.
15. Henry Koster, *Travels in Brazil*, 2nd ed., vol. 2 (London, 1817), pp. 208 ff.
16. André Rebouças, *Diário e notas autobiográficas* (Rio de Janeiro: Livraria José Olympio Editora, 1938), pp. 245–46.

9: THE LAST FRONTIER

1. Jaime Suchlicki, *Cuba: From Columbus to Castro* (Washington and New York: Pergamon-Brassey's, 1986), pp. 4, 28.
2. Ibid., p. 30.
3. Alexander von Humboldt, *The Island of Cuba*, tr. J. S. Thrasher (New York, 1856), pp. 218–19.
4. Curtin, *Atlantic Slave Trade*, p. 234, table 67; p. 217, table 65.
5. Suchlicki, *Cuba*, p. 43.
6. Curtin, *Atlantic Slave Trade*, p. 35, table 8; p. 234, table 67.
7. Thomas, *Cuba*, p. 169.
8. R. R. Madden, *The Island of Cuba* (London: 1849). Cited in Rice, *Rise and Fall*, p. 283.

10: DEFIANCE IN SPANISH AMERICA

1. Eugene D. Genovese, *From Rebellion to Revolution* (New York: Vintage, 1981), pp. 38–39.

2. Frederick P. Bowser, *The African Slave in Colonial Peru, 1524–1650* (Stanford, Calif.: Stanford Univ. Press, 1974), pp. 163, 159.
3. Ibid., p. 172.
4. Ibid., p. 216.
5. Herbert S. Klein, *African Slavery in Latin America and the Caribbean* (New York: Oxford Univ. Press, 1986), pp. 202–3.
6. Genovese, *Rebellion to Revolution*, p. 39.
7. Thomas, *Cuba*, pp. 37–38, 140, 204–5.
8. Esteban Montejo, *The Autobiography of a Runaway Slave*, ed. Miguel Barnet, tr. Jocasta Innes (Cleveland, Ohio: Meridian, 1969), pp. 45–48.

11: GUERRILLA WARFARE IN GUIANA

1. Curtin, *Atlantic Slave Trade*, p. 85.
2. Noel Deerr, *The History of Sugar*, 2 vols. (London: Chapman and Hall, 1949–50), vol. 1, p. 283.
3. Captain J. G. Stedman, *Narrative of a five years' expedition against the Revolted Negroes of Surinam, in Guiana, on the Wild Coast of South America, from the year 1772 to 1777*, 2 vols. (London, 1796).
4. Ibid., vol. 1, p. 287; vol. 2, pp. 289–90.
5. Ibid., vol. 2, p. 278.
6. Ibid., vol. 1, p. 69; vol. 1, p. 17.
7. Ibid., vol. 2, pp. 89–90; vol. 1, pp. 113–14; vol. 2., p. 108.
8. Ibid., vol. 1, pp. 227–28.
9. Ibid., vol. 2, pp. 173–74.
10. Ibid., vol. 2, p. 157; vol. 1, p. 331.
11. Ibid., vol. 2, pp. 112–17.
12. James Rodway, *Guiana* (London: T. Fisher Unwin, 1912), pp. 90–99.
13. Ibid., p. 119.
14. Richard Hart, *The Abolition of Slavery* (London: Community Education Trust, 1989), p. 62.

12: REVOLUTION IN ONE COUNTRY

1. Sidney W. Mintz in the introduction to Alfred Métraux, *Voodoo in Haiti* (New York: Schocken, 1972), p. 8.
2. J. Girord-Chantrans, *Voyages d'un Suisse dans différentes colonies d'Amérique pendant la dernière guerre* (Neuchâtel, 1785), p. 131.
3. Métraux, *Voodoo*, pp. 41–42.
4. Ralph Korngold, *Citizen Toussaint* (London: Gollancz, 1946), p. 42.
5. The source of such details is P. de Vaissière, *Saint Domingue, 1629–1789* (Paris, 1909), who cites official reports in the French Colonial Archives and other documents of the period.
6. The word "macandal" seems to have had or acquired various apposite meanings, such as "amulet," "poison," "poisoner," and "magician." See Métraux, *Voodoo*, pp. 35, 47–48.
7. J. H. Parry and P. M. Sherlock, *A Short History of the West Indies* (London: Macmillan, 1956), p. 162.
8. C. L. R. James, *The Black Jacobins* (London: Secker & Warburg, 1938), p. 65.
9. Ibid., p. 67.

10. Bryan Edwards, *An Historical Survey of the French Colony in the Island of St. Domingo, etc.* (London, 1797), p. v.
11. Ibid., p. 78.
12. Korngold, *Toussaint*, pp. 58–60.
13. Edwards, *St. Domingo*, pp. 116–17.
14. Korngold, *Toussaint*, p. 85; James, *Black Jacobins*, p. 100.
15. Other explanations that have been offered are that Toussaint got the nickname from a gap in his teeth; that a French commissioner, on learning of another Toussaint victory, exclaimed, "This man makes an opening everywhere!"; and that Toussaint sought a subtle association with Legba, the Voodoo god who guards and accordingly may open the Gate of Destiny. This last, given Toussaint's devout Catholicism and later campaign against Voodoo, seems unlikely in his choice of a name which he usually wrote, without an apostrophe, as "Louverture."
16. For the text of the letter, addressed to "My General, my Father, my Good Friend," see Korngold, *Toussaint*, p. 105.
17. Ibid., p. 111.
18. Ibid., p. 149.
19. James, *Black Jacobins*, p. 201.
20. See Korngold *Toussaint*, pp. 160–62, for this comment and others to the same effect from Edwards Stevens, the French historian Thiers, General de Lacroix, the French military historian Colonel Poyen, and even the otherwise hostile mulatto historian Madiou.
21. Ibid., p. 161.
22. Father and grandfather respectively of the two novelists, Alexandre Dumas père and Alexandre Dumas fils. James, *Black Jacobins*, p. 226.
23. Ibid., p. 203.
24. Korngold, *Toussaint*, p. 188.
25. James, p. 161.
26. Korngold, *Toussaint*, p. 195.
27. Ibid., p. 199.
28. Ibid., p. 215.
29. Ibid., p. 218.
30. James, *Black Jacobins*, pp. 288–89.
31. James cites evidence that Dessalines was encouraged by British representatives who told him that Britain would only trade with Haiti and protect its independence when the last of the whites there had "fallen under the axe." In this way, they hoped, the rupture between Haiti and France would, indeed, be final, and Haiti might the more easily fall under British influence or control. Ibid., pp. 307–8.
32. David Nicholls, *From Dessalines to Duvalier* (London: Macmillan; 1988), p. 36.
33. Ibid.
34. Ibid., p. 35.

13: Unquiet Islands

1. Williams, *Columbus to Castro*, p. 194.
2. Richard Ligon, *A true and exact History of Barbados* (London, 1672), p. 137.
3. Genovese, *Rebellion to Revolution*, p. 108.
4. Richard S. Dunn, *Sugar and Slaves* (London: Jonathan Cape, 1973), p. 258.
5. Ibid.
6. Hart, *Abolition of Slavery*, pp. 57–58.

7. Deerr, *History of Sugar*, vol. 2, p. 324.
8. Williams, *Columbus to Castro*, pp. 196–97.
9. Dunn, *Sugar and Slaves*, p. 259.
10. Deerr, *History of Sugar*, p. 322.
11. Bryan Edwards, *The Proceedings of the Governor and Assembly of Jamaica, in regard to the Maroon Negroes, . . .* (London, 1796), p. i.
12. Ibid., p. v.
13. Hart, *Abolition of Slavery*, p. 49.
14. Dunn, *Sugar and Slaves*, pp. 260–61.
15. Hart, *Abolition of Slavery*, p. 51.
16. Edwards, *Proceedings*, pp. viii–ix.
17. Ibid., p. xix.
18. Craton, *Sinews of Empire*, p. 228.
19. Bryan Edwards, *The History, Civil and Commercial, of the British Colonies in the West Indies* (London, 1793), vol. 2, p. 98.
20. R. C. Dallas, *The History of the Maroons*, 2 vols. (London, 1803), vol. 1, p. 145.
21. Ibid., vol. 1, pp. 172–73.
22. Ibid., vol. 1, p. 181.
23. Ibid., vol. 2, pp. 119–20.
24. Ibid., vol. 2, pp. 137–38.
25. Edwards, *Proceedings*, pp. 83–84.
26. Dallas, *Maroons*, vol. 2, p. 188.
27. Genovese, *Rebellion to Revolution*, p. 55.
28. Entry for March 22, 1816. Matthew Gregory Lewis, *Journal of a West India Proprietor* (London, 1834), pp. 226–28. "Buckra" was the Creole word for the white man.
29. Genovese, *Rebellion to Revolution*, p. 36.
30. Hart, *Abolition of Slavery*, pp. 63–64.

14: Against Peculiar Odds

1. Stampp, *Peculiar Institution*, p. 41.
2. Genovese, *Rebellion to Revolution*, p. 17.
3. Herbert Aptheker, *American Negro Slave Revolts* (New York: International Publishers, 1968), pp. 143–44.
4. Ibid., pp. 241–42.
5. Stampp, *Peculiar Institution*, p. 219.
6. Genovese, *Roll, Jordan*, p. 613.
7. *Southern Advocate*, January 29, 1830.
8. James Stuart, *Three Years in North America*, 2 vols. (Edinburgh and London, 1833), vol. 2, p. 123.
9. New York *Evening Post*, September 2, 1831.
10. Aptheker, *Slave Revolts*, p. 168.
11. Ibid., p. 171.
12. Ibid., p. 173.
13. Ibid., p. 189.
14. Letter from J. T. Callender to Thomas Jefferson, dated September 13, 1800. Papers of Jefferson, Library of Congress.
15. Ibid.
16. Aptheker, *Slave Revolts*, p. 222.

17. Ibid., p. 249.
18. New York *Evening Post*, February 27, 1811.
19. Aptheker, *Slave Revolts*, p. 270.
20. Ibid., p. 271.
21. Ibid., p. 272.
22. Ibid., p. 278.
23. Ibid., p. 280.
24. Ibid., p. 288.
25. Thomas R. Gray, *The Confessions of Nat Turner, the Leader of the Late Insurrection in Southampton, Va.* (Baltimore, 1831), p. 11.
26. Letter from Mrs. Lawrence Lewis to Mayor Harrison Gray Otis of Boston, dated October 17, 1831, in Samuel E. Morison, *Life and Letters of Harrison Gray Otis* (Boston and New York, 1913), vol. 2, p. 260.
27. Aptheker, *Slave Revolts*, p. 314.
28. Ibid., p. 358.

15: DISPERSED RESISTANCE

1. Leslie B. Rout, Jr., "The African in Colonial Brazil," in *The African Diaspora*, ed. Martin L. Kilson and Robert I. Rotberg (Cambridge: Harvard Univ. Press, 1976), p. 159.
2. Genovese, *Rebellion to Revolution*, pp. 60–64, 78–79.
3. Klein, *African Slavery*, p. 201.
4. Stuart B. Schwartz, *Sugar Plantations in the Formation of Brazilian Society* (Cambridge: Cambridge Univ. Press, 1985), pp. 158–59.
5. Ibid., p. 474.
6. Ibid., pp. 479–88.
7. Leslie Bethell, *The Abolition of the Brazilian Slave Trade* (Cambridge: Cambridge Univ. Press, 1970), p. 71.
8. Ibid., p. 72.
9. Rout, "African in Colonial Brazil," p. 165.
10. Ibid., p. 170; Schwartz, *Sugar Plantations*, pp. 476–77.

16: PARADOXICAL BARBADOS

1. Hilary Beckles, *A History of Barbados* (New York: Cambridge Univ. Press, 1990), p. 129.
2. Ibid., p. 105.
3. Ibid., pp. 142–46.
4. "Blacks in Britain," BBC 2 Television, Pebble Mill, January 7, 1991.
5. I am grateful to the distinguished Barbadian writer George Lamming for having brought this to my attention in a letter.
6. The Colonial Secretary told the House of Commons that daily wages for unskilled sugar workers were 30 cents in Barbados, 35 cents in Trinidad, and 48–60 cents in Jamaica. In Cuba, the minimum wage for such workers was 80 cents a day. Williams, *Columbus to Castro*, pp. 443–44.
7. Ibid., p. 116.
8. Selwyn D. Ryan, *Race and Nationalism in Trinidad and Tobago* (Toronto: Univ. of Toronto Press, 1972), p. 295.

17: THE PALM TREES OF JAMAICA

1. Bryan Edwards, *History of British Colonies in West Indies*, p. 227.
2. Philip Curtin, *Two Jamaicas* (Cambridge: Harvard Univ. Press, 1955), p. 240.
3. Ibid., p. 160.
4. Cited in F. G. Cassidy and R. B. Le Page, *Dictionary of Jamaican English* (Cambridge: Cambridge Univ. Press, 1967), p. 313.
5. In 1844, there had been 9,289 males and 6,487 females; in 1861, the figures were respectively 7,295 and 6,521.
6. Michael Kaufman, *Jamaica under Manley* (London: Zed Books, 1985), pp. 9–11.
7. *Encyclopaedia Britannica*, 1937 edition, vol. 12, p. 873. The author of the entry on Jamaica was Lord Olivier, who had been Governor of the island from 1907 to 1913.
8. Adolph Edwards, *Marcus Garvey* (London and Port of Spain: New Beacon Publications, 1967), pp. 27–29.
9. Kaufman, *Jamaica under Manley*, p. 50.
10. Ibid., table, appendix 7, p. 248.
11. Ibid., pp. 71–93.
12. Nutrition Advisory Council, 1975.
13. Trevor Monroe, *Jamaican Politics* (Kingston, Jamaica: Heinemann, 1990), p. 263.
14. Evelyne Huber Stephens and John D. Stephens, *Democratic Socialism in Jamaica* (London: Macmillan, 1986), pp. 251–69.
15. *Financial Times*, London, April 7, 1993.
16. Adrian Boot and Michael Thomas, *Jamaica: Babylon on a Thin Wire* (London: Thames and Hudson, 1976), pp. 50–53.

18: RACIAL POLITICS IN GUYANA

1. John Scoble, *Hill Coolies on British Guiana and Mauritius* (London, 1840), p. 20.
2. Alan H. Adamson, *Sugar without Slaves* (New Haven, Conn.: Yale Univ. Press, 1972), p. 46.
3. Ibid., p. 60.
4. *Colonist*, February 3, 1854.
5. Thomas J. Spinner, Jr., *A Political and Social History of Guyana, 1945–1983* (Boulder, Colorado, and London: Westview Press, 1984), p. 9.
6. Adamson, *Sugar without Slaves*, p. 263.
7. For more extensive biographies of Jagan and Burnham, see Spinner, *History of Guyana*, pp. 17–22, 28–29.
8. Raymond T. Smith, *British Guiana* (London and New York: Oxford Univ. Press, 1962), p. 173.
9. Spinner, *History of Guyana*, pp. 57–58.
10. Various small parties, with a combined total of a little more than one percent, received no representation.
11. Provided, for instance, by two programs from Britain's Grenada Television for its "World in Action" series: the first, transmitted one week before, and the second, three weeks after, the election.
12. For a detailed study of militancy among the bauxite workers, see Odida T. Quamina, *Mineworkers of Guyana* (London: Zed Books, 1987).
13. Jones was suspected of responsibility for the murder of a visiting United States Congressman, among others.

19: THE HEMORRHAGE OF HAITI

1. Nicholls, *Dessalines to Duvalier*, p. 38.
2. Métraux, *Voodoo*, p. 49.
3. W. W. Harvey, *Sketches of Hayti; from the Expulsion of the French, to the Death of Christophe* (London, 1827), pp. 167–68.
4. Ibid., p. 281.
5. James Franklin, *The Present State of Hayti* (London, 1828), p. 306.
6. John Candler, *Brief Notes of Hayti: With its Condition, Resources and Prospects* (London, 1842), p. 69.
7. Nicholls, *Dessalines to Duvalier*, pp. 72–73.
8. In Creole, *Lafiev la pa nan dra, se nan san li yé.*
9. *Doublure* may be translated either as "understudy," from the theater, or as "stand-in," from film-making. Though the political use of the word arose long before the birth of films, "stand-in" does seem more appropriate and vivid.
10. Proclamation of November 4, 1845. Nicholls, *Dessalines to Duvalier*, p. 81.
11. Ibid., p. 84.
12. *L'Avant-Garde*, June 15, 1882.
13. Robert I. Rotberg, *Haiti: The Politics of Squalor* (Boston: Houghton Mifflin, 1971), pp. 103–4.
14. In Creole, *Si mpa lan soup la, map craché lan soup la.*
15. Simon N. Fass, *Political Economy in Haiti* (New Brunswick, N.J., and London: Transaction Publishers, 1990), p. 7.
16. Rotberg, *Haiti*, p. 138.
17. The word *cacos* for the peasant guerrillas may have come from the name of a fierce little Haitian bird, called *taco*, or from *caraco*, a peasant garment. Nicholls, *Dessalines to Duvalier*, p. 284, note 3.
18. Ibid., p. 155.
19. Ibid., pp. 155–57.
20. Rotberg, *Haiti*, p. 148.
21. Nicholls, *Dessalines to Duvalier*, p. 189.
22. Rotberg, *Haiti*, p. 186.
23. Nicholls, *Dessalines to Duvalier*, p. 226.
24. Ibid., p. 233.
25. Rotberg, *Haiti*, pp. 242–43, 260.
26. Mark Danner, "Beyond the Mountains—II," in *The New Yorker*, December 4, 1989, p. 141.
27. Fass, *Political Economy in Haiti*, p. 5.
28. Danner, "Beyond the Mountains—III," in *The New Yorker*, December 11, 1989, p. 101.
29. Ibid., pp. 102–4.
30. Fass, *Political Economy in Haiti*, p. 31.
31. Danner, "Beyond the Mountains—I," in *The New Yorker*, November 27, 1989, p. 60.
32. Amy Wilentz, *The Rainy Season* (London: Jonathan Cape, 1989), p. 131.
33. Danner, "Beyond the Mountains—I," p. 66.
34. Ibid., p. 96.
35. Ibid., p. 98.
36. Wilentz, *Rainy Season*, pp. 334–38.
37. Ibid., p. 360.

38. Greg Chamberlain in *The Guardian*, London, June 29–30, 1991.
39. *The Guardian*, London, January 18, 1993.
40. *Financial Times*, London, July 5, 1993.

20: THE ROADS OF CUBA

1. Herring. *History of Latin America*, p. 400.
2. Thomas. *Cuba*, pp. 279–80.
3. Ibid., p. 376. Thomas considers incontrovertible the evidence presented by David Healy in *The U.S. in Cuba, 1898–1902* (Madison: Univ. of Wisconsin Press, 1963), pp. 26–27.
4. Thomas, *Cuba*, p. 419.
5. Ibid., pp. 429–32.
6. Ibid., p. 514.
7. Ibid., p. 523.
8. *New York Times*, April 29, 1927.
9. Thomas, *Cuba*, p. 736.
10. Herring, *History of Latin America*, p. 410.
11. Thomas, *Cuba*, p. 851.
12. Ibid., p. 856.
13. Carlos Moore, *Castro, the Blacks, and Africa* (Los Angeles: Center for Afro-American Studies, University of California, 1988), pp. 359–62.
14. Ibid., p. 20.
15. Ibid., pp. 22–25.
16. Victor Franco, *The Morning After* (London: Pall Mall Press, 1963), pp. 66–67.
17. *Crítica: Como surgio la cultural nacional* (Havana: Ediciones Yaka, 1961), p. 108.
18. *America Latina* (Rio de Janeiro) 7, no. 2. Cited in Moore, *Castro*, pp. 99–100.
19. Haynes Johnson, *The Bay of Pigs* (New York: Norton, 1964), pp. 184–85, 296.
20. Moore, *Castro*, p. 131. Moore himself inteviewed a number of the students.
21. Thomas, *Cuba*, p. 1408.
22. Moore, *Castro*, p. 167.
23. Ibid., p. 253.
24. Ibid., p. 256.
25. Ibid., pp. 260–61.
26. *Casa* (Havana), March–April 1969. Quoted in ibid., pp. 258–59.
27. Moore, *Castro*, pp. 292–93.
28. Ibid., p. 315.
29. Observations of the author during a visit to the island in the late sixties.
30. Louis A. Perez, Jr., *Cuba: Between Reform and Revolution* (New York: Oxford Univ. Press, 1988), pp. 357–71.
31. *The Guardian*, London, July 15, 1992.

21: AMERICA'S DEEP RIVER

1. Cited by C. Vann Woodward, *The Burden of Southern History* (New York: Vintage, 1960). pp. 89–90.
2. Samuel Eliot Morison and Henry Steele Commager, *The Growth of the American Republic*. 2 vols. (New York: Oxford Univ. Press, 1962), vol. 2, p. 43.
3. Paula Giddings. *When and Where I Enter* (New York: Bantam, 1985). pp. 17–29.
4. Morison and Commager, *Growth of American Republic*, vol. II, pp. 471–72.

5. Nicholas Lemann, *The Promised Land* (New York: Knopf, 1991), p. 16.
6. Elliot M. Rudwick, *W. E. B. Du Bois* (Philadelphia: Univ. of Pennsylvania Press, 1960), p. 201.
7. Ibid., p. 218.
8. Giddings, *When and Where*, p. 196.
9. E. U. Essien-Udom, *Black Nationalism* (New York: Dell, 1964), p. 385.
10. Charles V. Hamilton, *Adam Clayton Powell, Jr.* (New York: Atheneum, 1991), p. 58.
11. Giddings, *When and Where*, pp. 199–230.
12. Hamilton, *Powell*, pp. 121–22.
13. Lemann, *Promised Land*, pp. 71–73.
14. Morison and Commager, *Growth of American Republic*, vol. II, p. 968.
15. Ibid., p. 970.
16. Clayborne Carson, *In Struggle: SNCC and the Black Awakening of the 1960s* (Cambridge: Harvard Univ. Press, 1981), p. 38.
17. George Breitman, ed., *Malcolm X Speaks* (New York: Grove-Atlantic, 1990).
18. Archie Epps, ed., *Malcolm X: Speeches at Harvard* (New York: Paragon, 1991), p. 35.
19. Ibid., p. 37.
20. Ibid., pp. 41–42.
21. Harvard Sitkoff, *The Struggle for Black Equality, 1954–1980* (New York: Hill and Wang, 1981), pp. 213–14.
22. Ibid., p. 217.
23. Frank Levy, "Recent Trends in U.S. Earnings and Family Incomes," in *NBER Macroeconomic Annual*, ed. S. Fischer (Boston: MIT Press, 1989), pp. 100–4.
24. *The Guardian*, London, October 24, 1992.
25. U.S. Public Health Service. Cited in Andrew Hacker, "The Blacks and Clinton," *The New York Review*, January 28, 1993.
26. Bureau of Labor Statistics, cited in ibid.
27. U.S. Public Health Service, cited in ibid.
28. Elliot Currie, *Reckoning* (New York: Hill and Wang, 1993), p. 19.

22: BLACKS IN BRITAIN

1. Peter Fryer, *Staying Power* (London: Pluto Press, 1984), p. 11. I am indebted to Mr. Fryer's comprehensive book for much of the material in this chapter.
2. Ibid., pp. 22–23, where examples of such advertisements are quoted.
3. David Dabydeen, "Hogarth—the Savage and the Civilised," in *History Today* (London) 31 (Sept. 1981), pp. 48–51.
4. F. O. Shyllon, *Black People in Britain, 1555–1833* (London: Oxford Univ. Press for the Institute of Race Relations, 1977), p. 102.
5. Sir John Fielding, *Extracts from such of the Penal Laws, as Particularly relate to the Peace and Good Order of this Metropolis* (London, 1768), pp. 144–45. Original in italics.
6. December 30, 1786. Italics in the original.
7. The site of this disaster would become the settlement of Freetown, with the arrival of more than a thousand black loyalists from Nova Scotia in 1792.
8. Cugoano, *Thoughts and sentiments* . . . (London, 1787), pp. iii, 103.
9. Ibid., pp. 121–22, 133–35.
10. For more details on both men, see Fryer, *Staying Power*, pp. 214–27.

11. *Cobbett's Weekly Political Register*, June 16, 1804. Italics in the original.
12. John Locke, *Essay Concerning Human Understanding* (Oxford: Clarendon Press, 1975), pp. 606–7. Italics in the original.
13. Fryer, *Staying Power*, p. 151.
14. Footnote added to the 1753 reprint of Hume's essay "Of National Characters." The reference to the Jamaican black was to Francis Williams, who was born to free blacks around 1700 and taken up, as the subject of social experiment, by the Duke of Montagu. Sent to England, Williams studied Classics at a grammar school and then Mathematics at Cambridge, but was not provided, on his return to Jamaica, with the advancement that the Duke sought for him. Instead, he conducted a school at Spanish Town for a number of years.
15. *Spectator*, June 6, 1868.
16. *The Times*, October 11, 1825.
17. *Athenaeum*, April 13, 1833.
18. *Manchester Guardian* June 18, 1919.
19. R. J(ohnstone), "Memorandum of Certain Occurrences in the Period between 5th July and 14th August 1919," Public Record Office, Colonial Office 137/733.
20. Claude McKay's autobiography, *A Long Way from Home*, 1937 (New York: Arno Press and New York Times reprint, 1969), p. 76.
21. *Current Affairs*, December 5, 1942.
22. *Evening Standard*, London, June 21, 1948.
23. "Blacks in Britain," BBC 2 Television, Pebble Mill, January 7, 1991.
24. Sheila Patterson, *Dark Strangers* (London: Tavistock, 1963), p. 82. This was among several examples cited.
25. "Blacks in Britain."
26. J. H. G. Griffith, *Coloured Immigrants in Britain* (London and New York: Oxford Univ. Press, 1960), p. 21.
27. "Blacks in Britain: The Rise of Racism," BBC 2 Television, Pebble Mill, January 8, 1991.
28. Fryer, *Staying Power*, p. 379.
29. Patterson, *Dark Strangers*, p. 148, footnote.
30. Paul Foot, *Immigration and Race in British Politics* (Harmondsworth: Penguin, 1965), p. 126.
31. Patterson, *Dark Strangers*, pp. 420–21, table D.
32. *Smethwick Telephone*, March 13, 1964.
33. Fryer, *Staying Power*, p. 384.
34. *The Observer*, London, April 21, 1968.
35. John Solomos, *Race and Racism in Contemporary Britain* (Basingstoke: Macmillan Education, 1989), pp. 80–81.
36. "World in Action," Grenada Television.
37. *The Observer*, London, February 25, 1979.
38. See, for instance, Maureen Cain, *Society and the Policeman's Role* (London: Routledge & Kegan Paul, 1973).
39. Published as *Police against Black People* (London: Institute of Race Relations, 1979).
40. *The Brixton Disorders 10–12 April 1981: Report of an Inquiry by the Rt. Hon. The Lord Scarman* (London: HMSO, 1981).
41. *The Times*, London, July 10, 1981.
42. *Brixton Disorders*, para. 2:38.
43. Geoffrey Dear, *Handsworth/Lozells, September 1985: Report of the Chief Constable, West Midlands Police* (Birmingham: West Midlands Police, 1985), p. 69.
44. *Daily Telegraph*, London, September 14, 1985.

45. "Black and Blue: 1981 Remembered," Open Space, BBC 2 Television, April 8, 1991.
46. *The Guardian*, London, July 8, 1993.
47. *The Guardian*, London, July 15, 1993.
48. *The Guardian Weekend*, November 20, 1993.

23: THE BAJAN CAGE

1. George Bernard [Gordon Bell], *Wayside Sketches: Pen Pictures of Barbadian Life*, 2nd ed. (Barbados: Nation Publishing Co., 1985), pp. 5–6, 10.
2. Beckles, *History of Barbados* pp. 206–7.
3. *Barbados Advocate*, February 14, 1991.
4. Address by George Lamming to Guild of Undergraduates on International Students Day, Cave Hill Campus, November 17, 1983. The text has not been published, but Mr. Lamming kindly provided me with a copy of it. Mr. Sandiford would himself become Prime Minister in 1987.

24: TRAUMATIZED GUYANA

1. *The South American Handbook, 1991* (Bath, England: Trade and Travel Publications, 1991), pp. 1103–7.
2. *Stabroek News*, Georgetown, February 24, 1991.
3. Spinner, *History of Guyana*, p. 206.
4. *Daily Gleaner*, Kingston, Jamaica, March 22, 1991.
5. *Stabroek News*, Georgetown, February 26, 1991.
6. *New World Quarterly* (Georgetown), vol. 2, issue 3 (1966), pp. 10–11. Published by the New World Group.

25: THE MASK OF TRINIDAD

1. The disparity between the two islands is such—Trinidad, with 1,864 square miles, has a population of 1,195,000; Tobago, with 116 square miles, one of only 45,000—that it is permissibly convenient to talk of Trinidad on its own as an abbreviation for both.
2. The journalist himself told me of the incident and the remark.
3. Selwyn Ryan, *The Disillusioned Electorate* (Port of Spain: Imprint Caribbean, Ltd., 1989), p. 72.
4. Ibid., p. 71.
5. Ibid., p. 189.
6. Selwyn Ryan, "Popular Attitudes towards Independence," in *The Independence Experience, 1962–1987*, ed. Selwyn Ryan (St. Augustine, Trinidad: Institute of Social and Economic Research, University of the West Indies, 1988), pp. 224–26.
7. Unpublished; a copy of the text was provided by Pat Bishop.
8. Gordon Rohlehr, *Calypso and Society in Pre-Independence Trinidad* (Port of Spain: Gordon Rohlehr, 1990), p. 2.
9. Trevor Farrell, "The Development Experience: A Commentary," in *Independence Experience*, pp. 103–5.
10. Earl Lovelace, "The On-Going Value of Our Indigenous Traditions," in *Independence Experience*, p. 335.
11. V. S. Naipaul, *The Middle Passage* (London: André Deutsch, 1963), p. 29.

26: The Jamaican Beat

1. *The Sunday Record*, March 17, 1991.
2. The equivalent of roughly US$43.
3. *The Sunday Record*, March 17, 1991.
4. *Daily Gleaner*, March 26, 1991.
5. Kaufman, *Jamaica under Manley*, pp. 114–15.
6. M. G. Smith, *Culture, Race and Class in the Commonwealth Caribbean* (Mona, Jamaica: School of Continuing Studies, University of the West Indies, 1984; reprinted 1990), p. 75.
7. *Sunday Gleaner*, March 24, 1991.

27: The Dilemma of Identity in Martinique and Guadeloupe

1. *The Caribbean Islands Handbook*, 1991 (Bath, England: Trade and Travel Publications, 1990), p. 386.
2. Figures for 1987. Helen Hintjens, "France in the Caribbean," in *Europe and the Caribbean*, ed. Paul Sutton (London: Macmillan Education, 1991), p. 47.
3. *Cahier* is difficult to translate. It means an exercise book, and the sense here is almost of a folder. I have chosen "Notebook" as the most suitable.
4. *Return to My Native Land* (as John Berger and Anna Bostock, who translated the poem, chose to translate the title) (Harmondsworth: Penguin, 1956), p. 51.
5. F. Constant, "La politique française de l'immigration antillaise de 1946 à 1987," *Revue Européenne de Migrations Internationales*, vol. 3, no. 3 (1987), p. 19. Cited by Hintjens, "France in the Caribbean," p. 44.
6. Alain Anselin, *L'émigration antillaise en France* (Paris: Editions Karthala, 1990), pp. 8–9. French Guiana is included.
7. Composed by Ipomen Leauva. I am grateful to Advocate Fred Hermantin of Pointe-à-Pitre, Guadeloupe, for a literal translation from the Creole.
8. Luc Reinette, *ABC de L'Economie Guadeloupéenne* (M.P.G.I., May 1986), pp. 135–39. The car statistics are for the year 1984; the champagne statistics, for 1983. The advertisement appeared in March 1985.

28: A Haitian Space

1. Michel-Rolph Trouillot, *Nation, State, and Society in Haiti, 1804–1984* (Washington, D.C.: Woodrow Wilson International Center for Scholars, 1985), p. 1.
2. Ibid., p. 3.

29: Brazil and the Color of Invisibility

1. Publicity material produced by the state government of São Paulo.
2. The estimate of 48 percent came to me unofficially from a researcher in the São Paulo state government. Even if my informant exaggerated for some reason, the existence of a large black population in the city is beyond doubt.
3. *Jornal do Brasil*, Rio de Janeiro, August 18, 1990.
4. Centro de Articulaçao de Populacões Marginalizadas (CEAP), *Extermínio de Crianças e Adolescentes no Brasil* (Extermination of Children and Adolescents in Brazil), Rio de Janeiro, 1989, p. 41.

5. Amnesty International, *Torture and extrajudicial execution in urban Brazil* (London, June 1990), p. 4.
6. Joaquim Nabuco, *O Abolicionismo* (London, 1883), p. 252. Cited in Thomas E. Skidmore, *Black into White* (New York: Oxford Univ. Press, 1974), p. 24.
7. Abdias do Nascimento, "Racial Democracy" in Brazil: Myth or Reality? (Ile-Ife, Nigeria: University of Ife, 1977), p. 7.
8. Skidmore, *Black into White*, pp. 47–48.
9. Ibid., pp. 192–96.
10. Literally, "The Great House and the Slave Quarters," but published in English as *The Masters and the Slaves*.
11. When I interviewed him in August 1990, he was the Coordinator of Postgraduate Studies at the University of Rio.
12. *Folha de São Paulo*, February 13, 1977. Cited in Abdias do Nascimento, *Brazil: Mixture or Massacre?* (Dover, Mass.: Majority Press, 1989). p. 112.
13. *Jornal do Brasil*, Rio de Janeiro, June 26, 1955. Cited in ibid., p. 112.
14. *Jornal de Noticias*, Rio de Janeiro, February 12, 1901. Cited in ibid., p. 111.
15. "Estao de guarda . . ." by H. Martins and Darci de Oliveira. Cited in Ana Maria Rodrigues, *Samba Negro, Espoliaçao Branca* (Black Samba, White Exploitation) (São Paulo: Editora Hucitec, 1984), p. 37.
16. Thales de Azevedo, *Democracia Racial: ideologia e realidade* (Petrópolis: Editora Vozes, 1975), p. 53.
17. Rodriguez, *Samba Negro*, p. 43.
18. *International Herald Tribune*, August 1, 1990.

30: THE WASTELAND OF THE AMERICAN PROMISE

1. Ronald Segal, *The Race War* (London: Cape, and New York: Viking, 1966), pp. 262–63.
2. *USA Today*, November 11, 1991.
3. Zeev Chafets, *Devil's Night and Other True Tales of Detroit* (New York: Vintage, 1990), p. 19.
4. Ibid., p. 69.
5. See Henry Louis Gates, Jr., *The Signifying Monkey* (New York: Oxford Univ. Press, 1988), pp. 68–72, for a treatment of "the dozens" and "signifying" as a game of verbal challenge.
6. *The Guardian*, London, March 30, 1993.
7. Lemann, *Promised Land*, p. 31.
8. *New York Times*, October 20, 1991.
9. *New York Times*, November 14, 1991.
10. See, for instance, Jonathan Kaufman, *Broken Alliance: The Turbulent Times between Blacks and Jews in America* (New York: Scribner's, 1988).
11. November 21, 1991.
12. Published as *America's Receding Future* by Weidenfeld and Nicolson, London, 1968, and as *The Americans* by The Viking Press, New York, 1969.

31: A SEAT ON THE CANADIAN TRAIN

1. "Train to Montreal" in Dionne Brand, *Sans Souci and Other Stories* (Stratford, Ontario: Williams-Wallace, 1988), pp. 18–19.
2. Thomas F. Johnston, "Colour Prejudice in Canada," in *Anthropological Journal of Canada* 16, no. 2, pp. 3–9.

3. Agnes Calliste, "Canada's Immigration Policy and Domestics from the Caribbean: The Second Domestic Scheme," in *Socialist Studies* 5 (Toronto: Cross Cultural Communication Centre, 1989), p. 138.
4. Ibid., p. 141.
5. Ibid., pp. 142–43.
6. Ibid., p. 146.
7. Pamela M. White, Statistics Canada, Ottawa, *Ethnic Diversity in Canada* (January 1990), p. 33.
8. "A Minority Report," *Sunday Star*, Toronto, November 3–December 22, 1985.
9. Mordecai Richler, "A Reporter at Large," *The New Yorker*, September 23, 1991.
10. *Canadian Review of Books* 19, no. 7 (October 1990), p. 14.

32: An Ear for Music

1. Richard Jobson, *The Golden Trade or a Discovery of the River Gambra and the Golden Trade of the Aethiopians* (London, 1623), p. 105.
2. Eileen Southern, *The Music of Black Americans* (New York: Norton, 1983), pp. 10–14. This book is a major source of material for this chapter.
3. Edward Bowdich, *Mission from Cape Coast Castle to Ashantee* (London, 1819), pp. 449–52.
4. Southern, *Music of Black Americans*, p. 41.
5. *Memorable Days in America: Being a Journal of a Tour to the United States by W. Faux, an English Farmer* (London, 1823), p. 420.
6. Cited in Southern, *Music of Black Americans*, p. 123.
7. Ibid., p. 191.
8. Ibid., p. 334.
9. After the name of the alderman, Joseph Story, who had originated the project.
10. *The Penguin Encyclopedia of Popular Music*, ed. Donald Clarke (London: Penguin, 1990), p. 600.
11. Southern, *Music of Black Americans*, p. 363.
12. *Penguin Encyclopedia of Popular Music*, p. 1145.
13. LeRoi Jones, *Blues People* (London: MacGibbon & Kee, 1965), p. 80.
14. Dizzy Gillespie with Al Fraser, *To Be or Not to Bop* (New York: Doubleday, 1979), p. 207.
15. Ibid., p. 208.
16. "The Century of Jazz," Part 3, p. 4, in *Jazz fm*, 3 (London: Observer Publications in association with Jazz FM).
17. *Penguin Encyclopedia of Popular Music*, p. 931.
18. Ibid., p. 577.
19. John Storm Roberts, *Black Music of Two Worlds* (London: Allen Lane, 1973), pp. 72–74.
20. Chris McGowan and Ricardo Pessanho, *The Billboard Book of Brazilian Music* (London: Guinness Publishing, 1991), p. 25.
21. Ibid., p. 36.
22. Roberts, *Black Music*, pp. 71–92.
23. Nestor Ortiz Oderigo, "Negro Rhythm in the Americas," *African Music*, vol. 1, no. 3 (1956).
24. *Penguin Encyclopedia of Popular Music*, pp. 758, 1002–3, 1094.
25. Ibid., pp. 1031–32.
26. Roberts, *Black Music*, p. 110.

27. Rohlehr, *Calypso and Society*, pp. 360–61.
28. *Penguin Encyclopedia of Popular Music*, p. 975.
29. Ibid., p. 91.

33: THE INNOCENT EYE

1. E. H. Gombrich, *The Story of Art* (London: Phaidon, 1962), p. 440.
2. John O'Dwyer and Raymond Le Marge, *A Glossary of Art Terms* (London and New York: Peter Nevill, 1950), p. 107.
3. Edmund L. Fuller, *Visions in Stone* (Pittsburgh, Pa.: Univ. of Pittsburgh Press, 1973), p. 3.
4. E. P. Richardson, *Painting in America: The Story of 450 Years*, Detroit Institute of Arts exhibition (Cornwall, N.Y.: Cornwall Press, 1956), p. 389.
5. Transcript of his 1952 broadcast on Jamaican Radio.
6. Selden Rodman, *Where Art Is Joy* (New York: Ruggles de Latour, 1988). Unless otherwise specified, the various Haitian paintings cited are reproduced in this major source.
7. Angela Gross Collection, Christie's East Sale Catalogue, New York, May 15, 1991. Lot No. 38.
8. Ibid., Lot No. 5.
9. Sidney and Fahimie Marks Collection, Christie's East Sale, New York, May 19, 1992. Lot No. 26.
10. Biographical details of more than 100 Haitian artists up to the early seventies may be found in Eleanor Ingalls Christensen, *The Art of Haiti* (Philadelphia: Art Alliance Press, 1975), pp. 63–72.
11. Sidney and Fahimie Marks Collection, Lot No. 15.
12. Sheldon Williams, *Voodoo and the Art of Haiti* (London: Morland Lee, 1969), pp. 99–100.
13. Patricia Bryan, "Towards an African Aesthetic in Jamaican Intuitive Art," in *Arts Jamaica*, July 1985. p. 6.
14. *Daily Gleaner*, Kingston, September 13, 1934.
15. *John Dunkley*, The National Gallery of Jamaica, catalogue for an exhibition of his paintings and sculpture, December 1976–February 1977; *Jamaican Art*, *1922–82*, The National Gallery of Jamaica and The Smithsonian Institution Traveling Exhibition Service.
16. Cited in *Jamaican Art*, p. 22.
17. José Roberto Texeira Leite in "Negros, Pardos, e Mulatos na Pintura e na Escultura Brasileira do Séc. XVIII," in *A Mão Afro-Brasileira* (Tenenge, Brazil: Fundação Emilio Odebrecht, 1988), p. 14.
18. Amélia Zaluar, "*Gabriel, mestre de arquitectura fantástica e sue casa-escultura*," in ibid., pp. 210–13.

34: VOICES

1. Robert A. Hall, Jr., *Pidgin and Creole Languages* (Ithaca, N.Y., and London: Cornell Univ. Press, 1969), p. xiii.
2. One is a provincial form of standard French, spoken by the long established, socially prominent families of New Orleans and its environs; the other, Cajun, a dialect derived from French rural speech of the seventeenth century, and spoken by the

predominantly white descendants of immigrants from Acadia (hence Cajun) in Nova Scotia, Canada, at that time.

3. The tilde (-) is the phonetic sign for nasalization, which is common in the French-derived creole languages.

4. Hall, *Pidgin and Creole Languages*, p. 60.

5. Ibid., pp. 75–78.

6. Ibid., p. 92.

7. The Concise Oxford Dictionary, Clarendon Press, Oxford, 1990.

8. Ibid.

9. Frederic G. Cassidy, *Jamaica Talk*. (London: Macmillan, 1961), pp. 75, 116, 124, 131, 143, 191.

10. J. L. Dillard, *Black English* (New York: Vintage, 1973), p. 24.

11. Edith Efron, "French and Creole Patois in Haiti," in *Caribbean Quarterly* 3 (1954), pp. 199–200.

12. Loreto Todd, *Pidgins and Creoles* (London: Routledge & Kegan Paul, 1974), p. 66.

13. Dillard, *Black English*, pp. 27–30.

14. Ibid., pp. 45–46.

15. John Mason Brewer, *Dog Ghosts and Other Texas Negro Folk Tales* (Austin: Univ. of Texas Press, 1958), p. 14.

16. Zora Neale Hurston, *Their Eyes Were Watching God* (New York: Negro Universities Press, 1969), p. 10.

17. Ibid., p. 37.

18. Ibid., pp. 69–70.

19. Ibid., p. 111.

20. Ibid., pp. 122–23.

21. Ibid., p. 286.

22. Paule Marshall, *Brown Girl, Brownstones* (London: Virago, 1989), p. 24.

23. Ibid., p. 300.

24. Ibid., p. 307.

25. Ralph Ellison, *Invisible Man* (New York: New American Library, 1964), pp. 64–65.

26. James Baldwin, *The Fire Next Time* (Harmondsworth: Penguin, 1964), p. 42.

27. Edward Brathwaite, *The Arrivants* (London and New York: Oxford Univ. Press, 1990), pp. 260–61.

28. *The Langston Hughes Reader* (New York: Braziller, 1958), p. 89.

29. For a detailed analysis of the themes, see Gates, *The Signifying Monkey*, pp. 220–38.

30. Boston, 1861, p. 210.

31. Kenneth Ramchand, *The West Indian Novel and Its Background* (New York: Barnes & Noble, 1970), p. 259.

32. Anne Walmsley, *The Caribbean Artists Movement, 1966–1972* (London and Port of Spain: New Beacon Books, 1992), pp. 56–57.

33. *Black Women Writers*, ed. by Mari Evans (London: Pluto Press, 1985), pp. 344–45.

34. Paule Marshall, *Praisesong for the Widow* (New York: Penguin/Plume, 1983), p. 135.

35. Ibid., p. 39.

36. Ibid., p. 248.

37. Ibid., p. 256.

35: THE OUTSTRETCHED ARM

1. Albert Speer, *Inside the Third Reich* (London: Weidenfeld and Nicolson, 1970), p. 73.
2. "Will to Win," made by Catalyst Television for the BBC Pebble Mill, and transmitted in September–October 1993.
3. Frantz Fanon, *The Wretched of the Earth*, tr. Constance Farrington (London: MacGibbon & Kee, 1965), p. 41.
4. "Will to Win."
5. Ibid.
6. C. L. R. James, *Beyond a Boundary* (London: Hutchinson, 1963), p. 206.

36: THE SOUL OF THE DIASPORA

1. Geoffrey Parrinder, *Religion in Africa* (Harmondsworth: Penguin, 1969), p. 21.
2. Ibid., p. 45.
3. Ibid., p. 86.
4. Montejo, *Autobiography of a Runaway Slave*, pp. 34–36.
5. Ibid., p. 80.
6. Joseph M. Murphy, *Santeria* (Boston: Beacon, 1988), p. 41.
7. George Eaton Simpson, *Black Religions in the New World* (New York: Columbia Univ. Press, 1978), pp. 58–59.
8. W. J. Hollenweger, *The Pentecostals* (Minneapolis: Augsburg, 1972), pp. 96, 107.
9. Simpson, *Black Religions*, p. 255.
10. John Thomas Nichol, *Pentecostalism* (New York: Harper & Row, 1966), p. 57.
11. Phil K. Hitti, *The Arabs* (Chicago: Regnery, 1967), p. 54.
12. Gayraud Wilmore, *Black Religion and Black Radicalism* (Garden City, N.Y.: Doubleday, 1972), p. 238.
13. Simpson, *Black Religions*, pp. 237, 244.
14. James H. Cone, *Black Theology and Black Power* (New York: Seabury, 1969), pp. 48–49, 27–28.
15. Joseph R. Washington, Jr., *Black and White Power Subreption* (Boston: Beacon, 1971), pp. 141–42.
16. Simpson, *Black Religions*, p. 155.

INDEX